THE ATHLONE HISTORY OF
MUSIC IN BRITAIN

General Editor Ian Spink

Volume 5
THE ROMANTIC AGE
1800–1914

The Athlone History of Music in Britain

General Editor IAN SPINK
*Professor of Music, Royal Holloway College,
University of London*

1 The Middle Ages*
Editor MARGARET BENT
*Professor of Music,
Brandeis University*

2 The Sixteenth Century*

3 The Seventeenth Century*
Editor IAN SPINK

4 The Eighteenth Century*
Editor ROGER FISKE

5 The Romantic Age 1800–1914
Editor NICHOLAS TEMPERLEY
*Professor of Music,
University of Illinois
at Urbana-Champaign*

6 The Twentieth Century*
Editor ARNOLD WHITTALL
*Reader in Music,
King's College,
University of London*

*In preparation. Information on request
from the publishers.

Music in Britain

THE
ROMANTIC AGE
1800–1914

edited by
NICHOLAS TEMPERLEY

THE ATHLONE PRESS
LONDON

First published 1981 by The Athlone Press Ltd
90–91 Great Russell Street, London WC1B 3PY

© Athlone Press 1981

Distributor in the USA and Canada
Humanities Press Inc
New Jersey

British Library Cataloguing in Publication Data
The Romantic age 1800–1914. – (The Athlone history of music in Britain; 5)
1. Music – Great Britain – history and criticism
I. Temperley, Nicholas
180'.941   ML285
ISBN 0 485 13005 X

Phototypeset in VIP Baskerville by
Western Printing Services Ltd, Bristol

Printed and bound in Great Britain
at The Pitman Press, Bath

FOREWORD

It is now over seventy years since Ernest Walker published *A History of Music in England* and almost thirty years since it was revised and enlarged by Sir Jack Westrup. It served its purpose well—it had to, for with the honourable exception of Henry Davey's own revision of his *History of English Music* (1921) there was really nothing else. In some ways the two works complemented each other rather as Burney and Hawkins did in the eighteenth century. Both were remarkable for their time, but much has happened during the intervening years—particularly since 1950—that seems to call for a reappraisal of the whole subject; one that takes into account the results of recent research and presents in an authoritative manner a new synthesis that is both broad and deep. The hope is that the six volumes of *The Athlone History of Music in Britain* will answer this need.

Not only are there another thirty years of British music to chronicle: our whole approach to the past has undergone a change. We tend to see musical history less in terms of masterpieces, more in terms of artifacts the significance of which extends beyond whatever their status as works of art might or might not be. Reinterpretation is inevitable, and from this point of view English music in the nineteenth century demands a new look; not in the hope of finding an English Beethoven or Wagner (or Berlioz or Mussorgsky) but, perhaps, to see why there was none and what there was instead. Moreover, there is now much more that needs to be said about the music of earlier centuries than there was a generation ago. The intervening years have seen a massive upsurge of interest in, and appreciation of, early music, the reasons for which need not be gone into any further except to observe that musical scholarship has played an important part. Publications such as *Musica Britannica* and *Early English Church Music* are both a cause and an effect of this phenomenon. Begun in 1951 as an 'authoritative national collection of the classics of British music', the former produced almost forty volumes in its first twenty-five years, while the latter, aiming 'to complete the publication in modern editions of all early sacred music in Britain from the Norman Conquest to the Commonwealth', numbered more than twenty volumes in its first fifteen years. The research and scholarship

that underlies this tremendous advance has, at the same time, given
rise to many valuable studies of the music and its various contexts. The
moment now seems ripe to draw all this together on a scale that will
permit both the fine detail as well as the broad picture to be revealed.
Our method, therefore, has been to divide the time from the middle
ages to the present into coherent periods (except for the medieval
volume each roughly a century) and to entrust each to a specialist
editor who in turn has enlisted the help of other specialists to cover the
field. Lacking, for better or worse, a single viewpoint, an attempt has
been made to maintain consistency of approach from one volume to the
next in so far as it seemed sensible and practical to do so. The first part
of each volume deals with music and musicians in society, the second
with the music itself considered under such headings as church music,
theatre music, domestic music etc., as appropriate. Volume editors
have assumed responsibility for the detailed planning of their own
volumes, my role as general editor being mainly confined to initial
planning and final imprimatur. The task has had its pains and its
pleasures. Of the pains nothing need now be said; of the pleasures I
must mention my meetings and discussions with volume editors, and
my dealings with the editorial staff of the Athlone Press despite trau-
matic upheavals since the project was first mooted in 1974.

IAN SPINK

CONTENTS

vii

CONTENTS

PART IV Writings on Music

CONTRIBUTORS

STEPHEN BANFIELD is a Lecturer in Music at the University of Keele, and is a specialist on solo song in England in the early twentieth century.

NIGEL BURTON is a Lecturer in Music at the University of Reading, a specialist in the music of Sullivan, and a keen singer and conductor.

GEOFFREY BUSH is Visiting Professor of Music at King's College, London, known as a composer, writer, and editor; he is an authority on Sterndale Bennett.

BRUCE CARR is Assistant Manager of the Detroit Symphony Orchestra, and was on the editorial staff of *The New Grove*.

VINCENT DUCKLES, Professor of Music and Head of the Music Library at the University of California at Berkeley, is known as a writer and music bibliographer.

MICHAEL HURD is a free-lance composer and author, whose many books include biographies of Boughton and Gurney.

D. W. KRUMMEL is a Professor of Library Science and of Music at the University of Illinois, known as an authority on bibliography and music printing.

ANDREW LAMB is a writer who has specialized in lighter music, particularly operetta and other popular theatre music.

RICHARD MIDDLETON is Senior Lecturer in Music at the Open University, Milton Keynes; his research and writing lies mainly in the field of popular music.

JOHN PARRY is a concert pianist who has made available much little-known piano music of the period 1820–1914, including that of Sullivan.

BERNARR RAINBOW, after a long career as organist and choirmaster, is now director of the Curwen Institute; he is known as a writer on music education and liturgical music.

NICHOLAS TEMPERLEY is a Professor of Music at the University of Illinois, known as a writer on parish church music; he has revived music of Pinto, Loder and Pierson.

DONALD H. VAN ESS is a Professor of Music at the State University of New York at Brockport who has carried out research on English brass music.

G. LARRY WHATLEY is a Professor of Music at Brevard College, North Carolina, and the author of a dissertation on Tovey as a music theorist.

PERCY M. YOUNG is a composer, lecturer and broadcaster, widely known through his literary works, which include studies of Elgar, Sullivan, and Grove.

ACKNOWLEDGEMENTS

The Editor wishes to thank the many librarians, too numerous to mention individually, who have helped with enquiries; and to acknowledge advice and suggestions from Gerald Abraham, Geoffrey Bush, Bruce Carr, Roger Fiske, Nigel Fortune, Lawrence Gushee, H. Diack Johnstone, A. Hyatt King, D. W. Krummel, Andrew Lamb, Robin Langley, O. W. Neighbour, Michael Pope, and John Silantien. He is also grateful to the University of Illinois for financial support; to his research assistants, Carl Manns and Aaron Appelstein, and secretary, Valerie Woodring; to Ruth Burnham for her expert assistance in typing out the manuscript; to Denys Parsons for checking many references in the British Library; to the general editor, Ian Spink, for much constructive criticism; and to Arnold Dewey, formerly of the Athlone Press, for his understanding and encouragement.

* * *

ABBREVIATIONS

A	alto(s)	*MGG*	*Die Musik in Geschichte*
anon.	anonymous		*und Gegenwart*
b.	born	MS(S)	manuscript(s)
B	bass(es)	*MT*	*The Musical Times*
Bsn(s)	bassoon(s)	n.	footnote
Btne	baritone (instrument)	n.s.	new series
c.	*circa* (approximately)	Ob.	oboe(s)
Cb.	double bass(es)	Oph.	ophicleide(s)
ch.	chapter(s)	orch.	orchestra
Ch.	choir (organ manual)	Org.	organ
Cl.	clarinet(s)	p(p).	page(s)
Cnt(s)	cornet(s)	*P*	instrumental parts
col.	column	Ped.	pedal(s)
comp.	compiler(s), compiled by	Perc.	percussion
Cond.	conductor	Pf.	piano (instrument)
cpld	coupled	Picc.	piccolo(s)
d.	died	qtd	quoted
Diap.	diapason(s)	r	*recto* (front of leaf)
DNB	*Dictionary of National*	R.H.	right hand
	Biography	repr.	reprinted
ed.	editor, edited by	rev.	revised (by)
Euph.	euphonium	S	soprano(s)
ex(x).	example(s)	*S*	complete score
facs.	facsimile	ser.	series
ff.	and following pages	St.	stopped
fig.	figure	Supp.	supplement
fl.	*floruit* (flourished)	Sw.	swell (organ manual)
Fl.	flute(s)	Sxn(s)	saxhorn(s)
fol.	folio (leaf)	T	tenor(s)
Gt.	great (organ manual)	t.s.	*tasto solo* (bass alone)
Hn(s)	horn(s)	tr.	translator(s), translated by
K	keyboard reduction of	Tr.	trumpet(s)
	instrumental work, or	Trb.	trombone(s)
	of accompaniment	Tri.	triangle
L.H.	left hand	unacc.	unaccompanied
Man.	manual	unis.	in unison

ABBREVIATIONS

v	*verso* (back of leaf)	Vla(s)	viola(s)
v.	verse	Vn(s)	violin(s)
Vc.	cello(s)	vol.	volume(s)

A system of abbreviated references has been used in endnotes and music examples. References to works listed in the bibliography are by the author's surname, with initial if necessary. When there are two or more works by the same author, an abbreviation of the title is added in small capitals. These abbreviations are resolved in the bibliography itself. A work without an author is referred to by its first words as listed in the bibliography.

Sources of individual musical works are referred to by the abbreviations *S, K* or *P* (explained above), followed by the publisher (place of publication is London unless otherwise stated) and date of publication, or a full citation in the case of a manuscript.

In music examples, tempo and expression marks in parentheses () are carried over from a point in the music preceding the quoted passage.

INTRODUCTION

NICHOLAS TEMPERLEY

In the years from 1800 to 1914, the power and wealth of Great Britain were at their height: it was the time when the British people had their greatest opportunity, both in the mass and as individuals, to influence the rest of the world. It was also, by general agreement, a period when European music reached one of its peaks. Yet the part played by British musicians in this development was relatively modest.

Up to a point, this is not a matter for surprise. There is little positive correlation in history between political or economic power and artistic achievement: indeed, it has been argued that the opposite is true.[1] Yet the total debasement that some writers have professed to find in Victorian* music, if it really existed, would seem to require further explanation. But did it really exist? The position we will take in this book is that Victorian music, like any other, covers a full range of quality: it may include much that is very bad, but it also includes much that commands respect and some that is superlatively good. The debasement of Victorian music, then, has been exaggerated by the intervening generations, for reasons that will be fully explored. Forces hostile to British musical achievement were already oppressing composers in the nineteenth century, and they survived to undermine their reputations after death.

Similar forces beleaguered the other Victorian arts also. Now that they have largely subsided, we are inclined to treasure the artistic legacy of the nineteenth century. The early part of the century has long been recognized as a high point in English painting and poetry; the Edwardian period, in drama; fiction throughout the period is highly regarded; and in recent years many secondary authors have been

---

*The word *Victorian* has to do a double duty in this book. Sometimes it is used precisely to mean 'of the period 1837–1901', sometimes—as here—more loosely to mean 'of the period covered by this volume but more especially of the period 1837–1901'. We hope that the context will always show which meaning is intended. A similar ambiguity sometimes attaches to the words 'England' and 'English', though 'Britain' and 'British' have been used whenever Scotland, Wales, or Ireland is explicitly included.

1

reassessed and found worthy of respect. Victorian architecture and artifacts of all kinds are now protected by museums, preservation societies, and private collectors.

Music is a long way behind in the process of rehabilitation. The reason is not far to seek. Anybody can look at paintings, pottery, or buildings, or take books out of a library, but before music can be reassessed it must be performed, and before it can be performed there must be collaborative effort, financial investment, and education of the performers, generally with little reward other than personal satisfaction. So Victorian music must undergo a longer period of pioneering exploration than the other arts. This volume is designed to advance the work and to guide future adventurers. An adequate reassessment needs performance, not once but many times, not just of any Victorian music but of music carefully chosen with full understanding of its significance and its relation to other music of its period.

Another reason for reviving Victorian music is simply to enjoy it. True, there is a large quantity of continental music of the same period that is not only far more accessible than British music but also, in many cases, better. But British music has its own flavour, partly by association but partly by actual differences of style, which can give it a unique appeal, and not merely to British audiences. In the case of songs or operas there is a novel satisfaction in hearing romantic music of good quality with English words as originally set by the composer, rather than mere translations of German or Italian. And there is a frankly patriotic pleasure in demonstrating that Britain, as much as Germany, Italy, or France, has a long *and continuous* tradition of musical creation that can be recalled with pride.

But this book has an equally important goal that has nothing to do with the revival of music in performance. It is simply to bring about a better understanding of music and the musical life of nineteenth-century Britain: not to enjoy, but to know. After all, music is a part of human life, though its links with other parts are mysterious and often difficult to establish. It certainly was a large and important part of British life in our period; and if its importance has been neglected by most general historians, we can scarcely blame them when even musicologists have taken little account of it. We hope that this book will not only remove some of the prejudices and misconceptions that exist about Victorian music, but also reveal aspects of Victorian musical activity whose very existence has hardly been appreciated. It should do this both directly and through the revivals and recordings that we hope it will foster. Today's performers and listeners are more attuned to history than ever before, and the historical significance of a piece of music has become, through programme notes, record jackets, and radio talks, almost a part of its aesthetic message.

We hope that we have succeeded not only in establishing the facts about Victorian musical life, but in explaining them: more particularly, in explaining why the great and flourishing musical activity was seldom matched by the quality of original art music produced. We open, indeed, with a chapter which grapples with this very problem, followed by chapters discussing two means through which the nineteenth century saw a vast increase in the dissemination of music: education and publication. The third medium (performance) has no chapter to itself, but pervades the book. It seemed hardly necessary to assemble statistics to document the increase and diversification in the public performance of music in Britain between 1800 and 1914.

In dealing with the music composed in Britain in this period, we recognize two classes of music: one functional, or for popular entertainment, the other aspiring to high art by virtue of its intellectual and emotional content. It is often said that the split between these two classes originated in the nineteenth century or was a product of industrialization. But this is surely an error. The split was quite as clearly present, for example, in sixteenth-century England: plainsong and faburden, metrical psalm tune, broadside ballad, folksong intabulation, and dance music provided for functional and popular needs, while a highly developed polyphonic art music, with different goals and values, flourished at the same time. What was new in the nineteenth century was the control of functional and popular music by commercial interests on a more and more formidable scale, supported by the growing wealth of, in turn, the upper-middle, lower-middle, and working classes. Sheer growth in numbers of those who had the time and money to be entertained by professional musicians stimulated mass production and marketing techniques, and these in turn allowed the successful promotion of music of poorer quality than would have been acceptable in earlier periods. 'There never was a grosser system of puffery than that now established among music-sellers—genius and learning have no possible chance', exclaimed *The Athenaeum* in 1833.[2] If Britain led the world in industrialization and the social changes that ensued, it is logical to suppose that Britain led the world also in the production of bad commercial music, and indeed this may well have been the case. This is not to say that all popular music of the nineteenth century was bad. On the contrary, it will be maintained in more than one chapter that British popular music was as good as any in Europe by the turn of the century.

Popular and functional music, whether good or bad, is worthy of serious attention from those who would understand the whole musical life of any period. So we have not followed the example of most histories of nineteenth-century music by ignoring it. We describe and analyse it not as if it were unsuccessful art music, but for what it is, and for what it tells us about the society that produced it. When we judge its quality, our judgement is based on its vitality and its success in expressing the values of its audience.

Functional music is music that is primarily intended to assist some other action—working, dancing, marching, worshipping—and so is not greatly concerned with listeners. In this category we have placed parish-church and nonconformist music (but not cathedral music),* ballroom dances (as opposed to stylized dances for concert use), military band music, and so on. *Popular music*, on the other hand, is meant to be listened to, whether in theatre, seaside pavilion, public house, drawing-room, or street; but it aims only to please its audience in ways that are familiar to all members, and avoids any kind of intellectual challenge that would draw attention to the music as art. Both functional and popular music were transformed, in nineteenth-century Britain, by commercialization. The change was most radical in the case of working-class popular music. At the beginning of the period the working classes were making their own music, while at the end of it their music was supplied by a large, commercially organized population of professional entertainers.

In dealing with *Art music*, we adopt a different and more traditional approach. Where the music seeks to appeal to the taste of cultivated audiences familiar with the greatest European art music of the time, and to engage the attention and intellectual response of those audiences, it is analysed and judged by the standards to which it aspires. Victorian art music has been passed over, derided or denigrated by many writers, while others have interpreted the music of the years after 1880 as amounting to an 'English musical renaissance' following a period of darkness and degradation. We have not taken such judgements for granted, but have tried to make fresh ones. Sometimes the older views have been largely confirmed; often they have been modified or reformulated with different emphasis. The late Victorian 'renaissance' idea, for instance, holds well enough in the case of orchestral and chamber music and oratorio; but in opera, songs, partsongs and cathedral music the honours are spread more evenly over the century, and in piano and organ music the height of British achievement is now

*Cathedral music, though strictly speaking only an accompaniment to worship, had for long been treated as an artistic performance.

4

seen to come at the beginning of the period, the later decades showing a decline.

In retrospect it may be thought that the 1830s, not the 1880s, were the most dynamic decade (musically speaking) in our period. Within ten years of the great Reform Bill (1832), political movements for the reform of education, cathedral administration, and theatre licensing had got under way, with far-reaching effects on music: the Oxford Movement had been launched (1833); the first national opera house for the performance of English operas had opened (1834); the Sacred Harmonic Society (1832), Society of British Musicians (1834), Purcell Club (1836), Bristol Madrigal Society (1837), Musical Antiquarian Society (1840) and Motett Society (1841) had been formed (the Handel Society followed in 1843); the first chamber concerts had been given in London (1835) and the first one-man piano recital (1837); the first weekly musical journal had been launched (1836); the first Tractarian choral services (1839) and the first full-sized surpliced parish choir (1841) had been heard; the first scholarly collection of English folksongs had appeared (1838). These developments between them stimulated Michael Balfe, John Barnett, William Sterndale Bennett, Edward Loder, Robert Pearsall, and Samuel Sebastian Wesley to some of their best efforts—indeed several of these composers enjoyed their only really creative phase in these years. These, with Hugo Pierson and George Macfarren, were the English Romantics, of the same generation as Berlioz, Chopin, Mendelssohn, Schumann, and Wagner. For a short time it looked as if Englishmen could play as great a part in musical romanticism as they had in literary romanticism a generation earlier. Schumann and Berlioz were favourably disposed to such a development. But the decades that followed brought a decline, a disappointment of high hopes. Many of the new institutions failed; the English opera schemes faltered; Barnett, Bennett, and Wesley became disillusioned; Pearsall and Pierson settled abroad; interest in folksong, plainsong, and early English music sagged until it was revived at the end of the century. And after 1900, when Elgar, Parry, Stanford, Delius, and Vaughan Williams had made their mark, there was indeed a new surge of creativity which placed Britain once more on the 'musical map of Europe'.

Throughout the period covered in this book, the whole of Ireland was part of the United Kingdom, and indeed several of our leading composers, as well as our most famous music critic, were Irish protestants by birth and upbringing. If Ireland, Wales, and Scotland are not often mentioned in the book, the same is true of the English provinces: for the fact is that British music was overwhelmingly centralized in London, as much in the nineteenth century as in the twentieth. Only at the occasional provincial festival did another city, for a few days, borrow some of the musical glamour and vitality of the capital.

But if the rest of Britain tended to be a musical backwater, London itself was well in the mainstream of European music. It was nothing if not cosmopolitan, and it shared with Paris the honour of being the most highly prized city in the world for musical performance. If you had been acclaimed in London, success was yours. Although European musicians did not generally look to London for new developments in composition, they looked to it for performance opportunities, for generous patronage, for large enthusiastic audiences, and for open-minded and liberal acceptance of what was new. Nor was the traffic entirely one way. John Field's music was published all over Europe; Sterndale Bennett was recognized by Schumann in his teaching as a leading representative of the 'modern school';[3] Balfe's operas were almost as popular in Paris as in London; Pierson's *Faust* music was widely played in Germany; Sullivan's light operas and several English musical comedies had long runs in European capitals at the turn of the century; Elgar was hailed by German critics as the new genius of the day.

Nor should it be forgotten that for North America, particularly in the earlier part of our period, Britain was the leading *producer* of music,[4] even as it was the leading *consumer* of music from the Continent. Any successful work by a British composer played in London was quickly taken up in New York and Philadelphia, and even continental music generally reached them via London. Many English musicians made successful tours of the United States, and some, such as G. K. Jackson, Edward Hodges, and C. E. Horn, remained to occupy leading positions there—just as German and Italian musicians had for so long been settling in London. In Australia, British music had an unquestioning and admiring market.[5] Finally, it must be remembered that British folksong was an inspiration to many European composers in the nineteenth century—though here we are speaking of the 'national airs' of Ireland and Scotland, for it was believed that England had no folksong of its own.

The nationalist phase in musical history did not reach Britain until the end of our period, and hardly plays much part in our story. Britain, almost alone among European countries, had avoided revolution, substituting its own brand of peaceful 'improvement' and dynamically adapting its ancient institutions to the rapidly changing needs of the times. Musical nationalism on the Continent was usually linked with the assertion of national identity against political or cultural domina-

6

tion by another people. No such conditions existed in England (Ireland was another matter). The nationalism of Vaughan Williams, when it came, was not politically radical; indeed it coincided, at least chronologically and to some extent emotionally, with the imperialism and protectionism of the Edwardian years. It was a delayed romantic reaction to the bourgeois materialism that had prevailed. It was indeed associated, far more closely than the other movements of musical nationalism, with the revival of early music: to Vaughan Williams, folksong was above all ancient (Elizabethan or earlier), and it merged in his mind with the harmonic and melodic styles of the sixteenth century.

In the absence of nationalism, then, British art music of the nineteenth century was generally in the idiom of continental music, primarily German (or Italian in the case of pre-Wagnerian opera). What other idiom was possible, after all? It should not be assumed that this is a matter of 'imitation'. It is more a matter of a common language, noticeable in comparing Brahms and Parry, Mendelssohn and Sterndale Bennett—but also Field and Chopin, where the British composer clearly had the priority. In cathedral music, and a few other areas, there is a naturally English style that is not in the least nationalistic; and here, if we observe striking similarities to continental idioms, we have more reason to conclude that they are the result of one-way influence. But the time for basing value judgements on the detection of such influences is surely past. Short of direct plagiarism, a work should be judged for what it makes of the styles and materials it uses, not for where they come from, and such has been our standard in this book. Clearly there is nothing reprehensible about a general resemblance to the style of Mendelssohn, Brahms, or any other great composer.

It is not surprising to find in the nineteenth century a great development of published writing about music, to cater for the steadily growing informed public. Writing on music theory, aesthetics, and speculative criticism was an old tradition, and in these departments the British followed in the wake of the Germans, only occasionally producing an original contribution. But regular musical criticism of the journalistic kind was a creature of the nineteenth century, and here London periodicals were well to the fore, providing a well-informed and internationally-minded coverage of the musical life of Europe that was rivalled only in Paris. Another development peculiar to the romantic age was the rise of musical antiquarianism, leading eventually to the scholarly discipline of musicology: and here we have many little-known facts to put forward, revealing beyond all doubt that Britain was the innovator in many important aspects of musical historiography. These developments are dealt with in the fourth and last part of this book.

PART I

Music in Society

Chapter 1

THE ARTIST AND SOCIETY

STEPHEN BANFIELD

The Unmusical Nation

England has no music. It has never produced a first-rate composer, and accepts only such music as has already been decided to be good in Italy and Germany. They seem to have great delight in these things, but not original appreciation; and value them as showy commodities, which they buy at great price for pride.
Emerson[1]

The catchphrase *Das Land ohne Musik* apparently dates only from 1914, but the idea would seem to be immemorial. It has reared up widely since the eighteenth century, and, despite attempts to burn off its many hydra-heads by terminal documentation,[2] still lies twitching under the crushing weight of England's post-Wagnerian composers. Its alarming potential may be explained by its being part of a wider attitude to the overall dominance of a cosmopolitan art-music heritage in Western civilization, which under certain historical conditions can become more of an encumbrance than a stimulus to indigenous culture—as it is to the United States, still embarrassed about its own music. (We have a similar diffidence in ourselves as *le pays sans cuisine*, and it is thriving on much the same social factors as did its musical equivalent 150 years ago.) Nevertheless, the attitude can be narrowed to England's 'two centuries of imitative negligibility' between the death of Purcell and the rise of the modern 'cohort of composers', as diagnosed by Bernard Shaw,[3] or to the nineteenth century in particular, when, faced with the dazzling impact of foreign genius from Mozart and Beethoven to Wagner, it was most prevalent.

Was England unmusical in the nineteenth century? And if so, in what ways? Emerson, in basing his pronouncement on the lack of 'a first-rate composer' and on the characteristic view of music as a marketable commodity, touched upon factors to which we shall return; elsewhere he commented on the inhibiting circumscriptions of etiquette:

11

A severe decorum rules the court and the cottage. When Thalberg the pianist was one evening performing before the Queen at Windsor, in a private party, the Queen accompanied him with her voice. The circumstance took air, and all England shuddered from sea to sea. The indecorum was never repeated. Cold, repressive manners prevail. No enthusiasm is permitted except at the opera.[4]

Etiquette was also infamous for permitting a young gentleman to grace a keyboard performance with a few 'accompaniments' upon the flute whilst forbidding him from playing a keyboard instrument himself—it was a maiden's prerogative— in society. Male keyboard virtuosos such as Thalberg and Liszt were idolized inasmuch as they brought an alien thrill to that society; to the ladies they possessed something of the erotic aura of the twentieth-century pop singer, whilst to the men appreciation of their pyrotechnics was about as passive and vicarious as is the modern middle-class husband's admiration for the professional footballer. Appreciation of Liszt's compositions was quite another matter: the critic Francis Hueffer claimed to be still almost alone, except for Walter Bache, Alexander Mackenzie, and the young Frederick Corder, in preaching their gospel after Liszt's death in the late 1880s.[5] Hueffer had also sadly to recall, in illustration of the notion of a technical grasp of music as not befitting a gentleman, how 'at the meeting convened for the discussion of the Royal College of Music, and graciously presided over by the Prince of Wales at St James's Palace, the speakers, including such men as Mr Gladstone, the late Lord Iddesleigh, Lord Rosebery, and the late Archbishop of Canterbury, almost without exception prefaced their remarks upon music by saying that they knew nothing whatever about music!'[6]—though here at least and at last was a musical institution being set up by the State, and liberally endowed to boot.[7]

But there are several factors to be extricated. One is the element of malicious glee with which examples such as the foregoing are multiplied, generally (and I do not claim exemption) devoid of context. How much more fragmentary a nationwide musical consciousness was in Britain than in other European countries is a more searching question. Another factor is that we measure the cultural diffusion of music in the last century against that of our own, and not surprisingly find differences. Ingredients which we have long taken for granted were not always present. The very sense of 'culture' as I have applied it above is an essentially modern—post-Enlightenment—concept.[8] Conventionalized concert life, a corpus of comparative critical and historical commentary, the availability of published copies of musical works, and even an established canon of 'classics' evolved slowly; but the fact that they were evolving at all during the nineteenth century was due to

12

changes in the whole fabric of society whose pressures on music must be sympathetically understood before any evaluations can be made. England was in the European van as first industrial nation, and music, less institutionalized than in France and spared the *Kapellmeister* drudgery which persisted in Germany and Austria throughout the nineteenth century, was mercilessly exposed to the demands of a competitive, brisk, hard-headed, rapidly developing commercial society, and there were musical slums as well as brick ones among the attendant evils. Moreover, it is hypocritical to expect the nineteenth century to have accorded music the exalted position which it holds in post-romantic society. If we find it impossible to understand why, for instance, decorous Victorians treated theatrical or operatic musicians as stars yet refused to regard them as socially acceptable, or why Delius's father, an intelligent, ex-German Bradford wool merchant, who enjoyed playing in amateur string quartets and fostered musical events for his community, should have disowned his son once he decided to make music his livelihood, it is because we have treated music as an absolute value rather than as a variable in the cultural equation. Substitute, as I have already done once, sport for music, imagine a modern intellectual's first reaction if his son were to announce his serious intention of becoming a professional footballer, and the syndrome begins to sound more familiar: in each case the aspirant would be damning himself to become the public's pampered puppet.

The position of music in nineteenth-century England was actually a good deal healthier than most people would expect. Quite apart from such flourishing institutions as the Italian opera, the provincial festival, and the amateur choral society, the concert life of the capital flourished throughout our period, and in the course of the century many of the growing industrial towns also attracted ambitious concert seasons.[9] The foundation of the Philharmonic Society in 1813 placed first-class orchestral music within the reach of the wealthier bourgeoisie as well as the aristocracy, and from 1835 onwards there was a rapid development of specialized concerts of the modern type, including the chamber concert and the solo recital.[10] Admittedly the forces of conservatism were profound, and remained so: most composers other than Beethoven, Mendelssohn and Gounod had to wait a long time for acceptance (and sometimes, as with Schumann, Liszt, Wagner and Strauss, even for a hearing), and the aristocracy's dogged and dilettantish delight in Handel and the late baroque repertory was represented by the Concert of Ancient Music, a series which 'by the early 1830s . . . was the laughing-stock of the press',[11] but which lingered on

13

in semi-demise until 1848. Admittedly, too, there was slight encouragement of 'native talent' as far as instrumental music was concerned. The 'British Concerts' of 1823 lasted only one season; the Society of British Musicians, founded in 1834 and providing at least a proving-ground for many young composers, attracted very little notice or prestige; the New Philharmonic Society, founded in 1852, soon ran into financial difficulties. But despite all this, a valuable recent study[12] has shown that before 1850 concert life in London was more comprehensive and in some senses more advanced than that of Paris or Vienna. Even if, between the decline of the tradition of gentlemanly amateur participation and the rise of bourgeois professionalism, there is seen a dangerous hiatus into which Mendelssohn was easily pushed and where Spohr already frolicked, it was soon offset by the terrific explosion of musical events—including the performance of British works—in London in the 1830s and 1840s. But still Britain was producing no 'first-rate composer'. Why?

Although the question may be unanswerable, it will certainly be helpful to examine the very distinctive role played by art music in nineteenth-century Britain.

Music as the Handmaid of Society

The social history of English music provides a fascinating and stimulating study, particularly in the nineteenth century. To the great industrial society, with education and improvement as key-words, music could be of crucial assistance. John Turner, whose *Manual of Instruction in Vocal Music* had appeared in 1833, 'was prepared to maintain that a more general diffusion of vocal music among the industrial population of these islands would "contribute largely to the rooting out of dissolute and debasing habits"',[13] and this Platonic view of music's function was echoed again and again. Emphasis on the moral element in music was nearly always in the specific context of singing (Fuller Maitland notes that as late as the beginning of the twentieth century there was, 'among the poor', a semantic distinction, as found earlier in Jane Austen, between 'music'—instrumental music—and 'singing'),[14] for the words, consisting either of psalmody or oratorio or specially-written ditties for teaching, were to be of an uplifting and strengthening character. Participation in musical activities would also give bored villagers an alternative to the pub.[15] Thus a good deal of the art-music diet of Victorian consumer society can be accounted for by observing not what the leisured classes themselves liked—when they had musical tastes—but what they wished the working men to imbibe: partsongs, cantatas and, above all, oratorios were composed, performed and published (primarily by J. A. Novello, whose cheap octavo editions appeared from 1846) in this light; later on the brass band and music festival movements added further vast repertories. Organ arrangements of symphonic works had much the same ends in view. Even in Parry's choral settings of Milton (and of himself) and solo settings of the classics of English sixteenth- and seventeenth-century poetry, there is a strong residual air of the synonymity of moral and cultural purpose. The breadth of musical experience inevitably suffered as a result. Matthew Arnold, when in *Culture and Anarchy* he pointed out that 'plenty of people will try to give the masses, as they call them, an intellectual food prepared and adapted in the way they think proper for the actual condition of the masses',[16] saw the foolishness of drawing art down to the level of the man-in-the-street rather than drawing him up to its level; but Reginald Nettel was more sympathetic to the utilitarian view of art, for he had seen its not unfruitful consequences in his own background:

The history of music in the Potteries is the history of a commercial society in the throes of an artistic urge. Their minds were by reason of circumstance denied the conception of pure art held by a Shelley or a Beethoven, but it was possible for them to attain the 18th-century conception of art, the art of Wedgwood, Handel, Bach, or Dr Samuel Johnson. Indeed, the Wedgwood tradition had never been allowed to die in the Staffordshire Potteries.[17]

Stanford, Parry, Coleridge-Taylor, Elgar, and Vaughan Williams all ministered to the art of Wedgwood.

The position of music in leisured society was more complex, because slowly shifting. Between the aristocracy and the aspiring middle classes there was, at the beginning of the century, a fairly rigid division of taste and accomplishment.[18] In general, the aristocracy, to whom social appearance at an event was of more significance than the music, espoused Italian opera and, in the Concert of Ancient Music, the works of composers twenty years dead. The Three Choirs Festival and seasons at Bath and Brighton, as well as London, were patronized. Gentlemen performed as amateurs. The middle classes were either professional musicians, such as constituted the Philharmonic Society, or non-participating, more or less affluent bourgeoisie. They cultivated English opera and, increasingly as the century progressed, the Viennese classics of Haydn, Mozart, and Beethoven and contemporary works of Spohr and Mendelssohn. Only Handel—or at least the *Messiah*—was a universal phenomenon, cherished by both sides (as well

15

as being a working-class bastion). But by 1850 the division had largely dissolved. This was partly due to the decline in the influence of the aristocracy.[19] More significant, however, was the continual upward aspiration of the *nouveau riche* bourgeoisie, gradually invading aristocratic cultural territory, especially once the adoption of the practice of reserving high-price seats at concerts, universal by 1840, allowed them to mingle with full financial credentials, until, well before the middle of the century, the two began to merge into an affluent élite. Lionel Trilling sees Palmerston, who, although 'an aristocrat and by heritage a Tory', had turned Whig in the struggle over the Reform Bill of 1832, supporting it to prevent a more drastic reform, as 'the very symbol of the new union' of financial interests.[20] Similarly, tastes for Italian opera and the German (and, to a lesser extent, French) art-music repertory were compatible by the middle of the century. Weber[21] makes a distinction, if not a very convincing one, between 'popular' and 'classical' concerts and their audiences, the former embracing the virtuosos—Paganini, Thalberg, and so on—Rossini, popular orchestral programmes and commercial ventures, the latter gravitating towards the Viennese classics and chamber music. But despite the continual creation of new 'taste publics'[22] caused by the kaleidoscopic shifting—always upwards—of middle-class sectors, there was little serious conflict of musical interests in the middle and later nineteenth century. Music's function as a social grace was to bring together and smooth over the differences in origin and outlook between the aristocracy and the middle classes, and, since the merger was still on a casual social foundation, the more casual and unresistant the music, the better. In a society that expected music to serve its ends and gratify its pleasures, the foreign composer with a colourful, eye-catching name was preferred to the Englishman with a potentially ear-catching contribution to make.

Romanticism and the Individual: The Two Worlds

Music, however, cannot live by social grace alone. One wonders how many Victorian concert-goers were aware that outside their narrow social orbit was a world of entirely different horizons, to which music ought rightly to belong: the world of tremendous intellectual developments, in which Britain was playing a key role. William Rutland's study of Thomas Hardy contains an enlightening introductory chapter, 'The Background to Hardy's Thought', outlining the considerable influence which major nineteenth-century writings exerted upon him:

the list includes Darwin's *Origin of Species* of 1859, the *Essays and Reviews* of 1860, J. S. Mill's *On Liberty*, which he knew almost by heart, Swinburne's *Poems and Ballads* (1866), his friend Leslie Stephen's agnostic writings, Comte, Schopenhauer, Strauss's *Das Leben Jesu*, Leopardi, and Fitzgerald's *Omar Khayyam* of 1859.[23] But how many English composers active in the nineteenth century knew of these? The 'intellectual aristocracy' of Darwin and Huxley[24] had no musical member until Vaughan Williams, Fuller Maitland, Barclay Squire, and R. O. Morris appeared. Conversely, most of the great minds and men of letters, including Wordsworth, Lamb, Tennyson, the Arnolds, father and son, and, as we have already seen, Gladstone, were unmusical. Ruskin's aesthetic pronouncements upon music[25] suggest only the vaguest metaphysical acquaintance with it. Brunel, despite marrying William Horsley's youngest daughter and hence presumably being personally well acquainted with Mendelssohn, seems to have cemented no musical accomplishments beyond a fondness for the opera.

Thus music, living a life below stairs in the social complex, had few, if any, points of contact with the intellectual and artistic turmoil of the other world. It was precisely in the smoothness and precocity of England's material development, avoiding revolution in the 1790s, 1830, and again in 1848, and consequent prosperity, that the cause of her music's impotence lay. If, instead of reflecting society or serving in it as professors and directors of institutions, more composers had had the vision and courage to wish to reform, sublimate, or fly in the face of it, England's musical history might have taken a different course, or at least have developed earlier. They would have had to steel themselves for conflict—they would have been alienated personalities, individuals pitted against the mass, perhaps individuals at war with themselves—but conflict was of the essence of romanticism, and even where conflict tore the romantic artist apart, art repeatedly managed to spring up in the ruins. The lives of Crotch, Sterndale Bennett, Mackenzie, and Stanford, however, lacked the confrontations of strong opposing forces that engender creative tension; so does their music. Romantic expression lay largely dormant in English music for the greater part of the century. John Barnett's *Lyric Illustrations of the Modern Poets*, a collection of twelve solo vocal works published in 1834, was a rare and courageous attempt to express poems by Byron, Shelley, and Wordsworth in music, which provoked a thoughtful review by Chorley in the *Athenaeum*,[26] but Barnett lacked the ability to match the two arts and in no way set an example that could be followed. Superficially romantic opera plots too can be discounted: the melodramatic paraphernalia of *Maritana* and *The Bohemian Girl* consists at best of second-hand

Byronisms, and at worst reads like an anthological parody of overworked devices. Byron's only fertile influence was on the Continent, whither Pierson, who had set several of his poems to music in his *Thoughts of Melody* as an undergraduate at Cambridge, was indeed to emigrate.[27]

It is extraordinary how late this crippling sterility of vision was diagnosed. It took a German, Robert Papperitz, a Leipzig teacher who knew Sullivan as a student, to explain it:

You Englishmen, who come here and show such promise, become utterly spoiled when you get back to commercial England. Compare Sullivan with Brahms. Of the two I think Sullivan had the greater natural musical talent; but Brahms will not write a note he doesn't think worthy of his gift . . . As for Sullivan, he settles in London, and writes and publishes things quite unworthy of his genius. He is petted by royalty, mixes in aristocratic circles, acquires expensive tastes which oblige him to prostitute his talents for money-making works. As a consequence, his modes of expression deteriorate, and England and the world are robbed of the fruit of his God-given gifts.[28]

—though Chorley, sadly with no literary success, had endeavoured to explore the legitimate points of opposition between the artist and society in a series of novels published somewhat earlier in the century. Bernard Shaw, in arguing brilliantly for a socialist interpretation of *The Ring*, recognized in Wagner's association with Mikhail Bakunin and the Dresden uprising of 1849 an ideological commitment which was to have astounding creative repercussions, but looked in vain (except in himself) for similar signs of awareness in the English musical intelligentsia:

Had Wagner been the mere musical epicure and political mugwump that the term 'artist' seems to suggest to so many critics and amateurs—that is, a creature in their own lazy likeness—he need have taken no more part in the political struggles of his day than Bishop took in the English Reform agitation of 1832, or Sterndale Bennett in the Chartist or Free Trade movements.[29]

—whereas Bax, to whom the essence of romanticism was to have one eye focussed on the unattainable, with the other surveyed Parry, Stanford, and Mackenzie and reluctantly dismissed them as 'all three solid reputable citizens and ratepayers of the United Kingdom, model husbands and fathers without a doubt, respected members of the most irreproachably Conservative clubs, . . . [who] in Yeats's phrase had "no strange friend". Of this I am sure.'[30] Bax himself had a number of 'strange friends', including several Irish poets and at least two mistresses. His music is similarly free from social restraint.

Early Romanticism and its Aftermath

There were, nevertheless, before the age of Bax and Shaw a number of isolated musical personalities in whom the visionary seeds of romanticism, though ultimately stifled, had been planted. They were all outsiders in one sense or another. One of them, Hugo Pierson, could only appease his creative conscience by self-imposed exile. His father having been an Oxford don and a royal chaplain, he suffered on the one hand parental disapproval at lowering himself to be a musician, and on the other the repeated slights of reviewers who sneered at his works as products of an aristocratic, amateurish incompetence: 'To those of his own class, above all his father, a musician was not a gentleman; to those in the profession, a gentleman was not a musician. In Germany [where he settled from 1839] he found no difficulty in being both.'[31] A restless, irritable creature who struck up an uneasy acquaintance with Mary Shelley and a *menage à trois* with the Burmeister-Lysers, a 'husband-and-wife literary team'[32] (whose female half he later married), in Dresden, he was the only Englishman other than Hatton to tune in to Goethe's *Faust*—and to the refractory Part II at that. His stature as a composer is not great, but at least one feels that he had something original to say, unlike so many of his English contemporaries (such as Sterndale Bennett) who stayed—or returned—home. Others, particularly the expatriate Irish, having developed a certain cosmopolitan fortitude, were prepared to suffer in London. Ireland in the early 1800s had declined from its eighteenth-century cultural heyday, and was not to point the way to a tenable British musical romanticism until the end of the Victorian era. Meanwhile, anyone attempting to create a livelihood 'within territories marked off for foreign occupation',[33] notably opera, was doomed to a degree of alienation, from which Balfe, Wallace, and Field all suffered.

Two Englishmen of importance were further alienated by temperamental instability. Mary Cowden-Clarke has given an intimate portrait of her father, Vincent Novello, in which she tells how all through his life he suffered severe fits of debilitating depression.[34] He was, moreover, the son of an immigrant (from Italy), a passionate lover of the theatre and idolizer of actresses, and, as a Roman Catholic, automatically cut off from a large sector of English society. His friendships with Keats, Shelley, Charles and Mary Lamb, Leigh Hunt, and Hazlitt might seem to weigh against this alienation, but for the fact that there was a strong breeze of the radical underworld in his literary circle; Leigh Hunt actually served two years' imprisonment for an editorial in *The Examiner* insulting the Prince Regent.[35] Vincent Novello's services

19

to the cause of Haydn and Mozart in England, to the publishing of old English music, and, through his sons and daughters, to English musical life in general, were great; the paradox of his own equivocal position in English society is typical. Of more significance as a composer was Samuel Wesley. He suffered lifelong eccentricities and periodic bouts of mental derangement sometimes attributed (though with little evidence) to his having fallen down a hole in 1787, and like Novello, though only for a time, he was a member of the Roman Catholic Church, for which he wrote some of his best music. He also took pains, from the first decade of the nineteenth century onwards (his edition of *The Well-Tempered Clavier* appeared from 1809), to propagate the music of Bach in England at a time when this implied insurrection against Handel (although Mendelssohn's influence was later to add a sentimental mystique to the movement). Wesley had no qualms about the degree of belligerence to be mustered in the waging of his battle against the musical establishment:

I look upon the State of Music in this country to be very similar to the State of the Roman Church when the flagrant Abuses and Enormities had arisen to such a Height as to *extort* a *Reformation*.

It is high Time that *some* Amendment should take place in the Republic of Musick, and I know of no engine equally powerful with the immortal and adamantine Pillars of Sebastian's Harmony. I really think that our constant and unremitted question to *all* who call themselves friends to excellence should be 'Who is on our side—who?'[36]

At least Wesley, with his satisfyingly bilateral appreciation of the issues of the Reformation and, judging from his terminology, of the American Constitution, was no 'mere musical epicure and political mugwump'.

In 1810 Samuel Wesley fathered an illegitimate son, Samuel Sebastian, who inherited his erratic temperament and brought to it a fiery creative and critical genius which the elder Samuel had lacked. Throughout his life S. S. Wesley was to be in conflict with his environment—that of a cathedral organist—because he possessed the restless vision of a social and musical reformer. A stormy succession of appointments at Hereford, Exeter, and Leeds led to his publication of *A Few Words on Cathedral Music and the Musical System of the Church, with a Plan of Reform* in 1849. Although by no means perfectly balanced, it is a critical document of the utmost importance in that its author had the courage to dream passionately of a musical environment in which the creative artist need no longer be either a servant or an outcast. The key to his discourse is integration: musicians should be integrated into a society that is prepared to pay Landseer a thousand guineas for draw-ing a horse; cathedral music should be integrated into an educational plan that already involves the working classes in choral appreciation. He advocates a salary of £500–£800 for the cathedral organist, to enable him to fulfil his duties exclusively: 'He should be prohibited from ever giving a single lesson of the popular kind . . . , and be compelled to devote himself exclusively to the high objects of his calling; and to enable him to do this, he should have awarded to him just enough to dispel anxiety in pecuniary affairs . . . . The artists pointed to are *bishops* of their calling—men consecrated by their genius.'[37] The reper-cussions spread beyond the Church:

Before our Palestrinas can find a home at Cathedrals, the difficulties of musical composition must be appreciated, and our artists allowed to rank with men of true eminence in other walks of life. . . . It seems scarcely becoming the generosity of a great nation, that the artist who expends his health, devotes his talents to the service of the public, should be consigned to poverty when no longer able to work for his daily bread.[38]

Wesley's achievement consists in having composed works worthy of a bishop of his calling amidst the disgraceful conditions against which he was inveighing.

This phase of militant romanticism in English music came to an abrupt end around 1850, in counterpoint with the stormy progress of Catholicism and its music.[39] The Oxford Movement of high-church regeneration, which Newman himself dated from July 1833, the date of Keble's Assize Sermon on 'National Apostasy',[40] was engendered partly in reaction to the doctrinal underminings of the Higher Critic-ism, and partly in a similar spirit of historical enquiry. Some of its protagonists remained within the Anglican fold; others, like Newman, went over to Rome. The presence of pockets of real or suspected 'popery' scattered throughout London and the provinces, coming in an era when Jacobins and Chartists were causing the establishment to assert itself with particular weight and energy, was capable of arousing witch-hunt hysteria. As late as the 1870s, Stainer was once accosted in the organ loft of St Paul's by an irate intruder who insinuated that he had obtained the post through being not a fine organist but a high churchman.[41] Music was, for once, at the forefront of political and social undercurrents.

For a few brief years the Oxford Movement was passionately con-cerned, as was no other, with helping the working man to develop a musical experience which would transcend his environment, rather than with feeding him material appropriate to it. However, bourgeois

21

conformity won the day. Political revolution had already been averted in 1848, and a description by Hogarth of the Philharmonic Society audience's behaviour at a concert on 11 April, the day after severe Chartist demonstrations in London, leaves no doubt as to its political bias, for it 'did not fail to express the loyal feeling of British subjects. At the end of the first part, "God Save the Queen" was performed by orchestra and chorus, and received with a degree of enthusiasm rarely witnessed. At the words, "Confound their politics!" the whole company burst into acclamations of triumph, accompanied with the waving of hats and handkerchiefs, which drowned the sound of the voices and instruments'.[42] And although the continuing anti-popery demonstrations, and especially the Pimlico riots, give evidence that the populace could hardly be made to feel at ease immediately, by 1851 Prince Albert was looming large in people's hearts as a symbol of security, and his Great Exhibition in Hyde Park was the dominant focus of public attention, though not undertaken without considerable fears of and precautions against demonstrations or worse. It marks the century's turning-point and the inception of mid-Victorian immovability. By 1855 Tennyson, in *Maud*, felt acutely the need for a war, and Wagner, infamous as a revolutionary theorist but little scrutinized as a composer or conductor, was given a tough time at the hands of the Philharmonic Society that year.

If the epigonic aristocracy at least possessed a genuine feeling for style, the new bourgeoisie, lying like a dead weight on English culture, could rise no higher than its caricature, fashion. Illustrations of some of the furniture and statuary from the Great Exhibition bear grotesque witness to this. So does the posthumous idolatry of Mendelssohn. Popular enough in England even during his lifetime, after his death in 1847 he fell prey to the middle classes' romanticized view of the artist. In 1853 the daughter of a clergyman of Jewish descent, Mrs E. S. Sheppard, published anonymously a best-selling three-volume novel entitled *Charles Auchester: A Memorial*, on which she had been working since the age of sixteen. She had sent the manuscript to Disraeli, who, forwarding it to his publisher, wrote back to her, 'No greater book will ever be written upon music'.[43] Despite fashioning herself, the narrator, as a pubescent boy, she is quite incapable of disguising from twentieth-century minds the sublimated erotic yearning towards the handsome, infallible hero Seraphael who is of course Mendelssohn, whom she sets up on an apotheosized pedestal, and in dealing with whose career and personality she allows her starry imagination the freest of play. Execrable as a novel, the work is valuable as a document of middle-class attitudes to art music. Unable to see anything admirable in music as a servant of commerce and entertainment—the theatre is spoken of with particular aversion—with a kind of false romanticism the muse is deified at the opposite pole, hermetically sealed from society and even from personality. Auchester's teacher scrutinizes him at length, with views explored elsewhere in conversation:

When thou hearest the folks prate about Art, be certain thou art never tempted to make friends there; for if they be wise in any other respect, they are fools in this, that they know not when to keep silence and how. For Art consists not in any of its representatives, and is of itself alone. To interpret it aright we must let it make its own way, and those who talk about it gainsay its true impressions, which alone remain in the bosom that is single and serene.[44]

Mendelssohn, through little fault of his own, sterilized British musical endeavour throughout the 1850s and 60s. The weak points in his music—a lack of dramatic confrontation, due to material too classical and continuity of mood and texture too baroque, and moments of sentimental religiosity—became the norm in England (even if occasionally—as in Sterndale Bennett's Chamber Trio, op. 26—the strengths as well as the weaknesses of his style show through). Whilst older composers like Macfarren, whose comic operas *Robin Hood* (1860) and *She Stoops to Conquer* (1863) combine a residual Italianate grace with genuinely English dramatic wit, remained high and dry above his influence (or at least, like S. S. Wesley, kept their heads above water), the young were awash. Sullivan's *Tempest* music (1861) and Parry's three early string quartets (1867–8) bear witness. However, Parry had read *Charles Auchester* in 1865 and, although it was fascinatingly influential, was perceptive enough to find it 'foolish and mistaken'.[45] With the help of Edward Dannreuther, his musical aspirations were before long to take a very different turn.

The Later Phase of Romanticism

For about thirty years after the middle of the century, the development of English musical romanticism was stunted by over-serious attention to the problems of the ever-expanding bourgeoisie. How were they to develop a wide culture, which needed to be ever widening as the franchise expanded after the second Reform Bill of 1867? In his inaugural lecture as Professor of Poetry at Oxford in 1857,[46] Matthew Arnold, whose original writings are the finest touchstone of this concern, recognized that the old order of the aristocracy, with its

23

stylishness and feeling for 'Hellenism' (the classical culture), was passing away; that his era was

> Wandering between two worlds, one dead,
> The other powerless to be born[47]

because the English middle class had not yet awakened 'from its intellectual sleep of two centuries';[48] it was in command of economic and, increasingly, political power, but was culturally crippled by its fatal surfeit of 'Hebraism', the Puritan legacy of narrowing moral zeal. It was motivated only by *ideas*, and an art adequate for those ideas was not yet in being. It was, in short, philistine, a term which quite rightly reminds us of Schumann—both Arnold and Schumann (and Dickens in *Our Mutual Friend*) were adopting, via Heine, a term of derogatory slang applied to anti-intellectual townspeople in German university circles. But whereas Schumann took the logical step of countering philistinism with his *Davidsbündler*, of pitting himself and his initiates against the mass, Arnold was incapable of such a radical stance, and so, between 1850 and 1880, was English music. Since the combat between classes, cultures, *ethos* and *pathos*, Apollo and Dionysus, criticism and imagination, was tending to be evaded in England, the forces of philistinism and creative inertia came into silent occupation. Pacifism produced no new synthesis of class and culture. Arnold's dream of a union of Hellenistic all-round awareness of 'the best that is known and thought in the world'[49] with bourgeois Hebraistic zeal became less, not more, realistic as the century wore on. Hellenism came to seem a vestigial legacy of the age of Goethe and Jefferson, and the hope of an integrated consciousness receded.

In George Eliot's novel *Daniel Deronda*, published in 1876 and set ten years earlier, music and society are as strongly opposed as ever. But the work marks a major step forward in perception in that there is now no question of music accommodating itself to society's demands. Eliot has encountered Wagner and Liszt: the artist, she now realizes, has an inner aristocracy of soul which will ever conflict with but need no longer be stifled by the pressures of the Establishment. The pianist Klesmer, founded not as has often been supposed on Liszt but on Anton Rubinstein (though Dannreuther, whom she got to know probably only after *Daniel Deronda* was written, also fits the role in many respects), is the embodiment of the liberated musician. Jewish, cosmopolitan, intellectual, domineering yet capable of great tenderness, he shows how music must begin to take itself seriously in England. The novel must have done much to help change attitudes, as here for the first time, and before an enormous reading public, the injustices which music had suffered at the hands of society were exposed with the compelling bite of irony. There is a scene of splendid confrontation[50] in which an obscure philistine politician, Mr Bult, who 'had no idea that his insensibility to counterpoint could ever be reckoned against him', unwittingly insults Klesmer by praising him for being more than 'a mere musician'. Klesmer's reply is blunt:

> No man has too much talent to be a musician. Most men have too little. A creative artist is no more a mere musician than a great statesman is a mere politician. We are not ingenious puppets, sir, who live in a box and look out on the world only when it is gaping for amusement. We help to rule the nations and make the age as much as any other public men. We count ourselves on level benches with legislators. And a man who speaks effectively through music is compelled to something more difficult than parliamentary eloquence.

Catherine Arrowpoint, daughter of the country household in which he is staying, is thus led to committed recognition of 'the wrath of the artist', and the two decide to marry. Catherine's mother is shocked, for 'while Klesmer was seen in the light of a patronized musician, his peculiarities were picturesque and acceptable; but to see him by a sudden flash in the light of her son-in-law gave her a burning sense of what the world would say'. Catherine is disinherited but does not care; the scene ends with Klesmer's utter worthiness in all but social standing being implied by a nicely ironic contrast:

> 'It's all very fine', said Mr Arrowpoint, when Catherine was gone; 'but what the deuce are we to do with the property?'
> 'There is Harry Brendall. He can take the name.'
> 'Harry Brendall will get through it all in no time', said Mr Arrowpoint, relighting his cigar.

But in *Daniel Deronda* another conflict is beginning to loom larger than class: the novel's 'problem' is the position of the Jews within English society. Towards the end of the century the idea of race was replacing that of class as a fixation and a cultural watershed, and in music as well as literature the timely airing of the Jewish consciousness was overlaid by one much more far-reaching: that of the Celt. Here again was an issue on which Arnold had been prophetic yet short-sighted. In 1867 he had published *On the Study of Celtic Literature*, elaborating on Ernest Renan's *The Poetry of the Celtic Races* of 1856; he also advocated a chair of Celtic literatures at Oxford. Interest in Celtic culture grew considerably during the second half of the century, its theological ramifications (as in the writings of John Rhys on the origins of Christianity in Britain) forming a sort of corollary to the Higher Criticism of the first half. Interest peaked with the founding of the

Pan-Celtic Society in 1899.[51] To Arnold, the Celt was a perfect foil to the fact-obsessed Anglo-Saxon philistine; yet he still hoped that Celtic qualities could be integrated into a creative and intellectual world of classical balance and light. It was not to be. Celtic and Norse literature, having been crucial in sparking off the romantic movement in the previous century with Ossian and Percy's *Reliques*, fulfilled the same function of stimulating the anti-classical imagination when Wagner, more than any other single figure, breathed new life into the movement with *The Ring* and *Tristan*, beside which Arnold's *Tristram and Iseult* paled. It was a naturalized German and pupil of Weber, Julius Benedict, who wrote the first successful English romantic opera on Celtic themes—*The Lily of Killarney* (1862), and it was not until the 1870s—long after Wagner's dark tones and powerful symbols had begun to revolutionize English and French literary sensibilities—that English composers began to appreciate the possibilities of an art rooted in native soil. Parry, like Arnold, was unable to relinquish his natural classicism, and despite an early devotion to Wagner preferred to adopt Prometheus as symbol in his attempt to set English music free. Hamish MacCunn, however, made considerable headway in the later 1880s as Wagner's most noteworthy British follower, with his choral ballads and overtures on Scottish themes, and when Elgar began to explore fresh, Northern subjects in *King Olaf, The Black Knight, The Banner of St George*, and *Caractacus*, and Gerontius eventually appeared bearing a curious similarity to both Parsifal and Amfortas, the late but vivid flowering of English musical romanticism was assured. That it was during the following forty years so often to view the Celtic fringes rather than the heart of England as its spiritual home, and a Celtic twilight as its natural colouring, is in part ironic, but consistent with the nature of the romantic movement in its earliest phases; the Celt had ever been a vibrant geographical symbol of the artist's independence and alienation.

To pursue the quintessential achievements of romanticism in English music would lead far into the twentieth century. The many Irish, Scottish, and Cornish works of Bax, the Arthur-Machen-inspired primaevalities of John Ireland, Warlock's Yeats song cycle *The Curlew*, the multitude of Housman and de la Mare settings, and on a more abstract level the later music of Elgar, the concertos of Walton, the elegiac works of Bridge and at least some of Vaughan Williams's symphonies all form a legitimate part of the romantic canon. However, the dividing line between romantic and modern is puzzling, and the ambience of, say, Holst is perhaps most profitably viewed from the latter standpoint.

Not until the end of the nineteenth century could England point to a native composer of a stature commensurate with the greatness of the first industrial nation. No amount of re-evaluation can amend the fact that Elgar was the first great English composer after Purcell. The situation was not without paradoxes. Musical eminence was regained precisely as political greatness was beginning to wane; the one sometimes appeared as a celebration of the other in the works of Elgar (notably the Cello Concerto and parts of the Second Symphony) and, rather tardily, in the Seventh Symphony of Bax. Furthermore, it was with the acceptance of the conflicts inherent in the composer's relationship to society that the doors to musical self-expression were opened, not with their reconciliation (which had by the end of the century proved illusory). These conflicts were still both a strength and weakness. The point is that they were now being allowed to germinate more freely; there was in effect an upsurge of integrity.

The question of class was, with the growth of mass communications, no longer such a burning cultural issue, but to the individual it could still be an acute problem lying behind his art. Both Parry and Elgar had to come to terms with, and make music out of, a divided pedigree. Parry's naturally liberal imagination was thwarted and all too often crushed, in his prose as in his compositions, by a sterile aristocratic lineage. Where the two interact, his music takes wing with an outsider's nostalgic recognition of loneliness, such as informs the more lyrical passages of *A Vision of Life* and his Sturgis songs 'Through the Ivory Gate' and 'Looking Backward'. Elgar suffered all his life from a double class allegiance: his father was a shopkeeper, and yet he felt naturally drawn towards the aristocracy into which he married. He probably only dimly understood the warring forces within himself, forces which perversely caused him to play off highly serious work against commercial banality, with a daemonic sense of frustration at their incompatibility. His most profound moments were when he accepted his alienation from society and even from his friends, in the 'Enigma' Variations, *The Dream of Gerontius* with its Roman Catholic vision of the soul *in extremis*, and above all *The Music Makers*, which explores the oracular isolation of the artist through Arthur O'Shaughnessy's ode:

> O men! it must ever be
> That we dwell, in our dreaming and singing,
> A little apart from ye.

But if Elgar and Parry managed to maintain some sort of poise between their conflicting tendencies and surroundings, others did not, and it is in this same late-Victorian and Edwardian period that the thin

27

line between pressurized creativity and collapse most often gave way. If the artist was struggling for economic survival yet unable to renounce his freedom by undertaking salaried employment or hack work, all classes, including the poor, were equally inimical to him. He was *déclassé*; he belonged nowhere. Gissing, 'born in exile' as he saw himself, has given us a terrifyingly real picture of this world in *New Grub Street*. Here bohemianism is not a romantic panacea but the living hell of a *fin-de-siècle* failure. Elgar had experienced it; Rutland Boughton (who closely resembled Gissing, [52] in that both flew in the face of reason and self-esteem by marrying sluts whom they had attempted to rescue from squalor, only to plunge them into a deeper mire), Josef Holbrooke, and even Granville Bantock and Havergal Brian were all to a greater or lesser extent similarly pathetic bohemian failures. For whereas in literature it was possible to make a living out of serious creative work, in music it most certainly was not. Bantock, Holst, Howells, and Stanford had to teach; Brian was a journalist; Ivor Gurney, in his few brief years of freedom, sponged off his friends and family, probably unaware that he was doing so; only Bridge and Walton were fortunate enough to find patrons. Bernard Shaw and Lord Howard de Walden rescued respectively Boughton and Holbrooke from starvation, but they were unable to breathe creative life into them. This was a hard lesson to learn: that the composer, although he had to do battle with society, did not always win. The battle was almost impossible to fight without mercenary support, and it is perhaps a sobering thought that nearly all the successful English composers active around the turn of the century or the first world war, including Parry, Vaughan Williams, Quilter, Balfour Gardiner, Bax, and Ireland, enjoyed such support in the form of a private income, however small.

So it was that Britain, in developing a modern industrial society without the revolutionary confrontations which most other countries experienced, bred an age—and one generation in particular, the mid-Victorian one—of composers who were content for music to remain subservient to society; that during this period even the most perceptive of minds (that of Arnold) hoped for the growth of a culture which would allow the hitherto conflicting viewpoints of the artist and society to coexist painlessly; but that such a culture came no closer as the century progressed, and only when English composers joined their romantic brethren in other countries and other arts in accepting the opposing forces and the inherent alienation as a source of creativity could artistic regeneration take place and England produce a 'first-rate composer'.

Chapter 2

MUSIC IN EDUCATION

BERNARR RAINBOW

The earnest optimism which led the Victorians to see their century as the age of progress, and the energetic determination which character-ized so many of their achievements, were equally present in their endeavours in the field of musical education. When the century began, no formal provision for musical tuition was made in the country's ancient universities; there was as yet no national conservatory; and in the neglected schools of the land the music lesson had still not regained the place in the curriculum which it had lost at the Reformation. During the next hundred years, shamed by the general educational progress of their continental neighbours, increasingly aware of their disgraceful reputation as an unmusical nation, and eventually per-suaded that musical talent was not after all the monopoly of foreigners, the people of Britain were prompted to create for themselves a national system of musical education.

The Universities

At Oxford, the William Heather Chair of Music was established in 1626. By the eighteenth century, however, the invariable practice was to appoint one of the college organists as professor, with debilitating results. Apart from playing at university ceremonies, the professor's only duties at a meagre and unchanging salary of £12 per annum were to compose choral odes marking particular occasions and to examine degree exercises.

Applicants for degrees in music until the middle of the nineteenth century were required only to submit as an exercise a choral work with orchestral accompaniment and undertake its public performance at their own expense. Acquaintance with the musical writings of Boethius nominally remained a statutory requirement, but candidates underwent

29

no written examination. They received no test of general education, and were not required to reside in a college or to observe the university terms which applied to candidates for degrees in other faculties. Given such circumstances, the lack of esteem accorded to music as an academic discipline within the university becomes more understandable. It was demonstrated by an embargo, still operating in the 1830s, which excluded doctors of music from the 'sacred scarlet semicircle' of doctors within the Sheldonian Theatre at Commemoration.[1]

The first to attempt to improve music's status at Oxford was William Crotch, who was elected professor in 1797, when he was only 22. In the following year he inaugurated a popular series of lectures on music, illustrated by the Music Room Orchestra and his own performance at the piano.[2] Crotch explained that he had made his principal object 'an endeavour to raise the taste'.[3] In 1804, he was invited to lecture at the Royal Institution in London; and deciding that his future now lay in the metropolis, he resigned all his Oxford appointments, except the professorship, and moved to London in the following year, returning to Oxford only when professorial duty demanded his attendance.[4]

Crotch's resignation as organist of Christ Church in 1805 at last broke the tradition linking the professorship with college organ lofts. In 1848 he was succeeded as professor by Henry Bishop, whose career had been centred in London as a composer of theatre music. Bishop regarded his new appointment as a sinecure, its annual salary well earned by his 'appearing only at Commemoration to play the ramshackle old organ'.[5] He gave no lectures and made no attempt to enhance the musical life of the university. During his professorship the Music School at Oxford was 'used as the museum of the Oxford Architectural Society'.[6]

A number of circumstances combined to make Frederick Ouseley's appointment to the chair in 1855 propitious. In addition to his doctorate in music, Ouseley already held the Oxford degree of M.A. and was a member of convocation. Moreover, as a former gentleman commoner well known for his musical prowess and a baronet who was also now a priest in the Church of England, he commanded the respect of university magnates and was thus able to obtain support for reforms hitherto unattainable.[7]

Within a few months the music faculty was substantially reorganized. As a first step, and under a revised statute, a *viva voce* examination was introduced for all degree candidates. This was replaced in 1862 by a written examination. Finally, in 1870, examinations by three external examiners were introduced involving harmony and counterpoint, fugue, canon, formal analysis, and musical history, in addition to the submission of exercises as before. Candidates were soon aware that Ouseley's 'wide store of musical reading, coupled with his wonderful memory' enabled him to detect cribbed exercises of a kind that might perhaps have eluded his predecessors.[8]

Although not himself in residence, and committed by the new regulations to lecturing only once a term, at his death in 1889 Ouseley was acknowledged to have transformed the musical scene at Oxford.[9] His successors were able to build upon that foundation. John Stainer's appointment in 1889 was followed by a vigorous attempt to modify the effects of Ouseley's conservatism, by the provision of more detailed guidance for external students working for degrees, and by unsuccessful attempts to introduce residential courses in music. The latter goal was not, however, reached until 1911, by which time Stainer had been succeeded first by the dynamic Hubert Parry (1900) and then by Walter Parratt (1908).[10] In his inaugural lecture, Parratt paid tribute to Ouseley's achievement in establishing degree examinations which had 'needed but little alteration at the hands of his successors'.[11] The general pattern of the degree syllabuses introduced at Oxford under Ouseley was in fact to dominate the musical examination system—and later the teaching—of British universities generally until the middle of the present century.

The situation at Cambridge during the period under review was roughly similar. The chair of music was founded in 1668, and in the eighteenth century had generally been occupied by college organists; the position carried no salary. Charles Hague (professor 1799–1821) was a local violinist, composer, concert promoter, and bookseller. John Clarke-Whitfeld, his successor, was a distinguished composer, but he did not reside at Cambridge and treated the chair as a sinecure.

The turning point for music at Cambridge was the appointment of Thomas Attwood Walmisley as professor in 1836. His contribution to the university's musical life was outstanding. Sympathetic, genial, and a fine organist,[12] in general education and culture he was far in advance of most English musicians of the day.[13] During his latter years he discharged all the principal musical duties of the university, playing as many as eight services each Sunday in the three principal college chapels and at the University Church. Additionally, his choral and orchestral activities and the illustrated lectures which he undertook voluntarily all attracted loyal support. In 1850 Walmisley was able to write: 'Music is not cultivated to any great extent by members of the University, but I believe that a taste for the art is rapidly increasing among us.'[14] Upon his death in 1856, with no natural successor at hand

31

at Cambridge, William Sterndale Bennett was elected to the chair following an open poll of the Senate.[15]

Bennett's appointment came a year after Ouseley's at Oxford. A national figure with an established continental reputation as pianist and composer, he pressed for the further examination of candidates presenting degree exercises. The degrees conferred at Cambridge, he maintained, 'should be equal in reputation to those of the sister university'.[16] A system of examination akin to that adopted at Oxford was then introduced. In 1875, during George Macfarren's succeeding professorship, an attempt to introduce residential tuition for degree candidates was unsuccessful; but residence was made compulsory at Cambridge under the revitalizing influence of Charles Stanford, professor from 1887 to 1924.[17]

In Ireland, the chair of music at Trinity College, Dublin, was first occupied by the Earl of Mornington between 1764 and 1774, after which it lapsed. The chair was next filled in 1845, and passed in 1861 to Robert Prescott Stewart, organist of Christ Church Cathedral and Trinity College, Dublin, and conductor of the University Choral Society since 1846. A man of wide culture as well as an accomplished musician, Stewart gave 'excellent lectures' which marked the beginning of important reforms.[18] A new regulation in 1871 required candidates for degrees in music to pass a preliminary examination in elementary classics and mathematics. (A similar regulation was made only in 1877 at both Oxford and Cambridge.)[19] Also at Stewart's instigation, from 1871 Dublin introduced a regular course of undergraduate instruction in music.[20] He was succeeded by Ebenezer Prout (1894) and Percy Buck (1910).

At his death in 1807, General John Reid had left funds for endowing a chair of music at the University of Edinburgh, coupled with the foundation of an annual concert in his memory. From the annual revenue of the bequest, sums were available to provide a minimal annual salary of £300 for the professor with additional amounts for an assistant, toward 'class expenses' and to finance the annual concert.[21] John Thomson, the first professor, was an acquaintance of Mendelssohn and had studied at Leipzig. Although he was a salaried member of the academic staff of the university, his short term in office (1839–41), like those of his two immediate successors, was uneventful. John Donaldson's appointment in 1845 heralded a strenuous attempt to achieve better conditions. A music lecture room equipped with an organ and 'some excellent acoustical apparatus' was fitted up,[22] and Donaldson organized well-attended voluntary lectures and choral rehearsals.[23] There was as yet no music faculty as such. Under his successor, Herbert

Oakeley, the Reid Concerts, hitherto comprising largely ballads and operatic excerpts, were developed as regular symphony concerts,[24] and in 1890 the Senate was eventually persuaded to accept a proposal for a faculty of music with a full curriculum and degrees.[25]

Account must also be taken of the growth of university education itself. Between 1800 and 1914 more than a dozen British universities were founded. Not all of them, however, established chairs, gave tuition, or conferred degrees in music during that period.

London University received its charter in 1837; but disagreement over the feasibility of matriculation for music candidates delayed the establishment of music degrees until 1876, when the organization of their syllabuses was placed in the hands of William Pole—the professor of *Engineering*. A Fellow of the Royal Society, Pole was also a doctor of music; yet his appointment shows the university's anxiety over music's intellectual respectability. The study of acoustics was consequently made prominent in syllabuses otherwise similar to those of Oxford and Cambridge. Stainer was called in to assist as external examiner. London had no professor of music until 1902, when Frederick Bridge, organist of Westminster Abbey, was appointed.[26] His role, like that of his successors until the middle of the present century, was confined to examining external degree candidates, whose instruction was often undertaken at a London conservatory.

A music faculty and residential degree were instituted at Manchester in 1891.[27] At Durham a chair in music was established in 1897, but the degree was and remained 'external'.[28]

At the University of Birmingham a chair of music was endowed in 1905 on condition that it should be first awarded to Sir Edward Elgar. Elgar held the professorship, however, only for three uneventful years: he was succeeded by Granville Bantock (1908–33). Under Bantock a 'regular system of training' was introduced in conjunction with the Birmingham and Midland Institute School of Music, of which he had been principal since 1900.[29] At Queen's College, Belfast (1845), a lectureship in music was created in 1902 allowing music to be taken as part of the course for the B.A. degree. Similar provision was made from 1908 at University College, Reading.[30] At Aberystwyth, Joseph Parry had been active as a lecturer from 1871 to 1880 (and at Cardiff after 1888), but a regular course of instruction at degree level was not established until the School of Music at Aberystwyth was endowed in 1914.

As one looks back on the period as a whole, a number of issues combine to form an overall pattern of advance. During the eighteenth century, musical activity in British universities was largely limited to the public performance of degree exercises, ceremonial odes, and the regular service music of particular college chapels. Later professors and lecturers were to build upon that slender foundation by encouraging the growth of university music societies and performing groups. In such ways the general musical tone of the university as a whole was first fostered.

But music long failed to gain respect in university circles because it was considered unworthy of the serious attention of a gentleman. Crotch's innovatory lectures, later to be imitated in other universities, were addressed to general audiences with a view to removing such prejudices. Not until men of wider culture, such as Crotch and Walmisley, occupied chairs of music was reform feasible. With the appearance of the socially impeccable Ouseley and the internationally esteemed Sterndale Bennett it was attained. And under the vigorous championship of Parry and Stanford, the acknowledged leaders of a national musical renaissance, opposition was eventually disarmed. Although the shadow of the organ loft—perpetuated in Ouseley's enduring syllabuses—lay heavily across university music throughout the period under review, successive professors introduced less rigid attitudes toward the treatment of harmony or counterpoint, and the study of musical history was revolutionized between the days of Crotch and Parry.*

All these developments took place against a background of general change brought about by two royal commissions appointed in 1858 and 1878 to investigate university affairs. The range of studies was consequently broadened; written examinations commonly replaced empty *viva voce* encounters; the professoriate was increased and became largely residential; fellowships were awarded on merit; women students were admitted and religious tests abolished. The nineteenth century marked a turning point in the history of British universities. Music was eventually able to share in the increased facilities for higher education which resulted.

The Conservatories

The prototype conservatory, and the origin of the term itself, is to be found in the Neapolitan *conservatorio*, an institution for the shelter and instruction of orphans and abandoned children. The most ancient, Santa Maria di Loreto, was founded in Naples in 1535, followed by

*As late as 1943, Jack Westrup, a future professor of music at Oxford, was to write, 'Music in universities has in the past been too closely linked with the organ loft' (W. Shaw, ME, 60).

three similar establishments there before 1590. In each of them, the boy inmates received musical training to equip them to earn a livelihood, tradition linking the practice with the school of music founded at Naples by Tinctoris in the fifteenth century. Four similarly ancient orphanages for girls existed in Venice under the general name of *ospedali*, thorough training in music again being provided.

The first European country outside Italy to found a national music school was France, where the Conservatoire national de musique was established in 1793 as part of the aftermath of the French Revolution. Following that example, other conservatories were formed in Prague (1811), Brussels (1813), and Vienna (1817). In Britain the indifference of government and the antipathy of industry and commerce combined to delay the endowment of a similar institution. An impediment almost as substantial was the active opposition of professional musicians themselves. Obliged to rely upon teaching for much of their livelihood, individual musicians were not disposed to welcome the establishment of a central school.

A case in point was the academy for piano pupils opened in London in 1817 by Johann Bernhard Logier. Under the name 'chiroplast', Logier had patented a system using brass supports and finger guides to control the position of the hands of beginners at the keyboard. A chart below the music desk of the piano indicated the name and written symbol for each note on the keyboard. Thus equipped, groups of pupils at separate pianos then worked together from Logier's *Companion to the Royal Chiroplast*, a pioneer collection of graduated studies designed to be played simultaneously by pupils at various levels of attainment.[31]

Despite his unorthodoxy, Logier was no mere charlatan; all his pupils were well grounded in harmony and thorough-bass.[32] The hostile criticism and abusive pamphlets regularly levelled against his academy in fact voiced the conviction of professional musicians that his activities threatened their own livelihood. For the same reason, a formal proposal by Thomas Forbes Walmisley to found a national conservatory in association with the Philharmonic Society soon after the society's formation in 1813 was also rejected.[33] The intervention of independent authority was required before this defensive reaction could be overcome.

Eventually, in 1822, the necessary initiative was taken by a member of the aristocracy, Lord Burghersh—himself an amateur musician and the composer of several operas and choral works—who gathered the support of other aristocratic music lovers and announced a fund for the endowment of a Royal Academy of Music in London. George IV was persuaded to act as patron. The institution was to provide free residential accommodation and training for forty male and forty female students. When public subscription proved insufficient to finance so ambitious a scheme, an unpretentious house was leased in Tenterden Street, Hanover Square, to accommodate only ten students of each sex paying ten guineas toward their board and lodging. A 'most severe' examination was held to select the first entry, one further student being admitted at the patron's choice as 'King's scholar'.[34]

The Royal Academy was opened on 24 March 1823, under Dr William Crotch, already professor of music at Oxford. Most of his staff of eighteen were foreign musicians working in London. Formal regulations laid down the course of study:

The first object in the education of the students will consist in a strict attention to their religious and moral instruction. Next, the study of their own and the Italian language, writing, and arithmetic, and their general instruction in the various branches of music, particularly in the art of singing, and in the study of pianoforte and organ, of harmony and composition.[35]

As all the pupils were between the ages of ten and fourteen in those early days, their general education was undertaken by the institution. Boys and girls followed separate timetables, the boys beginning their day with prayers at 6.30 a.m., followed by the girls at 7.00 a.m. The whole day was divided into hourly periods each devoted to lessons, rehearsals or practice, with breaks only for breakfast, midday dinner, and supper. Four sessions of 'scholastic instruction' were included, the day ending with prayers at 9.00 p.m. The sexes were carefully segregated throughout. The earliest timetables reveal the following range of musical subjects: harmony and composition, singing and sight-singing, piano, violin, cello, oboe, clarinet, horn, trumpet, harp—the last of these, with dancing and (strangely) piano tuning, being prescribed only for the girls.[36] As further students were enrolled, this range was increased and the timetable made more realistic.

All instrumental practice then was undertaken communally under the supervision of an usher or monitor, several students practising in the same room simultaneously. The first annual report of the organizing committee defended this policy on the grounds that 'in all the conservatoires of Italy, from which the most able professors have sprung, this is the usual custom'.[37] Dr Burney's earlier account of the Italian conservatori confirms that claim;[38] and William Gardiner was thus to describe the scene at the Royal Academy in the early 1830s:

In a large apartment were near twenty pupils, strumming on as many pianofortes, producing an incessant jingle. In the singing room they were solfaing in every kind of voice. Such a Babel I never wish to hear again. We then visited the violin department, the horrid scraping of which I could not endure. The horns were in a double closet, the oboes and flutes in the garret, and the trumpets in a cockloft under the skylight. In a small out-office in the yard the drummer was at work, and near him the trombone . . . On the cellar-steps [another youth was] pumping away on his bassoon with all his might in the dark.[39]

The early years of the Academy were marred by tentative organization and financial difficulty. To bolster the inadequate income from donations, less able fee-paying, non-residential students were soon of necessity admitted. A petition to the government for a supporting grant was for long unsuccessful, the institution being nursed along by sundry fund-raising enterprises and by regularly increasing student fees. On more than one occasion the professors waived part or all of their salaries to save it. Meanwhile, under Crotch's genial but undynamic lead, the young students' progress depended largely upon the individual ability of a few teachers.[40]

In 1832 Crotch was succeeded as principal and teacher of composition by Cipriani Potter. Hitherto a distinguished teacher of piano at the Academy, and the conductor of the student orchestra, Potter was to exert beneficial influence upon a new generation of British musicians. His teacher, Joseph Woelfl, not only made Potter an accomplished pianist but also equipped him with an understanding of symphonic structure and orchestration which placed him far ahead of his contemporaries in Britain. Those attainments were to shape his teaching at the Academy, where he established a new school of pianism and became the first influential teacher in this country to elucidate the principles of orchestration, symphonic analysis, and extended composition.[41] One of Potter's pupils who eventually succeeded him as principal of the Royal Academy, George Macfarren, declared that Potter accomplished more than any man of his day for the advancement of music in England.[42]

With the death of Burghersh (by then Earl of Westmorland) and the retirement of Potter in 1859, Charles Lucas became principal and the Academy entered a new phase of its precarious existence. Most of the original circle of aristocratic supporters had now died or lost interest in the institution. In the cause of economy, residence and general education were no longer provided and student numbers had fallen seriously. At length, early in 1865 an independent committee of the Society of Arts met to enquire into the state of musical education at home and abroad.[43] With the flourishing state of continental conservatories revealed, the future of the ailing Royal Academy was debated at length, many of the committee believing it moribund. Proposals to reorganize and move the institution to new premises in the basement of Burlington House, or alongside the School of Design at South Kensington, were seriously discussed.

While debate continued, Lucas resigned his principalship and the post passed to Sterndale Bennett, then professor of music at Cambridge. The crisis at the Academy was to continue for the next seven years; but Bennett insisted that no move take place, and from 1869 student recruitment steadily improved and the institution's future became more secure.[44] Meanwhile a growing demand was evidenced by the emergence of various independent music schools in London. The London Academy of Music (1861), the National College of Music (1864), the London Organ School (1865), and the College of Church Music (1872)—later to become Trinity College of Music—were among these.[45] But the greatest challenge to the Royal Academy came with the establishment of the National Training School for Music, in 1876.[46]

As early as 1854 the Prince Consort had been interested in the foundation of a new music college in London. The Society of Arts had always supported the proposal; and something of this situation can be detected in the Society's dealings with the Academy after 1865. When the Academy refused to accept reorganization, the project to found a new college at South Kensington was formally adopted in 1873.[47] It was housed in a new building flanking the Albert Hall (now the Royal College of Organists). Eighty-two free scholarships were provided. Arthur Sullivan was with difficulty persuaded to act as principal with a board of eminent professors.[48]

The school opened in 1876, its premises rent-free and its scholarships endowed only for the next five years. By that time, it was believed, the Academy would agree to merge with the flourishing new conservatory. But that aspiration was disappointed in 1878 when Macfarren, Bennett's successor as principal, refused to relinquish the Academy's charter.[49] Immediately the future of the National School was itself placed in jeopardy; and new plans were formed to replace it with a more permanently endowed Royal College of Music distinguished by the presidency of the Prince of Wales.

Unlike the National Training School, the Royal College of Music was to accept fee-paying students from the outset.[50] Its organization and the fund-raising campaign necessary to ensure permanence for the new institution were placed in the hands of George Grove, a brilliant and versatile man whose earlier career in civil engineering had been followed by the secretaryship of the Crystal Palace, and who was at that time also engaged upon the compilation of the great *Dictionary of Music and Musicians* which bears his name.[51]

In 1883, the Royal College was opened with Grove as its first director and fifty maintained scholars, besides exhibitioners and fee-paying students not less than nine years of age. The original prospectus announced the following range of studies: harmony, counterpoint and composition, organ, piano, harp, strings, wind instruments, and singing. From among these, pupils compulsorily chose one principal and one subsidiary subject, also attending weekly choral, orchestral, and chamber music classes, harmony and sight-singing classes, and lectures on musical history and the construction of instruments. Accommodation for scholars with maintenance grants was provided in some twelve boarding houses.[52]

The opening of the Royal College was marked by a royal gesture of reconciliation between the two national conservatories, Grove and Macfarren both receiving knighthoods.[53] The two institutions have preserved their independence and a healthy rivalry to this day; and under Mackenzie's principalship from 1887, the Academy's curriculum and management were reorganized along more modern lines.[54]

By that time, in contrast to the earlier period at the Academy, when an embargo placed upon Alfred Day's unorthodox system of teaching harmony[55] had led to George Macfarren's resignation from the staff,[56] independent initiative was less frowned upon. Oscar Beringer at the College and Franklin Taylor at the Academy each taught a new, dynamic style of pianism based upon powerful finger action. Later teachers were to rely instead on physiological study of the entire muscular frame—an approach eventually refined by Tobias Matthay at the Academy. The techniques of string playing were similarly analysed, to produce sundry individual 'methods'; and the teaching of singing was to be systematically reformed after the introduction of the laryngoscope under Manuel Garcia in 1855.

New purpose-built premises were provided for the College in 1886 and for the Academy in 1911. Before the century ended, local conservatories were established in the provinces, including those at Birmingham (1886), Glasgow (1890), and Manchester (1893). Also founded at this time were the Military School of Music at Kneller Hall (1857), the Royal Normal College and Academy of Music for the Blind (1873) and the College (later Royal College) of Organists (1864), the last of these being only an examining body.

Music in General Education

The revival of music teaching in schools was a consequence of the reform of popular education as a whole. From 1800 onward, as the lessons of the French Revolution were learned and the work of Pestalozzi and other continental educationists became more widely known, the countries of northwestern Europe began to develop a sense of responsibility toward the education of their children.

Such old-established schools as existed in Britain early in the nineteenth century had been neglected and largely inefficient during the past hundred years. Besides the ancient 'public' schools and endowed grammar schools there were also the charity schools, most of them founded during the reign of Queen Anne; the local elementary schools maintained by the churches; the Sunday schools first introduced by Robert Raikes in 1780; and countless dame schools run by elderly women for infants. In all of these the lesson programme was extremely narrow, and the quality of teaching depended solely upon chance. Of the children of the labouring classes, meanwhile, more were put out to earn wages than attended any of these schools. A few pioneering private schools on Pestalozzian lines had only insignificant effects on this general situation.[57]

Compared with her continental neighbours, Britain was slow to accept state responsibility for education. The first government grant toward popular education was not made until 1833. Six years later a special committee of the Privy Council was appointed to supervise its administration. Largely through the zealous guidance of its secretary, Dr J. P. Kay (later Sir James Kay-Shuttleworth), a policy of reform and development was put into operation involving the widening of the school curriculum and the training of a new generation of teachers.

It was through the activities of this committee that the music lesson was at length formally admitted to the schools of Britain.[58] The arguments presented at the time in support of music as an element in general education now appear less than compelling; but they were highly relevant to existing social circumstances and thence became sufficient to persuade contemporary authority. Foremost among those arguments, and emphasized by recurrent criticism, was the need to improve congregational singing in the nation's churches. Then, it was claimed, a nation which had learned to sing would have discovered a means of cheering and stimulating domestic life, so providing an alternative attraction to the beerhouse and promoting the contentment of the artisan. Popular song, Kay declared, thus became 'an important means of forming an industrious, brave, loyal and religious people'.[59]

40

Such arguments, while they relied more upon the edifying nature of the song texts to be employed than upon music itself, became more persuasive at a time of growing Chartist unrest and the birth of the temperance movement.

For the means of bringing about the desired transformation, Kay turned to the method devised by Guillaume Wilhem for use in the *commune* schools of Paris and the public singing classes then flourishing there. Wilhem's system, specially adapted for English use by John Hullah, was first introduced in 1840 at the new teacher-training institution founded by Kay at Battersea. A year later it was also employed in a series of massed singing classes opened with government approval for practising teachers and run by Hullah in London's Exeter Hall. Although inexperienced as a teacher, Hullah possessed natural aptitude in that direction and his early classes quickly became highly successful.

A year later, it was announced, at least fifty thousand children of the working classes in London had begun to receive instruction in music at school from Hullah's pupils.[60] As the movement grew and further trained pupils took up teaching appointments in provincial towns and the surrounding countryside, singing classes for both children and adults became nationwide; and the seeds were set for that remarkable nineteenth-century phenomenon, the amateur choral society.* The resulting improvement in the status of music-making in public estimation was to provide support for the continuance of singing lessons in the nation's schools.

On the other hand, as a contemporary critic pointed out,[61] because of inadequacies in the imported method of teaching adopted, many of Hullah's adult pupils and most of the children concerned never passed beyond the earliest stages in learning to read from notes. The Hullah–Wilhem system depended upon the use of 'continental' solfa in which the syllables, *do, re, mi, fa, sol, la,* and *si,* were permanently related to the key of C major. Alphabetical note-names were not employed at all—C was always *do*, D was *re*, and so on. Because of this policy, when keys other than C were introduced, the solfa syllables ceased to convey a clear sense of note-relationship; and only those pupils whose natural talent and determination were sufficient to enable them to overcome the difficulties inherent in the use of 'fixed' solfa were able to proceed confidently.

During the next twenty years teachers in schools grew increasingly disenchanted with this method, turning in growing numbers to a

*The rival singing classes established by Joseph Mainzer in London, Edinburgh, and Manchester also contributed to this end, as did the later growth of the tonic solfa movement.

different system devised by a Congregationalist minister, John Curwen, which employed tonic-based or 'movable-*do*' solfa.[62] As he was always anxious to acknowledge, Curwen's tonic solfa system had its origins in the teaching method evolved by Sarah Glover, the daughter of a Norwich parson.[63] He relied at first upon his publications and meetings of Sunday School teachers and philanthropic institutions to make the system more widely known. By 1860, tonic solfa had become sufficiently widespread to form a serious rival to the government-sponsored Hullah method, most teachers preferring to use it for their classes.[64] After the Education Act of 1870, which introduced compulsory schooling and established school boards to administer local, rather than national, educational policy, tonic solfa replaced the Hullah system as the accepted method of teaching singing in most of the new elementary schools.

The principal aim of the school music lesson continued to be learning to sing from notes. The musical value of what was sung at first received less attention. School songs in the mid-nineteenth century had their prototype in the 'moral songs' first made popular by W. E. Hickson's *Singing Master* (1836), a collection of secular melodies with improving texts compiled to provide a repertoire less daunting for young singers than unrelieved hymns. A great improvement was made by Stanford in a little collection of national songs drawn largely from William Chappell's *Popular Music of the Olden Time* (1850–9) and entitled *A Song Book for Schools* (1884). This was later developed into the *National Song Book* (1906) which enjoyed an immense circulation and became a classic collection for school use. Other school song books drew on newly revived folksongs, classical songs, or specially composed songs by British composers.

While all these developments were taking place in schools supported by the state, the situation in independent schools, including the ancient 'public' schools for the sons of the gentry, at first remained static. Lord Chesterfield's damning observation that music wasted a man's time and took him into odd company—itself an unacknowledged quotation from John Locke—seems to have made an indelible impression upon the upper classes in Britain.[65] Although several schools, including Eton and Winchester, invited Hullah to demonstrate his method in the 1840s, music lessons were first introduced at a new type of boarding school established as a result of the Oxford Movement.[66]

The new schools, notably those founded by Nathaniel Woodard, were planned around a school chapel where daily services were to be held. To make the chapel service accord with the dignity and solemnity so highly esteemed by Tractarians, music masters were promptly appointed, to act as organists and to train both a selected choir and the rest of the school to sing competently. The first example of this practice took place at Radley in 1847, to be followed at Lancing (1848), Hurtspierpoint (1849), Bradfield (1850), and later elsewhere.

That policy was not immediately adopted in existing public schools, where professional choirs sang the chapel service, as at Eton and Winchester, or where the school attended services at a neighbouring church, as at Harrow and Westminster. The first of the older public schools to appoint a music master was Uppingham.[67] Edward Thring, the headmaster at the time, was noted for his encouragement of the arts and crafts; and in 1865, perhaps at the suggestion of his German wife, he appointed Paul David, the son of a celebrated German violinist, to develop music in the school.

At Harrow, the boys themselves took the initiative in 1862 by engaging the services of John Farmer to teach the piano unofficially.[68] Soon afterwards Farmer began independently to organize informal house singing amongst the boys, composing for their use his famous Harrow School Songs, and thus starting a tradition which has become a permanent feature of life at the school. But Farmer was not recognized as a member of the staff at Harrow until some years later.

The example of Uppingham and Harrow was slowly followed elsewhere, important pioneer work also being undertaken by W. S. Bambridge at Marlborough (1864), A. E. Dyer at Cheltenham (1875), Joseph Barnby at Eton (1875), Louis Parker at Sherborne (1877), and E. Rendell at Dulwich (1887). Not the least achievement of these men was to persuade their respective headmasters that music should contribute to general education, and not be regarded merely as an 'extra' confined to private tuition.[69] Before the century ended, most public schools had established choirs and orchestras as well as developing their chapel music. These activities to some extent compensated for a general lack of more formal class music teaching there.

The situation in those girls' schools, founded after mid-century, which formed an approximate equivalent to the boys' public schools, was entirely different, because modest musical skill had always been considered a desirable accomplishment for young women in polite society. Indeed it was said in 1874: 'Music hardly comes within the scope of a boy's education, at least in this country; while it is almost compulsory on girls, whether they have the talent for it or not.'[70] After 1860, once a new pattern of education for girls had been established and demonstrated at Cheltenham Ladies' College and the North London School for Girls under the pioneer headmistresses, Miss Beale and Miss Buss, music found a ready place in it.[71] As further high schools for girls were established during the last decades of the nineteenth century, singing lessons and instrumental teaching alike formed natural parts of the curriculum. Particular attention was given to music in the schools of the Girls' Public Day School Trust. It was in one of these, Streatham Hill High School, that Stewart Macpherson became director of music early in the present century. Some of his first experimental teaching in the new field of 'musical appreciation' was undertaken there in conjunction with Mary Agnes Langdale, while Marie Salt invented and introduced the Percussion Band during his directorship. The formation of the Music Teachers' Association, an organization designed to develop and improve the teaching of music in and out of schools, in 1908, was also due to Macpherson's initiative.[72]

Any comparison between the musical situation in independent schools, on one hand, and state schools, on the other, will be misleading unless account is taken of certain fundamental differences in their circumstances. At the time in question, independent and endowed grammar schools alone provided secondary education. The school-leaving age in elementary schools was fixed at ten years in 1880, rising to eleven in 1893 and twelve in 1899. Only in 1918 was school attendance made compulsory between the ages of five and fourteen. The kind of musical activity developed in each of the two types of school was therefore inevitably influenced by the ages of the pupils concerned. Moreover, where music teachers were appointed in independent secondary schools (and they were seldom, if ever, to be found in grammar schools for boys at this time), they were generally specialists who had received their musical training at a college of music or a university. On the other hand, music in the elementary schools was taught by ordinary class teachers whose musical knowledge and skill were commonly limited to basic matters included in a general teacher-training course. For these reasons, elementary schoolchildren were taught only class singing and note-reading, while those in secondary schools were more frequently involved with non-classroom activities such as individual instrumental lessons and choral and orchestral rehearsals. Instrumental music was not introduced in elementary schools during the nineteenth century.

Eventually, indeed, many of the more ambitious musical activities first introduced in independent schools were to be taken up in schools supported by the state. A start was made in 1905 with the introduction of violin classes—a venture made possible by a London music firm which supplied instruments by hire-purchase at low rates, and organized classes in elementary schools throughout the country. By 1910 a massed 'orchestra' numbering several thousand elementary schoolchildren playing violins was able to perform impressively at the Crystal Palace.[73]

If improvement in musical education was slow, it was well on the way in 1881, when a writer was able to refer to 'the efforts which are being made in this latter half of the nineteenth century to redeem this country of the reputation of being the Great Un-Musical Power of Europe'.[74] A generation later, music had found an accepted place in the weekly programme of schools of all kinds, and the musical recovery of the nation had begun.

Chapter 3

MUSIC PUBLISHING

D. W. KRUMMEL

London entered the nineteenth century as a centre of music publishing second only to Paris. Indeed, the modern conception of music publishing—involving not only the printing but also the distribution, promotion, and development of a functionally distinctive 'catalogue' of musical editions—seems to have begun in London soon after 1650 with John Playford. As for the modern technique of music printing, involving the punching of pewter plates rather than movable type, this too was developed in London, around 1700. In 1914 London was still one of the centres of music publishing, as it is today, sharing its leading position with half a dozen other cities. During the years between 1800 and 1914, activity in London, and in Great Britain in general, was flourishing and even burgeoning, the total output probably running to something near a million titles.

This very productiveness is one of the factors which has served to frighten away scholars, for several reasons. Our source materials are simply too profuse. In addition to the editions themselves—hard enough to consult in the absence of any attempt so far at a bibliographical record—we are faced with an indeterminately large assortment of manuscript records, composers' letters, and other archival documents. A small fragment of these have been transcribed or cited in articles or memoirs, and more are known to exist. But many times more than this are assumed to be unlocated or otherwise unavailable at this time. Contemplating the music itself, we are also led to entertain vague fears that some Gresham's Law may be at work, the publishers in their fertility having contributed to the badness of most of the music. Finally, the bulk interferes with our efforts to formulate a purpose and a plan for our survey. The massive dossier of facts which quickly becomes available—concerned as it is with the contracting, printing, promotion, distribution, and use of published music, and involving as it does the interrelationships between composers, printers, business agents, and

46

performers, in a mixture of evidence ranging from statistical extractions to amusing anecdotes—all this needs to be fitted together toward some meaningful end.

By way of opening up the field, this chapter will suggest three overriding trends in English music publishing between 1800 and 1914: first, the growing complexity of the music publisher's activity, as reflected in the increasing quantity and diversification of his output; second, the advent of copyright as one of his important business considerations, involving specifically in our period such matters as performance rights and international protection; and third, the increasing dichotomy between art music and popular music, which will be reflected in the institutions of the royalty ballad and the illustrated cover, and will inevitably be caught up in the Victorian predilection for moralizing.

The Growth of Music Publishing

Let us enter our field with a tour of the publisher's premises. Around 1846, the London firm of D'Almaine issued their eight-page booklet entitled *A Day at a Music Publisher's*, purportedly in response to the frequently asked question: 'By what process is music engraved and printed?' The text begins with a description of the premises at 20, Soho Square. The building is described as spacious and lavish, redecorated by the Adam brothers in the 1780s and including such works of art as the Hudson portrait of Handel. The ground floor is given over to a pianoforte saloon and other rooms for musical instruments, also to three sales rooms for printed music. It is hard to tell exactly what happens in the 'Town Department', as opposed to the 'Wholesale and Country Department' and the 'Foreign Department': the first two seem to involve only editions which appeared under the D'Almaine imprint, while the description of the third speaks of publications 'which circulate to all parts of the civilized globe', but also mentions the firm's 'constant communication with every foreign musical dept.'. The basement houses a stock room, another one for storage of lithographic stones, and 'The Tudor Room' devoted to instructional materials (still downstairs rather than upstairs, notwithstanding the observation that the firm's music education catalogue has been 'long unrivalled'). Also down here are the 'plate cellars', with 'several hundred tons' of well organized and tightly bundled plates, and a catalogue 'which enables any party wanting a particular piece of music, to select from the mass at once'.

D'Almaine was proud of its ability to handle all three methods of music printing. Music engraving, first, involves pewter plates able to 'throw off upwards of two thousand impressions'. Movable music type, second, is 'very unsightly, and is only useful to those whose capital is too limited to produce extensive works on pewter'. D'Almaine's, however, have only recently developed a 'new and very superior mode' of printing music, still secret but due to be seen very soon in Sir Henry Bishop's forthcoming edition of Handel's works. The third printing method, lithography, is reserved for music titles; and already by this time the firm is working with chromo-lithography. Such are the 'many curious processes through which the favourite Concerto, or Ballad, may pass, ere it can be placed on a lady's music desk'.

D'Almaine was one of perhaps a dozen major firms around 1850. Several shops may have been larger and more lavish, while many were no doubt more modest. The premises of comparable major firms of 1800 were presumably somewhat smaller and less assuming—but perhaps not by much; those of comparable firms in 1914 were larger, more elegant, also more industrialized in their work rooms—but again probably not much. Yet the changes in music publishing between 1800 and 1914 will be seen to be drastic indeed. Rather than find this situation curious, it is more useful to believe that cultural enterprises like music publishing demand style but not pretence; the music belongs in the foreground, the capital in the background. The music publisher's power depends on his ability to see the musical repertory changing hands; his success depends on his ability to see money changing hands. Thus what we witness happening to musical life represents half of our story; the other half is the trade secret.

The increasing complexity of music publishing, while plausible and evident, is therefore something we can rarely document. We are not entirely helpless, however. From the music registrations at Stationers' Hall, for instance, we can develop some statistical totals (Table 1). Of course we cannot really trust them; but we can interpret, extrapolate from, and pad them, on the basis of convincing arguments, to give us some insights into the magnitude of our topic. Projecting plausible totals to fill in the lacking years, for instance, we still come up with a total approaching two hundred thousand items for the whole period. But surely there were many editions which never found their way to Stationers' Hall. Established works in the public domain were issued in new editions, for which no protection was appropriate. New works were issued in several forms at once: for high or low voice, in various instrumental arrangements, extracted from larger works or collected into anthologies. There were also the piracies—at least the established

48

Table 1. Annual Totals of Music Copyrights

1800: 159			1860:2987	1880:4432	1900: 7114
1801: 115			1861:3481	1881:4469	1901: 8063
1802: 196		1842: 550	1862:2792	1882:3523	1902: 8198
1803: 152		1843:1031	1863:2833	1883:4506	1903: 8667
1804: 112		1844:1137	1864:2904	1884:3810	1904: 7929
1805: 115		1845: 931	1865:2270	1885:3116	1905: 9113
1806: 86		1846:1936	1866:2699	1886:4444	1906: 8092
1807: 151		1847:1604	1867:1851	1887:4433	1907:10744
1808: 92		1848:1240	1868:1945	1888:4016	1908: 9779
1809: 113		1849:1074	1869:2182	1889:5083	1909:10331
1810: 152		1850:1142	1870:2456	1890:3625	1910:11121
1811: 135	1831: 159	1851:1129	1871:2461	1891:3878	1911:10418
1812: 105	1832: 200	1852:1315	1872:3025	1892:6472	1912:11577
1813: 121	1833: 272	1853:1319	1873:3628	1893:6560	1913:11325
1814: 111	1834: 173	1854:2626	1874:6077	1894:6830	1914:11436
1815: 105	1835: 151	1855:2304	1875:2571	1895:5795	
1816: 128		1856:2239	1876:5604	1896:6604	
1817: 188		1857:2581	1877:4369	1897:6735	
1818: 272		1858:4092	1878:4743	1898:7493	
		1859:3424	1879:5186	1899:6952	

Totals for 1808–18 are taken from William Hawes's transcript at the Newberry Library, Chicago (MS 6A.36) which lists the works deposited at Stationers Hall. Totals for 1831–5 are from the relevant copyright reports in the *Lists of Additions made to the Collections of the British Museum* (London 1831–5). Totals for 1842–56 are from the Annual Returns to Parliament, the figures for 1845–8 and 1852–6 specifying 'pieces' and for 1842–4 and 1849–51 specifying 'works'. Totals for 1857–1914 indicate the number of domestic depository copies received at the British Museum from Stationers Hall, and were assembled by A. Hyatt King on the basis of the Registers of the Copyright, through whose kind permission they are reproduced here.

publishers were always complaining that there were—although naturally we have no idea how many. We also have the evidence of several contemporary music catalogues: Clementi's of 1823 running to 217 pages, Cocks's of 1840 to 304 pages, the D'Almaine auction of 1867 to 294 pages, Metzler's of 1866 to 240 pages, Novello's of the 1890s to 364 pages, Ashdown's 'Yellow Catalogue' of the same decade to 727 pages. The circulating library catalogues from mid-century were also enormous, although many of the entries were probably for manuscript copies or imports. It is perhaps not too far wrong to propose that the total production for our period was near to a million items, in other words that only one in five items ever was entered as such at Stationers Hall. We would seem to be on even firmer grounds in proposing that Britain's annual production of printed music—like that of most countries of the western world—increased between fifty and a hundred times over the course of our period of study.

We also know that there were many more publishers in 1914 than in 1800; also that there were many more people to buy their music. This large public was also more diversified musically. For instance, the output in 1800 consisted mostly of songs or keyboard music, with some church and chamber music. By 1914 most publications were intended for special audiences: a whole new field of instructional music for beginners, using different schemes in regular or solfa notation; more instruments and more different ensembles, ranging from amateur to professional; more choral groups of varying size and competence; more bands, of various kinds from military to the Salvation Army; more songs, with a variety of different messages. (The appeal to different social and cultural levels, in fact, added a whole dimension to the publisher's search for and service to his audiences). There is also the rise of miniature scores and other editions specifically intended for listeners rather than performers—a development in England tantalizingly suggested by Berlioz* as early as the 1850s. Thanks to faster transportation and communication, there were better hopes for London publishers to serve an outlying audience, if also fewer prospects for the survival of provincial publishers; and there was greater pressure to export music as well as greater competition from imported music. Finally, thanks to a more flexible printing technology (and recalling our visit to the D'Almaine's shop) there were new production methods for the music publisher to call on. (Curiously, most of these, in England and elsewhere, were still based ultimately on the cumbersome old practice of punching on engraved plates.) The publisher after about 1840, in any event, was no longer likely to be his own engraver and press-man; freed of the burden of preparing his copies, he could thus devote more time and effort to the tasks of building and marketing the catalogue. Evidence of the proliferation of published music is abundant, but we still lack the trade secrets, the details of exactly how this changed the music publisher's life and times.

Music Copyright

The modern conception of copyright dates from the famous Queen Anne statute (8 Anne c.19 (1709)). At first this was held to apply to writers and literary publishers who worked with the letterpress prin-

---

*'Vous voyez là des Anglais suivre de l'oeil, sur de petites partitions-diamant, imprimées à Londres pour cet usage, le vol capricieux de la pensée du maître.' Berlioz, 274. The precise meaning of 'petites partitions-diamant' is unclear; nor are there any known London publications from the years just before 1851 which would appear to fit this description. See also Howes EMR, 45.

ters. Music was not registered in any quantity until the firm of Longman & Broderip began the practice in about 1780. In its broad principles, the British copyright law was later revised only twice, in 1842 and in 1911. Both revisions extended the period of protection, the first from twenty-eight to forty-two years, the second to a period of fifty years from the death of the creator or the last of the creators. Among the provisions of other laws which concern music was one in 1884 which for the first time required a copyrighted publication to bear notice of its registration in the form of the words 'Entered at Stationers Hall'.

The history of performance rights does not begin with the establishment of the Performing Right Society in 1914. Dramatic performances, for instance, were controlled as early as the so-called Bulwer-Lytton Act of 1833 (3 & 4 Will. IV.c.15); the 1842 act extended the protection to music (5 & 6 Vict.c.45). Ten years later the interdependence of rights over printing and rights over performance became obvious, through the case of Novello v. Sudlow. For a concert of the Liverpool Philharmonic Society, William Sudlow purchased one copy of *Novello's Part-Song Book*, and copied the music of Benedict's 'The Wreath' on lithographic stone; from this copies were made for the two hundred and fifty members of his chorus. Novello brought suit, and while Sudlow argued that the copies had been lithographed and not printed, and then given out and never sold, the judge ruled in favour of Novello.[1]

The next chapter in the story of performance rights is devoted to the Authors', Composers', and Artists' Copyright and Performing Right Protective Society. Its existence was dreaded as early as 1876, and recalled with fear some fifty-five years later by the fearless-looking William Boosey. Any unauthorized public performance whatever of copyright music was subject to a fine of £2 for each performance of each song, be it in a music hall or a church or anywhere else, in London or in the country. The enforcement was assigned to the infamous Harry Wall, whose unpleasant task it was to seek out the performance, then sue the performer for having 'caused or permitted' the performance of a work 'without permission in writing'.[2] He carried out his work with diligence; one writer lamented: 'His method is designedly to keep the victims unconscious of their danger, and then to pounce upon them, backed by the authority of a Society of the very existence of which they were previously unacquainted.'[3] To be sure, the generally circumspect Henry Lunn of the *Musical Times* seemed to feel no compunction in intimating that 'whispers . . . had reached us that freedom from the Society's clutches may be obtained by those who kindly supply information of copyright work being placed in programmes.'[4]

51

Control over musical publication and performance can be counter-productive; and almost always it can be more expensive than it is worth. The use of copyright to control street music was once proposed, but happily never put into practice. More serious was the problem of itinerant pedlars, who sprang up following the 1902 copyright act, and became such a nuisance as to necessitate the formation of the Musical Defence League in 1902,[5] which, following the 1911 copyright law and the international performance rights movement, led to the formation of the Performing Right Society.

International protection posed a special problem, or more specifically, two problems: protection of English music in foreign countries, and protection of foreign music in England. While the two ought to reflect some reciprocity, in fact this was obtainable only through negotiation, then legislation, and finally enforcement. Generally England exported a good deal of music to but imported very little from the colonies and the United States (at least up to the ragtime craze at the turn of the century), whereas with the Continent, Germany and France especially, the situation was the other way round. In 1853, for instance, Novello opened an office in New York, which however lasted for only a few years. The problem was presumably greater than a single office could control. Editors could complain about American piracy, but little could be done, except in rare instances. One such incident did occur in 1884, involving a book called *The Song Folio* which had been published in Detroit. Of its 116 songs, 110 were protected by English copyrights, 39 of them Boosey's; and when Samuel Townsend sold a copy of this book in Derby, Boosey brought an action and easily won the case.[6] Such confrontations were rare, and ultimately no doubt more trouble and expense than they were worth. More lucrative, more spectacular, and more complicated were the famous battles over Gilbert and Sullivan's comic operas: the first performance of *The Pirates of Penzance* at Paignton in Devon on New Year's Eve, 1879, specially arranged so as to assure U.S. protection; the splendid decision by one New York judge, that 'copyright or no copyright, commercial honesty or commercial buccaneering, no Englishman possesses any rights which a true-born American is bound to respect';[7] and the general secrecy and espionage required for the first performances. American composers were among those to speak out for international protection in America. A collection of such statements appears in the 1887 *Musical Times*, including messages from Dudley Buck, George W. Chadwick, Hugh Archibald Clarke, Arthur Foote, Waldo Selden Pratt, and Theodore Thomas. Such efforts no doubt encouraged the enactment of American legislation in 1891.

Relationships with the Continent were less contentious but more complicated. As early as the days of Haydn and Beethoven, a kind of protection had been worked out, at least within the limitations of the honesty of the parties concerned. George Thomson's national song collections, for instance, are not known in the annals of international music copyright litigation, although the arrangements were done mostly by famous continental composers. Robert Birchall soon after 1800, and the firm of Boosey a generation later, were well known for their foreign catalogues, the former re-emerging in recent years as the producer of the best extant authentic editions of several Beethoven works.[8] In the time of Mendelssohn and Chopin, the practice of joint publication seems to have worked quite well. Even a court decision in 1854,* invalidating the foreign copyrights held by British publishers, seems to have had small effect on the overall picture. It did manage to wipe out Chopin's London publisher, Christian Rudolf Wessel; while the firm of Boosey, having lost *Rigoletto*, *La Traviata*, and *Il Trovatore*, was forced to sell its stock at reduced prices and to look for new specialities. Before long, however, German and French firms were either setting up shop in London (as Schott and Enoch did), or arranging for a British firm to serve as their agent (as Peters did with Augener, beginning in 1873). In turn, Arthur Sullivan set up the firm of Bosworth in Leipzig around 1870, for the purpose of advancing his musical interests on the Continent, although before long this firm had settled in London.

The Divided Market

'A publisher of serious music *needs* the performance royalties, and a publisher of popular music *earns* the money.'[9] The modern copyright dictum leads us into the dichotomy between art music and popular music. The very idea of such a dilemma is a nineteenth-century phenomenon; and music publishing is clearly central to its emergence. It arises as a logical extension of the romantic notion that a composer opts for ignominious wealth, or for impecunious glory. This option becomes operative through the involvement of the music publisher, who in turn will have decided in his own conscience whether he should go in for quality and poverty, or trivia and worldly success. There are perhaps some elements of truth to such rules. But there is more to the failure of a music publisher than the seriousness of his repertory, just as

*Jefferys v. Boosey, 4 H.L.C. 815, 10 Eng. Rep. 681 (1854).

there is more to popular music publishing than making a profit: skill and industry, timing and luck are required as well, while financial and musical success in one generation can quickly turn into disaster during the next. In any event, music publishers, in their rare moments of commentary on their colleagues, seldom passed judgement using the criteria of seriousness or popularity. But meanwhile there were events around the mid-century which pointed to a more democratic audience for musical editions. Apart from those pervasive forces which shaped the growth of the English urban classes in general, two specific events in the history of English music publishing are an important part of our discussion: the rise of the royalty ballad and the increasing attention to illustrated music covers.

The origins of the royalty ballad are obscure. Many of London's very first song sheets from the 1690s, for instance, already refer to performers—*The Conjurer's Song, in the Indian Queen, sung by Mr Leveridge*, and the like. One important date has yet to be established: when was a singer first paid a royalty for singing a song, thereby promoting and helping to sell it? The citation of the singer's name in the nineteenth century is usually evidence of a royalty arrangement, but not necessarily: London singers, for instance, are often named on American piracies from around 1800. By the 1840s, in any event, the royalty ballad seems to have been well established in England. The next landmark date is 1866, for the first ballad concert. But it is hard to believe that publishers were not by this time, in various subtle ways, influencing the content of public programmes in favour of their repertories. St James's Hall, for instance, was controlled mostly by the Chappells; and so Boosey's, limited to Wednesday performances there, decided to make theirs distinctly British in order to promote their speciality.

The royalty system, meanwhile, depended on the famous 'artistes': once a song was established, it was assumed, lesser singers would pick up the music in order to advance their own careers, and thereby further promote the music itself. This led one adroit composer and publisher, W. M. Hutchinson, to shun the famous singers and pay out his royalties in smaller portions to a number of the less well-known. The system survived his attack, and in time was no doubt a major factor in the rise of the English music hall. Among the best known singers were Clara Butt, Plunket Greene, Sims Reeves, and Antoinette Sterling, who introduced Sullivan's 'The Lost Chord' and Molloy's 'Love's Old Sweet Song'. (George Mozart, in spite of his name, seems to have failed to reach the first rank; John MacCormack was among the operatic lions whose career began with royalty ballads.) Charles Santley was both composer and singer, as was Edward Lloyd, famous for 'The Holy

54

City'. Hatton and Balfe were probably the most successful composers, while Longfellow was conspicuous among the poets.

Among the by-products of the royalty system was the practice of paying royalties to composers rather than outright fees. The composers were obviously the beneficiaries, although the publishers stood to gain as well. No doubt they remembered well such instances of the old arrangement as the fine tale of how Chappell paid no more than £100 for Gounod's *Faust*, and thus Boosey's, witnessing the success of this work, paid £1,000 the next year for the composer's less than spectacular *Mirelle*.[10]

The illustrated music cover could be, and often was, viewed as evidence of an appeal to vulgar tastes. One writer, for instance, complained that the windows of music shops were filled with respectable piano music, incongruously placed next to 'glaringly illustrated comic songs,' and suggested that the only appropriate solution was for the music publishers' catalogues—if not the publishers themselves, and in effect the whole world of music—to be separated into two classes.[11]

English music illustration is slowly coming to be studied today, if not quite as extensively as its American counterpart. Interest was aroused at the turn of the century by collectors like W. E. Imeson, publicized through such a pleasantry as Sacheverell Sitwell's *Morning, Noon, and Night in London*, and furthered by A. Hyatt King's more recent scholarship. While Renaissance and baroque music editions often have handsome illustrated title pages, the modern tradition should be traced back no further than the decoration of caption titles on song sheets during the 1820s. The rise of lithography and the appeal to popular audiences during the 1830s resulted in the half-page title citation expanding to a full page; by the 1840s and 1850s, music illustration had reached its fullness with the advent of chromo-lithography. The flamboyant Louis Jullien was among the major promoters of music illustration, and the practice reached its artistic high point with the fine workmanship of John Brandard in the 1860s and Alfred Concanen in the 1870s and 1880s. The vulgarization and decline of music covers dates from the last years of the century, aggravated by the advent of cheaper paper, recourse to photography, and the use of faster but less fastidious printing technology. (This seems to have taken place about the same time in America, whereas in Germany and Italy there was a trend toward more artistic and progressive decoration, at least on prestigious musical editions.)

Under such conditions, the spirit of Victorian moralizing could hardly be far away. Bad taste makes money: whether true or false, or however refined or qualified, this principle was probably accepted no more cynically, or pervasively, by British music publishers of our period than by their predecessors or their continental colleagues. But when the Victorians realized it, the reaction in print was both profound and spirited.

Guilt seems to have been a national necessity. Chopin's unhappiness with the fancy titles which Wessel added to his piano music was a fact that British commentators never allowed their readers to forget, notwithstanding some comparable events on the Continent. Stanford, looking back from 1914, saw the royalty ballad as the villain: he reserved his respect for 'the type of publisher who has an eye to the dignity which some good music gave to his catalogue, even if the cost took longer to recoup'.[12] (His example of a good British publisher was Birchall, who had recognized Beethoven's genius; and his influence encouraged Stainer & Bell to promote serious music by British composers.) 'We remember the time when it was the boast that concerts were "patronized by Royalty,"' lamented one 1867 *Musical Times* editorial; 'now they are patronized by the "Royalty" system.' Bells issued Samuel Wesley's *Service*, but only one cathedral ever bought a copy, and so 'the plates were eventually melted down . . . to be re-stamped with a set of Quadrilles'[13]—a remark almost worthy of Macaulay. Publishers were naturally quick to blame the public, and vice versa. The music used at the celebrated Novello–Leigh Hunt 'musical evenings', for instance, was never published, according to Mary Cowden Clarke: it was unprofitable, being 'much too far in advance of the then existing public taste for music'.[14]

America quickly came to epitomize bad taste, in its music and also in its titles for music, while Germany epitomized good taste. One writer, to be sure, expressed some fears that continental opera was in for bad days ahead, by virtue of its being largely in the hands of music publishers;[15] but for the most part serious English musicians viewed Germany as the place where 'good' music could be published. But might it not be that the German publishers were simply more aggressive, while the British were more cautious? Or perhaps the Germans had a better market; for instrumental music in particular, where no text in a particular language was essential, they had developed a world-wide coverage.

Inevitably the composer came to be caught up in the moralizing. The legend of Edward Loder, composing a song a week in order to make his miserable living, becomes the more poignant as we remember that his publisher was D'Almaine, whose impressive offices we visited earlier. It was natural enough for the composer to view the publisher as the villain who had failed to contribute to his support. Stanford ranks as the fiercest of those who bit the nearest hand in sight. His polemics are perhaps best counteracted by the stories of Berlioz's warm friendship with both J. B. Cramer and Frederick Beale; by Gounod's reference to Thomas Patey Chappell as a 'prince among publishers'; by recalling the many kindnesses extended to Sterndale Bennett by Charles Coventry; or, above all, by the 'Nimrod' variation in Elgar's 'Enigma' Variations, in which the composer paid the most gratifying of compliments to A. G. Jaeger, his editor at Novello's.

The British music publisher was caught up in two larger nineteenth-century trends, one musical and the other economic. The first was the increasingly historical nature of the repertory. Around 1800, when most music was still ephemeral, it was the rule that major music publishers should disappear within a period of a few years, whether through mergers or internal withering. John Longman and Francis Broderip, together making up the leading firm of the 1790s, each combined with different partners after the break-up of the firm in 1798. Both were off the scene by the 1810s. Later the concept of the musical monument, of permanent value to several generations of purchasers, allowed for long-term investment, and probably lengthened the life of publishing firms.

The second trend, then, is the economic one, having to do generally with the accumulation of wealth in nineteenth-century England, and specifically with the merchant's need to plan his capital investment. We have a few interesting records of the transactions. A cross-section of Birchall's contracts with composers is preserved in the Newberry Library, Chicago, for instance;[16] while the auction records for later musical properties offer some interesting reflections on popular tastes. The D'Almaine auction of 1867 shows most songs and short selections fetching between £15 and £50; Arnold's *Cathedral Music* going for £91.11s; Crouch's popular songs, 'Dermot Astore' and 'Kathleen Mavourneen', fetching £168 and £532, respectively; and, close behind the latter as the second highest price of all, at £502.10s, the piano tutor (1858) of Henri Frederick Hemy. (The fact that Metzler, the purchaser, thought so highly of this now-forgotten treatise—and that some unidentified underbidder thought nearly as much—suggests that its text may be worth studying.)

Related to such economic conditions—however faintly we understand them—is the technological development over the course of the century. The prime example of this activity is provided by Novello, specifically J. Alfred the son, who, arriving on the scene in the 1840s, inherited his father's highly respected but probably none too lucrative catalogue; acquired several dubious sight-singing properties, which brought with them a momentum toward mass production; revived the virtually obsolete practice of printing art music from movable type; and thus set in motion the process by which the prices for popular vocal works declined from pounds and guineas to shillings. The impact of this event was mixed. It enabled Alfred to spend his last forty years in lavish retirement in Italy, leaving his firm established as Britain's principal music publisher; but it seems to have had very little effect on other publishers, their pricing, their technology, or their repertory. Did it not also contribute significantly to the 'freezing' of the repertory of classical music around the corpus of established masterworks, whose composers' names were emblazoned on the decorative border of Novello's famous octavo covers?

Music and money are thus inextricably intermixed in the basic dilemma of the music publisher. Through his recognition of musical values and trends, he comes to be aware of those works which are part of the long range history, and hence of the nature of a capital investment, and those which are appropriate to the shorter trends of musical consumption and capital turnover. His success depends on his reconciling himself to his chosen position on the spectrum stretching from one extreme to the other. At one end are those firms which are obviously out for the quickest capital turnover with no concern for the quality of the music (and, by almost any sensible definition, some of the worst can be identified). At the other extreme are firms like Stanley Lucas, Weber & Co., which during the 1870s and 1880s created an ambitious catalogue of chamber music by native composers, several Berlioz works, large choral works, and sedate song editions, many of them by George Macfarren. Here was a London firm which specialized in issuing that very music which British composers complained about having to go to Germany to publish.

At this point, our interpretative scholarship becomes intertwined with the moralizing habits of our subjects. Can we actually propose that most of the works in the Lucas Weber catalogue (Santley's third Mass, or Prout's Magnificat, for instance, or Benedict's G Minor Symphony, op. 101) were superior to the royalty ballads, in musical terms; or in terms of their enhancement of English cultural life; or in any other terms? While Lucas Weber survived in business for barely two decades, most of the royalty-ballad publishers did no better. If we consider only the publishers who did survive for a number of decades, our record is no clearer: Novello favoured serious music while Chappell favoured popular music, especially after 1850; Augener and Boosey, Metzler and Cramer had something of a mixture in their catalogues. Interpreting the history of Victorian music publishing—whether of the publishers individually, or of their practices, or of the period in general—is not easily separated from musical criticism; and perhaps it should not be separated. Less controversial is the conclusion that the music publisher of the nineteenth century was indeed the successor to the Renaissance humanist prince who patronized the art of music.

PART II

Popular and Functional Music

Chapter 4

POPULAR MUSIC OF THE LOWER CLASSES

RICHARD MIDDLETON

Folk Music or Popular Music?

In true folk-songs there is no show, no got-up glitter, and no vulgarity . . . and the pity of it is that these treasures of humanity are getting rare, for they are written in characters the most evanescent you can imagine, upon the sensitive brain fibres of those who learn them, and have but little idea of their value. Moreover, there is an enemy at the doors of folk music which is driving it out, namely, the common popular songs of the day; and this enemy is one of the most repulsive and most insidious. If one thinks of the outer circumference of our terribly overgrown towns, where the jerry-builder holds sway; where one sees all around the tawdriness of sham jewellery and shoddy clothes, pawn-shops and flaming gin-palaces; where stale fish and the miserable piles of Covent Garden refuse which pass for vegetables are offered for food—all such things suggest to one's mind the boundless regions of sham. It is for the people who live in such unhealthy regions—people who, for the most part, have the most false ideals, or none at all—who are always struggling for existence, who think that the commonest rowdyism is the highest expression of human emotion; it is for them that the modern popular music is made, and it is made with a commercial intention out of snippets of musical slang. And this product it is which will drive out folk music if we do not save it.[1]

Hubert Parry's distinction is a familiar one, but it is riddled with ambiguities. Many of these derive from conflicting usages of the term 'popular music'. What did Parry mean by it? What does it mean to us? Does it refer to stylistic type, aesthetic value, size or perhaps social class of the audience, mode of dissemination? The question is particularly difficult for the nineteenth century, since, as far as folk/popular music is concerned, the period is very much one of transition, standing between the folk music, as it clearly is, of earlier times and what is equally clearly the mass entertainment of the twentieth century. The huge amount of relevant material and the paucity of research into it—which for the

63

scholar are the most striking characteristics of the subject—add to the difficulties of framing adequate definitions.[2]

We can at least be clear that the conventional folk/popular distinction will not do. (I am referring here to a distinction of type, not to the kind of value distinction which Parry makes—though I shall have something to say about this later.) The assumption by earlier generations of folklorists that folk music is necessarily rural and utterly separate from urban culture has been exploded by the work of numerous recent scholars.[3] Folksong has always been in close touch with the ways of the towns; 'the idea of the "folk" as an autonomous social category alien to book learning and mechanical industry, and evolving their own unwritten culture in isolation, is a sentimental abstraction.'[4] At the same time, the popular music, and even the middle-class and art music, of the towns has often been influenced and infiltrated by the songs of the countryside; and such theories as that of *versunkene Kulturgüter* (submerged cultural goods), according to which all folk music consists merely of bastardized versions of written urban material, have also been discredited. The truth is that rural and urban 'popular' music have always been intimately related. The Hungarian, János Maróthy, has therefore proposed abandoning 'folk' and 'popular' and describing all the common, everyday music of the lower classes, whether of country or town, by the all-embracing 'mass music'. This is preferable, but has the disadvantage, at least as far as the nineteenth century is concerned, of suggesting the omission of one topic—the assimilation of bourgeois music by working people—which is an important aspect of the subject. Maróthy himself points out, valuably, that 'mass music' has a historical dimension—it is not changeless, as sentimental folklore imagines—and, moreover, its periodization is related, in terms of stylistic change, to that of 'official' music history. This is certainly important in the nineteenth century: for example, there is a transition from eighteenth-century objectivity to nineteenth-century sentimentality and passion in both popular and art traditions; both middle-class music—Gilbert and Sullivan, for instance—and the broadside ballad and music hall betray the Victorian liking for parody; and so on.

As a temporary solution I propose to avoid the problem of defining 'folk' and 'popular' altogether and simply describe the material under discussion, namely, the common, everyday music of the lower classes. 'The music of the working classes' would be almost as accurate, except that the audience for much of the music extended into the lower middle class too. 'The music of the working class'—that is, of the mass of working people who were beginning to feel themselves defined by belonging to a single large proletarian class—raises additional problems, since not all workers, especially in the country, saw themselves in class terms.

The prime historical fact lying behind this music is of course the growth of industrialization, together with the resulting increase in urbanization and the decrease in the proportion of the population living in the countryside. These changes had major effects on the styles and forms of popular music. There are three principal themes. Firstly, there is a transition from rural folk music, disseminated chiefly orally, to a mainly written urban popular music. This change is already in progress at the start of our period. Secondly, there is a move away from composition, often anonymous, by amateurs or small-time professionals, usually in the context of a limited locality, towards a fully professional system, operating on a national and even transatlantic basis, with eventually 'star' singers, the 'industrial' production of songs and all the other trappings of mass entertainment. This is a move towards 'the exclusive concentration of the artistic faculty in single individuals and its resulting suppression in the masses' (Marx-Engels), and, while it is characteristic of the whole period, it is most striking and far-reaching in its effects after about 1850. Thirdly, it may be worth stressing that the period coincides with the establishment of the working class as an identifiable and self-aware group, conscious of its own distinctiveness. It is impossible, therefore, to avoid thinking in class terms. However, working-class culture could not exist in isolation, for the period also sees the full flowering of the capitalist system and of the power and influence of the bourgeoisie. Not surprisingly, then, middle- and working-class genres and styles increasingly intermingle, leading in the Edwardian era to the beginnings of the 'classless' mass culture of the twentieth century. Nevertheless, working-class self-awareness and solidarity, in the midst of this move towards a classless culture, does result in a new 'collective' style, a new folk music perhaps, which in some ways is an unexpected continuation of the old—and in others is perhaps a forerunner of the 'collectivity' of twentieth-century Afro-American-derived popular styles, such as rock music. This paradox is central to nineteenth-century popular music.

The Decline of Rural Folk Music

Without necessarily accepting wholesale the aesthetic judgement involved in Parry's words, quoted at the beginning of this chapter, we can agree with him about the decline of rural folk music and its replacement by other genres. His words were written for the inaugural meeting of the Folk Song Society in 1898, which, ironically, coincided with the golden age of music hall, at which his contempt was undoubtedly directed.

By 1901 the proportion of the population living in towns was seventy per cent; in 1801 it had been twenty per cent.[5] Britain was transformed into a country in which the urban environment, especially that of the industrial towns, with its new work patterns, social relationships and communications, was the norm. This process, together with the accompanying spread of literacy and book culture, affected not only town dwellers but also country people—both in their ways of living and in the sources and nature of their culture—and it undoubtedly caused the decline of rural folk song.* The chronology of the decline is less certain. A. L. Lloyd dates its beginning about 1790.[6] The early collector, Baring-Gould, found (c. 1880–90) that the men under fifty knew no folk songs.[7] Similarly, Sharp (c. 1900) discovered that only those born about 1840 or earlier sang the old songs[8]—which suggests that young people first started to reject them completely around the 1860s—and Alfred Williams (1914–16) found them confined to the very old.[9] Sharp also writes that the old songs were still alive in 1860–70[10] (but perhaps mainly among the middle-aged and old). Flora Thompson, writing about Oxfordshire village life in the 1880s, tells of a traditional ballad, 'The Outlandish Knight', sung by a man in his eighties which was 'out of date, even then, and only tolerated on account of his age'. The young men sang mostly recent music-hall songs, while even those a little older seem to have largely abandoned the old tunes in favour of comic and sentimental town songs.[11] In the north, the Society of Antiquaries of Newcastle-on-Tyne, looking for traditional ballads in 1855, found they were 'half a century too late'.[12] It seems, then, that a decline which set in at the beginning of the century speeded up considerably after 1850. The creation of new rural songs, as distinct from performances of the old, declined more quickly still. Relatively few appeared in the first half of the century; 'The Lincolnshire Poacher', popular equally in country and in town, seems to have been one of the rare exceptions. After 1850 the creation of new songs seems to have more or less ceased.[13]

Of course, geographical differences make these generalizations less than universally applicable. The old music naturally survived longer in the remote areas of Ireland and Scotland than in rural parts of England. In Scotland this includes not only song but the instrumental traditions: fiddle dance-music and the pibroch and marches of the

*But Cecil Sharp, amazingly, seems to doubt this. See Sharp, 4th edn., 150–2, 175–5. For a reply to Sharp, see Lloyd sɛ, 52–3.

pipes, still vigorous throughout the nineteenth century. Nevertheless, by 1900 these regions had joined the general decline.

The rural song still current in the nineteenth century was a curious mixture of historical layers. It had already been affected by urban styles to some extent during the seventeenth and eighteenth centuries, growing smoother, rounder, and more graceful in shape, more lyrical in mood, more regular in rhythm and structure, and, often, tonal rather than modal (for example, 'Searching for Lambs', 'I sowed the seeds of love').[14] Nevertheless, older songs, wilder in shape, more often modal or pentatonic, and less orthodox in rhythm, also survived (for instance, 'The Cutty Wren', and many of the big ballads). All types suffered in the decline, but, musically speaking, the threatened loss of older elements in the face of the advance of new urban styles was the most significant feature.

Such new styles entered country life in various ways. Ballad sellers journeyed through the countryside peddling broadsides and, later, cheap songbooks.[15] The same songs were also heard at country fairs and race meetings. Travelling theatre companies took more 'cultivated' songs, drawing-room ballads, and music-hall songs with them,[16] and minstrel troupes also worked in rural areas with much the same kind of music.[17] City street bands visited country towns and even the villages.[18] Improved communications meant that more country people travelled to the towns (quite a number, for instance, to the Great Exhibition of 1851).[19] Many girls went to the city to become domestic servants, taking urban songs back with them when they returned. At the same time, the country gentry often liked to imitate the 'cultured' ways of the towns, including the music, and their servants carried the songs and styles away.[20] By the late nineteenth century, moreover, still better communications, together with the nationwide spread of commercial entertainment, meant that far more country people than before were within reach of urban pubs, music halls, and theatres. Perhaps this is where the young contemporaries of Sharp's sad old folk singer obtained their 'thicky comic zongs', and why they wouldn't 'hearken to my old-fashioned zongs'.[21] Such old singers, to the extent that they knew any town songs, tended to be a little further behind in their taste, preferring Henry Russell's 'Woodman, spare that tree' and 'Cheer Boys Cheer' and Thomas Bayly's 'The Mistletoe Bough' to the later music hall.[22] The young men, on the other hand, seem to have been pretty well up to date as far as the music-hall repertory was concerned.[23] Certainly, by the 1890s the music-hall hit 'Ta-Ra-Ra Boom-De-Ay' swept through the countryside almost as quickly as through the towns.[24]

The spread of urban taste also affected the performance of rural songs to some extent, encouraging harmonic thinking, instrumental accompaniment, and part-singing.[25] And it often led to the 'modernization' of the traditional tunes themselves. The celebrated collection, *Popular Music of the Olden Time* (1855–9), published by the antiquary William Chappell (1809–88), contains mostly such modernized versions—not surprisingly, since Chappell used almost entirely written sources. Comparison of a modernized tune with its traditional counterpart provides a good illustration of the effects of urbanization on folk music. Example 4.1 is Chappell's version of 'The Miller of Dee'; example 4.2 shows a version sung to the same words, and collected from a Sussex singer in 1906 by Vaughan Williams. Dorian or aeolian mode turns into minor key, harmonic implications appear (see bar 13), and the melodic shape becomes more regular, with the use of predictable sequence (bars 2–3, 6–7, 9–12). The syncopation in bar 11 disappears. Sharp gives other comparisons of the same type, including 'The Vicar of Bray' and 'Polly Oliver'.[26] Both of these, together with 'The Miller of Dee', were often used, in their modernized versions, for nineteenth-century urban song-making.*

Ex. 4.1   'The Miller of Dee' as published in 1859

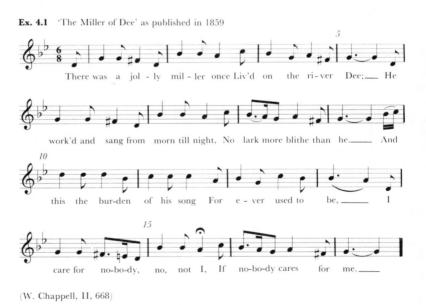

(W. Chappell, II, 668)

*See, for instance, Vicinus IM, 290–1 for an entertaining parody of 'The Miller of Dee' originating among Sheffield steel-workers c. 1835 and entitled 'The Jolly Grinder'.

Ex. 4.2 'The Miller of Dee' as collected in 1906

(Sharp, 4th edn., 146)

The words of 'The Miller of Dee' paint such an idealized picture of rural life that they are probably urban 'pseudo-folk'; and indeed changes in rural society and taste meant not only that modernized versions of old tunes penetrated the countryside but also that folk-like songs were often accepted and sung as genuine folksongs. William Shield's 'The Ploughboy' is an obvious example. Another interesting one is the early music-hall song (c. 1850), 'Villikins and his Dinah',[27] which is a *parody* of the folk-ballad form but uses a variant of a traditional tune; it was offered by country singers to early collectors as a folksong. Much the same is true of 'Joe Muggins',[28] a music-hall parody of 'Lord Lovel'.[29]

But the traffic was not all one way. Indeed, genuine rural folk tunes survived to some extent in the towns. Further research is needed here—into the tune repertories of street singers for example; but it is clear that we should not underestimate the persistence of rural tunes—both as individual songs to some extent and, more widely, as an influence within other genres—in the face of their undoubted decline as an identifiable tradition. Certainly, for reasons which are not well understood, the persistence of folksong style seems to be stronger in Britain than in any other West European country.[30] Some tunes were put to new words to form 'industrial folksongs' (see below). Some survived in their original form. Lloyd lists several in the catalogue of one London broadside printer, whose business survived until the first decade of this century,[31] and other publishers' lists are similar. Henry Mayhew, researching for *London Labour and The London Poor* (c. 1850), was told that ' "Barbara Allen" 's selling yet', and that other traditional ballads were sung also in the streets—though only occasionally by then.[32] The early collector Frank Kidson heard Leeds mill-girls (probably in the 1880s) singing 'The Knight and the Shepherd's Daughter' at fairs.[33] Other folk tunes survived actually within the music hall. George Leybourne sang 'Polly Put the Kettle On', which derives from a country dance called 'Jenny's Bawbee', and Arthur Lloyd sang an eighteenth-century dumpling-seller's street cry called 'Diddle Diddle Dumpling, My Son John' (both c. 1870). The traditional ballad, 'A Frog he Would A-Wooing Go', survived in the halls at least until the 1850s.[34]

The Broadside Ballad

The major urban popular song form among the lower classes in the first half of the century was the broadside ballad. Most towns had their own broadside printers and writers, the most important centres being Birmingham, Manchester, Preston, Newcastle, Glasgow, and of course London, which had several printers, including the famous James Catnach.[35] Many broadsides contained non-musical material: religious tracts, news, murderers' 'confessions', and so on. But many were ballads and songs, of various kinds. The quantity produced was phenomenal. One London publisher had over five thousand ballads. Some (usually contemporary murder or trial ballads) sold over a million copies.[36] Some writers are known: Joseph Mather (1737–1804) of Sheffield, John Freeth (1731–1808) of Birmingham, Reuben Holder (b. 1797) of Bradford, Samuel Laycock (1812–93) of Oldham, 'Blind Willie' Purvis (1752–1832) of Newcastle, the Wilsons (father and two sons) of Manchester.[37] Most are anonymous. This period saw the peak of broadside production, stimulated by the need for news and entertainment of the growing urban working class—and increasingly of rural workers too.

After about 1850 it began to decline, in the face of competition from the music hall, mass-circulation newspapers, and cheap songbooks. It survived longest in the more conservative countryside: while in the 1850s there were still about two hundred singers in London, according to Mayhew, and at least seven hundred throughout the country,[38] by the 1880s the broadside was all but dead in the towns.[39]

The classic description of the broadside-seller's art is Mayhew's.[40] Most were singers also, and some fiddlers as well. Often they worked in pairs or groups. Their material tended increasingly away from the noble, elevated, religious and traditional, typical of the broadsides of earlier periods, towards the secular, everyday, topical, scurrilous, satirical, sensational. Current scandal, political events, and crime became especially popular, prefiguring the mass Sunday newspapers of the twentieth century. The singing style seems to have been similarly sensational, moving away from the 'objective', controlled, almost ritualistic approach of the traditional folk singer, which denotes a known audience and a communally accepted culture, to an extravagant, high-pitched, 'shouting' style, revealing the singers as *sellers* to unknown passers-by who must be attracted.[41] The seeds of the singer-audience relationship of the music hall, and even of later mass entertainment, are found here.

It is more difficult to be sure of the tunes used—this because the ballads were always sung to well-known tunes, which were never printed on the broadside and only rarely indicated by name. Further research in this area would be of great interest, though the difficulty is in discovering which tunes were well-known and popular at any particular time. From what we know, it seems that early in the century mostly folk, and Scots and Irish pseudo-folk tunes, together with a few patriotic songs of the Dibdin/Shield variety, were used.[42] We know that Catnach, for one, paid men to collect tunes from country taverns.[43] Later more 'cultivated' tunes from drawing room, theatre, and music hall increased in popularity. We have seen that early on some folksongs were themselves printed on broadsheets, and several contemporary sources make it clear that as the century went on, middle-class and music-hall songs were reproduced complete also. For instance, Mayhew's informants in the 1850s seem to have sung mostly songs of this kind,[44] and he was told that fewer ballads were now written expressly for street sale, rather than being taken direct from concert room and music hall, than ten years previously.[45] Minstrel songs were also printed on broadsides (or their melodies used for new words); and indeed 'nigger minstrel' troupes, or 'Ethiopian serenaders', sang on the streets as well as in concerts.[46] By the 1860s few non-music-hall songs were being printed on broadsides at all.[47] This is all further evidence to support the view of a shift in tune type for *newly written* ballads.

The variety of tune type which resulted is reflected in every broadside collection. In that held by Manchester Public Library, for example, we find traditional songs such as 'Barbara Allen' and 'Henry Martin', modernized folk ('The Miller of Dee'), Scots and Irish songs, minstrel songs, drawing-room ballads, and music-hall songs, mostly of London origin.

For new ballads, popular traditional tunes, probably modernized, included 'Polly Oliver', 'The Miller of Dee', 'The Bold Trooper', 'All Among the Leaves So Green-O', 'A-Hunting We Will Go', 'The Brisk

Young Bachelor', 'Derry Down', 'Dives and Lazarus', and 'Lilliburlero'. Favourite Scots tunes seem to have been 'Nae Luck About the Hoose', 'The Ball o' Kirriemuir' (or 'Castles in the Air') and 'The Campbells are Coming' (mentioned by one of Mayhew's informants, who used it for 'The Pope he is Coming; Oh Crikey, Oh Dear!').[48] 'Rory O'More', 'The Bold Dragoon', 'Irish Molly', 'The Rakes of Mallow', and 'The Wedding of Ballyporeen' were commonly used Irish tunes.

However, it was composed tunes which gradually became the most popular. The comic song, 'The King of the Cannibal Islands', was often used—for instance to a Lancashire strike ballad of 1853 called 'The Cotton Lords of Preston' (ex. 4.3). The smooth stepwise melody, the tonic-subdominant-dominant thinking, the use of regular repetition and sequence: all signal the literate composer. Some ballads had quite literate verses too, among them 'Manchester's Improving Daily',[49] which was partly written by Alexander Wilson (see above).

Ex. 4.3 'The Cotton Lords of Preston' (1853)

Have you not heard the news of late A - bout some migh - ty
men so great? I mean the swells of Fish - er-gate, The Cot - ton Lords of
Pres - ton. They are a set of stin - gy blades, They've lock'd up all their
mills and shades, So now we've no - thing else to do But come a sing - ing
songs to you.

(R. Palmer, 313)

Again the tune is a cultivated one, 'The Good Old Days of Adam and Eve', similar in type to 'The King of the Cannibal Islands'. Frank Kidson collected a ballad from an East Riding singer, called 'Time to Remember the Poor', which is also quite literary in tone. The tune is minor, with modulations and chromatic passing notes.[50] In the West Midlands, Dibdin's 'The Warwickshire Lad' seems to have been popular.[51] Early music-hall tunes also became widely used—particularly those of the burlesque type: 'Villikins and his Dinah', 'The Rat-catcher's Daughter', 'Billy Barlow', 'Pretty Polly Perkins', 'All Round My Hat'.

Industrial Folksong

The words of most broadsides were the work of professionals; but some were written by ordinary workers, and many of these are now often termed industrial folksongs. (Later in the century—after about 1860—they were often printed in cheap songbooks; some were never printed at all, but circulated entirely orally.) The early folksong collectors did not know of the existence of these songs; and they did not look. We owe what is in fact a new chapter in our knowledge of folk music to recent research—in England, notably by Ewan McColl and A. L. Lloyd. Lloyd has explained why they should be considered folksongs despite the fact that many are not anonymous, and that written dissemination was important.[52] They were made by workers themselves out of their own experience, and are intimately related to the collective culture of their locality and class. They were passed on mainly orally, and were often subject to variation in the process. Their language is earthy, usually dialect—rarely 'literary'. Their spirit is different from that of rural folksong, of course, becoming more aggressive, realistic, down-to-earth and class-conscious. But it seems to have been felt that there was a relationship between the new kind of group solidarity which they reflected and the traditional collectivity of the rural communities; and so the industrial song-makers, instead of creating new tunes, generally turned to traditional English folk tunes, or Scots and Irish tunes, or local music-hall tunes of a kind that lay close to folk tradition. The resulting sense of cultural continuity, characteristic of oral culture, is well illustrated by 'Jone O'Grinfilt', comic hero (but also protest figure) of a group of early nineteenth-century Lancashire ballads, who was turned into the purely comic 'Johnny Green' by the Wilsons of Manchester in the 1840s, then, in the 1880s, into the contented, almost sentimental 'Wayver of Wellbrook' of the dialect writer, Ben

73

Brierly[53]—and, during the same period, perhaps also into the comic 'John Willy' of the music-hall singer, George Formby senior. 'John Willy' lived on into the 1920s and 30s in the songs of Formby's son, the great George Formby.* In the midst of a century that tended to force the working man to become more and more individualistic, literate, and bourgeois, industrial folksongs represent an important counter-trend.

As far as we know, the most important groups to produce industrial folksongs were the textile workers of Yorkshire and Lancashire and the miners of the north-east. To some extent both existed before the main period of the industrial revolution and comprise pre-proletarian working-class groups. At the same time they brought with them into the nineteenth century elements of the traditional folk culture in which, as small, early industrial groups, they had participated. The earliest recorded miners' songs are the celebrated 'Collier's Rant', first printed in 1793;[54] 'Walker Pits';[55] and 'The Bonnie Pit Laddie', with its dance rhythm (it was probably danced originally) and lydian sharp fourth (ex. 4.4). All these are still known and sung in the north-east. The Lancashire weavers had 'The Bury New Loom',[56] first printed in 1804, which combines the sexualization of tools and working techniques (common in rural song) with a quite new delight and pride in the complexities of industrial machinery.

Ex. 4.4 'The Bonny Pit Laddie'

The bon-ny pit lad-die, the can-ny pit lad-die, The bon-ny pit lad-die for me, O!
He sits in a hole as black as the coal An' earns the bright sil-ler for me, O!

The bon-ny pit lad-die, the can-ny pit lad-die, The bon-ny pit lad-die for me, O! He

sits on his crack-et and hews in his jack-et, An' brings the bright sil-ler to me, O!

(Lloyd CAY, 40)

*I am indebted to Mr Ed Hayward of the BBC for the suggested tie-up with the Formbys.

Soon, the progress of industrialization brought problems, and with them a new mood, often one of protest. 'The Weaver and the Factory Maid' (c. 1820?), collected by A. L. Lloyd in 1951, tells of the love of a hand-weaver for a girl who has 'gone to weave by steam', and it was sung to a mixolydian tune in 5/4, a tune of the 'Barbara Allen' family. (It is worth noting that in traditional English rural tunes additive metres, in particular 5/4, are quite common; in urban popular styles, on the other hand, they tend to be smoothed out into regular metres.) 'The Handloom Weaver's Lament' (c. 1820), sung to 'A-Hunting We Will Go', berates the 'tyrants of England'.[57] But the most famous Lancashire protest song is one of the Jone O'Grinfilt set, written about 1815, reprinted many times up to the 1860s, and variously known as 'The Poor Cotton Weaver', 'The Hand-Loom Weaver', or 'The Four-Loom Weaver'.[58] Two tunes have been collected, one by Frank Kidson in Cheshire, the other more recently by Ewan McColl in the Pennine village of Delph.[59] McColl's dorian tune, another 'Barbara Allen' type, might easily be a rural folk tune of the seventeenth or eighteenth century (ex. 4.5).

Ex. 4.5 'The Poor Cotton Weaver'

(McColl, 4)

Contemporary miners' songs on similar topics are many.[60] Among the best and most popular were 'The Best-Dressed Man of Seghill',[61] dating from a strike of 1831, and 'The Coal-Owner and the Pitman's Wife',[62] dating from an 1844 strike, and sung to a variant of the old 'Henry Martin' tune.

From the middle of the century on, industrial folksong was increasingly influenced by small-time professional entertainers and the early provincial music hall. In the north-east such men as Joe Wilson (1841–75), J. P. Robson (1808–70), George Ridley (1835–64), and Ned Corvan (1830–65) were active as song writers and performers. Many of their verses show the effect of music-hall comic song, and often the tunes chosen were music-hall tunes. However, they could also produce—usually for more serious topics—songs in a folk style. Joe Wilson, author of the comic 'Keep Your Feet Still, Geordie Hinnie',[63] also produced 'No Work',[64] set to the tune 'Pretty Polly Perkins', which, though originally a music-hall folk parody, lies close to folksong in musical style. Wilson's 'The Strike'[65] uses a variant of a Northumberland dance tune; and 'Aw Wish Yor Muther Wud Cum' (together with 'Aw Wish Pay-Friday Wud Cum'[66] by a miner and part-time professional called Anderson) is set to a folk tune called 'The Whistlin' Thief'. All these songs date from the 1860s and 70s. In Lancashire a school of dialect poets, led by Sam Laycock, was prominent. As well as more ambitious literary works, Laycock wrote ballads in folk style, such as 'The Shurat Weaver'.[67] This dates from the cotton shortage which resulted from the American Civil War, and is set to the traditional Irish tune, 'Rory O'More'. It could even happen that a music-hall song lacking any trace of folk idiom was 'folklorized'. J. B. Geoghegan's 'Down in a Coal Mine' (1872) has a tune of a common music-hall type—regular in rhythm and phrase structure, its melodic shape strongly conditioned by tonic-dominant harmony—but it was adopted by miners themselves as a song of pride in their trade, circulated orally, and by the time it was collected by Lloyd (in 1951?) had acquired a melody deriving from the traditional Irish tune, 'The Roving Journeyman'.[68] (In much the same way, when the tonic solfa pioneer, John Curwen, visited Wales in 1864 he found that newly-written tonal hymn tunes were being transformed by congregations into modal melodies.)[69]

The struggle within industrial folksong between traditional and modern musical tendencies was also affected by the Irish potato famine of the late 1840s. This resulted in a massive influx of Irish peasants into English and Scottish industrial areas, and with them came their rural song, which merged with the local traditions, infusing them with new vigour. A common type within Irish song at this time was the 'Come-All-Ye' form (so called because this exhortation often appeared in the text). With its 6/8 rhythm, modal cast, and simple structure, usually *ABBA*, this became the characteristic British industrial type.[70]

Thus it is that as late as the 1880s and 90s we can find a ballad-maker like Tommy Armstrong (1848–1919), of Tanfield Colliery in County Durham, creating songs on topics of local interest, either humorous or

serious, in much the same way as bards of small, closely knit, predominantly oral cultures always have. Some of this remarkable man's
songs resulted from contests between improvising poets; such is his
'The Oakey Evictions'.[71] Others were written for contemporary strikes
or disasters: 'The Trimdon Grange Explosion' (1882), for instance.
Many simply resulted from everyday events and thoughts: for example,
'The Row Between the Cages'.[72] Many entered oral tradition and have
been collected in different versions. Armstrong used early music-hall
tunes of a folk-like type or, more often, folk tunes, either traditional or
recent.

   To a large extent, however, Armstrong represents the end of a
tradition. The story of industrial folksong in the early decades of the
twentieth century seems generally to show a decline in the significance
of the songs to their communities, and an increasing reliance on 'modern' kinds of tune. These were now usually of music-hall type (a type
itself losing vigour by this time). Even traditional tunes were regular-
ized in urban manner. The folk tune, 'The Mode o' Wooing' (ex. 4.6),
is turned into a much squarer and tonally less ambiguous melody (note
the dominant instead of subdominant in bar 4) for the Durham ballad,
'The Blackleg Miners' (ex. 4.7). On the other hand, the song's four-
square, march-like rhythm, with emphatic accents, especially in its
'smashing' conclusion (♩ ♩ c̄), fits the list of characteristics of industrial
folksong which has been developed by Maróthy.[73] He calls this
rhythmic scheme *wuchtige Viertel* ('heavy crotchets') or 'workers' *giusto*'.
The other pattern which we have seen to be popular he calls 'industrial
six-eight'. More characteristics listed by Maróthy, such as modality
and the use of repetition and variation in simple structures, are also
illustrated in 'The Blackleg Miners'. Others are rhythmic variation,
syncopation and polyrhythm, and the use of refrains rather than the
extended lyrical forms characteristic of middle-class song. The result is

Ex. 4.6 'The Mode o' Wooing'

(Bruce & Stokoe, 104)

Ex. 4.7 'The Blackleg Miners'

Oh, ear-ly in the eve - nin', just af-ter dark, The black-leg mi -ners

creep te wark, Wi' their mole-skin trou-sers and dor-ty short, There go the black- leg mi-ners.

(Lloyd FSE, 387)

a synthesis of folk and middle-class styles which, however, is turned to a new, proletarian purpose, as indeed it is in 'The Blackleg Miners'. Musically, it is not hard to prefer 'The Mode o' Wooing' to 'The Blackleg Miners'—or, indeed, 'The Poor Cotton Weaver' or 'The Trimdon Grange Explosion' to 'Moses of the Mail'. But folk and popular music is never just a matter of musical values; it is too deeply embedded in social milieu for that. For the workers involved, as Maróthy suggests, perhaps the late industrial folksongs were felt to reflect not so much a decline as a changing world.

The Dissemination of Middle-Class and Art Music

We have already seen something of the dissemination of middle-class music among working people. Certainly in the towns this became an important element in musical life. On the broadsides Dibdin, Shield, and Bishop were increasingly joined by 'Come into the Garden, Maud', 'Alice, Where Art Thou' and the songs of Thomas Bayly, Henry Russell, and Stephen Foster.[74] It should be remembered too that broadside 'chaunters' were by no means the only street vocalists: more 'educated' performers, both soloists and groups, were also common, singing drawing-room ballads, minstrel songs, and glees.[75] Industrial song was not immune from this influence: J. P. Robson's 'Pitman's Happy Times' (c. 1840), for example, was set to the sentimental parlour ballad, 'In the Days When We Went Gipsying'.[76] Moreover, 'official' labour anthems, such as Ernest Jones's 'Song of the Lower Classes' or Jim Connell's 'The Red Flag', usually employed 'literate' (i.e. 'improving') tunes. The music hall played its part in the dissemination of 'educated' music too, middle-class ballads increasingly featuring on its programmes. 'Light classics' (Rossini overtures, or songs from Flotow, Balfe, and Sullivan) were not uncommon; indeed, some of the artistically more ambitious early halls put on complete (though unstaged) ballet and opera extracts. At the same time many songs originating in the music hall—such as Harry Clifton's 'uplift songs': 'Work Boys Work', 'Pulling Hard Against the Stream', etc.—made their way into the drawing room. By the end of the century the two repertories often overlapped. Art music was also disseminated widely among the working and middle classes by military and brass bands (see Chapter 7) and through the sight-singing movement and mass choral singing (see p. 41), both of which played a large part in swinging many working people towards a literate musical culture.

Another way in which literate music circulated among the lower classes was through the performances of street instrumentalists. Many contemporary sources describe such performers, usually with disapproval and descriptions of pained ears. Mayhew assessed their number in London at one thousand, and listed hurdy-gurdy players, fiddlers, bell players, Irish and Scottish pipers, bands (small and large, English and German), harpers, barrel organs, concertinas, and oriental 'tom-tom' players.[77] This was in 1850 or thereabouts. Things were much the same in 1881, when F. J. Crowest described street organs and pianos, hurdy-gurdies, bands (wind, string and mixed, many of them German), 'tom-toms', cornets, fiddles, zithers, harps, tin whistles, concertinas, bells, jew's harps, and a motley assortment of percussion and improvised instruments.[78] Standards of performance also varied—from the tolerable to the unbearable. Throughout the century attempts were made to control street instrumentalists by law. But however annoying such performers might be, their repertory—mostly popular middle-class and operatic songs, dances and marches, hymns, oratorio extracts (especially Handel), and light overtures*—must have had a considerable impact on the musical taste, and hence the cultural consciousness, of the urban poor. 'The mechanical organs and pianos, which penetrate into the remotest slums and alleys, spread musical culture even among the dregs of the people. They are, in effect, so many perambulating *conservatoires* teaching the masses the most accepted music of the day.'[79] Later in the century the disc musical box, invented in 1886 and marketed under many trade names (Symphonion, Polyphon, etc.), performed a similar function, its interchangeable discs

---

*A typical barrel-organ repertory of 1881, described in *Chambers' Journal*, comprised selections from Lecocq's comic opera of 1872, *La fille de Madame Angot*, and from a Handel oratorio, the Row Polka, 'Adeste fideles', the music-hall song 'Champagne Charlie', the 'Marseillaise', a sailor's hornpipe and the 'Blue Danube' waltz. Pearsall vpm, 192, 194.

providing the latest favourite tunes in pubs, hotels, and public rooms. Often a penny-in-the-slot mechanism was fitted, so that not only the gramophone was anticipated—this began to take over the field of mechanical reproduction in the Edwardian period—but also the juke-box of the mid-twentieth century.[80]

Music Hall

Despite the existence of all the other strands in nineteenth-century popular music, the principal source of musical entertainment for most urban working and lower-middle-class people in the second half of the century was the music hall. In any case, as we have already seen, the development of the hall intertwines with these other strands at many points. Music-hall reminiscence, anecdote, and social history are plentiful;[81] little time need be spent on these. What *is* in short supply, particularly for the earlier period, is adequate musical research, both into the songs themselves and into performance styles. Any conclusions reached here are fairly tentative.

The origins of music hall are diverse: the theatre, mostly the popular theatre of travelling showmen but also 'stars' like the great clown, Grimaldi, active up to 1828; the pleasure gardens of London (Marylebone, Ranelagh, Vauxhall, etc.), where middle-class ballads and comic songs could be heard;[82] middle-class glee clubs and harmonic societies; the rather bohemian song-and-supper clubs (the Cyder Cellars, the Coal Hole, Evans's),* patronized mainly by the raffish man-about-town, continuing the tradition of glee and partsong singing but adding more disreputable songs;[83] and a variety of 'free-and-easies' which sprang up in taverns and pubs to provide informal entertainment and group sing-songs. As they developed, these 'free-and-easies' took over influences, material, and performers from the other establishments already mentioned. The first custom-built music hall, the Canterbury Arms in London, was opened by Charles Morton, 'Father of the Halls', in 1852. During the 1850s and 60s similar establishments sprang up throughout London and most provincial cities. By 1860 there were more than two hundred and fifty halls in London and at least three hundred in the rest of the country. The 1870s saw a rash of expansion and rebuilding. Early halls, basically small rooms for eating and drinking with a rudimentary stage at one end, made way for large,

*Celebrated descriptions of the Coal Hole (under the pseudonym 'The Black Kitchen') and Evans's ('The Cave of Harmony') appear in William Thackeray's *Pendennis* and *The Newcomer* respectively.

comfortable theatres, with galleries, an orchestra pit, proscenium arch, and a well-equipped stage. Eating and drinking declined in importance. The 'Palace of Variety' had arrived. By the 1890s chains of halls, associated with businessmen like Oswald Stoll, Edward Moss, and Richard Thornton, were developing. These Empires and Hippodromes had huge, plush auditoriums, twice-nightly shows, touring troupes of performers, and an emphasis on respectability. At the same time, smaller halls of an older pattern continued in poorer districts.

In the early days, audiences were basically working and lower-middle class, with a sprinkling of upper-class bohemians and 'slummers'. By the time of the Golden Age (1890–1914) the big city-centre halls were much more classless—or rather their respectability catered for a mixture of all classes. The mass audience of twentieth-century popular culture was appearing. At the same time, provincial differences, which existed earlier, were disappearing, under the influence of better communications and the touring system, and a national audience was emerging. The methods of producing songs underwent similar changes. Many of the early performers wrote their own, as well as adapting material from elsewhere (the street, the drawing room, the theatre). By the 1870s most songs were newly composed by specialist professionals, who sold their creations to particular singers. By the 1890s we can see the outlines of a Tin Pan Alley mode of song production, just as the singers, with whom the songs were associated much more than the composers, were becoming stars in the twentieth-century sense, the best-known of them earning several hundred pounds a week.

The musical programmes of the early halls seem to have varied considerably with the type of hall, its location, and the character of its audience. Some were no doubt rough and bawdy. Some, like Morton's, were relatively refined. One middle-class eye-witness, travelling in Lancashire, reported (1842) that 'the operatives of Manchester have shown their taste and capability for higher enjoyments than smoking and drinking. I have gone into the concert-rooms attached to favoured public-houses which they frequent, and have never been in a more orderly and well behaved company. The music is well selected, the songs perfectly unobjectionable.'[84] Disraeli's fictional picture of such a 'Temple of the Muses', in *Sybil*, is similar. 'It's almost too much, the enthusiasm of these people,' says the proprietor; 'I believe they look on me as a father.'[85] Certainly operatic excerpts, glees, and partsongs were common, often mixed with drawing-room ballads, old patriotic songs (Arne, Carey, Dibdin, etc.), comic songs, current street ballads, and a few folksongs.

81

The most characteristic specifically music-hall songs of this early period are the comic songs, parodies and burlesques of such singers as Sam Cowell, Charles Sloman, and Sam Collins. We have already met 'Joe Muggins' and 'Villikins and his Dinah', which use variants of folk tunes. Cowell's 'Billy Barlow'[86] has an aeolian tune of folk-like cast, but also has audience-addressing ascents which seem to suggest the new context. 'The Rat-Catcher's Daughter'[87] has a comic *parlando* tune, arpeggio-based, which remained a common music-hall type into the twentieth century. Also popular, by way of contrast, were songs of patriotism and uplift. For these a march-like or hymnic style was favoured. Henry Russell's 'Cheer, Boys, Cheer' harks back to eighteenth-century patriotic style (though it was immediately parodied as 'Beer, Boys, Beer').[88] Again this style continued to be a music-hall staple, as did the dotted-rhythm march style of Harry Clifton's 'Work, Boys, Work' (ex. 4.8), which adapts its source in much the same way as the contemporary revivalist gospel hymn.

Ex. 4.8   Harry Clifton, 'Work, Boys, Work' (c. 1867)

Work, boys, work and be con - ten - - ted, So long as you've e-nough to buy a meal, Ev'ry man you may re-ly, Will be wealth-y by and by, If he'll on-ly put his shoul-der to the wheel.

(Chilton, 165)

By the 1870s the more 'artistic' pieces had largely disappeared—with the exception of the drawing-room ballad—and characteristic song types had been established: the sentimental song (closely related to the middle-class ballad), the cockney song, the patriotic song,* the minstrel song, and above all the 'swell' song. During the

*The most celebrated was G. H. McDermott's 'We don't want to fight, But by Jingo, if we do,' expressing the anti-Russian mood of the people during the Balkan crisis of 1878.

1860s, 70s, and 80s the 'swell' or 'masher' song, sung by the *lions comiques* (George Leybourne, G. H. McDermott, Albert Vance, Arthur Lloyd), was the most characteristic type, its portrayal of the idleness and good living of the 'toff' satisfying working-class escapist fantasies. At the same time this genre was parodied, and by contrast working-class realism celebrated, by the female 'serio-comics'. The most famous 'swell' song was Leybourne's 'Champagne Charlie' (ex. 4.9); the music (by Alfred Lee) illustrates many of the pervasive characteristics of music-hall style. The verse is diatonic, completely chordally-based, with simple sequence, organized, as it often is, round the circle of fifths. The chorus, with its arpeggio-based, dotted-rhythm march style, invites audience participation.

This kind of, shall we say, simplified, even diluted development of eighteenth- and nineteenth-century bourgeois song became a basic reservoir for a national music-hall language. But even in the 1870s some provincial distinctions survived, particularly in the north-east, where, as we have seen, strong folk traditions influenced the local halls. We have already noted Joe Wilson's use of folk tunes. His contemporary, Ned Corvan, often used music-hall tunes—but equally often folk tunes as well.[89] Even George Ridley's 'Cushie Butterfield'[90] and 'Blaydon Races',[91] set to the music-hall melodies of 'Pretty Polly Perkins' and 'Brighton' respectively, have such a regional identity and achieved such a strong oral currency that they relate to the folk traditions as much as to the world of commercial entertainment. These were all local working men, turned small-time professional; their 'concert rooms' and 'theatres' were often rough and ready. Note that they continued the street-song tradition of adapting existing tunes, rather than using new music, as was usual in music-hall practice by this time.

By the end of the century such men, along with provincial distinctions in music hall, had largely disappeared. So for the most part had the 'swell' song (though occasional examples of a related kind—'The Man Who Broke the Bank at Monte Carlo', 'Burlington Bertie from Bow'—continued to appear). But the other song types reached maturity, pouring from the composers' pens to meet the demands of the extraordinary profusion of singers.

The masters of the cockney (or 'coster') song were Albert Chevalier and Gus Elen. Elen's 'If It Wasn't for the 'Ouses in Between' (ex. 4.10), a gentle satire on the pastoral myths of the town-dweller, is perhaps the best example, with a more varied melodic shape and richer harmonies than many music-hall songs.

Leslie Stuart wrote mostly for musical comedies, but his songs for the blackface music-hall singer, Eugene Stratton, fuse the sentimental

Ex. 4.9   Alfred Lee, 'Champagne Charlie' (1867)

(*K*: Sheard, 1867)

Ex. 4.10 Edgar Bateman and George Le Brunn, 'If It Wasn't for the 'Ouses in Between' (1894)

(P. Davison, 192)

ballad and the minstrel song, the combination of an underlying harmonic simplicity, chromatics, rich sevenths and added sixths providing a readymade pattern for the twentieth-century escapist romantic ballad. 'Lily of Laguna'[92] is a very good example.

Waltz rhythm, with its audience-lifting lilt, was popular for songs of nostalgia ('The Miner's Dream of Home'),[93] sentiment ('After the Ball'),[94] romance ('Joshua'),[95] and comradeship ('Comrades'). Indeed the waltz-song remained immensely popular as a type well into the twentieth century. As so often in music hall, harmonic simplicity usually is the key (ex. 4.11).

Ex. 4.11 Felix McGlennon, 'Comrades' (1888)

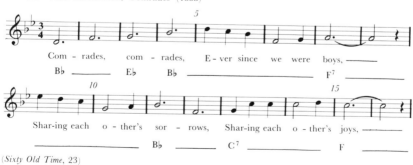

(Sixty Old Time, 23)

85

The *parlando* comic song kept its popularity ('Daddy Wouldn't Buy Me a Bow-Wow', 'Where Did You Get that Hat?'),[96] as did the Scots song (Harry Lauder: 'Roamin' in the Gloamin', 'I Love a Lassie',[97] etc.), the patriotic song ('Sons of the Sea', for example), and, perhaps most important of all, the song of group conviviality and togetherness, usually deriving from march or dance rhythms and centring on a 'sing-along' chorus ('Down at the Old Bull and Bush', 'Pack Up Your Troubles', 'Any Old Iron', 'I'm 'Enery the Eighth', etc.). Of these the rather *risqué* (at the time) 'Ta-Ra-Ra Boom-De-Ay'[98] may owe its naïve exuberance to its American origin, which in any case certainly points to a future pattern in popular music.

In cold notation, many music-hall songs can easily seem uninteresting and lacking in character. This points to a central fact: the importance of the performance, as against the material, a tradition which runs back to W. G. Ross's macabre song-and-supper-room ballad, 'Sam Hall',[99] and culminates in the work of Marie Lloyd, most celebrated of music-hall singers. Her most popular songs are in fact very ordinary, but there is common agreement about the genius of her delivery, and the intimacy of the artist-audience relationship she created.[100] As T. S. Eliot wrote, 'Marie Lloyd's audiences were invariably sympathetic, and it was through this sympathy that she controlled them. . . . It was . . . this capacity for expressing the soul of the people that made Marie Lloyd unique, and that made her audience, even when they joined in the chorus, not so much hilarious as happy'.[101] A contemporary description of one of her performances, at the London Pavilion about 1907, illustrates Eliot's meaning:

A dainty little figure, Parisienne in its *chic*, its clothes, and its manner, steps out, and again the cheers ring out. It is Marie Lloyd, the greatest artiste of her type and day, the spirit of London and of the old music-hall, incarnate. The tune of her song has a certain sparkle, the words have a certain point, but it is the curiously attractive, husky voice, the flash of the eyes, the wonderful, restrained gesture, the marvellous play of the hands that betrays the great artiste. The ditty has something to do with the adventures of a simple London girl in 'gay Paree'—'Paree' is always gay in music-hall land—and is sufficiently banal; it is the personality of the singer that counts, and again the cheers ring out as with a final mischievous wink and nod the singer darts off to change.

The orchestra repeats the chorus a trifle perfunctorily; a bell rings, the chorus is abruptly abandoned, and a new tune is struck up. From the thunderous welcome it receives it is a favourite, and again the singer twinkles on to the stage.

This time she is London, the incarnate cockney, the 'gamine' of the greatest city in the world. Gone is the *chic* Parisienne, with her demure naughtiness, her

86

piquant point, and in her place is all Mile End Road, Whitechapel and Covent Garden. The song itself is little or nothing, the air has the usual catchiness, but the art of the singer epitomises and embalms a type—a type known to every member of the audience. Every gesture, every intonation, every 'aside' is utterly and absolutely right; there is a polish, a finality, that stamps the work as that of a consummate artiste. And a consummate artiste is 'Our Marie', as the gallery boys call her.[102]

This technique, this appeal, this relationship, are built on an acceptance of secure class definitions and an awareness of common life styles; as T. S. Eliot puts it, Marie Lloyd was 'the expressive figure of the lower classes'.[103] This aspect of music hall is what makes its real nature so difficult to analyse now. It also seems to be characteristic of all urban popular song, and in fact helps to set off such song from traditional rural folk music, where the singer is more of an objective presenter of collectively familiar subject matter. At the same time, the music-hall singer-audience relationship perhaps performed a 'collectivizing' role of its own, celebrating a shared experience within the cultural confusion of urban life. 'The working man who went to the music-hall and saw Marie Lloyd and joined in the chorus was himself performing part of the act; he was engaged in that collaboration of the audience with the artist which is necessary in all art and most obviously in dramatic art.'[104] After the first world war and its effects on the social system, together with the rise of mass entertainment, such a shared experience would no longer be possible in the same way.

Pointers to the Future

By the Edwardian period the repertories of music hall, theatre, and middle-class drawing room often overlapped. Many of the same performers played the halls, ballad concerts, theatres (pantomime, revue, light opera, and musical comedy) and seaside pierrot shows and concert parties. Increasingly, the most popular songs, the 'hits', were heard by everybody, and those traditions which could not be accommodated to this trend, such as industrial folksong, declined. The emergence of the classless mass culture of the twentieth century is quite clear. With it came mass marketing, born in America's Tin Pan Alley and built on the 'plugging' of formula-songs* and the mass production of cheap sheet music. By 1914 Britain had its own Tin Pan Alley around

*For instance, American songs written for the Spanish-American War of 1898 were exported to Britain for the Boer War, with great success.

London's Charing Cross Road. At the same time the early gramophone, which carried many music-hall songs and popular ballads as
well as truncated 'classics' and operatic excerpts, was contributing to
the steady 'massification' of musical taste too—as well as foreshadow-
ing the media revolution of later twentieth-century popular culture.

The seeds of the decline of music hall were already visible. The attack
from outside came from the revue and the dance hall—shortly to be
joined by the cinema, already in embryo subverting the halls from
within in the form of the bioscope and cinematograph. Musically, the
critical event was the arrival from America of ragtime. Of course,
American tunes were nothing new in Britain; from the early minstrel
troupes, some eighty years before, to the mature music hall, many of
whose songs ('After the Ball' and even seemingly English songs like
'Down at the Old Bull and Bush', 'Nellie Dean', and 'Goodbye Dolly
Gray') were American in origin, the transatlantic dimension of British
popular music had been strong. Towards the end of the nineteenth
century particularly, British music hall and American vaudeville
became closely linked. But ragtime was something new in the peculiarly 'American' nature of its style. J. B. Priestley, hearing ragtime in
the Bradford music halls of his youth, saw it 'drumming us into another
kind of life in which anything might happen . . . Out of this ragtime
came fragmentary outlines of the menace to old Europe, the domina-
tion of America, the emergence of Africa, the end of confidence and any
feeling of security, the nervous excitement, the frenzy of modern
times.'[105]

From 1912 on ragtime swept all before it in Britain. That year saw
the visit of the American Ragtime Octette and the arrival, from
America, of a revue called *Hello Ragtime!* The popularity of the style
grew over the next few years alongside the success of subsequent
ragtime-oriented revues (*Hello Tango!*, *Keep Smiling*, and so on). In 1913,
according to the stage paper *The Era*, there were a hundred and thirty
American ragtime groups touring the British music halls, together with
countless British imitators. With ragtime came new dances, notably
the foxtrot and the tango (also other animal dances, like the turkey-trot
and the bunny-hug). We see the beginnings of mass social dancing,
previously confined mostly to the upper and middle classes, but to
become so widespread in the twenties and thirties. By the time of the
war, ragtime was fully established within popular music in Britain, and
was preparing the ground for the next invader—jazz.

However, ragtime had been heard—and recorded—in Britain well
before all this (the first known British ragtime recording appears to
date from 1898).[106] 'Coon-songs' and 'cakewalks' had been music-hall

favourites certainly since the 1890s. 'Classic' piano ragtime made little headway in Britain, for our ragtime imports were filtered through New York's Tin Pan Alley. Instrumental 'novelties' and ragtime songs, many of which—'Alexander's Ragtime Band', for example—had little connection with ragtime beyond the title, were more the staple fare. It is interesting that, whereas purely instrumental music seems to have been of relatively little significance in the popular music of the lower classes through most of the nineteenth century, now instrumental pieces grew in popularity (alongside the rise of popular dancing, of course); the important role of the dance band in the twenties and thirties is prefigured. Piano ragtime playing was not common, but bands—embryonic dance bands (especially after 1912) and military and brass bands—took up the music, and ragtime banjo players were particularly numerous, perhaps the best-known being Bert Bassett and Ollie Oakley. So alongside songs like 'Bill Bailey' and 'He'd Have to Get Under' were heard 'Temptation Rag', 'Grizzly Bear Rag', 'At a Georgia Camp Meeting', and 'Eli Green's Cakewalk'.[107]

Among the most popular ragtime songs, sung by the American Ragtime Octette and in *Hello Ragtime!*, were 'Hitchy-Koo' and 'Waiting for the Robert E. Lee'.[108] The latter is a good example of the style, with its rather mechanical but, at the time, immensely exciting half-beat syncopations, its simple harmonies, and its circular, nodal melodic shapes, with internal repetition and variation, and suggestions of the pentatonic scale, so different from the lyrical lines of nineteenth-century ballad and music-hall song, and reminding one instead of 'primitive' folksong (ex. 4.12).

In retrospect the second half of the nineteenth century can easily seem a Golden Age in British urban popular music, despite the fact that from a purely musical point of view it compares badly with traditional folk music. For popular music is more than just music. This period produced an enormous amount and variety of types of popular music; the variety may be unmatched before or since. Secondly, the songs had a great impact on the collective mind and memory, an impact not just of the music itself but of all that was bound up with it, including associations and performance styles. Many of these songs are widely remembered today, retaining a particular significance within our radically different popular culture. Perhaps this is because of a third aspect, the fact that the period was a transitional one and had the vigour which stems from the creative tensions of such periods. Earlier, the popular song of the towns had not achieved a completely distinct identity; subsequently, in the twentieth century, the character of popular music has been absorbed into the total culture of a mass society, losing much

Ex. 4.12 Lewis F. Muir, 'Waiting for the Robert E. Lee' (1912)

(*Sixty Old Time*, 130)

of its specificity in the process. This pattern seems typical of the
development of popular musics within mass societies. A group or class
emerges, achieves an identity, then is absorbed into the larger culture.
This certainly happened with the Afro-American styles of ragtime,
blues, and jazz, with the popular styles of Latin-American cities, and
more recently with the rock music of young whites in America and
Western Europe. When one looks at the historical position of late-
nineteenth-century popular music, a fourth factor in its importance
emerges: the cultural balancing act which is performed. There is an
energy, a vulgarity, a stress on personality which is typical of popular
music, which is new and which is exciting, but there is still a folk-like
intimacy in the artist-audience relationship which would shortly disappear.

By the Edwardian period the creative tensions in nineteenth-century
popular culture seem to be declining in energy; the new to be triumph-
ing over the old; the bourgeois, the modern, the commercial, the mass,
to be replacing folk and working-class traditions. Only a few great
artists, like Marie Lloyd, could hold back the tide a little. Their demise,
as Eliot pointed out, seemed to signal the absorption of the lower classes
into the passive, rootless individualism of mass society.[109] And yet,
unexpectedly perhaps, the same conflict has reappeared in twentieth-
century popular music, the role of 'the folk' being taken over largely by
Afro-American sources, which, from ragtime onwards, have dominated the significant developments, in Britain as elsewhere. Parry was

90

wrong to make his sweeping generalizations about the value of popular song, but he was right to stress the importance of the conflict; and ironically, in the age of rock we can see that the fight for the oral and the primitive was by no means as hopeless as he suggests. The century which started with the decline of rural folk song ended with the musical emergence of that twentieth-century folk hero, the Negro.

Chapter 5

MUSIC OF THE POPULAR THEATRE

ANDREW LAMB

The second half of the nineteenth century was a period when the music of the popular theatre had an increasing significance for the general public. As we have seen, it was the age during which music hall developed from its origins as public-house entertainment into the organized productions of the variety theatre. It was also the age that saw the development of comic opera and operetta as genres of international significance. Between these two extremes in the popular musical theatre—extremes in both musical substance and the social class of their audiences—lay a considerable body of theatrical entertainments that incorporated musical numbers into a light-hearted framework. Musicians were cheap to hire, and an orchestra was a standard part of a theatre's equipment. Thus a musical piece was commonly included in a theatre's programme, even if only one item in the evening's fare.

Burlesque (1830–1890)

During the first half of the century musical productions fell readily into the category of *burletta*, a term that for legal reasons was used by London theatres to describe a wide variety of comic or farcical pieces with interpolated songs.* The burlettas at the Olympic Theatre achieved particular success, largely owing to the personal magnetism of the theatre's leading lady and sometime manageress, Lucia Vestris. Her performances in breeches roles were greatly admired, and she was the idol at once of the bucks in the boxes and the humbler occupants of pit and gallery.[1] Vestris was fond of introducing into her pieces any song she considered suitable for her talents, however incongruous it might

*See also Chapter 13.

92

be. (She was far from unique in this particular aspect of the popular musical theatre.) However, the bulk of her scores were put together by the theatre's musical directors, who included Charles Edward Horn (1786–1849) and John Barnett (1802–90). Horn's song 'Cherry Ripe' was one of Vestris's greatest successes (see p. 123). Example 5.1 is from Barnett's 'Love's Review', sung by Vestris in the burletta *The Conquering Game*, by William Bayle Bernard (Olympic 1832).* The song depicts Field Marshal Love reviewing the various units of his army of female types.

Many of the works that came under the general description of burletta fell more specifically into the categories of *extravaganza* or *burlesque*. The two terms were not always clearly differentiated, though James Robinson Planché, a particularly significant purveyor of these genres, defined burlesque as a broad caricature of a serious subject whereas extravaganza was the 'whimsical treatment of a poetical subject'.[2] Beginning with *Olympic Revels; or Prometheus and Pandora* (Olympic 1831), Planché turned out for Vestris a succession of satirical pieces written mostly in rhyming couplets and full of clever puns, catchy songs, and extravagant tableaux. The appeal of Planché's burlesques lay in 'putting modern sentiments and expressions into the mouths of characters from antiquity' and 'having the acting perfectly natural and familiar, so that the contrast between the absurdity of the thing said and the propriety of the everyday behaviour should greatly heighten the effect'.[3] The songs were generally popular tunes of the day fitted with verbal parodies, for example 'A Fine Old English Gentleman' which turned up as 'A Fine Young Grecian Gentleman' sung by Vestris in *The Golden Fleece; or Jason in Calchis, and Medea in Corinth* (Haymarket 1845). This particular burlesque also contrived to have the classical Greek chorus portrayed by a single actor.[4]

During the late 1850s and the 1860s burlesque came into particular prominence as the major type of musical entertainment in the area between comic opera and music hall. The range of targets had by now widened. The objects of the fun might be Greek or Roman mythology, events in British history, the plays of Shakespeare, the novels of Scott, or some current theatrical or operatic success. Within the overall satire there was the opportunity to make passing fun at some current topical incident, some politician, or some theatrical performer. Where the Olympic burlesques had relied more on pleasing the eye with elegant dresses and extravagant scenes, the burlesques of the 1850s and 1860s were more hearty, rumbustious entertainments. Planché's successors

*The theatre and year following each work are those of the first production.

93

Ex. 5.1 John Barnett, *The Conquering Game* (1832): song, 'Love's Review'

(Tempo di Marcia)

(*K*: Collard & Collard, c. 1833)

had not his natural wit, and prominent burlesque writers such as Henry J. Byron, F. C. Burnand, and William Brough relied even more heavily on a sequence of often excruciating puns. *The Rise and Fall of Richard III; or A New Front to an Old Dicky* (Royalty 1868) was one Burnand piece whose subtitle indicated the general level of the humour. However, there were also the bright and gay songs and dances, the shapely forms of actresses in 'trouser' roles, and the spectacular transformation scenes. Performed with manifest zest and enjoyment, the burlesques at the Royal Strand Theatre in particular attracted large audiences. Many ran for several months and a few achieved subsequent revival.

The musical content of the burlesque was undoubtedly subservient to the words, and the score was usually not original but largely made up of familiar airs. In Burnand's *The Latest Edition of Black-Eyed Susan* (Royalty 1866), a highly successful example of the genre that ran for four hundred performances, the score provided by the musical director Theodor Hermann had a music-hall style song 'Pretty See-u-san, don't say no', but also included a trio using the music of Balfe's 'In the gipsy's life' from *The Bohemian Girl*,[5] while later a character entered singing 'Captain Crosstree is my name' to the tune of 'Champagne Charlie' (music by Alfred Lee: see ex. 4.9), a current hit of the music halls.[6] Indeed many music-hall successes reached the theatre-going public by being introduced into burlesques with altered words.[7]

Some attempts to provide burlesques with entirely original scores were made at the Royal Strand Theatre. Burnand's *Windsor Castle* (Royal Strand 1865) had a score by Frank Musgrave that even achieved the distinction of publication in vocal score, and the same collaborators also worked together on *L'Africaine; or The Queen of the Cannibal Islands* (Royal Strand 1865) and *Der Freischütz; or A Good Cast for a Piece* (Royal Strand 1866). (It was, of course, the subjects and conventions of grand opera that were burlesqued: satirical treatment of their *scores* would be likely to fly above the audiences' heads.) For long musical director of the Royal Strand Theatre, Musgrave was a self-taught musician of limited technique but with the ability to produce what appealed to the public.[8] At a time when Offenbach's *opéras bouffes* were first achieving great popularity, Musgrave even managed to attract the description of 'Offenbach of the Metropolis'.[9] However, this would appear to have owed more to associations with the term 'burlesque' than to musical quality.

For the time being the idea of composing completely original scores for burlesques appears not to have caught on. When the recently built Gaiety Theatre staged an ambitious burlesque *Columbus; or The Original*

Pitch in a Merry Key (1869), the music 'by the best composers available' included numbers from seven Offenbach scores as well as from *Norma, Faust, La Traviata* and other sources.[10] The Gaiety gradually became recognized as the new home of burlesque, with a more glamorous style of production free from some of the animal spirits of the Royal Strand productions and populated by characters who set their sights higher in the social scale. During the 1880s the Gaiety stalls were packed with young men of the 'jeunesse dorée' who, after an evening admiring the pretty young actresses, would meet them at the Stage Door for supper at Rule's or pay a visit to the fashionable night clubs of the time—the Gardinia in Leicester Square and the Corinthian in York Street, St James's.[11]

Over the years, too, some original songs provided for Gaiety productions by the resident musical director, Bavarian-born Wilhelm Meyer Lutz (1829–1903), achieved considerable success, and the music of the Gaiety productions became no longer so clearly subservient to the words. By the mid-1880s it had become customary to provide original scores, and the Gaiety burlesques became an increasingly significant source of popular songs and dances that achieved currency beyond their immediate theatrical origins. The scores were now published complete in vocal score, with successive printings incorporating as 'additional numbers' the new songs that were substituted as the run of a show progressed.

The overall shape of the Gaiety burlesque score of the late 1880s was basically that of a three-act comic opera embracing songs, duets, trios, ensembles, choruses, and dances. However, there was minimal musical development, the songs were often of music-hall banality, the part writing was rudimentary and the vocal ranges undemanding. Lutz provided the bulk of the scores. His 'Pas de quatre', danced in *Faust Up to Date* (Gaiety 1888), was a particularly successful number that in time became established as the signature tune of the Gaiety. Its infectious rhythm and melody have remained familiar into modern times (ex. 5.2). Another 'hit' was his song 'Hush! the Bogie', first introduced during the run of *Ruy Blas and the Blasé Roué* (Gaiety 1889) and carried over into *Carmen Up to Date* (Gaiety 1890). However, the Gaiety scores also included interpolated songs and dances not only by established theatre composers such as Edward Solomon (1855–95) but also by up-and-coming young song writers. Among those who achieved their first big success with songs for Gaiety burlesques were Lionel Monckton (1861–1924) and Sidney Jones (1861–1946). The latter's 'Linger Longer Loo' from *Don Juan* (Gaiety 1893) proved a popular success not only in Britain and the Empire but also in the United States and

Ex. 5.2   W. Meyer Lutz, *Faust Up to Date* (1888): Pas de quatre
Allegro moderato

(*K*: Ascherberg, c. 1889)

Europe. Toulouse-Lautrec sketched the Parisian *diseuse* Yvette Guilbert singing the song,[12] and the Viennese dance composer C. M. Ziehrer used it in his *Barrison-Marsch*.[13]

Musical Comedy (1890–1914)

During this period the Gaiety had come under the control of a young impressario named George Edwardes. Under him the Gaiety burlesque established many of the characteristics that were to typify British popular musical theatre for a quarter of a century. The substitution of new numbers during the run of a piece, for example, was just part of the tradition of the 'new edition', whereby a particular show was kept fresh by the introduction of new dresses and new routines as well as new musical numbers. Satisfied customers could thus happily pay a return visit to a production knowing that they would see not only something enjoyably familiar but also something new.

Edwardes had a keen instinct for satisfying popular taste, so that he was perfectly placed to direct theatrical tastes when the whole London popular musical theatre underwent one of its periodic changes of fashion in the early 1890s. At one extreme the genuine music halls were being obscured by the large variety theatres. At the other Gilbert and Sullivan had suffered their most celebrated quarrel, and Sullivan's chief comic opera rivals—Clay, Cellier, and Solomon—were all at or near the ends of their careers (all three died between 1889 and 1895). In burlesque, too, death and illness had robbed the Gaiety of its most popular performers. Thus the time was ripe for experiment, and Edwardes provided it with *In Town* (Prince of Wales' 1892). Musically the format was essentially that of the Gaiety burlesque, with a score by F. Osmond Carr (1858–1916) that was the usual sequence of simple comic songs, dances, and ensembles. Gone, however, were the traditional puns of the burlesque. The plot—such as it was—was a topical one, and instead of tights for the ladies and eccentric dress for the men there were exquisite *haute couture* frocks and Savile Row suits.

Edwardes continued the experiment with *A Gaiety Girl* (Prince of Wales' 1893) with music by his protégé Sidney Jones. The result again proved highly successful. *A Gaiety Girl* ran for well over a year and was then taken on a world tour under the musical direction of Granville Bantock, who on his return collaborated on a book about the experience.[14] Some idea of the impression created by the new formula may be gained from a contemporary press report which, having stressed that the plot was not the strong point of the piece, went on to describe it as 'sometimes sentimental drama, sometimes almost light opera, and sometimes downright "variety show"'.[15] Edwardes himself, perhaps genuinely perplexed as to how to describe his new formula, had simply used the term *musical comedy*, a loose description that had often been used previously for any light-hearted piece with musical numbers. Here, however, it was attached to a noticeably different style of entertainment, and when that new style captured the public's imagination the term came to be used specifically for a work of the new genre.

With *A Shop Girl* (Gaiety 1894) Edwardes finally allowed his new style to supplant burlesque at the Gaiety. The emphasis on youthful female glamour was highlighted by the title, and Edwardes followed it with a sequence of 'girl' pieces including *The Circus Girl* (Gaiety 1896) and *A Runaway Girl* (Gaiety 1898). Lionel Monckton's march song 'Soldiers in the Park' ('O, listen to the band!') from *A Runaway Girl* is remembered and played to this day.

Meanwhile, at his other principal theatre, Daly's, Edwardes had been establishing a variant of the formula. By comparison with the nature of the Gaiety pieces, the Daly's variety boasted a more substantial and consistent plot and more ambitious and extended musical writing that was indeed nearer to comic opera. *An Artist's Model* (Daly's 1895; music by Sidney Jones) set the pattern for the 'musical play'—a term that tended to be used (though by no means consistently) for works of these more substantial qualities. The work to which Daly's and the new genre owed most was *The Geisha* (Daly's 1896), which combined oriental colour with topical brightness and a score by Jones (with interpolations by Lionel Monckton and others) that combined charming ballads, catchy songs, and stirring choruses, all imbued with a thoroughly musicianly substance. *The Geisha* ran at Daly's for two years and toured Britain and the Empire for many more. Abroad it achieved an international success greater than that of any other work of the British popular musical theatre—including *The Mikado*. It achieved more performances on German stages than any German-language work of the time,[16] and was published in vocal score in German and Italian. A Russian performance features prominently in Chekhov's story *The Lady with the Little Dog*.

The success of Edwardes's musical comedy formula inevitably brought imitations from other managements, above all *Florodora* (Lyric 1899), with which Leslie Stuart (1864–1928) repeated the success he had achieved with music-hall songs such as 'Soldiers of the Queen' (1895), 'Little Dolly Daydream' (1897) and 'Lily of Laguna' (1898). By the end of the 1890s British musical comedy had established itself not only as the dominant form of popular musical theatre throughout the English-speaking world but also as the most successful European school of operetta of the time. Around the turn of the century one could see *The Circus Girl* at the Theater an der Wien and *Florodora* at the Bouffes Parisiens, while *The Geisha* conquered the world.

Though European enthusiasm for the British musical comedy and musical play proved short-lived, the success that had been achieved so far was only a foretaste of the popularity that was to be attained in English-speaking countries during the first decade of the twentieth century. The Edwardian era saw perhaps the greatest output of music for the British popular musical theatre of any decade. There was a great boom in theatrical entertainment, and the glamorous, romantic musical comedy was in the forefront. The leading ladies and gentlemen were popular idols, their activities eagerly followed in fashionable periodicals. Picture postcards perpetuated the memory of their leading roles, and glossy monthly publications such as *The Play Pictorial* devoted individual issues to scenes and performers from the latest London success. Several chorus girls actually did achieve in real life the traditional operetta or musical-comedy transition from poor upbringing to marriage into the aristocracy: for example Rosie Boote, who became the Marchioness of Headfort, and above all Gertie Millar who, after the death of her first husband Lionel Monckton, married the Earl of Dudley.[17]

In the quest for colour and novelty, the musical comedy and musical play (the distinction between them became ever less clear) rang the changes on geographical settings. Japan, China, Ceylon, Germany, Holland, Denmark, and the Balkans were all used, as well as Devon, the Scottish Highlands, and other places less readily identifiable; but the music remained essentially the same—a mixture of light opera and variety elements in varying proportions. The scores were often the work of a pair of composers—usually a collaboration between an experienced and technically proficient theatre musician such as Caryll, Jones, or Howard Talbot and a specialist musical comedy song writer such as Monckton or Paul A. Rubens. New numbers were provided as a show went into a 'new edition', though leading performers also felt free to introduce any other song that had taken their fancy—often the latest American vaudeville hit. Vocal scores, with colourful title pages, sold in large numbers, as did sheet music editions of individual songs. For the first time the major songs could also be preserved for posterity in their original interpretations through the medium of the infant gramophone record.

Most prolific of the Edwardian musical comedy composers was Ivan Caryll (1861–1921). Belgian by birth, he had come to London as a young man and become musical director and adaptor of French operettas for various theatres before settling at the Gaiety in the early 1890s. Adapting to fashionable musical styles was something that Caryll took in his stride, and he managed to integrate himself in turn into the world of comic opera, Edwardian musical comedy, and finally ragtime-influenced American popular music. His luxurious cosmopolitan life style was doubtless partly responsible for his need to pour out an endless stream of music for various theatres.*

For the Gaiety in particular Caryll contributed to a string of successes. But his contributions were increasingly overshadowed by Monckton's. The latter had the advantage of being married to the theatre's

*For a most entertaining description of Caryll, see Wodehouse and Bolton, pp. 102–4.

leading lady, Gertie Millar, and for her in particular he created many striking numbers (for which he often wrote his own lyrics). 'Moon-struck' from *Our Miss Gibbs* (Gaiety 1906) is the best remembered. In the more ambitious works for other theatres he demonstrated his admiration for Sullivan, most obviously in his double choruses. Inevitably Monckton lacked Sullivan's technical resource; but he put his natural talents to considerable effect. *The Arcadians* (Shaftesbury 1909), one of three productions on which he collaborated with Howard Talbot, remains the work by which the whole Edwardian musical comedy genre is best remembered. Other masterpieces were *A Country Girl* (Daly's 1902) and *The Quaker Girl* (Adelphi 1910); both, apart from the inevitable interpolations, were entirely Monckton's own work. As a fluent popular melodist, particularly in waltz time, Monckton had no equal among British theatre composers. His talents as a whole entitle him to a far more eminent position in the international ranks of operetta composers than posterity and British reticence have granted him.

Monckton's chief rival as a melodist was Paul A. Rubens (1875–1917). A man of considerable natural talents, he could and on occasion did throw off a new number at a few minutes' notice. He wrote additional numbers for many shows; but for others he was not only sole composer (in itself a rarity in an age of collaboration) but also sole book author and lyricist. His best work is *Miss Hook of Holland* (Prince of Wales' 1907), a lighthearted work full of captivating, expertly shaped melodies, and a considerable international success in its day. A victim of illness throughout his short life, he lacked the application and consistency of Monckton. But even in his less successful works one can readily find examples of the freshness of his invention. In *Dear Little Denmark* (Prince of Wales' 1909), another work that was entirely Rubens's own, the simple charm of the duet 'I'm in love with you' contrasts effectively with an entrance number for a gout-riddled grand duke that displays an Offenbachian sense of theatrical effect. Some of his more immediately striking tunes were not without vulgarity; but he was able to display a genuine depth of feeling that increased as his illness gained hold. Popular theatre music has produced few things more satisfyingly evocative than the haunting 'Violin Song' from *Tina* (Adelphi 1915), a work on which he collaborated with Haydn Wood, or 'Bohemia' from *The Happy Day* (Daly's 1916) on which he collaborated with Sidney Jones. Example 5.3 shows how Rubens could write particularly effectively in pensive or dreamy mood. (The number is sung by Bandmaster van Vuyt, a role created by the future Wagnerian tenor Walter Hyde.)

American-born Howard Talbot (1865–1928) was responsible for the

Ex. 5.3 Paul A. Rubens, *Miss Hook of Holland* (1907): song with chorus, 'Little Liqueurs'

(*K*: Chappell, 1907)

scores of several big successes, either alone or in collaboration. *A Chinese Honeymoon* toured the provinces for two years before reaching the Royal Strand Theatre in 1901 and becoming the first musical comedy to run for a thousand consecutive performances. However, Talbot was not primarily a melodist, and it was in providing musical substance to collaborations with Monckton and Rubens that he was most successful. In *The Arcadians* he achieved a popular success with the lugubrious 'My Motter', while his musical good taste was admirably demonstrated by the delightful duet 'Half-Past Two'. But it was perhaps in his concerted numbers that Talbot put his inventiveness and technical proficiency to best effect. The opening choruses and first-act finale of *The Blue Moon* (Lyric 1905), one of his collaborations with Rubens, are particularly fine.

Though both Jones and Leslie Stuart composed a good deal in Edwardian times, neither recaptured the success of earlier days. Stuart owed much of his early success to a rhythmic individuality—a sort of jaunty moto perpetuo—that pervaded not only 'Little Dolly Day-dream' and 'Lily of Laguna' but also 'Tell me, pretty maiden', the most popular number from *Florodora*. After a while the novelty inevitably faded. Stuart suffered considerably from the operations of the pirate music publishers who flourished in the early years of the century. Yet he made and frittered away a fortune; and after trying his luck in the United States, he ended his days reduced to touring in music halls and revue, playing selections of his most popular songs at the piano.[18]

Jones, for his part, had his roots firmly in the musical climate of nineteenth-century comic opera, and he never came to terms with the Edwardians' need for a brasher, more readily assimilated style. The most successful of his later works was *King of Cadonia* (Prince of Wales' 1908; additional numbers by Frederick Rosse); but his masterpieces remained *The Geisha*, *San Toy* (Daly's 1899), and the comic opera *My Lady Molly* (Terry's 1903). Stubborn and retiring by nature, Jones adhered to the ideal of completing his scores unaided by the harmonizers and orchestrators who had become an accepted part of the scene.

The standard London theatre orchestra of the time consisted of up to thirty, sometimes forty musicians—a small body of strings, perhaps two flutes, an oboe, two clarinets, a bassoon, two horns, two cornets, two trombones, and percussion. One musician who gained considerable experience as a deputy in various theatre orchestras of the time was Eric Coates, then a young viola player at the Royal Academy of Music. In his autobiography Coates describes the cramped, sweaty conditions in which the musicians worked; but he also writes with affection of the conductors under whom he played, particularly

Howard Talbot, Edward Jones of the Vaudeville Theatre, and Barter Johns of Daly's. He also remarks on the interest and admiration with which he studied the work of the specialist orchestrators such as I. A. de Orellana who finished off the scores of the less thoroughly trained composers of the day.[19] This breed, incidentally, was by no means a peculiarity of the London scene. Gaston Serpette 'helped many a French composer with his orchestration',[20] and Arnold Schönberg and Alexander von Zemlinsky are known to have spent time orchestrating the operettas of others in Vienna.

Pantomime, Ballet, and Revue (1830–1914)

Light musical entertainments had, of course, always been particularly plentiful at Christmas time. It was during the early part of the nineteenth century that the tradition of the *Christmas pantomime* really became established, so that by 1830 all the theatres in London were vying with each other with their own pantomime opening on Boxing Day.[21] Originally the pantomime had consisted of a short opening based usually on some sort of nursery tale, followed by a transformation scene in which the characters were transformed into the figures of Harlequin, Pantaloon, Columbine, Clown, and Lover, who engaged in the traditional Harlequinade. However, all this began to change with the success of Planché's fairy extravaganzas. Such works as *Puss in Boots* (Olympic 1837), *The Sleeping Beauty in the Wood* (Covent Garden 1840), and *Beauty and the Beast* (Covent Garden 1841) were obvious precursors of the pantomime as we now know it. Gradually the pantomime opening sequence lengthened until it, and not the Harlequinade, became the principal element.[22] Eventually the Harlequinade disappeared altogether.

The pantomime was always closely related to the extravaganza in its extravagant scenic effects, punning humour, prominence of the female 'principal boy', and emphasis on popular tunes of the day. During the latter part of the century pride of place always went to the pantomime at the Theatre Royal, Drury Lane, spectacularly staged and making effective use of leading music-hall stars such as Vesta Tilley, Dan Leno, and Harry Fragson. *Beauty and the Beast* (1890) had an original score by Procida Bucalossi (c. 1837–1918) that achieved some success; but usually the music was arranged from various sources by the musical director of the time—Karl Meyder in the 1870s, Oscar Barrett (c. 1846–1941) in the 1880s and James Glover (1861–1931) from the mid-1890s.

Besides pantomime, Edwardian families were also able to enjoy various seasonal entertainments using a specially written score of simple songs, duets, and choruses that could readily be appreciated by children. J. M. Barrie's *Peter Pan* (Duke of York's 1904), with music by John Crook (c. 1847–1922), is still played today, and there were also popular stage adaptations of Lewis Carroll's *Alice in Wonderland* (Prince of Wales' 1886) with music by Walter Slaughter (1860–1908) and Charles Kingsley's *The Water Babies* (Garrick 1902) with music by Frederick Rosse (1867–1940).

Somewhat outside the field of theatre proper were the large variety theatres. Music hall turns made up the bulk of an evening's entertainment; but *spectacular ballet* was for many years a star attraction at the Alhambra and Empire. At the Alhambra,[23] dominating Leicester Square with its dome and Moorish facade, the ballet tradition dated back to the 1860s, when the theatre was still a genuine music hall with tables in the pit. At that time the style of the ballets was largely dictated by the law which prevented a theatre with a licence for music and dancing from presenting a dramatic entertainment. A ballet of the *Giselle* type was thus out of the question, and the emphasis was very much on spectacular effects. *The Watteau Fête* (1866) featured a 'prismatic torrent', a crystal curtain made up of thousands of pieces of glass which threw kaleidoscopic reflections of every colour on to the forest scene behind, while for *The Titanic Cascades* (1866) the theatre's publicity proclaimed 'a picturesque ravine down which the real torrents pour'—the latter produced by one hundred and fifty tons of water stored in tanks above the stage.

The music for these ballets was, as usual, composed or arranged by the resident musical director—J. W. Hird until 1866, succeeded by Jules Rivière (1819–1900). When, in 1872, the Alhambra reopened with a theatrical licence, the position was taken over by Georges Jacobi (1840–1906). Jacobi, a musician of talent, composed the music for more than sixty ballets over a period of twenty-six years, though for Queen Victoria's Diamond Jubilee in 1897 the score of *Victoria and Merrie England* was specially commissioned from Sullivan.

It was in 1887 that the Alhambra first came under direct competition from the Empire Theatre[24] on the adjacent north side of Leicester Square. Opened in 1884, it at first failed to find a winning formula; but the appointment of George Edwardes as managing director launched the theatre on a prosperous era. The Empire became famous not least for the promenade at the rear of the auditorium, which was the most celebrated picking-up point in the world. But no less celebrated in their different way were the variety programmes themselves, with spectacularly staged ballet a prominent feature. Edwardes recruited a first-rate team consisting of designer C. Wilhelm, maîtresse de ballet Katti Lanner (daughter of the Viennese dance composer Joseph Lanner) and, as musical director, the French operetta composer and conductor Hervé. In 1889 Hervé was succeeded by Léopold Wenzel, and for fifteen years the team of Lanner, Wilhelm, and Wenzel created a succession of spendid ballets, particularly after the arrival of Adeline Genée as *première danseuse* in 1897.

Genée's first appearance was during the run of *Monte Cristo* (1896), a work which exemplified the more serious and traditional ballet that was one of the two pillars on which the Empire's ballet policy rested. The first ballet newly created for her, *The Press* (1898), typified the more topical style, with a wider range of dances, that had been introduced as a direct counterpart of musical comedy. After an introductory sequence in which the Spirit of the Liberty of the Press (danced by Genée) appeared to William Caxton, the action portrayed some stages in the production of a newspaper, and then there was a varied sequence of dances introducing over a hundred London newspapers and periodicals of the day. As there was little classical training of male ballet dancers in those days, men were usually restricted to comic roles, while the more serious male roles were danced by women *en travesti*. The casts were large, as was the orchestra. The published piano score of *The Press* lists an orchestral complement of over sixty players, including as principal first violin Lorenzo Barbirolli, the father of Sir John. Wenzel's scores incorporated vocal passages and made effective use of his large orchestral forces.*

By the end of the Edwardian era tastes in popular theatrical entertainment were again changing. For several years the British musical theatre had had little to fear from foreign competition, and only the occasional importation such as Kerker's *The Belle of New York* (Shaftesbury 1898) and Messager's *Véronique* (Apollo 1904) had seriously challenged native supremacy. However, the English version of *The Merry Widow* (Daly's 1907) surpassed even that theatre's previous tremendous successes and heralded a new era in Viennese operetta that was confirmed by Oscar Straus's *A Waltz Dream* (Hicks' 1908) and Fall's *The Dollar Princess* (Daly's 1909). In ballet, too, the public began to succumb to the Russian dancers who came to London, at first singly or in pairs and then in 1911 with the full Diaghilev company. The traditional style of ballet as staged at the Alhambra and the Empire thus began to look decidedly old-fashioned. Yet the material that really instituted a new era in London musical theatre came neither from

*Several of his original scores are now preserved in the Bibliothèque de l'Opéra in Paris.

Austria nor from Russia. Rather it came from North America, in the lively popular songs that had been reaching the British ear through the music hall, through interpolation in musical comedies or, increasingly, through *revue*.

Revue had originated in France as a series of sketches representing a satirical review—often annual—of current events and theatrical productions. A compère or commère was an inseparable part of the entertainment, introducing the items and interpolating explanatory or cynical remarks. In London, revue-style sketches had commonly been incorporated into burlesques, although an occasional production was more specifically in revue form, for example *Under the Clock* (Court 1893; music by Edward Jones), a one-act burlesque of English literary and theatrical personalities. During the early years of the twentieth century revues began to appear more often as part of the evening's entertainment at the large variety theatres such as the Empire and Coliseum. George Edwardes was again in the forefront with *Rogues and Vagabonds* (Empire 1905), which took over the French idea of the commère and introduced some of the latest hit songs from America.

Thus it was that in due course such commercial American ragtime song hits as 'Everybody's doing it', 'Alexander's Ragtime Band', 'Row, Row, Row' and 'Waiting for the Robert E. Lee' reached the British public through revues at the leading variety theatres. *Everybody's Doing It* (Empire 1912), *Kill That Fly!* (Alhambra 1912), and *Hello, Ragtime!* (Hippodrome 1912) were titles that indicated the fast-moving presentation and snappy topicality of the breed. They were in fact little more than chains of variety acts, often featuring American performers. There was no dramatic development and seldom more than a vague thematic link. But, thanks to the appeal of the songs and routines, the fashion caught on. The Palace Theatre presented *The Passing Show* (1914), while the Ambassador's Theatre reverted nearer to the original French model with the one-act *Odds and Ends* (1914) which was followed by the full-length *More (Odds and Ends)* (1915)—titles that reflected the piecemeal nature of the entertainment. The scores were often attributed to the resident musical directors—Cuthbert Clarke (1869–1953) at the Empire, Herman Finck (1872–1939) at the Palace, and Edward Jones (c. 1859–1917) at the Ambassador's—but they were now no more than a sequence of songs, chorus numbers, and incidental music. This was the province of specialist song composers—often American—though there were British successes in Finck's 'We'll Make a Man of You' ('On Sunday I walk out with a soldier') from *The Passing Show* and James W. Tate's 'Broken Doll' from *Samples* (Playhouse 1915).

107

For a time the British musical comedy and imported Viennese operetta survived alongside. But the imminent eclipse of the Edwardian musical style was well symbolized by the designation of Rubens's *After the Girl* (Gaiety 1914) as a 'revusical comedy'. Only in the special conditions of the first world war, when safe, escapist entertainment was in particular demand, did traditional British musical styles gain a temporary reprieve. The 'romantic musical play' *The Maid of the Mountains* (Daly's 1917), with music by Harold Fraser-Simson (1872–1944) and James W. Tate (1875–1922), ran for three years and 1352 performances, though this was already exceeded by the achievement of the 'musical tale of the east' *Chu Chin Chow* (His Majesty's 1916), with music by Frederic Norton (1869–1946), which ran for 2238 consecutive performances—a record that was to stand for forty years. By the time their runs were ended, the floodgates were already open for the inflow of American theatrical entertainment that was increasingly to dominate the British popular musical theatre.

Chapter 6

BALLROOM AND
DRAWING-ROOM MUSIC

NICHOLAS TEMPERLEY

Dance Music

Dancing was a pastime enjoyed by all classes of society, except those who disapproved of it on religious grounds (these included some Evangelical Anglicans as well as dissenters). But it was a strictly segregated activity in the early decades of the nineteenth century. At Almack's, the most fashionable of the London assembly rooms, the distribution of tickets was controlled by a committee of noblewomen on socially exclusive lines, while at the rooms opened at Cheltenham in 1816 the rule was most explicit: 'That no clerk, hired or otherwise, in this town or neighbourhood; no person concerned in retail trade, no theatrical or other public performers by profession be admitted'.[1] A second 'layer' of dance halls was maintained for wealthy business men, while other assembly rooms were open to anyone who could pay a shilling and was properly dressed.[2] In 1845 the 'tea dance' (*thé dansant*) was introduced for the newly genteel. At the lowest end of the social scale, dancing took place in taverns, warehouses, and the open air.

In view of this stratification it is a little surprising to discover that in 1800 much the same dances and music were used at all levels, at least in England. The *country dance*, universal since Playford's time and before, remained the staple for even the most aristocratic balls. Every year throughout the eighteenth century and well into the nineteenth, new country dance tunes were published for the old figures, generally for a band of violin, flute, harp and keyboard; for melody instrument alone; or for keyboard alone (ex. 6.1). The tunes had names, and the leading lady 'called the tune'. By way of variety there was an occasional 'French country dance' (contredanse), a cotillion, or an early version of the waltz. Scottish and Irish dances were becoming more fashionable. The minuet, which had once been the favourite court dance, was

109

Ex. 6.1 Country dance, 'The Duke of York's Birthday' (1807)

(Astor, 2)

almost obsolete, though still danced ceremonially at royal balls and at Almack's. All these dances were performed with the partners barely touching one another, and most demanded intricate footwork.

Into this traditional and provincial setting came the first harbinger of modern ballroom dancing, the *waltz*, in its newer form in which the partners clasped each other with unaccustomed intimacy. It came, together with the quadrille, from Paris, which was not only the centre of fashion but the undisputed capital of dance. According to Byron it first became popular in England in the year of the battle of Austerlitz (1805); Burney, writing for Rees's *Cyclopaedia* at about the same time,

110

still spoke disapprovingly of 'foreigners' he had seen waltzing. By 1812 it was clearly on the way in. Neither the enthusiasm that some felt for it, nor the disapproval it aroused in others, was entirely musical, as Byron's lines show:

> Endearing Waltz!—to thy more melting tune
> Bow Irish jig, and ancient rigadoon.
> Scotch reels, avaunt! and country-dance, forego
> Your future claims to each fantastic toe!
> Waltz—waltz alone—both legs and arms demands,
> Liberal of feet, and lavish of her hands;
> Hands which may freely range in public sight
> Where ne'er before—but—pray 'put out the light'.[3]

In the next hundred years, a growing portion of the British population would learn to love the waltz, until at last it entered the music halls. But it long retained an aura of slight impropriety. In *Daniel Deronda* Gwendolen Harleth at a grand ball would only dance in the quadrille: 'I shall not waltz or polk with anyone', she announced, to her mother's dismay but with the approval of her clerical uncle.[4]

The *quadrille* was much less daring, and in consequence more readily accepted. Captain Gronow recalled that in 1814,

the dances at Almack's were Scotch reels and the old English country-dance; and the orchestra, being from Edinburgh, was conducted by the then celebrated Neil Gow. It was not until 1815 that Lady Jersey introduced from Paris the favourite quadrille, which has so long remained popular . . . The 'mazy waltz' was also brought to us about this time; but there were comparatively few who at first ventured to whirl around the *salons* of Almack's.[5]

A quadrille was a set of movements, generally five, each with its own rather elaborate figures and steps; it was danced by four couples in square formation. The most popular set was the one originally introduced by Lady Jersey, consisting of five figures: Le Pantalon, L'Été, La Poule, Le Trénis, La Finale (later Le Trénis was often replaced by La Pastourelle). A variant was The Lancers, introduced at Dublin in 1817 but not widely popular before mid-century. Judging by published sets of quadrilles, the only essential features of the dances were the two beats of each bar and the 4- and 8-bar phrases (ex. 6.2); simple and compound time were used interchangeably for the same figures. Thus it was easy to make a set of quadrilles out of the most popular tunes of an opera, and many sets were so made. Others were named after some prominent person, recent event or other topical subject. There were even the 'Landslip Quadrille', after the landslip at Lyme Regis in Christmas 1839, and the 'Stabat Mater Quadrilles' (1842) by James

W. Davison (later music critic on *The Times*), based on tunes from Rossini's *Stabat Mater* (this last provoked a certain amount of protest).[6]

The waltz and quadrille soon took over from the country dance in fashionable circles, though one country dance, the Sir Roger de Coverley, was still often used to wind up a ball. In humbler surroundings the country dance survived longer, as we learn from Dickens's description of Mrs Fezzwig's ball, held in her husband's warehouse, accompanied by a fiddler with a music book: 'Away they all went, twenty couples at once; hands half round and back again the other way; down the middle and up again; . . . old top couple always turning up in the wrong place; new top couple starting off again, as soon as they got there; all top couples at last, and not a bottom one to help them!'[7] The old dances survived in the slums as well as the villages, as is shown in an illustration of 1872.[8]

The novelties in the nineteenth century were all dances that had had a folk origin in a foreign country; appealed to aristocrats for their lively character, first in Vienna or Paris and then in London; and would ultimately trickle down through the ranks of British society. The *galop*, a simple dance in fast 2/4 time, had its London debut in 1829, when it was introduced at the King's ball at St James's Palace; the *polka*, in a slightly slower 2/4, appeared at a ball given by the Duke of Wellington in honour of the Queen's birthday in 1844.[9] Others such as the mazurka, polonaise, redowa, and schottische had less spectacular success. For royal state balls no further innovations were permitted for the rest of our period: the first ball of George V's reign, in 1911, consisted of 3 quadrilles, 15 waltzes, 3 polkas and a galop.[10] By this time enthusiasm for dancing had waned in aristocratic circles, and it was considered bad form for a gentleman to be too good at it. According to an eye-witness at the turn of the century, 'a far higher standard of dancing was to be found at the football, cricket, tennis clubs and other subscription balls organised by the upper middle classes'.[11]

Certain novelties were beginning to come in from the United States such as the Military Schottische or Barn Dance (1888), the Washington Post (1894) and the Cake Walk (about 1900); the rhythms of ragtime were creeping in. But until the first world war it was still usual to engage a small string orchestra to play the music for a dance, with or without a piano.

The contribution of British composers to the repertory of British dance music was modest. Country dance collections, compiled generally by dancing masters, were made up mostly of adapted materials, or of anonymous new dances closely modelled on older ones in style (ex. 6.1). In the Victorian period the new dances, all of continental origin, were danced chiefly to music by continental composers, a great deal of it adapted from operas, ballets, and concert pieces. The Catalogue of Ewer & Co.'s Universal Circulating Music Library for 1860 listed, in all, 51,801 musical works available on loan to subscribers. There were 494 sets of orchestral dances and marches (compared to 463 other orchestral works), of which 117 were by Charles d'Albert (1809–86) and 75 by Johann Strauss (1804–49); 390 dance sets for piano duet compared with 3285 other piano duets; and 1584 dance sets for piano solo compared with 12,428 other piano solos. Of the 1584 sets for piano solo, the most by any one composer were, once again, those by d'Albert, which numbered 237, including 70 quadrilles, 68 waltzes, 53 polkas, and 20 galops. Not a single one of the 78 composers or compilers can be identified as British by birth: but several, including Henri Laurent, John Weippert, and d'Albert himself, had settled in Britain.

D'Albert was born near Hamburg, the son of a French cavalry officer who died in 1816; his mother brought him to England, where he studied both music and dancing. In his successful career as a provider of dance music the main landmarks were such favourites as 'The Bridal Polka' (1845). But the great bulk of his music is adapted. Native British composers of dance music included Stephen Glover, C. H. R. Marriott, and the Coote family. Their music is quite undistinguished; the scoring is generally coarse but effective. The full-size dance band of the period was little different in make-up from the classical orchestra (ex. 6.2). Military bands frequently played at balls, and the *valse militaire* was a popular form. The *Mabel Waltz* by Dan Godfrey senior (1831–1903) was written for a ball given by the Brigade of Guards for the Prince and Princess of Wales in 1863: in Andrew Lamb's opinion it 'must have been the most popular English waltz of the century'.[12]

Closely associated with dance music were the *promenade concerts* that began in London in the late 1830s and later spread to the spas and seaside resorts. The idea of listening to music while freely walking about was not new; it had been the practice in the pleasure gardens of Marylebone, Ranelagh and Vauxhall. But the fashion for pleasure gardens waned after 1800 (though Vauxhall stayed open until 1859), and when the promenade concerts arrived they came from Paris. Philippe Musard (1793–1859), a French violinist and conductor whose orchestra had been in demand for masked balls, began a series of promenade concerts in 1833, which were uncommonly successful and consisted largely of dance music. In 1838 concerts 'after the manner of Musard's' were announced at the English Opera House, and several others followed; in 1840 Musard himself came to London and conducted a series. In all these the programme was largely made up of

113

Ex. 6.2 C. H. R. Marriott, 'The Merry Quadrilles' (1857): No. 1

*Sounding notes

(B. Williams, No. 14)

waltzes, quadrilles and galops, but there was also an occasional overture or symphony movement. Musard was closely followed by the
inimitable Louis Jullien (1812–60), who was engaged at Drury Lane
Theatre in the summer of 1840. His showmanship brought huge
crowds to the scene. They heard massed bands, choruses, orchestras
with strange additional instruments, and saw many gimmicks and
special effects; but they heard entire Beethoven symphonies and even

114

Berlioz's 'Harold in Italy' in the midst of all the dance music and ballads. To conduct Beethoven Jullien ostentatiously put on white gloves and took up a jewelled baton; to heighten the effect of the storm in the 'Pastoral' symphony he had dried peas rattled in a tin box. And his own style of conducting was a spectacle in itself, initiating the vogue of the virtuoso conductor.[13] He rescored many of the classics he performed, and with every season introduced some outrageous novelty. The climax was reached at the Great Exhibition of 1851 when his 'Great Exhibition Quadrilles' were performed by 207 players.[14]

There were many other series of promenade concerts in late Victorian London. From 1895 the term took on a new meaning with the foundation of the Queen's Hall Promenade Concerts under Henry J. Wood (1869–1944), which, though aiming at a wide middle-class audience, concentrated almost exclusively on classical art music.

The lighter side of the promenade concerts was reflected in the music of the resort orchestras. The oldest tradition was at Bath, where the Pump Room Orchestra had played every season since 1704. Other prominent orchestras were to be heard at Bournemouth, Brighton, Eastbourne, Harrogate, Llandudno, Margate, Scarborough and Torquay; in seaside towns they generally played on the pier, or in a pavilion near the sea front. A direct link with Jullien existed at Llandudno, where another Frenchman, Jules Rivière (1819–1900), who had come to London in 1857 to work with the famous showman, in 1871 began 'Rivière's Promenade Concerts' with an orchestra of 80, often supplemented by a chorus or a military band. He took his orchestra on tour around the leading resorts, and from 1887 settled as conductor of the Pavilion Orchestra at Llandudno, which soon became famous, and would later be the first stepping stone in the conducting career of Malcolm Sargent.[15] At Bournemouth, the Winter Gardens Orchestra, originally formed to play in the Pavilion by adding a small string section to the local band, blossomed under Dan Godfrey junior (1868–1939) into the Bournemouth Municipal Symphony Orchestra.

Though many of the resort orchestras aspired from time to time to play 'serious' music, their chief function was inevitably to provide entertainment of an undemanding kind. Their programmes were made up of dances and marches, overtures and operatic medleys; most included vocal music, which took the form of ballads of a type to be described in another section, or of popular glees and part-songs. In vocal and instrumental music alike, the favourite form, year in and year out, was the waltz. It turned up in selections from symphonies, like the second movement of Berlioz's *Symphonie fantastique*, or from operas, like the 'Bijou' song from Gounod's *Faust*; in suites of waltzes by Strauss,

Waldteufel, or Lehár; in waltz songs like 'Oh where, oh where has my little dog gone?' (1847), 'My bonny lies over the ocean' (1881), 'Daisy, Daisy' (1892), or 'You, me, sympathy' (1912); and in brilliant waltzes for the piano like Brahms's or Liszt's. One of the more successful British composers of waltzes, Alfred Gwyllym Crowe (1835–94), seems to have been the inventor of a kind of waltz cantata which became popular in London and the resorts. One such was *The Rose Queen*, performed at the Covent Garden Promenade Concerts in 1883; another was named *The See-Saw*. The texts of these pieces are bland, totally free of anything remotely disturbing. Their 'plots' lack any kind of conflict or tension; their music is pleasant, tuneful, and entirely predictable.

In the Edwardian period and the years immediately before the War, British dance music did at last produce a few works of international popularity, just before it was overtaken by the new American influences. Among the most successful waltzes of this period were Archibald Joyce's 'Remembrance' (1909) and 'Dreaming' (1911), Sydney Baynes's 'Destiny' (1912), and Charles Ancliffe's 'Nights of Gladness' (1912). Example 6.3 shows the beginning of 'Destiny': a brief, attention-getting introduction is followed at once by the sinuous waltz tune, warmly scored for cellos, violas, and clarinets in unison: it returns as a rondo theme with contrasting sections between. Dance band scores at this date featured a 'piano conductor' and were designed to suit bands of varying size and make-up: the wind and percussion parts were generally optional. At many modest dances, no doubt, the 'band' was reduced to violin and piano.

Drawing-Room Music

Printed sheet music for the drawing room exists in enormous quantities from the nineteenth century—more, probably, than from all other periods put together. The drawing room or parlour can be taken as the representative milieu for the music under discussion, even when it was performed in public concerts; and it was this milieu that gave it its distinctive character.

The main body of consumers of this music was of course that ill-defined and fluctuating entity, the middle class. The degree of wealth and social standing implied by a house containing one room set aside for leisure activities was also approximately that required for the acquisition of a piano, the employment of a music master, and the purchase of a library of sheet music. As the population having this potential steadily increased, so did the quantity of music published to

Ex. 6.3 Sydney Baynes, waltz, 'Destiny' (1912)

*Sounding notes

117

(*P:* Watson, Wilcock, 1912)

cater for it. Publishers found after a while that they could turn a profit even from a relatively unsuccessful work, so large was their market. The economics of the matter have been dealt with in Chapter 3.

But the music cannot be clearly distinguished from upper-class music. On the contrary, the middle class generally wished to associate itself with the aristocracy, and in music as in many other things they adopted the values of those who had been the traditional arbiters of fashion and taste. Drawing-room music appealed also to the higher nobility, as we can tell from collections maintained in great houses,* and the upper classes were doubtless much more influential in determining its character than their numbers alone would suggest.

On the other hand drawing-room music is rather sharply distinguished from working-class popular music of the kinds described in Chapter 4. That music tended to reflect pride in membership of the working-class community, and to emphasize regional or proletarian dialects, jokes, characters, and traditions. In drawing-room music we find, not an aggressive assertion of class status, but an underlying assumption that all who are involved in the music—composer, performer, listener—enjoy a certain standing, leisure, and cultivation. In the subjects treated and their settings we find a remoteness from

---

*For example, a collection of some 30 volumes of bound sheet music compiled from 1780 to 1860 by successive Duchesses of St Albans, and now in the Music Library of the University of Chicago.

familiar, everyday situations in which the finer shades of class distinction might be identifiable. In the language of songs there is an absence of all the distinguishing marks of working-class music: no dialects, no vulgarity, no low humour. The language does not, however, make use of upper- or middle-class slang, but instead falls back on a bland, faintly archaic poetic diction, often with 'thee' and 'thou' and words like 'ere' and ''tis': the language sometimes called 'Wardour Street English'.

It is the same with the musical language. Drawing-room music is clearly distinct from the virile, pungent style developed in the music halls, but it is not so blatantly different from high art music. The consumers recognized the high social status of the musical language of European art music, and they wanted a kind of music that audibly partook of that status. But, because the players and singers of drawing-room music were amateurs of modest accomplishment, it must be technically undemanding. And because they and their audience looked on music as a social, not an intellectual accomplishment, and used it only as an ornament to an occasion whose primary function had nothing to do with music, drawing-room music was intellectually undemanding also. It was often a pale reflection of the music of the great composers of an earlier generation. Nevertheless, as we shall find, it could often be the vehicle of strong emotion.

It is clear that drawing-room music was an adjunct to the rapid rise in status of the newly rich, above all by means of advantageous marriages. Few young ladies were minded to put a love of serious music before their desire for a good match. Mary Bennet in *Pride and Prejudice*, 'having, in consequence of being the only plain one in the family, worked hard for knowledge and accomplishments, was always impatient for display' of her talent as a pianist. At a large party at Sir William Lucas's she followed her younger sister at the keyboard: but alas!

Elizabeth, easy and unaffected, had been listened to with much more pleasure, though not playing half so well; and Mary, at the end of a long concerto, was glad to purchase praise and gratitude by Scotch and Irish airs, at the request of her younger sisters, who, with some of the Lucases, and two or three officers, joined eagerly in dancing at one end of the room.[16]

The male attitude to the matter was satirized by George Eliot through the mouth of Mr Brooke in *Middlemarch* (the time portrayed is 1829):

There is a lightness about the feminine mind—a touch and go—music, the fine arts, that kind of thing, they should study those up to a certain point, women should, but in a light way, you know. A woman should be able to sit down and play you a good old English tune. That is what I like; though I have heard most things—been at the opera in Vienna: Gluck, Mozart, everything of that sort.[17]

Lucy Honeychurch, in *A Room with a View*, was serious in her love of music, but her choice of Beethoven's Opus 111 Sonata at an amateur concert met with the disapproval of the vicar.[18] Young ladies singing or playing were expected to charm but in no way to disturb or challenge their listeners.

Drawing-room music, then, was clearly functional, and was appropriately dominated by the female sex. Gentlemen, if they played at all, played a subordinate role; in the early nineteenth century they might 'accompany' the young ladies on a violin or flute, instruments which were traditionally excluded for women. The piano, the harp (to a declining extent), and the voice were the vehicles of feminine musical accomplishment, and hence became the chief media of drawing-room music; string quartets and the like were relegated to rare groups of dedicated male amateurs, playing for their own edification. This was true on the continent also: a Parisian journalist in 1835 pointed out that 'the piano today shares popular favour with singing, and that is true because, though I do not wish to offend other instruments, the two specialities are exclusively the province of women'.[19]

Gentlemen were not expected to play the piano in the drawing room: the only male pianists were professionals, providers, not consumers of piano music. It was taken for granted that published piano music was for ladies to play. A review of Weber's *Concertstück* complained of a passage demanding a stretch of eleven notes, 'written, we presume, for those ladies who have an extra joint to their fingers'.[20] So drawing-room music nearly always included a lady or a pair of ladies at the piano. More often than not, the singer was also feminine. Bass or baritone songs are quite rare in our period. The vocal line, whether of high or low range, was written in the treble clef, and the spacing of the accompaniment generally suggests that the voice line was conceived at the written pitch, not an octave lower.

Victorian ladies looked to Paris to learn what they should do, and a good deal of sheet music published in London either came from Paris or pretended to come from there. The taste for 'good old English tunes' was old-fashioned and provincial. French titles were often used for German or English piano pieces: even composers of the integrity of Mendelssohn, Schumann, and Sterndale Bennett frequently gave French titles to pieces that had no other French association whatsoever. And much music that came to London from Paris had reached Paris from Milan or Naples, if it was vocal, or from Vienna, Leipzig, or Berlin if it was instrumental. Especially in the case of instrumental music there was no need for London publishers to commission English composers, for they had quite enough material coming in from the continent, and could freely reprint it in the absence of effective copyright. Some publishers did, however, employ hack composers, primarily to make instant piano arrangements of the latest orchestral or operatic successes.

An amateur piano solo in a Victorian drawing room, then, was likely to be a medley, fantasia, or rondo based on popular songs, mainly operatic; a set of variations on a well-known tune which might be in origin a ballad, operatic aria, or instrumental melody; a dance or set of dances; or, perhaps, a 'piece' of some kind, such as a nocturne, romance, song without words, or caprice. Sonatas were sometimes played, but on the whole they were too serious, although a sonata movement might pass for a 'piece'. And in all probability the composer would be foreign.

Nevertheless, a great many composers of British stock produced and published drawing-room piano music—in fact most did so, the chief exceptions being the 'high romantic' group who set themselves against popular music as a matter of principle. Two composers of the early Victorian period, Edward Bache (1833–58) and Sydney Smith (1839–89), achieved unusual success along these lines. Bache's four 'Mazurkas de Salon', op. 13, and his 'Souvenirs d'Italie', op. 19, were highly thought of,[21] as were Smith's 'La harpe éolienne' and 'Le jet d'eau' which, as Barclay Squire put it, were 'extremely popular with the numerous class of performers whose tastes are satisfied by a maximum of brilliancy combined with a minimum of difficulty'.[22] Walter Macfarren (1826–1905), brother of George, was another accomplished composer of salon pieces.

The Ballad

If it was hard for British composers to compete with foreign virtuosos in popular piano pieces, in the realm of song the native product held its own alongside the imports. However popular the songs of Rossini, Auber, Gounod, or Offenbach had been in Paris, when they were brought to London they could never quite compete with the English ballads for the favours of the drawing room. Similarly, the *ballad* is the one element that makes English operas of the period distinctly different from their continental models. There was, indeed, an intimate relationship between public performance and private consumption in the life

121

history of the ballad, which goes far to explain its commercial success. Wiley Hitchcock, perceiving the same phenomenon in the United States, has invented the apt term 'concert-household song' to describe it.[23] The ballad is worth closer study: it was not the only form of drawing-room music, but it was the most typical and significant one.

In public concerts, until at least 1840, singers were invariably accompanied by an orchestra, even when a piano was used in the same programme for solos or chamber music: the time of song recitals was still far off. The songs they sang, and their style of singing them, were much the same as in the theatre. But a well established procedure was to publish a song with piano accompaniment, and at the same time to launch it in public by having it sung by a famous singer with orchestra. It made little difference whether the public performance was at a concert or in a stage piece. Ballads were 'introduced' haphazard into any public performance, even an oratorio.[24] During a performance of Mozart's 'Marriage of Figaro' in 1827, 'just in the midst of the lively dialogue . . . the band without rhyme or reason struck up the symphony of [Charles Edward Horn's ballad] "I've been roaming"'.[25] Even when the subject of the song was nominally related to the opera or play, it was really designed for subsequent sale in the music shops for use in the drawing rooms. The 'shop' ballad was still very much alive in the time of Gilbert and Sullivan, though they introduced it with greater finesse than their predecessors. Some so-called 'operas' were little more than ballad concerts strung together on a perfunctory dramatic thread: an example was Edward Loder's *Francis the First* (1838) which included his popular ballad 'The Old House at Home' and others that he had already composed and published before the stage piece was produced.* The *ballad concert*, proper and so-called, was introduced by Charlotte Sainton-Dolby in 1866, and survived into the era of broadcasting.

Because the popularity of a ballad would depend chiefly on its success at the public performance, publishers were willing to pay well-known singers a fee for introducing them in operas or concerts: hence the term *royalty ballad*.[26] The composer gained at best a small initial fee, unless he controlled the public performance of the song, as did Hook at Vauxhall Gardens or Bishop at Covent Garden Theatre. Experience soon showed that the public had limited tolerance for any sort of innovation, and it was this that decisively separated the ballad from serious art. Even composers of considerable invention and

---

*Victorian operas are sometimes called 'ballad operas'. But they were not, like the real ballad operas of 1728–40, made up of already well-known songs adapted to new words. Instead, they included a number of new songs of popular type, in the hope that they would become widely known as separate songs.

resource, like Barnett, Loder or Sullivan, had to conform to the limitations of popular taste when they made ballads.

Efforts to define the Victorian ballad in histories and reference books have generally been too restrictive. It had few limitations of mood or of subject matter: almost the whole range of human experience and emotion was covered, though, to be sure, the treatment was generally shallow, conventional, or even mendacious. Not all ballads were sentimental: some were grisly, humorous, or cynical. Nor was there any set musical form. Most ballads were strophic, but the rondo form was not uncommon (as in 'Cherry ripe'), while some songs written in operatic or art-song forms entered the ballad domain through their use and popularity (like Braham's 'The Death of Nelson' or Sullivan's 'The Lost Chord'). Finally, not all ballads were 'bad', either in their poetry or their music. Provided that they did not challenge conventional morality or demand intellectual effort, ballads could be superbly finished works of art, appealing to the sensitive as well as the philistine. Few would deny such standing to songs like 'Cherry ripe', 'Annie Laurie', or 'Come into the garden, Maud'. Turner calls Tosti's 'Goodbye!' 'a prime example of the art ballad';[27] Sullivan's 'The Lost Chord' is a ballad of highest artistry, however dated its sentiment. The only quality common to all successful ballads was easy accessibility. Harold Simpson wisely treated the term as encompassing 'any song of whatever nature or sentiment that is of a popular type'.[28]

A strong element in the popularity of many ballads was the assertion of British character, especially against other national stereotypes: the frivolity of the French, the licence of the Italians, or the over-seriousness of the Germans. In their texts ballads often reveal the way ordinary middle-class English people saw themselves. Songs like 'Home, sweet home', 'Rock me to sleep' or 'That is love' explicitly deny or belittle the values of sexual love, for example, setting up instead the ideals of family loyalty and mother love. 'The Soldier's Tear' and 'Excelsior' depict a blind patriotism and valour that set aside all temptations, including love. Many ballads re-assert older or purer virtues which, it is implied, have been lost in the modern urbanized society, or are threatened by continental influences, but which the listeners want to believe they have preserved in themselves: 'Even today we hear Love's song of yore,/Deep in our hearts it dwells for evermore' ('Love's Old Sweet Song'); 'Sick of the hollow, the base, the untrue,/Mother, dear Mother, my heart calls for you!' ('Rock me to sleep'). Many invoke settings of childhood, of simple English country life, of the English sailor's life at sea, of the age of chivalry, of the more backward Celtic parts of Britain, of distant countries thought to be unsullied by modern European ideas, or even of destitution and incurable disease. (The one setting never used is that of the drawing room.) Almost identical feelings are invoked in American ballads of the same period, and the words of 'Home, Sweet Home' were by an American.

Many of the earliest ballads were *national airs*, which set up certain features of style to be recognized as Scottish, Welsh or Irish. The national air satisfied a demand of the Romantic for music that seemed 'natural', and hence sublime. Authenticity was less important than a certain strangeness or crudity in the musical idiom; and while there were no musical forgeries on the scale of the Ossianic swindle, there was a certain element of deception in the collections of 'Scottish airs' and so on, which appeared in abundance after 1800. George Thomson's *Select Collection of Original Scottish Airs* (begun in 1793) allied the words of Burns to tastefully modified Scottish tunes, which were supplied with incongruous accompaniments by Haydn, Pleyel, Beethoven and others. Edward Jones in 1801 published *The Bardic Museum: or, Musical, Poetical, and Historical Relicts of the Welsh Bards and Druids*. Similarly James Power, of Dublin, brought out from 1808 *A Selection of Irish Melodies*, for which Thomas Moore altered Irish folksongs collected by Edward Bunting, wrote new words to go with them, and had them harmonized by John Stevenson and later by Henry Bishop. There were also many collections of songs of foreign nations. In such productions it is difficult to say where adaptation ended and composition began. Moore's *Irish Melodies*, in the words of Michael Turner, 'formed the foundation stone of Victorian balladry with their melting melodies married to sentiments of unimpeachable respectability'.[29] A number of them reached ballad level in popularity: 'Oft in the stilly night', 'The minstrel boy', 'The harp that once through Tara's halls', 'Believe me if all those endearing young charms', and above all, 'The last rose of summer' (1813), which spread fast not only through Britain and America but also through Europe, where it was used by Mendelssohn and Flotow. Its opening phrase had the nostalgic I–IV–I harmony; its third phrase modulated to the relative minor, a key that was chosen (in preference to the dominant) in a surprisingly large number of later ballads. The style of Moore's *Irish Melodies* was imitated in hundreds of other ballads of Irish or Scottish flavour, the most popular from the Victorian period being Lady John Scott's 'Annie Laurie' (1838) and Annie Macleod's 'Skye Boat Song' (1884). Continental composers from Berlioz to Brahms also responded to the fascination of these Celtic artifacts, while in America Stephen Foster and a host of less celebrated composers clearly took them as a model for their own popular songs.

In all this development there is a glaring absence of interest in English, as opposed to Scottish or Irish, 'national melody'. Indeed some writers, even into the twentieth century, persisted in claiming that England lacked any folk song of its own.[30] When the first scholarly edition of English folk song appeared in 1838 (the first part of William Chappell's *A Collection of English National Airs*), Henry Chorley declared that 'a far better argument is to be found [here] in support of England's claim to the possession of a national music than many will have thought possible'.[31] English folksongs were still in common use, for example in productions of Shakespeare's plays and of the ever current *Beggar's Opera*, or as nursery rhymes and country dances. But they had little impact on the drawing-room ballad, perhaps because they were too close to home, both in subject matter and in musical idiom, to have the necessary romantic appeal.

If the essence of ballads is their popularity, there is little point in choosing obscure ones for discussion.* Let us begin, therefore, with the most popular of all, 'Home, sweet home', which seems to have won a permanent place in the Anglo-Saxon consciousness and is said to have 'done more than statesmanship or legislation to keep alive in the hearts of the people the virtues that flourish at the fireside, and to recall to its hallowed circle the wanderers who stray from it'. [32] Bishop at first published it as a 'Sicilian Air', later admitting that he composed it. He used it as a theme song in *Clari* (1823).† Its staggering success as a ballad, which reached its height in the 1850s after Jenny Lind had made it her own, needs explanation. The words are evidently the essence of 'balladry' as it has been understood here, but the tune seems lacking in distinction and indeed strangely repetitive: its melodic form can be represented as $AAA'A'BA'$, and even then B is not very different from A, and the whole thing repeats for the second verse. Every phrase has the same harmonic scheme, I–IV–I–V–I. True, there is an effective rise to the upper tonic for the third and later phrases, but that hardly seems enough to make a melody immortal. Turner calls it 'a vacuum of a tune which nostalgia rushes to fill. There is just enough melody to support but not dominate the yearning of the words.'[33] But the same might be said of hundreds of other ballad tunes that never took the public fancy. Though the precise reasons for its success are likely to remain elusive, it might be said that the total predictability of the tune makes it a total reinforcement of the sentiment in the text. Its harmonic scheme is the Schenkerian basis of all tonal music, but repeated many

*Most of the ballads discussed here are to be found in Michael Turner's anthology, *The Parlour Song Book* (London 1972).
†See below, p. 294.

times *without extension*: one literally never leaves home, never faces adventure or challenge. The music gives the very same feeling of safety and protectedness that home itself provides, more especially the home of childhood in which the parents take all cares from one's shoulders. This profound repose, with the emphasis on the major tonic chord and the melody hovering round the mediant, can be found in other settings emphasising fatherly or motherly protection: the March of Priests from 'The Magic Flute'; 'How willing my paternal love' from *Samson*; Agatha's preghiera from 'Freischütz'—the two last, like 'Home, sweet home', in E major. But whereas these pieces vary the repose by interesting melodic or harmonic resource, 'Home, sweet home' remains static from first note to last. The marriage between music and text is perfect.

In Michael Balfe's 'I dreamt that I dwelt', from *The Bohemian Girl* (1843), it is easier to observe the technical means by which the song acquires its magic. The words by Alfred Bunn detach themselves easily from the opera, and neatly express the hopes of a Victorian middle-class girl—wealth, social status, admiration, and a constant lover. The setting of the first two lines in E flat major induces a dreamlike state by means of static harmony and a hypnotic accompaniment figure; but the melody has an unusual construction in which a three-note phrase is gradually 'collapsed' towards a unison. In the third line, the three-note phrase begins higher, and it expands instead of contracting, while maintaining the level of its highest note; at the same time the harmony takes an unexpected turn. The gleam of G major, where nothing more enterprising than G minor was expected, could be paralleled in many a song by Schubert, Bellini, or Meyerbeer; in an English ballad it has just that acceptable degree of surprise or sophistication that could find the song a place in the public memory. The return of the main melody is extended to a conventional operatic conclusion, but the highest note, G, is happily reserved for the last cadence. This is a fine example of a ballad which, though plainly popular in its appeal, has also touches that raise it to the level of art. Considered as an art song, however, it has two faults: the banal version of the tune that serves as introduction and conclusion, and the pause on the penultimate dominant chord (presumably allowing for a cadenza) that is a trademark of the Victorian ballad, designed as a signal for applause.

A ballad from an equally successful opera of the 1840s, 'Yes! let me like a soldier fall' from Vincent Wallace's *Maritana* (1845), appeals instead to the fantasies of the male Victorian. The hero asks only to die an honourable death in battle, 'to blot out ev'ry stain', maintaining the 'ancient chivalry' of his 'proud race'. Trumpets and drums are prominent in the orchestral version, and are imitated in the piano accompaniment, though the martial rhythms recede in the middle of each verse and are replaced by a triplet broken-chord figure *pianissimo*. Over this the voice effectively comes in loud: 'I [he] like a soldier fell'. The structure of this song, though just as easy to grasp as that of 'I dreamt', has nothing in common with it (illustrating the point about the lack of any formal stereotype). It is in five four-bar phrases, all independent melodically—the last extended to a two-bar cadence. There is no return of the opening phrase. The second phrase cadences on the relative minor, the third on the dominant of that key, the others all on the tonic. The instrumental interlude of eight bars is also independent, and does not state the main tune; only its cadence resembles that of the vocal melody. The whole song is preceded and followed by a drum roll. Wallace does little to please the sophisticated in this song, and he ruins his chances with them when in the second verse he adds an extra trumpet call following the words 'Tho' o'er my clay no banner wave,/Nor trumpet requiem swell'.

The success of 'Three fishers went sailing' (1857) was due to entirely different qualities, both textual and musical. The text, by Charles Kingsley, is a conscious evocation of the traditional folk ballad, telling a story of stark tragedy: women and children await the return of three fishermen during a storm, and see their corpses washed up on the beach. Sentimentality is out of the question here, for no expression of grief could seem exaggerated in such a context. The popular appeal is a more primitive one, and is reinforced by the note of proverbial truth sounded in the refrain (ex. 6.4). The composer, John Hullah, found a highly appropriate musical analogue to this text, which pleased both Kingsley and Charlotte Dolby (later Sainton-Dolby), for whom the song was written. His setting is quite dry, his accompaniment made up of detached chords throughout, with no effort to depict storm or wave, no search for harmonies appropriate to grief, and only the most restrained word painting at the word 'moaning'. His harmony, more particularly for the refrain, is of the kind then known as 'ancient'—made up of common chords, chiefly in root position, with 4–3 suspensions instead of dominant sevenths at cadences,* and emphasizing diatonic chords on the second, third, and sixth degrees of the scale rather than secondary dominants or chromatic chords such as provided the normal harmonic fare of the time. In this song the opening vocal melody is quite subordinate to the memorably simple refrain, which is also the basis of the introduction.

An illuminating commentary on the interpretation of this song has

*The cadence in the example does include a decorative dominant seventh, but the main harmony is a plain 4–3 suspension on the dominant.

Ex. 6.4 John Hullah, ballad, 'Three fishers went sailing' (1857)

(S: Addison, Hollier & Lucas, [1857])

been left by Antoinette Sterling, a leading ballad singer who made it one of her chief standbys:

Although I had never been to sea in a storm, and had never even seen fishermen, I somehow understood that song of 'The Three Fishers' by instinct. On reading the poem over for the first time no one could know from the opening that the men would be drowned. Therefore it was a story. But there is a natural tendency to anticipate an unhappy ending; hence it was customary to begin the song so mournfully that everybody realized from the very start what the end was going to be. Madame Sainton-Dolby, for instance, used to sing it sorrowfully from the first note to the last. I had never seen or known of anyone who was drowned, but that mysterious instinct was so strong that I could not foreshadow the finish. When, therefore, I started, I always made the first verse quite bright. I must believe it was the true way, since both the poet and composer endorsed my rendering of it.[34]

It was perhaps naïve to assume that nobody would anticipate the tragic ending, even at a first hearing, but Sterling certainly hit on an excellent mode of heightening the suspense, founding it upon an *illusion* of uncertainty into which the audience would willingly enter. Her 'mysterious instinct' was not, as she thought, for the life of the sea, but for the emotional state of her listeners, who were only too eager to imagine themselves experiencing an elemental drama as far removed from their own lives as it was from hers.

Sterling also contributed to the success of 'The Lost Chord' (1877), Sullivan's maligned masterpiece. When she asked him to set Adelaide Procter's words for her, she found he had already done so, and he willingly allowed her to introduce the song, which she did with immediate and lasting success. The text is a tribute to the power of music, romantic in expression but not itself peculiar to the romantic period. The lost chord had Aristotelian powers of soothing pain and sorrow; it 'seemed the harmonious echo/From our discordant life'; and it suggested the divine: 'It may be that only in Heav'n/I shall hear that grand Amen'. Sullivan chose a varied-strophic setting (*AA'BA"*); the main tune was provided with three very different accompaniments, in much the same skilful manner as in his setting of the hymn tune ST ANNE for *Church Hymns* (1874).[35] The introduction suggests a traditional 'learned' voluntary based on piled-up suspensions to illustrate the opening verse (My fingers wander'd idly/Over the silent keys'). The last phrase of the verse, leading towards a conventional ending, is extended by an unusual form of interrupted cadence and a four-bar coda (ex. 6.5). Here is introduced the chord on the flat seventh (E♭), which is surely the 'lost chord' of the text: it never recurs in the song, even at the end of the last verse where the promise of hearing the chord again in heaven is mentioned. This chord, which was the ultimate

Ex. 6.5 Arthur S. Sullivan, 'The Lost Chord' (1877)

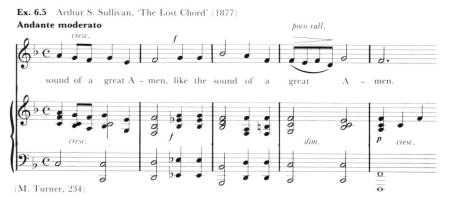

(M. Turner, 234)

'ancient harmony' to the Victorians, had also been used by George Macfarren in his setting of the same poem (ex. 6.6). (Compare also ex. 8.2.) Sullivan introduced it on the insignificant words 'like the', probably because he saw no practical way of using it for the word 'Amen' itself, in a *popular* song which must have a predictable cadence. In the third verse Sullivan used an astringent form of dissonance with an inverted tonic pedal, followed by strong chromatic harmonies suggesting S. S. Wesley, which were surely aimed at the connoisseur; but the grand climax in the last verse could be understood by everyone. Sentimental this song undoubtedly is, but it is a powerful piece of work none the less. Clara Butt was not far wrong when she said 'there is something of the grandeur of Beethoven in it'.[36]

A ballad of purest escapism was Frederic Clay's 'I'll sing thee songs

Ex. 6.6 George A. Macfarren, 'A Lost Chord' (1866)

(*S:* Metzler, [1866])

130

of Araby', which was introduced in his cantata *Lalla Rookh* (1877),*
with a text by W. G. Wills remotely derived from Thomas Moore's
dramatic poem. The lush images of the text are effectively matched in
the harmonies. The four-bar phrase (ex. 6.7, bars 6–10) used as introduction and interlude, and later modified for a vocal coda, is entirely
over a tonic pedal, as is the first vocal phrase, perhaps representing the
comfortably stable home base from which one can afford to take trips
into the exotic. The music proceeds through a hackneyed series of keys
(G major, A minor, B minor), but the harmonies after the climax on G
are more original and quite enterprising. Clay was evidently a musician
of some resource. The rhythm so well suited to the word 'Araby' in the
first line is less apt when it returns at 'on thee break' and 'wonder
wakes'. But it happily forms the basis for the introduction-and-coda
phrase, and thus the most evocative word of the text becomes the
musical motto of the song. Clay is using more than the usual amount
of artistry to lull the audience into the beautiful dream world they
desire.

The Victorian ballad was one of the most characteristic musical
expressions of its age. As long as it is treated as a debased kind of art
song, or alternatively as a snobbish-genteel version of popular
working-class music, its qualities will not be recognized or understood.
In one sense the emotion or sentiment of most ballads is false, in that it
was manufactured and calculated to cater for a promising market. But
in another, more important sense, it is true. Of the thousands of ballads
written and composed, a small number gained great popularity; and
this popularity means that the songs concerned had somehow called
forth the feelings of those who bought, sang, and heard them. Sentimentality is the expression of emotion exaggerated out of proportion to
the matter at hand. The apparently exaggerated emotion of such a song
as 'The Lost Chord' has its source not in the scene depicted, but in the
pent-up feelings accumulating in the breasts of middle-class Victorians, whose social conventions restricted so many natural outlets of
emotion. In this larger sense the emotion of the best Victorian ballads is
genuine, and we need not be ashamed to respond to it. Even such a
hardened critic as Bernard Shaw had to admit to being moved by a
revival of Wallace's opera *Lurline* in 1888: 'There are several moments
in the opera in which the string of hackneyed and trivial shop ballad
stuff rises into melody that surges with genuine emotion.'[37] Triviality is
certainly a fault of most ballads. But when the real feeling below the

---

*Example 6.7 shows how the song is introduced by recitative-like material in the cantata, and
gives indications of scoring from the autograph full score. The sheet music version begins at the
asterisk in bar 5.

surface is able to speak through an adequate composing technique, ballads can evoke a powerful response, even in an audience of our own time.

Ex. 6.7 Frederick Clay, *Lalla Rookh* (1877): ballad, 'I'll sing thee songs of Araby', with preceding recitative

sing thee songs of A-ra - by _____

(*S:* Washington, Library of Congress, [MS] ML96. C7; *K:* Chappell, [1877])

The Edwardian period saw new departures in the popular ballad. Harold Simpson, himself a ballad lyricist, made an acute and detailed survey of the ballad scene in 1910. Among new developments he drew attention to the ballad cycle, introduced by Landon Ronald;[38] the 'short song', also usually appearing as one of a group;[39] and what he called the 'light humour ballad', often launched as part of a burlesque or musical comedy.[40] But the most successful and significant ballads of this period were love songs, often of a more emancipated and passionate kind than those of the Victorian era. Lyrics expressing personally amorous feelings were coupled with surging melodies, rich harmonic support, and a lush style of pianistic writing which (like that for string dance bands) brought to popular music developments that had reached art music half a century earlier. 'Because' (1902), by 'Guy d'Hardelot' (Helen Rhodes, 1858–1936), was typical of the new style of popular love song, and it is a favourite to this day at American wedding receptions. Its second phrase ends with a dissonance resolving by a descending leap, sung no doubt with *portamento*, that was a pronounced cliché of the period. In 'I hear you calling me' (1908), by Charles Marshall, this is made the main feature of the song, and ingeniously varied at the beginning of each of the three verses. This and other points in the song show considerable artistic subtlety, derived from art song, even if the effect today seems trite through its over-familiarity from later imitations. A much more simple and direct but equally popular example of the same genre is Arthur Tate's 'Somewhere a Voice is Calling' (1911): it, too, uses the 'descending-leap' cliché, at the word 'falling'. The first eight measures of this strophic song (ex. 6.8) give a good idea of the style that won Edwardian hearts. In form it differs

133

little from ballads of a hundred years earlier, but its unrestrained emotionalism was something relatively new in middle-class popular music.

Ex. 6.8   Arthur Tate, 'Somewhere a Voice is Calling' (1911)

Dusk, and the sha - dows fall - ing O'er land and sea;

Some-where a voice is call - ing, Call - ing for me!

(*S:* Larway, 1911)

134

Chapter 7

BAND MUSIC

DONALD H. VAN ESS

Military Bands

The military band appeared rather late in English history. The first full band was formed in 1678, according to the records of that year, which for the first time show an allocation for instruments (other than fife and trumpets) for military use: 'Provision furnished out of His Majesty's great wardrobe for a war against France . . . for ten hautboys and four drummers.'[1] The instrumentation of the early bands, composed mainly of oboes, was a result of Charles II's attempt to imitate the French bands which had greatly impressed him during his exile in France.[2] In the course of the eighteenth century the military bands were expanded considerably, and for the first time brass instruments made their appearance. The Articles of Agreement of the Royal Artillery of 1762 state: 'The regiments musick must consist of two trumpets, two French horns, two bassoons and four hautbois or clarinets.'[3] The Royal Artillery band was already larger than other regimental bands.

The tense political atmosphere during the Napoleonic period gave greater impetus to the rise of military bands in England. Not only was there a rapid growth of regimental groups but, beginning in the last decade of the eighteenth century, the number of provincial volunteer bands grew steadily throughout the British Isles. Shortly before 1800, the British bands (emulating their Prussian and French counterparts) modified the traditional oboe-bassoon-horn band by adding clarinets, flutes, a trumpet, and a serpent (a bass instrument related to the ancient cornett). The clarinets now became the dominant 'core' of the ensemble (as in ex. 7.1). In the early years of the nineteenth century the size of the English bands continued to be much like that of their predecessors, largely due to a War Office regulation (1821) which limited regimental bands to ten players; the exception was the Royal Artillery Band which numbered thirty-nine.[4]

In the 1830s the full brass family was added to the line-up of instruments, again in emulation of the French, who had made out-standing progress in the development of new instruments. At this stage the brass section of the English military band was relatively small: several trumpets, cornets, horns, trombones, bass horns, ophicleide, and serpents. The brass group, like the woodwinds, was gradually expanded, and by the 1880s it encompassed the four tonal registers. From highest to lowest instruments, it included: cornets, trumpets, flügelhorns, E-flat tenor horns, French horns, baritones, euphoniums, trombones, and basses. This instrumentation, with the exception of the tenor horns, baritones, and flügelhorns, continued in the twentieth century.

The woodwind family also developed rapidly during this period, especially in the Royal Artillery Band. In 1839 the band numbered a total of forty-eight players; of this figure twenty-six were woodwinds, consisting of piccolo, flutes (2), oboes (2), E-flat clarinets (3), B-flat clarinets (14), and bassoons (4).[5] Like the brass, this section of the military band was enlarged considerably by the 1880s, mainly with the addition of the saxophones (alto, tenor, soprano) and the alto and bass clarinets. Finally, the percussion was also increased from two to four players as a rule, and now equipped with a wider range of accessories to meet the demands of an expanded repertory.

As the military band advanced from its purely functional existence in the eighteenth century to a concertizing, public-entertainment role in the nineteenth, attention was directed to the refinement of its tonal character. The change in the quality of sound by the late nineteenth century was due in part to the improvement of instruments, and specifically of the elements which influenced intonation and playing technique. Of course, both English and continental instrumental groups—orchestras, military bands, recreational brass bands—shared in the benefits derived from the new inventions. These included the Böhm flute (c. 1846) and analogous improvements to the reed instru-ments, which resulted in greater ease and flexibility of fingering, an extended range, and purer intonation. The brasses experienced the most dramatic changes: from the old natural instruments, which were confined to playing hunting-call figures, to the modern valved forms, which offered great flexibility and colour, ascending and descending scale passages, chromatic notes, and freedom of modulation. The valve system was adapted to all existing brass instruments such as the bugle (thereafter known as the soprano saxhorn in England and the flügelhorn in Germany), the trumpet, the French horn, and the cornet (in England it was at first called the cornopean). These valved instru-ments created a wealth of expressive possibilities, which were first brought into the orchestral field by Berlioz and into the military by Wilhelm Wieprecht (1802–72), the leading figure in Prussian band music.

An important milestone for the development of British military band music was the establishment of the Royal Military School of Music. The founding of this institution, commonly referred to as Kneller Hall, took place in 1857, when the War Office acquired the mansion of Sir Godfrey Kneller at Twickenham for the purpose of training instrumentalists and directors for army bands.[6] Within the general context of army reform following the Crimean War (1853–6), there was growing pressure to raise standards of performance (which were below those of many European bands) by providing a disciplined professional training. Most of the earlier bandmasters had been civilians imported from the Continent: Kneller Hall provided the regiments with skilled British-trained directors. A further advance was made in 1881 when regimental directors were required to pass the Kneller Hall bandmasters' exam.

The chief functional form of music for military band was, of course, the *march* (ex. 7.1), which necessarily remained much the same in general character throughout our period, with changes only in harmonic style and instrumentation. Marches were organized in phrases of eight, sixteen, and other multiples of four bars, and frequently had contrasting sections known as *trios*, often in the subdominant key. (Though these were intended to lead back to a repeat of the main section, by the later nineteenth century a march often ended with the trio in performance.) The *quickstep*, in fast 6/8 time, lent itself equally well to marching (see ex. 7.2). As regimental bands began to be used also for concert purposes, they were provided in the late nineteenth century with waltzes, divertimentos (usually potpourris of marches and waltzes), and arrangements of standard orchestral and operatic works. Original British music for military band, going beyond the strictly functional, may be regarded as negligible.

Concert Bands

Following the Napoleonic era, English wind-music activity shifted from the military to the public realm. After Waterloo many of the regimental and volunteer bands that had been formed during the patriotic fervour of the 1790s were disbanded. Others continued into civilian life, often merging with church bands (which in many towns had been made redundant by the introduction of an organ) or with

Ex. 7.1 Charles Griesbach: *12 Military Divertimentos for a Full Band*
(c. 1795): No. 1, March

(*P:* Smart, c. 1795)

surviving town waits. The earliest of these purely civilian or recreational groups date from 1814–30 and include the Black Dyke Band (started 1816), Besses O' the Barn (1818) (originally 'Clegg's Reed Band'), Stalybridge Old Band (1814), Bolton Old Band (1815), and Bramley Old Band (1828).[7]

Understandably, the military influence was very much in evidence in these first post-war bands. For example, Stalybridge had a typical 'military' composition: four flutes, four clarinets, two bassoons, one trumpet, two horns, bugle, serpent, bass horn, and drums.[8] The Blaina Band (Monmouthshire), formed about 1823, was one of the first all-brass bands, and was composed of twenty-three players. By 1850 the transition to all-brass bands was well under way. By 1900 the movement had spread throughout England and numbered over 20,000 amateur brass players.[9] Without a doubt the popularizing of the brass instruments by the touring John Distin family was a major influence in this trend from reeds to brass. The Distins, led by the father, John (1793–1863), who had been a trumpeter with the Grenadier Guards and in the Band of George IV, formed a brass quintet in 1836 which for several years toured extensively in England, Scotland, and Ireland. Later, in Paris (1844), they visited the famous instrument maker Adolphe Sax, who equipped them with his new 'saxhorns'. These bugle-like instruments, which ranged in size from the high soprano to the bass, later became (with some modifications) the principal instruments of the brass band. Upon their return to England the Distins became the sole selling agents for Sax's instruments and continued to perform and tour until about 1855.[10]

The existence of the all-brass band, a peculiarly English development, was partly the result of philanthropic efforts to mitigate the evils of industrialization. Various industrialists attempted to improve the working conditions of factory labourers by establishing recreational bands and choral groups. For example, the Blaina Band had its beginnings under the aegis of Brown's Ironworks. A travelling member of the company procured a set of brass instruments in Amsterdam for the firm's employees.[11] The advantage of brass over reed instruments was that they were more easily mastered. Undoubtedly, the invention of the cornopean in the 1830s helped the movement on its way. Its ease of fingering and blowing and its lyrical qualities were particularly appealing to the working-class amateur bandsmen. Its role was similar to the clarinet's in the military band; that is, its main function was to carry important melodic passages, and it was thus given considerable emphasis in scoring and arranging.

The year 1845 marked the beginning of the brass-band contest movement, which has continued up to the present day. The first contest took place at the home of Sir Clifford Constable as part of an elaborate festival which, in addition to brass bands, included medieval games, falconry, archery, and tournaments.[12] The Partington Band, one of the five bands participating in the contest, employed three cornopeans, two keyed bugles, a trumpet, two trombones, an ophicleide, and three serpents. The music, all arrangements of semi-serious works, was similar (apart from its instrumentation) to that offered at the prom- enade concerts then coming into vogue in England. It included a selection from 'Mozart's Twelfth Mass', the *preghiera* from Weber's 'Freischütz', a selection from Rossini's 'Barber of Seville', Handel's 'Hallelujah Chorus', and a pot-pourri of country airs. Despite the lack of original brass music, this contest and the many that followed were important for placing the bands in a concert setting. The first contests were held in the open air. They attracted a predominantly working- class audience which was to grow in size and in musical understanding over the years. Furthermore, the contests were important for encourag- ing performance skills, musicianship, and a balanced instrumentation. At the Belle Vue (Manchester) festival of 1853, the *Manchester Guardian* reported that 'these working-class amateurs were little less skilful than the best professional players'.[13] This contest attracted eight bands with an audience estimated at sixteen thousand, which was typical of the tremendous following given to brass-band contests in the latter part of the century.

In 1854, Enderby Jackson (1827–1903), a leading figure in the early history of the movement, established the procedure of requiring all participating bands in contests to perform a designated test piece.[14] This not only provided a more accurate measure of musical achieve- ment; it also tended to hasten the standardizing of instrumentation in printed music.

The London festival of 1860 marked a geographical expansion in the brass movement, which now included southern England. The audience of some twenty-seven thousand heard approximately 115 bands take part in the contest and a massed band concert conducted by Jackson. The gigantic band of 1,390 players presented the 'Wedding March' by Mendelssohn, the national anthem, the 'Hallelujah Chorus', and 'The heavens are telling' from Haydn's *Creation*. The instrumentation of this band resembled the modern ensemble: soprano cornets, first and sec- ond cornets, E-flat althorns, first and second althorns, B-flat baritones, tenor and bass trombones, euphoniums, E-flat contrabasses, B-flat contrabasses, and percussion.

The next figure of importance in the movement was John Henry Iles (b. 1871).[15] Perhaps his most noteworthy contribution was his plan of commissioning British composers to write test pieces for the National Festival contests. His work in organizing a progressive series of graded contests for all levels of brass bands, instituted in 1900 at the Crystal Palace, brought the contests to the national level.[16]

Most of the music listed in the early catalogues consists of operatic works and popular dance favourites arranged for brass band. (The principal catalogues of the 1870s were *The Bandmaster Brass Band Journal* and *Distin's Brass Band Journal*, later known as *Boosey's Brass Band Journal*.) Shortly afterwards, original pieces began to appear: for example, 'The Chromatic' (1880), 'The Adventurer' (1885), both by J. Sidney Jones (b. 1832), and 'Air Varié' (1889) by Warwick Williams (b. 1846).

The two pieces by Jones are of the same style and genre: both are quicksteps. 'The Chromatic' consists of a short introduction, followed by five related sections of sixteen bars each (*AA'BB'*): the beginning of the first is shown in example 7.2. Its chromaticism is unusual, but in all other respects this music departs but little from its functional ancestors, the military quicksteps of the eighteenth and early nineteenth centuries. The instrumentation is the standard one for the period: four cornets, ripieno cornet, four saxhorns, euphonium, tenor and bass trombones, baritones, and percussion.

'Air Varié', dating from 1889, is one of the first works for brass band in which a solo instrument is given opportunity for technical display. A solo euphonium is called upon to play difficult passages throughout

Ex. 7.2   J. Sidney Jones, march, 'The Chromatic' (1880)

(Sounding notes for all instruments)

(*P: Bandmaster*, No. 106 (1880))

141

three sets of variations. The first is in 3/4 time, E flat major, and is constructed around quaver arpeggio figures; the second variation is based on triplet semiquavers; the third is in common time, G flat major, and offers the soloist a brief tonal flourish of rapid semiquaver figures. In its imitation of light military band pieces, this music, and many others like it, fulfilled the amateurs' needs; but the dearth of invention and monotony of tone colour did little for the artistic development of the medium.

Salvation Army Bands*

A special function pertained to the bands of the Salvation Army, founded by William Booth in 1865. The Army directed its evangelical efforts to some of the poorest parts of the cities, and soon felt the need for outdoor music to accompany processions, attract the attention of passers-by, overcome hecklers, and provide the cheerful kind of moral uplift that was the Army's speciality. At first woodwinds were used; brass was added in 1877, drums in 1880, and during the next two decades the woodwind instruments were gradually dropped.[17] In 1890 the Salvation Army meeting at the Crystal Palace boasted 'the biggest band in the world', with ten thousand instruments—brass, tambourines, and other percussion.[18] Bands quickly spread throughout the movement, and became a well-known spectacular feature of the parades and meetings. The first Salvation Army Massed Band Festival was held at Clapton in December 1899, with five hundred bandsmen out of the ten thousand and more who were then serving in Salvation Army bands in the United Kingdom alone.[19]

A leading personality in the development of Salvation Army music was Richard Slater (1854–1939), a professional violinist who received the call to join the Army in 1883.[20] He was at once put in charge of a new music department, and in the next few years he rapidly built up the choirs and bands of the movement and supplied them with music, both adapted and newly composed. The chief medium for disseminating the music was *The Musical Salvationist*, which began publication in July 1886.[21] Both staff and solfa notations were used, and the bulk of the music consisted of 'songs' or hymns to be used at the meetings, in which the instruments simply doubled the voice parts. Many Salvation Army hymns, indeed, were influenced in their style by the military march (see ex. 8.9). Salvation Army bands also played recreational music, despite the opposition of the Founder: the first piece of this type was a march

*Section added by the Editor

142

called 'Roused from my slumber' (1885) which Slater adapted from an operatic excerpt.[22]

A constant champion of the Salvation Army bands was Bernard Shaw, who revelled in the massed sonorities of the trombones. In 1905 he was invited to the Festival at Clapton and wrote a technical report for the benefit of the Army. In October 1941 he wrote in a letter to *The Times*: 'Had the Albert Hall, the BBC Orchestra and The Salvation Army's International Staff Band been within Handel's reach the score of *Messiah* would have been of a very different specification. The music would not, and could not have been better, but the instrumentation would have been very much richer and more effective.'[23]

Brass-band music of the nineteenth century was popular in aim, in the sense that it catered to large numbers of unsophisticated players and listeners, mostly of the lower classes of society. Yet it rarely responded freely to popular tastes. Whether under military, philanthropic, or religious auspices, it represented not so much what the masses wanted to play and hear as what their social superiors felt they ought to play and hear. Perhaps it is this paternalistic quality that robs brass-band music of the vitality one feels in, say, music-hall songs of the same period. The idiom is generally derived from the 'safe' style of the art music of an earlier generation.

By 1900 the brass band was beginning to secure recognition as a valid medium for art music, and would soon stimulate leading composers to apply their creative gifts to it, beginning with Elgar and Holst in the late 1920s. The first landmark in this change was the appearance in the 1880s of music originally composed for the medium, however limited its scope and significance. For, as Elliot points out, 'as long as the all-brass ensemble was confined to arrangements of music conceived in terms of other media, it was employing a foreign tongue without possessing the natural advantages of a native, while its own rich and resourceful language remained undeveloped—indeed, largely unsuspected.'[24]

Chapter 8

PAROCHIAL AND NONCONFORMIST CHURCH MUSIC

BERNARR RAINBOW

Although the nineteenth century witnessed the composition of choral music for parochial and nonconformist use on a prodigal scale, this chapter will be only incidentally concerned with the earnest activities of those minor composers whose new anthems, settings, and choruses were presented Sunday by Sunday to the Victorian church and chapel goer. To review that mass of ephemeral material would be both wearisome and misleading; for the enduring achievements of church musicians working outside the cathedrals in the nineteenth century lay in rediscovery and reform rather than in extended composition, in the provision of music for congregation rather than choir.

The Church of England

Changes in parochial church music in the early nineteenth century were directly stimulated by the success of the Methodist and Evangelical movements. Bishop Beilby Porteus, in his *Charge to the Diocesan Clergy of London* in 1790, urged reforms whose intention was, at least in part, to win back defectors to Methodism by making Anglican music equally attractive: he mentioned that 'many of those who separate from our communion understand perfectly well the use and force of this commanding instrument of devotion, and apply it with success'.[1] He therefore commended the musical training of some of the most promising children in each parish till by degrees a large part of the congregation had been instructed from their youth.[2]

Parochial Psalmody Corrected (1790), a book published by Henry Heron, organist of St Magnus the Martyr, London Bridge, shows how sistsistc.

---

the bishop's proposal was adopted in one London parish. That similar steps were taken to teach singing in other church schools is demonstrated by the prefaces to collections of psalms and hymns published elsewhere for local use, such as *Psalms of David* (1790), compiled by Dr Edward Miller (1735–1807), organist of Doncaster, with the Evangelical vicar of Doncaster, George Hay Drummond.[3]

The first Evangelicals had been clergy strongly influenced by John Wesley, and like him, choosing to remain within the Church of England. While adhering generally to church law and discipline, they determined to stimulate greater fervour, spontaneity, and congregational participation in the prayer-book services. Music provided an obvious field for reform in that respect: and some of the first efforts to improve parochial church music in the nineteenth century thus took place under Evangelical leadership. Congregations were encouraged to stand during the singing of the metrical psalms, to add their voices to those of the choir, to abandon the drawling pace previously adopted, and to employ modern tunes—many of them, like DARWALL'S 148TH, already familiar in Methodist circles. At the risk of litigation, some Evangelical clergy in the north of England began, early in the century, to augment congregational psalmody with a few hymns—a practice whose legality was not established in court until 1820.[4] Collections for local use including both psalms and hymns were published in increasing number after the second decade of the century.

Another reform desired by some Evangelicals, notably at York, was the introduction of *congregational chanting*, a custom unknown to English worship either before or after the Reformation. It became common in the early decades of the century for the canticles to be chanted in parish churches, and also the Gloria Patri at the end of a spoken psalm, since these texts were repeated often enough to be learned by heart.[5] Benjamin Jacob's *National Psalmody* (1817) and several collections published in the 1820s included chants, and gave pointed versions of the canticles. It was a different matter for congregations to chant the psalms, however, with no guidance other than the colons printed at mid-verse in the prayer-book psalter. Thus at about the same time that efforts began to be made to improve and regulate cathedral chanting,* additional momentum was provided by parochial demand: and eventually, in 1831, the first printed psalter[6] appeared with all the psalms fully pointed. But in the same year J. A. Latrobe, outlining the current state of parochial music in his ponderous book, *The Music of the Church*, noted that the custom of chanting the psalms was 'generally confined to Cathedrals'.[7] While regretting its general absence in parochial

*See pp. 176–9.

145

churches, Latrobe felt that chanting did not readily accommodate itself to the united voices of the people, a belief that was shared by many throughout the Victorian period.

All these attempts at musical reform were local in origin and, lacking national impetus, influenced only individual parishes whose clergy felt the need to improve their music. But in the changed atmosphere which followed the passing of the first Reform Bill of 1832, Parliament at length acknowledged a measure of responsibility for national education by making a modest grant toward the maintenance of the country's schools. In the wave of new interest in elementary education which resulted, the first two school textbooks specifically designed to teach children in this country to read music appeared. Significantly, both books were presented to the public as means to improve congregational singing in churches. John Turner's *Manual of Vocal Instruction: chiefly with a View to Psalmody* (1833) and Sarah Glover's *Scheme for Rendering Psalmody Congregational* (1835) overtly stated their purpose in their titles.

Both books made their appearance as the Anglo-Catholic revival known as the Oxford Movement began. As a result, the reintroduction of music teaching in schools which their appearance heralded, and the new resolve to conduct church services with more appropriate dignity stimulated by Pusey, Newman, Neale, and their disciples, were brought together to produce a new and unique feature of Anglican parochial worship—the surpliced chancel choir.[8]

Found hitherto only in cathedrals, the chapel royal, and certain college chapels in the universities, surpliced choirs were introduced in a few isolated parish and district churches in England and Ireland during the first half of the nineteenth century at the instigation of individual priests. The example which was to provide a model for wide emulation in other Anglo-Catholic churches was established at Margaret Chapel, St Marylebone, by the incumbent, Frederick Oakeley (1802–80), in 1839. Standing on the site of the present church of All Saints, Margaret Street, Margaret Chapel attracted devout congregations to its daily service and became the most influential of London's churches in demonstrating new standards of reverence.

Oakeley's choir was not introduced in imitation of cathedral practice—to sing while the people listened—but to lead the congregation's own singing. Accordingly, music was chosen which all could manage and which, so far as could then be established, had been employed in much earlier times. Working by rule of thumb, Oakeley and his young organist, Richard Redhead (1820–1901), compiled *Laudes diurnae* (1843), the first Anglican psalter for use with the plainsong tones, to

146

complement the Tudor versicles and responses, dignified hymn tunes, and such other solemn congregational music as they were able to assemble.[9] Redhead also composed several new hymn tunes of sober cast which survive in general use today.

With the spread of new standards of musical churchmanship after 1839, scholarly editions of early liturgical music were to appear, including Edward F. Rimbault's *Order of Chanting the Cathedral Service* (1843) and John Bishop's *Order of Daily Service* (1844); but a more substantial contribution was made by William Dyce (1806–64), the Scottish painter and amateur musician who had played a leading part with Rimbault in founding the Motett Society in 1841.[10] During 1843 and 1844 Dyce published a sumptuous edition of Marbeck's *Book of Common Prayer Noted*, adapting the original music where necessary to accommodate the textual revisions made since 1550. The publication provided high churchmen with a simple musical setting of the Eucharist which has been employed, however inexpertly, ever since. Rimbault followed with a cheaper would-be facsimile edition of Marbeck in 1845.

An important feature of Dyce's book was his scholarly investigation of the conventions of Latin plainsong, summarized in a substantial preface and appendix. Previous attempts to chant the psalms in English to the plainsong tones, being based simply on arithmetical syllabic distribution as exemplified in Oakeley's *Laudes diurnae* (1843) or W. B. Heathcote's *Oxford Psalter* (1845), had consistently led to false emphasis. Dyce now revealed how observed differences in the accommodation of Latin syllabic quantity could point the way to reconciliation of verbal and musical accent with English words.[11]

The task of preparing a new plainsong psalter following the syllabic rules laid down by Dyce in his appendix was undertaken by the Reverend Thomas Helmore (1811–90), whose *Psalter Noted* was published in 1849 after extensive trial in the chapel of St Mark's College, Chelsea, where Helmore was precentor and a remarkable choral tradition had recently been established.[12] Two years later the psalter, together with the canticles and other service music, was republished as *A Manual of Plainsong* (1851), a book widely adopted in Anglo-Catholic churches as a means of encouraging congregational participation in the choral service. Helmore's attention then turned to the preparation of a Gregorian hymnal with the same end in view, a task undertaken jointly with John Mason Neale (1818–66), who translated the texts, and a small committee. *The Hymnal Noted* appeared in two parts in 1851 and 1854, and contained just under one hundred ancient hymns and their tunes, drawn mostly from the Sarum Gradual.

By 1846, the movement to establish surpliced choirs in local churches had become sufficiently widespread to support its own magazine, *The Parish Choir*, published under the editorship of Robert Druitt, a medical man who had also founded the Society for Promoting Church Music. The paper's avowed aim was 'to find out, publish, popularise, explain and recommend the adoption of that system of music most suited to the genius of the English Prayer Book'.[13] From its pages the early progress of the movement and the arguments upon which its musical policy depended may be traced.

A point at issue, it seems, was the use of plainsong. While conceding that the Gregorian tones might seem 'strange to modern ears', Oakeley believed that they provided an ideal medium for congregational chanting and that 'they take wonderfully with the poor'.[14] Most ardent Anglo-Catholics agreed with him, an article in *The Ecclesiologist*[15] maintaining that in the use of the tones, rather than in Anglican chants or metrical psalmody, lay the key to congregational participation. The editor of *The Parish Choir* was less sanguine. Although he encouraged William H. Monk (1823–89) and Charles C. Spencer to contribute articles on Gregorian music to the journal and was himself an advocate of plainsong, Druitt warned his readers that the 'severe and majestic simplicity' of the Gregorian tones would no doubt grate harshly upon ears more accustomed to animated chants and dancing hymn tunes. He urged that some middle ground be taken to allow people's taste to improve before they were expected to admire the severer music of a remote period.[16] The debate was to continue indefinitely; but meanwhile the use of plainsong had become an established badge of Anglo-Catholicism.

The dividing line was made more pronounced by the existence among more traditional high churchmen of an independent movement to introduce surpliced chancel choirs in parish churches. The model here was not, understandably, Margaret Chapel with its Tractarian overtones, but Leeds Parish Church, where the vicar, Walter Hook (1798–1875), had been persuaded by influential parishioners in 1841 to introduce an endowed choir of professional competence. The advice of John Jebb (1805–86) was consulted on musical policy.[17] Samuel Sebastian Wesley was appointed organist in the following year; and daily 'cathedral' services were held at the church with regular anthems, settings of the canticles, harmonized choral responses, and the psalms sung to Anglican chants. Long exasperated by adverse working conditions and lack of support in his previous cathedral appointments at Hereford and Exeter, Wesley took fullest advantage of the favourable circumstance at Leeds to provide lavish music; but since neither he nor Jebb approved of congregational chanting,[18] the services were exclusively choir-centred. Here, then, was presented another model, for hazardous emulation in churches where there was no sympathy with plainsong—associated as it was with Tractarian principles. Moreover, in 1843 John Hullah made his telling observation: 'Congregations generally do not sing at all . . . It is not genteel to sing in church.'[19] Most 'respectable' churchgoers, it seems, were not averse to accepting a largely passive role throughout the service.

It is noteworthy that the opening of a new or restored church was made the occasion for introducing a surpliced choir at Leeds. An explanation for the rapid spread of surpliced chancel choirs during the next thirty years lies in the outburst of church building and restoration which took place then. Between 1840 and 1874 no less than £25,548,703 was raised for the purpose.[20] It was in those new churches, invariably built according to neo-mediaeval specification with deep chancels, that a robed choir seemed to form an essential feature, and there were no existing local traditions to overcome. Consequently, choirs were often introduced 'for no better reason than that the congregations wished to be in the fashion, and did not care to be beaten by their neighbours who possessed one'.[21] The repertory of these new choirs, uninfluenced by any central musical policy such as Anglo-Catholics accepted, was drawn from a wide variety of sources which will repay further examination.

Prayers, versicles and responses, and the prose psalms were customarily read, parson-and-clerk fashion, in most churches until mid-century; but after that time, as the clergy became more musically aware and popular resistance to 'popish practices' grew less acute, the adoption of intoned prayers and versicles justified the adoption of choral responses—usually those attributed to Tallis. In larger town churches whose organists had been trained in cathedral lofts, Anglican chants were often employed at least for Venite and the Gloria Patri after the psalms. Pointed psalters were seldom used, choir and people following local tradition as recorded in the organist's own marked copy.

S. S. Wesley's *Psalter with Chants* (1843) was designed to put an end to such casual treatment of the psalms at Leeds. John Hullah also published a *Psalter with Chants* (1844) for the use of choristers who had graduated from his Exeter Hall Singing School. But the first book to be widely used, and one whose appearance may be taken to mark the wider acceptance of chanting the prose psalms, was William Mercer's *Church Psalter and Hymn Book* (1854). Other pointed psalters, particularly those by Stephen Elvey (1856), Ouseley and Monk (1862), and James Turle (1865), each attracted devotees. The most generally adopted book, however, and one surprisingly still in use in some quarters to this day, was *The Cathedral Psalter*, brought out by Stainer, Turle, and Barnby in 1875. By that time, even village churches began to aspire to the full choral service sung by a surpliced choir.

The metrical psalm, meanwhile, still held a place in the people's music; and of the books with tunes for church use, Goss's *Parochial Psalmody* (1827) and Crotch's *Psalm Tunes for Cathedrals and Parish Churches* (1836) exerted beneficial influence by discarding unworthy material. But by mid-century, earlier resistance to the use of hymns as unhealthily reminiscent of nonconformist 'enthusiasm' had been largely overcome, and there appeared a large number of general collections drawing on wider sources, including Catholic hymns (both mediaeval and post-Tridentine), German chorales, and Methodist and Congregational hymns. There was also a great burgeoning of newly written hymns and hymn tunes. All these trends were to merge with the publication of *Hymns Ancient and Modern* (1861). It was first regarded as distinctly 'high' in tone, but in its later and more comprehensive editions (1875, 1889), it won the approval of all but the extreme high and low church parties.

More ambitious choirs undertook anthems and settings of the canticles. Many early-nineteenth-century parochial psalmody collections included anthems in the 'country psalmody' tradition described in Volume Four. In the early Victorian period, simple cathedral anthems of the sixteenth and seventeenth centuries were republished in cheap octavo editions by Novello & Co. and in *The Parish Choir*. Excerpts from the oratorios of Handel, Haydn, and Mendelssohn soon followed, to be augmented by English adaptations of easier motets by Italian composers. But by 1860 when, as one rhapsodic writer put it, 'the gradually-spreading desire of elevating our Church services became too evident a sign of the times to be disregarded by any composer of power and prominence',[22] many organists who had not attained cathedral rank could no longer resist the opportunity to write easy music for parish church use. More than fourteen hundred anthems written by 221 English church composers born after 1800 were proudly listed by M. B. Foster in 1901.[23]

As the nineteenth century proceeded, the influence of continental opera encouraged the development of an affectedly intense style, not only in anthems and services, but in hymn tunes of an emotional type which appeared in considerable numbers in the Appendix (1868) to *Hymns Ancient and Modern*. The reform of hymnody, following this lapse, was begun by the poet laureate, Robert Bridges (1844–1930), in his *Practical Discourse on some Principles of Hymn-Singing* (1899) and demonstrated in his *Yattendon Hymnal* (1899). It was taken further by Ralph

Vaughan Williams, whose editing of *The English Hymnal* (1906) introduced a new modal, folksong quality, a number of serviceable French
and Welsh melodies, and several impeccable tunes of his own. Other
fruits of the research and scholarship which marked the turn of the
century were Briggs and Frere's revision of Helmore's *Manual of Plainsong* (1902) and Robert Bridges' investigation of the principles of good
chanting.[24] Bridges' determined efforts to rid churches of the 'Anglican
thump' led to 'speech-rhythm' chanting and the production, a generation later, of a new type of pointed psalter.

From the constantly growing mass of material thus assembled, individual churches were able to make a choice according to their standards of churchmanship and taste. The astonishing disparity of situations is reflected in the accounts of visits to many different churches
published by F. J. Crowest (1881),[25] Charles Box (1884),[26] and J. S.
Curwen (1885).[27] At that time it was possible to encounter extreme
Evangelical churches which still 'echoed with the shoutings of flocks of
school children' in the absence of a trained choir.[28] Yet, at another
church was to be found 'a Mass by Schubert, or Mozart, or Cherubini,
rendered as such works frequently are in our London churches with
orchestral accompaniment'.[29] And while one writer declared that
churches in which a plain service was held were comparatively deserted
while those with a choral service overflowed with congregations,[30]
another firmly stated, 'The better the choir the worse the congregational singing'.[31] The latter generalization, however, must be considered in relation to Hullah's observation, as true in 1914 as it had
been when first uttered in 1843: 'It is not genteel to sing in church.'

Music for Anglican Parish Churches

In the early part of the nineteenth century, when many country
parishes still had west-gallery choirs and bands, elaborate fuging tunes
and anthems were still being composed for them by unschooled country
singing teachers. One of the last printed collections of this type of music
was *Sacred Music* (1838), compiled by Shadrach Chapman of Draycott,
Somerset. Excerpts from one of the long anthems in it, entitled 'A War
Piece', are given in example 8.1. As barrel organs and later harmoniums replaced the village bands, country church music was
brought into the mainstream:[32] the last church bands survived in a few
west-country churches in the 1890s. Meanwhile, town churches had
replaced the charity children in the organ gallery with a large choir of
boys (or women) and men in the chancel, instituted regular choir

practices, and, in many cases, employed a professional organist and choirmaster.

During the second half of the nineteenth century these conditions encouraged professional composers to provide easy church music for local choirs, and many technically undemanding anthems and services were written. Several of the composers concerned wrote mainly for the cathedrals; Stainer, who wrote inferior music for parish choirs before going to St Paul's, later regretted having done so at the request of earnest incumbents. For the rest, two examples of pieces by less exalted composers, both of them intended for parish choirs, will sufficiently illustrate the shift from sobriety to intemperance that took place in a single generation after mid-century.

Ex. 8.1   Shadrach Chapman, *A War Piece* ('O God thou has been displeased')
(1838)

(a) Verse. TB [unacc.]

(b) **Symphony**

(S. Chapman)

The first is an introit by Monk which conveys an atmosphere almost Pre-Raphaelite through its conscientious adherence to the manner of a past age. It appeared in *The Parish Choir* in October 1850 and reflects the ideals of the early period of the choral revival (ex. 8.2). The second is a passage from an anthem by Herbert H. Woodward (1847–1909), published in 1882, which enjoyed long popularity (ex. 8.3). Comparison of the two pieces and the apparently contradictory aspects of romanticism which they exemplify is revealing. Monk, it seems, looked to the past because it represented for a Tractarian the epoch of a catholic liturgy. Woodward appears to have embraced a fashionable contemporary idiom because it made possible a direct appeal to the subdued emotions of the respectable. An unconscious Mendelssohnian allusion also helped.

The Anglican hymn tune also underwent great changes in the Victorian era. In the early decades of the century the prevailing type of tune was the feebly decorative 'Methodist' tune (represented in ex. 8.7: a fine example, still in Anglican hymnbooks despite all the efforts of reformers to get rid of it, is HELMSLEY, which dates from 1769). The early Victorians reacted in favour of the plainer style of the early metrical psalm tunes, and provided a number of conservative but vigorous and forthright examples that have lasted well. Among these are Monk's MERTON (1850), Gauntlett's ST FULBERT (1852), Redhead's

Ex. 8.2 William H. Monk, 'Let your light' (1850)

(*Parish Choir*, No. 58. Note values halved)

METZLER'S REDHEAD (1859), and Henry Smart's REGENT SQUARE (1867). More romantic and emotional in style are two indestructible favourites, Gauntlett's tune for 'Once in royal David's city' (1849) and Monk's for 'Abide with me' (1861).

With the 1860s and the appearance of *Hymns Ancient and Modern*, a more frankly emotional type of tune began to be fashionable. John Bacchus Dykes (1823–76), high-church vicar of St Oswald, Durham, was a pivotal figure who introduced the new style of tune which was to dominate the scene for at least two generations. Written in the style of a partsong and depending as much upon harmonic as melodic structure, Dykes's tunes were on that account relished even when they contained many repetitions of the same note. RIVAULX (ex. 8.4) demonstrates those qualities. No fewer than fifty-six of his tunes appeared in the 1875 edition of *Hymns Ancient and Modern*. Joseph Barnby (1838–96) developed the harmonic style introduced by Dykes to the point of lushness. Strongly influenced by Gounod, the emotional surge of Barnby's CLOISTERS reveals qualities which were to be carried to extravagant depths in his own anthems and services. Arthur Sullivan devoted much time and energy to the editing and composing of hymn tunes, anthems, and services. His best-known tune is the perennial ST GERTRUDE for 'Onward, Christian soldiers' (1871); with its echoes of

Ex. 8.3 Herbert H. Woodward,
'The Radiant Morn' (1882)

the brass band it is a long way from the liturgical ideals of the Oxford Movement, and approaches those of the Salvation Army.

The leaders of the 'English musical renaissance' contributed some fine tunes: Parry's LAUDATE DOMINUM, which had formed part of his anthem 'Hear my words, ye people' (1893), Stanford's AIREDALE (1904), and Basil Harwood's LUCKINGTON (1905) were tunes that helped to bring breadth, vitality, and genuine emotion back into currency. Above all, Vaughan Williams's splendidly congregational SINE NOMINE, written for *The English Hymnal* (1906), set a high standard for true melodic hymn writing.

Ex. 8.4   John Bacchus Dykes, RIVAULX (1866)

(*Hymns A & M* (1875), No. 164. Note values halved)

The Church of Scotland and the Nonconformist Churches

Nonconformist congregations generally were little concerned with gentility. Vigour was seldom lacking in their singing; shortcomings were due to lack of skill, not diffidence. The nineteenth century brought many determined attempts to correct that situation—events different in kind from those taking place in the Anglican communion, but equally effective in creating a turning point.

In the Church of Scotland (Presbyterian) a movement to establish choirs to lead the people's voices in the metrical psalms (in the absence of organs) had taken place during the second half of the eighteenth century.[33] Local singing classes with the same aim were also held in some areas at that time; but the first major step toward reform was taken when Robert Archibald Smith (1780–1829), a Scot born and brought up in England, was appointed precentor of Paisley Abbey in 1807. Concentrating upon training the abbey choir to a high standard, Smith was able to demonstrate that the 'discordant bawling and drawling' (of the old way of singing with 'lining out') were neither necessary nor desirable. Under his guidance the psalmody at Paisley was brought to 'a state of perfection hitherto unknown in Scotland'.[34] Among his important publications in the field of church music were *Devotional Music* (1810), *Anthems in Four Parts* (1819) and, particularly, *Sacred Harmony of the Church of Scotland* (1828). Many of his tunes were of the decorative type popular among the Methodists, harmonized with fluent passages of thirds and sixths (see ex. 8.7). But a few were more distinctively Scottish in character, such as the still popular MARTYRDOM (1825), described by Smith as an 'Old Scotch melody' but also claimed as the work of Hugh Wilson (1766–1824), an Ayrshire sundial designer.[35]

A further contribution of a different kind was made in 1842 when Joseph Mainzer (1801–51), the celebrated pioneer teacher of sight singing, accepted an invitation from the Lord Provost of Edinburgh to establish classes in the Scottish capital. An expatriate German, Mainzer had already organized popular singing classes in Paris (1834), London (1841), and many parts of England. Between 1842 and 1847 he held equally successful classes for both adults and children in Edinburgh, extending his activities in 1843 by touring the country.[36] His *Standard Psalmody of Scotland* (1845) brought back to currency a number of forgotten tunes from the 1564 psalm book; and in his *Music and Education* (1848) he sought to persuade the civic dignitaries of Edinburgh that there was a place for music in the general education of future citizens. An enthusiastic and skilful teacher, Mainzer also founded an Association for the Revival of Sacred Music in Scotland. His good influence upon Scottish psalmody was considerable.[37]

Lengthy debate during the 1860s and 70s slowly led to the grudging admission of the organ into the Church of Scotland; and with the twentieth century came common acceptance of a single hymn book, *The Church Hymnary* (1901), edited by Stainer. By that time, too, Anglican chants were used and there was often little to distinguish the musical part of the service from that in the Anglican Church.[38]

The breakaway Free Church of Scotland (instituted 1843) also held psalmody classes in many parts of the country. Thomas Legerwood Hately (1815–67) was appointed precentor to the Free Church Assembly after 'disruption' in 1843. His *Free Church Psalmody* (1844) and *National Psalmody* (1848) helped to banish many of the more meretricious tunes then current.[39] Similar classes were held in the countryside around Aberdeen, where William Carnie had begun to hold classes in 1854. The Psalmody Improvement Association which he founded brought together large numbers of local precentors and provided the means to carry reform still further. Carnie's *Northern Psalter* (1870) contained over four hundred tunes previously issued by him in penny sets from 1859.[40] But perhaps the greatest advance was made after the introduction of tonic solfa to Scotland following John Curwen's visit to give a series of lectures in 1855.[41]

Throughout the eighteenth century the Congregationalists had established a strong tradition for the vigorous singing of psalms and (especially) hymns, of which those of Isaac Watts held a pre-eminent position. During the century that followed they were to be responsible for several notable drives to improve the singing in their churches. In this movement the new methods of sight-singing played a prominent part. In the 1830s John Waite (1807–68) evolved a system of numerals to indicate the degrees of the scale, first for his own congregation at Ilminster, Somerset, and then further afield, using as his textbook his own tune book, *The Hallelujah* (1842, 1852) with harmonies by Henry Gauntlett (1805–76).[42] John Curwen (1816–80), the leading exponent of the tonic solfa system, was another Congregationalist minister, whose work was initiated by the Congregational Church itself in asking him to investigate the best method of teaching singing in Sunday schools.[43]

Other reforms were associated with particular chapels. One of these was begun at the King's Weigh House Chapel, London, by the minister, Dr Thomas Binney, who encouraged the formation of regular psalmody classes there. One of his sermons was published as *The Service of Song in the House of the Lord* (1849) and enjoyed wide circulation. In his preface to *Congregational Church Music* (1853), compiled anonymously for use at the chapel, he voiced a plea for simple congregational music: 'If, indeed, it be the *duty* of the congregation to sing, it must be its *right* to be furnished with such music as it *can* sing.' The collection was designed to go with *The Congregational Hymn Book* compiled by Josiah Conder in 1836. The tunes are, indeed, simple and melodious. Elaborate fuging and repeating tunes, such as had been commonly sung by rehearsed choirs earlier in the century, were banished. In a supplement of 1864, chants and anthems were added; but the preface by 'The Compilers' emphasized that these were meant for the whole congregation to sing: 'These "anthems" have, indeed, little in common with our splendid cathedral compositions, save the name, for which "prose-tune" might be substituted, as better defining their character. . . . As few existing anthems were found to suit this purpose, Mr [Lowell] Mason's assistance was called in.' Many of the anthems were by Mason, others by John Goss, still others were simplified arrangements from cathedral sources; all were entirely homophonic. This type of *congregational anthem*, probably a Methodist invention, was to find great favour in nonconformist circles in the later nineteenth century. An anonymous example from the 1864 supplement (beginning as in ex. 8.5) appeared in several later collections.

Ex. 8.5   Anonymous congregational anthem, 'O love the Lord' (1864)

(*Congregational Church Music* (1864))

Another local scene of reform was the Union Chapel, Islington where, under the ministry of Henry Allon and with Gauntlett as organist, the congregation attended singing rehearsals regularly, beginning in 1847 with hymns, going on to chants in 1856 and anthems in 1859. Their book, *The Congregational Psalmist* (1858), had 330 tunes, including many German chorales and others new to the Congregational tradition. When J. S. Curwen visited the chapel in the 1880s he found a large proportion of the people singing with copies of the music in their hands, while no less than eight hundred copies of the anthems, chants, and hymns were provided for the use of visitors.[44]

Various strands were brought together in *The Congregational Church Hymnal* (1887), sponsored officially by the Congregational Union of England and Wales, and edited by George S. Barrett with the musical assistance of E. J. Hopkins (1818–1901), organist of the Temple Church, and of Josiah Booth (1852–1930), organist of Park Chapel,

Crouch End. The first part, consisting of hymns with chants, was almost as eclectic as the 1889 edition of *Hymns Ancient and Modern*, but it retained some tunes of specifically Congregational origin and added new ones combining the new harmonic resources with the robust assertiveness characteristic of nonconformity. One of the most popular of these was Booth's COMMONWEALTH (ex. 8.6), composed for the hym-

Ex. 8.6 Josiah Booth, COMMONWEALTH (1887)

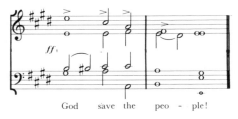

(G. Barrett, No. 655)

160

nal, which serves as a reminder of the strong ties linking nonconformity to political radicalism. Lloyd George declared that he had heard it sung 'with great effect by many thousands and tens of thousands at Liberal gatherings throughout the country'.[45] The second part of the *Hymnal* consisted of litanies and chants. In the third part were sixty-four anthems, all entirely or largely homophonic; eight collects; and twelve canticles and other liturgical pieces. A Magnificat and Nunc dimittis composed expecially for the work by J. Baptiste Calkin (1827–1905) had 'easy alternative Glorias' in case the regular ones were found 'too difficult for congregational use'. Thus had the Congregational Church adopted almost all the musical practices of the Church of England, but had still avoided monopolization by trained choirs.[46] For this achievement, there is little doubt that the sight-singing movement was largely responsible.

The Baptists were less disposed by tradition and teaching than other nonconformist bodies to place high value on music in worship; indeed opposition to singing of any kind in public worship, which had prevailed among them in the seventeenth century, was not quite dead at the end of the eighteenth. In some Baptist congregations, however, elaborate choir music had developed along similar lines to that in Anglican country churches, accompanied by instrumental bands. A great centre for such music was the valley of Rossendale in Lancashire. But 'the orchestra was at last undermined by the organ in chapel after chapel' until by the mid-century few of the old bands were left.[47]

In their music the Baptists generally followed the Congregationalists. Their most popular hymn book, John Rippon's *A Selection of Hymns* (1787), was conceived as a supplement to Watts. The musical edition (1795), probably prepared with the assistance of Thomas Walker (1764–1827), used tunes of Anglican, Methodist, and Congregationalist origin, including a number of very elaborate ones that demanded choirs. The widely adopted *Baptist Tune Book* (1860) was avowedly 'an adaptation of *Congregational Church Music*', and suited the more congregational style that now prevailed. Something of the general picture in the later nineteenth century may be gathered from a visit to Charles Spurgeon's famous Metropolitan Tabernacle in the 1880s. The singing was led by a precentor, but the vast assembly was beyond his power to control. There were no congregational singing classes. Spurgeon had produced *Our Own Hymn Book* (1866) and evidently 'was anxious that every man, woman and child in the place should sing'. But his attempts to regulate the singing were limited to such observations as 'Dear friends, the devil sometimes makes you lag half a note behind the leader. Just try if you can't prevail over him tonight, and keep in proper time.'[48] With the publication of *The Baptist Hymnary* (1879) other hymnals were largely superseded, but musical standards remained low. Even after 1900 some Baptist churches in country districts still employed a precentor wielding a pitch-pipe, though town churches were equipped with organs and had begun to share with other nonconformist bodies the use of Anglican chant and anthem.[49] The officially authorized *Baptist Church Hymnal* appeared in 1900 with over seven hundred tunes, chants, and anthems.

Throughout the nineteenth century the Methodists retained their reputation as 'a singing people'. Wesley's injunction that all should sing was still observed; but as the Methodists established centres of worship, at first in barns, then in modest chapels, something of the early fire was lost. Bands of instruments were formed to guide the singing, giving way to harmoniums by mid-century. Organs had appeared in a few town chapels before 1800, and became more common (where they could be afforded) after the Conference of 1820 had approved them.[50]

The tune books prepared under the Wesleys' authority in the eighteenth century continued in use,[51] and new books generally adhered to their principles: religious music could take advantage of the best music of concert and theatre ('plunder the carnal lover', as Charles Wesley had put it) by imitating its style and by actual adaptations; men's and women's voices should be exploited, together and separately; there must be no obscuring the text by overlapping entries. The long popular tune ECCLES (c. 1840, ex. 8.7) was composed for a hymn of Charles Wesley's by Richard Boggett (c. 1810–79), who was choirmaster of the chapel at Kippax, near Leeds:[52] it is typical of its kind, with diatonic harmony, often largely a duet in thirds and sixths between soprano and tenor, four-square cadences, and repetition of the last line of text (the *piano* phrase was probably for women alone).

John Wesley had also allowed anthems, of an appropriate character for all to sing: Martin Madan's 'Before Jehovah's awful throne' and Edward Harwood's 'Vital spark of heavenly flame' were included in his *Sacred Harmony*, 2nd edition (1787) and were great standbys in Methodist circles in the early nineteenth century. They were like extended hymn tunes, with metrical texts, homophonic, often in several sections like a glee; such compositions were sometimes called *set pieces*, and though theoretically congregational they were choir pieces in nineteenth-century usage.[53] Prose anthems were also allowed, often of a much simpler character than their Anglican prototypes. Occasionally

Ex. 8.7   Richard Boggett, ECCLES (c. 1840)

(E. Booth, No. 235)

such simplicity could be moving, as in a modest Funeral Anthem composed by Thomas Jarman (c. 1788–1862), choirmaster of the chapel at Clipston, Northants. (ex. 8.8): it appeared in *The Northamptonshire Harmony, containing a greater variety of Tunes, Anthems and Set Pieces than has hitherto appeared* (London, c. 1820).

163

Ex. 8.8 Thomas Jarman, funeral anthem (c. 1820)

(Jarman, 92)

The many local collections were largely superseded by *The Methodist Hymn Tune Book* (1877), sponsored by the Methodist Conference, edited musically by the Anglican organists George Cooper (1820–76) and E. J. Hopkins. By that time, in the opinion of many Methodists, their psalmody was in decline. 'We hear complaints', said one writer, 'of a departure from the simplicity and bare spirituality of Wesley's services, of a lack of warmth in the congregation, and a disposition to hand over the singing to a choir.'[54] These were no doubt natural consequences of the increased sophistication of many of the movement's urban followers, now no longer drawn mainly from among the poor to whom Wesley had first ministered. Certainly by the end of our period the music in the larger Wesleyan chapels included anthems, Anglican chants, even a few plainsong hymns, which would have caused alarm a century earlier.

The Calvinistic Methodists were descended from the early secession of George Whitefield and the Countess of Huntingdon from the Wesleyan body. In English town chapels, such as that at Bath, their services were almost indistinguishable from those of Evangelical Anglicans. In Wales, where they became the predominant sect in the nineteenth century, in many places joining forces with the Congregationalists, a genuinely popular form of hymnody prevailed, and the chapels of Welsh mining towns became famous for choral music. Some of their best tunes were based on traditional Welsh folksongs. To this tradition we owe the magnificent tune ST DENIO, now often associated with the hymn 'Immortal, invisible'; it was based on a folksong 'Can Mlynnedd i' nawr', and first appeared as a hymn tune in the Welsh-language collection, *Caniadau y Cyssegr* (1839), compiled by John Roberts (1807–76).[55] Another tune of this kind is TON-Y-BOTEL or EBENEZER (*English Hymnal* no. 108).

The revival movement reached England in 1807, when the first camp meeting was held on Mow Cop, on the border of Staffordshire and Cheshire, under the influence of the American revivalist Lorenzo Dow (1777–1834). The movement was organized as 'The Society of Primitive Methodists' in 1812, and they soon earned the nickname of 'Ranters' because of their unrestrained singing. Their hymns and tunes were largely American in origin and were of the kind known as 'folk hymns' and 'spirituals', often combining verse in simple language with folksongs originating in the British Isles but reintroduced from the Southern United States.[56]

A new impetus arrived in 1873–5 with the first tour of the American evangelists Dwight Moody (1837–99) and Ira Sankey (1840–1908). The 'gospel hymns' they used at their meetings were compiled from the experience of many years in America, but they struck a relatively new note in Britain. They 'may be said to have carried the more emotional and less cultivated element of religious people off its feet . . . The new melodies penetrated even the music halls and were whistled by the man on the street'.[57] For they were more thoroughly popular in style than anything that had been used before for religious music. The words, and the ideas behind them, were simple and straightforward, without literary conceits, often sounding a note of comfort for those whose lives were hard; the tunes were entirely predictable; the rhythms march- or dance-like; the harmonies obvious, generally going no further than tonic, dominant, and an occasional subdominant. The most popular collection was *Gospel Hymns* (six numbers, 1875–91) compiled by Sankey and P. P. Bliss.

The chief British revival movement of the period was the Salvation Army, founded in 1865 as the East London Christian Mission.[58] With the distinctive addition of brass and percussion instruments* the Army won an equal success by much the same means as Moody and Sankey, and their songs, whether of American or British origin, were in very much the same style (ex. 8.9). They usually included a catchy chorus or refrain, in which anyone with a grain of music in him could easily

*See above, p. 142.

165

Ex. 8.9 Anonymous Salvation Army song, 'If the Cross' (c. 1900)

Allegro moderato ♩ = 104

(*Salvation Army Hymn Book*, No. 69)

join, and they often derived some of their good cheer from martial rhythms reinforced by the trombones and drums.

The Roman Catholic Church

Until the Catholic Emancipation Act of 1829, Roman Catholics in Britain remained a barely tolerated minority worshipping in back-street chapels, many of them indistinguishable from neighbouring houses. After Emancipation that situation continued for a time. But now, new churches were built; and to serve them, Vincent Novello, also founder of the publishing house, issued cheap editions of the masses of Haydn, Mozart, Weber, and Hummel together with those of Samuel Webbe (1740–1816), thus starting a tradition for the use of Viennese masses in Britain which was to linger throughout the nineteenth century. Yet many of the new churches had not the financial resources to engage suitable choristers. A movement in 1849 to introduce music lessons in catholic schools with a view to producing boy choristers met with little success;[59] and another movement to reintroduce general

166

plainsong, led by Augustus Pugin, the celebrated architect,[60] met with vigorous resistance.[61]

From 1849, however, vernacular hymn singing was fostered by the Frederick W. Faber, founder of Brompton Oratory. Faber's hymns were associated with weak, sugary tunes of a kind which became even more popular after the appearance of Henry F. Hemy's *Crown of Jesus* hymnal (1864). This musically unfortunate development was to set the tone of parochial music for at least two generations.[62] When Richard Terry (1865–1938)* edited the new *Westminster Hymnal* for general catholic use in 1912, he dared not scrap much of the inferior material which had by that time been taken to the hearts of congregations throughout the land.[63]

*For Terry's achievements in Roman Catholic choral music, see below, pp. 210–13.

PART III

Art Music

Chapter 9

CATHEDRAL MUSIC

NICHOLAS TEMPERLEY

The nineteenth century saw a great revival in English cathedral music. So much is this so that a large part of the existing musical tradition can be traced back no further than the Victorian period. This includes the harmonized 'ferial' responses, the style of singing, chanting, and organ playing, the placing of hymns in the services, the structure of some of the services (such as choral communion), and much of the musical repertory. There was a complete transformation of performing standards, an awakening appreciation of the glories of early cathedral music, both Anglican and Roman Catholic, and a marked rebirth of creative vitality. The period produced one of the greatest composers of the entire history of English cathedral music, Samuel Sebastian Wesley.

The beginning of the nineteenth century was a low point in the worship of the Church of England, despite its continuing monopoly of legal, financial and constitutional privileges. On Easter Sunday, 1800, there were only six communicants at the morning celebration in St Paul's Cathedral.[1] Choral music was also at a low ebb, and there were very few foundations that could provide even a barely adequate performance of the choral services.[2] The abuses in cathedral administration that had diverted endowments away from their intended musical purpose (and into the pockets of deans and canons) were ended in the 1840s, but it was not until the 1870s that a thoroughgoing reform of the choral services took place.

Meanwhile there was a strong movement to introduce choral services in parish churches, and by the mid-Victorian period many parochial choirs equalled, and some even surpassed, those of the cathedrals, both in standard of performance and in the broadening of the repertory. Many boys' public schools and colleges of various kinds also conducted choral services.[3] There was thus a rapid growth of the market for Anglican choral music, which stimulated both the

171

reprinting of old music and the composition of new. Much choral music of the Edwardian period was written with schools and parish churches in mind more than cathedrals. As it is often impossible to distinguish cathedral and parochial music in this period, all liturgical music for trained and rehearsed choirs is covered in the present chapter.

The end of our period also saw the reinstatement of trained choirs in Roman Catholic cathedrals, most notably that of Westminster, which was in the forefront of the revival of Renaissance church music.

The Anglican Choral Foundations and their Reform

At the coming into existence of the United Church of England and Ireland on 1 January 1801,* the choral foundations of the Church consisted of twenty-two English, four Irish, and four Welsh cathedrals; a few collegiate parish churches; the chapel royal; and the 'royal peculiars' of Westminster Abbey and St George's Chapel, Windsor. Ten new English cathedrals were founded during our period, though only one, that of Truro (1887), was provided with a completely new building. Episcopal cathedrals were built at Glasgow (1873) and Edinburgh (1870) and later endowed for choral services. The Temple Church, London, was opened for daily choral services in the 1840s; St Michael's College, Tenbury, was founded in 1856.[4]

The statutes of the ancient foundations had set up adequate funds for the support of choral services, but over the years these had been reduced to the bare minimum necessary to pay the organist, lay-clerks and choristers—less in some cases, as at Llandaff, which had neither choir nor organ. A typical cathedral choir in the early nineteenth century had ten or twelve members, but the attendance of the lay-clerks or vicars-choral was so bad (chiefly because they had to hold another job to earn a living) that there was often only one alto, one tenor, and one bass present, sometimes even less than that. The men did not attend rehearsals at all. Torrington in 1791 feared he 'would live to see when none will be present at a cathedral service, but a reader, a verger, and 2 singing boys; who will gallop over it in a few minutes'.[5] Gauntlett in 1837 described the singing of an anthem at St Paul's, when only three men (two altos and a tenor) were present. 'The organ with its "thunderstop" carried all before it . . . whilst by a process, called by musicians of the old school, "playing the thoro'-bass", the number of unnecessary notes thrust into poor Hayes' score created quite an

*It lasted until the disestablishment of the Church of Ireland in 1871.

172

uproar.'⁶ Organists indeed made a regular policy of playing loud throughout the anthems and services to cover up gaps in the singing.⁷

The low state of the choirs was not only due to financial inadequacy: moral support was also lacking. Deans and canons were frequently non-resident and took no interest in the music; the precentor, the clergyman nominally in charge of music in cathedrals of the old foundation, was often 'a man totally incompetent to distinguish one note from another', even as late as 1891.⁸ Congregations were often discouraged from attending. At St Paul's in about 1813 one had to bribe the verger to obtain a seat in the choir;⁹ in 1865 only five or six persons attended weekday services at Carlisle.¹⁰

The reform of the cathedral choirs has sometimes been loosely attributed to the Oxford Movement, but it was really part of a much wider series of reforms that swept the country after the passing of the Reform Bill (1832), leaving no institution untouched and making the Church answerable to the public for its legal privileges and share of the national income. The more flagrant financial abuses were swept away by the Dean and Chapter Act (1840). The Oxford party was generally opposed to these changes, and particularly to the fact that they were imposed by the secular authority; its mission was to purify the Church from within.¹¹ The Cathedral Commissioners conducted a thorough investigation of the running of the cathedral foundations, which they reported in 1854;¹² some of their recommendations were put into effect. But almost another generation passed before cathedral chapters had been sufficiently influenced by the newly responsible attitudes to carry out a really effective overhaul of the system.

None of the early pioneers of cathedral reform were Tractarians. Maria Hackett, who devoted her life to the championing of choirboys and succeeded in shaming many cathedral chapters into making proper provision for their care and education, acted chiefly from humanitarian motives, as did the low-church wit and rationalist, Sydney Smith. John Jebb, whose *Choral Service of the United Church of England and Ireland* (1843) was a merciless indictment of abuses, was a traditional high churchman who wished, not to alter, but to perfect the existing musical traditions. This goal was shared by Samuel Sebastian Wesley, whose tract *A Few Words on Cathedral Music* (1849) was an outlet for the bitterness that had accumulated in his mind after many years of frustration at the hands of cathedral chapters. Frederick Ouseley, whose churchmanship was similar to Jebb's, placed his own wealth at the service of the Church by founding St Michael's College at Tenbury, to be a model school for the study and performance of church music. But he would not have Gregorian chants.

By the late 1860s the tide of opinion in favour of reform was considerable, and the inadequacies of cathedral choirs had been exposed by the high choral standards attained at Tenbury, at the Temple Church, and at unendowed parish churches such as Leeds or St Andrew, Wells Street, London. At this time some second-generation Tractarians entered into positions of authority on cathedral bodies, often by the nomination or direct influence of Gladstone, who became prime minister in 1868. At St Paul's the heroic age of reforms began with the installation of Robert Gregory as a canon in 1868, and of Richard Church as dean in 1871. John Stainer was appointed organist (March, 1872) and began calling regular rehearsals of the choir. At his demand the numbers were increased to twenty boys and eighteen men, and their salaries were raised. Days off and holiday periods were allowed, but regular attendance was insisted on at all other times. The foundation stone of a new choir school was laid in 1874.[13] Weekly choral celebration of communion was begun in 1873, and in general a much fuller programme of choral services was adopted, with ritual observance of the Church year.[14] Cassocks and surplices were adopted in 1872–3.[15] Similar reforms took place in other cathedrals at about the same time, or very soon afterwards.[16]

Entirely new kinds of cathedral service were brought in, in addition to the choral celebration. In 1858, at Westminster Abbey, Sunday evening services in the nave were tried out, and proved immensely popular; they included hymns sung by the congregation, which was also encouraged to take part in the chanting of the psalms; a well-known preacher was usually engaged.[17] This innovation was the work of the Evangelical party. It was imitated at St Paul's later in the same year, with equal success, and at York Minster in 1863;[18] many other cathedrals followed. A special voluntary choir usually performed at these services.

A later Victorian invention, the Festival of Nine Lessons and Carols, had its origin in an unlikely quarter, the temporary wooden building used at Truro before the present cathedral was built. Carol services (evensong with sermon and carols) had been held in several cathedrals on Christmas Eve, but in 1880 the service of nine lessons and carols was drawn up by Edward Benson, the bishop of Truro, and used there for the first time.[19] A derivative form of the Festival has become a national institution through its annual broadcast from King's College Chapel, Cambridge, but few are aware of the time and place of its birth.

The Music of the Liturgy

It is sometimes stated that the music of the liturgy has been retained in a continuous tradition from the Reformation to the present except for the Commonwealth period. It is true that the priest's part in the prayers and versicles has remained more or less unaltered, being derived from traditional plainsong as adapted by Marbeck (1550) to the English text. The *responses*, however, have varied greatly from time to time and from place to place. Settings by Tallis, Byrd, Tomkins and Smith have been revived in recent times, but were not in general use in the nineteenth century, though a version believed to be Tallis's was often sung. A remarkable diversity of music for the responses and litany existed in the early nineteenth century, and was put on record.[20] During the early Victorian period, efforts were made to standardize the musical practice of cathedrals. Henry Gauntlett took the opportunity to compose a setting with bold modern harmonies (ex. 9.1): he claimed to 'have done that which Tallis did, used the best harmonies I could, and in my best manner'. The setting that prevailed was chiefly that of St Paul's cathedral. As harmonized by John Stainer in *The Cathedral Prayer Book* (1891) it became the standard music for the responses when no special setting was in use. It included a special harmonization of the sixth response after the creed (invented either by Stainer or by his predecessor at St Paul's, John Goss), ending in D major and marked 'Soft and slow', which forms a kind of romantic coda to the choral prayers. Stainer also wrote a 'Sevenfold Amen' (1873) for use after the consecration prayer, which was adopted in many cathedrals and churches. Another Victorian innovation was the 'Ely Confession', a setting of the general confession in which each phrase was first mono-

Ex. 9.1 Henry J. Gauntlett, responses (1852)

(Gauntlett)

toned by the minister and then answered by the choir, sometimes on a monotone but sometimes in a harmonized tune.[21]

The use of the organ to accompany prayers and responses became more and more common in later Victorian times. J. S. Curwen wrote in 1880: 'There is an ambition among some players to use greater freedom in accompanying than a mere doubling of the voice-parts allows; to employ the organ, in fact, as Handel and Mendelssohn employ the orchestra to accompany their choruses.'[22] At least nine full-length books on the subject were published between 1880 and 1920. Many of them gave successions of chords, often chromatic, for accompanying a monotone. Madeley Richardson, organist of Southwark Cathedral, went further: 'It is often thought sufficient to play a succession of chords indiscriminately . . . Monotone accompaniment should be genuine music, with unmistakable evidence of design of its own. . . . It should include the elements of musical form—rhythm, melodic outline, and recurrence', ignoring the rhythm and meaning of the prose text (ex. 9.2).[23]

Ex. 9.2   A. Madeley Richardson, organ accompaniment for prayer on monotoned F (1907)

(M. Richardson, 118)

The *chanting of psalms* underwent greater changes than any other aspect of cathedral music in our period. Antiphonal chanting, verse by verse, had been abandoned almost everywhere in the eighteenth century because of poor attendance and incompetence. But even without this, there was little chance that all the singers would sing the words together: it was lucky if they even began and ended a verse together.[24] This cannot be a matter for surprise, since choirs never practised the psalms, and pointed psalters were unknown. The organist, unbelievable though it may appear, played the chants through in more or less strict time throughout the psalm, so that a long recitation would have to be sung very rapidly, while the rest of the verse had to be dragged out. Various printed collections show this proceeding in actual musical notation (ex. 9.3). In many cathedrals the syllables were distributed by the 'rule of three and five' (counting from the end of each half-verse), completely disregarding verbal accent, and this was actually recommended by Edward Hodges, an experienced church musician, in 1822, and by Rimbault as late as 1844.[25] It was in use at Lincoln and Norwich in 1834, when, however, three other modes of syllable distribution were recorded: one at York, another at Canterbury (and St Paul's), the third at Bangor (and Chester).[26]

Ex. 9.3 Lord Mornington, chant, fitted to the words of the Venite by Richard W. Beaty (1825)

*This tempo indication is given for the chanted canticles in Benjamin Jacob's *National Psalmody* (1817)
(Beaty, I)

As early as 1804 John Marsh suggested that the organist and choir of a cathedral should agree on the pointing of all the psalms, and underline the last syllable to be sung to the reciting note in each verse.[27] From 1831 onwards pointed psalters appeared in print, but the demand for them was chiefly stimulated by the introduction of congregational chanting in parish churches.[28] Many cathedral choirs continued in the old slovenly ways, and the psalm singing at Norwich was described as 'reckless gabbling' as late as 1860.[29]

Reform soon followed; psalms were practised at rehearsals, antiphonal chanting was reinstated. In the new, Victorian style of chanting, each verse was clearly divided into an unmeasured and a measured part. The first was to be sung in more or less the rhythm of speech, the second in strict time, though considerably faster than in the Georgian method. Because of the difficulty of suddenly switching from free to strict rhythm, Victorian musicians placed an 'accented syllable' near the end of the recitation, which began the strict-time part of the chant. Thus one heard first a monotoned prose passage of indefinite length, then a strict-time performance of all the chords of the chant (including the first) with one or two syllables to each. The idea of marking an accented syllable was probably first tried out by Stephen Elvey, organist of New College, Oxford, in his *Psalter* (1856). It was given authoritative stamp in *The Cathedral Psalter* (1875) (ex. 9.4), which was soon in very wide use, and it was continued with little modification in *The New Cathedral Psalter* (1910). Meanwhile the seeds of a second revolution in psalm chanting had been planted, in Francis Pott's *Free Rhythm Psalter* (1896). The new principle, which was stimulated by developments in the Roman Catholic Church, was to chant in the natural rhythm of slow reading, fitting the chords to the words with a complete disregard for their written durations. Robert Bridges was the spearhead of this movement,[30] but it was first tried out in public schools and parish churches and made little impact on cathedral practice until after the first world war.

Ex. 9.4 Explanation of pointing (1875)

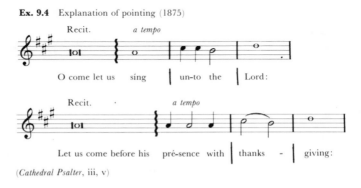

(*Cathedral Psalter*, iii, v)

178

In the midst of these radical changes the *Anglican chant* itself, astonishingly, had undergone little alteration. It had achieved its set form, of ten (or twenty) chords in a set rhythm of semibreves and minims, well before 1800, and remained in this form throughout our period. Hundreds, perhaps thousands, of new chants were composed. William Crotch in later life devoted much thought to the form, which he even used as the basis of composition teaching at the Royal Academy of Music; he wrote a set of fugues based on chants; and one of his chants exhibits both his gift for simple melody and his learning, for each section is the retrograde of another section, in all four voices (ex. 9.5). Some Victorian chants are exquisite miniatures of expressive harmony (ex. 9.6), and will bear twenty or thirty repetitions when sensitively chanted by a good choir. Variety was often provided by the organist. Even the conservative Goss illustrated such words as 'storm and tempest' in his accompaniments.[31]

Gregorian chants, advocated strongly by the Tractarian party from the 1840s onwards, were never widely used in cathedral services, although some cathedrals by 1900 were using Gregorian chants at one or two weekday services each week.

Ex. 9.5 William Crotch, double chant in G

(Bennett & Marshall)

Ex. 9.6 John Stainer, double chant in E minor

(*Cathedral Psalter*)

179

Two other kinds of music heard in cathedral services must be mentioned. The *metrical psalm* or *hymn* had been used in cathedrals since Elizabethan times, and its traditional place was before and after the sermon. With the reforms of the 1870s, this custom frequently was superseded, but hymns began to appear at other points, especially where high-church views prevailed: office hymns, processional hymns at festivals or for special services, communion hymns during the people's communion. The *organ voluntary* had an equally long history, not only as a way of 'playing the congregation in' (or out), but as a liturgical survival in the middle of morning and evening prayer, usually before the first lesson. A voluntary at this point was quite usual in cathedral services from Elizabethan to Victorian times, and as late as 1885 Frederick Bridge, organist of Westminster, said it was still not unknown though 'now, happily, almost obsolete'.[31]

Services and Anthems: Repertory and Performing Practice

In the early nineteenth century choir music was still performed out of hand-copied partbooks. The cheap octavo editions pioneered by Novello & Co. from the 1830s onwards were prompted chiefly by the growing parish-church market, and it was not until the 1860s that most cathedrals gave up their partbooks and began singing from printed scores.[33]

The repertory of the earlier period can be judged from surviving partbooks and from the printed anthem wordbooks issued by many cathedrals. For services a valuable repertory list of nineteen cathedrals was printed in 1824.[34] A sample of music lists for five Sundays in 1857, from a number of cathedrals and other churches, was published in the *Musical Remembrancer* and has recently been reprinted.[35] From about 1880 onwards most cathedrals issued weekly music lists. A systematic study was made by E. H. Fellowes and P. C. Buck in 1898, and its results were later printed in summary form.[36]

These sources show a predominance of music between fifty and one hundred years old at the time, with a fair representation of earlier music back to the Reformation. No dramatic increase in the performance of early music is perceptible before 1914. Instead there is a modest increase in the proportion of recent music, by such composers as Garrett, Lloyd, Parry, Stainer, Stanford and Sullivan. There was also a notable increase in the use of excerpts from oratorios, translated Latin motets and masses, and the like. This practice had begun in the late eighteenth century almost simultaneously at York and at St George's,

180

Windsor, with the use of parts of *Messiah*.* Handel was joined in nineteenth-century service lists by Haydn, Mozart, Spohr, Gounod, Brahms, Dvořák, Schubert, Bach and many others. Some cathedrals also resorted to simpler and more popular music, especially in the earlier part of the century when their choirs were not equal to the performance of genuine cathedral music. John Clarke in 1805 complained of 'the absurd, if not profane, introduction of Jackson's Hymns, in siciliana movements! The Denmark Hymn [Madan's 'Before Jehovah's awful throne']! The Sicilian Mariners Hymn! Pleyel's German Hymn! The Portuguese Hymn ['Adeste, fideles']! &c. &c. &c. as substitutes for anthems'.[37]

The later nineteenth century saw a huge increase in the quantity of 'cathedral' music composed. Novello's *Collection of Words of Anthems* appeared in 1889 with over 1,500 anthems; between that time and the appearance of an enlarged edition in 1898, 'no less than 400 new anthems' had appeared.[38] A great deal of this music, however, was largely for the parish-church market, and is little represented in cathedral service lists. But in certain parts of the service, cathedral choirs were compelled to be up-to-date in their selection because few early settings existed. This was true, for example, of the service for men's voices. The introduction of a weekly day off for choristers created a sudden need for this type of service; as a result, many of the leading composers produced examples, some commissioned by publishers and some by cathedral chapters.[39] The revival of the Benedictus, which had practically fallen out of use between 1650 and 1850, prompted a number of composers to add a setting of this canticle to morning services they had composed earlier, or even to services written in previous generations.[40]

Above all, the late Victorian high-church 'choral celebration' of communion required new music. It included a number of elements that had not traditionally been sung at all, such as the Sursum corda, Lord's prayer, Gloria in excelsis and blessing. In some cathedrals there were outright interpolations, such as processional hymn, introit, offertory hymns or prayers, Benedictus qui venit, Agnus Dei (during the communion of the clergy), and final antiphon.[41] (The use of the Agnus Dei at Lincoln was challenged in court, but allowed by the Privy Council in 1890.)[42] No complete traditional settings of such a service were in existence. As more and more cathedrals adopted it, those who preferred old music were compelled to select and adapt; the only hope of a solution that was artistically satisfying was to compose an entirely new

*A few adapted Latin motets by Tallis, Palestrina and Carissimi, and some of Garth's adaptations of Marcello's Latin psalms, were already in the repertory.

setting, and this was what many composers did. A manual in 1901 recommended twenty-five 'concerted' choral communion services; seven were adaptations of continental masses, the rest were by modern English composers, all published during the previous thirty years. (Five of these, mostly published in the 1870s, were designated as 'without *Benedictus* [*qui venit*] and *Agnus Dei*'.)[43] After introits were first introduced at York in about 1866, for several years the choir relied almost entirely on introits by one contemporary composer, George Macfarren.[44] These had been composed at the suggestion of the organist, Edwin G. Monk, to texts selected by him. They are miniatures, mostly in a modified ternary form. Macfarren, who was not a church musician, used this occasion to try out some highly original harmonies, often resulting from the ruthless pursuit of contrapuntal technique, and some imaginative text setting.

Contemporary sources are almost unanimous in their sense of a general improvement in the musical standards of cathedral services between 1870 and 1890. We have already seen that there was, indeed, a great improvement in the attendance, dedication, and discipline of choirs, in professional standards of singers and organists, and in support by cathedral clergy. Cathedral music was seen to be an efficient and well-run affair, free of the neglect and abuse that had become scandalous in earlier years. Beyond all this, however, there was a change in the style of performance, which brought cathedral music into conformity with the contemporary standards and conventions of the concert hall.

For a long time, the style of performance, as well as the music performed, had been out of date. It perpetuated traditions of the eighteenth century, which had once governed secular music as well. The Georgian style of singing anthems and services (described in detail in Volume Four) was very different from anything heard in church today. It centred on the glorification of the solo voice, as did the verse and solo anthems that formed the bulk of the repertory. The written melodic line was broken up by ornaments of all kinds; improvised cadenzas were customary at the end of each movement of an anthem; even in the choral sections two or three solo voices would often predominate.

Little change in this performing style took place in the early nineteenth century: if anything the tendency may have been towards greater elaboration. A lay-clerk of Norwich Cathedral, writing in 1880, recalled how different the services had been in 1840–50: 'Then everything was done in the most florid style, viz., grace notes, cadenzas, "shakes" (single, double and triple), while time was not much considered. Indeed, some of the treble solos were nearly sung *ad libitum* . . . In the anthems I have heard three boys making "shakes" simultaneously, and not only the boys but the lay-clerks used to "shake" most extensively . . . Such things are not allowed now.' The organist and choirmaster at Norwich from 1819 to 1877, Zechariah Buck, made the shake (or trill) one of the main features of his training of choristers' voices.[45] Indeed, an authentic performance of cathedral music composed before about 1860 should certainly include added ornaments in solo passages.

The new Arnoldian ideal emphasized discipline, and the merging of the individual voice in a unified choral texture. A number of choir-training manuals were published from about 1880 onwards,[46] often placing special emphasis on the development of a 'pure' tone in the boy's voice, to replace the operatic style formerly encouraged.[47] It seems clear that the characteristic singing tone and style of the present-day cathedral choir, regarded as typically English, had their origins in this period.

Services and Anthems: Late Georgian (1800–1830)

In the first part of the nineteenth century, the 'classical' anthem and service continued to prevail.* *Services*, because of their longer texts, avoided extended contrapuntal passages, except perhaps in the Gloria Patri, and tended to sound perfunctory. There might be changes of tempo and metre at conventional points in each canticle. *Full anthems* began and ended with a section for full chorus with some counterpoint, but normally contained a 'verse' section in the middle. *Verse anthems* were largely for soloists, with only a brief concluding section for chorus. The *solo anthem*—a verse anthem with only one soloist—remained in vogue. Accompaniments in 'full' sections were still sometimes written for figured bass, with occasional 'symphonies' written out in full. These traditions had been formed in the baroque period, and they now continued with little outward change, while the melodic and harmonic style was gradually transformed.

A representative composer of this period was John Clarke, later Clarke-Whitfeld (1770–1836), organist of Hereford Cathedral and later Professor of Music at Cambridge. A cultivated man who moved in literary circles,[48] he was affected by the romantic movement, which in musical terms at this date meant the style of Haydn and Mozart. His

*The *Treasury of English Church Music*, an otherwise excellent anthology, unfortunately includes no anthem, properly so called, composed between 1765 and 1833.

full anthem 'The heavens declare' (1805) is very obviously influenced by Haydn's chorus in *The Creation* beginning with the same words. In the verse anthem 'Bow down thine ear, O Lord' (1805) Clarke began with an aria for tenor, using appoggiaturas, chromatic harmony, and pauses (implying cadenzas) in the expressive manner of Mozart, and a form that clearly owed much to the sonata-allegro, or the corresponding operatic aria (ex. 9.7). Clarke's contrapuntal choruses are solid and correct, but rarely inspired. The same is true of his opposite number at Oxford, William Crotch (1775–1847), who came to life only in more homophonic passages with emotive texts (such as 'How dear are thy counsels', described in Volume Four).

The only composer of this generation who could express himself naturally in counterpoint was Samuel Wesley (1766–1837). His music for the Anglican cathedral service, though it has never been performed with any frequency,* is more extensive than is generally realized, consisting of about thirty anthems as well as the Service in F (1824). It does not reach the level of his best Latin church music (see below, p. 210) but there are passages showing a self-confidence and boldness rare enough in the period, for instance in 'I said, I will take heed to my ways' (1800).

A new kind of cathedral anthem was also beginning to emerge: short, quiet and tender, generally in a single movement for full choir. Today it is apt to sound 'Victorian' and to be despised as sentimental, but it had much earlier roots, and was the vehicle of strong and genuine emotion before it became trivialized through overuse. The composer most prominently associated with this new style was Thomas Attwood (1765–1838), who had been a pupil of Mozart and a composer for the theatre before he settled down as a church musician. He was organist of St Paul's Cathedral from 1798 until his death. His first essays in the new idiom were published in 1814: instead of the usual biblical texts Attwood chose to set three collects,† and the tone of the three works was that of musical prayer. In one of them, 'O God, who by the leading of a star' (ex. 9.8), he began with a touching tune for the treble voices, conceived in four-bar phrases which he extended slightly by the flowing movements of the lower parts. In 'Turn thee again' (1817) the form is ternary and the harmonies have become distinctly sugary, with much use of the tonic pedal. Yet there is no doubt of the genuineness of feeling

---

*'Sing aloud with gladness' and 'When Israel came out of Egypt' are adaptations of his Latin motets, not made by Wesley himself.

†An earlier example of a collect set in a simple tender vein is 'O Lord, we beseech thee' (1805) by Joseph Pring (1776–1842) (*Musical Times* no. 1563, May 1973). It is, however, in a style imitative of the seventeenth century.

Ex. 9.7 John Clarke-Whitfeld, verse anthem, 'Bow down thine ear, O Lord' (1805)

(J. Clarke, III)

185

Ex. 9.8 Thomas Attwood, collect, 'O God, who by the leading of a star' (1814)

(Attwood. Note values halved)

behind this piece. It was written for the funeral of Princess Charlotte of Wales, whose death in childbirth had deprived the country of its one hope of deliverance from a succession of unpopular kings, sons of George III, and was deeply mourned. Later examples of Attwood's tender style are the hymn 'Come, holy ghost' (1831)[49] and the anthems 'Turn thy face from my sins' (1835)[50] and 'Let the words of my mouth' (1835). The latter is in sonata form with contrasting melodies, with a coda strongly recalling that of Field's third Nocturne in A flat (1814).

It is tempting to put down these developments of style to external influences, and more particularly to such a work as Mozart's motet *Ave verum corpus*, K.618.[51] While these were almost certainly a factor, there was also an indigenous influence at work in the kind of music that was fashionable in London hospitals and proprietary chapels and later in parish churches, under the influence of the Evangelical movement.[52] Such a work as Richard Cecil's 'I will arise'[53] had just the same appeal as Attwood's short anthems.

Services and Anthems: Early Victorian (1830–1870)

The Oxford movement and the genius of S. S. Wesley tend to take up most of the space allotted to the early Victorian period in any history of cathedral music. But the change that quietly renovated the cathedral style after 1830 was largely independent of either, and was well in advance of the great improvements to come in standards of performance. As Fellowes put it: 'If the facts are carefully examined it will be seen that after the very lean period, extending over a hundred years, which . . . [preceded it], a great revival took place in the early years of Victoria.'[54] Among its causes were the romantic movement, the growing influence of Evangelicals in the Church, and the pressure for public accountability, which gave rise to the feeling that choirs were singing not for the dean and chapter only, but for the congregation. The change in style was not radical, but it was far-reaching. Outward forms were mostly preserved, but the expression of religious feeling became more direct and intense. There was a movement away from the formality of Georgian music, either through the revival of earlier styles or by the imitation of modern secular idioms.

The view that recent styles were unsuitable for church music had been bluntly stated by Crotch:

I should tremble for the fate of the sacred style, if modern music in general, or much of that now composed for the church, were to be adopted a hundred years hence. Few productions of the present day will ever become fit for divine service at all. The rust of antiquity will never constitute sublimity.

He advised young composers to model themselves on the music of the sixteenth century.[55] His views were actually enforced through the

Gresham Prize, donated by Maria Hackett annually from 1831 for the best anthem or service.[56] Crotch was the most eminent of the three judges, and was assisted by two other conservative musicians (William Horsley and Richard Stevens). Inevitably the prize compositions tended to be archaic in idiom.[57] Many of them contained deliberate examples of modal harmony, such as the triad on the flat seventh which, for a while, became almost a cliché of cathedral music. Another common archaism was the opening unison 'incipit' suggesting plainsong, used even by Attwood in his Service in D (1831) and anthem 'Enter not into judgement' (1834). Other composers who emphasized such links with the remoter past were Vincent Novello (1781–1861), William Monk (1823–89), and Frederick Ouseley (1825–81). They succeeded best in a simple homophonic texture (see p. 154, ex. 8.2); when they attempted sixteenth-century counterpoint the result was generally wooden and unconvincing.

The exception was Robert Pearsall (1795–1856). Although he was never connected with a cathedral, he wrote a substantial amount of cathedral music, some of which was published after his death;[58] it was occasionally performed at Bristol, Exeter and elsewhere. As in his madrigals, he succeeded at times in building a convincing personal idiom upon a mixture of Victorian and Elizabethan elements. His anthem 'Let God arise' ends with an extended fugue containing all manner of learned devices, and reaching an effective climax; his Venite in C contains a successful canon by inversion; his 'O clap your hands' is based on a plainsong *cantus firmus*. In his services he incorporated sections of Gregorian chant, sometimes harmonized in faburden style.

The other and more important feature of early Victorian cathedral music was the tendency towards bolder, more direct emotional expression. Regarded by Crotch as a serious defect, which caused him to reject Walmisley's and Wesley's entries for the Gresham Prize, this trend would eventually prevail and, taken to excess, would lead to the theatricality of the later Victorian period. At first, however, it was restrained by some of the surviving disciplines of Georgian style, and there could be a fine balance between form and expression. Sometimes a mood of quiet penitence was set, with just enough counterpoint to provide musical interest without obscuring the text, as in 'In my distress' (1861) by Edward Hopkins. Sometimes a stronger impulse was released. Such an outburst as William Monk's in 'Blessed are they' (1861) (ex. 9.9) carries conviction: the yearning dissonances seem to express genuine feeling, the unexpected change to the major mode at bar 45 gives an appropriate touch of hope. The passage quoted is followed by a more conventional fugato, but this does not destroy the

Ex. 9.9   William H. Monk, 'Blessed are they that always keep judgement' (1861)

(Novello & Co. CTA. Note values halved)

powerful impression made. The anthem is in a single movement and preserves one mood throughout, as do many of the better works of the time. First-rate services are few: the demand for sustained passages of praise and joy was seldom adequately met by composers of this period.

John Goss (1800–80), organist of St Paul's cathedral from 1838 to 1872, came into his own late in life as a cathedral composer. His best works all date from after 1850, when the conservatism of his earlier style was transformed by new encouragements or inspirations. 'If we believe', written for the Duke of Wellington's funeral at St Paul's (1852), is an intimate expression of the grief that gripped the nation at the passing of the old hero. It is a full anthem in one movement, almost entirely taken up with the single sentence, 'If we believe that Jesus died and rose again, even so them also which sleep in Jesus will God bring with him'. The point of imitation (ex. 9.10, (a)) is an eloquent one; it is treated with freedom, slowly building emotional force, and the music eventually moves from D minor to D major (ex. 9.10,(b)) expressing comfort in sorrow in a way that is worthy of Brahms. After a cadence there is a surprising afterthought with a different text, 'Wherefore

189

comfort one another with these words': for these five bars only, the tempo changes to a slow 3/2, and the harmonies form a plagal cadence with the minor subdominant: a moving conclusion.

Ex. 9.10 John Goss, 'If we believe' (1852)

(*Treasury*, IV, 62. Note values halved)

Several other anthems of the highest quality were written by Goss, particularly 'The wilderness and the solitary place' (1862), 'O taste and see' (1863), and 'O saviour of the world' (1869).[60] One of his last, 'The Lord is my strength' (1872), shows no abatement of his lyrical gift.

Of all the composers who were overshadowed by Wesley he is the most underrated.

Another important composer of the period was Thomas Attwood Walmisley (1814–56), godson and pupil of Attwood, Cambridge professor and organist, and son of a successful composer who outlived him to edit a posthumous volume of his cathedral music.[61] He is rightly best known today for his Evening Service in D Minor (1855),[62] which is, indeed, exceptional in his output.[63] It continues the 'archaic' tradition begun in the 1830s. Many of the verses are sung in unison by the tenors and basses, in phrases that suggest the ancient psalm tones and dwell on a dominant 'reciting note'. They are generally treated as the bass of the organ harmonies, which are resourceful extensions of the 'learned' contrapuntal style so much admired by Crotch and Samuel Wesley. The upper voices often reply antiphonally, with modal harmony. However, these romantic invocations are set in various keys; there is a specially notable change from B flat to G major at 'And his mercy endureth' in the Magnificat, enhanced by the chord of E minor and, shortly after, that on the flat seventh. The verse 'He rememb'ring his mercy' constitutes a drastic, barely acceptable contrast of style, recalling the honeyed Mozart-Attwood idiom in a hymn-like passage of square four-bar phrases.[64] The Gloria that follows restores the severe style of the opening. Antiquity is once again called to mind in the final Amen of the Nunc dimittis, on an imperfect cadence.

Walmisley's other, earlier services are relatively dull. He provided a few examples of the short full anthem: the best is 'From all that dwell below the skies', written to a metrical text. Its main climax depends for its effect upon modulation from the flat submediant back to the tonic, with the German sixth as pivot chord—a device which Walmisley used often and somewhat uncritically. Of his full-length anthems the best is 'If the Lord himself' (date unknown). Its first two movements continue the tradition of using elaborate organ accompaniments to depict storm and stress, the bass being played on the manuals with 16-foot stops. Over this Walmisley erected a vigorous contrapuntal choral texture, with crossing of parts, and, in the second movement, a dramatic bass solo with two-octave compass (ex. 9.11).

William Sterndale Bennett (1816–75) has been chiefly represented in cathedral lists by the short four-part chorus 'God is a spirit' from *The Woman of Samaria* (1867). But although he had no professional link with a cathedral, a considerable portion[65] of his rather slender output of compositions was written for cathedral choirs. Foremost among them is the splendid 'In thee, O Lord, have I put my trust' (1857), the first part of which was based on the introduction, for strings alone, of the

191

Ex. 9.11 Thomas A. Walmisley, 'If the Lord himself' (c. 1845?)

(Walmisley)

composer's first symphony, composed in 1832. The work presents contrasting sections of polychoral homophony and counterpoint in eight real parts, with admirable attention to text rhythms and meaning. 'Lord, who shall dwell', composed for the opening of the new chapel at St John's College, Cambridge in 1856, was one of the first of a type that would soon become common, the *hymn-anthem*, with a chorus based on a well-known hymn tune, in this case ST MARY'S. 'Remember now thy creator' succeeds in capturing a pleasant Mendelssohnian idiom: it appeared first as a treble duet sung at the Three Choirs Festival in 1848, and in 1855 the composer added a second, choral movement that reworked the same material. His pupil Charles Steggall (1826–1905) wrote a setting of the same text[66] that began in a manner reminiscent of Bennett's anthem (to say the least), but it continued with a long section for unison choir with organ accompaniment—'While the sun, or the light, or the moon, or the stars be not darkened'. This descends gradually from F to B flat (with some intervals of harmony), illustrating 'and all the daughters of music shall be brought low' and successfully casting a spell of quiet awe. There had never been a passage quite like this in English church music before, but it was perhaps Steggall's only flash of inspiration.

No composer in this period had higher ideals than Ouseley, who dedicated his life and fortune to the perfection of the cathedral service. He wrote five ambitious services, of which the grandest, in C (c. 1856), was for eight voices throughout and included settings of *all* the canticles including alternates. He wrote also several anthems for eight or more voices, notably 'O saviour of the world' (1865),[67] taking endless pains to avoid consecutive octaves or fifths, even at the cost of awkward part writing. His personal brand of antiquarianism favoured the Restoration period; 'How goodly are thy tents' (1861), for example, contains both prominent hemiola rhythms and the old 'English ending' with false relation between sharp and flat sevenths. He was never able to rid himself of these self-conscious or pedantic considerations, so that spontaneous feeling rarely comes through in his works.

Samuel Sebastian Wesley

The figure of Samuel Sebastian Wesley (1810–76) towers above the lesser men of his time, and now begins to look pre-eminent in the cathedral music of the last 250 years. For this reason, and also because his style was strikingly individual and even opposed to the general trends of his period, he demands separate treatment.

He was the natural son of Samuel Wesley, who instructed him in organ playing and composition, winning early recognition as a choir-boy and as a composer. From 1826 to 1832 he held organistships at various London churches, and in 1832 began his long career as a cathedral organist, which took him to Hereford, Exeter, Winchester and Gloucester, with an interlude between Exeter and Winchester at Leeds parish church (1842–9), which had a full 'cathedral' choir. His relations with deans and chapters were generally strained, because he criticized their lack of support for music while himself neglecting his duties. He felt not only displeased with conditions, but dissatisfied with the position of a cathedral organist, which he did not feel measured up to his abilities; private teaching he also thought 'degrading'. He wanted an academic appointment, and applied for one several times without success.

By all accounts Wesley, like his father, was incomparably the greatest organist of his generation.[68] His music for organ, like his songs, partsongs and piano music, is by no means insignificant, but from a fairly early period he concentrated his main creative energies on church music. His famous anthem 'The wilderness and the solitary place' was composed for the opening of a new organ at Hereford on 6 November 1832, and was then submitted for the Gresham Prize.[69] The judges pronounced it 'a clever thing, but not cathedral music'; Gauntlett, however, praised it highly.[70] In fact it was to prove one of the greatest landmarks in the history of English cathedral music. Other of his best anthems also date from this early period, including 'Blessed be the God and father' (for Hereford) and 'O Lord, thou art my God', submitted for his Oxford doctorate in 1839. At Exeter he began his Service in E, which he completed at Leeds; there he wrote several more anthems and prepared collections of chants and psalm tunes. In 1853, while at Winchester, he published *Twelve Anthems* by subscription. In later life much of his time was occupied with composing and harmonizing hymn tunes, which he eventually published in *The European Psalmist* (1872).

Wesley was indifferent to both the movements which we have identified as the prevailing ones in the cathedral music of his time. He was no antiquarian, despising both early English church music and Gregorian chants; and he had nothing but scorn for the emotionalism of Dykes and Barnby. He admired Bach, and regarded his own father as one of the few representatives of the 'pure style'. But he had a violent dislike of equal temperament and the 'German organ', and little to say in praise of any of his own contemporaries. In his compositions he worked out his own methods and styles, and in truth they are not closely comparable to anything else, though they sometimes show a kinship with the style of Spohr.[71]

His greatest achievements are in his anthems. The great Service in E Major, though it is full of splendid music, is too long for the ordinary services of the Church; Wesley discovered that he could not spread himself in a freely artistic setting of the canticle texts without going beyond the normal limits of length. In his anthems he was free to choose texts of appropriate length, and allowed himself much licence in this proceeding, putting together verses from many different parts of the bible, mixing the bible and prayer-book translations of the psalms, and incorporating parts of the liturgy or even metrical psalms. The resulting texts provided imagery, dramatic contrasts and climaxes as he desired them, and avoided dead or perfunctory passages.

In short full anthems, such as 'Wash me throughly'[72] or 'Thou wilt keep him in perfect peace',[73] Wesley was able to produce profoundly beautiful effects simply by skilful management of four or five voices in full harmony. The manner derived partly from the Mozart–Attwood tradition; the Roman Catholic influence, absorbed through his father, was a fruitful new element here, and word-setting was comparatively unimportant; a ternary or rondo form with quiet coda was the usual arrangement. The lovely opening phrase of 'Thou wilt keep him in perfect peace' was a favourite of Wesley's; he used very similar phrases in 'I am thine, O save me' and in 'The face of the Lord'. The harmony of the fourth bar, a diatonic ninth on the mediant, was almost a trademark of his style. He made great use of such diatonic dissonances, often with unusual spacing between the voices. On a slightly bigger scale, but still essentially in a single choral movement, is the six-part 'Cast me not away'.[74] The largely contemplative mood is interrupted by a dissonant climax at 'the bones which thou hast broken may rejoice' (bars 54–8), where, as so often with Wesley, great advantage derives from the placing of the basses near the top of the compass—a device learned from Handel. (A well-known anecdote associates this piece with a fishing accident suffered by the composer in 1847.[75])

In medium-length anthems of three or four movements Wesley was also highly successful. In one of the best known, 'Blessed be the God and father' (1833),[76] the main feature is the verse for treble solo and treble chorus. At first impression it seems Mendelssohnian, but it is really typically Wesleyan in its deftly uneven phrase structure. 'The Lord is my shepherd' (c. 1865?) opens with Wesley's special blend of recitative and arioso, carefully tailored to the rhythms of the text. In 'The face of the Lord' (c. 1850) the opening movement is for chorus, and is a superb example of Wesley's talent for subtle effects of harmony, rhythm and dynamics (ex. 9.12). In the opening phrase the high quartet is set off against the low bass line, and is then left alone for the second phrase, with its totally unexpected modulation to D minor and ending on an unaccompanied unison D, 'to cut off the remembrance of them from the earth'. To secure imitation without obscuring this text Wesley boldly shortened the text for the three lower voices, though the resulting verbal phrase has little meaning in this context. Next is a phrase dwelling on the comforting nearness of the Lord (an idea frequently evoking warm harmonies from the lonely Wesley), and on the 'broken heart', whose astringent harmony is set off by open spacing and by oblique motion against the held A and F in the upper voices. Then a dramatic homophony ('And saveth such'), followed by a general rest (reminding one of Purcell's funeral sentences, perhaps), and repeated on a different chord, leads to a rich five-part cadence in the dominant major. After this a long dominant pedal underlies the chromatically harmonized 'afflictions of the righteous', and the movement ends in G major with the same phrase that begins 'Thou wilt keep him in perfect peace', to the text 'But the Lord delivereth him out of all'.

But Wesley's most remarkable contributions to cathedral music lay in his large-scale anthems, so large that they are rarely performed in their entirety and are known only from movements that have been extracted from them (often with the composer's sanction) and become popular as short anthems or introits. In these longer works Wesley achieved a magnificence that has rarely been surpassed in English cathedral music, in spite of the weak movements that nearly all of them contain. The first and one of the greatest was 'The wilderness and the solitary place' (1832). It retains much of the traditional form of the verse anthem, beginning with a quartet, a bass aria recognizably of the ritornello type, and another quartet, before the chorus enters for the final sections, one of which is fugal. But throughout, Wesley shows boldness and freedom from harmonic cliché. The imposing opening phrase is harmonized I–VI–I⁶, like the beginning of 'The Magic Flute'. The bass solo is an early example (in England) of independent pedals; it too recalls 'The Magic Flute' (the chorale for the two armed men), relies on strong diatonic harmony, including the baroque sequence on descending fifths, and has a striking Neapolitan sixth at the cadence (bar 91). Imaginative accompaniment colours the text of the next quartet ('For in the wilderness shall waters break out'), in a phrase that is repeated in a cycle of keys (E, A♭, C and again E). Then follows a passage more dramatic than was customary ('And a highway shall be there') leading straight into the *fortissimo* choral entry 'And the ransom'd of the Lord', which soon opens out into a long fugue. After the

196

Ex. 9.12   Samuel Sebastian Wesley, 'The face of the Lord' (c. 1850)

15

ALTOS DIV.

Ma-ny are the af - flic-tions of   the   righ-teous.

Ma-ny   are the af-flic-tions of the righ-teous.

Org.   Ma-ny are

(*S:* Novello, Ewer, [c. 1850]. Note values halved)

preparation on the dominant Wesley, in one of his strokes of genius
generally associated with inspiring texts, delays the return to the tonic
with a modulation to C major and back. The key transition in itself was
not unusual—Walmisley could have managed it—but the sequence
and spacing of the chords, and the position of the passage at the climax
of a long and arduous fugal movement, make it electrifying. The
supertonic seventh in bar 265, in particular, shows Wesley's personal
touch. The triad on the flat seventh just after may be taken as a
concession to the 'sublime' tastes of the Gresham adjudicators, but it
also contributes a great deal to the splendour of the passage. The
anthem ends with a quartet in E major, in glee-like style, with chromatic harmonies, which might be too sickly if sung alone, but which is
entirely appropriate by way of relaxation from the excitement that has
preceded it. The full choir joins only in the final plagal cadence.

As fine as any of Wesley's long anthems is 'Let us lift up our heart',
with the bass aria 'Thou, O Lord God' described eloquently by Fellowes.[77] 'Ascribe unto the Lord' (c. 1852) begins with what Fellowes
rightly called a 'master stroke': a choral phrase 'Let the earth stand in
awe of him' sung first *fortissimo*, then repeated *pianissimo* a fourth lower.
The section 'As for the gods of the heathen' recalls Bach's mocking
crowd scenes with its discords, declamatory imitation, and descending
chromatic scales. The longest of all is 'O Lord, thou art my God'
(1839). Wesley handled its extended form with effortless ease, suggesting its large scale early by means of a substantial organ introduction
and by beginning again in the tonic after the first movement. Once
more Wesley wound up a long Handelian *fugato* with a dramatic

198

CATHEDRAL MUSIC

outburst and modulation, this time to the appropriate words 'Lo, this is
our God, this is the Lord; we have waited for him'. It seems to express
the Church of England's awakening from long slumber.

Wesley is an isolated figure. His music draws eclectically from many
sources, but is a unique amalgam that defies comparison or imitation.
Unmistakably his best efforts were inspired by the uplifting nature of
certain texts from the English bible, and it was the renewed consciousness of the Word fostered by the Evangelical revival that lay behind his
life-giving touch.

Services and Anthems: Late Victorian and Edwardian (1870–1914)

Several historians have identified a low point in English cathedral
music in the middle part of Victoria's reign. According to Hadow the
primary fault was 'the tendency to softness and sentimentalism, which
meant really the use of cheap and shallow formulae',[78] but that does not
explain much. Fuller Maitland, followed by Fellowes, attributed the
trouble to over-reliance on foreign influences, particularly those of
Spohr, Mendelssohn and Gounod.[79] He did not explain why foreign
influences should cause a decline in quality. The 'bad' period was
followed, according to the conventional view, by a 'renaissance' at the
hands of Elgar, Parry and Stanford, although only the last-named of
this famous trio contributed substantially to the cathedral repertory.
To cater for this interpretation Fellowes inserted a 'mid-Victorian'
period between the 'early Victorian' and 'late Victorian and neo-
Edwardian' periods, and placed in it the music of Garrett, Barnby,
Stainer and Sullivan. ('Mid-Victorian' presumably means, roughly,
1860–80.)

It may be that the time has come to revise this interpretation.
Enough has been said to show that the early Victorian period can be
regarded as one of the summits of English cathedral music. Even if the
presence of S. S. Wesley is regarded as fortuitous, he was supported by
a number of other composers of ability, whose music was a response to
an intense religious revival, and showed a balance between austerity
and emotionalism peculiarly suited to the genius of the Anglican
Church. In the period that followed, the balance was tipped on the side
of emotionalism, and the turning point came about 1870.

There is plenty of evidence that the antiquarian impulse that we have
noted in early Victorian church music was on the wane. The change

can be seen in the decline of the movement for congregationally chanted Gregorian psalm tones;[80] in the discontinuance of the publications of the Motett Society and the Musical Antiquarian Society, which remained the only scholarly collected editions of early English church music until *Tudor Church Music* began publication in the 1920s; in the disappearance of early English church music from Novello's *Musical Times* supplements;[81] in the shift in the content of *Hymns Ancient and Modern* between the 1861 and 1875 editions.[82] The new taste is exemplified in the first volume of a new series, *Novello's Collection of Anthems*, beginning in 1876: it contained only recent music, above all six anthems and adapted motets by Gounod (out of twenty-six in all). The first piece in the whole collection was Gounod's 'Come unto him', whose style differed from the cathedral music of the preceding period so strikingly that it was quoted by Fellowes as an example of 'harmful influence'.[83] It was a style in which the expression of feeling was unrestrained by the reticence hitherto found in Anglican music.

The 1870s witnessed, as we have seen, a remarkable improvement in the performance of cathedral music, which, far from contradicting the decline in quality of composition, goes some way towards explaining it. For the reforms that brought about the rapid rise in choral standards were based on goals and methods imported from outside the cathedral walls: from the concert hall and, to some extent, the theatre. People who had heard choirs and orchestras conducted by Sir Michael Costa could no longer tolerate the slovenly and perfunctory singing of unreformed cathedral choirs. Conducting and rehearsal techniques were introduced; organists, choirmasters, and choir singers sought professional training and qualification; institutions to regulate these quickly came into existence (the College of Organists, 1864; Trinity College, London, 1872). It was inevitable that external stylistic influence would be brought in along with external methods and standards.

So the imitation of secular styles (opera, cantata, or partsong), and of foreign composers, was an almost involuntary consequence of the vigorous efforts to improve performance. It certainly was not in any way wrong in itself. It had happened before—for instance in the Restoration period. Yet its consequences at this time were not altogether happy. The late-romantic musical ideal brought all resources to bear on the maximizing of emotional effect, and this did not accord well with a religious liturgy and tradition that emphasized dignity and restraint. Cathedral and even parish choirs were now expected to give a 'performance' to rival that of a concert or oratorio society; the organ was called in to add all kinds of orchestral colour. In the hands of Stanford and his successors, this new tradition eventually produced some excellent and even some highly original music. But something essential had gone out of the cathedral choir, never to return. English cathedral music lost its distinctiveness, or, as some would say, its insularity.[84] It gained a knowledge of the world, which could not be discarded when later composers, such as Charles Wood, began in their turn to look back with regret on past innocence.

One of the oldest composers to contribute to the new style was Henry Smart (1813–79),. who belongs to this period rather than the early Victorian: most of his cathedral music dates from after 1860.[85] As one of the first English organists to gain a thorough mastery of pedal technique, he was well equipped to bring about the transformation of the anthem into a concert piece. Some of his earlier anthems, such as 'Grant, we beseech thee' (1863), are relatively severe, but in a work such as 'Lord, thou hast been our refuge' (1878), written for the festival of the London Church Choir Association, but dedicated to the Sub-dean of St Paul's, he expanded into the full opulence of the late Victorian style. Smart's Service in F (1868)[86] was one of the most popular settings of the century. In quoting a long unison passage from the Te deum that builds to a substantial climax (bars 67–126), Bernarr Rainbow has remarked that it 'demonstrates the importance of the role played by the organ . . . while the voices are limited to a chant-like part. Here, it appeared to Smart and his contemporaries, was presented "the living kernel of the Gregorian chant without its husk"'.[87] One might well say the same about Stanford's and Wood's adaptations of early musical styles.

In John Stainer (1840–1901) we have a man who was himself an antiquarian—indeed it is arguable that his work as a musicologist was of more permanent value than his composition. Yet there is little trace of the influence of early music in his cathedral style, which exploits the full range of contemporary harmonies for direct emotional expression. More than that, he made use of dramatic devices alien to the cathedral tradition and to English canons of taste, as in the representation of the risen Christ appearing to Mary in 'They have taken away my Lord' (1875) (ex.9.13), clearly influenced by Catholic continental composers like Gounod. The incarnation clause in the Nicene Creed of the Service in E Flat (1874) is also painfully vulgar, being set as a tenor solo over repeated chords in 12/8. Fellowes quoted some instances of Stainer's woefully inadequate settings of splendid words.[88]

The danger of vulgarity came from the demand for music that would demonstrate in the most concrete way the greatly increased expenditure and effort that had been invested in choirs, cathedral and parochial. The desire for 'improvement' of church choirs was more a

Ex. 9.13 John Stainer, 'They have taken away my Lord' (1875)

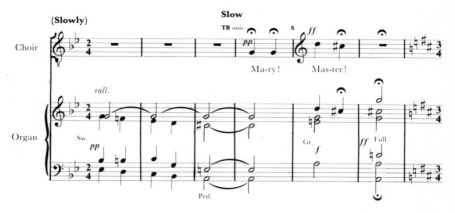

(Wienandt & Young, 273. Note values halved)

part of the general drive for material progress in all facets of life than a purely religious impulse. Joseph Barnby (1838–96) was especially prone to vulgarity. His main professional activity was as a conductor of choral societies, and he brought this experience to bear on his conduct of the musical services at London parish churches and at Eton College. The opening of 'King all glorious', which he called 'a motett for soli and chorus' but which was published in Novello's anthem series, begins with a loud organ fanfare, quickly diminishing from *ff* to *pp* to herald a tenor solo over repeated chords in 9/8. The 8-bar phrase is repeated by the chorus *ff* with the tune sung in octaves by 1st trebles and tenors:[89] the effect is entirely theatrical, suggesting a choral scene in an opera of

Meyerbeer or Verdi. Theatricality might be expected in the work of Sullivan (1842–1900), and commentators have perhaps unfairly combed his cathedral music for echoes of the Savoy operas. One of his earliest anthems, 'We have heard with our ears' (1865), still belongs to the 'antiquarian' phase, beginning with an intonation of the eighth Gregorian tone, which is also the basis of the opening movement and of the excellent final five-part fugue. A middle section, 'How thou hast driven out the heathen', treats an unusual melodic phrase as the basis of a *fugato*. In his later work, however, Sullivan followed the trend of the times. So also did the Belgian organist Berthold Tours (1837–97) who, through his position as musical adviser to Novello & Co., occupied an influential position in the cathedral music market. His compositions are taken seriously by Wienandt and Young, but it is difficult to see in them any more than effective catering to the demands of the hour, as in 'Sing, O heavens', which uses ADESTE FIDELES as its culminating 'big tune'.[90]

An exceptional work of this period is the Communion Service in F by Hugo Pierson (1815–73), who was wholly removed from participation in cathedral services, being permanently resident in Germany. It was published in 1870 on commission from Simpkin, Marshall & Co., and although parts of it are perfunctory, it has a beautiful Agnus Dei that is like no other English cathedral music. Its closest models are the Latin motets of Liszt.[91]

Charles Hubert Hastings Parry (1848–1918), a student of Pierson's and one of the leading musicians of his age, provided only occasional music for the church service. His large-scale anthems 'Hear my words, ye people'[92] (1893) and 'I was glad' (for the coronation of Edward VII, 1902) are very much on the lines of his cantatas, so popular at provincial festivals and competitions in this period. 'Hear my words' was, indeed, composed for a festival of the Salisbury Diocesan Choral Association. Thus, like many of the larger late Victorian anthems, it was meant to be sung not by a cathedral choir but by a massed gathering of amateur parish choirs. It aims, aptly enough, at grand and massive effects; the organ writing, particularly in the introduction, is symphonic, and was equally well adapted to an actual orchestra; motives in the accompaniment are used to integrate the work; and the concluding movement is a rousing hymn tune, making the most of the contrast between a professional quartet and a unison choir of hundreds of voices. This tune is sung in the anthem to the words of Sir Henry Baker's hymn 'O praise ye the Lord', and it soon became the standard tune for this popular hymn in ordinary use. Late in life Parry composed a set of six motets, the 'Songs of Farewell' (1916–18); but, though

203

deeply emotional, these are hardly cathedral music, and only one of them ('Lord, let me know mine end') has a biblical text. The best known of the group is 'My soul, there is a country',[93] but the finest is perhaps the five-part setting of Campion's hymn 'Never weather-beaten sail', with its touching mood of longing for release from the world, so characteristic of the period.

In Parry's contemporary Charles Villiers Stanford (1852–1924) we have a composer for whom the cathedral service was one of the central facts of life. As an Anglo-Irish protestant he was devoted to the Church of England. He was very much one of the newer type of cathedral composers, bringing a cosmopolitan and professional training to bear on his task. He patently modelled his style on the more conservative continental protestant romantics, above all Brahms. Like Parry, he wrote symphonically for the organ; he abandoned the old sectional tradition of the English anthem, welding his pieces into integrated forms by development and recapitulation and by motivic construction. Like Parry also, he wrote his share of grandiose works for diocesan and provincial festivals, and late in life contributed 'Three English motets' (1913) of touching personal feeling. But unlike Parry he made it his business to provide working models of services and anthems for cathedral use.

It is especially due to Stanford that the service setting regained its full place beside the anthem as a worthy object of artistic invention. The daily canticles, particularly the Te Deum, present technical problems for the composer, and their texts are too long to allow much in the way of development and imitation. Stanford got through the texts quickly and with little repetition, generally in a tuneful, treble-dominated style, with sectional variety of key, tempo, metre, and rhythm; and he allotted to the organ the chief responsibility for making a coherent musical work. In the Te Deum from the early Service in B Flat (1879), for example,[94] the opening unison chorus phrase, though derived from a traditional Gregorian intonation, forms a perfect symphonic motive. It is anticipated in the introduction (added for the 1902 coronation service); links the opening phrase to the second section in the dominant; forms the organ bass for the homophonic chords at 'Holy, holy, holy', recalled at the final 'O Lord, in thee have I trusted'; recurs in various transformations as the melodic germ for other passages—'The glorious company of the apostles', 'Also the Holy Ghost', 'When thou tookest upon thee' and so on; appears in triumphant recapitulation at 'Day by day we magnify thee'; and is converted into a running accompaniment in the next section, 'Vouchsafe, O Lord'. There are less obvious motivic connections linking the other canticles to the Te Deum, while the distinctive 'Dresden Amen'* first heard in the Gloria of the Jubilate is recalled at several points in the Communion Service, always with judgement and taste. Modulations are well planned and enterprising. The result, as most often with Stanford, is a thoroughly satisfying artistic experience, but one that is perhaps lacking in deeply felt religious impulse. Never does he, like Wesley, cast aside all principles of musical structure to respond directly to the imperative demands of the text. And this, in religious music, makes him the lesser man of the two.

Stanford's later services, in A (1880), F (1889), G (1903), and C (1909), are his generation's most important and lasting contribution to the cathedral repertory. They have stood up to a great deal of repetition; the one in C, in particular, has a solid simplicity that has made it a favourite with parochial as well as cathedral choirs. The Magnificat of the G Major Service (ex. 9.14) is original in its pictorial evocation of the Virgin Mary, sitting perhaps at her spinning wheel, as she sings the opening words.[95] Such use of a persistent figure of accompaniment for combined pictorial, emotional, and harmonic effects is a measure of the depth of secular influence on cathedral music in this period.

In his anthems Stanford was only marginally less successful than in the services. 'The Lord is my shepherd' (1886), one of the earliest and best, is also unified by thematic transformations; it is largely built on three-bar phrases, for Stanford, unlike such predecessors as Henry Smart, was acutely conscious of the need to avoid certain 'Victorian' trademarks, of which the most prominent were decorative chromaticism, square phrase lengths, and false verbal accents. Few English composers have been more scrupulous in choosing musical phrases to suit the natural rhythms of English, both in their note-lengths and in their pitches: Fellowes cited the opening phrase of the B-flat Magnificat as a perfect example.[96]

The pitfall of squareness is most obviously present in the setting of metrical texts, which, in common with others of his generation, Stanford increasingly chose for his anthems (indeed the distinction between an anthem, a 'motet', and a sacred partsong had become thoroughly blurred by this time). He responded to this technical challenge with unfailing resourcefulness, nowhere better than in his late anthem for Advent, using the old Wesleyan hymn 'Lo! he comes with clouds descending'. The trochaic lines generate several motives, and, when the composer wants them to, can provide a marchlike rhythm ('See in solemn pomp appear'); but his deft variation of phrase lengths, generally following the natural emphasis of certain words, keeps an onward

---

*Stanford's use of this theme followed Mendelssohn's in the 'Reformation' Symphony, but anticipated Wagner's in *Parsifal*.

Ex. 9.14 Charles V. Stanford, Magnificat in G (1903)

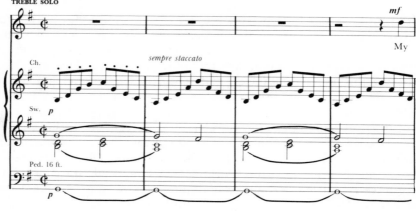

(*S:* Houghton, [1903])

momentum throughout this joyful piece. Conversely, Stanford would often pick out words from a prose text which lent themselves to rhythmic repetition, as in a striking passage from 'And I saw another angel' (ex. 9.15), strongly supported by the symphonic organ. He has cleverly linked two rhythmical prose passages (Revelation vii, 9 and 12) by setting them to the same music, made all the more memorable by

206

Ex. 9.15 Charles V. Stanford, 'And I saw another angel' (1890)

(*S:* Novello, [1890]. Note values halved.)

207

its use of that still electrifying device, the triad on the flat seventh, which bursts into some relatively conventional counterpoint. The repetition fits nicely into a well balanced musical form (*ABCB*). Such consummate skill has been equalled by few in the history of our cathedral music.

Almost as important for his contributions to the repertory of service settings was Stanford's pupil and successor Charles Wood (1866–1926). He was particularly fond of evening services, of which he produced over twenty—perhaps because in his lifetime fewer and fewer cathedrals were able to maintain daily choral matins. After three early examples in D, C minor and E flat (1898–1901) he returned to the task later in life, eventually covering all the principal keys, as well as several of the modes. The well-known Evening Service in the Phrygian Mode (1923) was added to an earlier communion service.[97] Another notable setting is the 'Collegium Regale' Service in F, written for the choir of King's College, Cambridge. Most of the later services, indeed, were written for college choirs, and they require a refined, exquisite style of singing for best results, as do his intimate short introits like 'O most merciful' and *Expectans expectavi* ('This sanctuary') (ex. 9.16). Some of Wood's music shows a second wave of antiquarianism that reached its height in the music of Vaughan Williams and Holst. Having a more developed understanding of the nature of the modes than his Victorian predecessors, Wood could achieve a purity of style that to some listeners was indistinguishable from Palestrina's or Byrd's. A large proportion of his thirty or more anthems are of the hymn-anthem type; some, including one of the most popular, 'O thou sweetest source', are little more than a set of richly harmonized variations on an old tune. He drew not only on the Gregorian psalm tones and mediaeval office hymns, but also, even more, on the early metrical psalm tunes. His treatment of them, however, is still romantic in its evocation of the primitive.

Another contemporary who was addicted to the hymn-anthem was Basil Harwood (1859–1949), but he is best known for his Service in A Flat (1892), a melodious work that is utterly conservative in style, especially in its return to the relentless 4-bar phrases of Smart. Edward Bairstow (1874–1946) also made his greatest mark in hymn-anthems like 'The king of love', 'Blessed city, heavenly Salem', and 'God, who at sundry times'. His usual method was to use a biblical text for an introductory section that reaches a climax with the entry of the hymn, which often appears in three verses of rising splendour, reminiscent of the finales of Bruckner's symphonies. An exceptionally fine work of Bairstow's is 'Let all mortal flesh keep silence' (1925),[98] which, in

208

Ex. 9.16 Charles Wood, *Expectans expectavi* ('This sanctuary') (1919)

(*S:* Deane, 1919)

Long's view, places him 'head and shoulders above' all his contemporaries except Vaughan Williams.[99]

Two emigrant composers of the late Victorian and Edwardian period made valued contributions to the repertory. Thomas Tertius Noble (1867–1953) made a mark with his Service in B Minor (1899)[100] before emigrating to the United States in 1912, and Healey Willan

(1880–1968) published several anthems before he went to Canada in 1913. John Ireland (1879–1962), not primarily a church musician, produced before the first world war two successful works in the Stanford tradition, the Communion Service in C and the anthem *Greater love hath no man* ('Many waters cannot quench love').[101] The latter was published in 1912, but the horrors of war gave a fuller meaning to its text, making it one of the most popular anthems of its period.

Roman Catholic Cathedral Music

It was not until near the end of our period that the Roman Catholic Church in Britain was able to compete on equal terms with the Anglican cathedral. The celebration of mass had been made legal in 1791, most of the civil disabilities of catholics were removed in 1829, and the catholic hierarchy in England, headed by the Archbishop of Westminster, was restored in 1850. But the Church lacked the resources to support elaborate music. Its largely Irish congregations were poor, and, of course, it did not possess the accumulated endowments of the Established Church. In Ireland itself the resources were also inadequate: the Pro-Cathedral in Dublin had no professional organist until 1827.[102]

During the earlier part of the nineteenth century the only places where catholic services of a high musical standard could be heard were the London embassy chapels. Vincent Novello, who had succeeded Samuel Webbe as organist of the Portuguese Chapel in about 1797, soon made it a fashionable resort for music-lovers, catholic and protestant alike, who came to hear a professional quartet perform the masses of Haydn and Mozart. His friend Samuel Wesley was temporarily converted to catholicism largely as a result of his admiration for the music at the embassy chapels. Wesley confessed that one of his greatest musical treats was to accompany unison plainsong at the organ of the Portuguese chapel. Plainsong, however, was gradually being replaced by concerted music of recent date.[103]

Wesley himself wrote a large number of settings of the catholic liturgy which are among the most important English music of their period.[104] Between 1780 and 1783 he composed a series of antiphons in a style similar to Webbe's, but in 1784 came an ambitious *Missa de Spiritu Sancto* which he dedicated and presented to the Pope. It is an elaborate work for soloists, chorus and orchestra, in the style of an earlier generation of Italian composers such as Leo, Porpora, or Pergolesi, whose music had been frequently performed at the Concert of

Ancient Music since 1776. A work on a similar scale was his motet *Confitebor tibi* (1799), composed presumably for some occasion.[105] It is still basically in the Italian late baroque style, with many operatic arias, *fugato* choruses, and *cantus firmus* movements, but with a wealth of original invention and a surprising mastery of orchestration. At the turn of the century Wesley was also developing a more severe style for unaccompanied motets, clearly showing his absorption of the music of Byrd and Palestrina. Among these are *Levate capita vestra* (1798), *Anima nostra* (1798?) and *Te decet hymnus* (1798). His best-known works, *Exultate Deo*[106] (1800, originally with orchestral accompaniment) and *In exitu Israel* (1810, written for a concert performance) mix this style with Handelian counterpoint, as do the fine motets *Tu es sacerdos* (1814) and *Constitues eos principes* (1814) (ex. 9.17). Wesley continued occasionally to contribute Webbe-like music for the embassy chapels. He also wrote between 1799 and 1807 a number of Latin hymn and psalm settings for three male voices, perhaps for use by the Concentores Sodales, a private singing club (one of his settings of *Dixit Dominus* was certainly written for this body in 1806). Late in life he returned to Latin religious texts, perhaps for purely personal satisfaction, as in his moving unaccompanied motets *Omnia vanitas* (1824–7) and *Tu es sacerdos* (second

Ex. 9.17 Samuel Wesley, *Constitues eos principes* (1814)

(*S:* Novello, 1974)

setting, 1827).[107] Wesley's music has not been much appreciated by English catholics. After his death the few works that remained alive were performed in Anglican cathedrals, adapted to English texts.

In the 1830s the best catholic music in London was to be heard at the Bavarian chapel, Warwick Street, and at the English chapel of St Mary, Moorfields, according to a writer in *The Athenaeum*. The chief musical fare was still the masses of the Viennese masters, sung by leading operatic singers.[108] From 1849, Brompton Oratory became a centre of catholic music under F. W. Faber, whose hymns were sung congregationally there; the choral music followed the trend on the Continent towards a more and more theatrical style, and was almost entirely continental in origin.

During the 1860s Cardinal Manning attempted to ban female singers from the choirs of catholic churches. His order was not universally obeyed, but at Brompton Oratory a fine choir of men and boys was formed, and began to sing the works of Palestrina and Carissimi as well as those of Haydn and Mozart.[109] Some provincial catholic churches developed highly successful choirs in the later nineteenth century, for example the one at St Mary, Richmond Hill, Leeds, which had twenty-five boys and fifteen men, all voluntary, in about 1890.[110] Birmingham Oratory, too, had a respected choral tradition.[111]

Westminster Cathedral was opened in 1901, and Cardinal Vaughan's ambitious plans for its services included a large musical establishment for the daily performance of choral mass and office. He placed the music in the charge of Richard Terry (1865–1938). A former chorister at King's College, Cambridge, Terry had been received into the Catholic Church in 1896, and as music master at Downside Abbey had attracted attention by his revivals of sixteenth-century polyphony: his performance of Byrd's five-part Mass on 21 March 1899 was the first for three hundred years.[112] At the cathedral Terry needed a vast quantity of music for the constant choral services, and he edited large numbers of masses and motets of the later Renaissance and early baroque periods. The Pope's *Motu proprio* of 1903, outlawing most music of recent date, lent authority to his policy, and he took full advantage of the resources available to give superb performances of much unknown early music. Of the works of Palestrina alone, he performed twenty-seven masses, nearly sixty motets, twenty-one offertories, and thirty-five magnificats, 'an achievement quite without equal anywhere in the world'.[113] Later he placed greater emphasis on English music, and the effective revival of Tudor church music owes far more to Terry than to any Anglican activities. As one of the editors of *Tudor Church Music* he produced in print, from 1924 onwards, music that had been regularly performed at Westminster Cathedral for twenty years or more. The choral establishment at the cathedral was soon subject to financial pressures. In 1906 the number of men in the daily choir was reduced from fourteen to nine, and in 1912 to six; during the war only one man remained.[114]

The brilliant developments at Westminster were not particularly conducive to contemporary composition, though Terry did mount the first London performance of *The Dream of Gerontius* and, in 1923, the cathedral commissioned Vaughan Williams's Mass in G Minor. Edward Elgar, the most prominent catholic musician of his day, composed little for the Church after his early motets and litanies, written for St George's catholic church, Worcester, where he was organist from 1885 to 1889. Of these, his *Ave verum corpus* was among the first contemporary English works officially recommended for use in the archdiocese of Westminster (in 1907).[115] It is an attractive and devotional piece, but hardly in the same class as the composer's masterpieces of later date. Stanford wrote far more Latin liturgical music than Elgar, including a Requiem, *Te Deum*, *Stabat Mater*, Mass in G, and three motets published in 1905.[116] These pieces were more antiquarian in style than his Anglican church music: the motet *Coelos ascendit hodie* (op. 51, no. 2)[117] successfully revived the polychoral style of the late sixteenth century.

Chapter 10

ORATORIOS AND CANTATAS

NIGEL BURTON

The Handelian Aftermath

The musical life of nineteenth-century Britain was governed not by opera, as in the rest of Europe, but by oratorio.

The causes of this apparently improbable exception lay deep within the nation's history. By 1914 Stanford had concluded that 'as Luther discountenanced painting and so killed for centuries in Germany an art for which Dürer and Cranach had laid the soundest of foundations, so did the Puritans destroy music in this country. Its rescue depends upon the foundation, support and sure continuance of a National Theatre, and a National Opera'.[1] But this was an oversimplification, for although the Puritans were against liturgical music and the theatre, they were never opposed to music itself. Consequently oratorio, a form that was sacred but not liturgical, unstaged and yet dramatic, was an ideal compromise for a nation whose Established Church sought to combine and resolve both Catholic and Calvinist traditions in its worship and theology. Handel's oratorios were first intended to be staged, but the Bishop of London ruled against the staging of sacred dramas: his successor confirmed the ruling when another attempt to stage an oratorio was made in 1835. Most Methodists and Nonconformists opposed even concert performances of oratorios in Handel's day, and for a long time continued to view them with suspicion; but by the Victorian period they were as enthusiastic as Anglicans in their support. The Sacred Harmonic Society, which gave frequent oratorio performances throughout its existence from 1832 to 1882, was largely supported by Nonconformists.

In 1800 Handel's oratorios were a national institution, evoking strong patriotic feelings (more than ever in time of war) and reaching out to all but the lowest classes of society, especially at the great festivals in Westminster Abbey and in provincial cathedrals, though some Anglican clergy objected to the 'desecration' of sacred buildings

214

for this purpose. England's long-established foreign policy of opposing whichever happened to be the strongest continental power abetted the natural tendency of English art to react tardily (if at all) to continental developments. The few oratorios by English composers that enjoyed even modest success tended to be heavily Handelian, or alternatively (after 1800) modelled on Haydn's *Creation*.[2] The only oratorio which has survived, however precariously, from the century which followed Handel's death, is *Palestine* (London 1812),* by William Crotch (1775–1847).[3] Perhaps it is no coincidence that it was composed (between 1804 and 1811) when Napoleon's Continental System was at its height.

Despite its merits, *Palestine* suffers from two serious drawbacks: excessive length and an appalling libretto. (These observations, as will be seen, apply to many of the works which follow.) Crotch arranged his text from a poem by Reginald Heber (1783–1826) which had won the Oxford medal for English poetical composition in 1803. In doing so he followed eighteenth-century precedents, for it was not yet usual to select words 'entirely from the Holy Scriptures'—*Messiah* itself had been exceptional in this respect. The poem's subject, so far as it had one, was the history of Palestine from the Red Sea crossing to the Ascension, and it reads like the competition piece it was:

> Hence all his might, for who could these oppose?
> And Tadmor thus and Syrian Balbec rose;
> Yet e'en the works of toiling genii fall,
> And vain was Estakhar's enchanted wall.

Crotch evidently considered that verse such as this would nurture those 'sublime' qualities which he conceived to be the embodiment of musical perfection. These, as we have seen, were to be found in the most dignified masters of the past: Palestrina, Byrd and Gibbons, J. S. Bach and Handel.[4] *Palestine* provides ample evidence that he was better informed regarding contemporary musical developments than most of his English colleagues, yet he deliberately cast the work in a Handelian mould because he believed that by doing so he could appeal not merely to his own generation, but to posterity. The undeniable validity of his assumption now seems remarkable, but it was justified by the stylistic time-lag which existed in many branches of music between English and continental developments.

Today, however, it is clear that *Palestine* is a magnificent ruin. Its marble statuesque beauty is covered in dust, as the quotation from the

---

*Places and dates in parentheses following the name of a work are of its first performance. Where the place is Gloucester, Hereford, or Worcester, the occasion was the Three Choirs Festival.

opening chorus shows (ex. 10.1). The roots of this chorus can be traced
to Purcell, as those of the treble aria 'Ye faithful few' lead back to Lully.
The Handelian numbers now seem the feeblest, if only because they
can still be compared directly with their superior archetypes: the last
four numbers, for instance, ape their equivalents in *Messiah*. The large
fugal choruses, such as 'Worthy is the Lamb', betray Crotch's lack of a
thorough musical training (the penalty of his celebrated precocious-
ness), and demonstrate his inability to curtail a piece before he had

Ex. 10.1 William Crotch, *Palestine* (1812): chorus, 'Reft of thy sons'

(Larghetto)

(*K*: Author, [1812])

wrung every last possible conclusion from his material. This was a damaging failing, for it had an adverse bearing upon the work's proportions. That he never deviated from his stoically eighteenth-century aesthetic outlook is shown by the two finest movements: the powerful chorus 'Let Sinai tell', a dramatic expression of the doctrine of the affections, and the once well-known quartet 'Lo! star-led chiefs', which is animated by the rococo manner of Johann Christian Bach.

The most modern music is found in the overture: stylistically its three sections (Larghetto-Allegro-Andante) reflect Gluck, Samuel Wesley, and Haydn respectively. The end of the second (fugal) section briefly captures the atmosphere of Beethoven's Fifth Symphony. The comparative stylistic freedom of this overture is significant: the German masters who dominated English music were (with the exception of Mozart) primarily instrumental composers, and this may explain why, of Crotch's large-scale works, his organ concertos (especially the third in B flat major) stand a better chance of revival than his oratorios and odes. For the rest, Crotch set a pattern followed by many English composers: he was essentially a miniaturist (as his glees and anthems prove), and his musical compositions were far less influential than his musical teachings.

In attempting to assess the work of Crotch's contemporaries and successors, it is best to state immediately that a favourable revision of previous historical judgements is not really possible. Most of the music involved is overwhelmingly Handelian in origin, though Mozart's operas and Haydn's *Creation* appear as secondary sources of inspiration. So strong are these influences that aesthetic evaluation frequently consists of merely tabulating a work as either a good or a bad neoparody.

The Crucifixion and the Resurrection (Hereford 1822) by John Clarke-Whitfeld (1770–1836) can be cited as an example of the former category. It demonstrates a feature common to this school: a great many of the large Handelian choruses are in D major, whilst the movements most suggestive of Haydn are in B flat major. The work's essential refinement is epitomized by the duet 'Daughters of Jerusalem' (for alto or treble, and tenor) in which the composer effectively fuses his thorough knowledge of the English Church tradition with an elegance derived (as in *Palestine*) from J. C. Bach.

But the moribund condition of the Church tradition could not be disguised, and some works, such as *Job* (Foundling Hospital 1813) by William Russell (1777–1813), made no attempt to do so. Like so many minor composers who were tempted by oratorio, Russell's talents were simply not equal to the scale of the task. Moreover, he could hardly have chosen a worse subject than Job, since he allowed its succession of disasters to occasion a string of totally unremarkable arias, sung by the hero to his maker. Hence the work's narrow stylistic base (a colourless and predictable emulsification of Handel, Haydn, and Mozart) is perfectly revealed by its structure, with fatal consequences.

Such depressing triviality is partially relieved by the enjoyable vulgarity of *The Seventh Day* (London 1834) by Sir Henry Bishop (1786–1855). But by far the finest oratorio of the period after *Palestine* is *The Omnipresence of the Deity* (published 1829) by John Barnett (1802–90), though ironically it was never performed. Like Bishop's, Barnett's style is operatic, albeit far more grand and self-assured, and in his love of effects he anticipated Pierson's *Jerusalem* fairly closely. The external influence upon this line of composers was Spohr, whose *Last Judgment* enjoyed an enormous popularity in Britain until it was overtaken by Mendelssohn's *Elijah*.

Despite a work of such promise, however, English oratorio was still far from self-sufficient. Sadly, its only hope lay in a fresh infusion of life from the Continent; happily, the advent of that new force was not to be long delayed.

The Mainstream: I

On 26 August 1846 the first performance of *Elijah* took place at the Birmingham Festival. This event did more than anything else to drag British choral music belatedly into the romantic era. Mendelssohn was to exert a vital and beneficial influence on the course of Victorian music: his style, whatever its faults, flexed sufficient musical muscle to effect several immediate and long overdue improvements.

The first significant work of this transitional period was *The Martyrdom of St Polycarp* (Oxford 1854, composed as a D.Mus. exercise) by Frederick Ouseley (1825–89). Internal musical evidence would suffice to date this oratorio fairly accurately, for while several numbers are overtly Mendelssohnian, the older Handelian style still predominates. The conventional wisdom which claims that Crotch's innately conservative teachings harmed the succeeding generation of composers in general and Ouseley in particular is undeniably correct (Crotch advised his pupils to model their music on 'no one after Greene or Boyce'). But in addition to this, Ouseley was one of the first British composers to fall into the trap of transferring the results of his musicological researches untreated into his own compositions; for instance, the Chorale (no. 4)—'supposed to be sung by the Christians in the fields'—consciously attempts to imitate J. S. Bach, though unintentionally its most striking feature is its bizarre part-writing (the result, no doubt, of following 'the rules' as he understood them).

Yet Ouseley's odd stylistic mixture is somehow the source of a new-found sense of warmth. Such things as the sudden lapse into Meyerbeer in the middle of the March of the Pagans (no. 5)[5] and the unruffled serenity of the double chorus in which the Christians and Pagans confront one another (no. 14: 'He taught impiety') are no less touching than inapposite; in fact they illustrate a fundamental truth concerning the nature of Victorian oratorio: these works, secular and sacred alike, reflect a society permeated at every level by acceptance of conventional Christian doctrine. For too long they have been evaluated by the criteria of twentieth-century criticism, in the light of which they inevitably appear naïve and unsophisticated. Only as the nineteenth century recedes further into the distance is it possible to view its achievements with the balanced intuition which must surely inform all truly sympathetic artistic judgements.

Mendelssohn's influence was finally absorbed into the mainstream of English music in the compositions of William Sterndale Bennett (1816–75). It was not simply a question of direct imitation, because Bennett's early works prove conclusively that his personal style happened largely to coincide with Mendelssohn's. But his failure to develop it properly accounts for the lifelessness of his two main choral works, both written comparatively late in life: *The May Queen* (Leeds Festival 1858) and *The Woman of Samaria* (Birmingham Festival 1867).

Bennett was a leading Bach enthusiast, and this affected the structure of *The Woman of Samaria*, which he described as 'a sacred cantata'. The distinction between cantata and oratorio was always inclined to be blurred in this period, but broadly speaking the two forms characterized the two strains of religious music, the pictorial and the didactic, respectively. Bennett's use of the term 'cantata' was deliberately retrospective, however; presumably he saw the work as a legitimate nineteenth-century English development of an eighteenth-century Lutheran tradition. At any rate, the moments which suggest this are by far the most lively: the 'Alla Chorale' setting of 'Abide with me' at least displays a spark of individuality, and the C major 9/8 orchestral opening of the chorus 'Therefore with joy' succeeds in catching the rhythmic impetus of a Vivaldi-Bach ritornello. Best of all is the opening number for sopranos only, in which the chorale melody 'Nun freut euch lieben Christen g'mein' is sung in duple time against a triple accompaniment (ex. 10.2).

The May Queen is the prototype of the Victorian *secular cantata*,

Ex. 10.2 William Sterndale Bennett, *The Woman of Samaria* (1867): opening chorus

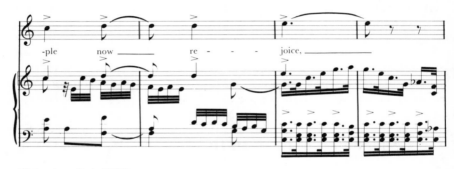

(*K*: Lamborn Cock, [1867])

although in view of its insipidity its long and undisputed popularity now appears remarkable. Much has been made of the libretto by Henry Chorley, whose literary efforts were certainly in a class of their own. Chorley managed to produce a poem in which dramatic urgency was refined down to the barest acceptable minimum:

> What! you, my lord, in vile array?
> What would your plighted lady say!
> You, to a village girl descend?
> Shame! from our presence! hence! amend!

and Bennett responded with a score whose virtues were emphatically negative.

It is no accident that *The May Queen* comes across in performance as a work of the same genre as *Acis and Galatea*. The early nineteenth-century secular cantata's links with the eighteenth-century serenata* eventually hampered its dramatic and pictorial development, and many minor composers exhausted their energy in attempting to overcome its inbuilt inertia. However, they usually managed to earn a living in the process, and those who worked as doggedly as John Francis Barnett (1837–1916) (nephew of John Barnett) could claim with justice that their drudgery had eased the paths of those who followed them.

Barnett's music ultimately died because of its self-effacing politeness. Although he managed to update his style in some of his later cantatas such as *The Wishing-Bell* (1893) and *The Eve of St Agnes* (1913), his best work was *The Ancient Mariner* (Birmingham Festival 1867). At a time when literary considerations were beginning to weigh more heavily on composers' minds, Barnett remained curiously insensitive to the problems of word-setting (ex. 10.3). This quotation comes from the opening chorus, which, in accordance with the unwritten rule applied to most secular cantatas, also closes the work. It is interesting to note that the festival choruses helped to keep the male alto tradition alive, for one chorus ('The bride hath paced into the hall') has a footnote appended to the effect that 'only half of the altos should be employed, and they should, if possible, be female voices'. Barnett's most pretentious work was the oratorio *The Raising of Lazarus* (New Philharmonic Concerts, London 1873). It is hard to believe that only seven years separate its neo-Mozartian writing from Parry's *Prometheus Unbound*.

Ex. 10.3 John Francis Barnett, *The Ancient Mariner* 1867 : opening chorus
(Allegretto, ma tranquillo)

The ship was cheered, the har-bour cleared, Mer-ri-ly did we drop
Be-low the Kirk, be-low the hill, Be-low the light-house top.

(*K*: Hutchings & Romer, [1867])

Mention must be made of Henry Smart (1813–79) if only because his music does not warrant the harsh treatment which has often been meted out to it ('It is conventional to take a gloomy view of an age in which ... Henry Smart was even counted as a composer at all').[6] As his well-known hymn tune REGENT SQUARE shows, Smart's style was bluff, open-handed and energetic—qualities usually regarded as essen-

*Macfarren's *The Sleeper Awakened* (1850) was actually so called; Loder's *The Island of Calypso* (also 1850) was called an 'operatic masque'. Both would have been called cantatas ten years later.

tially English. His cantata *The Bride of Dunkerron* (Birmingham Festival 1864) benefits from his knowledge of Weber (see the passage 'Wake the wild harp')[7] and Mendelssohn's more vigorous writing (the orchestral introduction, for instance, recalls the *Ruy Blas* overture). His word-setting contrasts favourably with Barnett's, and anticipates Sullivan's.

Taken together, the works so far discussed in this section trace the gradual emergence of the early Victorian choral-orchestral style. Since this followed the long Handelian aftermath, it was inevitably conditioned by Teutonic models, yet it managed to preserve the nation's basic musical instincts intact. Its most eloquent exponent was George Alexander Macfarren (1813–87) in whose hands it reached its mature and finite form.

Macfarren's oratorios and cantatas belong mainly to the second half of his long career, and their volume alone represents a labour of immense dedication. His iron determination earned him a reputation for harshness, although Joseph Bennett was probably right when he wrote: 'I believe, in spite of his apparent hardness, tears were never very far from his sightless eyes.'[8]

So far as oratorio was concerned, Macfarren's musical personality was tougher than any of his predecessors', and in his finest work, *St John the Baptist* (Bristol Festival 1873), he succeeded where they had all failed: by sheer artistic will power he forged a personal idiom strong enough to rely essentially on its own merits. At its heart lay a unique sense of modulation (it could be called 'key extension'—a term which implies an anticipation of Elgar). Like Haydn before him, Macfarren delighted in setting himself difficult technical problems and then solving them triumphantly. Rather than follow the usual procedure of modulating gently from phrase to phrase, he changed gear from bar to bar, even from chord to chord, but in such a way that the music's diatonic logic, instead of being compromised, seemed all the more unassailable (ex. 10.4).

Few composers have written better for massed choral voices, though Macfarren's weaknesses tend to show in the solo numbers, for he was a dramatic composer, not a lyrical one. But he manages to portray his characters and situations vividly: Herodias, for example, never appears, but the use of her motif (see no. 12) throughout Part II makes it clear that she is the source of evil at Herod's court. Macfarren's psychological musings in the 'argument' foreshadow the 'intellectual' approach of Parry:

The aim of this short oratorio [it would be considered full-length by modern standards] is to depict the Baptist in all his greatness—greatest of all in his

Ex. 10.4 George A. Macfarren, *St John the Baptist* (1873): opening chorus

(*K*: Stanley Lucas, Weber, [1874])

constant self-abnegation . . . Contrasted to his grand figure is the effeminate, voluptuous character of Herod acting as much from passionate impulse to good as to evil.

In short, although the charge of unjustified neglect is made too frequently to arouse much interest, it must be pointed out that Macfarren's choral works definitely constitute one of those areas of Victorian music which merit performance as well as description. The other large-scale works are all late: *The Resurrection* (Birmingham Festival 1876), *Joseph* (Leeds Festival 1877), *King David* (Leeds Festival 1883), and the 'St George's Te Deum' (Crystal Palace 1884). Of the cantatas the most successful were *May Day* (Bradford Festival 1857) and *The Lady of the Lake* (Glasgow Festival 1877).

Individualists

No authentic native renaissance was possible until the flood tide of Mendelssohnian influence waned, yet during the mid and late century there emerged several composers whose musical personalities were strong enough to work independently of the stylistic mainstream, even though they could not hope to alter its direction.

Of these the greatest and most perplexing was undoubtedly Henry Hugo Pierson (1815–73). Previous critics of his ambivalent style have naturally been at variance, and most of their disparate judgements contain elements of truth. Newman described him as 'a musician who is at the same time poet and thinker',[9] which was true, since the basis of Pierson's very considerable talent was his intellect. But despite (or perhaps because of) this, his music suffers from technical insecurity, and amateurishness is a charge from which he cannot entirely be acquitted. Time after time he will begin a piece brilliantly only to dissipate his energy in a welter of ostensibly unrelated ideas, though the music is nearly always informed by an inherent psychological continuity. Now presumably some listeners can detect this whilst others cannot, which probably explains why Pierson's admirers find his works immediately memorable, whilst his detractors are completely untouched by them. All this leads to at least one interesting conclusion: that of all the major composers of the nineteenth century, the one with whom he is in closest spiritual affinity is Berlioz.

The sacred* oratorio *Jerusalem* (Norwich Festival 1852) shows that Pierson's sweep of vision and grandeur of conception were unrivalled by any of his contemporaries. (The other new work at Norwich that year was the colourless *Israel Restored* by William Bexfield (1824–53), which won the critics' preference.) The scriptural text of *Jerusalem* is a mixture of history and allegory: it opens with Christ's prophecy of the destruction of the city and concludes with the vision of the New Jerusalem contained in the Revelation of St John. In the fact that it propounds few philosophical absolutes lies the key to the musical style, which never consists of music *qua* music since it is entirely dependent upon its extramusical dimensions. The beauty of moments such as example 10.5 from the chorus 'How shall I pardon thee for this?' shows why it is hard to be uncharitable to the composer.

Pierson's greatest achievement was his setting of the Second Part of Goethe's *Faust* (Hamburg 1854), which was regularly performed with the play in Germany for many years.[10] This would have been a difficult task for most composers, but he was ideally suited to it: his temperament was perfectly attuned to the expression of broad and complex intellectual issues by means of a multiplicity of interrelated musical miniatures. There are many fine moments in the score (which was obviously heavily influenced by Schumann's work on the same subject), among which Ariel and the Chorus of Fairies and the Chorus of Invisible Spirits of the Elements may be cited. Most outstanding of all

*The term 'sacred' was applied to an oratorio when its words were entirely derived from scripture.

Ex. 10.5 H. Hugo Pierson, *Jerusalem* (1852): chorus, 'How shall I pardon thee for this?'

(*K*: Novello, [1852])

is Euphorion's death: the nobility of Helena's grief at her son's demise is moving enough in itself, yet when it it is fused with an implicit expression of her passionate love for Faust, the impact is overwhelming.

So England exported Pierson, whom she could ill afford to lose, but she imported Michael Costa (1808–84) and Julius Benedict (1804–85). Although she lost by this transaction, both 'imports' have been unfairly treated by posterity. Benedict's greatest 'sacred' achievement was the oratorio *St Peter* (Birmingham Festival 1870), a work strongly reminiscent of Weber (his teacher) and Henselt. Yet Costa's career was probably the more influential: as a conductor his approach may have been old-fashioned, but at least he managed to implant some basic standards where none had existed previously. His *chef d'oeuvre* was the oratorio *Eli* (Birmingham Festival 1855), a work to gladden the hearts of all who love Victorian curiosities. Never before or since can the church and the opera house have joined hands in such amazing but vital incongruity. Costa's real self emerges against his will in the passages of refined early Verdi and Meyerbeer (with lavish use of the brass), but he constantly attempts to disguise it beneath a coat of applied Spohr and Mendelssohn in a naïvely touching effort to be reverent. This Janus-like attitude does not preclude the gestation of some very fine music (ex. 10.6). Costa's second oratorio was *Naaman* (Birmingham Festival 1864), but by that time the Church had tightened its grip, and his operatic vitality succumbed.

The composers of sacred music who modelled themselves on Gounod and Wagner produced their best results when writing specifically for the church service. *Rebekah* (London 1870) by Joseph Barnby (1838–96) is an unbalanced work: thirty-one of its one hundred and seven pages are fugal, and it never attains the composer's highest standard. John Stainer (1840–1901) has two sacred cantatas to his credit: *The Daughter of Jairus* (Worcester 1878) and *St Mary Magdalen* (Gloucester 1883). The former is the more satisfactory, although the systematic employment of chromaticism for expressive purposes is more marked in the latter. Both these works, however, are studies for Stainer's masterpiece, *The Crucifixion* (St Marylebone Parish Church 1887), a classic and almost faultless composition if accepted on its own terms.

The Mainstream: II

During the last forty years of the century the taste for choral works of a pictorial and descriptive type reached and then passed its peak. As a fashion it served English music well, for it offered composers the chance to discover which styles and methods best suited their individual talents. The increasing sense of self-confidence which resulted was an artistic manifestation of the growing magnitude of British imperial power.

The expansion of the Empire created a vogue for the exotic which composers were not slow to exploit. One work which enjoyed a phenomenal success was *Lalla Rookh* (Brighton Festival 1877) by Frederic Clay (1838–89). It owed it to the famous solo 'I'll sing thee songs of Araby',* a number completely at odds with the naïve orientalism of the

*See above, p. 130–1.

Ex. 10.6 Michael A. Costa, *Eli* (1855): aria, 'Hear my prayer, O God'

(*K*: Addison, Hollier & Lucas, [1856])

227

rest of the work: the ultimate destination of the 'Slow March of the Cortège' (no. 8) turned out to be Albert Ketèlbey's *Chinese Temple Garden*.

This vein found a more refined expression in the Moresque from *On Shore and Sea* (London International Exhibition 1871) by Arthur Sullivan (1842–1900). Of Sullivan's two secular cantatas, the earlier, *Kenilworth* (Birmingham Festival 1864), was the more impressive, though like Bennett's *May Queen* it was saddled with a libretto by the indefatigable Chorley. The inclusion of Shakespeare's 'How sweet the moonlight sleeps upon this bank' gave Sullivan his only real chance, and he seized it avidly. This duet is an early instance of his unique gift for word setting: by careful placing of the external accents, he was somehow able to penetrate to the deeper levels of a poem in the way Schubert had before him.

It took him a considerable time to establish his mature oratorio style. His difficulties arose from inherent temperamental contradictions: he suffered simultaneously from a misplaced anxiety to adopt the 'correct' musical models, and from a complacency bred of the spontaneous nature of his genius. He made a reasonable beginning with *The Prodigal Son* (Worcester 1869), one of the shortest mid-Victorian oratorios; its best number was the multi-sectional chorus 'O that men would therefore praise the Lord', in which he drew effectively on his knowledge of the verse anthems of Purcell and Handel to create an impressive series of related and heightening musical climaxes (an ability which was to stand him in good stead in the first-act finales of his comic operas). In general, though, he seems to have taken greater trouble over the construction of the libretto than over the music, in which, amongst other influences, the first traces of Gounod are evident.

Gounod's music made a marked impression on British choral composition from the 1860s onwards, although *The Redemption* (Birmingham Festival 1882), which he wrote specifically for this country, compares unfavourably with his masses and *Mors et Vita*. Just as Mendelssohn's imitators harmed his reputation by misrepresenting his style, so Gounod's followers performed their mentor a similar disservice. Sullivan was not a major offender in this respect, but the one large-scale work in which Gounod's influence did prove harmful turned out to be his worst. This was *The Light of the World* (Birmingham Festival 1873), of which Queen Victoria prophesied that it 'was destined to uplift British music'.[11] It did so by virtue of its elephantine proportions, if nothing else, but Sullivan clearly felt few genuine creative impulses when composing it, and in this sense it stands apart from his other major sacred works. The didactic nature of the text was unsuited to his long-term aims (he had been attracted to the subject of the Prodigal Son by the allure of its local colour),[12] and in order to allow his dramatic talents fuller scope he turned, logically, to extra-biblical subjects.

Of *The Martyr of Antioch* and *The Golden Legend* (Leeds Festival 1880, 1886) Percy Young remarks that 'in the general context of choral music of that era both works represented a departure from the overriding convention of religiosity', and he adds that Elgar was influenced by their 'boldness of conception'.[13] This is undoubtedly true. In purely structural terms the former is the more pioneering and uneven work of the two, and like many of Sullivan's 'serious' compositions has been virtually buried beneath a deluge of hostile criticism. It would be senseless to make inflated claims on its behalf; but anyone who has taken the trouble to glance at the score will be aware that it contains many episodes of individual beauty. The apotheosis ('Margarita's immolation') is as uplifting as Sullivan intended it to be (it takes as its precedent the fourth-act finale of Rossini's 'William Tell'—one of the most prophetic passages of early-nineteenth-century music, as Wagner's operas testify).

Finally, there came *The Golden Legend*, for a long time considered the composer's masterpiece by respectable musical opinion. Fuller Maitland attests to its significance by acclaiming it as the first native work to create a furore 'at all comparable to that caused by [*Messiah* and *Elijah*]'.[14] It was in fact a late florescence of the Handelian school, which was based on the visible and demonstrable aspects of Christianity and rooted in one of the two authentic national religious traditions.

Its high-church counterpart had been assiduously fostered by the Oxford movement. By contrast, it emphasized the contemplative and devotional religious virtues and expressed the subjective mysticism inherent in Arminian Anglicanism and Roman Catholicism. The musical language of late romanticism was its ideal aesthetic medium, as several European composers had already discovered: two major representative works specifically written for English audiences were George Henschel's *Stabat Mater* (1894) and Gounod's *Mors et Vita* (1885).

The apogee of this tradition was *The Dream of Gerontius* (Birmingham Festival 1900) by Edward Elgar (1857–1934). Elgar's religious faith and musical temperament uniquely qualified him to write such a work. He had patiently hammered out his highly personal style during his long apprenticeship and by 1900 had four secular cantatas and an oratorio to his credit. Of the former, *Caractacus* (Leeds Festival 1898) stands out as the most ambitious: in so far as he was unafraid to court popularity or to flaunt his patriotic fervour, Elgar was Sullivan's spiritual successor rather than a man of the academically respectable 'renaissance', and *Caractacus* is the natural sequel to his predecessor's 'Festival Te Deum' (Crystal Palace 1872) and two Imperial Odes (1886, 1887). No work better demonstrates Elgar's mastery of the orchestra. Here again, the links with Sullivan are obvious, although Elgar thought in rich, composite textures founded upon his supreme knowledge of the idioms of string writing, whereas Sullivan's orchestration emphasized instrumental individuality with an inbuilt bias in favour of the woodwind. On the debit side are the Eigen-Orbin scenes, not so much for being ineffectual, but because they are out of place. They display an inability to compose genuine love music, which may explain Elgar's reluctance to venture into operatic territory (*Caractacus* was the closest he ever came to it).*

Elgar's style is characterized by its constant state of emotional flux which he achieved by an intuitive application of Wagner's modulatory technique. But the stained-glass harmonies of *Gerontius* owe as much to the organ music of César Franck as to *Tristan* or *Parsifal*, and in general the oratorios contain more of the Wagnerian manner than its matter. In his attitude to key relationships, Elgar resembles Tchaikovsky (Wagner's antithesis): keys for him were sources of colour, and these colours were related, in their turn, to specific emotional states.

In his early oratorio *The Light of Life* (Worcester 1896) Elgar displayed the enormous potential of this approach. The oratorio's subject is Christ's healing of a man blind from birth. Its brevity accentuates its forcefulness: blindness (the outward sign of evil) is set against sight (the outward sign of goodness): an ethical scheme which allows Elgar to represent its antagonisms by the juxtaposition of intense blackness and dazzling brightness. In the first full chorus, light suddenly blazes out of the darkness with searing energy (ex. 10.7). 'It is here', wrote Basil Milne, 'that the music is lifted to an imaginative plane that at once sets the work apart from all that uniform mass of music which until 1896 had represented the English oratorio tradition.'[15]

After *Gerontius*, Elgar conceived the idea of a trilogy of oratorios upon the subject of the foundations of Christianity. The third work, *The Last Judgement*, was never written—a fatal omission as it turned out, for it was as though *The Ring* had been truncated at the end of *Siegfried*. The parallel is an apt one, since *The Apostles* (Birmingham Festival 1903) and *The Kingdom* (Birmingham Festival 1906) are episodic works held together by a framework of leitmotifs which generate an ever-increasing, but unfulfilled, momentum of musical interest.

The reversion to biblical oratorio proved mistaken. Morover, there is

*Apart from *The Spanish Lady* (sketches only).

Ex. 10.7 Edward Elgar, *The Light of Life* (1896): first full chorus (no. 6) an uncharacteristic element of miscalculation about *The Apostles*, the first work of the trilogy. The music strives after an unnatural modernity, and many of the consequent technical difficulties are superfluous. But the characterization is interesting: Judas is portrayed as a frustrated intellectual who becomes the victim of his own inquisitiveness; Mary Magdalene as a cynical sophisticate who belatedly awakens to the latent evil in her nature. One of the finest moments depicts her humility as she washes Christ's feet with her tears—this episode is deeply affecting. But taken as a whole *The Kingdom* is the stronger work of the two, principally because its closer-knit text supports music of a more symphonic character.

The thirty years which led up to *Gerontius* were probably the most productive in the entire history of British choral music and space permits only a glance at the other men involved. *Ruth* (Worcester 1887) by Frederic Cowen (1852–1935) and *The Rose of Sharon* (Norwich Festival 1884) by Alexander Mackenzie (1852–1935) both enjoyed a considerable vogue in their day, though Young's assessment of their merits is accurate: 'Mackenzie, like Cowen, was at his best with exotic or fantastic ideas, but his skill in orchestration was unmatched by any substantial sense of musical logic.'[16]

Charles Harford Lloyd (1849–1919) and C. Lee Williams (1853–1935) deserve honourable mention. The former's work, of which *A Song of Judgment* (Hereford 1891) is typical, never descends to the trivial or the shoddy. Williams drew his inspiration from the glee tradition, as the best pages from *A Harvest Song of Praise* (Tewkesbury 1894) show.

The last significant composer in the Sullivan-Elgar tradition was Samuel Coleridge-Taylor (1875–1912). His music, like Sullivan's, is conservative and eclectic, though less individual. All his life he battled against cultural and financial insecurity, and this meant that once he had hit upon a successful formula he was tempted to repeat it again and again. *The Atonement* (Hereford 1903), his most ambitious work, was heavily influenced by Elgar, though the chromaticism of its main motive, 'Christ Triumphant', is indebted to the Tchaikovsky-Rachmaninov school. In *A Tale of Old Japan* (Queen's Hall, London 1911), Coleridge-Taylor predictably employed faint reminiscences of *Madame Butterfly*. This was the finest of his late works, for his technical mastery grew steadily throughout his career. But he never recaptured the spontaneity of his masterpiece, *Scenes from the Song of Hiawatha* (1898–1900),* for which he is remembered today. The famous perfor-

*Part I: Royal College of Music 1898. Part II: North Staffordshire Festival 1899. Part III: Albert Hall 1900.

232

mances by Malcolm Sargent and the Royal Choral Society at the Albert Hall institutionalized the work and brought colour into many suburban lives: 'I used to have to leave the hall in my costume complete with war paint and caused quite a stir on Charing Cross Station', recalled a chorus member recently.[17] In effect this was the last really successful English secular cantata ever written, and it should never have been allowed to fall from the concert repertoire. It was, however, the swan-song of the nineteenth-century pictorial school: by 1900 it had already been overtaken by the march of great events.

The 'Renaissance'

'From the last decade of the nineteenth century onwards the word "renaissance" has been applied to the changes which had come over English music about that time and its appropriateness has never since been seriously questioned', wrote Frank Howes, adding immediately however that 'a modern writer, Arthur Jacobs, dismisses the term as a "comic overstatement without any serious attempt at computation".'[18] The new indigenous school of composers which arose in the 1880s proved that English music was in its healthiest state since the death of Purcell; but the term 'renaissance', with its inescapable overtones of the artistic glories of fifteenth-century Italy, now seems a little exaggerated.

The work which (by general agreement) inaugurated this new era was *Prometheus Unbound* (Gloucester 1880) by Charles Hubert Hastings Parry (1848–1918). Hubert Parry occupies a large position in the annals of British music, rather than a great one, and *Prometheus Unbound* may be considered as the prototype of his choral compositions. Like most crusading works written in a spirit of self-conscious zealotry it has not survived. Shelley's text was an unsuitable vehicle for music, and reading it remains a more uplifting emotional and intellectual experience than studying the score. Rather than keep solely to the poem's lyrics, Parry laudably decided to remain true to its dramatic spirit and so included long passages of narrative blank verse. Not surprisingly, he found them heavy going. It was well known that he was a disciple of Wagner, yet he failed to turn that composer's influence to good account. He did not realize that the essence of Wagner is melody, and found to his cost that no amount of rhetoric, bombast, intellect, discords, or declamation could manufacture genuinely dramatic music if a sense of line was lacking.

Yet in spite of its drawbacks, *Prometheus* possesses one quality which

233

Parry hardly ever recaptured in the same measure: enthusiasm. For all its unsuitability, the text inspired him and imparted its elemental energy to the music. The critics may have reacted in a variety of ways to the first performance, but most of them agreed about the work's finest moments: the female Chorus of Spirits 'From unremember'd ages we', Jupiter's solo 'Pour forth heav'n's wine', the entire last scene, and the Chorus of Spirits 'Life of life', in which the influence of Brahms shows through in the contours and dispositions of the vocal writing (ex. 10.8).

But although Parry may have spoken with a new native voice, in one sense he closely resembled his predecessors: he was essentially a miniaturist, and this explains why a piece like *Blest Pair of Sirens* (London Bach Choir 1887) has survived whilst works such as *A Vision of Life* (1907) and *The Love that Casteth Out Fear* (1904) are totally defunct. It is no coincidence that the works which stand the best chance of revival are the most concise: *L'Allegro ed il Pensieroso* (Norwich Festival 1890: an effective setting of Milton's poems which develops and integrates the style of *Prometheus*), *Ode on the Nativity* (Hereford 1912) and *The Chivalry of the Sea* (London Bach Choir 1916: influenced by Stanford's Newbolt settings). Finest of all is *The Glories of our Blood and State* (Gloucester 1883), in many ways Parry's most impressive work. Its sense of nobility in the face of suffering is achieved by sparseness of style and deliberate musical understatement, and since orchestral showmanship of any kind would have been quite out of place, the scoring for once is highly effective.

The oratorios are less successful. Shaw called *Judith* (Birmingham Festival 1888) 'a hard blow to bear'[19]—a judgement which erred on the side of charity. *Job* (Gloucester 1892), however, is a work of great dignity and character; its style is heavily influenced by *Die Meistersinger*, and the hero's demeanour is frequently reminiscent of Hans Sachs. Like Wagner, Parry often wrote his own librettos: he did so to good effect in *King Saul* (Birmingham Festival 1894) but then set the result very badly. This was the outcome of an overconcern with ethics, a bad habit picked up from the 'serious' works of Brahms. Parry thought of himself as an intellectual revolutionary, whereas in fact several of his predecessors (particularly Macfarren) had possessed greater intellectual vigour. He was a genial man and a fine human being, and these qualities are consistently reflected in his music, even though they cannot ensure its survival. We are still close enough to him to experience the benefits of the revolution he did so much to bring about in English music and for which we owe him all honour. But gratitude, however well deserved and genuine, will not now float works which, in effect, served a more or less functional purpose. His fatal weakness was that his personality lacked the essential element of drama, with the result that in the majority of his choral works the ethics stand poised, ever present, waiting to swoop down upon the music.

Ex. 10.8 C. Hubert H. Parry, *Scenes from Shelley's Prometheus Unbound* (1880): chorus of spirits, 'Life of life'

(*K*: Novello, [1882])

Parry's great contemporary and partner in his reforming mission was Charles Villiers Stanford (1852–1924). Both men wrote far too much music, though Stanford unquestionably possessed the more natural talent of the two.

As far as his choral compositions were concerned, his secular pictorial works were better wrought than his sacred abstract ones. The early oratorio *Eden* (Birmingham Festival 1891), admittedly not one of his best works, nevertheless accurately mirrors his musical personality: the workmanship is superb, but the materials slight. The tenor solo for the Angel of the Earth 'What new delight, ye angels?'[20] is a case in point—Stanford's scores contain hundreds of pages of such excellently prepared but flavourless music, which induces neither protest nor boredom, yet leaves no impression on the memory. His enharmonic modulations search for the hidden secret of endless melody, but the result merely sounds like a sight-reading test. The work also raises the question of the extent to which the redeployment of pre-seventeenth-century styles has benefitted modern music. The plainsong writing in the prelude, for instance, does not in any way act as a seminal force, and the mock-Palestrinian section 'We thy love-kindling fire'[21] is simply irritating (had its mentor seen it, he would have rubbed his eyes in disbelief). Innovatory composers are frequently burned out by their destiny, and Stanford, whose musical gifts were innately conservative, was unlucky to live at a time when such a role was forced upon him. When composing *Eden, The Three Holy Children* (1885), the *Stabat Mater* (1907), and (to a lesser extent) the Requiem (1897), he instinctively threw an inner lever marked 'oratorio' and steered himself away from the true expression of his personality as it had manifested itself in his church music and his songs.

His temperament was far less intellectual and metaphysical than Parry's, and although he was not a great dramatic composer he could at least be described as a narrative one. *The Revenge* ('A Ballad of the Fleet', Leeds Festival 1886), justifiably one of his most popular works, clearly instances this. As Tennyson's narration gathers pace, so the music matches it with an instinctive and parallel sense of expanding excitement. Fuller Maitland was right when he observed that 'the contrast between the dignified and sonorous Spanish characteristics and the bluff and gallant demeanour of the Englishmen must stir the blood of the most convinced pacifist'.[22] Stanford had the gift of being able to create and sustain an atmosphere, and here as in *The Songs of the Fleet* (1917) the inescapable presence of the sea permeates the inner essence of the music.

The works in which he was most true to himself were those in which

236

he attempted to put aside pretence, and wrote, albeit self-consciously, as an Irishman. Perhaps the greatest achievement in all his music is the coda of the choral ballad *Phaudrig Crohoore* (Norwich Festival 1896), which foretells the hero's death in the 1798 rebellion. The sudden change of mood from rollicking braggadocio to overladen nostalgia perfectly captures the inherent contradictions of the Irish temperament. But at a deeper level it testifies to the truth of Ireland's tragedy: permanent, historically immutable, always ready to intrude its disturbing emotions when least expected.

Stanford was a natural orchestrator, and the vivid quality of his aural perception is nowhere reflected more clearly than in the pages of this score. Example 10.9 shows a unique approach towards blending and contrasting the *obbligato* qualities of several instruments.

But despite moments of such beauty, little of the music so consciously written as the harbinger of change could hope to survive—indeed, its composers probably understood subconsciously that it could not. In any case, survival was not its purpose; its role was catalytic, and as such it fulfilled itself. The choral tradition had always been the heart of English music, and was therefore the most likely breeding-ground for the inevitable revolution. The achievement of Parry and Stanford was in reality a reformation; the substance of the renaissance they sought was to follow them.

Towards Modern Times

The truth of this assertion is validated by the cantata *Everyman* (Leeds Festival 1904), the masterpiece of Henry Walford Davies (1869–1941). In it the new and the old are mixed kaleidoscopically, but the former is the prophetic and predominant element. *Everyman* achieves many of the aims of the Vaughan Williams school, but without recourse to obtrusive musical propaganda. It takes its text from an ancient English source and revivifies it, and it foreshadows the renewed interest in Tudor, mediaeval, and folk music which has been so prominent a feature of twentieth-century British music. If it had a message for future generations, it was that music must nearly always evolve if it is to be great. Evolution was probably the supreme idea of the nineteenth century, and although it was natural for twentieth-century composers to disregard it, they did so at their peril.

Surprisingly, in view of Davies's distrust of opera, it was Wagner who exerted the strongest influence on the score. The mystical chromaticism of the opening motto theme (symbolizing our fear of death and

Ex. 10.9 Charles V. Stanford, *Phaudrig Crohoore* (1896) (*S*, p. 49)

(*S:* Boosey, [1896])

238

our reconciliation to it) probably derives ultimately from that source, as does the following moment from Everyman's Farewell, which looks back to a greater farewell in *Die Walküre* (ex. 10.10). In 'God speaketh', the chorus takes on the role of a single person in the manner of the *turba* of traditional Passion music. By contrast, the sense of irony in 'The Appeal to Riches' is quite a new element, and at such moments Davies closely anticipates Holst. The work's spiritual apex is 'The Song of Knowledge', in which the influence of Elgar is paramount.

Ex. 10.10 H. Walford Davies, *Everyman* (1904): 'Everyman's Farewell'

(*K*: Riorden, 1904)

Of Davies's later choral works *The Song of St Francis* (Birmingham Festival 1912) is the most interesting. Although he never repeated the success of *Everyman*, his stylistic horizons broadened continually: whereas the earlier work predicted Holst and Britten, the later one is closer in affinity to Walton and Stravinsky. All in all, his decision to give up composition in favour of broadcasting was a highly regrettable one for English music.

Martin Cooper has described this generation of composers as 'the last . . . for whom music remained essentially vertical'.[23] This was certainly true of Frederick Delius (1862–1934) whose entire style was based on the principle of harmonic intuition. Delius's major choral work was 'A Mass of Life' (Munich 1908), a setting of a German text from Nietzsche's *Also sprach Zarathustra*. It opens with a challenging hymn to the Will which testifies to the composer's unquestioning acceptance of the poem's philosophy; the words and music interreact to produce an incandescence of magnesium brightness. The aesthetic kernel of the Mass is its third movement 'In dein Auge schaute ich jüngst, O Leben'; its third section is a remarkable double fugue 'Das ist ein Tanz über Stock und Stein',[24] a whirling dithyrambic apotheosis of this medium's nineteenth-century romantic usage. The movement's final section introduces Zarathustra's *Mitternachtslied* 'O Mensch! gib Acht! Was spricht die tiefe Mitternacht?'

Delius kept *Zarathustra* by his bedside as other men kept their bibles, and one might say that at some point in his career he had to write such a work. But for that very reason it is not typical of his music as a whole. Here his unremitting control of his materials refutes the decadence of which he is often accused. The apparent contradiction between the softness of so much of his music and the hardness of the man is probably best reconciled by his fundamental hedonism. His art is unique in that, simultaneously, it uncompromisingly celebrates the aristocratic principle, and indulges in uninhibited nostalgia.

This last quality marks Delius's best known choral work, *Sea Drift* (Essen 1906). In it, the poet Whitman, as a mature man, reflects on a poignant experience of his boyhood. It would be difficult to find a more perfect expression of nostalgia than the opening choral entry. At the words 'lilac scent' the music is suddenly so perfumed that the aural sensation is almost as strong as the physical sensation it attempts to recreate. The baritone solo part is testing. The quality of Delius's choral and vocal writing depended largely on coincidence: he composed intuitively by reacting to sensations, and performers of his music can only succeed if they do likewise.

There are times when the sense of despair in *Sea Drift* becomes so profound that it feeds on itself and leads to the unbearable thought that it is incurable ('O reckless despairing carols').[25] In this the work artistically reflects the mood of its generation. Yet Delius's philosophy was always one of hope and courage, and his music shows that by accepting anguish we gain the strength to conquer it. And in this discovery lies the final vindication of this century of British music, throughout which, because of the nation's previous musical history, choral works had frequently been in the van of progress. It had been an era of magnificent toil, strife, and struggle, and it culminated with the promise that a truly self-sufficient national art would, at last, be born.

Chapter 11

GLEES, MADRIGALS, AND PARTSONGS

MICHAEL HURD

In the composition of works suitable for part-singing, the link between the glories of Elizabethan times and the work of twentieth-century English composers is perhaps stronger than in any other type of music. Even when English creative vitality was at its lowest ebb there were composers of sufficient talent to supply a voracious market with glees, 'madrigals', and partsongs in abundance. And because these works were short, intellectually undemanding, dependent more on spontaneity than on cunning, and assured of a tolerable structural coherence by the verse that underpinned them, literally hundreds of minor composers were able to make their contribution with confidence and relish. The art of writing music for part-singing flourished throughout the eighteenth and nineteenth centuries. It may not have been a great art, but it was genuine, popular, and lively, and therefore deserves sympathetic consideration.

The primary impetus to all this activity arose in the eighteenth century with the formation, both in London and in the provinces, of gentlemen's clubs devoted to wining and dining and convivial song: the Madrigal Society, founded in 1741; the Noblemen and Gentlemen's Catch Club, 1761; the Anacreontic Society, 1766; the Glee Club, 1783; and the Concentores Sodales, 1798—a club which differed from the others in that its membership was restricted to composers only.

Of these the most influential was probably the Catch Club, for in 1763 it instituted annual prizes for three categories of part-music: catches, canons, and glees. The stimulus to composition (culminating in 1787 when John Wall Callcott submitted nearly 100 glees for consideration and thereby precipitated a change in the rules, so that 'no composer should send in more than three compositions for one prize'!) was out of all proportion to the cost of the prize medals.[1] William Barrett calculated that by 1886 nearly 25,000 glees had been published,[2] and this is confirmed by Baptie's list of nearly 250 individual composers,[3] many of whose compositions run into the hundreds.

Inevitably much dross was produced. But though it is scarcely possible to attempt an exhaustive study, one thing becomes evident after even the most cursory inspection: the general level of work was surprisingly high, and there is much that can be performed today without apology.

One further consideration is also important: the musical style adopted by these composers did not materially change for nearly seventy years. What Samuel Webbe was writing in the 1770s is not markedly different from what William Horsley was publishing in 1840. Though this conservative trait may in part be attributed to England's artistic insularity, it must also be due to the conditions that prompted the composition of these works. The clubs, by their very nature—convivial rather than speculative—imposed a basic style, from which it was well nigh impossible, and certainly inadvisable, to depart.

By the middle of the century, however, the prevailing musical style had changed—doubtless because the conditions which prompted the music had themselves changed: the semi-private, aristocratic club giving way to middle-class choral societies intent on public performance. The new style remained in fashion for some fifty years; again, typically, resisting change until the challenge of competitive festivals led to the infiltration of more obviously virtuoso techniques.

Within the confines of this strongly traditionalist ethos, three distinct types of musical form occupied the composers of music for part-singing: the glee, the madrigal, and the partsong. In drawing a distinction between them, however, it must be clearly understood that the Victorians themselves used all three terms very loosely indeed and were particularly indiscriminate in their use of the word 'glee'. Almost anything that was not a catch or a round could be so described. Even as late as 1821 it is possible to find publications such as W. Blackman's *Harmonic Cabinet* blithely enlisting the chorus 'Fear no danger' from Purcell's *Dido and Aeneas* and Thomas Ford's ayre 'Since first I saw your face' as glees. And it is quite certain that glee clubs, whatever their avowed purpose, made no distinction in what they actually sang. If it moved in parts, they sang it.

The three forms, then, grew up more or less concurrently. From 1750 to 1830 the glee held the dominant position, gradually dying out towards the middle of the nineteenth century. The madrigal flourished most effectively after 1830, particularly, as we shall see, at the hands of one composer. The partsong existed in all but name alongside the earliest glees, and then, from about 1830, began to dominate the scene both in quality and in quantity.

In defining the term *glee*, nineteenth-century musical historians are agreed on one thing: that it is essentially a composition for three, four, or five male voices (some permutation of alto, tenor, and bass) intended to be sung one voice to a part.[4] Thereafter, an element of uncertainty creeps into the various definitions.

Henry Davey, for example, declares that the glee 'is "set through-out", the music not being repeated to successive stanzas'.[5] This seems a fair comment on the practice of the times. He further states that 'the best glee-writers frequently chose picturesque and dramatic words which suggested many short sections rather than one homogeneous movement; and their works accordingly are of a kind which has been well described as a *musical mosaic*. This is, however, by no means invariably the case; and some glees exhibit masterly continuity and construction.' Again, example seems to bear out both dictum and caveat.

William Barrett goes further, and, in describing George Berg's 'On softest beds at leisure laid', which won the Catch Club's prize for the best glee in 1763, says: 'This glee is for three voices, and is a typical specimen of the form which the glee was required to assume, and which was accepted as the indicative model of all compositions of the same class. Alternate passages, lively and slow, to suit the sentiment of the words, are the rudiments of those contrasted movements which were to form one of the distinguishing features of the glee.'[6]

His later comments on individual works, however, allow that 'continuity of thought and treatment, and a sufficiency of development consistent with the design of the form of composition' may also be found.

George Alexander Macfarren, writing in 1868, was sufficiently convinced of the prevalence of the 'musical mosaic' feature to use the idea in disparagement of glees in general;[7] while Fuller Maitland makes it 'an important feature of all genuine glees', and adds that 'short solo passages for a single voice are present in many of the best specimens'.[8]

A study of what glee-composers actually wrote does in fact suggest that these elements, though not invariably present, were indeed a frequent feature of glee construction and must therefore be taken into account in any definition of the form.

The *madrigal*, on the other hand, describes any partsong that deliberately harks back to Elizabethan techniques of imitative points unfolding in a seamless contrapuntal texture. Modal scales may or may not be used.

The *partsong* may well incorporate elements of glee and madrigal styles and textures, but it is more likely to be in strophic form and have the air of a song laid out in four (or more) parts—the 'tune' dominating, however interestingly the accompanying parts may be contrived. Unlike the glee, it is typically for mixed voices, singing as a chorus.

The Glee

Although the word 'glee' is used as early as 1659 in Playford's third set of *Ayres and Dialogues*, it is not clear why a mediaeval term of Saxon origin (*gligge*, meaning 'music') should have been adopted in the first place. In the convivial atmosphere of the tavern or coffee house the double meaning of the word may perhaps have had a special appeal—though composers were careful to describe their glees as 'cheerful' or 'serious'. And it is perhaps reasonable to suppose that the spirit of antiquarianism that was to give birth to Ossian, Chatterton, and all the paraphernalia of Gothic romanticism should find a deliberate archaism attractive. One thing is certain: by the middle of the eighteenth century the term was firmly established and described a specific form of music found nowhere but in Britain and (a little later) in North America.

The credit for giving that form its classic shape is generally[9] ascribed to Samuel Webbe (1740–1816), who published nine volumes of *Catches, Canons and Glees* (1764 onwards) and composed over two hundred glees. His 'Glorious Apollo' (really a harmonized song) had the distinction of opening the evening's programme at each meeting of the Glee Club from 1790 onwards.

As a typical example of Webbe's full-scale type of glee we may instance 'When winds breathe soft' (1784?), described by Barrett as 'the noblest product of its composer, a truly grand conception'.[10] It is in essence a dramatic scene, depicting during the course of a hundred and fifty-four bars the changing moods of the sea. There are six sections:

1. 'When winds breathe soft' (repeated)
   Andantino   4/4   E   40 bars
2. 'A stronger gale the troubled wave awakes'
   Moderato   A (modulating)   52 bars
3. 'When, in an instant, he who rules the floods . . .
   In pleasing accents speaks his sovereign will'
   Andante   2/2   E   17 bars
4. 'Hush'd, hush'd are the winds'
   Larghetto   4/4   B   9 bars

5. 'Now say that joy elates the sailor's breast'
  Allegretto   6/8   E   32 bars
6. (coda) *Largo*   4/4   E   4 bars

Webbe's approach is frankly pictorial. Simple dotted-quaver figures, trills, and common-chord melodic shapes serve to suggest the waves at rest, and later, when combined with brisker rhythms, more vigorous quaver runs and a little mild chromaticism, the 'mounting billows' themselves. Similar devices serve for the rest of the programme. Textures vary throughout (the full five-part ensemble being reserved for moments of natural climax) and there is a degree of free imitation. Though the first sections employ similar figures, there is no real attempt to unify the work by musical means—it moves in response to the changing mood of the words.

'When winds breathe soft' is, in short, a piece which achieves its effects simply and naturally. It may be argued that its phrases are short-winded and too closely pegged to cadential patterns, and that the passage from section to section is sometimes abrupt (particularly when a change of key is involved), and that the entire piece is tonally unadventurous. Indeed these are charges that may fairly be levelled against Webbe's work generally. But what matters is that the overall effect is pleasing, apt, and serviceable. As a 'classic' glee it lacks only one feature: the presence of virtuoso solo passages, such as may be found, for example, in William Horsley's famous 'Cold is Cadwallo's Tongue' (1801).

Webbe's example remained potent for as long as the glee was taken seriously as a musical form. Choose at random, and the consistency of approach is remarkable. 'Fill high the grape's exulting stream', which won Reginald Spofforth (1770–1826) a prize medal in 1810 and is, as its title suggests, an example of the 'cheerful' glee, is constructed along similar lines, though on a much less elaborate scale. It falls into two parts; an opening 4/4 section of fifty-nine bars, beginning in E flat major and modulating to B flat at bar 28, but returning immediately to E flat; and a contrasting quicker section in 6/8 time, consisting of thirty-one bars wholly in E flat major. Spofforth achieves the necessary contrast by means of varied texture as much as by change of rhythm and speed. The opening section offsets passages in which pairs of voices (AA against TB) echo each other in neat fanfare-like phrases. The modulation to B flat is followed by a brief quasi-fugal passage, before the music settles into a sonorous conclusion, in which minim chords in the upper voices drift lightly over a rumbling bass line that moves downwards through the span of a tenth (B♭ to G) as an effective

246

pictorial illustration of the words 'Pour oceans with unbounded soul'. The second section of the glee ('Fill high, till laughing o'er the brim/The sparkling treasure loads the bowl') makes a feature of sustained pedal notes held in one or two voices (in octaves) against a flowing melodic line moving in parallel sixths or thirds.

In some respects, however, Spofforth's glee heralds the coming partsong. The number of sections is reduced to two, the top voice is more dominant, the structures tend to be binary; and Spofforth's melodies are generally breezier and less constrained than Webbe's.

By 1830, when Thomas Forbes Walmisley (1782–1866) published 'Music, all-powerful' (ATTB), the model was still Webbe. Walmisley's splendid glee falls into four sections:

1. 'Music, all-powerful o'er the human mind'
   Moderato   4/4   F   21 bars
2. 'At her command the various passions lie'
   Più moto   4/4   to D minor   32 bars
3. 'Soft through the dell the dying strains retire'
   Tempo primo   4/4   F   16 bars
4. 'Oh! surely harmony from heaven was sent!'
   Andante cantabile 3/4   F   40 bars

The opening section is largely chordal, enlivened with a degree of quasi-imitation, and a nicely judged 'pictorial' bass line at the words 'Fierce anger's furious rage disarm'. The second section begins imitatively with bold, trumpet-like figures, but moves to a series of effective rising sequences for the words 'She stirs to battle, or lulls to peace', and a degree of mild dissonance to express 'And bids the world's harsh clangour cease'. Section 3 forms a linking passage in preparation for the last and longest section, which consists of a harmonized tune that would not disgrace Samuel Sebastian Wesley. Indeed, the melodic spaciousness and the subject matter of the words curiously foreshadow Parry's *Blest Pair of Sirens*, and it is perhaps arguable that his concept of the 'choral ode' owes something to these earlier, humbler forms.

Henry Bishop (1785–1856), who was composing glees almost into mid-century, adopted the same approach, and such excellent pieces as 'I gave my heart to sorrow's hand' betray their date only by an increased harmonic richness and a slightly more sentimental melodic line. (Many of Bishop's best glees were originally composed as part of a stage piece: these are discussed in Chapter 13.) Even by 1878, the year in which Henry Hiles (1826–1904) won the Manchester Gentlemen's Glee Club prize with 'Hushed in death', the formula was the same. But by that time it can no longer be said that the glee was a living entity. Indeed in 1852 Edward Holmes had asserted that 'the glee . . . had no longer any active existence, and may now almost be said to be extinct. In clubs, harmonic societies, and convivial meetings, glees are still heard, though scarcely any new ones are written'.[11]

The multi-sectional glee (often reduced to a mere two sections, usually on a slow-fast plan) was not, however, the only formal shape popular with Webbe and his successors. Many examples follow a distinct rondo plan—Webbe's delightful 'Do not ask me, charming Phyllis' is an early example. The main returning section is itself in binary form, modulating from G major to D major and back, and consists of an elegantly harmonized tune given out in block harmony so that the words, which hover agreeably on the verge of indelicacy, may be heard clearly. Both contrasting sections are in G minor and offer a slight variation of texture. Similar structures can be found throughout the glee's history. This type of one-movement glee merges impercept-ibly into the partsong.

While it would be difficult to lay a claim to greatness for any individual glee, collectively they form a remarkable body of work. They were intended as practical entertainment, for instant enjoyment. Their composers were minor musicians with a flair for melody and a reason-able competence in handling the harmonic and structural small-talk of the period. They did not strive to be original, but merely to fill the passing moment. The wonder is that so much of what they wrote can still be performed with pleasure and effect.

Certain composers stand out, and their names have already been mentioned. Others who might well be added to a select list include William Shield (1748–1829), Richard J. S. Stevens (1753–1837) and John Goss (1800–80). Dozens more might be added of those who, perhaps by virtue of a single felicitous composition, deserve a place in what Novello & Co. charmingly termed the English 'Glee Hive'.

The Madrigal

In any consideration of English part-writing it is important to remember that the madrigal tradition never quite died out in this country. Throughout the seventeenth and eighteenth centuries at least a handful were reprinted and therefore presumably sung and enjoyed. Moreover, it is arguable that the rounds, canons, and catches (many of them of great technical ingenuity) that so delighted composers and performers during this period were themselves linked, as poor relations, to the great tradition.

A more positive interest in the Elizabethans arose in the middle of the eighteenth century. The foundation of the Madrigal Society of London in 1741 undoubtedly gave an edge to the movement and prompted individual composers to attempt 'madrigals' of their own. Those composed in the eighteenth century (by such as Lord Mornington, several members of the Linley family, John Callcott, and Thomas Battishill) tended to be little more than glees decorated with a few overlapping imitative points: an example is 'Let me careless and unthoughtful lying' by Thomas Linley senior (1725–95), published posthumously in 1800. Rather more pertinent is 'Flora now calleth forth each flower' (1783) by John Stafford Smith, a resourceful musician and a scholar deeply interested in the music of the past. Though the influence of glee structure is still very evident, the use of imitative points is sufficiently consistent to suggest a true madrigal.

In the nineteenth century, interest in the madrigal became much more widespread, and a real appreciation of the madrigal technique began to be developed. The donation of a silver cup to be awarded by the Madrigal Society for a composition in the style of the great madrigalists, with particular reference to imitative counterpoint, helped the process. The competition was announced in 1811. Among the thirteen unsuccessful candidates for the prize[12] was Samuel Wesley, whose madrigal 'O sing unto my roundelay' shows considerable understanding of the style. The prize was awarded in 1813 to 'Awake, sweet muse' by William Beale (1784–1854), who made several contributions to the madrigal revival: of these 'Come let us join the roundelay' proved particularly popular. It is in fact a species of ballett, complete with fa-la-la's and a cheerful, neatly harmonized tune. It contains, however, a degree of imitation, and is particularly notable for its rhythmic freedom—which includes a sudden and very effective dive into triple time.

A similar sensitivity to the true spirit of the madrigal can be seen in 'Sweete flowers, ye were too faire' (1839) by Thomas Attwood Walmisley (1814–56). Here the imitative points are carried out consistently and fluently and, for once, seem emotionally related to the words. Most important of all: the melodic lines have a truly madrigalian breadth and sense of direction (reflected also in the work's harmonic drive). Walmisley composed another excellent madrigal, 'Slow, slow, fresh fount' (1840).

From these examples it may be seen that by the middle of the nineteenth century many English composers had come to appreciate the essential nature of their madrigal heritage. And if credit for this deeper understanding is to go anywhere, it must be laid at the door of one man: Robert Lucas Pearsall.*

He was born in Bristol in 1795, and though he wrote music from an early age he was trained first as a lawyer. Ill health took him abroad in 1825 and he began to study music seriously under Josef Panny in Mainz. Apart from brief periods in England he lived in Germany, studying in Munich and Vienna and composing assiduously. In 1836 he inherited family estates at Willsbridge in Gloucestershire, but sold them in the following year and eventually settled in the castle of Wartensee on Lake Constance, where he was able to indulge mediaeval fantasies on a suitably grand scale. He died, from apoplexy, in 1856.[13]

Apart from one or two more ambitious efforts, the bulk of Pearsall's work was for unaccompanied voices on a small scale. He was a keen antiquarian, and his experience of English madrigals (largely through contact with the Bristol Madrigal Society, founded in 1837) led him to compose the words and music of a number of works that effectively imitate the style and spirit of the Elizabethans.

Certain of these works are indeed remarkable. Two eight-part madrigals, 'Great god of love' (1839) and 'Lay a garland' (1840) (ex. 11.1), achieve a splendid sonority, and they not only look like Elizabethan music, but almost sound like it. Both are propelled forward by effective suspensions, carefully woven points of imitation, and melodies projected in long flexible lines. Similar qualities enliven the six-part 'O ye roses' (1838). The simpler textures of 'I saw lovely Phillis' (a sort of ayre, 1837), and 'No no, Nigella' (a ballett, in eight parts, 1836) are also extremely well managed and give the feeling of a style genuinely reborn, and not merely resurrected.

But it is not possible to claim an equal felicity for all Pearsall's madrigals. His melodic ideas can be short-winded, and the lines can lack a genuine rhythmic spring. A forward harmonic drive is not always in evidence, and the melodic lines do not always create the harmony as they unfold, but move rather within the confines of an academic harmonic plan. Even more unsettling is his attitude to words. Many of the texts he wrote himself, and though they are in a madrigalian style, replete with pastoral conceits and amorous fancies, they are curiously empty of real feeling, and sometimes even of real meaning. In other cases he simply reset a text used by one of the Elizabethan madrigalists. His setting of 'Sing we and chaunt it' is not unworthy of Morley's.

Outside the strict madrigalian style Pearsall behaved more like the

---

*The 'de' sometimes attached to his surname is completely bogus, and was never used by the composer himself (Hunt, 4).

GLEES, MADRIGALS, AND PARTSONGS

Ex. 11.1 Robert L. Pearsall, 'Lay a garland on her hearse' (1840)

(*S:* Novello, 1873)

average Victorian composer than is generally supposed. Such part-songs as 'Purple glow the forest mountains', 'O who will o'er the downs so free' and 'Why with toil thy life consuming' contain delightful passages, but an equal number that reveal the routine sentimentalist. Certain pieces, however, directly benefited from his madrigalian studies—the one-movement glee 'When Alan a Dale went hunting', for example, moves briskly with passages of free imitation and a lively sense of drama. But even faith in Pearsall's antiquarianism receives a jolt when confronted by his 'realization' of 'Sumer is icumen in', complete with an ingenuous preface in which he states: 'Owing to the author's wish to work his subject rigorously even at the expense of effect, his harmony is monotonous and full of faults. The melody being happily conceived and bearing a genuine old English character, I have attempted to make it acceptable to modern taste.'

Pearsall, far from being the un-Victorian genius that some commentators have implied, would seem in reality to have been very much part of his age. Working as a dilettante, and able to indulge antiquarian whims of considerable psychological interest, he managed to produce a limited amount of very fine music. His real importance (which must not be underestimated) is that he awoke his contemporaries to the possibilities of the true madrigalian style, and in particular to the importance of a clean harmonic palette.

In the Victorian period the madrigal revival was in full swing, and many local madrigal societies were formed.[14] Among composers who took the composition of madrigals seriously were Frederick Ouseley and Edward Taylor: examples of their efforts have survived in manuscript.[15] Besides Walmisley, many of the leading composers of the day contributed at least one published example: Walter Macfarren's 'Good night, good rest' (1863), Sullivan's 'When love and beauty' (from *The Sapphire Necklace*, 1863), Parry's 'Fair daffodils' (1866), and Stanford's 'To Chloris' (1900) are all true examples of the genre. The Madrigal Society's prize, which had not been awarded between 1813 and 1880, was placed on a permanent footing in 1881. From then onwards two prizes were awarded (the first called the Molineux Prize), annually from 1881 to 1889 and then about every three years from 1891 to 1929.[16] As a result there was a constant flow of new madrigals in the last decades of our period. All this activity has led one writer to speak of the 'English Romantic Madrigal' as a genre in itself.[17]

All too often, however, it was merely the superficial aspects of the style that were imitated, the spirit notably absent. Examples range from Henry Leslie's six-part 'Charm me asleep' (c. 1879), which might better be described as a partsong using points of imitation chosen with little regard for Herrick's words, to W. S. Rockstro's five-part 'O, too cruel fair' (c. 1884), which courted authenticity by deriving its material wholly from plainsong!

The prizes may have encouraged composition, but they do not seem to have tapped a creative spring. A typical example is Philip Armes's five-part 'Victoria', which won the Molineux Prize and the Society's Medal in 1897, and is remarkable only for short-winded, wooden phrases (though it cannot be said that the words, by Alfred Austin, poet laureate of the day, offered much by way of inspiration). Similarly lacking in genuine impulse are W. J. Westbrook's five-part 'All is not gold' and Henry Lahee's six-part 'Hark how the birds', both of which won Bristol Madrigal Society prizes in 1865. Not even the stimulus of a 'royal' occasion made any appreciable impact. John Stainer's five-part madrigal 'in imitation of The Triumphs of Oriana' shows careful workmanship but is as unconvincing as its title, 'The Triumph of Victoria' (1887). Thus, when the true spirit of the madrigal does make itself felt and the composer combines a sure technique with a genuine feeling for words, the outcome has the added distinction of rarity. One such example, published in 1893, is Charles Wood's splendid five-part 'If love be dead'.

It seems, then, that despite Pearsall's valiant effort of historical imagination, the nineteenth-century madrigal remained something of an anomaly.

The Partsong

The chief characteristics of a partsong are: that it is a setting of words to be sung either by a group of soloists or by a choral group; that the upper part tends to dominate, so that the overall impression is of a harmonized song, even though the accompanying parts may themselves be lively and independent; and that its formal shape is determined only by the dramatic or atmospheric needs of the words—the most likely outcome involving some form of verse repetition. Thus identified, it will be seen that such works have enjoyed a long and almost unbroken history in this country.

The glee composers of the second half of the eighteenth century had plenty of precedent for setting verse in this way. They frequently included part-music by earlier composers in their programmes. And though they habitually bestowed the title 'glee' upon their own compositions, it did not always bear the restricted meaning given to it in this chapter. What they so often wrote—what, indeed, the verse forced them to write—was a partsong.

The range of possibilities was considerable. In Samuel Webbe, for instance, we can move from the breezy tunefulness of 'Glorious Apollo' to the solemn counterpoint of 'The death of fair Adonis I deplore'. Some examples, in fact, seem deliberately modelled on the Elizabethan ayre: Spofforth's charming 'My dear mistress hath a heart' is one. Others exhibit all the characteristics of late eighteenth-century song: Jonathan Battishill's enchanting 'Amidst the myrtles', for example.

As with the glee proper, the general standard of craftsmanship is high, within the modest limits the composers set themselves. Indeed, these 'harmonized airs' are more satisfying than the average classic glee, simply because their structure is, by definition, simple and spontaneous. Composers who could write a shapely tune and harmonize it decently found in the partsong an ideal outlet—one through which even a modest talent might shine.

Similar virtues are to be found in the partsongs of the nineteenth century. But here we begin to become aware of a definite parting of the ways between those composers who were content merely to supply fodder for the rapidly proliferating choral societies, and those who, using the same materials and aiming at the same market, nevertheless contrived to produce music that was both genuinely felt and put together with a degree of imagination and cunning. Among the former, most notable are John Liptrot Hatton (1809–86) and Henry Smart (1813–79); among the latter, Julius Benedict (1804–85) and George Macfarren (1813–87).

If the capacity to reflect the quality of a poem in music were sole criterion of a composer's ability, then both Smart and Hatton might rank high. Both responded with deadly accuracy to fourth-rate verse and facile emotions. Though their music is well laid out for voices, and must therefore be admitted 'effective', it is also too obvious. Phrase answers phrase with leaden predictability. Rhythms plod along with merciless regularity. Modulations admit no surprises and open up no new horizons. Harmonies tread a familiar path. In almost every aspect, theirs is music that follows the line of least resistance.

And yet—it cannot quite be dismissed. It was, in its time, exceedingly popular, remaining in print well into the twentieth century and manifestly filling a need. And isolated examples still have a certain charm. Smart's ''Tis break of day', with its trim hunting-horn motifs, is one such example, as is Hatton's deftly humorous 'He that has a pleasant face', which neatly echoes the convivial glees of the previous century. But finest of all, and enshrining a complacent sentimentality, both of words and music, that actually transcends itself, are Arthur Sullivan's 'The long day closes', and Joseph Barnby's 'Sweet and low'. In their own dreadful way they are masterpieces, and any history of nineteenth-century music that fails to take them into account is blind to a crucial aspect of the period.

Fortunately this was not all that the earlier years of Victoria's reign had to offer by way of partsong. Though he wrote little part-music, Sterndale Bennett produced at least one minor masterpiece: an SATB setting of Marlowe's 'Come live with me and be my love' (1846), which handles Mendelssohnian small-talk in a way that is fresh and charming.

A similar Mendelssohn influence can be felt in the partsongs of Julius Benedict. Despite his German upbringing Benedict demonstrates an enviable sensitivity to the English language, not only with regard to actual word-setting, but also in choice of poem. Among the finest are a set of *Six Choral Songs* (1862): they include three settings of Beaumont and Fletcher ('Old May', 'Invocation to Sleep', and 'Dirge for a Faithful Lover'), two of Barry Cornwall ('A Night Song', and 'A Drinking Song'), and one of Thomas Heywood ('Sylvan Pleasures').

Benedict's is a genuinely subtle art. Though 'Invocation to Sleep'

255

begins with a broad, quasi-operatic tune in more-or-less block harmony, unobtrusive imitations begin to creep in and soon spread the interest throughout the four-part texture. One series of entries provokes a very purposeful set of modulations that move to a nicely-judged climax. Throughout, the music delicately paints pictures of the words, so that the overall impression is extremely evocative. In 'Dirge for a Faithful Lover' the word-painting is carried to even greater effect, not only through the melodic shapes, but also through the harmony, which is suitably chromatic. 'Sylvan Pleasures' is perhaps more commonplace, but as a light, airy scherzo it is not unworthy of Mendelssohn himself. Even 'A Drinking Song' has a rhythmic bounce and operatic boldness that lifts it well above the average setting of similarly routine words. Benedict, in short, is a composer to be reckoned with.

So too is George Macfarren. Between 1850 and 1864 he wrote a series of Shakespeare partsongs: fifteen in all, published by Novello in two sets. They are, without doubt, among the finest products of the period—varied, fresh, and imaginative. Admittedly they are not free of the sort of weaknesses that seem endemic in nineteenth-century English music—the tendency to lapse into facile melodic clichés at cadence points, a too ready acceptance of note-for-note verse repetition (regardless of the text), a too frequent reliance on 'pathetic' harmonies. And modern taste may also find the repetition of words and phrases somewhat arbitrary. But the debilities are not obtrusive, and are outshone by one prime virtue: these are partsongs that are singularly adventurous in the matter of texture. Indeed, Macfarren is one of the few composers of the period who seems to be able to think in terms of living sound, as opposed to mere notes on paper.

Examples abound. 'When daisies pied' leans effectively on open-fifth drones and a nice distinction between loud and soft. 'Fear no more', perhaps the finest of the entire group, opens with its tune in the tenor line, against drowsy sustained pianissimo chords which turn, in the third verse, into a kind of banjo accompaniment of repeated quavers. A delicious, Mendelssohnian account of 'You spotted snakes' (ex. 11.2) swings magically between major and minor versions of the same simple phrase at the words 'Philomel with melody'. 'Hark, hark, the lark' effectively separates the syllables of 'winking' and 'arise'—in the latter case as a perfect foil to a simultaneous legato setting of the same words as a pedal in the tenor part. Macfarren's Shakespeare settings make the first tentative steps towards the kind of orchestral style in vocal writing that came to fruition at the end of the century in the partsongs of Elgar.

Just as glees had formed a staple item in comic operas of the late eighteenth and early nineteenth centuries, so, in the Victorian period,

Ex. 11.2   George A. Macfarren, 'You spotted snakes' (1870?)

(*S:* Novello, [1870?])

any full-length opera was expected to include at least one partsong (or 'madrigal', as in Barnett's *Fair Rosamond*): sometimes, as in Loder's *Raymond and Agnes*, it was called 'quartet' or 'quartettino'. A usual place for it was near the end of the last act. Macfarren's *She Stoops to Conquer* (1864) has an effective though dramatically irrelevant example in Act II, 'The cuckoo sings on the poplar tree'. Sullivan continued the tradition with some fine examples in the Savoy operas: 'I hear the soft note' (*Patience*), 'O, many a man in friendship's name' (*Iolanthe*), 'Strange adventure!' (*The Yeoman of the Guard*), and so on, not to mention the superb 'madrigals', 'When the blooming buds of

May' (*Haddon Hall*) and 'Brightly dawns our wedding day' (*The Mikado*).

Many of these stage partsongs and 'madrigals' were sung with accompaniment, like many of Bishop's stage glees earlier in the century; and indeed accompaniment was becoming more usual for partsongs in general. Holmes in 1852 looked back to the time before 1800 when glees were sung unaccompanied, even in dramatic entertainments; 'now ... we sing much better music, but always accompanied'.[18] While it is certain that partsongs were ideally unaccompanied in late Victorian times, most were published with at least an optional accompaniment for rehearsal or amateur performance, and some even had independent accompaniment.

At the same time that these stage and concert varieties of partsong flourished, a more idealized type, still conceived for voices alone, was reaching a height of creativity in the late Victorian period. Its success depended on sensitive understanding of poetry, and this quality was possessed in good measure by Parry and Stanford, the most important partsong composers of the period. Both were men of wide culture, and both (Parry particularly) responded to English poetry with the utmost sensitivity. The bulk of their work covers the period between 1890 and 1918. Parry's most important collections were *Six Lyrics from an Elizabethan Song Book* (1897), *Six Modern Lyrics* (1897), *Eight Four-Part Songs* (1898), *Seven Partsongs for Male Voices* (1903–10), and the great cycle of six *Songs of Farewell* (1916–18) which, though described as motets, can equally be regarded as serious partsongs. Stanford's marginally larger output includes three sets of *Six Elizabethan Pastorals* (op. 49, 1892; op. 53, 1894; op. 67, 1897), three sets of *Four Partsongs* (op. 47, 1892; op. 106, 1908; op. 110, 1908), one of *Three Partsongs* (op. 111, 1908), and two of *Eight Partsongs* (op. 119, 1910; op. 127, 1912).

Superficially Parry would seem to be the less interesting composer. Unlike Stanford he seldom made experiments. The textures of his partsongs are generally uniform and unadventurous—though this is not to say that they lack variety within the basic approach. But, as in all his works, it is not the surface appearance that matters. What Parry offers is a remarkable depth of feeling, a sense of space and power, and a total artistic integrity.

Parry's successes seem directly related to the quality of the poetry he set. Thus Tennyson ('There rolls the deep'), Shelley ('Music when soft voices die'), and Bridges ('Since thou, O fondest and truest') provoke a much more impressive response than Thomas Moore ('How sweet the answer') and Arthur Benson ('Home of my heart'). The better the poem, the better the music. And it is this feeling for the English language that assures his partsongs a quality that is seldom found. For each line in a Parry texture is a *complete* response to the words, regardless of whether its role in the overall plan is simply that of accompaniment. In Parry there is no 'filling in'. Though basically subordinate to a homophonic texture, the individual parts have a Bach-like integrity.

Music thus organized is extremely rewarding to sing. And when it is allied to a rich, Brahmsian harmonic vocabulary, and an instinctive understanding of how vocal textures can be laid out to make the maximum impact, it is small wonder that choirs have found, and still find, a special pleasure in his work. Because each song makes its mark as a totality (there is nothing piecemeal about his approach, even when handling verse forms) it is difficult to illustrate the spaciousness and grandeur of his style through a brief quotation, but perhaps the opening of 'O Love, they wrong thee much', from the 1898 set (ex. 11.3), may serve to suggest its essential nobility.

By comparison Stanford's work is apt to seem a trifle calculated and even opportunist. He was a consummate craftsman and had at his finger tips a far greater range of technical possibilities than Parry would ever have deemed necessary. With absolute assurance he could encompass the unadorned homophony of 'Heraclitus' (op. 110, no. 4), the delicate impressionism of 'The Blue Bird' (op. 119, no. 3) and the deft canonic imitation of 'Sweet love for me' (op. 49, no. 4). But his very facility seems to militate against a distinctive style. Stanford, it would seem, set words aptly, but with a kind of indifference. He wielded a formidable technique and never wrote less than effectively, but seldom found an emotional reason for using his skills. One can admire his work, but not feel deeply involved by it.

The best of Stanford undoubtedly lies in the three sets of *Elizabethan Pastorals* (eighteen songs in all). These have a lightness and humour that is very appealing. They offer considerable variety of texture—from the SA, TB duets of 'Corydon arise' (a delightful conversation-piece) to the dramatic homophony of 'The Knight's Tomb'. They are, as is only to be expected, expertly laid out for the voices: satisfying both to sing and to listen to.

If none of Parry and Stanford's contemporaries achieved anything like their consistency of style and expression, it was not for want of trying. Many laboured mightily in these fields, for the end of the century saw a great upsurge in the demand for partsongs of all shapes and sizes. One reason for this was the growth of the competitive festival movement. As early as 1860 John Curwen had organized competitions in choral singing at the Crystal Palace, as a way of publicizing his tonic solfa system.[19] After 1880 the idea caught hold strongly. In 1885 the

Ex. 11.3   C. Hubert H. Parry, *Eight Four-Part Songs* (1898): No. 2, 'O Love, they wrong thee much'
Moderato

(*S:* Novello, 1898)

singer Mary Wakefield established what was soon to become a highly successful festival at Kendal. Similar festivals arose elsewhere, reaching their height of popularity in the 1920s. Choral singing was a natural ground for friendly competition, and the demand for suitably testing works was vastly increased. At the same time the competitive challenge stimulated an advance in choral composing techniques (though whether it actually improved the quality is another matter). This movement, together with an all-round increase in the formation of local

260

societies dedicated to singing (including such highly polished and influential groups as Lionel Benson's famous Magpie Madrigal Society, founded in London in 1885—a group for which Parry and Stanford wrote many pieces), made the composition, and publication, of partsongs a highly profitable industry.

In any event, there proved to be no dearth of material. It ranged from the genuine masterpiece, such as an Elgar might contribute, to vapid nonsense: George Garrett's 'Home is home, however lowly' (1897) is an example of the kind of thing a perfectly respectable musician could perpetrate, given half a chance! Certain minor composers stand out as making restrained, effective, and thoroughly 'useful' contributions. Walter Macfarren (1826–1905), brother of George, is one; Frederick Cowen (1852–1935) is another—though his partsongs drift too often into mere prettiness, or sink under the weight of turgid rhythms: few are as purposeful as 'Bring me a golden pen' (1911). But the major part of what was written, perhaps not surprisingly, has proved ephemeral. The great exception was Elgar.

He wrote, in all, some thirty-four partsongs, of which most were published in groups (not exactly cycles in the strict sense). The most important individual songs are 'My love dwelt in a northern land' (1890), 'Evening scene' (1906), 'Go, song of mine' (1909), and 'Death in the hills' (1914). 'As torrents in summer' (1896) can be added to the list, even though it was extracted from the cantata *King Olaf*, in which it had formed the final section. The important sets include: *Five Partsongs from the Greek Anthology*, op. 45 (1903), *Four Partsongs*, op. 53 (1907), *Two Partsongs*, op. 71 (1914), and *Two Partsongs*, op. 73 (1914). Most of these were written at the very height of his powers, and they are the small-scale utterances of a great man.

Even the partsongs he composed in the 90s hint at what was to come. 'As torrents in summer' and 'My love dwelt in a northern land' may look, on paper, fairly typical of their period, but they *sound* magnificently grand and passionate—as if a Parry had suddenly been released from gentlemanly reticence. And to this capacity for emotional intensity Elgar was soon to add a delight in treating voices almost as if they were orchestral instruments, thereby creating textures of great subtlety and complexity, which call for a degree of virtuosity that speaks volumes for the standard of the best choral singing of the day (a standard he had personal experience of and was keen to exploit).

Elgar's mature partsongs are notable for their wide range of harmonic colour, including sustained chromaticism, enharmonic change at strategic emotional and dramatic points, and even an occasional experiment with bitonality ('There is sweet music', op. 53, no. 1). He

261

used a very wide tessitura in *all* voices (and all may be called upon to display an equal virtuosity); a vast increase in dynamic range; and a quasi-orchestral detail in the interpretive markings on individual parts. It is quite startling, even by twentieth-century standards, to see four notes in a single two-bar phrase marked *allegro moderato, ff, allargando, sf, diminuendo* (to *piano*), *crescendo* (to *forte*), with the final tied note finished off with a *staccatissimo* sign ('O wild west wind')! Add to these features a delight in *divisi* effects, which can appear even in ostensibly four-part settings—as, for example, the splendidly evocative opening of 'Love's Tempest', which gradually swells from two parts to a shimmering eight-part dissonance at the word 'ocean'—and it can be appreciated that Elgar treats the writing of partsongs virtually as a branch of his symphonic art.

Elgar's rhythms are dynamic and unpredictable, his treatment of phrase lengths extremely fluid, his word-setting sensitive, though not slavishly subservient to the language—he often prefers to strike out for the overall meaning of the poem, and leaves minor details to look after themselves. In his hands ordinary academic devices, such as imitative points, take on a genuine expressiveness: they are there because the drama of the moment demands their services (for example, the splendid climax achieved through varied imitations in 'O wild west wind'). He is also a master of musical scene painting—from the simple onomatopoeic suggestion of raindrops ('The Shower', bar 12) to the rhythmically complex 'storm' texture of 'Love's Tempest'.

But, above all, it is the sense of emotional urgency and total commitment that lifts his partsongs above the work of his contemporaries. Save in one or two bread-and-butter instances (such as 'How calmly the evening', written in 1907 in response to a *Musical Times* commission) he set words to music because he believed in them, and set them as partsongs because this was the medium through which he could best express his thought. Sometimes the depth of self-expression is so profound and concentrated as to equal anything he wrote in any other medium. The song 'Owls' (op. 53, no. 4) is just such a work: a bleak and haunting setting of his own desolate words, revealing the inner man with visionary intensity.

Elgar's partsongs are thus the culmination of the Victorian tradition—a high water mark beyond which few composers would venture. Indeed, among his immediate contemporaries only Delius was able to add anything new—a slender contribution of five partsongs in which the words are almost ignored *as words* and used for their sound value to create, in perfect consonance with his subtly drifting chromaticism, miniature tone-poems. Significantly, two pieces ('To be sung of a summer night on the water', 1917) are wordless. What he was capable of in more orthodox settings can be seen in 'The splendour falls on castle walls' (1924)—though even here it is the wordless bugle-calls that capture the essence of Tennyson's poem rather than the actual setting of his words. Delius's partsongs, it need scarcely be added, are the very devil to sing: their incessant semitonal shifts make demands that Elgar's practical musicianship would have rejected instantly.

Lesser contemporaries wrote much, but produced little of permanent value or even historical interest. Samuel Coleridge-Taylor (1875–1912) shared something of Elgar's emotional intensity and technical expertise, but too often placed his talents at the service of inferior words—'Sea Drift' (1908), for example, has considerable musical merit, but the words are purest fustian. Moreover, even when the words are acceptable, as in his setting of Shelley's 'Song of Proserpine' (1912), he was apt to sentimentalize them with sugary harmonies.

The partsongs of Granville Bantock (1868–1946) are technically very efficient, even adventurous, but so low in musical ideas as to leave little impression. A similar absence of personality dogs those of Josef Holbrooke (1878–1958), but Rutland Boughton (1878–1960) fared better. Certain experiments with 'choral variations' ('The Berkshire Tragedy', 'King Arthur', 'William and Mary', 'Widdicome Fair', 1905) are effective, though at times a little wooden and contrived, lacking the poetic edge that was to illumine later works, such as the *Six Celtic Choruses* (1914), and the fine, virile cycle *Child of Earth* (1927). Boughton's feeling for partsong came more clearly into focus in the extensive choral sections of his operas.

For the rest there is little to say. Edward German (1862–1936) produced partsongs of great technical efficiency, though few with the charm of 'Orpheus with his lute'—extracted, in many different arrangements, from his incidental music to *Henry VIII* (1892). With the exception of certain pieces by Holst and Vaughan Williams, the English partsong tradition was not taken up again with much conviction until the arrival of Gerald Finzi, and then Britten. But this is to speak of another period and a very different world.

The Christmas Carol*

A word might be added here about the Christmas carol, which in its late Victorian revival was a kind of specialized partsong. The traditional folk carol, associated with waits, broadsides, and begging, was

*Section added by the Editor.

263

not quite dead when it and its ancient forbears were discovered by antiquarian scholars, harmonized for four-part choir, and made a part of the post-Dickensian festive Christmas, outside the direct influence of the Church. (Efforts to spread carol singing to other seasons have not caught on.)

The pioneering collections of traditional English Christmas carols published by Davies Gilbert (1822) and William Sandys (1833) were followed in 1853 by Neale and Helmore's *Carols for Christmas-Tide*, which provided new words to twelve tunes from the recently discovered Swedish sixteenth-century collection *Piae cantiones*. One of these, 'Good King Wenceslas', quickly became *the* English carol, and has kept that position despite criticism and the appearance of countless rivals. It set a fresh example in that it was secular and folksy in style, and definitely not a hymn.

The next landmark was the publication of *Christmas Carols New and Old* (1871) by Henry Bramley and John Stainer. Its forty-two carols were increased to seventy in the second edition (1878): of these, twenty-eight had traditional words and twenty-two traditional tunes.[20] This marked the popular rediscovery of the English folk carol. The tunes, as arranged by Stainer, became Victorian partsongs, but often with a breezy freshness that caught some of the true spirit of the words. His versions of 'The First Nowell' and 'God rest you merry' are still widely used, as is Arthur H. Brown's harmonization of 'When Christ was born of Mary free' (retained in *The Oxford Book of Carols*, no. 178). The new pieces in the book were mostly of the *Hymns Ancient and Modern* kind: a composer such as Dykes could not as yet get far enough away from the church choir to write a truly secular carol. But Goss's 'See amid the winter's snow' quickly became a favourite, and was soon joined in the Christmas repertory by other Victorian pieces originally written as hymns, like 'Once in royal David's city' (tune by Gauntlett, 1849), 'It came upon a midnight clear' (Sullivan, 1870) and 'Hark, the herald angels sing' (adapted by W. H. Cummings in 1856 to a chorus by Mendelssohn written in honour of Gutenberg).[21] 'For carol singing had now become popular.'[22] After Bramley and Stainer, many other collections appeared; more carols were imported, revived, or composed, and were used for festive singing in the Christmas season in schools, at home, and in village halls; middle-class 'waits' sang them on their neighbours' doorsteps. It would be some time before carols of secular flavour would be admitted in church.*

Besides those already mentioned, two very different carols of the partsong type, originating from our period, deserve special attention.

*For the origin of the carol service, see p. 174.

One is Pearsall's magnificently opulent arrangement of the mediaeval German hymn *In dulci jubilo*, written in 1836 for solo octet and eight-part chorus. It is virtually a cantata, with several different treatments of the tune in elaborate counterpoint, but it still retains the spirit of the old tune, and in simplified forms it has won a permanent place in the carol repertory. It was the only carol that was sung at the Christmas Eve carol service at King's College Chapel, Cambridge, every year from 1919 to 1957.[23]

The other outstanding original carol is 'In the bleak midwinter', a poem by Christina Rossetti (written before 1872). It was sufficiently churchy to be inserted in *The English Hymnal* (1906) with a new tune by Gustav Holst that superbly matched the intimate melancholy of the poem. It was also sufficiently secular to be included by the same editors (Percy Dearmer and Ralph Vaughan Williams) in *The Oxford Book of Carols* (1928), whose preface began with a splendidly challenging statement: 'Carols are songs with a religious impulse that are simple, hilarious, popular, and modern.'

Chapter 12

SONGS

GEOFFREY BUSH

Milton's view of voice and verse as 'two harmonious sisters' would certainly be endorsed by twentieth-century British composers, for most of whom the choice of a satisfying text is as important as the actual composition of the music. Not so the Victorians. They set to music a prodigious amount of inferior poetry; but this was due not only to defective literary taste but to the fact that song writing (with single copies costing the customer around two shillings a time) was a strictly commercial proposition. Words had to be chosen which the composer (or the publisher) believed were likely to have a wide popular appeal. Provided these were then treated simply as a peg on which to hang a good tune, and provided the composer happened to be a master of melody, no great harm was done; we can still enjoy the songs written by Thomas Arne for the eighteenth-century pleasure gardens. But as soon as a composer starts to pay attention to the words—to interpret the meaning and the emotional nuances of the poem he is trying to set—a song becomes a dual work of art; it cannot be judged on the merits of the music alone, but on the sum of both its parts. Even in the case of Schubert, it is arguable that his last settings of Heine offer a profounder musical experience than the song cycles to texts by the greatly inferior Wilhelm Müller.

The Earlier Romantics

The first composer we are to consider possessed both outstanding melodic gifts and a taste for good poetry—Mozart's pupil Thomas Attwood (1765–1838). His songs are characterized by a beautifully-shaped and genuinely expressive melodic line. One of them, 'Let me die' (1810), was even put forward by the editor of *The Harmonicon*, William Ayrton, as the source of Horn's 'Cherry ripe'.[1] There is some resemblance, certainly—sufficient, we are told, for an action to be brought against Horn for breach of copyright[2]—but the song is a lovely piece of lyrical writing on its own account. As in most of the songs of Attwood and his contemporaries, there is not a great deal of independent interest in the accompaniment (ex. 12.1).

Ex. 12.1 Thomas Attwood, 'Let me die' (1810)

Agitato ma non troppo presto

Let me die! let me die! the de - lu-sion is o'er, Hope's

beau - ti - ful vi - sion can cheat me no more!

(*S:* Monanzi, 1810)

The poets chiefly favoured by Attwood were Walter Scott and Thomas Moore: his setting of the 'Coronach' ('He is gone on the mountain') (1811) from *The Lady of the Lake* is particularly fine. The texts of four of his songs are taken from Moore's 'Lalla Rookh', which attracted the attention of a great many other composers as well; *The Monthly Magazine* for October 1817 reviewed no less than nine songs which were all settings of extracts from Moore's poem, which had been published the same year.

Besides being a poet, Moore (1779–1852) was a singer and amateur composer. As he himself readily admitted, he had to have professional assistance in writing down his songs and preparing them for publication, and this process often led (in his opinion) to their true character being distorted:

The truth is, that, not being sufficiently practised in the rules of composition to rely on the accuracy of my own harmonic arrangements, I am obliged to submit my rude sketches to the eyes of a Professor [i.e., professional], before they can encounter the criticisms of the musical world; and as it but too often happens that they are indebted for their originality to the violation of some established law, the hand, that corrects their errors, is almost sure to destroy their character, and the few little flowers they may boast are generally pulled away with the weeds.

The songs that chiefly suffered were those in which he had been 'wandering from home in search of discords and chromatics'; among the simpler songs which required no emendation he lists 'Farewell, Bessy' (1807), whose artless refrain (ex. 12.2) is really rather touching.[3]

Ex. 12.2   Thomas Moore, 'Farewell, Bessy' (1807)

(Moore VM)

The primacy of melody is also maintained in the songs of John Clarke (1770–1836), who by adding another barrel to his name in memory of a maternal uncle became in 1814 John Clarke-Whitfield. He, too, set words taken from 'Lalla Rookh', but perhaps his finest song is the canzonet 'One struggle more'.* This is a setting of Byron, another poet destined to become very popular with composers. Clarke-Whitfield could seldom resist introducing decorative or illustrative touches into

*This and several other songs discussed in this chapter may be found in Musica Britannica, volume 43.

his accompaniments; as a result songs that begin strongly often seem to lose their way amid agreeable irrelevancies.

If Clark-Whitfeld's greatest achievement was due to the inspiration of Byron, that of George Frederick Pinto (1785–1806) was due to Alexander Pope. This is 'Eloisa to Abelard', which was published posthumously under the editorial supervision of Samuel Wesley. Several others of his sixteen surviving canzonets[4] are worthy of serious attention, among them the serenely pastoral 'Invocation to Nature', one of a set of six published in 1804. Another in the same set, 'The Distress'd Mother', is an early example of the quintessential theme of the Victorian ballad. (A young girl who has been seduced and deserted is thrown out by her cruel parents to die with her baby in the snow—a situation which Pinto exploits for all it is worth.)

Some of the most prolific composers of ballads were capable of, and occasionally aspired to, better things. In the earlier part of the century, the principal names (excluding those who were first and foremost composers of opera) were Charles Edward Horn (1786–1849), John Barnett (1802–90), John Liptrot Hatton (1809–86), and George Alexander Macfarren (1813–87). The first three all published collections of songs with a high artistic purpose and some considerable merits. They justified their departures from the norm in prefaces which exhibit real or assumed diffidence, and (in one case) a powerful and very genuine sense of grievance.

The most ambitious collection was John Barnett's *Lyric Illustrations of the Modern Poets* published in 1834. In an 'Advertisement' the composer claimed that as the twelve songs 'were written for my own gratification and amusement, I had no idea of ever introducing them to the public until they were heard by some of my musical friends* who advised me to print them'. In 1877 the composer revised and reissued the collection with three additional songs. In the preface to this second edition he described what had happened to the first. 'My work appeared and was bitterly abused by the very Musical Profession and Press who, but a short time before, had been urging young Composers to gird up their loins and attempt the rescue of the Art [of English Song] from its fallen estate.' Nor was that all. 'The celebrated Tenor, [John] Braham, expressed his desire to sing "Queen Mab" at the Philharmonic Concerts . . . I therefore hastened to "Instrument" the Song, which was forwarded to the Directors with a recommendation from the great Tenor, but, it was returned to me almost immediately, *unopened*.' Discouraged, Barnett abandoned the idea of writing a companion volume; but when he came to re-issue the original collection, yet

*Identified in the 1877 edition as John Hullah, Macfarren, Henry Smart, and Samuel Wesley.

269

another blow was in store. 'The work itself was no longer extant. The Music Seller, into whose hands it had fallen, had "melted down" the music plates, and the same pewter on which my songs were engraved may probably be now supplying impressions of Music Hall and Christy Minstrel Songs.' In a footnote he inveighed against publishers who allowed insufficient time for a work to establish itself in the repertory, and broke up the plates if profits came in too slowly (a state of affairs not unknown today).

In the final version of the collection there are fifteen songs; the major poets represented are Shelley (eight settings), Byron (two), and Wordsworth (one—a rather fine 'Descriptive Canzona: Ossian's Glen'). There are four in which Barnett indulges his taste for the dramatic; these are on the grand scale and are described by the composer as scenas. ('Darkness' to words by Byron is a characteristic example.) But the cream of the collection, a masterpiece by any standards, is his setting of Shelley's 'I arise from dreams of thee'. There is a total identification of music and poetry; and the voice and piano—perhaps for the first time in our history—are truly equal and independent partners. It should be in the repertory of every tenor and soprano who cares for English song.

Hatton was rather more fortunate with his *Songs, and Other Poems by Herrick, Ben Jonson and Sedley* which he published in 1850, since one of them, his setting of 'To Anthea', was an instant success and has remained a favourite to this day. This, too, is quite simply a masterpiece, though the accentuation of the words 'under that cypresse tree' is open to criticism. Curiously, Hatton wrote two different versions of the passage in which this line occurs (modulating to different keys). He seems never to have made up his mind which one he preferred—pardonably, because their merits are equally balanced. There is nothing else in the set which quite equals 'To Anthea', though 'The Hag', a brilliant witches' ride, comes close to it. 'The Teare' and 'To Blossoms', also to words by Herrick (who is the source of seventeen of the nineteen texts), are very agreeable songs, lacking only the final touch of inspiration. In his preface Hatton apologized for the brevity of some of the songs, and indeed for publishing them at all:

The songs forming the contents of this Volume were written at different times and under varying circumstances—Some few of them were composed previous to my departure to America in the Autumn of the year 1848 and presented as little Souvenirs to several of my friends on leaving England—The rest with one exception I wrote entirely for my own amusement during the time I was away—and all of them were composed without any view to their publication. This statement I think it necessary to make in order to account for the fragmentary and scraplike form of some of them.

Like Barnett, Hatton saddled a 'friend' with the responsibility of urging him to issue the collection in print.

A single composition may occasionally become so popular that it distracts attention from the rest of a composer's output. In exceptional cases it may, paradoxically, cause his name to be forgotten. Nowadays most people think of 'Cherry ripe' (1825), another Herrick poem, as a traditional tune, whereas of course it was the work of a highly professional composer of songs and stage music, C. E. Horn. This song, too, one can only describe as a masterpiece—which certainly cannot be said of his rather weak cavatina 'I've been roaming' which rivalled 'Cherry ripe' in popularity during the composer's lifetime.

Macfarren was a much more considerable composer than Horn, but he seems to have taken remarkably little trouble over his songs—possibly because he regarded them simply as a commercial undertaking, possibly because of a defective literary taste. On the rare occasions when he chose to exert himself he showed himself able to produce first-class work. In particular there are two lovely songs with clarinet obbligato, published in 1867 with a dedication to an admired contemporary performer on that instrument, Henry Lazarus (1815–95). The first, an ebullient setting of Thomas Heywood's 'Pack, clouds, away', was deservedly popular—its opening phrase was embossed in gilt on the front cover of H. C. Banister's biography of the composer. The lack of musical interest in the piano part has sometimes been objected to, but precisely the same criticism could be levelled at Schubert's 'Der Hirt auf dem Felsen'. Even finer is its companion piece, a restrained but deeply touching setting of Shelley's poem, 'The Widow Bird'. One other remarkable production is a group of four songs 'from the story of Alee and Shems en Nahar, in Lane's new translation of the Arabian Night's Entertainments' (1867). Macfarren's (mainly) strophic settings and Lane's prose translations are not entirely compatible—though the composer chose passages which were lyrics in the original Arabic; nevertheless all the songs are worthy of attention and the third, 'Separation', is a composition of real distinction.

Many of the most popular songs of the Victorian era were taken from the romantic operas of Henry Bishop (1786–1855), Julius Benedict (1804–85), Michael Balfe (1808–70), William Vincent Wallace (1812–65), and Edward Loder (1813–65). Some of Bishop's best songs are to be found in a series of stage entertainments consisting of spoken dialogue and separate musical numbers concocted from Shakespeare plays by Frederick Reynolds in 1816–21.* Since (unlike such works as *The Bohemian Girl* and *The Night Dancers*) these so-called operas have no chance whatever of stage revival, their contents must be allowed to survive as songs or not at all.

Bishop, a most able composer, raised the level of his own music to match Shakespeare's words, just as he lowered it to match the trash provided by his usual librettists (in both cases, as Bernard Shaw remarked of Rossini, as a matter of business). The simpler and more lyrical settings, such as 'By the simplicity of Venus' doves' and 'Come, live with me', are really beautiful things, and the orchestral accompaniments do not lose too much by being transferred to the piano in the composer's own transcription. (Bishop kept the alterations to the minimum, as example 12.3, from the cavatina 'Take all my loves', will

Ex. 12.3   Henry R. Bishop, music for *Twelfth Night* (1820): cavatina, 'Take all my loves'

(*K*: Goulding, D'Almaine, 1820)

*See Chapter 13.

272

show.) The faster and more elaborate movements, 'Lo, here the gentle lark' for example, and 'Bid me discourse', are quite a different story. An accompaniment consisting of an endless series of detached chords—perfectly satisfactory when played by strings—rapidly becomes intolerable on the piano.*

There is virtually nothing of interest to be found in the songs written outside the context of the stage by Wallace or Benedict. Balfe is another matter. His most ambitious effort was a group of six songs and a duet (c. 1855) to words by Longfellow, and these had a wide circulation in the composer's own day. They smell a bit too much of the footlights to be wholly successful as songs, but the serenade 'Goodnight! goodnight! beloved' deserves occasional revival. There are two settings of other poets which are worthy of a more permanent place in the repertory: 'The Sands of Dee', which allows Kingsley's poem to speak for itself instead of seeking to illustrate the tragedy with a series of melodramatic or picturesque effects; and Tennyson's 'Come into the garden, Maud'. The latter has long been an object of derision among those who have never sung it, or heard it sung, properly. But, as John Webster wrote in his preface to *The White Devil*, 'detraction is the sworn friend to ignorance'. The only valid criticism that can be levelled against Balfe's exciting and passionate song is his cavalier treatment of the text. One possible explanation of this is that he was so familiar with the words that he set them to music by heart, only to have his memory betray him. This is a not uncommon experience among composers who have thought for a long time about a particular poem before setting it to music.†

Of the five operatic composers under consideration Loder has been the most harshly treated by posterity. He has been judged by his worst products. In 1835 he was driven by poverty to contract an artistically disastrous agreement with his publishers, D'Almaine & Co., to produce a new song (or some equivalent composition) *every week*; consequently his best work lies buried under a heap of commercially-orientated trivialities. One solitary song was rescued (and reissued) by Ernest Walker—'I heard a brooklet gushing' (1850), a setting of a translation by Longfellow of Wilhelm Müller's 'Wohin' which actually challenges comparison with Schubert. But it is not a 'single . . . and almost unbelievable effort'[5] as Walker supposed; equally admirable are 'Invocation to the Deep' (to words by Felicia Hemans) and 'Robin

*'Arrangement' is a word of fear, unpleasing to the scholar's ear: but arranging the accompaniments of these songs in a more idiomatic form seems the only way to rescue them from oblivion.
†But correcting Balfe's misquotations is a very simple matter. The repetition of only a single note will enable the singer to substitute Tennyson's original 'Queen rose of the rosebud garden of girls' for the meaningless 'Queen of the rosebud, Garden of girls.'

Hood' (to words by George Soane). The latter has a melody of unforced, almost noble simplicity (ex. 12.4). Then there is the group of nine *Sacred Songs and Ballads* (1840–2) dedicated to Sterndale Bennett. These, set to scriptural paraphrases, were originally issued separately by D'Almaine, perhaps under the terms of their contract with the composer. The variety and high standard maintained throughout the collection are most impressive. Particularly striking are 'My soul is sorely vexed' (whose agitated mood contrasts admirably with the gentle confidence expressed in 'Oh! refrain thy voice from weeping'); 'Give thanks unto the Lord', a sturdy melody in triple time; and two very intense songs—'My days are past', which contains some remarkable chromatic modulations, and 'The Lamentation', in F sharp minor.

This collection of Loder's is not unique. Songs to sacred texts were much in demand for domestic consumption during this period. One of the best sets was (scarcely surprisingly) composed by S. S. Wesley (1810–76): *The Collects for the First Three Sundays in Advent* (1851), paraphrased by W. H. Bellamy. The accompaniment of the third collect, 'Lord Jesu Christ', though marked 'piano forte', seems closer to organ music in texture; unusually, a bass voice is specified. The second, 'Most blessed Lord', has a much more pianistic accompaniment; the vocal line (which is assigned to a treble voice) culminates in a soaring Amen. Wesley's settings of Byron, notably 'By the rivers of Babylon we sat down and wept', are also very fine.

The German Influence: Sterndale Bennett and Pierson

William Sterndale Bennett (1816–75) and Henry Hugo Pierson (1815–73) were at various times friends, collaborators, and rivals. They can be considered jointly responsible for bringing English song within the orbit of the German lied.

Bennett began to plan a set of twelve songs to be issued with English and German texts as early as 1837; but the first group of six did not appear until 1842 and the second—though advertised in 1844—was not published complete until 1856. This was no doubt due in part to Bennett's tendency to procrastinate, but also to the difficulty of obtaining satisfactory translations. These were essential to Bennett's plan, for he intended his songs to be equally viable in English and German.*'On the one side, they would show the German public that England, too, could produce good music—music that was not provincial, but dis-

---

*Two of Bennett's texts were original German poems. Uhland's 'Maienthau' was translated for Bennett by Pierson as 'Maydew' (op. 23, no. 2).

SONGS

Ex. 12.4 Edward J. Loder, 'Robin Hood' (1844?)

(**Moderato con espressione**)

(*S*: Novello, *Albums of English Song*, No. 5 [c. 1890])

275

played a full command of the style that was central in European music at the time. . . . At the same time they would show the English music-lover how English poetry should be set to music in the approved German manner.'[6] The first to be written was 'Gentle zephyr', probably in 1837; but it later underwent a revision so comprehensive as to alter the whole character of the song. (Apart from innumerable changes of detail, the original tempo was speeded up from *moderato con espressione* to *allegro leggiero*.) The final version is as fresh and individual as any of the early piano pieces. Equally characteristic but in a different mood are 'To Chloe in sickness' (op. 23, no. 4, words by Burns) and 'Indian love' (op. 35, no. 1, words by Barry Cornwall). Both songs are masterly; sorrow is expressed simply, lyrically, and without a trace of sentimentality. Two other Barry Cornwall settings, 'Dawn, gentle flower' (op. 35, no. 3) and 'Sing, maiden, sing' (op. 35, no. 6) both have their merits. The latter's splendidly uninhibited climax more than compensates for what has been over-harshly described as Bennett's 'liking for the 6/8 jog-trot' in imitation of Mendelssohn.[7]

It is the quality rather than the quantity of Bennett's work which makes him a significant figure in the history of English song: Pierson (born Pearson) is of major importance on both counts.

Possibly because of his self-imposed exile in Germany, possibly because of what we would now describe as his upper-middle-class origins, Pierson has tended to be dismissed by English writers as a musical amateur, an eccentric in the Berlioz mould but without Berlioz's talent. But then, until recently, so was Berlioz. Even critics who purported to be admirers of the French composer were given to apologizing for his irregular phrases, his deplorably unexpected twists of harmony, his taste for weird instrumental combinations and extravagant literary programmes, and his alleged inability to sustain a musical argument for any length of time. On examining the music, one discovers the last-mentioned criticism to be entirely baseless, while the other features are the very quintessence of Berlioz's mature style. It is impossible to say whether the same is true of Pierson's large-scale choral and orchestral works without hearing them in performance. But it is certainly true of his songs, which are imaginative in conception, masterly in execution, and responsive to every nuance of the poet's meaning.

His gifts are already well in evidence in the songs he wrote while still an undergraduate at Cambridge, including a set of Shelley songs, and in the 6 *Lieder von Robert Burns* published in Leipzig as op. 7 in 1842. Despite his residence in Germany, Pierson returned again and again to English poetry; among his best work are three Shakespeare songs published in 1864, and there are spendid settings of poems by Moore, Byron, and Tennyson, including the latter's 'Claribel' (ex. 12.5) which has been described (incorrectly, for it has many rivals) as 'undoubtedly his best song'.[8]

Ex. 12.5   H. Hugo Pierson, 'Claribel: Elegie' (c. 1860)

(**Andante cantabile, tranquillo assai**)

(S: Schuberth (Leipzig), [1861])

Towards the end of his life Pierson published a selection of thirty of his songs in two volumes, the first headed *Liebeslieder* and the second *Romanzen und Balladen*. These titles provide three very convenient subdivisions under which one may consider his work. Among the love songs 'Take, O take those lips away' (op. 26, no. 3: first published c. 1852) is outstanding. This deeply expressive setting uses a two-verse text taken from John Fletcher's play *The Bloody Brother* (instead of the familiar single verse found in *Measure for Measure*). Of the romances, Tennyson's 'The White Owl' (op. 95: 1868) shows a delightful sense of humour and Byron's 'She walks in beauty like the night' (op. 33, no. 1) an attractive lyrical simplicity. The ballads are more controversial; they have been described as 'clattering "knights-in-armour" romance which is apt to sound out-of-date and slightly ridiculous today . . . they contain some extraordinary features . . . but they cannot be taken seriously as wholes.'[9] 'The Cavalier's Nightsong' (op. 69)* could be put forward in refutation of this view; it sweeps impetuously along with scarcely a breathing space from start to finish, and demands to be 'taken seriously as a whole' or not at all.

The Later Romantics

Neither Bennett nor Pierson ever wrote 'a little song-cycle, German fashion'; probably the first attempt was Sullivan's *The Window, or The Songs of the Wrens* (1869). This was first planned as a triangular collaboration involving Sullivan, Millais, and Tennyson, but like so many triangular situations ended in divorce. Millais never finished the illustrations, and Tennyson attempted (unsuccessfully) to forbid the publication of the work in 1871 in order to suppress the poems to which he had by then taken a dislike. The words are indeed weakly ambiguous (it is at times impossible to tell whether Tennyson is writing about birds or human beings), but much of the music is Sullivan at his best.

The first half of the cycle consists mainly of nature pictures, of which the loveliest, 'At the Window', will stand very well on its own. The second half concerns a proposal of marriage sent by letter, and the tense wait for the loved one's reply. Tennyson's not very inspiring text is

*Originally a German poem entitled *Sturmritt*.

Ex. 12.6 Arthur S. Sullivan, *The Window* (1869):

No. 9, 'The Answer' ('Two little hands that meet')

(Tennyson & Sullivan)

handled with particular sensitivity in no. 9, 'The Answer' (ex. 12.6: the reference here is to the loved one's seal, two crossed hands, which must be broken before the verdict can be read). Unfortunately the finale of the cycle is a disappointment. Sullivan attempts to compensate for some rather dreary moralizing about the married state with a display of fireworks, but one is more conscious of the sticks coming down than of the rockets going up.

Before writing *The Window* Sullivan had already composed several fine songs: 'Arabian Love Song' (1866) to words by Shelley, 'Sweet day, so cool' (1864) to a deplorable Victorian adaptation of a poem by

279

George Herbert,* and 'I heard the nightingale' (1863) to words by Chauncy Townsend. Still better are the five Shakespeare songs (1863–4) which include the superb 'Orpheus with his lute'. It is deeply to be regretted that such a master of melody virtually gave up serious song writing in later years. 'By about 1870 Sullivan seems to have found an outlet for a certain part of his make-up in ballads, and most of the songs from then on are of this type.'† Few of his contemporaries were able to resist the ballad either. Another of Gilbert's collaborators and a personal friend of Sullivan, Frederic Clay (1838–89), wrote virtually nothing else—with enormous success. And they keep cropping up in the work of a number of composers who were capable of better things: Arthur Goring Thomas (1850–92), Frederick Cowen (1852–1935), Maud Valérie White (1855–1937), Liza Lehmann (1862–1918) and even Alexander Mackenzie (1847–1935). No doubt they, like Loder, found in ballads one of the few ways of earning a living by composing.

Mackenzie's undoing was his seemingly complete lack of literary discrimination. Even when setting reputable poets, he was drawn irresistibly to their worst productions: *two* versions of Tennyson's 'What does little birdie say'. But when Mackenzie had the luck to stumble on a really fine poem, for instance Christina Rossetti's 'When I am dead, my dearest', he could do work as good as any in the entire century. Yet the three Rossetti songs, op. 17, are flanked by two other sets, op. 16 and op. 18, of which one can only say that the poverty of the words is well matched by the poverty of the music. Shakespeare, as so often, produced a good response, the three songs op. 35 (written before Mackenzie became a full-time teacher and administrator) being superior to the *Three Sonnets* (op. 50) which belong to his period at the Royal Academy. Best of all is the truly lovely setting of the Latin cradle song 'Dormi, Jesu' for voice, violin, and piano, from opus 12; it leaves one torn between delight and vexation that he so seldom put his talents as a song writer to such splendid use.

Cowen is a simpler proposition. He is credited with nearly three hundred songs, but although some of the nimbler, gayer ones are attractive, they have little positive character. Diligent research has unearthed only one song worth reviving (although others may still be waiting to be found). This is a setting of Longfellow's 'Thy remembrance', in which Cowen walks the narrow dividing line between sensitivity and sentimentality with tact and assurance.

At first sight, Thomas would seem to have made no more significant

---

*A later edition restores Herbert's original, but at some cost to the verbal accentuation.
†Dr David Mackie in a letter to the author.

a contribution to English song than Cowen; but he is important in that he introduced a new influence, French music, to counterbalance the German. Thomas studied in Paris, and his best songs are settings of the poetry of Victor Hugo. These plumb no depths, however; they are elegant, sensuous, feminine—the sort of music Massenet might have written had he become a naturalized Englishman. 'Je ne veux pas autre chose', dedicated to Jean de Reszke (a singer who looms large in the pages of Bernard Shaw's music criticism), is a characteristic example. Of his English songs, mostly to very inferior words, 'Time's Garden' (with cello obbligato) might possibly be recommended—but only to those with an insatiable taste for musical marshmallows.

Liza Lehmann and Maud Valérie White were still more versatile: they wrote songs in English, French, *and* German.* As a (very accomplished) professional singer, the former was of course familiar with the principal European languages; the latter was born in Dieppe and studied in Vienna. In her German songs in particular Lehmann successfully evoked a wide variety of moods; 'Die Nachtigall' (Bodenstedt) is simple and lyrical, 'Im Rosenbusch' (von Fallersleben) light and witty, 'Lieb' Liebchen, leg's Händchen' (Heine) depicts agitation, and 'Wohin mit der Freud' (Reinick) is an irresistible waltz. She seldom made the mistake of challenging greater song-writers on their own ground. White's Heine settings, unfortunately, come into competition with Schumann and Wolf; unfortunately, because in themselves such songs as 'Im wunderschönen Monat Mai' and 'Wenn ich in deine Augen seh'', both written early in her career, are quite delightful. Her masterpiece in this genre is 'Die Himmelsaugen', a great song by any standards; the single arch of melody rises to a climax of the utmost expressiveness over the chord of C, E flat, G, B flat and D. White's French songs are essentially light music; her favourite poets are Hugo and Sully Prudhomme, and her favourite texture is a vocal line doubled by the piano at the octave below with the harmony sandwiched in between. The songs in her own language are a good deal less consistent, her choice of poet being the determining factor. Herrick was a notable source of inspiration: 'To music, to becalm his fever' and 'To God' (which has a vivid contrasting section to the words 'Beat me, bruise me, rack me, rend me') are simple, serious, and moving. Tennyson and Shelley also aroused her sympathies. Her most ambitious, though not wholly successful, effort is 'My soul is an enchanted boat', an extended scena to words from *Prometheus Unbound*. Her less pretentious songs are

*Among the few songs of Ethel Smyth (1858–1944) are settings of Eichendorff and Regnier. It is ironic to reflect that a better-than-average recital programme could be made up entirely of *mélodies* and *Lieder* written by English composers.

preferable; in 'To Mary' (Shelley) and 'I sometimes hold it half a sin' (Tennyson) she deploys a very genuine melodic gift within a more suitable, because more restricted, framework. The well-known 'King Charles' (Browning) is probably the best of a bad bunch of later ballads.

Lehmann has been woefully underestimated, possibly because there seems something ludicrous to twentieth-century minds about a song cycle to words from the *Rubáiyát* of Omar Khayyám, entitled *In a Persian Garden*. (It was this work—really a cantata for four solo voices*—which established her reputation among her contemporaries.) It is true that she wrote much that was trivial, but serious landscapes like 'A widow bird' (Shelley) and 'Dusk in the valley' (Meredith) do not deserve their neglect. Some of her lighter songs are really very neat: 'I will make you brooches' ('Gipsy Love-Song': R. L. Stevenson) has a most attractive coda, and 'I know a bank' ('Titania's Cradle': Shakespeare) can sound charming, provided it is given a performance of the utmost delicacy. It will probably come as a surprise to many that Lehmann also published, in 1899, a song cycle in the grand manner to words from Tennyson's *In Memoriam*. This is an impressive achievement. The ten songs are thematically linked, and there is an extensive interlude between the sixth and seventh for piano solo. Most of the movements are dark and dramatic, but welcome and well-judged relief is provided by settings of 'Wild bird, whose warble' and 'Sweet aftershowers'. The cycle ends grimly: a passing-bell is heard tolling in the piano part while the voice proclaims 'Thou art just'. But there is an epilogue which can be used to bring the work to a more hopeful conclusion. This recapitulates a consoling melody originally heard in the third movement to the words 'If sleep and death are truly one'. An objection to using this epilogue—which the composer wisely indicates may be omitted—is that it employs for the only time in the work a speaking instead of a singing voice. Song and melodrama are best kept apart: this Lehmann seems to have realized when setting Jean Ingelow's poem 'The High Tide on the Coast of Lincolnshire, 1571', a rather more convincing experiment which uses a reciter throughout.

Liza Lehmann has been unlucky in that her *In Memoriam* was over-shadowed by another and greater Tennyson cycle published the previous year: *Maud* (1898) by Arthur Somervell (1863–1937). Somervell's opening song 'I hate the dreadful hollow' is electrifying; minor ninths at the words *blood* and (at the climax) *death* bring vividly before us the terrors and tensions which lie just beneath the surface of Tennyson's

*Stanford's cycle of op. 68 to words from Tennyson's *The Princess* and Somervell's *Wind Flowers* (1903) belong to the same unusual genre.

seemingly calm, uncomplicated world. Somervell shows great resource in providing contrasts of mood and texture throughout the remaining eleven movements of the cycle: 'O let the solid ground' is a joyous portrayal of youthful passion; 'Birds in the high hall garden' is an exquisite lyric; and 'Dead, long dead' is a horrifying description of a corpse disturbed by the sounds of the living world still audible within the coffin. The emotional climax of the cycle is the penultimate song 'O that 'twere possible'—very short, but full of deep inner feeling. Both the prophetic text and the music of the finale are likely to prove over-rhetorical for some tastes, but the work's underlying psychological unity is satisfyingly expressed in musical terms by the recapitulation of themes from the second and eleventh movements.

Somervell wrote nothing else of the calibre of *Maud*, though there are four other cycles for voice and piano, rather less closely knit. *A Shropshire Lad* (1904) has its admirers, but Housman's irony and gritty pessimism are quite beyond the composer's reach. Somervell is happier with the poems of Burns and Browning, and his setting of 'Young love lies sleeping' by Christina Rossetti, from the cycle *Love in Springtime* (1901), is, in its gently lyrical way, decidedly attractive. Somervell also had a gift for writing lullabies; one enchanting example (out of many) is his version of Thomas Dekker's 'Golden Slumbers'.

Parry and Stanford

The first thing that strikes one about the songs of Hubert Parry (1848–1918) is their extraordinary consistency. Ten books of *English Lyrics* were published in his lifetime, and ten more posthumously, containing seventy-four songs in all;* of these, fully a third are first class. Not one of them falls below a commendable standard of craftsmanship, and even the less inspired songs invariably contain points of interest, such as the final cadence of 'The Faithful Lover' (words by A. P. Graves: *English Lyrics* I.5) and the subtle sonorities given to the piano in the closing bars of 'The Witches' Wood' (Mary Coleridge: IX.3). Parry was exceptionally sensitive to words. It is instructive to compare his setting of Thomas Heywood's 'Ye little birds that sit and sing' (VII.3) with Stanford's. Parry throws away the last syllable of *warble* on the weakest beat of the bar, whereas Stanford hammers it out on the strongest. This sensitivity works both for and against Parry. As long as he is setting the classics of English poetry, he is as likely as not to

---

*Of his earlier songs much the best are the *Four Sonnets of Shakespeare* (1873–82). There are two vocal lines, one for the English words and one (the original) for Bodenstedt's German version.

respond with a masterpiece; but when he turns to lesser writers like Graves, Julian Sturgis, and Mary Coleridge (whom he preferred, for some reason, to the living poets who were really his equals) the weakness of the words is mirrored in the comparative weakness of the music. There are exceptions to this of course. Parry never wrote a song cycle as such, but the ninth book is devoted entirely to settings of Mary Coleridge. No single one of these is anything like as good as his best work, yet taken as a whole the songs have a coherence which commands respect.

Parry's first volume (1881–5: settings of Sidney, Shelley, Scott, and Shakespeare) is exceedingly fine; and it is possible to criticize him on the grounds that later volumes, despite their excellences, show no evidence of any further development. As against this, he rarely repeated himself. One or two characteristic procedures recur, perhaps, a little too often—but so they do in the works of most composers. One such is the droop of a fifth or more at the end of a phrase, of which a familiar example is to be found in 'To Lucasta on going to the wars' (III.1: 1895), at the words 'Tell me not, sweet, I am un-KIND'. In every other respect his songs are remarkable for their variety. He prefers the through-composed song to the strophic; where verses are repeated, he adopts the principle of 'perpetual variation'. There is seldom much in the way of preludes or postludes for the piano—'Lay a garland on my hearse' (V. 4: 1902) is a magnificent exception—but the accompaniments are usually imaginative, and never less than unobtrusively effective. (This will surprise nobody who knows Parry's second piano sonata.)

The emotional range of Parry's songs is tremendous. At one end of the scale there is the profoundly tragic setting of Massinger's 'Why art thou slow' (XI. 7), at the other the delicately witty treatment of Herrick's 'Julia' (VII. 5). In between there are all manner of other moods: lyrical (V. 7, 'A Welsh Lullaby'; VII. 1, 'On a time the amorous Silvy'), dramatic (XII. 4, 'When the sun's great orb'), passionate (X. 1, 'My heart is like a singing bird'), sad (VIII. 4, 'Dirge in Woods'), rumbustious (II. 4, 'Blow, blow thou winter wind'; VIII. 6, 'Grapes'), delicate (XII. 5, 'Dream Pedlary'), ironical (V. 2, 'Proud Maisie') and reflective (III. 2, 'If thou wouldst ease thine heart'). This list is far from exhaustive. One of the loveliest songs of all is the deeply felt setting of 'Take, O take those lips away' (II. 2: 1881), to which one feels that Hugo Wolf himself would have been proud to sign his name. Notice the touching way in which the piano completes the phrase which the voice has left hanging in mid-air (ex. 12.7).

Charles Stanford (1852–1924), at his best, was a very fine song-

Ex. 12.7 C. Hubert H. Parry, *English Lyrics*, *2nd set:* 'Take, O take those lips away' (1881)

(*S:* Stanley, Lucas, Weber, 1886)

writer; at his worst he was horrid. Most of the horridness is to be found in the series of songs (much admired in his own day) about life in Ireland.* This seems to have had the same kind of nostalgic attraction for Stanford that life under the linden tree had for Mahler—to be enjoyed, in both cases, from a safe distance. The emotions in these poems by Moira O'Neill and others are thoroughly bogus and expressed for the most part in embarrassingly feeble dialect verse. It would be worth while rescuing from these collections two amusing patter songs, the familiar 'Bold unbiddable child' (op. 140, no. 5) and 'The Sailor Man' (op. 174, no. 2); also two landscapes, 'The Fairy Lough' (op. 77, no. 2)—the subject of a detailed analysis in the biography of Stanford written by his chief interpreter, Plunket Greene[10]—and

An Irish Idyll (1901), *Cushendall* (1910), *A Cycle of Irish Songs*, op. 139 (1913), *A Sheaf of Songs from Leinster* (1914), and *Six Songs from 'The Glen of Antrim'* (1920).

285

'A Soft Day' (op. 140, no. 3). Both songs put simple means to very effective use. But whereas in the former the repeated juxtaposition of two chords (D major and the first inversion of F) is arguably overdone, in the latter the grouping of crotchets in twos in opposition to the basic triple metre perfectly expresses the lagging rhythm of the refrain: 'and the rain drips, drips, drips, drips from the (l)eaves'.

Stanford's English songs are not consistent, but even if one does not include cycles for solo, chorus, and orchestra (like the popular *Songs of the Sea*), there still remain after careful sifting at least twenty as fine as anything by Parry, which is to say as fine as anything in the whole history of English song. Stanford is particularly good at the larger canvas. The example usually given is his early setting of 'La belle dame sans merci' (1877), but although the motivic development is most skilfully done—everything is generated by the first four notes of the song—the magic and mystery essential to Keats's miraculous poem are missing. Far more convincing is the second set of *Songs of Faith* (op. 97, 1908), to words by Walt Whitman. In 'Tears', the intensely dramatic centrepiece, the rapidly shifting moods of the poem are vividly portrayed without destroying the coherence of the song as a whole. The climax 'O then, the unloosen'd ocean Of tears!' is overwhelming. Other songs on the same grand scale are 'Prospice' (Browning) and 'The Battle of Pelusium' (Beaumont and Fletcher), in both of which Stanford maintains a tremendous rhythmic drive from start to finish. If one compares these with his music for children, one begins to get some idea of the vastness of Stanford's range. 'The Little Snowdrop' (from *The Elfin Pedlar*) and the Stevenson settings in *A Child's Garland of Songs* (1892) are models of economy, miniatures written on the head of a pin.

Two little-known groups of songs contain some of Stanford's best work: *Three Songs* of Robert Bridges (op. 43, 1897) and *Five Sonnets from 'The Triumph of Love'* (op. 82, 1903), which begin and end with a really fiery display of passion. But perhaps the composer is at his most attractive when he is being either simple and lyrical, or else light and witty. Excellent examples of the former are 'To Carnations' (Herrick), 'There be none of beauty's daughters' (Byron), and 'Golden Slumbers' (Dekker) which surpasses even Somervell's lovely setting; and of the latter 'Dainty Davie' (Burns), 'Phoebe' (Thomas Lodge), and 'Spring' to words originally written by Tennyson for Sullivan. In this second type of song vocal lines of real melodic distinction are supported by delicate staccato accompaniments.

In his early days Stanford (who studied at Leipzig) wrote two sets of German songs to poems by Heine. Rather more surprisingly, the last of *Six Songs* (op. 14, 1882), is in French: 'Le bien vient en dormant'. This is the sort of song which is so captivating that the minute it is over one wants it to begin all over again. In particular the refrain 'tout dou— tout doucement' (in the English translation 'Heigh ho, heigh ho the day') is delicious. Another fine composition off the beaten track is the *Six Biblical Songs* (op. 113, 1909). These may well be regarded as the successors of the sacred songs which were so much a part of the early Victorian domestic scene; but since each song was planned to end with a well-known hymn in Stanford's own arrangement, and moreover requires a large organ for adequate performance, it would be more logical to class them with his church music, as hymn-anthems.

Unlike Stanford and Parry, Elgar (1857–1934) and Delius (1862–1934) are not generally thought of as song composers. In the case of Elgar this view is soundly based; there is only one major work for solo voice, the *Sea Pictures* (1899), and that is accompanied by orchestra. There is no evidence in this cycle (for all its merits), or in the handful of early songs for voice and piano, that Elgar cared much for the medium or anything at all for good poetry. All the same, nothing a master writes can be entirely devoid of interest, and anyone who cares to examine the set of *Three Songs* (op. 16, 1895) is likely to be very agreeably surprised. (This contains the delightful 'Shepherd's Song', the only one of Elgar's that has achieved enduring popularity.) Delius is quite another matter. He wrote songs—the total numbers more than sixty—throughout his working life as a composer, although the majority of them were written before the turn of the century.[11] He chose poems of high quality from many languages, principally (under the influence of his friend Grieg) Scandinavian ones, though he seems generally to have set them in translation. As with Elgar, one of his songs has surpassed the rest in popularity: 'Love's Philosophy'. This is one of a consistently attractive set of *Three English Songs* (all to words by Shelley) published in 1892. Harmony is not allowed to predominate over melody (which is liable to happen in later works like the four *Old English Lyrics* published in 1919). Accompaniments are pianistic and skilfully varied, and the climaxes of Shelley's poems are matched with equally powerful and passionate music. Only a captious critic would complain that the composer's love of feminine phrase endings occasionally conflicts with the poet's prefer- ence for masculine ones. Outstanding among songs in other languages are 'Twilight Fancies' and 'Il pleure dans ma coeur'. The former, which makes splendid use of a distant horn call magically evoked in the accompaniment, is a setting of a poem by Björnstjerne Björnson in German translation; the latter, whose economy of means is as masterly as it is unexpected, is the first of the Three Songs to poems by Verlaine published in 1910.

287

Chapter 13

THEATRE MUSIC: 1800–1834

BRUCE CARR

Music in the Theatre

'Few indeed are the people who do not derive pleasure from music; and, by the lower orders, music is seldom heard to such advantage as at the theatre.' So wrote Thomas Holcroft in 1805;[1] his assessment may well serve as a guide to the period, for hardly a theatrical production of any type was put on in London without including some music. In fact it was Holcroft's own *A Tale of Mystery* (Covent Garden 1802,* music by Thomas Busby) that inaugurated the vogue for melodrama which, before it lapsed into tired formulas, would provide some of the most fruitful native models for more extended and elaborate kinds of dramatic music. Not until the late fifties could a critic such as Edward Morley of the *Examiner* openly scorn the 'unhallowed union of music with the drama', and only then, in Phelps's fourteenth season of managing Sadler's Wells (1857–8), did that union break down enough to dissolve.[2]

The ubiquity of music on the stage was partly the result of the Licensing Act of 1737, which provided for the censorship of dramatic productions, confirmed the King's Theatre's monopoly in the performance of Italian opera, and restricted the use of English spoken drama on the London stage to the two 'patent' theatres, Drury Lane and Covent Garden. The King's Theatre stood socially above and apart from the others as the chief theatrical haunt of the aristocracy. During this period several new productions of Italian operas were mounted there every year:[3] beginning with *La clemenza di Tito* (1806) most of Mozart's major operas were done, including *Die Zauberflöte* as *Il flauto magico* (1811), and many of Rossini's followed, beginning with *Il barbiere di Siviglia* (1818). The only opera by an Englishman was *Zenobia* (King's 1800), by the Earl of Mount Edgcumbe (1764–1839): another

---

*Theatres and years in parentheses after the names of works are those of the first production. The place is London unless otherwise stated.

288

peer, Lord Burghersh (1784–1859, founder of the Royal Academy of Music), wrote six Italian operas, privately staged in Florence.* Giovanni-Battista Velluti, the last castrato *primo uomo* to appear on the London stage, sang in Meyerbeer's *Il crociato in Egitto* in 1825. In 1832 a new departure was made with the first performance in England of an opera in German, *Der Freischütz* (King's 1832), produced by a touring company with Wilhelmine Schröder-Devrient as primadonna: *Fidelio* followed later in the same season.

Ballets and *divertissements* were also given at the King's Theatre, usually by way of an afterpiece to the opera. The music was generally either imported from the Continent or provided by a composer on the staff. The only English composer who was involved to any extent was Henry Bishop, who was responsible for several ballet scores (1806–9).

The other London houses, known as the 'minor theatres', were legally excluded from presenting straight tragedy or comedy (except for the Little Theatre in the Haymarket, which was licensed for the summer months when the larger theatres were closed). Until the passing of the Theatre Regulation Bill of 1843, the monopoly of Drury Lane and Covent Garden limited all the rest to the genres of 'illegitimate' theatre: melodrama, farce, burletta, English opera, ballet, pantomime, and spectacle, all dependent to some degree on music. Nor did the major theatres limit their repertories to the legitimate drama, for their audiences made it clear that they wanted to see exciting modern plays and to hear new music attractively performed. James Winston, for example, noted in his diary the uproar caused at Drury Lane in 1820 when the management tried to substitute an old Dibdin farce for Soane's play *The Innkeeper's Daughter* (Drury Lane 1817)—which could not be performed because Tom Cooke's music for it was lost.[4]

Music in the theatre was not only omnipresent but also extensive and elaborate, for theatrical evenings were long, beginning at 6.30 or 7 o'clock and sometimes lasting past midnight. The main piece came first, a full three- or five-act drama, comedy, or opera; it would be followed by one or more afterpieces—an interlude, farce, petite comedy, or short ballet. At the conclusion of the main piece (or sometimes during its last act, depending upon the hour), the doors would be opened to holders of half-price tickets, among them members of the 'lower orders'. Seating capacity in each of the two major theatres fluctuated around three thousand; partly in response to the increased numbers of the audience, orchestras grew somewhat larger and a great deal louder than they had been in the previous century. There were

*Burghersh's English opera, *Catherine*, was performed in the 'small theatre at the Italian opera house' by R.A.M. students on 6 November 1830. *Harmonicon* (1830), 525.

twenty intrumentalists on the Covent Garden payroll in 1760 and twenty-four on Drury Lane's in 1775;[5] Covent Garden employed thirty-one musicians in 1818 (eighteen string players, six woodwind, five brass, and two percussion), and a list of Drury Lane's 'band' in about 1825 contains thirty-four positions: sixteen string players, eight woodwind, six brass, and four percussionists.[6] Extra musicians were—usually grudgingly—hired for the more elaborate operas and other spectacles, but theatrical orchestras continued to grow, reflecting changes in musical style: Adolphe Jullien employed sixty-six instrumentalists for his opera season at Drury Lane in 1847.[7]

Music on the English stage during this period, however, was never important enough to challenge the primacy of the drama itself. Like the scenery, the writing, and even the acting, music was ancillary to the story in the perception of most theatrical people. The music followed the theatre's forms, genres, and conventions, and it is studied most revealingly through them. Beyond the basic divisions into 'legitimate' or 'illegitimate', main piece or after-piece, theatrical works were categorized—and advertised—by dozens of not always helpful descriptions.[8] Such categorization of dramatic types was hardly rigorous, of course, but it did govern the thinking of actors, managers, playwrights, composers, and audience alike. Notice was taken whenever boundaries were crossed, as they often were, and the musical consequences were often important. The operatic versions of Shakespeare, for example, drew large audiences and outraged the chronicler Genest.[9] Musical works were regularly cut down from main piece to afterpiece, as when *The Sexton of Cologne* (Covent Garden 1836), an 'operatic romance', was made into a 'melodrama' by omitting all the songs.

Henry Bishop (1786–1855)

An excellent pool of examples to illustrate practices characteristic of English musical theatre (as it was experienced at the two 'major' establishments) is to be found in the numerous stage-pieces of Henry Bishop. Not only are his works readily available—a very large number were published in vocal score and almost all the manuscripts are in the British Library—but Bishop was by far the dominant theatrical composer of the second and third decades of the century. The son of a London shopkeeper, he studied music under Francesco Bianchi, who facilitated the production of his earliest stage work (all ballets) at the King's Theatre and at Drury Lane. His first big successes came with the operas *The Circassian Bride* (Drury Lane 1809) and *The Maniac; or,*

The Swiss Banditti (Drury Lane company at the Lyceum Theatre, 1810), and at the beginning of the 1810–11 season he was appointed music director and composer to Covent Garden. The music he wrote there during the next fourteen years, especially his ballads and glees, caught the public fancy, and its sale as sheet music made him famous and wealthy.

A dispute over salary prompted his transfer in 1824 to Drury Lane, where Elliston paid him £20 per week.[10] But here his attempts at more ambitious kinds of composition in the wake of Rossini's and Weber's popularity, and particularly the disastrous opera *Aladdin* (1826), produced in opposition to Weber's *Oberon* at Covent Garden, marked a decline in his fortunes, though not his fame. His enormous productivity slackened: after *Aladdin* he composed only nine more original pieces. He continued as a theatrical conductor, back at Covent Garden in 1829, again at Drury Lane beginning in 1831 (Capt. Polhill paid him £10 per week),[11] and finally again at Covent Garden during Lucia Vestris's first season as manager in 1839–40. But after 1834 he seems to have been unable—or unwilling—to compete with the younger generation of dramatic composers headed by Loder, Barnett and Balfe. He never composed another work for the stage.*

As he moved out of the theatrical world, Bishop in 1839 published his glees, in a collected edition which suppressed the titles of the stage works in which most of them had first been sung. 'To have annexed the name of the Opera from which each piece was taken, would have been giving it that theatrical feature which I deemed it better to avoid, and I know well that in private societies it has often formed an objection to the performance of such pieces', he wrote.[12] He directed the Concert of Ancient Music during its last nine seasons (1840–8), and in 1842 became, at the instigation of its patron Prince Albert, the first musician to be knighted by a reigning monarch.† His fame rested on his theatrical music; he was the most successful English dramatic composer between the death of Storace and the rise of English romantic opera, and his reputation was surpassed only by Balfe's and Sullivan's during the rest of the century.

From 1805 to 1840 there were just over one hundred and twenty-five theatrical works presented on the London stage whose musical content Bishop composed or materially influenced. About twenty-five of these were revivals or adaptations of musical dramas by other composers, works as old as *The Beggar's Opera* and as new as *La sonnambula*; the rest

---

*The Fortunate Isles (1840) was largely pasted up from patriotic airs and earlier Bishop works.

†The previous musician-knights had all been so honoured by Lords Lieutenant of Ireland: William Parsons in 1795, John Stevenson in 1803, and George Smart in 1811.

may conveniently be divided into five categories according to the amount and type of music they contain. A dozen works are modern legitimate tragedies, comedies, or historical plays with minimal musical involvement. Five Shakespeare plays, revived with music between 1816 and 1824, comprise a second group. Thirdly, there are about twenty-five modern 'musical dramas' with varying numbers of songs and glees, including seven dramatizations of works by Sir Walter Scott. The fourth and largest group contains the more than thirty operas, operettas, and other 'operatic' pieces so described in playbills or scores. The fifth category is a miscellany including ballets, pageants and other occasional pieces, and melodramas properly so-called, which have music throughout, or in which the crucial dramatic points are underscored with music. There are about twenty-six of these pieces: seven occasional works, seven ballets, and about a dozen melodramas.

(1) The music in a *legitimate drama* might amount to as little as a single ballad or as much as four or five songs and choruses. Often the music was literally incidental, i.e., an incident of the action, as a ceremonial chorus or singing-lesson duet; sometimes, however, it was used for characterization or comment. The only principal characters in the legitimate drama who sang were heroines in comedy, or sometimes comic heroes if the music was simple.

(2) The musicalization of *Shakespeare* is a special case, and is connected particularly with the dramatist Frederic Reynolds.[13] These five plays had an overture and from ten to twenty vocal numbers each, with at least two and as many as eight of them arrangements by Bishop of earlier Shakespeare settings by Arne, Battishill, Stevens, and others. All the lyrics were Shakespearean or traditionally Shakespearean, although most were transplanted from sonnets or from plays other than the ones in which Reynolds placed them; only rarely were the musical numbers integrally connected to the plot. Solos and duets predominated, but most of the plays had about five choruses or glees, often at the ends of the acts. One or more of the principal female roles might be taken by a singer, but male singers were more likely to personate secondary or supernatural characters (Amiens, Antipholus of Ephesus, Oberon); *Twelfth Night* and *Two Gentlemen of Verona* had no male soloists.

(3) A *musical drama*, if a main piece, was almost always in three acts, each of which closed with an ensemble or finale, and the first act always began, after the overture, with a glee or chorus. In all there would be some ten to twenty musical numbers including several choral or concerted ensembles.

(4) Only in an *opera*—or more likely an operatic afterpiece—might the principal male role require a singer; an opera's principal female

character was always a singer, but a musical drama's might or might not be. *Aladdin* was almost alone among Bishop's main-piece operas in having no main character who does not sing. In general it can be said that operas were musically more ambitious than musical dramas.

(5) The musical practices of *ballets* and *pageants* are self-evident, and except for one work (the burletta *Harry-le-Roy*, Covent Garden 1813, which had sung recitatives) these are the only pieces by Bishop with music throughout. The *melodrama* requires more careful attention, to avoid confusion with modern usage of the term. Melodramas were almost always afterpieces, whose distinguishing feature was the extensive use of action music: to accompany entrances and exits, to substitute for words in the case of dumb characters both animal and human, and to underscore and heighten any dialogue, action, or emotion of particular importance to the plot. The pieces of action music (also called 'melodrames' or simply 'melos') are of course exactly analogous to early film music, even to the fact of their having been published in the sheet-music piano scores of the work. Bishop usually also wrote a few glees and choruses for these staged melodramas, but no solo music aside from a simple ballad or comic song.

The Musical Genres

The 'lower orders' who heard music to such advantage at the theatre would have been willing to categorize its various forms just as they did the drama's: there were overtures, airs and ballads, display pieces, glees and choruses (including ensemble finales), and instrumental music (including melodrames, marches, and dances). Here again Bishop can provide the examples, for although his works are generally more elaborate than the average, they exhibit both the best and the worst in all genres of stage music for the first three decades of the century.

Theatrical *overtures* were almost always multi-movement pieces. Usually they began with a *maestoso* introduction—sometimes surprisingly effective—which led, through a transition section, to an Italian Allegro in the style of Spontini which comprised the overture's principal movement. It was followed by a slower movement for a soloist, playing a melody either newly composed (ex. 13.1) or appropriately selected (a 'national air' relevant to the locale of the drama). A modulatory half-cadence and fermata led to the closing rondo movement, again possibly on a relevant subject, and—especially in the case of Bishop who had little talent for music without words—often tiresomely

Ex. 13.1 Henry R. Bishop, *The Miller and His Men* (1813): Overture, 2nd movement, 'Arietta'

(*S:* London, British Library, MS Add. 27703; *K:* Goulding, D'Almaine & Potter, 1813)

trivial. The pattern was variable: the 'Overture alla scozzese' to *Guy Mannering* (Covent Garden 1816) is in seven sections, while for most of his more important operas in the 1820s (*The Law of Java, Maid Marian, Clari, Cortez*, and *Aladdin*) he wrote single-movement overtures with slow introductions. In a few early overtures (*The Knight of Snowdoun, John du Bart*) Bishop attempted instrumental tone-painting.

Airs and *ballads* were, for a large portion of the theatre-going public, the most memorable items of the evening, and a successful song could keep an otherwise unsatisfactory piece on the stage for most of a season. Some of these songs have even survived the 150 years since they were first heard. One example is Charles Edward Horn's 'Cherry ripe' in *Paul Pry* (Haymarket 1825), called a 'cavatina' probably because it was not, like the typical ballad, strophic in form. Even more famous is Bishop's 'Home, sweet home' in *Clari* (Covent Garden 1823). Bishop's own native ballad style was not strikingly better than many of his contemporaries', but he wrote hundreds of such tunes, and some are quite attractive in a sub-Mozartian way (see ex. 12.3), or in a sturdy 'English' manner. Unfortunately, his melodic charm is often vitiated by a curious 'tonic-bound' quality, as in 'In my bower' from *Aladdin*, and several much worse examples. Frederick Corder noted that 'a song by Bishop when it is not of his best is a truly melancholy thing'.[14]

294

Display pieces were always composed for a particular singer, and unless they proved especially successful in performance, they tended to fall out of use once the original singer was no longer acting the part. Few such works of Bishop are now remembered: one is 'Lo, here the gentle lark' (first sung by Catherine Stephens in *The Comedy of Errors*, Covent Garden 1819), which has the additional advantage of a text by a recognized poet. Anne Maria Tree was another favourite singer, for whom Bishop wrote 'Bid me discourse' (in *Twelfth Night*, Covent Garden 1820) and 'Should he upbraid' (in *Two Gentlemen of Verona*, Covent Garden 1821). These and similar antique-flavoured da-capo arias, with plodding Handelian chords and coloratura vocal writing, established a 'Shakespearean' song style to which Edward Loder, for example, acknowledged a debt in his *Songs of the Poets* (1841).

Like ballads, display pieces could be transplanted by their original performers to other stage works. Thus Edward Pearman, who was by 1825 acting Figaro in Bishop's 1818 adaptation of Rossini's *Il barbiere*, sang 'The Description of a Play' which Bishop had written for him as the valet Jocoso in *Clari*, and the fact was advertised in the playbill. This insertion perhaps compensated for the omission, now that Mrs Dickons was no longer in the role, of Rosina's scena 'Away, deceiver! let us part forever', which she sings after being told by Doctor Bartolo that her lover Lindoro is merely an agent of Count Almaviva. This bravura piece, cast in a rudimentary four-part (recitative-cantabile-recitative-allegro) form (ex. 13.2), is a characteristic example of Bishop at his most 'operatic'. Bishop was, in fact, a rather clever imitator, and anxious to give the public what he thought they wanted. The aria 'Tyrant, I come', from *The Law of Java* (Covent Garden 1822), obviously reflects the growing popularity of Rossini in the early twenties. It was to be expected that *Aladdin* should try to capitalize on the mania for Weber: 'The hour is here', sung by Charles Horn as Aladdin's 'uncle' Mourad anticipating the boy's retrieving the magic lamp from the cave, is a good example of Caspar-inspired bravura.

Very early in his theatrical career, Bishop wrote that he had 'ventured to carry out to a greater extent [in *The Maniac*, 1810] . . . a more elaborate system of concerted music than for some years previously had been attempted by English composers.'[15] This effort prompted him to develop the *glee*, the standard eighteenth-century form of social and convivial music, into an integral theatrical form with more elaborate vocal writing and an indispensable instrumental accompaniment. The form was ideally suited to Bishop's short-breathed genius, and his melodic grace, rhythmic life, appropriate word-setting, and easy harmony won him success both on stage and around the drawing-room

295

Ex. 13.2   Bishop (after Rossini), *The Barber of Seville* (1818): scena, 'Away, deceiver! let us part'

Larghetto Andante

(*K:* Goulding & D'Almaine & Potter, 1818)

296

piano (ex. 13.3, 'The tiger couches', from *The Maniac*). Both contemporary and later critics praised the skill with which Bishop could characterize classes of people on stage; Macfarren was particularly perceptive when he wrote that Bishop's talent was 'of a theatrical, not a dramatic nature, enabling him to represent groups but not persons, dispositions but not feelings, customs but not passions; your forester, your toper, your gypsey, your bandit, your serenader, and your

Ex. 13.3   Bishop, *The Maniac* (1810): glee from Act I finale, 'The tiger couches'

We spring up-on him to sup-ply

-ply, we spring up - on him to sup-

-ply, we spring up - on him to sup-

we spring up-on him, we spring up-on him

-ply, we spring up - on him to sup-

-ply, we spring up - on him to sup-

(*K*: Goulding & D'Almaine & Potter, 1810)

mourner.'[16] (Gervase Hughes makes a similar point about Arthur Sullivan.[17])

With more ambitious forms than the glee, such as the extended *finale*, Bishop was less successful. Planché's account of the gallery's crying 'cut it short' during pieces like the finales of his and Bishop's *Cortez* (Covent Garden 1823) has often been quoted.[18] But the cries were not entirely unjustified: the lengthy first finale of *The Maniac*, which Bishop probably had in mind when he spoke of his 'more elaborate system of concerted music', is simply an inserted multi-movement, descriptive cantata on the subject of fishing, occupying an entire scene of the opera but of no importance whatever to the plot. Bishop did, however, manage to write several real *action pieces*, though few are as appealing as the one in the operatic farce *December and May* (Covent Garden 1818). This sextet, in which a clownish old merchant secretly abets the elopement of his ward so that her dowry will be forfeit to him, has a melodic and harmonic integration that makes it one of Bishop's very best concerted dramatic ensembles. Evidently because of a poor performance the farce was greeted with a storm of abuse; it was played only twice more, and the sextet was never published. If it had been, or if Bishop could otherwise have found success with such music, perhaps the action pieces and finales of his more ambitious operas from the twenties would not have been so forced and tedious.

300

Instrumental music had been used on the English stage for centuries in obvious ways, to accompany processions, dancing, and other incidents. What was new in the nineteenth century was the *melodrame*, used to accompany actions and events which would not seem to require music to enhance their realism. Many melos were mere scraps (rushing scales, arpeggios, diminished-seventh chords), but others were longer, and the models for these came of course from the ballet. Of the approximately twenty-five melos in *The Miller and his Men* (Covent Garden 1813)—a work so popular that a toy theatre version is still being manufactured—almost half amount to simple musical punctuation. Several more are independent tunes, ranging from pastoral to agitated, and they seem to have no more systematic interconnection than have the isolated vocal numbers of a regular musical play. But a few are clearly related motivically to one or another of the four pieces of concerted vocal music in the score, and these provide some of the most interesting moments. Surprisingly, Bishop did not develop this line of musical integration further until much later, and then in only a few works.

Recurring Tunes and Motives

The basic conservatism of most English music at the beginning of the nineteenth century may suffice to explain why theatrical composers initially adopted only the most intuitive procedures in melos and melodramatic music. Drama itself was encountering strong resistance from critics and other writers, as it worked to evolve from a theatre of language and situation to one of action and emotion; a more sophisticated, systematic use of music to increase the emotional impact of the play took some time to develop. One of the most fruitful techniques to emerge was the use of recurring tunes and motives, unleashing the psychological power of reminiscence, and it emerged most clearly on the English stage in 1823 in Bishop's *Clari*. The idea was not new: both Grétry's *Richard Coeur-de-Lion* (1784, adapted at both major London theatres in 1786) and Cherubini's *Les deux journées* (1800, adapted by Holcroft and Attwood as *The Escapes*, Covent Garden 1801) feature a recurring ballad. But in each case the song is an element of the physical mechanics of the plot, like a birthmark or a signet ring. In *Clari*, the tune 'Home, sweet home' serves as the psychological agent of Clari's moral salvation, reminding her of her equivocal position in her noble lover's household, and prompting her to return to her humble home and beg her parents' forgiveness. Bishop set the song both for single

301

voice and for chorus, in different time signatures (4/4, 6/8, 3/4),[19] and in several melos, mostly for solo flute; these are especially prominent in the third act during the grief-stricken soliloquy of Clari's father. The tune's refrain also is woven into the coda of Clari's third-act scena 'Droop not, poor castaway'. But the theme-song technique seems to have earned no critical notice either favourable or not, and Bishop used it only once again, in *Yelva* (Covent Garden 1829), which it failed to keep alive beyond two performances.

More subtle use of recurring music had to wait for the influence of Weber, whose *Freischütz* swept London in the late summer and autumn of 1824 in seven different English adaptations, of which the last and most faithful was by Bishop. Bishop made effective use of a melody from the opening glee of his (and Cooke and Horn's) *Faustus* (Drury Lane 1825)[20] at two later points in the drama; equally interesting is *Aladdin*, whose Act II finale (the lamp-stealing scene) includes several tunes repeated from earlier in the opera. But the most surprising of Bishop's works for its use of recurring music is *Manfred* (Covent Garden 1834). In this, his last entirely new theatrical piece, Bishop's procedure became for a moment what can only be called leitmotivic.

Manfred was of course the best modern play for which Bishop ever wrote music—even after Byron's original drama was altered for staging by the rearrangement of several scenes, the cutting of over six hundred lines, and even the borrowing of a few verses from Byron's *The Giaour* to make a finale.[21] The result is almost unclassifiable in contemporary theatrical terms: it is too legitimate for melodrama and too spectacular for tragedy. The principal actors do not sing, and all the music is connected with supernatural beings or events. Bishop seems rather consciously to have integrated much of the music: an octave-long descending scale forms a prominent feature of many of the numbers, particularly some (not all) of those which involve infernal or evil agencies, for example the scene of the Six Spirits (I:1), the Witches' Malediction (I:4), the Witches' Carnival (I:5), and the Spirits' Chorus 'Crush the worm!' (II:4). The influence of Weber is quite strong; in fact Bishop, instead of writing an overture for the piece, borrowed Weber's *Beherrscher der Geister* Overture.[22] But the most striking part of Bishop's *Manfred* is its finale. Byron's original equivocal ending ('[Manfred's] soul hath ta'en its earthless flight;/Whither? I dread to think—but he is gone.') is mitigated first by a voice from above which forgives Manfred before he dies, and then by a patched-on choral finale* which produces an impressive *Geisterdämmerung*:

*From *The Giaour*, lines 632–5, 374–5, 384–5.

(*Thunder, lightning, and snow arise. Rocks fall, and discover at the back the Palace of Arimanes.*)

> EVIL SPIRITS: Thus as the stream and ocean greet
> With waves that madden as they meet,
> Thus join the fiends whom mutual wrong,
> And fate, and fury, drive along.

(*The good spirits suddenly appear. As they do, the evil spirits retire, abashed.*)

> GOOD SPIRITS: Sullen it plung'd, and slowly sank;
> The calm wave rippled to the bank,
> And all its hidden secrets sleep,
> Known but to Genii of the deep.

Bishop's music for this magnificent display of machinery must be called truly inspired. For the chorus of evil spirits, he chose the stormy tune of the Fourth Spirit, and for the good spirits' final benediction he used once again the Third Spirit's song—which he had already clearly identified with water, in the Witch of the Alps's invocation under the sunbow. This is surely a leitmotivic conception, and if the tune has not quite the sweep of 'O herrstes Wunder, herrlichtes Maid!' it is nonetheless effective, and certainly remarkable for its date and composer.

Bishop's Contemporaries

Manfred had much success but no successors. A few months before it opened, while John Barnett's *The Mountain Sylph* with its elaborate concerted action pieces was proving itself the most attractive new English opera in many seasons, the reviewer for *The Athenaeum* had issued Bishop this challenge:

> We are not disposed to forget the merits of one who, for so many years, honourably held the place of champion . . . nay, who may keep it yet, perhaps, if he is inclined to fight for it. . . . Let him then up, and . . . put on his musical gloves.[23]

If *Manfred* was Bishop's response, it was nevertheless also a swan-song; he could never have progressed further into the new styles of dramatic music. In fact his basic musical sense was in many ways anti-dramatic. Even his musical strengths were no longer useful. *The Athenaeum* accurately observed that Barnett was 'certainly inferior to Mr. Bishop in the art of giving a descriptive character to his music', but Bishop's undeniable descriptive gift was always more literary than pictorial: an elaborate simile like 'The tiger couches in the wood, and waits to shed the trav'ler's blood, and so couch we' was far more inspiring to him than all

303

the machinist's singing birds in Mourad's first romance in *Aladdin*, and his music shows it. A near-perfect illustration of how the drama was changing is connected with Bishop's entr'acte for *The Dog of Montargis* (Covent Garden 1814). This descriptive piece 'endeavoured to express the occurrences which are supposed to take place between the 1st & 2^d Acts, viz: the departure of Captn Aubri for the Forest of Bondy, his murder, the action of the Dog, &c. &c.' But between the play's licensing for presentation and its publication, four pantomimed scenes were added to the beginning of the second act, portraying in vivid detail exactly what the music had endeavoured to express.[24] Eventually Bishop—like his continental contemporaries (and superiors) Cherubini and Rossini—abandoned the field to his competitors and devoted the rest of his life to non-theatrical music.

Until the 1830s, however, Bishop had little serious competition, and the works which survive of his fellow composers are musically of even less importance than his own. Among the older composers who continued to produce theatre pieces during the first third of the century, only Charles Dibdin (1745–1814) approached Bishop's popularity, and that only as a song-writer. Most were hacks like Charles Reeve (1757–1815) and Joseph Mazzinghi (1765–1844), whose activity at Drury Lane overlapped the beginning of Bishop's career there. Thomas Attwood (1765–1838) is a more interesting figure, having been a pupil of Mozart, but almost all of his thirty-four theatrical works are afterpieces, and most are pasticcios or collaborations; in any case he wrote very little for the stage after 1801.[25] The Irish tenor Michael Kelly (1762–1826) claimed a theatrical production of sixty-two works, second only to Bishop's in number;[26] according to Fiske, Kelly wrote only the melodies of his songs, and left harmony and orchestration to others.[27] The tenor John Braham (1774–1856) acquired a small reputation as a composer in the same way.

Bishop's close contemporaries included men like Jonathan Blewitt (1782–1853) and William Hawes (1785–1846), whose careers moved easily between the theatrical and other musical worlds. Hawes was a music publisher and organist, as well as master of the choristers at St Paul's cathedral (1812–46) and master of the children of the chapel royal (1817–46). For several years in the 1820s and 30s he composed music for the Lyceum Theatre, and he adapted more continental operas for the English stage than any composer except Bishop. Blewitt passed much of his career in Ireland, as an organist, teacher, and music director at the Crow Street Theatre, Dublin. He collaborated with Horn and Cooke on Moncrieff's Vauxhall Gardens burletta *Actors Al Fresco* in 1823, and later wrote much for the Surrey Theatre, including the original music for Douglas Jerrold's famous melodrama *Black-eyed Susan* (1839).

More important was another Irish tenor, the extraordinarily versatile Tom Cooke (1782–1848), who was for twenty years a principal singer and orchestra leader at Drury Lane, almost from his arrival in London in 1813. He composed (often in collaboration with others) or arranged the music for over sixty theatrical productions, including nine adaptations of continental operas (*La dame blanche*, *Masaniello*, *Gustave III*, *La juive*). Besides being a talented performer on half a dozen different instruments, he was famous for his jokes, and he seems never to have taken himself so seriously as Bishop did himself. An 1826 note to the Drury Lane acting manager James Winston reveals his compositional practicality: 'really there is so much music [required] in *Oberon* that I have exhausted all I can borrow, and as a last resource must request of you to let me have the key to get the books of *Flodden Field* [composed by Cooke in 1818].'28

The only other major figure of the period before 1834 was Charles Edward Horn (1786–1849), who after 1827 spent most of his life in the United States, where he produced eleven of his forty-four theatrical works. He was less gifted than Bishop but better trained (his father was Karl Friedrich Horn, music teacher to Queen Charlotte, and a close associate of Samuel Wesley), and equally ambitious musically. Beginning his theatrical career as a cellist and singer, he scored his first success with *The Devil's Bridge* (Lyceum 1812), but continued also to perform on stage. He composed and tried to interest London theatregoers in an all-sung English opera (*Dirce*, a translation of Metastasio's *Demofoonte*, Drury Lane 1821), but failed. His last production in England was an adaptation of Auber's *Le philtre* at the Olympic Theatre, where he was Mme Vestris's music director in 1831–2. During the later 30s and 40s he devoted his efforts more to oratorio, and to orchestral conducting, in New York and Boston—much as Bishop did in London and the English provinces.

In 1826 Covent Garden produced one of the greatest operas ever written to an English text, Carl Maria von Weber's *Oberon*.29 Despite the inept libretto by Planché, the wonderfully romantic score was a revelation of the power of music to rescue the English theatre from its current plight. The challenge would be taken up after 1834, but the intervening years represent one of the lowest points in the history of English musical theatre. Weber himself died in London soon after the first performance of *Oberon*; an attempt by another German composer, Ferdinand Ries, to follow his lead (*The Sorceress*, Adelphi 1831) came to very little; and between 1826 and 1834, as the critic William Hogarth

305

wrote in 1838, 'no English composer produced a single musical piece of the smallest importance . . .and the stage was supplied with importations from abroad'.[30] The practice of adapting continental operas for performance in English theatres was long established, but their frequency had declined by the end of the eighteenth century to less than one per season, and the rate slowed further through the first two decades of the nineteenth. But the Freischütz-mania of 1824 seems to have led to a flood of adaptations in the next several seasons: the rate averaged about five per season from 1824 to 1840.

Any direct influence these adaptations may have had on the development of English romantic opera is difficult to trace. They were of course not authentic translations in the modern sense (a sense which did not exist when they were made): before 1830 most included additional music inserted by the adaptor, and not until almost 1840 was it usual to include substantially all the original music. In the frequent case where the plot was already well known it is often more useful to compare the adaptation to its prior English version than to its continental musical source. Contemporary critics certainly did so: Genest notes of Bishop's adaptation of *Don Giovanni* (Covent Garden 1817) that 'this Op. is attributed to Pocock—he has borrowed the bulk of his plot from Shadwell's Libertine . . . and sometimes the very words—if he had borrowed more and omitted the songs, his piece would have been much better than it is'.[31] Just as at the King's Theatre,[32] temperamental singers and cost-conscious managers would insist that original music be suppressed or supplanted,[33] and the composer/adaptor exercised his judgement, too: Kelly entirely recomposed operas of Dalayrac and Méhul for English representation in 1802 and 1803, because they were 'not calculated' for the English taste, 'which, in the musical way, requires more Cayenne than that of any other nation in the world'.[34] Moreover, any direct link between English and foreign-language opera in London seems to have been discouraged: Lucia Vestris had only mixed success at the King's Theatre during her seasons there in the early 1820s, and conversely, when Malibran appeared in Bishop's adaptation of *La sonnambula* at Drury Lane in 1833 (she had been singing at the King's Theatre since 1825), one critic was moved to grumble that 'there seems to be something a little *infra dig*, in the appearance of so eminent a vocalist on the English boards, and in a merely English performance.'* The next generation was to see a determined effort to assert the validity and significance of English opera.

*From an unidentified review pasted to the back of a *Sonnambula* playbill: London, Victoria and Albert Museum, Enthoven collection.

Chapter 14

OPERA: 1834–1865

MICHAEL HURD

English Romantic Opera

The thirty years between 1834 and 1865 witnessed a remarkable revival in the fortunes of English opera. The sudden appearance of a number of composers who were not only determined to write opera in English, but also sufficiently gifted to make the attempt, conspired with the presence of various theatre managers sympathetic to their ambitions to bring about a situation in which the foundation of a genuine national school of opera seemed a distinct possibility. Though in the long run each venture failed to consolidate its early hopes, a body of work was produced that merits serious attention. It cannot, however, be argued that even the finest of these operas are comparable to the best that continental composers could offer—there were no Verdis or Wagners among them; but they are by no means inferior to what the average lesser continental master could produce, and in certain instances they are a great deal better. It is no exaggeration to say that a select handful of English romantic operas could be revived without embarrassment.

A number of factors helped to bring about the new situation. Probably the most important was the realization, following the success of Weber's *Der Freischütz* in London in 1824, that to be worth while, opera need not necessarily be in Italian. The commissioning of *Oberon* by Covent Garden and its successful production in 1826 further underlined the point. The old hegemony of Italian opera, though still accepted by the aristocratic patrons of Her Majesty's Theatre in the Haymarket (until 1837 the King's Theatre), and of the rival Royal Italian Opera set up at Covent Garden in 1847, was challenged, and the way made clear for the encouragement of serious opera in the vernacular.

Moreover, as Weber's operatic masterpieces suggest, the idea of 'national' opera was very much in the air, and though it was perhaps diluted in a country as self-contained and self-confident as Great

307

Britain, there is no reason to suppose that native composers were impervious to its summons. And once bitten with the notion, they were fortunate in having an active champion in the person of Albert, Prince Consort. It is not entirely fortuitous that the period under consideration coincides roughly with that between his marriage to Queen Victoria in 1840 and his death in 1861. The Queen declined to take the slightest interest in English music until her marriage, after which there was a marked change in her attitude: for Albert was an active moulder of her taste.

The patronage of the Crown undoubtedly encouraged the new middle-class audiences to regard theatrical performances with less suspicion than hitherto (the Georgian theatre had long been a byword for immorality); and opera in English, though perhaps not wholly beyond moral reproach, must have come as a welcome addition to London entertainment.

The emergence of a group of talented composers whose disposition was towards opera was, to a certain extent, a matter of sheer good fortune. Though none of them were necessarily more talented than the best of their immediate predecessors (such as Bishop), the prevailing social and artistic climate was more sympathetic, and they themselves were thus encouraged to be more daring.

Of these composers the most important were John Barnett, Michael Balfe,[1] Vincent Wallace, George Macfarren[2] and Edward Loder,[3] all born within the first fifteen years of the century. To this list should be added a composer who was English by adoption, Julius Benedict. Each of these, as well as a number of lesser lights, produced work of quality—work which in certain instances was not only to make an impression in Great Britain, but to enjoy considerable popularity abroad.

No definitive estimate has yet been made of the total number of English operas produced in this period. Eric Walter White[4] lists eighty or more, of various types, but this is almost certainly not the sum total of what this remarkably fertile period produced.

This operatic outpouring was channelled into a number of ventures that range in efficacy from the totally misconceived to the genuinely practical. First in the field was the rebuilt Lyceum Theatre, opened in 1834 as the 'English Opera House' under the management of S. J. Arnold, the son of the composer Samuel Arnold. Though he had commissioned an opera from Balfe (*The Siege of Rochelle*), problems arose and the contract was cancelled. The first new work produced was therefore Loder's *Nourjahad*, which was performed on 21 July. Rather more significant, however, was the piece that followed it: John Barnett's *The Mountain Sylph* (25 August), for this proved to be the first

English opera 'in the modern form, in which the music throughout illustrates the action, in which an extensive technical design embodies continuous dramatic expression.'[5]*

Arnold's venture ran, under varying degrees of financial stress, until 1841, when it was taken over briefly by Michael Balfe, whose *Keolanthe* was produced on 9 March. It was followed by a production of Loder's *The Deerstalkers* (12 April), and then a total collapse—which left Benedict and Macfarren stranded with partially complete operas on their hands.

In the meantime, the composer John Barnett rashly assumed the management of St James's Theatre and announced the production of Francis Romer's opera *Fridolin* for 1 December 1840. Its failure was speedy and spectacular. The theatre closed after a week.

Nevertheless, these ventures must have been sufficiently impressive to convince other managers that there was genuine operatic talent around, and a potential audience to appreciate it. Within a year of Arnold's first production, Drury Lane, then under the management of the ubiquitous Alfred Bunn (c. 1796–1860), had opened its doors to an English opera by Balfe—the very one that Arnold had commissioned.

The success of *The Siege of Rochelle*, first performed on 29 October 1835, was prodigious. It ran for some seventy nights, and when, in the next season, Balfe scored a similar success with *The Maid of Artois* (in which he cunningly provided a flattering part for his friend Maria Malibran) the future of English opera must have seemed assured.

The greater number of productions during the next twenty years must therefore be credited to the occasional enterprise of the various managers of Drury Lane and the Princess's Theatre. Apart from a brief period from December 1847 to April 1848, when the conductor, composer, and impresario Louis Jullien (1812–60) tried to establish an 'English Opera' at Drury Lane (he commissioned *The Maid of Honour* from Balfe, but went bankrupt before it could be produced), it was not until 1856 that another consistent attempt was made to create a National Opera. What the managements achieved, however, was considerable, and was rewarded with financial success on several notable occasions—as, for example, with Balfe's *The Bohemian Girl* (Drury Lane 1843) and Wallace's *Maritana* (Drury Lane 1845). The productions ranged from through-composed operas in English (Balfe's *The Daughter of St Mark*, Drury Lane 1844) to musical dramas in the traditional English manner consisting largely of songs and spoken dialogue. Balfe's reputation was such that in 1838 Her Majesty's Theatre

*The Mountain Sylph was not, however, 'the first English opera since *Artaxerxes* without spoken dialogue', as White states. See B. Carr.

commissioned him to write an Italian opera (*Falstaff*), a privilege hitherto reserved for foreigners and peers of the realm.

The year 1856 saw the beginning of the last, most artistically secure and therefore most successful attempt to establish a national opera. The prime movers were both singers: the soprano Louisa Pyne (1832–1904), and the tenor William Harrison (1813–68), who had sung principal parts at Drury Lane in first performances of operas by Balfe, Wallace, and Benedict. Their enterprise began at the Lyceum Theatre, moved to Drury Lane, and then, in 1857, settled at Covent Garden. Their stated intention was to stage opera in the English language, but this led them also to provide a home for new works by native composers. Altogether they produced fifteen new English operas, including six by Balfe, three by Wallace, and one each by Macfarren and Benedict. Individual efforts by several lesser composers were also given a hearing: *Victorine* (1859) by Alfred Mellon (1820–67), and *Ruy Blas* (1861) by William Howard Glover (1819–75), for example.

When the company collapsed in 1864, its affairs were taken over by the 'English Opera Company' which prolonged the experiment for a further two years, providing a platform for Macfarren's last opera *Helvellyn* (1864) and Benedict's operetta *The Bride of Song* (1864).

Stimulated by their example, Her Majesty's Theatre opened its doors to a select number of native works, including Wallace's *The Amber Witch* (1861) and Macfarren's *Robin Hood* (1860); but, being still wedded to the idea of Italian opera in the Italian language, it did not adopt any consistent policy of encouragement. When the theatre was burned to the ground in 1867, the company (under the management of J. H. Mapleson) moved to Drury Lane where, in 1874, Balfe's last opera, *Il Talismano* (translated into Italian), was produced posthumously.

Apart from a brief and inglorious 'Royal National Opera' scheme, launched in 1871 at the St James's Theatre with a revival of Balfe's *The Rose of Castille* and with Sullivan as conductor, and Richard D'Oyly Carte's ill-conceived 'Royal English Opera House' with Sullivan's *Ivanhoe* (1891), no further attempts were made during the rest of the century—unless the brilliant success of the Savoy Operas is to be counted as a 'national opera' taking root unawares. Although a considerable number of new English operas were produced, it was at the hands of such enterprising companies as the Carl Rosa, playing seasons in London, Manchester, and Liverpool, and on general tour. Throughout this period Italian opera continued to flourish, at Covent Garden and (until 1891) at Her Majesty's. However, *I masnadieri* (Her Majesty's 1847) was the only opera Verdi composed for London.

310

The Composers

By far the most prolific and successful of the half-dozen composers to make a significant contribution to English opera during this period was Michael William Balfe (1808–70). He was born in Dublin, the son of a dancing-master, and showed an early talent for music—both as a violinist (he was later to serve in the orchestra of Drury Lane) and as a composer. On the death of his father in 1823 he came to London as an articled pupil of Charles Edward Horn. Evidently endowed with great personal charm, he soon attracted the attention of an Italian nobleman, Count Mazzara, who took him to Italy (ostensibly because of his likeness to the Count's dead son) where he was able to pursue his composition studies and have his voice (a light baritone) professionally trained. In Italy he not only appeared in leading operatic roles, but also began to make a mark as an operatic composer, at Palermo and Milan.

Balfe eventually settled in London in 1833, thereafter pursuing a highly successful career as a composer. His contribution to the English operatic stage has already been outlined, but it should not be forgotten that his operas received considerable currency abroad and he remains one of the few British composers ever to be commissioned by a Paris opera house—*Les puits d'amour* (1843) and *Les quatre fils Aymon* (1844) being composed for the Opéra-comique, and *L'étoile de Seville* (1845) for the Opéra itself.

The key to Balfe's extraordinary success lies partly in the nature of his personality. He was undoubtedly a man of great charm, handsome, well-travelled, and socially at ease. With these formidable gifts allied to talent, ambition, and an instinct for theatrical effect, it is scarcely surprising that he became a complete man of the theatre.

What supports his operas is their unfailing flow of melodic invention. This may not be of the highest order (it is too often content with short-winded phrases for that), but it has a genuine warmth that is difficult to resist. Untroubled by any vestige of intellectuality, Balfe's melodies made an instant appeal and his audiences responded gratefully.

Charm and ease of manner may have been sufficient to gild the surface of his works, but could not, by their very nature, penetrate to any depth. Far too often he allowed his ideas to rest on trite, tonic-bound harmonic progressions. Far too often he was content with a pretty tune—regardless of dramatic appropriateness. Far too often did his sense of musical architecture take the line of least resistance, relying merely upon conventions of the most obvious and hackneyed kind.

311

He was capable of subtlety, as his Italian opera *Falstaff* (Her Majesty's 1838) shows—it is arguably his finest achievement. But he was more often than not content to accept the first thing that came to mind. Perhaps in this he showed a clear and cynical understanding of his audience, offering them precisely what they deserved, hoping that if the opera itself could not win lasting favour, at least individual songs might have a lucrative career as drawing-room ballads. His attitude to opera, perhaps more especially after the collapse of his sole venture as impresario in 1841, was nearer to that of the present-day purveyor of musicals; and when we come to examine the works themselves, it may perhaps become clear that it is as nineteenth-century musicals that they should be judged.

William Vincent Wallace (1812–65) was also Irish. His career, much to Berlioz's delight,[6] was colourful in the extreme and might best be described as that of an adventurer. Like Balfe he began as an orchestral violinist, but later developed as something of a virtuoso performer on the piano, as well as the violin. In this guise he worked in Australia, South America, the United States, Germany, and Holland, before settling in London in 1845. His first opera, *Maritana*, was produced in that year and scored an instant success. *Lurline* (Covent Garden 1860) also enjoyed considerable acclaim, but *Matilda of Hungary* (1847), *The Amber Witch* (1861), *Love's Triumph* (1862), and *The Desert Flower* (1863) were less well received. Some half a dozen operas were left incomplete at his death.

If Wallace lacked Balfe's easy spontaneity, he could, when necessary, rival him in melodic charm—as the fluent melodies of *Maritana* prove. Harmonically he was rather more adventurous and self-critical, and his capacity for realizing large-scale musico-dramatic structures (as in *The Amber Witch*) was greater. But, as might be expected from someone who followed such an erratic career, the cumulative effect of his operatic achievement is rather less than its individual high points might lead one to anticipate.[7]

Of all the composers under consideration, George Alexander Macfarren (1813–87) was clearly the most intellectual. Less facile than Balfe or even Wallace, and less capable of the kind of melodic invention that would make a lasting appeal, Macfarren nevertheless possessed a strong feeling for the theatre, and his operas are notable for a genuine flair for characterization in terms of music. (His father, George Macfarren, was a well-known dramatist, and provided him with the librettos for several of his operas.) His musical models were not the contemporary Italian and French operas that served Balfe and Wallace, but Mozart and other earlier composers, and accordingly his operas often

312

exhibit an ingenuity and thoughtfulness that goes far beyond the range of his more successful rivals.

It must also be observed that he pursued his operatic ambitions with considerable courage. A first effort, *El Malechor*, came near to production on several occasions, only to fall victim to the collapse of the several companies that had decided to stage it. The most successful of his six operas was probably *Robin Hood* (Her Majesty's 1860); but his operettas *Jessy Lea* (1863) and *The Soldier's Legacy* (1864), both written with accompaniments for piano and harmonium for the German Reed entertainments, were also deservedly popular. More than Balfe, Wallace, and almost any other composer of the time, he was fond of English subjects—which indeed suited his gentle style and place him more directly in line of succession to the ballad opera composers of the previous century.

By comparison, the career of Edward James Loder (1813–65) was dogged by misfortune. A member of a well-known Bath family of musicians, he came to London after studying in Germany under Ferdinand Ries, and made his mark with the opera *Nourjahad* (1834) which opened Arnold's new English Opera House.

Unfortunately the need to earn a living led him into various arduous and artistically unprofitable undertakings, including a large number of songs and ballads of the most insignificant kind. Some of these were even cobbled into an opera, *Francis I* (Drury Lane 1838), which met with the fate it deserved. Loder's lasting contribution to English romantic opera rests on two works: *The Night Dancers* (Princess's 1846) and *Raymond and Agnes* (Theatre Royal, Manchester 1855). Both are characterized by a vein of melody that is not only stronger than Balfe's or Wallace's, but is also much more distinctive and refined. In *Raymond and Agnes* he also shows considerable powers of musico-dramatic construction, as well as psychological insight into his characters. It was his, and English opera's, misfortune that circumstances combined with his own somewhat unstable temperament to prevent his talents from flourishing as they deserved.

The career of John Barnett (1802–90), though lengthy, was also something of a disappointment. His father was a Prussian of Jewish descent, and he is said to have been a cousin of Meyerbeer. He was a child prodigy, both as singer and composer, and he provided music for at least 20 stage works between 1826 and 1833. His serious work in opera began well enough with *The Mountain Sylph*, but fell away in subsequent operas: *Fair Rosamund* (Drury Lane 1837), and *Farinelli* (Drury Lane 1839). A fourth, *Kathleen*, remains unpublished and unperformed. From 1841 Barnett worked as a singing teacher in

Cheltenham and gave up any serious concern for the operatic stage. He would be relegated to the many 'also-rans' of the century were it not for *The Mountain Sylph*. This work, however, contains much that is both moving and genuinely dramatic, and has been praised by more than one discerning historian.[8]

Julius Benedict (1804–85) was born in Stuttgart and studied with Hummel and Weber. After working in Vienna, he went to Italy as conductor of the San Carlo opera house in Naples, for which he wrote two works. From 1835 until his death in 1885, London was his home, and he eventually adopted British citizenship. Of his five English operas, only the fourth, *The Lily of Killarney* (Covent Garden 1862), scored a lasting success—though others, in particular *The Gypsy's Warning* (1838) and *The Brides of Venice* (1844), made an impression in their day. Benedict's melodic gifts, though less obviously 'catchy' than Balfe's or Wallace's, were considerable and somewhat more refined, and his craftsmanship had something of Weber's polish.

A detailed account of the period might also find room for at least a passing mention of several lesser composers who made their operatic mark with perhaps one work. John Thomson (1805–41), the first Reid Professor at Edinburgh University, is such a contender. His *Hermann, or The Broken Spear* (1834) made some impact at the time—partly because of its picturesque Scottish subject (faintly echoed in the music). His talent was not much different from that of Barnett, though his premature death makes a strict comparison impossible.

Much the same comment can be made about the work of John Liptrot Hatton (1809–86), whose first opera, *Pascal Bruno* (1844), was premiered in Vienna, and whose second, *Rose, or Love's Ransom* (1864), reached Covent Garden. He was primarily a composer of ballads and partsongs, and his operas betray the fact all too clearly. Even more fleeting was the impression left by Henry Leslie (1822–96), despite three operas that all found London *premieres*. Nor can anything more positive be said of the work of George Rodwell (1800–52), who composed more than forty stage works. The operatic career of Henry Hugo Pierson (1815–73) took place wholly on the Continent.

Thus, a reasonable understanding of the operatic methods of the period can be gained from a study of selected works by the five main composers of the day: Balfe, Wallace, Loder, Macfarren, and Benedict. Though scarcely matching the best of their continental contemporaries, these composers at least managed to combine an understanding of operatic techniques with a genuine flair for vocal melody of an attractive, if ultimately superficial kind. Much of what they produced met the approval of audiences in their own day, and, in certain instances, of audiences for many years after. Perhaps their greatest misfortune was simply that their efforts provided ready targets for the deadly parody of Gilbert and Sullivan.

The Operas

In considering the nature, structure, and musical content of the English romantic operas, it must be remembered that the public of the day had come to accept as axiomatic that there were two kinds of opera. One, thought of as the higher, purer form, was in Italian and sung throughout, with recitatives linking the various set pieces. The other, the true native variety developed from the eighteenth-century ballad operas, was in English and had its set pieces linked by spoken dialogue. It was thought of as 'musical drama' or 'musical theatre' rather than 'opera'.

How deep this tradition ran can be seen from the behaviour of London's main home for Italian Opera—Her Majesty's Theatre in the Haymarket. When it commissioned Balfe to write an opera (*Falstaff*, 1838) the libretto was in Italian, even though the composer had proved his competence with operas in English from 1835 onwards. Years later, in 1858, when the theatre decided to mount a production of *The Bohemian Girl*, which had begun its triumphant career in 1843, it had to be translated into Italian as *La zingara*, and Balfe provided suitable recitatives for the occasion. The idea of English opera sung throughout clearly had a double fight to establish itself.

The second matter of background fact which stood as a barrier to opera in English was the absence of any strong, active school of modern dramatists to provide librettos. The strict division of the playhouses into legitimate and minor theatres, and the parcelling out of what they might or might not perform, imposed, in effect, a degree of censorship. The minor theatres, restricted as they were to hybrid forms of drama, tended to attract at best only third-rate writers. After Sheridan, whose last important play, *The Critic*, was produced in 1799, there were to be no dramatists of comparable distinction until Gilbert, Pinero, Wilde, and Shaw at the end of the century. Leaving aside the theatrically ineffective attempts at verse-drama by such major poets as Shelley, Byron, Tennyson, and Browning, the new contributions to the stage came in the form of melodrama from the pens of hack writers. (Bishop's setting of Byron's *Manfred*, treated in the last chapter, and Hullah's of Dickens's *The Village Coquettes*, which was largely destroyed by fire, are the only significant exceptions.)

It was to these hacks that composers were forced to turn. What they

315

received by way of librettos for fully-fledged opera was no worse than
the standard melodrama of the period, and it can be argued that a
certain skill was shown in contriving 'occasions for a song', but from a
dramatic and literary point of view the outcome was abysmal. Card-
board characters postured in wooden situations and expressed themselves in doggerel that would disgrace a Christmas card.

High on the list of operatic 'dramatists' were Edward Fitzball
(1792–1873), known (because of his fearsome melodramas) as 'the
Terrible Fitzball', and the impresario Alfred Bunn (c. 1797–
1860)—'the Poet Bunn', as *Punch* described him. These two, with such
writers as John Oxenford, George Soane, and Edmund Falconer, supplied most of the librettos of the period. A brief example from *Maritana*
(Fitzball) may stand as typical of the general standard. It begins with
spoken dialogue, which leads heavy-handedly from one excuse for a
song to another—thus showing how the individual numbers in an
opera were liable to be 'planted', like so many items of stage furniture,
rather than being allowed to grow naturally out of the emotional needs
of the drama. The choral prayer into which the dialogue leads was one
of the 'hit' numbers of the opera.

DON JOSÉ: Brava! brava! take the recompense your sweet song richly deserves.

MARITANA: Another golden quadruple! See, friends, I shall be affluent indeed!
Oh, thanks, thanks, signor! (*Chimes heard.*) Ah! the Angelus! Such good
fortune should admonish us to be double devout! (*They kneel.*)

OMNES: Angels, that around us hover,
               Guard us till the close of day;
               Our heads, oh! let your white wings cover,
               See us kneel and hear us pray!

Faced with such ineptitude, which pervades not only the detail but
the entire dramatic structure of the librettos, it is remarkable that the
composers were able to achieve as much as they did. Even so, they often
treated the words with contempt, repeating them and splitting up
phrases to provide pegs for their tunes regardless of syntax. The opening chorus of Balfe's *Satanella* is typical of this cavalier attitude to
word-setting:

                Donor of this lordly, this lordly, this lordly fête,
                Liberal of heart, liberal of heart and hand,
                Nobly born and truly, and truly, and truly great . . .

In all fairness it should be added that some of Balfe's bad word setting is
the result of adapting tunes first composed for verse in other languages.[9]

316

Another factor calculated to inhibit any genuine musico-dramatic aspirations is to be found in the publishing practices of the day. Publishers, not without reason, clearly felt obliged to hedge their bets when it came to printing the vocal score of an opera. Except in the case of an outstandingly successful work (and perhaps not even then), it was not likely that the expense of printing a score would be covered by its sales. To offset the loss, the publisher relied heavily on the opera containing a number of songs (and even duets and partsongs) that could be sold separately. With this outlook in view, scores were often printed in such a way that the same plates could be used to run off individual items. Sometimes, as in the case of the vocal score of Barnett's *The Mountain Sylph*, published jointly by Hawes, Cramer, Beale & Co., Addison & Co., and Keith Prowse & Co., the pages are double-numbered: the numbers printed at the top centre serving for the entire opera, and those printed at the sides serving for publication of certain likely songs and duets as individual items. The temptation to write songs that would enjoy a double life, tailoring their style and even their length to the occasion, must have been very great. It would need a composer of considerable integrity, and financial security, to strike out for set-pieces whose sole justification related to the opera. Perhaps the surprising thing is that so many of them did!

The majority of English romantic operas, then, arranged a series of songs, ensembles and choruses, with the occasional recitative or melodrame, on the framework of a spoken drama, contrived in such a way as to make the singing arise more or less naturally. The musical set-pieces could arise as expressions of the characters' inner thoughts and conflicts—the ideal, as it were, of true opera. Sometimes several movements form a connected scena or finale. But all too often, as the libretto example quoted above shows, the musical element was dragged in as part of the scene-painting—almost apologizing for its very presence.

Even in those operas that attempt some form of structural musico-dramatic unity, as for example Balfe's *Falstaff*, Loder's *Raymond and Agnes*, and Wallace's *The Amber Witch*, there lurks the suspicion that at least some of the numbers are being cast for the dual role of saleable drawing-room song and practical ingredient of the opera itself. In consequence it is very rare indeed that all the items in an opera point to one end and one end only: the gradual unfolding of character and story in terms of music. Whereas Verdi would occasionally adapt an old aria for a new character and situation (a practice almost as old as opera itself), the songs in these English operas were often planned from the first to avoid explicit reference to their dramatic context, and might be

317

switched from one character to another without serious incongruity.*
Only Macfarren seems actively aware of this aspect of opera as drama:
in *An Adventure of Don Quixote* (Drury Lane 1846) the Don's own melodic
lines have a bravura extravagance that differentiates them sharply and
very appropriately from those of the other characters in the story. But
subtlety of this order is the exception, and for the most part character
delineation in terms of music is carried on at only the most superficial
level—at cheerful moments characters sing quick, energetic music, and
at moments of sadness they sing quietly and lyrically, and that is as far
as it goes.

A brief analysis of one act of a dialogue-opera of the period may serve
to show the kind of structures that were possible within the basic
limitations of the genre. Balfe's *Satanella* (Covent Garden 1858), with
libretto by Edmund Falconer and Augustus Harris, is typical of its
kind, though it is perhaps more than usually dated by its reliance on
devils and fairies.

The story concerns Count Rupert, who contrives to lose his entire
fortune at the gaming tables on the eve of his marriage to Stella, who
consequently rejects him. Faust-like, he invokes supernatural aid, in
the shape of Arimanes and his female attendant Satanella. They strike
a devilish bargain and his fortune is restored. The Count now realizes
that he loves his faithful foster-sister, Lelia, but fails to recognize that
Satanella has fallen in love with him. When the time comes to honour
his bond, Lelia offers to join him in eternal damnation. Satanella,
overcome by this proof of true love, tears up the bond and is saved from
the wrath of Arimanes only by the resourceful Lelia, who hands her a
timely rosary.

It need scarcely be said that dramatic and psychological truth play
no part in this farrago, and it would therefore be asking too much of any
composer to do more than decorate it with music that is entertaining in
itself and more or less appropriate to the action. This is exactly what
Balfe did.

The first act is preceded by an orchestral 'preludio' beginning with a
march-like Quasi andante in C minor (20 bars), and proceeding to an
Allegro moderato (59 bars). Both ideas are borrowed from the finale of
Act IV, the Allegro moderato being based on Satanella's crucial aria:

> Oh! tenderness sublime!
> If thou, without a crime,
> Wouldst Heav'n for him resign,
> Thy Love surpasses mine!

*The operatic ballad as drawing-room music is discussed in more detail in Chapter 6.

The prelude leads without a break into an opening chorus 'Donor of this lordly fête' which rings the changes on various combinations of simple SATB partwriting in a basically ternary structure. Count Rupert immediately acknowledges this loyal greeting in a lengthy scena that combines solos, quartet, and choral commentary, and ends by returning to the music of the opening chorus. The quartet element is concerned with two contrasting musical ideas: Count Rupert's lyrical 'Thanks, thanks my friends', which also serves for Stella's musings ('This forest fête doth all enchantment prove'), and the patter mutterings of his friend Hortensius's disapproval: 'A mere coquette to honour thus, for shame!'

Dialogue then leads to Lelia's first song, 'Our hearts are not our own to give'—a typical two-verse ballad in E major, whose words suggest a generalized emotion rather than any revelation of the heroine's character as an individual, and whose music has a negligent jauntiness that betrays Balfe's indifference. After more dialogue there follows an extended scene, described as 'Concerted Piece and Chorus'. Here the structure is quite purposeful, moving through a succession of keys and moods, and employing changing speeds to underline the action as it grows to a climax. In it, Stella taunts Count Rupert, who plunges into his fatal gambling, and the scene culminates in a despairing ensemble:

> Of life I have no care,
> My friends have turned to foes.

The entire scene is lively and effective, despite the banal words and wooden situation, and Balfe shows considerable cunning in delaying the ultimate climax. There are other effective touches—the music of Count Rupert's rather hysterical drinking song, 'Here's to gold, mighty gold', becomes the background of Lelia's arietta 'My heart is shadowed by some coming woe'. A sense of genuine theatrical irony is thus neatly created.

After more dialogue and a brief strophic song for a minor character, Karl, there follows a 'scena and cavatina' for Arimanes, summoned from hell by the desperate Count Rupert. A mixture of aria and recitative, heavy with diminished sevenths and tremolandos, it makes an effective if predictable picture of stage demonology—vigorous rhythms, leaping vocal lines, staccato phrases, chromatic runs, and all manner of bravura effects. Count Rupert then returns with a defiant two-verse drinking song in 6/8 time.

The last few minutes of the act consist of a 'recitative and cavatina' for Satanella; the cavatina, sung against a background accompaniment of offstage spirits (murmuring 'Ah!'), turns out to be the 'theme' song of the opera. Typical of Balfe's lyricism, it is a tune that manages to be both chaste and faintly erotic, commonplace and haunting. A brief 'finale' repeats the cavatina, with the addition of interjections from Count Rupert, who is now completely under the demon's seductive sway.

Such is the content of Act I of *Satanella*, and it is typical of the whole opera and most of the operas of the period. Other works differ from this structural pattern only in matters of detail and degree. The general scheme of things is typical.

Those differences, however, are often very interesting. In Balfe himself, for example, it becomes clear that his whole style can develop a greater cutting edge when the kind of opera he is tackling differs from what was expected by the English stage. When an Italian opera was called for, as in *Falstaff*, the music is much more vigorous and ingenious. Harmonic schemes are more adventurous, the accompaniments more varied and individual, and the melodic line has a sense of purpose and refinement that raises it far above the kind of work he was generally content to offer. Example 14.1 is the opening of the Act II duet, 'Nell' orror di notte oscura', sung by Mistress Ford and Sir John Falstaff (Giulia Grisi and Luigi Lablache in the original production). It is worthy, surely, of Bellini (or John Field).

Balfe's French operas show a similar awareness of national characteristics. Indeed, throughout his career he exhibited a chameleon-like ability to modify his style, and his ambitions, according to the kind of opera he was writing—even to the extent of lowering his sights for his English-opera audiences. Undoubtedly disillusion played a part in shaping this accommodating attitude—for his early English operas, such as *The Siege of Rochelle*, have a sweep and enthusiasm that is not always evident in later examples.

In many ways Wallace, though never as fluent as Balfe, trod a more consistent path, and certainly allowed himself to experiment more wholeheartedly with different types of opera and different types of operatic story. For example, in *The Amber Witch* (Her Majesty's 1861), based on a novel (1843) by J. W. Meinhold, he attempted a grand opera on the Meyerbeer pattern—complete with extensive choral scenes, a cliff-hanging trial scene, and the usual mixture of historical approximation and romantic improbability. Although the libretto, by the music critic Henry Chorley (1808–72), is no better poetry than the average of the time, it does show some awareness of the need to reconcile musical form with dramatic shape. The second act, for example, neatly frames a passage of arias, recitatives, and duets with extensive choral sections that depict the machinations of the lovers' enemies. Brief choral inter-

Ex. 14.1 Michael W. Balfe, *Falstaff* (1838): duet, 'Nell' orror di notte oscura'
Andante cantabile

(*K*: Cramer, [1845?])

ruptions in the main duet create a genuine sense of theatrical tension, while at the same time helping to weld the act as a musical unity.

Both Loder and Macfarren showed a more subtle understanding of characterization in music than either Balfe or Wallace, and both handled the problems of ensemble with much greater resource. Instead of the individual vocal lines appearing to be contrived out of whatever notes happen to be available in the prevailing harmonic situation, there is a distinct feeling that each reflects the emotions of the character that sings them.

Macfarren's gentle lyricism is at its best in his several operas on specifically English subjects, such as Fitzball's adaptation of Gold-smith's *She Stoops to Conquer* (Covent Garden 1864). He was one of the few composers to make a point of treating such subjects—perhaps because his whole approach to opera was more in direct descent from the ballad opera of the eighteenth century. The trio between Squire Hardcastle, his niece Constance, and Tony Lumkin, from Act I (ex. 14.2), may serve to illustrate the nature of his talent and the degree of his skill in presenting simple dramatic action in terms of music, often with striking economy of means. The libretto, surprisingly by Fitzball, seems to have profited from Goldsmith's eighteenth-century reason-ableness: the doggerel is not too painful, and the cliché ('Lost! sad surprise!') not too obtrusive.

Loder's talent was much more full-blooded. Echoes of Weber, Bel-lini, Donizetti, Verdi, and even Beethoven and Chopin, pervade his work—though this is not to say that he has no personality of his own to express. His two finest operas, *The Night Dancers* (1846) and *Raymond and Agnes* (1855), have a melodic, harmonic, and orchestral distinction that

Ex. 14.2   George A. Macfarren, *She Stoops to Conquer* (1864): trio, Give me, if you please, my jewels'
(Allegretto)

have them, un - cle, pray. They may be lost for aught I know. Lost! I

fear it. Sad sur-prise. That he has lost them I'll bear wit-ness, I saw them

sto-len with my own eyes.

(*K*: Cramer, Weber, [1864])

is rare for the period. And in these two works his music is always a positive aid to the drama—even in *The Night Dancers*, where the claims of the 'saleable ballad' clearly take their toll. An example of his musico-dramatic skill can be seen in the Quintet from the sleep-walking scene in the finale of Act II of *Raymond and Agnes* (ex. 14.3). Modelled perhaps on the quartet 'Mir ist so wunderbar' from *Fidelio*, it is not so very far removed, either in quality or dramatic effectiveness, from that masterpiece.

Ex. 14.3 Edward J. Loder, *Raymond and Agnes* (1855): quintet, 'Lost, and in a dream', from Act II finale

(**Andante**)

325

eyes on phan - toms gleam, He's

lost and in a dream, His eyes on

eyes on phan - toms gleam, He's

lost and in a dream, His eyes on

on me gleam, Ah me! that look so

(*S*: Washington, Library of Congress, MS ML96. L59R3; *K*: Jeffreys, 1859)

327

A similarly wide range of awareness informs Benedict's style, which, though never as powerful as Loder's, shares in something of its resourcefulness. Ironically it was to him that the honour of writing the first really convincing 'Irish' opera fell. *The Lily of Killarney* (1862), based on Dion Boucicault's famous play *The Colleen Bawn* (1859), has moments of melodic Irishness (ex. 14.4) that might have been more readily expected of the two native Irishmen in our group of romantic opera composers.

Ex. 14.4 Julius Benedict, *The Lily of Killarney* (1862): air, 'It is a charming girl I love' (**Allegretto**)

It   is   a charm-ing girl I love, She comes from Ga-ry   o-wen;
She's   gent-ler than the turt-le dove, Her hair is brown and flow-ing!   Her

eye is of the   soft-est blue, Her breath as sweet   as   morn-ing dew, Her *tread** is light-er

than the fawn And   och', she's call'd the   Col-leen Bawn. Bo-ther - a - tion,   bo-ther-

- a - tion, Her like-ness I   ne-ver shall   see;   There is   but   one Col-leen Bawn, And

she   does not   love   me!

* 'Breath' in original
(*K*: Boosey, [1862])

The great strengths of the finest English romantic operas are to be found in their unfailing tunefulness and unabashed vitality. Though never approaching the emotional intensity and psychological insight of the major continental composers of the period, such works as Balfe's *Falstaff*, Loder's *Raymond and Agnes*, Macfarren's *She Stoops to Conquer*, and Wallace's *The Amber Witch* have positive virtues which suggest that under better conditions the British composer of the mid-nineteenth century might have produced work of genuine distinction. Even as it is, what they wrote deserves to be remembered in its own right and not merely as a source of parody or an object of nostalgia. If the operas of certain minor continental masters are thought worthy of the occasional serious revival, there is no reason why their English counterparts should not be honoured to the same degree.

Chapter 15

OPERA: 1865–1914

NIGEL BURTON

Sullivan: The Savoy Operas

One evening in November 1866 (the exact date will probably never be known), the dramatist F. C. Burnand (1836–1917) gave a supper party at his home. Burnand was a contributor to *Punch* and the author of several burlesques (an art form which usually implied the parody of French originals), and on this occasion his guests were entertained to an operatic version of *Box and Cox*, a farce by John Maddison Morton (1811–91), which had been rechristened *Cox and Box* and set to music by Arthur Sullivan (1842–1900).

From this apparently casual and insignificant event sprang a series of works unique in the history of the British theatre. The story of the Gilbert and Sullivan partnership has been told often enough elsewhere to obviate the necessity of repeating it here, but it is strange that nearly all Sullivan's critics and biographers* should have treated his operettas as one of two bisected halves of his creative output. The true appreciation of any great composer's music demands a knowledge of all its facets, and Sullivan is no exception: if the operettas are set within the conspectus of his entire art, their significance is automatically enhanced.

Parody was deeply rooted in the Victorian theatre, musically as well as dramatically. Sullivan's operatic career divides itself fairly sharply into three main periods, and the works of the first of these, up to and including *Patience* (1881), are dominated by pastiche, amusing lampoonery, and conscious impersonation. Often the extent to which these devices are employed slightly compromises the integrity of the results, but in each case it must be asserted that the ends justified the means. After all, Sullivan went on to create a tradition single-handed, and a composer can only forge a personal idiom by basing it, in the first instance, upon the music he already knows. In this sense it might be

*To his credit, Young is an exception: see Young s, especially p. 265.

said that Sullivan knew too much music, for his style was eclectic from
the beginning and remained so to the end. Operatically speaking, his
lingua franca had been formed by his work with Costa as organist at
Covent Garden, and it was natural for him to think in terms of the
accepted Italian classics of the day.

Parody, then, was a convenient crutch to him at the outset, though as
his self-confidence increased he relied on it less and less. But the
manner of its employment immediately lifted his operatic works on to a
plane high above the level of everday Victorian theatre music, and for
two reasons: he was a genius, and he had been impeccably trained.
Throughout his life, the continual process of subconscious refinement
of his talents was complemented by a gradual reconciling of the antithetical elements within his personality, which was extraordinarily
complex. Accordingly, it is wrong to dismiss the works of his last years
as neutral; rather, they should be seen as his most integrated accomplishments, despite their obvious shortcomings.

It must be admitted, however, that these processes would not have
advanced as far as they did had it not been for W. S. Gilbert
(1836–1911). There is little doubt that of the two men Sullivan possessed the greater artistic gifts, but Gilbert the stronger artistic determination. The librettist was the masculine dominant partner, the composer
the feminine submissive one (he needed an external source of strength
to fertilize his creative potential). Gilbert's talent was above all else
distinct: whereas Burnand's topsy-turvy wit was modelled on the fantastic style of Lear, Gilbert had the insight to perceive that such
humour, paradoxically, could only reach its *ne plus ultra* of absurdity if it
was subjected to the discipline of rigorous and consistent logic.

The finest work of the first period was unquestionably *H.M.S. Pinafore*. *Trial by Jury* (New Royalty 1875), written as a curtain-raiser to
Offenbach's *La Périchole*, established Sullivan as a musical humorist of
genius: the Judge's song was its most prophetic number (minimum
means achieving maximum effect). There followed *The Sorcerer* (Opera
Comique [London] 1877), an enjoyable but not wholly successful piece
in which each partner gained strength from the other, though they had
recourse to their respective pasts: Gilbert took the plot from one of his
short stories, and Sullivan wrote many numbers (especially the soprano and tenor solos) in his drawing-room ballad idiom. But in retrospect it is now clear that these early operettas all led to *H.M.S. Pinafore*
(Opera Comique 1878)—a crucial work, for the partnership had, in
fact, reached a crossroads: either it produced a major success, or it
perished. The mania *Pinafore* induced was entirely warranted, for just
as Wagner would have been assured a place in history had he died in

1849, leaving *Lohengrin* as his final legacy, so would *Pinafore* have retained its popularity and its stature if Sullivan had written no more operettas after 1878.

This is more than can be said for *The Pirates of Penzance* (Royal Bijou, Paignton 1879). Gilbert's libretto was workmanlike and reliable, even though it failed to recapture the champagne sparkle of its predecessor (one biographer aptly dubbed it '*H.M.S. Pinafore* transferred to dry land').[1] But Sullivan for once allowed parody to run riot—Schubert, Mendelssohn, Verdi, Gounod, Bizet, all were guyed. The best music in *Pirates* (as so often in these works) is found in the second act, most notably in the policemen's choruses, the Sergeant's song 'When a felon's not engaged in his employment', and the exquisite duet for Frederic and Mabel 'Ah, leave me not to pine'. As a whole, however, this piece contains more of the orange peel and sawdust of early Verdi than any of the other operatic scores, which may explain why it is often an initial favourite for aspiring amateur societies wishing to cut their teeth. *Patience* (Opera Comique 1881) is an essentially transitional operetta, and the only one of the series in which the librettist's brilliance overpowered the composer. Sullivan here was far more his own master than he had been in *Pirates*, but still too complacently so (perhaps subconsciously he sensed that the paramount satirical element gave the music little real chance). His main success was the vivid musical contrast between the collective depictions of male soldiers and female aesthetes.

Even so, the gulf which separates *Patience* from its successor is a wide one, and it is surprising that it has been so little remarked upon. With *Iolanthe* (Savoy 1882) the Savoy operas came of age. Only Gilbert could have conceived the idea of bringing Fairyland to Westminster, and Sullivan responded spontaneously to this fascinating libretto—now emphasizing its avuncular humanity, now blunting the sharper points of its satire—to produce a nearly perfect work. A new note of wistfulness is present: it was to characterize his style from this time on, though it is particularly apparent in the 'second period' works, of which *The Gondoliers* was the last. This vein in his music is always disturbingly eloquent of his personal loneliness, and it may not be an exaggeration to say that it owed its inception to the death of his mother in May, 1882: he started work on *Iolanthe* only three days after that event.[2] The ballad 'He loves' fully reveals this deeper plangency as its second verse rises to a climax of passionate entreaty.

The tendency towards introspection is furthered by *Princess Ida* (Savoy 1884). Too much emphasis has been placed upon this work's reflection of Gilbert's attitude to women, for his views were at least as enlightened as those of his contemporaries.³ But because its basis was so topical, *Ida* has dated, whereas the rest of the series (with the exception of *Utopia Limited* likewise) has not. The pity is that this is one of Sullivan's best scores; indeed from a purely musical point of view it may be accounted his second finest achievement. The second act is an outpouring of undiluted lyrical beauty that has no parallel within the bounds of British opera.

The Mikado (Savoy 1885) and *The Gondoliers* (Savoy 1889) can legitimately be considered together, for they are both the aesthetic heirs of *Pinafore*: their most pronounced element is the spirit of comedy. It is interesting that the more purely comic a libretto was, the more Sullivan's music veered towards eighteenth-century classicism (this was true of many nineteenth-century light opera composers, who in this respect were probably more influenced by Rossini than they realized). *The Mikado* will always be Sullivan's most popular work, and rightly so, but it is not his best. His career reached its apogee in *The Yeomen of the Guard*, for which *Ruddigore* (Savoy 1887) can in many ways be regarded as a preliminary sketch.

Ruddigore's artistic value is still underrated. Cohesive performances of this burlesque of a burlesque are rare, since their essential ingredients are painstaking care and subtlety. Its one real flaw is its ending: Gilbert's usual ploy of resorting to a sudden piece of devastating logic to effect an instant *dénouement* always involved an element of risk. And the fact that he regarded Sullivan's ghost music as too elaborate was potentially serious. It indicated that the emotional and temperamental disparity between the two men was widening with the passage of time.

It was in their one unique work that they both successfully reconciled the sentimental and satirical strains within their respective characters (the fact that Gilbert's serious and comic styles were more mutually antagonistic than Sullivan's has not been recognized sufficiently). The greatness of *The Yeomen of the Guard* (Savoy 1888) lies in its profound humanity: Point was the finest of all Gilbert's creations, and Sullivan never wrote more touching music than that which depicts the terrible fatality of the jester's dilemma (ex. 15.1).

The richness of the texture of *Yeomen*, its prevalent sense of inner warmth, could not have been achieved had Sullivan been exclusively a light-opera composer. Like Bishop and Macfarren before him, although he did not often depict single characters convincingly, he managed collective groupings and situations superbly. But the experience by which he had perfected these techniques had been gained in theatrical work of a very different nature from that which has so far been considered.

Ex. 15.1 Arthur S. Sullivan, *The Yeomen of the Guard* (1888): quartet, 'When a wooer goes a-wooing'
(**Allegretto grazioso**)

(*K*: Chappell, 1902)

Sullivan: The Incidental Music and 'Ivanhoe'

By 1890 Sullivan had written five sets of incidental music, all to Shakespearean plays. The first, *The Tempest*, was composed during his student days at Leipzig and immediately established his national reputation when it was performed at the Crystal Palace on 5 April 1862. Inevitably, it relied heavily on German models: the slow section of the Introduction contained traces of Beethoven, though the main influences were Schumann and Mendelssohn. It was in his unconscious reworking of the latter's fairy idiom that Sullivan was most himself: Ariel's music (especially 'Come unto these yellow sands') illustrates this, and in fact the spirit-world of *A Midsummer Night's Dream* animates most of his fairy music, *Iolanthe* included. One of the most surprising features of *The Tempest* is its anticipation of Tchaikovsky; Young notes this regarding the Introduction,[4] but the effect is even more marked in the emotional climaxes of the prelude to Act V, which in the context of the period are quite astonishing.

334

The next three sets of incidental music belong to the 1870s, and are primarily instrumental in character. *The Merchant of Venice* (Prince's, Manchester 1871) is one of Sullivan's most balletic scores, and in this respect stands between his two fully-fledged ballets, the early *L'île enchantée* (Covent Garden 1864) and the late *Victoria and Merrie England* (Alhambra 1897). *The Merry Wives of Windsor* (Theatre Royal, Manchester 1874) is an excellent work, though it is a pity that it consists of only four numbers, all reserved until the play's fifth act. The slow introduction to 'Windsor Park' evokes an atmosphere of Weber by moonlight, and anticipates Rowena's soliloquy to the moon in Act I, scene 2 of *Ivanhoe*. The music to *Henry VIII* (Theatre Royal, Manchester 1877) is energetic and enjoyable, but the scoring of the 'Processional March' is unusually garish in its overuse of the cornets.*

Macbeth (Lyceum 1888) dates from the same year as *The Yeomen of the Guard* when his mind was turning to higher things. It is probably his most intellectually concentrated work, and the deep consideration he gave to the text resulted in music of uncharacteristic austerity. Young provides a sympathetic criticism of the overture,[5] which fuses all the important motives from the individual numbers into a brilliantly concise exposition of the drama's psychological issues (in this it recalls Liszt's *Hamlet*). Incidental music was to the nineteenth century what film music has been to the twentieth; Walton's Shakespearean scores are probably the most outstanding British examples of the latter genre, as Sullivan's *Tempest* and *Macbeth* were of the former (they both deserve to be revived under appropriately lavish and realistic theatrical conditions).

'Taking into account all Sullivan's incidental music to the plays, it is to be regretted that no-one thought of encouraging him to undertake a Shakespearean libretto', says Young,[6] and most students of the composer's 'serious' music would emphatically agree. Scott's *Ivanhoe*, the subject Sullivan eventually chose for his long-projected grand opera, was by no means so ideal as it might have appeared to be: many of its characters were lifeless (particularly the nominal hero and heroine), and the scope of its action could not be conveniently condensed to meet the practical limitations of the stage.

The circumstances surrounding the initial run of *Ivanhoe* (Royal English Opera House 1891) and the causes of its failure have been rehearsed elsewhere.[7] It certainly contains some of the best music Sullivan ever wrote, which is sufficient in itself to justify its existence.

*Sullivan was always careful to stipulate whether cornets or trumpets were required; he scored for the former throughout his operettas, and for the sake of balance it is time their usage was restored.

The partial truth of Shaw's adverse strictures must be allowed, but Gilbert's opinion—he simply said he was not bored—should not be forgotten (in fact it should be endorsed: Gilbert may not have been musical, but he did possess a very sound theatrical instinct). However, the work's structure (three acts, each divided into three scenes, making nine in all) undermines its unity: the first scene of the second act, for instance, is enlivened by the familiar 'Ho, jolly Jenkin', but is completely at odds stylistically with the two scenes which follow it. The score is strongest when at its most Wagnerian (as in Act I, scene 1), although it seldom advances far beyond the idiom of *Lohengrin*. One exceptional moment occurs in Act II, scene 3 when Ulrica informs Rebecca of the grim fate awaiting her at the hands of the Normans (ex. 15.2). The effect produced is startlingly chilling.

Sullivan succeeded precisely where Scott had, most notably in his characterizations of Rebecca and the Templar. But *Ivanhoe* cannot be accounted entirely satisfactory even though he wrote it, 'so to speak, with his lifeblood'.[8] Therein lay the trouble—he tried too hard. Throughout the work one senses the strain imposed by the composer's conscientious striving to elevate his syntax. 'Never before had he been such a creature of moods, never so highly-strung. So alive was his brain to the importance of the work he was doing that he became obsessed with nervous qualms.'[9] In one sense he achieved more than he knew, for the composition of *Ivanhoe* so radically affected his style that it was never quite the same again.

Sullivan: The Last Years

It is generally agreed that Sullivan's inspiration suffered a decline after *The Gondoliers*, and that the works of his last years are less immediately appealing than the rest of his compositions. Like many composers who reach a 'final period', however, his idiom had undergone internal and imperceptible transformation to emerge, ultimately, as an instrument of hypersensitive refinement. Probably it had lost more than it gained, but not to the extent implied by the condemnation of so much of the music concerned.

Utopia Limited (Savoy 1893) provides evidence of an increasingly aphoristic vocabulary. By far the most sophisticated product of Sullivan's partnership with Gilbert, this work is the supreme embodiment of late Victorian British life. The civilized urbanity of the drawing-room music says it all: 'Sunshine. Parasols. Toppers. Rich, elaborate dresses. The scrunch of metal-shod wheels on the long drive. . . .'[10]

Here Gilbert's satire is at its most pungent, so much so that it earned the appreciation of Shaw, who also, with shrewd critical insight, drew a neat comparison between Sullivan's orchestral accompaniments and Mozart's.[11] Mozart was fundamental to the classical side of Sullivan's musical personality, and his influence is seen in numbers such as the

Ex. 15.2   Sullivan, *Ivanhoe* (1891): scena, Act II, scene 3

once   as   proud   as   fair,   Was

sport   of   conqueror's   wan - ton   mood.

(*S:* Chappell, [1891])

King's song, 'First you're born', and 'Although of native maids the cream' for the two young princesses (there is no trace in the vocal score of the delicious violin *perpetuum mobile* which decorates this duet).

The harsh criticism continually meted out to *The Grand Duke* (Savoy 1896) is in one sense justified, for in it the author and composer each reverted spasmodically to their older comedy veins, and the work is consequently flawed by moments of surprising coarseness. But for all that it remains the best English light opera of the decade, after *Utopia Limited*; it comes across as a far stronger stage-piece than Stanford's *Shamus O'Brien* (1896), if only because its tunes are more memorable. None of the other operettas Sullivan wrote during this period has lasted. *Haddon Hall* (Savoy 1892) is saddled with an impossible libretto by Sydney Grundy, but merits a full recording on account of its considerable quantity of good music. Unfortunately, this is less true of *The Chieftain* (1894) (an unnecessary reworking of *The Contrabandista*), *The Beauty Stone* (1898), and *The Rose of Persia* (1899). This last work admittedly enjoyed an initial success due to its mild oriental atmosphere, but now seems faded. For sheer strength, the incidental music to *King Arthur* (1894) shows what might have been if Sullivan, when in his prime, had realized his lifelong ambition of composing a grand opera upon this subject.

His career remains a unique one in our nation's musical history. Nothing succeeds like success, and one cannot escape the impression that it is the extent of Sullivan's triumph which has for so long been resented by 'respectable' musical circles. The point is too often missed that his operettas, if performed sympathetically (a condition which obtains, alas, all too infrequently), are not only delightful and amusing but also profoundly moving, because they are imbued with a deep and enduring sense of humanity. This is their source of life, their vital force; it reaches out to reality by means of apparent absurdity, and it should remind us, if there was ever the need, that our most popular composer was also a truly great one.

Light Opera: Sullivan's Contemporaries

Although Sullivan created a tradition single-handed, he cannot be said to have founded a school. His imitators were legion, but none of them possessed a sufficiently strong musical personality to effect any lasting or cogent development of his work.

Of his operatic contemporaries, two stand out: Frederic Clay (1838–89) and Alfred Cellier (1844–91). Clay is best regarded as a talented amateur, even though he did abandon the Civil Service to pursue a musical career. His 'grand comic and spectacular opera' *Don Quixote* (1878) shows that he knew his limitations and usually had the sense to work within them. There is a good deal of Offenbach in this score: the infectious rhythm of 'With loosen'd rein and flowing mane'[12] can be traced to that source, as can the sentimental vein of 'Love is oft a sea of trouble' which recalls Paris's 'Judgment' song from *La belle Hélène*. Clay's stage works are very much period pieces. There is a solid 'earthy' quality about his idiom with hints of cathedral influence.

As a composer, Cellier had more potential than Clay, but probably less self-discipline. This can partly be accounted for by the phenomenal success of his comic opera *Dorothy* (Gaiety 1886). He deliberately aimed the music at the taste of the middle-class man in the street, which he gauged to a nicety. The result served its purpose brilliantly: it was less highbrow than Sullivan, and it burst upon the theatrical world like a rocket, only to disappear. In its myriad waltz tunes it resembled *The Sorcerer* fairly closely. Cellier acquitted himself rather better in *The Mountebanks* (Lyric 1892); the libretto, by Gilbert, was the famous 'lozenge' plot which Sullivan had so consistently refused to set[13] (quite unjustifiably, in the event). It certainly had an invigorating effect on Cellier, imparting its alert and pointed humour to his musical style. *The Mountebanks'* greatest drawback is one seldom encountered in comic opera: it suffers from exessive length, for Gilbert's welter of dramatic paradoxes resulted in twenty-seven individual numbers and 186 pages of vocal score.

Edward German (1862–1936) very nearly succeeded in developing the tradition Sullivan had established, and might have done so had he been lucky enough to find the equivalent of a Gilbert. His best known work, *Merrie England* (Savoy 1902), is hampered by Basil Hood's rather thin libretto, but many of the lyrics are excellent in themselves, and the piece as a whole is successful in so far as it aims at being little more than a glorified pageant. German's style was quite distinct, especially in its sense of modulation: he had a tendency to slide into the mediant and submediant majors which was something of a mannerism (numbers such as 'That ev'ry Jack should have a Jill', 'The Big Brass Band', and 'When Cupid first this old world trod' can all be cited as evidence). Apart from this, his music is English to the core, all the more so because there is nothing self-consciously nationalistic about it: the lovely 6/8 dance in the introduction, the big tune in the first act finale, the glowing patriotism of 'The Yeomen of England'—these things strike a genuine note. The portrayal of Jill-All-Alone (whose character is a mixture of Iolanthe and Mad Margaret) greatly extends the work's emotional dimensions; her rhetorical dialogue with her cat in the opening number of Act II, when she is under sentence of death, is haunting and poignant (ex. 15.3).

Ex. 15.3   Edward German, *Merrie England* (1902): Act II, opening chorus (*k*, p.170)

(*K:* Chappell, [1888])

A Princess of Kensington (1903), in which German again collaborated with Hood, was a failure for the same reason that *The Emerald Isle** (1901) had been: in the latter Hood had aped Gilbert's methods in an attempt to coax the old magic out of Sullivan, and in the former he likewise copied the devices he himself had originated in *Merrie England*. This may explain why German turned to new partners for his next comic opera, *Tom Jones* (Prince's, Manchester 1907). As with Sullivan, time and practice had refined his style, and for sheer craftsmanship *Tom Jones* is his most impressive achievement: it captures the essence of

*Left unfinished by Sullivan, completed by German.

Fielding's sense of humour, and it breathes the languorous atmosphere of a Somerset summer. German always excelled in his writing for the soprano voice, and Sophia's solos are no exception: in 'Dream o'day Jill' (Act II), the placing of minor-key transitions in a major-key context gives rise to the music's artless simplicity, whilst, conversely, of all the postscripts to Marguerite's Jewel Song, the grandiose waltz 'For tonight' (Act III) is one of the most dazzling.

British Opera: The Old Tradition

As a nation the British have always tended to categorize their works of art as either edifying or flippant, and for that very reason those of the former variety have almost invariably proved less interesting and enduring than their more casual counterparts. Late-nineteenth-century British opera validates this assertion: there is surprisingly little cross-fertilization between its serious and comic schools (far less than on the Continent). Native composers responded to this dilemma by selecting their medium deliberately (often going against the grain of their talents in the process), and those who wished to have the best of both worlds did so by the expedient of taking each in turn. This explains why there was no genuine British equivalent of the Gounod-Massenet school, and it shows that Sullivan's unique success was due to the Gilbertian irony which forced him, quite against his artistic conscience, to compose works which directly reflected the spirit of his genius.

Other men were less fortunate: Frederic Cowen (1852–1935) is a case in point. His gifts, like Sullivan's, inclined towards light music, but he resisted nature more successfully than his greater contemporary. Cowen seems to have laboured under the delusion that he was a leader of the 'renaissance'—a role for which he could scarcely have been more ill-equipped (Howes was right when he defined Cowen's music as 'suburban').[14] Of his three significant mature operas, *Thorgrim* (Drury Lane 1890) is the most representative. Its appalling libretto (by Joseph Bennett, music critic of *The Daily Telegraph*) immediately raises the question of the extent to which music alone can overcome dramatic improbability, if not incompetence. An inherent theatrical instinct is, of course, a *sine qua non* for all would-be opera composers, and miracles can be accomplished in this respect *providing* the libretto contains at least one overriding or powerful idea, no matter how commonplace. Far too many British librettists of the period failed because, in trying to found a national school where none had previously existed, they sought refuge in complexity and ignored the rudimentary facts of operatic life. One need only compare their efforts with the librettos of any established continental master (Verdi and Massenet are good examples) for this unhappy truth to become apparent.

The legacy of Richard Wagner was a further problem facing all late-nineteenth-century operatic composers. It was not until 1870 that the first production of a Wagner opera ('The Flying Dutchman') took place in Britain, and even then it had to be translated into Italian as *L'Olandese dannato* (Drury Lane 1870); *Tannhäuser* and *Lohengrin* soon followed, also in Italian, at Covent Garden. The later music-dramas had to wait until 1882, when the Bayreuth company on tour gave a Ring cycle at Her Majesty's* and several were also produced at Drury Lane.[15] Many British composers, however, had seen Wagner productions in Germany and were thus ahead of their public and critics: some were totally under Wagner's spell.

Of those considered here only one, Delius, possessed a personal idiom strong enough to avoid being engulfed, and his operas, for all their beauty and originality, constituted a stylistic backwater. The rest reacted in different ways: some, like Hamish MacCunn and Ethel Smyth, accepted Wagnerian influence as an inevitability, and then exploited its varying features as most befitted their respective musical personalities. Others, who found it less psychologically congenial, blew hot and cold and usually arrived at an uneasy compromise. *Thorgrim* shows that Cowen was one of these. He failed to make up his mind whether to write a set-number opera or to attempt a quasi-Wagnerian synthesis. As a penalty for his evasion he was condemned to write in a musical no-man's land. *Thorgrim* is neither a romantic, nor a lyric, nor a grand opera; there are elements of all three about it, but they are at war with each other. To be fair to Cowen, many of the *ersatz* Wagnerisms were forced on him by Bennett, who intended the hero to justify himself as a second Siegfried, glorying in the magnificence of his will (instead he emerges as little more than an unreasonable thug). Space does not permit itemization of the many points in the score which burlesque specific moments in 'The Flying Dutchman,' *Tristan*, and *Götterdämmerung*; rather, two important conclusions should be drawn: first, that *Thorgrim* is not a *bad* work but a negative, colourless, and insipid one; and second, that in harmonic terms (like *Ivanhoe*) it does not advance beyond the Wagner of 1848. In both these observations it typifies its generation: British music was lagging behind the Continent in this field

*This event was the fatal blow to the long 'Italian tyranny' over grand opera in London. In 1892 the word 'Italian' was dropped from the name of the Royal Opera House, Covent Garden; Her Majesty's had closed in 1891 (Scholes MM, 244–5).

as in most others, and consequently many operas of this period will not bear contemporary revival, despite their undeniable virtues.

It would be totally unjust, however, to ignore the fact that Cowen did produce one opera worthy of resurrection. This was *Pauline* (Lyceum 1876), written at the age of twenty-four, before he was overtaken by delusions of grandeur. Although British opera had become dependent upon Teutonic models by the 1890s, the process had been gradual; during the 60s and 70s composers were still able to draw upon the authentic native tradition of Balfe and Wallace. Cowen did so in *Pauline* to his decided advantage. He was on strong ground here, and was ill-advised to leave it. This is an old-fashioned work, soundly based on a Bulwer Lytton play of unexceptionable moral precepts (love overcomes pride, and nobility the weakness of temptation), and it amply demonstrates the maxim that opera is of life, but larger than it:

BEAUSANT (*to the newly-wedded and distraught heroine*):
I'll taste those lips, ere I depart;
Resistance is in vain!

PAULINE: Fierce indignation fills my heart!
Base coward, wretch, refrain!

BEAUSANT: I shall not be by insult awed—

PAULINE: Help! Claude!

BEAUSANT: No help is near!

PAULINE: O for a husband's arm! Claude! Claude!

CLAUDE (*rushes on and hurls Beausant to end of the room*):
Pauline! thy Claude is here!

Thanks to the healthy influence of Gounod and Ambroise Thomas, Cowen's music is more sophisticated than the text implies. In later works his style lapsed into triteness (immediate repetition of initial melodic phrases was its trademark), but there is a youthful freshness about *Pauline* which lifts the piece out of the mire and touches it with distinction. There is more: a credible heroine, whose love for her husband really does shine through her music, making her archetypal of Victorian womanhood (ex. 15.4). It would be interesting to hear this sentimental and unproblematic opera once again. Its requirements for success are minimal: pretty sets, exquisite (but not necessarily expensive) costumes, and—imperatively—a cast which believes in its music.

The sweetness of French lyrical influences is so pronounced in the

Ex. 15.4 Frederic Cowen, *Pauline* (1876): from Act IV finale (*K*, p. 243)

(*K*: Boosey, [1877])

stage works of Arthur Goring Thomas (1850–92) that he may be described as an eclectic Francophile. He had much in common with Cowen, and his opera *Esmeralda* (Drury Lane 1883) is an ambitious but satisfactory sequel to *Pauline*; its libretto is a bowdlerized version of Victor Hugo's *Notre-Dame de Paris*, complete with happy ending. The composer disregarded Wagnerian substance entirely, wisely confining himself to sparing applications of its technique (though at second hand from Gounod's workshop). The predominant stylistic model is Bizet's *Carmen* (the gypsy music is an obvious link), but there are several secondary influences: the French ballet element in Tchaikovsky (opening chorus, Act I; introduction, Act IV), Auber (Act I ensemble for Gringoire, Clopin and chorus) and Massenet (Phoebus's aria 'O vision entrancing'). Surprisingly, there is very little Offenbach in the work (though Thomas's comedy opera *The Golden Web* (1893) more than remedies this omission) and the only really German-orientated music is

345

given to Frollo, presumably because Caspar (*Freischütz*) and Pizarro (*Fidelio*) suggested themselves as suitable prototypes of villainy. Behind all this there lies the revolution wrought by Rossini in French opera, which guaranteed the vocalist's supremacy: for example, the harmonies of the second verse of Clopin's Act I song ('Come my lads') are varied purely in order to support an increased amount of vocal *fioriture*. The opera is entirely lacking in English credentials. Thomas overreached himself: the length and scale of his works were out of proportion to his jewel-like talent. This defect had marred *Esmeralda*, but it fatally flawed *Nadeshda* (Drury Lane 1885). Even so, *Nadeshda* is more polished than *Esmeralda*; its equable style neither rises as high, nor falls as far. It has the merit of a book by Julian Sturgis, who was unquestionably the finest serious librettist of the late Victorian period, no matter how fusty his efforts might now appear. Thomas was not slow to take advantage of the many opportunities for pictorial opulence the opera's Russian setting offered, and if the indications in the vocal score are an accurate guide, his orchestration was both idiomatic and effective. In short, his contribution to British opera was conservative but not undistinguished, and as the beautiful Act III duet for Voldemar and Nadeshda proves, the strength of his potential charm still lies in his best music's essential endearment.

Whatever his demerits, Thomas was usually sure of his chosen ground, but with Alexander Mackenzie (1847–1935) this was not the case. Because his grammar and techniques were old-fashioned his place is in the nineteenth century, rather than in the emerging twentieth; only in his consistently scholastic attitude did he predict the future. The prelude to *Colomba* (Drury Lane 1883), Mackenzie's *magnum opus*, instantly illustrates this: it is firmly bound by its relationship to the prelude of Gounod's *Faust*. Of its two sections, the first, in F minor, is full of dark, crawling chromaticism; the second, in F major, presents a tune shaped and scored in a manner markedly similar to 'Avant de quitter ces lieux'. In its way this prelude is coherent and impressive, though it is significantly more pedantic than its prototype. The opening *parlando* chorus of Act I, 'Siori, buy', is a clever Italian pastiche, heavily indebted to Rossini's *buffo* writing; but it overstays its welcome, because Mackenzie obviously felt that the 'correct' thing to do was to construct a large-scale ternary movement. He made the mistake of setting nearly all the words in the exposition, however, and by the time *two* balancing sections were added, the whole structure had become unwieldy. Immediately this chorus ends, the sailors enter singing 'Heave ho!' to a motive reminiscent of Siegfried's forging song. So many styles have now appeared, all in the space of fifteen pages, that one is tempted to ask the real Alexander Mackenzie to stand up. When he eventually does so, it is clear that his kernel had been formed by his Teutonic training. One aria ('Flowers that bloom, blossoms that wither') shows how strong the influence of Joachim Raff was during the mid-to-late nineteenth century. Nor was his influence baleful, for his style was plastic enough to serve as a starting point from which other composers could step out in their own directions. The lesson Mackenzie learned from Raff was that of developing motives symphonically, though he mistakenly believed that melodies could be made into motives, a common post-Wagnerian blunder. He mitigated this somewhat in his next opera *The Troubadour* (1886), based on a mediaeval legend which engendered a mixture of 'back to the greenwood' and Weber (the work is permeated by the chivalric atmosphere of *Euryanthe*). When Mackenzie turned his hand to comedy in *His Majesty, or The Court of Vignola* (1897) he proved how unsuited he was to the genre. At the end of his career he produced *The Eve of St. John* (1923), quite a remarkable little piece, in which the standards set by Ethel Smyth helped him to tighten up his style. But in glimpsing so far into the future he was untrue to himself; the quartet 'Let the past be dead'[21] from *Colomba* finds him at his best, writing a real Victorian partsong, and of high quality. This music looks back, for the last time, through Balfe and Wallace to Bishop; it was the final link in a long chain from which the succeeding generation severed itself.

The Transition

Although the 'renaissance' which is said to have taken place in British music during the late nineteenth century affected the choral tradition more radically than any other, its gravitational pull dragged opera along in its train. The sum of its effects only partially weakened continental influences, but such adolescence was vital to the emergence of a new British operatic school. At any rate, works written exclusively along foreign lines enjoyed diminishing chances of success, let alone survival. The operas of Frederick Corder (1852–1932), of which *Nordisa* (1886), his '17th work', is the foremost, bathe the Wagnerian idiom in syrup before processing it in the most erratic manner of Berlioz and diluting the result down to trivial negativity with an applied anglicization. *Petruccio* (1895) by Alick Maclean (1872–1936) is better: it is one of the very few genuine English *verismo* operas, and follows faithfully in the footsteps of *Cavalleria rusticana*.*

*Grove (5th edn., V, p. 480) says it is 'after *Taming of the Shrew*', but this is not so: it merely contains a 'play within a play'.

Nearly all major upheavals in stage music have been marked by a desire to return to ancient Greek ideals, and the incidental music to the nineteenth-century revivals of Greek plays at Oxford and Cambridge by Macfarren, Parry, and Stanford merits attention. Macfarren's single effort was the best of all: his music for Sophocles' *Ajax* (1882) is in his usual direct and vigorous style. Its blood-and-thunder rhetoric is convincing, especially in the prelude, which depicts 'The Phrenzy of Aias'. Parry's finest Greek score was for *The Birds* of Aristophanes (1883); its best music is to be found in the three last numbers: the Introduction to Act III, the Entr'acte, and the well-known Bridal March and Chorus, the voice parts of which are entirely superfluous. His most ingenious achievement, however, is in *The Frogs* (1892), where his setting of the Frogs' 'Brekekekex koax koax' (as they cry out and clamour against Dionysus) sticks in the mind by virtue of being given in canon 4 in 1 at the unison.

Stanford's setting of Aeschylus' *Eumenides* (1885) contrasts sharply with Parry's approach: of the two men his theatrical sense was definitely the more highly developed. Nevertheless, his operas lacked staying power. There is just cause for disappointment over their failure, for although Stanford was not a natural stage composer he possessed sufficient skill to have endowed the repertory with at least one work of permanence. That he did not do so was due to various adverse factors, of which bad luck certainly was one. But there was more to it than that: throughout his career he displayed the ability to size up librettos and dramatic situations intellectually but not emotionally, and this proved to be his Achilles' heel. Given the high quality of his songs, his best chance lay in lyrical set-number operas, and his regrettable avoidance of this medium resulted from a lack of rigorous self-analysis. Like most of his contemporaries, he found the operatic road was thick with thorns, yet although he lacked the strength to beat them down he refused to cut them away one by one. He reacted impetuously, as if to say 'England is a land without opera; it is *my* mission to write one'.

In the event he wrote eleven, of which seven were published and performed. The first, *The Veiled Prophet of Khorassan* (composed in 1877 and performed at the Court Theatre, Hanover, in 1881) is an exposition of his strengths and weaknesses. The style is 'German-common-denominator': its mentors are Schumann and Brahms, with Beethoven and Schubert in the second line (it is not Wagnerian). Because the 'renaissance' composers placed less emphasis on the overtly pictorial than their high-Victorian forbears, there are fewer attempts at local colour than might be expected. Zelika's aria 'By the hill-embosomed lake' is a beautiful mood piece, however; behind its oriental atmosphere lie Schubert and Bizet, and throughout the opera Stanford adopts a pre-1848 motto-theme technique as opposed to regular leitmotifs (ex. 15.5: the accompaniment figure given here is always associated with the heroine).

Fuller Maitland spoke (unfortunately quite erroneously) of the 'strong evidence of Meyerbeer's influence'[16] in this work. Certainly it displayed high hopes of a promise never to be fulfilled. *Savonarola* (1884) was Stanford's least effective opera, for he allowed the vocabulary of *The Veiled Prophet* to run over dramatically weaker territory. He pulled himself together somewhat in *The Canterbury Pilgrims* (1884) which did at least sound as though an Englishman had written it. By means of a continual westward geographical progress he eventually arrived at his homeland in his most successful stage work, *Shamus O'Brien* (Opera Comique 1896). This, his only number opera with dialogue, was good, but not quite good enough. The crux of the matter was that its charm was too fragile; the appeal of Kitty's 'Where is the man that is coming to marry me?' is precisely the same as that of 'The Fairy Lough', which, whilst it makes a wonderfully individual art-song, cannot support a whole opera. To its detriment, the piece remains politically topical, and its best number, Mike's 'Ochone, when I used to be young' would appear to have been an afterthought.[17] The constant repetition of the refrain 'Oh boys, listen to Shamus' is maddening, and the moment in Act II when Nora raises Little Paudeen for Shamus to kiss is utterly bathetic. All this would be irrelevant if the work contained just one really memorable tune; but if the audience does come away from a performance singing anything, it is most likely to be the English folk-song, 'The Glory of the West'.

Stanford was unlucky that *Much Ado About Nothing* (Covent Garden 1901) was never given a real chance to establish itself. It contains some of his best operatic music, and Julian Sturgis's adaptation of Shakespeare was masterly. Little need be said of *The Critic, or An Opera Rehearsed* (1915), which is a poor man's *Ariadne auf Naxos*. If any one of these works deserves revival it is *The Travelling Companion* (1919). This was Stanford's finest operatic achievement, though its stature was largely due to the unique brilliance of the story, adapted by Henry Newbolt from Hans Andersen. This is not to decry the composer, whose music was never bad, only lacking in a dramatic force and power which the libretto here provided; it did so, moreover, by its reliance on twentieth-century anti-romantic criteria. For the creation of a truly British school of opera could not and did not occur until the ebb of the romantic tide, and it is to the works which enhanced that process that we must now attend.

Ex. 15.5 Charles V. Stanford, *The Veiled Prophet of Khorassan* (1877): aria, 'By the hill-embosomed lake'

(Adagio espressivo)

(*K*: Boosey, [1881])

The New Tradition

The first that did so was *Jeanie Deans* (Edinburgh 1894) by Hamish MacCunn (1868–1916), unquestionably the finest serious opera of the late Victorian period. The subject matter was ideally suited to Mac-Cunn's personal style, which is by no means easy to define, because as soon as one formulates generalizations concerning it, one can turn a page and find grounds for demolishing them. But he belonged to the new tradition by virtue of possessing a refreshingly personal idiom, in which a streak of Scottish nationalism was prominent. There is visible evidence here that the spadework of previous generations had at last succeeded in laying the foundations upon which a young composer could base himself, for the Teutonic influences in MacCunn are seen to be derived at second or third hand. Joseph Bennett's libretto was much better than usual; it was an adaptation of Scott's *The Heart of Midlothian*, the narrative strength of which somehow managed to percolate to its surface. It inspired MacCunn to write music which was basically simple, but extremely self-assured. The work's most refreshing aspects are that it does not constantly change style in the manner of a butterfly trying to make up its mind which flower to settle on, and that it entertains no wretched preconceived notions about what constitutes 'the grand style'.

MacCunn displayed considerable powers of musical characterization, especially of Dumbiedykes and Jeanie herself; her entrance[18] is accompanied by a beautiful oboe solo which anticipates the 'faery' music of Bax and Boughton. The harmonic language of the Constable's solo (ex. 15.6) looks back to *Siegfried* and forward to Holst. Dean's lament is very well executed; in both its key (B minor) and its slow insistent chords it anticipates Ellen's 'embroidery' aria from *Peter Grimes*. Act II, scene 2, set in the common room of the Tolbooth prison, contains two superb songs for Effie, Jeanie's sister. The second, a lullaby, is so daring in its harmony that it seems to foreshadow Prokofiev; example 15.7 shows the climax of the first, in which the imprisoned woman wistfully looks back to her childhood.

From the musico-dramatic point of view the strongest part of the opera is Act III, scene 2, in which Jeanie visits Dumbiedykes in order to solicit financial assistance for her (successful) attempt to plead with Queen Caroline for Effie's life. Anyone who has experienced the bracing crispness of a Scottish winter morn will be aware how perfectly MacCunn has captured its sensations. Dumbiedykes, not unreasonably, expresses amazement at Jeanie's mission; then, seeing that she is in earnest, begs her to marry him: 'Be Lady Dumbiedykes today!

351

Ex. 15.6 Hamish MacCunn, *Jeanie Deans* (1894): from Act I (*K*, p. 41)

(Allegro moderato)

FIRST CONSTABLE

(*K*: Matthias & Strickland, 1894)

Tomorrow travel as a lady should', and the measured restraint of the music shows how deeply he loves her. Her refusal (as so often, marked 'simply') disappoints not only him, but the audience, because (in the opera at least) the pair are so obviously well matched. The fact that it cannot be introduces a prophetic touch of twentieth-century realism, and the final orchestral ·outburst is a magnificent fusion of Dumbiedykes's conflicting emotions: it depicts a mixture of love, admiration, and fervent hope for her success, all tinged with sadness and regret, as well as the frustration that his great wealth and position are insufficient to gain him his heart's desire.

MacCunn's ability to conceive operatic scenes as single entities found even greater exposition in his other opera *Diarmid* (Covent Garden 1897). Although this vast Celtic poem would now be totally impracticable on stage, it is a staggering piece of work for a British composer of only twenty-nine writing in 1897. It shows that MacCunn was completely aware of all that was going on around him: the influence of Richard Strauss is considerable, and in several places the score anticipates Debussy's *Pelléas et Mélisande*.

The weaknesses which mar *Diarmid* are also reflected in the operas of Frederick Delius (1862–1934). The neglect and obscurity into which these works have fallen are partly attributable to Delius's attitude to the medium. 'I don't believe in realism in opera', he said in 1896, and later added: 'Realism on the stage is nonsense, and all the scenery necessary is an impressionistic painted curtain at the back, with the fewest accessories possible.'[19] Yet his scores abound with stage instruc-

Ex. 15.7 *Jeanie Deans:* Act II, song, 'Oh! would that I again could see'

(*K*: Matthias & Strickland, 1894)

353

tions of the most detailed and specific kind. This does not mean that they are to be interpreted literally; they are intended to act as an aid in helping to suggest the mood-picture the composer had in mind. But because most of the music, despite its individuality, cannot avoid Wagnerian reminiscences (especially of *Tristan*), its emotional and intellectual matrices are antithetical. At the change between scenes 1 and 2 of the second act of *Irmelin* (composed 1890–2), for instance, the score indicates:

The stage becomes darker and darker . . . It has now become quite dark. Nils gradually disappears in the gloom . . . Thunder is heard, heavy clouds obscure the stage . . . Through the flashes of lightning the castle of Rolf is discovered high up on an eminence, Nils also wearily trudging along driving his swine. The castle is lighted up inside . . .

Then, only one page later:

The scene changes to the banqueting hall of Rolf's castle.

Not only are these deliberately impossible directions derived from *Das Rheingold*: so is the substance of the music. The claim that Delius's operas were prophetic of future sparse twentieth-century developments is true, but they are irretrievably rooted in the nineteenth century for all that, and situations like this where the music cannot escape from its Wagnerian pedigree and cries out for realistic staging present would-be producers with a terrible dichotomy. How then to rescue these works? Perhaps in the cases of *Irmelin* and *Fennimore and Gerda* (where the problems are most acute) television production might well be the most satisfactory answer.

About the need for their rescue there should be little disagreement, though in one sense criticism of Delius is almost pointless, since his style is so highly personal that it forces the listener to choose between loving or loathing it. No more and no less than the rest of his music, his operas vindicate themselves by their unashamed appeal to man's love of beauty. His stage masterpiece is his 'music drama in six tableaux', *A Village Romeo and Juliet*, composed in 1900–1 and performed in Berlin in 1907. Its pathos is well-nigh unbearable. In this it is anticipated by *Irmelin*, his first opera and in some ways his most engaging. All the essential Delian qualities are there: the subconscious alignment of harmony and colour; limited power of characterization, since the only living characters are those which are symbolic; the use of dream sequences (in a manner not unlike Ken Russell's); a fusion of Wagnerian, Debussian, and Scandinavian influences; rudimentary employment of the leitmotif principle; and, as the ultimate source of it all,

Nature. This music acts like a narcotic. One longs for it never to end, yet the yearning is never satiated, no matter how much the senses are saturated (ex. 15.8).

Ex. 15.8   Frederick Delius, *Irmelin* (1890–2): Act III, introduction

(*K:* Hawkes, 1953)

The fundamental flaw in Delius's operas is their lack of drama, whereas the stage works of Ethel Smyth (1858–1944) are characterized by their unremitting dramatic force. Smyth's finest work was *The Wreckers*, composed in 1903–4 and performed at Leipzig in 1906 (as *Strandrecht*). It takes as its subject the evil inherent in religious fanaticism, and treats it with compelling power and clarity. The syntax of her style is derived largely from Brahms, though it is far more taut and steely than that source might imply: its predominant quality is its masculinity (an evaluation which might have displeased its author). Aesthetically and structurally the work is simultaneously indebted to Wagner and prophetic of Britten, and it can be regarded as a halfway stage between *Tristan* and *Peter Grimes*. It is linked to the former principally by its Cornish setting and reprise of the *Liebestod* idea, and to the latter by its implication that the morality of 'the village' is pitiless. The presence of the sea is inescapable in all three works, and is nowhere used to better effect than in the final scene of *The Wreckers*, where Smyth depicts it rising ever higher and higher, and finally bursting into the cave where the doomed Mark and Thirza sing their last rapturous duet. To give the lovers the only overtly lyrical music in the opera was a stroke of genius, for it makes a perfect foil to the bigotry of all the other characters. This contrast, on which the drama rests, is brilliantly captured at the moment in Act I where the entire village sings a fierce hymn inside the chapel off stage whilst Thirza denounces their zealotry to the audience in ferocious terms (ex. 15.9).

There is a further link with *Tristan* in the lighting of the beacon at the start of Act II, and with *Grimes* in the mounting climaxes of the first act

Ex. 15.9   Ethel Smyth, *The Wreckers* (1903–4): from Act I (*K*, p. 82)

(*S:* London, British Library, MS Add. 459 39–41; *K:* Universal (Vienna & New York), 1916.)
The hymn tune is the Lutheran Easter chorale, *Erschienen ist der herrliche Tag*.

finale. But the work of Smyth which carried British opera closest to its twentieth-century destiny was *The Boatswain's Mate* (Shaftesbury 1916). The libretto is by the composer after a story by W. W. Jacobs. From the very outset the character descriptions strike a note of the new realism: 'POLICEMAN: a country constable; blend of extreme density and self-importance, any age.' So also does the dialogue:

BENN (*to Mary Ann, sententiously*): No girl ought to speak disrespectful of her father.

MARY ANN: Decidedly such; but 'e don't 'appen to be my father; 'e's only my mother's second. Took 'im as a stop-gap, a neighbour said; 'Well,' says I, 'if that's a stop-gap give me an 'ole in the fence.'

The musical style, too, has changed appreciably; far more acidic and pungent than in *The Wreckers*, it frequently takes its cue from Ravel. To some extent this is explained by Smyth's decision to adopt a classical approach as being more suitable to comedy, but it also testifies to her awareness of contemporary continental developments. But it is the work's willingness to sacrifice the passing moment in the interest of the whole that brands it as modern. Greater emphasis is placed on musico-dramatic technique for its own sake, because the composer is not attempting to write a string of beautiful melodies or to clothe a poem in gorgeous sound, but rather to aim unerringly and insistently at dramatic veracity. The methods and aesthetics of the eighteenth century proved more adaptable to this purpose than those of the nineteenth. Part II of *The Boatswain's Mate* is written 'through' as symphonic music, whereas Part I follows standard comic-opera 'number and dialogue' procedure. The result is not unbalanced, however, for Smyth very sensibly used the dialogue to give the work pace, and then jettisoned it when it had fulfilled its task. Such methods paved the way for the new freedoms gained by twentieth-century musicians. A further sign that British opera was coming of age lay in the consistently professional demands made by this composer, which placed her music out of reach of amateur performance.

What finally marks this piece out as a genuine native product is its emphatic celebration of the British sense of humour. This was something to which no foreigner, however gifted, could ever aspire. Ethel Smyth had succeeded better than she realized; her operas were to reach out and touch the next generation, which witnessed the flowering of a truly national art.

Chapter 16

ORCHESTRAL MUSIC

PERCY M. YOUNG

The Philharmonic Society

In the German-speaking countries during the eighteenth century the orchestra at many courts was an accepted institution under the control of a suitably trained professional. In Britain there was one court (two, if the viceregal establishment in Dublin is counted), where—because of parliamentary control of revenues—investment in music was meagre. The orchestra thus was subject to the vagaries of middle-class opinion, and unprotected against the play of 'market forces'. When Haydn's 'London' symphonies were played under his direction at Salomon's concerts in the Hanover Square Rooms at the end of the eighteenth century it had seemed that a new dawn was breaking. On Haydn's final departure after the 1795 season, there was a certain cooling of public interest in orchestral music which was reflected in a decline in activity during the next few years. But the setback was slight. Salomon's concerts were revived in 1796, 1801 and 1808; similar subscription series were offered by other concert promoters in 1795–1800 and in 1807–12. In addition there was a healthy proliferation of individual benefits at which orchestral music was generally included. Those given by musicians such as Giambattista Cimador, the Cramer brothers, Charles Neate, Salomon, and Felix Janiewicz were quite adventurous in the choice of modern orchestral music. Even the 'Vocal Concerts', refounded in 1801, included symphonies and overtures in their programmes, while the Lenten Oratorios maintained the tradition, dating from Handel's time, of concertos inserted between the acts.[1] As a result not only were Haydn's and Mozart's symphonies regularly performed, but most of Beethoven's were given in London shortly after their first performance in Vienna.[2]

Thus when the Philharmonic Society was founded in 1813 it was not launched in a vacuum. George Hogarth's picture of 'orchestral destitution'[3] before 1813, copied by several later writers, is quite fictitious, and was no doubt inspired by a wish to enhance the importance of the Society whose history he was narrating. Nevertheless, the founding of the Philharmonic was an important landmark, for it was organized and run by professional musicians in relative independence of aristocratic patronage. It seems to have been foreshadowed by a more informal body known as 'The Harmonic', founded about 1800, which had sponsored mainly instrumental concerts at the London Tavern, financed by business men in the City under the leadership of a German merchant named Schick. It is said that Beethoven's Pastoral Symphony and Mozart's *Don Giovanni* had their first English hearing at these concerts.[4]

The new feeling of professional solidarity is expressed in one of the Philharmonic Society's byelaws, which laid down that 'there shall not be any distinction of rank in the orchestra, and therefore the station of every performer shall be absolutely determined by the leader of the night'.[5] The violinists who were members took turns to act as leaders, and they included the best players in London: Salomon, F. Cramer, Spagnoletti, Viotti and others. The same principle governed the selection of the 'conductor' who 'presided at the pianoforte'. 'No orchestra ever before exhibited so many celebrated leaders playing the subordinate parts. . . . It was not only the power and unity of the band that was remarkable, but also the consummate taste and judgement of every individual composing it.'[6] Adam Carse cites an array of contemporary praises for the quality of the orchestra, many from visiting foreign musicians such as Spohr, Weber, Mendelssohn and Fétis.[7] But two obstacles prevented the Philharmonic orchestra from becoming as fine a band as that of the Paris Conservatoire: the lack of a strong and undisputed conductor, and the lack of adequate rehearsal. Neither was remedied until the advent of Michael Costa as permanent conductor in 1846.

The main innovation in the early programmes of the Philharmonic was the introduction of chamber music and the exclusion (until 1820) of concertos. As far as orchestral music was concerned its main service was in providing better performances of classical music, especially Beethoven's, in whose interests none worked harder in this respect than George Smart. The Society also commissioned many important new works in its first three decades, not entirely excluding works by native composers and by such naturalized Englishmen as Clementi and J. B. Cramer.

Clementi's symphonies have only recently been rescued from oblivion. In addition to the two he published in 1787, there are fragments of more than a dozen later works,[8] of which four are sufficiently complete to be put together in reasonably accurate form.* They are ambitious works for a large orchestra, and Clementi intended them to crown his fame as a composer.[9] They failed to please at the time, and were soon forgotten, partly because he made them a vehicle for the same kind of uncompromising harmonies and learned counterpoint that he explored in his late piano works. But they make a considerable impression on audiences today. Cramer, a pupil of Clementi, composed eight piano concertos over a period of about thirty years (c. 1792–1825). It was not until the fifth (c. 1813) that he began to model his form on that of Mozart, whose concertos were well behind his symphonies in their introduction to the British public. Cramer's eighth concerto, in D minor, is experimental in form: it consists of a double exposition on a Beethovenian scale, which leads straight into the D-major slow movement, followed by a normal 'Rondo a l'Espagnola'. Cramer in his concertos avoided the temptations of reckless virtuosity and strove, often with success, to preserve a classical balance and restraint; but a certain dryness has militated against their survival.

In this form, however, there was one European master who was—technically, at least—British: John Field (1782–1837), also a pupil of Clementi. On 7 February 1799 Field presented himself as a composer at the King's Theatre, Haymarket, in a performance of his First Piano Concerto, in E flat. In keeping with the fashion of the day, he used an old and well-liked popular song, 'Within a mile of Edinboro' town', as the basis of the slow movement. The variations, at least in the form in which they were published in 1814, have some of the character of the nocturnes on which the composer's fame chiefly rests. His seven piano concertos are not least in importance among the works of his era. They reveal the poetic properties of the piano and also of the orchestra. Field was both eloquent and authoritative, as shown by the 'military' motives of the First and Sixth Concertos, and by the rhetoric introducing the soloist in the first movement of the Second Concerto. This work, possibly composed as early as 1802, admired and taught by Chopin, and in the repertoire of pianists from Clara Schumann to Pachmann, demonstrates Field's sense of wonderment in the superb placing of harmonic statements about which a feeling of mystery still holds (ex. 16.1). There is a similar extension of fancy in a transition from E flat to F sharp major in the first movement of the Third Concerto, which was dedicated to Clementi. In the first movement of the Fourth Concerto Field explores a rare, if not rarefied, ambience in a

*The recent edition by Pietro Spada (Milan, 1975–8) is unfortunately not reliable. (Hill.)

Ex. 16.1 John Field, Piano Concerto No. 2 in A flat major (1802?): 1st movement

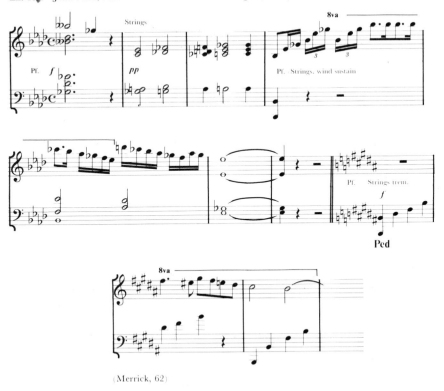

(Merrick, 62)

manner quite without parallel at the time (ex. 16.2). The first movement of the Fifth Concerto introduces instrumental effects more familiar at the end of the century than at the beginning. Entitled *L'incendie par l'orage*, this is an essay in realism evidently intended to challenge Steibelt's 'Storm Rondo', and makes use of tam-tam, a bell tuned to B flat to provide forty-five bars of pedal, and a second piano to sharpen the edge of the orchestral tone.

There was small encouragement for British-born composers to venture into the arena of the symphony proper, and few did so. Samuel Wesley's Symphony in B flat (1802) is a lone masterpiece, and may never have been performed. It is a long way from the four galant symphonies of his youth (1781–5): in four movements, serious, mature, emotional, and bearing the full weight and richness of the symphonic style of Haydn and Mozart. Wesley wrote two orchestral overtures

361

Ex. 16.2 John Field, Piano Concerto No. 4 in E flat major (c. 1810?): 1st movement

(Piggott, 162)

later in life. One of them is an impressive work in E major, possibly dating from as late as 1830.[10] It is scored for a large orchestra with three trombones, and is laid out on a spacious scale, often sustaining harmonies for many bars at a time while melodic instruments explore yearning dissonances (ex. 16.3); but the structure of the piece is not well founded.

362

Henry Bishop tried his hand at the classical style with a 'Grand Sinfonia' in C (really an overture), written in 1805. Many of his theatre overtures demonstrate his mastery of orchestration.* William Crotch composed several orchestral works in the early years of the century.[11]

Ex. 16.3   Samuel Wesley, Overture in E major (c. 1830?)

[**Allegro vivace**]

*See above, p. 217.

(*P:* London, British Library, MS Add. 35010, fols. 39–100. Clarinet parts editorial)

Of two symphonies one, in F, was played at the Philharmonic Society on 16 May 1814. Sometimes one sees the composer who might have been: the second subject of the first movement, with an easy, almost Viennese flow, may seem to anticipate the manner of Arthur Sullivan.

Cipriani Potter (1792–1871), the son of an orchestral player, belonged to a family long known as instrument manufacturers. His father, who played viola, helped to found and to play in the band of the Philharmonic Society. As a boy Potter had lessons from Thomas Attwood and the Salzburg-born Joseph Woelfl, and then from Aloys Förster at Vienna. Through the mediation of Ferdinand Ries he was here able to meet and to receive the commendation of Beethoven.

'Botter [sic]', wrote Beethoven to Ries, 'has visited me a few times, he seems to be a good fellow and has talent for composition.'[12] Before he went to Vienna, Potter had already appeared at Philharmonic concerts as pianist and composer. After his return he was for many years prominent in their programmes. In addition to his previous functions he was conspicuous as conductor. As pianist Potter had the distinction of introducing to the public the piano concertos of Mozart and Beethoven. His own works included four overtures (three on Shakespearean subjects), three piano concertos, much solo piano and chamber music, and at least ten (perhaps as many as fourteen) symphonies,[13] most of which were composed before he succeeded Crotch as principal of the Academy in 1832.

Potter was neither the first nor the last British composer to sacrifice his creative talents to the demands of education and administration. But this does not justify the ungracious treatment he has received from posterity, which has been due, no doubt, to his negligence in not writing an oratorio. In his own field he was outstanding. At any rate this was recognized by *The Harmonicon*, which greeted his G Minor Symphony of 1826 with laudable generosity: 'It . . . displays invention, the want of which is so oppressively felt in nineteen out of the twenty of those things called *new*, that are annually brought forward, in various shapes, and immediately consigned to oblivion.'[14] A contemporary of Spohr, Potter had a good deal in common with that composer, attempting to acclimatize the classical manner in an uncertain atmosphere where a new kind of bourgeois romanticism was evident. Although as symphonist Potter remained sternly non-representational he did not feel himself too much obliged to surrender his freedom to the conventions of formal procedure. The dramatic C Minor Symphony of 1826[15] starts from propositions drawn from *Sturm und Drang*, and later takes them through interesting areas of harmonic development. Potter did not feel the orchestra to be a large keyboard; his scoring, therefore, has, for that time in Britain, an uncommon spaciousness, of which a passage in the coda of the first movement of Symphony 'no. 4' in D major provides an example (ex. 16.4).

In the summer of 1855 Richard Wagner came to London to conduct a series of eight Philharmonic concerts, which, poorly patronized, were far from successful. At the fourth concert the Third Symphony of Charles Lucas (1808–69)—Potter's successor as principal of the Academy—was played under the composer's direction. At the sixth, Potter's G Minor Symphony of 1832, conducted by Wagner, was said by *The Athenaeum* to be 'the only item which could be said to impart any variety'. The next concert, attended by the Queen and Prince Albert, opened with George Macfarren's lively concert overture, *Chevy Chase* (1836).

Wagner described Potter as 'an old-fashioned but very friendly composer', whose symphony 'entertained [him] by its modest dimensions and its neat development of counterpoint'. Had Wagner known other works by Potter he would sometimes have recognized a kinship of spirit, most of all in the mythic propensities revealed in the grand opening C major sequence of fifty bars unfolded by full orchestra in the Overture *The Tempest* (1837). Wagner also enjoyed conducting

365

Ex. 16.4   Cipriani Potter, Symphony 'No. 4' in D major, dated 24 November 1834: 1st movement

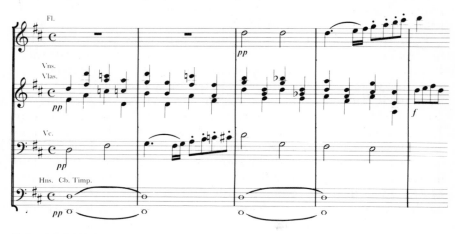

(*S:* London, British Library, MS Royal Philharmonic Society 326)

Macfarren's Overture 'on account of its peculiarly wild, passionate character'.[16]

George Macfarren (1813–87) was a serious and remarkably persistent composer of orchestral music. He wrote at least nine symphonies, four concertos for different instruments, and eight overtures, a record equalled by few English composers. Perhaps the best of his symphonies is No. 4 in A minor (1833); the one in C sharp minor (c. 1840), dedicated to Mendelssohn but modelled chiefly on Beethoven, was the most often performed. His overture *Hamlet* (1856) deserves revival. It begins with a romantic theme for cellos alone, followed by a contrasting theme with which it is ingeniously combined; the second subject, part of which is shown in example 16.5, is unusually lyrical for this composer, but typical of him in its deft handling of harmony and orchestration. The whole work is built with skill and consistency on these three ideas, with full exploitation of orchestral colouring.

One of the composers of the 1830s of whom much had been expected was William Sterndale Bennett (1816–75). When he was a Royal Academy student of sixteen, he played the solo part in his first Piano Concerto in D minor (1832). In the next four years he composed two more piano concertos—in E flat, dedicated to Potter, and in C minor, dedicated to Cramer—and five symphonies. The praise lavished on him by Schumann may now seem excessive,[17] unless one listens sympathetically to the urgency of the Third Concerto in C minor, which

Ex. 16.5 George A. Macfarren, concert overture, *Hamlet* (1856)

(*S:* Cambridge, Fitzwilliam Museum, MU. MS 1016)

Bennett presented at a Leipzig Gewandhaus concert on 19 January 1837. The soloist announces himself with the boldly Beethovenish gesture shown in example 16.6.

Ex. 16.6 William Sterndale Bennett, Piano Concerto No. 3 in C minor (1834): 1st movement

(*K:* Kistner (Leipzig), [1838])

Here was a British composer—a species whose existence had been generally unsuspected in the heartland of German music. During the years in which he was a familiar figure on the German musical scene, Bennett's reputation depended particularly on the delicate romantic fancy of the overtures *Parisina* (1835), *The Naiads* (1836), and *The Wood-nymphs* (1838); the clarity in the layout of the Fourth Piano Concerto in F minor—of which the slow movement, a barcarolle, remained in favour after the rest of the work had faded; and the efficient G Minor Symphony (1864). All these works were published by Kistner of Leipzig.

Bennett contributed the first British examples of the romantic *concert overture* (i.e., an overture with a poetic title but independent of any dramatic work), beginning with *The Tempest* (1832). Consideration of *The Naiads*, the most popular of his overtures, leads one to agree with Schumann that, despite similarities with Mendelssohn's *Melusina* (1833) and a certain monotony, it is a charming antidote to all that is prosaic. Bennett's scoring, conspicuous by the delicate handling of string and woodwind colouring, is almost pointillist in character. Melodically there is a grace of movement that anticipates Sullivan (who surely learned from Bennett how not to overpopulate a score with unnecessary notes), while sequential passages in 'development' sections are almost Elgarian. The G Minor Symphony—a more patently 'serious' work—shows more clearly Bennett's weakness as well as his strength. It is ambitious in design, with five movements. The minuet itself divides into four sections, one of which, the trio (*pomposo*), is for brass alone à la Meyerbeer. This venture into vulgarity is distressingly inert. Bennett's true métier was in water-colours. Yet there are moments when the shape of things to come is apparent. The second subject of the first movement lies somewhere between Schumann and Elgar.

After Mid-Century

The Great Exhibition of 1851 was a watershed in British life in many ways, not least in musical affairs, where there had been many evidences of a desire for change. Established institutions were, therefore, put on the defensive, particularly the Philharmonic Society. The timidity of the directors and the mutilation of the classics by Costa—conductor from 1846 to 1854—led some to the conclusion that it was a hopeless case. In 1852, therefore, a New Philharmonic Society, nursed into being by and on the reputation of Berlioz, came into existence under the leadership of Dr Henry Wylde (1822–90). Six years later, as a challenge to the New Philharmonic, the Musical Society of London was formed. Of all attempts to reform or to popularize (or to reform and popularize) instrumental music in a land suffering from choral saturation the most significant was through the opening of the Crystal Palace—left over from the Great Exhibition—in Sydenham. August Manns was engaged as musical director, and in 1855 began the Saturday Concerts which he was to conduct for more than forty years, and for which George Grove was to write programme notes which themselves helped to mould the taste of the British people in hitherto unknown regions of orchestral music.

In 1858 St James's Hall was opened: it was the principal auditorium in London until the building of Queen's Hall in 1893. In the same year the Hallé Orchestra was established in Manchester. By now other provincial institutions, notably the Birmingham and Leeds Festivals, and the Liverpool Philharmonic Society, were slowly beginning to offer more opportunity to native composers of orchestral music. One example is the moderately successful debut of Sterndale Bennett's pupil, Francis Edward Bache (1833–58), in Liverpool in 1855, with an allegro movement from his new piano concerto,[18] which unhappily has not survived.

One composer who did not fit the usual British pattern was Henry Hugo Pierson (1815–73), who first studied, and then permanently settled in Germany. Befriended by both Mendelssohn and Schumann,

369

he was more influenced by the musical thinking of the latter, as well as by Berlioz and Liszt. Like most composers of the period Pierson paid tribute to the Shakespeare cult in orchestral works which, composed for the most part in Germany, provided a striking contrast with what was being written in England. In the ambitious Symphonic Poem *Macbeth* (which contrasts violently with the earlier *Macbeth* Overture of Pearsall) there is a detailed programme, with lines from the play occasionally appearing over the score. Both in this work and in his *Romeo and Juliet* Overture there is to be heard a sometimes bewildering complex of urgent rhythmic figuration, of strings divided with Straussian ardour, of evocative wind solos, and energetic thrusts from multiple percussion. Something of this may be gathered from his presentation of the three witches in *Macbeth* (ex. 16.7). To many Germans his freshness of

Ex. 16.7 H. Hugo Pierson, symphonic poem, *Macbeth* (1859)
Andantino agitato

MACBETH (*sic*): What are these, So wither'd and so wild in their attire,

That look not like the inhabitants o' the earth, And yet are on't? Live you?

(*S:* Schuberth (Leipzig), [1859])

utterance and dramatic exuberance appeared innovatory. In the *Neue Zeitschrift für Musik* he was thus defined: 'Pierson belongs, if not to the most popular, to the most fertile group of modern composers.'[19]

In the first twenty-five years of its existence the Leipzig Conservatorium—founded in 1843—had more than a hundred British students on its roll. The reputation of the school in Britain in 1857 is indicated by a comment of a girl from Cheltenham who became a student that year: 'Everything was, and must be right because it was the way of the Leipzig Conservatorium. To question anything, to imagine the existence of any different or superior methods never could have occurred to me. All was accepted without question.'[20] A few months later the sixteen-year-old Arthur Sullivan, first Mendelssohn Scholar of the Royal Academy of Music, arrived there in a batch of students that included Edvard Grieg, from Bergen, and Dudley Buck, from Hartford, Connecticut. His quickness and deftness in handling musical material gave to his early scores a combination of academic propriety and imaginative insight. In 1861 his incidental music to *The Tempest*, played at the Conservatorium Graduation Concert, was received with acclaim, as it was a year later when—largely through George Grove's sponsorship—it was performed at a Crystal Palace concert.

Sullivan was fortunate to emerge when the major English festivals were anxious to vie not only with each other, but also with those in Germany, which they came to resemble. If this was one way of symbolizing British economic power (though the fees for native composers were modest) then it was a sensible investment. No one understood this more than Sullivan, who in the first phase of his career wrote a sequence of important orchestral works for the Crystal Palace, the Philharmonic Society, and several festivals. In 1866 his First Symphony—known later as the 'Irish'—and Cello Concerto were played at the Crystal Palace. Also in that year the Overture *In Memoriam*, a tribute to his father who had lately died, was performed at the Norwich Festival.[21] In 1867 the Overture *Marmion* was included in a Philharmonic Society programme. In response to another commission from Birmingham, where his masque *Kenilworth* had been performed in 1864, Sullivan wrote one of his most distinctive works, the Overture *Di ballo*, for the 1870 Festival. At this point, quite abruptly, Sullivan left the orchestral arena, his mastery in instrumentation being from now chiefly reserved for his theatre music and oratorios.

Sullivan was an eclectic composer, absorbing ideas from many sources, Irish, Italian, French, English—even Jewish as he once admitted—as well as German, and his theatre pieces and concert works

371

pointed the way towards an emancipation of the orchestra in a British setting, as is postulated by Adam Carse.[22]

When the young Sullivan was beginning his studies in Leipzig, a ten-year-old prodigy from Edinburgh, Alexander Campbell Mackenzie (1847–1935), was being taught the violin in the Thuringian town of Sondershausen, where there was a court orchestra much praised for its promotion of the new music of Berlioz and Liszt. The boy made such progress that at the age of fourteen he was taken on as a regular member of the court orchestra. In 1862 he went back to Britain and became a student at the Royal Academy. After completing a course there he went back to Scotland where he was active as violinist and teacher. But he was seized with a zeal for composition. In 1877 his Overture *Cervantes* was played in Sondershausen and soon afterwards, through the recommendation of Hans von Bülow, in Glasgow.

Mackenzie was a prolific composer of romantic disposition, and aware of a duty to promote national interests. But in consequence of his early training and the general attitude towards the incorporation of folk music into the main stream, those of his works which bear a Scottish label are all—as was fitting in the age of Queen Victoria—German-Scottish. There are, especially, three Scottish Rhapsodies, a Pibroch Suite for violin and orchestra, and a Scottish Piano Concerto, first played by Paderewski in 1897. The first *Rhapsodie écossaise*, performed at Glasgow in 1880, was one of the earliest British examples of the freely composed *orchestral piece*, which in its more ambitious form was called a *symphonic poem*. Mackenzie in his earlier years was far ahead of most British composers in respect of orchestral practices and techniques. Of his works of those years the 'Orchestral Ballad' *La belle dame sans merci* (1883) exemplifies a talent for transmitting literary ideas into vivid rhythms and sonorities. The slow introduction (*largo, mesto*) for cello and bassoon solo is almost Straussian; the succeeding Allegro con brio with a pentatonic thrust in 6/8 time over pedal fifths presents a distinctly North British knight-at-arms. In the second-subject group, in contrasting tonality, the clarinet melody running across a glinting landscape pictured by second violins *divisi a 3*, high chords for harp, and pizzicato violas and cellos, takes one into the neighbourhood of Elgar's *In the South*.

In 1894, to demonstrate that he was not exclusive in his nationalism, Mackenzie contributed a sprightly 'Nautical Overture', *Britannia*, to the repertory. The accession of Edward VII stimulated another work which led into an area otherwise apparently reserved for Elgar. The Orchestral Suite *London Day by Day* (1902), scored for large orchestra, containing gong, glockenspiel, and organ, included as third movement

'A Song of Thanksgiving (June 1, 1902)' (referring to the King's recovery from illness) with something of an 'imperial' theme predominant (ex. 16.8).

Ex. 16.8 Alexander C. Mackenzie, orchestral suite, *London Day by Day* (1902): 3rd movement

Lento espressivo

(*S:* Bosworth (Leipzig), 1902)

The 'R.C.M. School'

When the Royal College of Music came into existence in 1883, George Grove, the first Director, had assembled a talented professorial staff, of whom the best-known were Hubert Parry (1848–1918) and Charles Stanford (1852–1924), generally regarded as the main instruments of a 'renaissance of English music'. This somewhat simplistic assessment of their influence is due partly to the air of personal authority which each carried, to the compositions which brought them into prominence, and to the calibre of certain of their pupils.

Parry composed four symphonies—the 'English' (1889) being thematically the most interesting; two charming, slender suites for strings; a set of Symphonic Variations (1897); and, towards the end of his life, a Symphonic Poem, subtitled 'From Death to Life' (1914). The more ambitious of these works have been defeated by the intensity of their purpose, and are to be seen as companions to a philosophic treatise by Parry which remained in manuscript.[23] Of the purely orchestral works the Symphonic Variations stand out, forming a fine prelude to (and contrast with) Elgar's 'Enigma' Variations. They were first performed at a Philharmonic concert, and the spartan vigour of the work, the taut, intellectual organization of its architecture, and the urbanity of the gentler passages, accord well with the trust reposed by the composer in the influences of Purcell, Handel, and Bach. Parry's theme (ex. 16.9) stands at the confluence of these influences.

Stanford belonged to the prosperous Anglo-Irish middle class of Dublin at a time when this class began to realize that many of its members were destined to be to some extent victims of ineluctable historical developments. He was thus impelled by a nationalism in

373

Ex. 16.9   C. Hubert H. Parry, Symphonic Variations (1897)
Maestoso energico

(S: Novello, 1897)

which he could not fully believe; his 'Irish' music is deferential where it might have been expected to be assertive. In comparison with, say, Dvořák, he was a failure. He was—to use present-day terminology—unsure of his identity; yet it was precisely this that enabled him to sympathize with, and promote the interests of, Samuel Coleridge-Taylor, one of his most gifted pupils.

Into the life of teacher, administrator, and club man, he inserted the career of a composer. Gifted with an inordinate, possibly fatal, fluency and a composerly confidence, he wrote music in almost every genre. In the field of orchestral music alone there were seven symphonies, five Irish Rhapsodies (all post-1900), six concertos (three for piano, two for violin, and one for clarinet), as well as overtures, suites, and variations.

It was predictable that the third symphony, the 'Irish' (1887), should have been generally regarded as his most characteristic work. But it is particularly in this work that conflict between the constituent elements diminishes credibility. As Plunket Greene pointed out, 'the resemblance of the opening strain of the Lament movement . . . to that of the slow movement of Brahms's Fourth was easily spotted, but Stanford took it from a Lament in the Petrie Collection of Irish folk-songs.'[24] Stanford took other melodies from this anthology for his symphony, but, as Frank Howes writes, 'the total effect is like leaving and returning to Ireland for a holiday in Germany'.[25] Reviewing a Philharmonic performance of this symphony in 1893, Bernard Shaw referred to the 'return to nature' then in vogue, suggesting that it was being effected 'by the smuggling into academic music of ancient folk-music under various pretences as to its archaeological importance'. Stanford's music, he says, 'is a record of fearful conflict between the aboriginal Celt and the Professor'.[26]

Stanford's works exemplify the manner of his teaching, which was based on conservative ideals and directed against uncharted expeditions into the unknown. There is one work for orchestra which carries the lyrical impulse and the imaginative modesty that determine the quality of Stanford's best music for voices: the Clarinet Concerto of

1902. Consisting of one movement, within which there are three inter-linked sections based on two germ motives, it charmingly explores the expressive personality of the solo instrument.

In his notice of Stanford's 'Irish' Symphony Shaw drew attention to a considerable number of composers similarly pursuing 'naturalistic' or 'nationalistic' ideals. In this connection Hamish MacCunn (1868–1916), a Scotsman, and Samuel Coleridge-Taylor (1875–1912), son of a West African father and an English mother, came into early prominence with works that were startlingly effective. Both men studied at the Royal College of Music; in the end neither realized his full potential. MacCunn's *The Land of the Mountain and Flood* (1887) was one of the many concert overtures put into currency by Manns at the Crystal Palace. It was immediately successful, and MacCunn followed it with a number of works of patently Scottish inspiration, including the three brief *Highland Memories* (1897). In these pieces MacCunn in search of apposite, and unhackneyed, references shows a delicacy of observation that is almost impressionist (ex. 16.10). A year later Coleridge-Taylor's vivid Ballade in A Minor was performed at the Gloucester Festival and also at the Crystal Palace. This marked the beginning of a career—tragically denied its ultimate fulfilment—that began to bring home the inescapable consequences of the competitive nationalisms of the nineteenth century.

Ex. 16.10   Hamish MacCunn, *Highland Memories* (1897): No. 2, 'On the Loch'

(*S:* Augener, [1897])

Self-taught Masters of the Orchestra

At the time of Queen Victoria's Diamond Jubilee there were still only two orchestras with any kind of permanency (and the players would have contested that it was a curious kind of permanency that denied them security). But improvement was on the way. Henry Wood had instituted Promenade Concerts in the Queen's Hall in 1895. Three years later Granville Bantock undertook the conductorship of the band of the New Brighton Tower Pleasure Gardens, where he launched himself as a composer of frightening versatility and insubstantial consequence, as well as a number of his talented contemporaries. In 1904 the London Symphony Orchestra came into being, and Wood, Elgar, Bantock, and, in due course, Thomas Beecham, hammered home the theme that permanent orchestras were an essential part of a civilized community. The nationally and municipally subsidized orchestras that gradually emerged in Britain did so during the disappearance of the last of the old German court orchestras.

It was against the odds that two British composers, acknowledged masters of orchestral music, but non-Establishment figures, should appear at this time. One was Edward Elgar (1857–1934), the other Frederick Delius (1862–1934).

The story of Elgar in brief is of the rise to fame (though not to riches) of a small-town poor boy through his own exertions. It is not a *curriculum vitae* that fits any other major British composer of recent times. Born near Worcester, the son of a diligent if unremarkable music teacher and dealer, he learned the basic musical skills at home, and enhanced them by a long process of self-education. As a young man he played various instruments, the violin well enough for him to belong in due course to the more important festival orchestras of the region, and the organ as far as the services of the Roman Catholic church in Worcester required; and he directed ensembles of various abilities. Always ambitious to become a composer, Elgar wrote undistinguished pieces for local consumption until he was past thirty. In 1889 *Salut d'amour*, a pretty salon piece that was to become world-famous, was played at a Crystal Palace concert: another instance of Manns's support of unknown talent.

After his marriage Elgar tried, but failed, to earn a livelihood in London. He returned to Malvern, again to experience the confining restrictions imposed by the country music-teacher's routine. But, supported by the loyalty of friends and, increasingly, by the percipient confidence in him of August Jaeger, of Novello's, he wrote a series of works in the choral-cantata manner favoured by Victorian musical societies, which went through local channels into the regional round, and thence into the national pool. Some orchestral works began to catch attention, by felicity of expression and technical expertise. In 1897 an *Imperial March*, first played at the Crystal Palace, seemed splendidly to capture the euphoric national mood. Two years later the 'Enigma' Variations—original and allusive pieces relating to particular persons within the Elgar circle—were accepted and directed by Hans Richter (1843–1916), who was, to date, the greatest conductor to have established himself in Britain. With the accolade of Richter's praise Elgar could then be said to have arrived. That there is scant justice in the musical world is demonstrated by the fact that Granville Bantock's 'Helena' Variations—a splendid work which should for its interest be compared with the 'Enigma'—were also first performed (by the Liverpool Philharmonic Society) that year, and promptly forgotten.

Elgar, however, went on to produce a sequence of orchestral works that took him far ahead of any other British composers. The first four of the *Pomp and Circumstance* Marches and the Overture *Cockaigne* were directed at the wider public, while the *Introduction and Allegro* for strings, composed for the newly constituted London Symphony Orchestra (with which Elgar maintained a lasting friendly relationship), typified the composer's inspired practicality by its perfect realization of the medium.

During his early years Elgar had more than once determined to write a symphony, but was always deterred by the thought of the penury that composition of such a work would ensure. In 1898–9 he was working on a symphony on the subject of General Charles Gordon, the hero of Khartoum.[27] In 1904 an Elgar Festival took place at Covent Garden in acknowledgement of the composer's all-round achievement and his wide popularity. The extravagant concert overture *In the South* was first performed during this festival in place of the symphony which might have been expected. It was another four years before the First Symphony, in A flat, was given its first performance by the Hallé Orchestra in Manchester under Richter, to whom the work was dedicated. There is evidence that the Second Symphony, in E flat (1911), was in part conceived before the First. The elegiac second movement is, like 'Nimrod' of the 'Enigma' Variations, a characteristic song without words, eloquent as a national song (ex. 16.11). Between the two symphonies was the Violin Concerto. The last major orchestral work written by Elgar before the outbreak of the 1914–18 war was the symphonic study *Falstaff*. Comparison of this with previous works based on Shakespearean themes by other composers shows how far Elgar had brought the orchestra into modern times.

It is not unusual for the reputation of an artist to fluctuate. That of Elgar was at one time subjected to criticisms which reflected either strong personal prejudices or transient aesthetic or social opinion.* A degree of warrantable revisionism in respect of the Victorian and Edwardian eras has assisted in establishing a more objective approach

---

*For instance, he was dismissed as a mere 'master of orchestral decoration' in a book by Charles Stanford and Cecil Forsyth published in 1916 (Stanford and Forsyth, 317).

Ex. 16.11   Edward Elgar, Symphony No. 2 in E flat major (1903–10): 2nd movement

(S: Novello, 1911)

to the arts of those periods. This, however, does not, except marginally, account for the present assessment of Elgar as one of the last great Romantic composers and the preeminent British master of symphonic form. This rating has been won on merit, for the pleadings of specialists have for the most part followed the enthusiasm of the musical rank and file. It is a tribute to Elgar's imaginative genius that his major works have a particular appeal to the young.

More than those of many composers, Elgar's symphonic works comprehend and develop ideas from many and disparate regions of his thought. His extant sketchbooks show how he was captured by themes and fragments of themes whose personalities only became apparent after long deliberation. What appears in a sketchbook as almost trivial is quite transfigured by symphonic development and the appositeness of orchestral colouring and dynamic subtleties. Nowhere is this more true than in the First Symphony, where the opening theme grows into a work of compelling significance, illustrating the initial instruction—*nobilmente e semplice*. The 'heroic' idea inherent in the jettisoned 'Gordon' Symphony is refined into an Aristotelean concept in the extant symphonic works of Elgar.

The case of Delius in some respects is similar to that of Elgar, even though each held the music of the other at a respectable distance. In the

378

long term Delius is counted among British musicians, albeit he was neither British by descent nor concerned to retain British sympathies. He was born in Bradford, where his father—an immigrant from Germany—was a wool merchant. At first it was not his intention—still less his father's—that he should become a professional musician. However, music came to absorb more and more of his interest, and when all other attempts to induce him to follow a business career failed he was despatched to Florida to superintend an orange grove.

So far from dissuading him from the pursuit of music, this unlikely experience gave Delius the stimulus he needed to liberate his own musicality, which was closely linked to an acute visual sensibility. Friendship with an organist in Jacksonville (who gave him some lessons), appreciation of an exotic landscape and a non-European native culture, furnished him with ideas that were duly refined into musical form. From Florida Delius went to Leipzig—with reluctant consent and a subsistence allowance from his father—to enrol as a student in the Conservatorium. In the eighteen months spent there Delius composed some modest orchestral pieces. One, *Hiawatha*, is of interest on account of the work on the same subject composed at the same time by Coleridge-Taylor.* Another, *Florida*, attracted a favourable opinion from Grieg (with whom Delius had become acquainted in Leipzig). Grieg tried to persuade Manns to include this four-movement suite in a Crystal Palace concert, but Manns was unresponsive, having—he said—too many other works in rehearsal at the time. One suspects, perhaps, that Manns was by now finding himself a little out of his depth. Ten years later he could, and did, appreciate Elgar's *Bavarian Highlands* music, which he readily performed on a Saturday afternoon; but when he saw the score of Delius's Symphonic Poem *Life's Dance* in its original (1898) form he declared it to be 'ultra-modern' and beyond his understanding.

After a contretemps with his father concerning his future, Delius felt that it would be preferable to be relatively poor in France than in England. In any case the atmosphere there was thought to be conducive to artistic creativity. Delius therefore took up his residence in France, where he spent the remainder of his life. Progress as a composer was slow. *Florida* was performed in 1888. Five years later, through the generosity of an uncle, the tone-poem *Sur les cimes* was played at Monte Carlo, and in 1897 another tone-poem, *Over the Hills and Far Away*, in Elberfeld. In 1899, a few weeks before the premiere of the 'Enigma' Variations, a concert of Delius's music (paid for by himself) was given in St James's Hall, the conductor being Alfred Hertz of Elberfeld. In

*See above, p. 232.

the next ten years Delius composed most of the works—operatic, vocal, and orchestral—on which his reputation came to depend. The dedications of *Appalachia* to Julius Buths (also a friend and advocate of Elgar's music), *A Mass of Life* to Fritz Cassirer, and *Paris* to Hans Haym, indicate the encouragement then given to Delius by German conductors, who, it should be said, tended to regard Delius as a German.

The subsequent advance of Delius's music in Britain was due almost entirely to the creative insight and irresistible advocacy of Thomas Beecham, who more than any other individual enabled its unique virtues to be made manifest. Apart from occasional recollections of England in such works as *Brigg Fair* (variations on a Lincolnshire folksong) and *North Country Sketches*, Delius's connections with Britain in later life were slender. Nonetheless he was created a Companion of Honour and a freeman of the city of Bradford.

It is perhaps fitting that the two most durable orchestral composers of the period of the 'renaissance' should, in the professional sense, have been outsiders. In one way Elgar may be taken to be a German symphonist, except that he was born English. Although as patriotic as the next man, Elgar did not consider that folksongs were of significance to a composer, who should be their provider and not their purveyor. 'I write the folksongs of this country', he said.[28] This remark made to Troyte Griffith is an expression of the sense of assurance shown in Elgar's works. Such certainty was not to be found in the music of other British composers, and came strangely from Elgar's modest, provincial, Victorian background. But it was this environmental fact that made him aware of the importance of the common touch. It was once thought that this rendered his music commonplace, if not, indeed, common. Taking the long view, however, one may conclude that this is the point at which Elgar met the great classical composers to whose company he is now admitted.

Like Elgar, Delius was—in Forsyth's terms—a master of 'orchestral decoration'. Unlike Elgar he responded more particularly to what was uncommon. Much more even than Elgar he was a self-made composer, owing little to anybody in particular but everything to the spirit of his own times rather than to past conventions. Out of the scattering elements of late romanticism he fashioned a style that was singularly effective in conveying the changing shapes of landscapes, and, perhaps, related patterns of human feelings.

Chapter 17

CHAMBER MUSIC

GEOFFREY BUSH

From Chamber to Concert Hall

In the first part of the century, chamber-music making was principally a domestic affair. In higher society it was dominated by the piano, played almost invariably by ladies,[1] and the most characteristic form in 1800 was the 'accompanied sonata' (for piano with subordinate instrumental parts, usually flute or violin and cello) which was becoming rapidly trivialized. There was also around 1800 a vogue for violin duets: Viotti's were the best known. The string-quartet party, popular in the later eighteenth century, was maintained here and there in the nineteenth, especially in circles led by professional musicians such as Vincent Novello, or in middle-class families such as that of the Leicester stocking-manufacturer William Gardiner.[2] George Haddock remembered that at Leeds in the 1830s there were 'at least a dozen of our first and most influential families at which weekly quartet meetings were held'.[3] The atmosphere at such gatherings was serious and intense, the players dedicated; but it is not surprising that the chief fare was the music of the Viennese classics. Any English composer writing a string quartet was performing an act of selfless dedication to his art, without hope of advancing his reputation or gaining any reward. Several well-known composers, among them Bishop, T. A. Walmisley, and Ouseley, wrote one or two early quartets and then abandoned the form for life. The piano continued to dominate domestic music making for most of the century. John Hullah wrote in 1877: 'Music in the house, purely as well as partly instrumental, has long been and is long likely to remain largely dependent on the pianoforte, deservedly called "the family orchestra".'[4] In his seventy-nine-page book *Music in the House* he devoted only half a page to the entire violin family.

But chamber music was gradually making its way on to the concert platform. The Philharmonic Society included chamber works as well as orchestral music in its early programmes, and this, though not strictly

381

an innovation, helped to spread a knowledge of classical chamber music after 1813. Public concerts devoted entirely to chamber music began in 1835, on the model of Baillot's *soirées musicales* in Paris, and were instantly successful, soon spreading to provincial towns as well.[5] A still more specialized series offered by the Beethoven Quartet Society from 1845 performed nothing but the cycle of Beethoven's string quartets.[6] At about the same time the Society of British Musicians, founded in 1834 and mainly populated by students and former students of the Royal Academy of Music, provided some encouragement to British composers to try their hand at chamber music. At least seventy-seven chamber works received their first performance there before 1850.[7]

Such small groups of dedicated musicians, largely men, listening to chamber music with a rapt attention whose novelty aroused comment in the press,[8] saw themselves as guardians of the classical tradition in times of declining taste due to commercial interests.[9] The preferred style, therefore, was a conservative one. Mozart, and to a lesser extent Haydn, were the most admired models for composers in the first few decades of the century. In chamber music with piano a powerful influence was that of the 'London pianoforte school' led by Clementi, Dussek, and Cramer.*

There was one composer whose gifts might have enabled him to absorb these influences and forge a truly personal style; but—English music has suffered more than its fair share of these tragedies—he died young. This was George Pinto (1785–1806), a composer who is only now being rescued from neglect. He was a friend of John Field; but whereas Field was a pianist who played the violin, Pinto was a violinist who played the piano. His contemporaries were so impressed with his promise that they spoke of him (as they had spoken of Thomas Linley junior before him) as the English Mozart. His chamber works comprise four sonatas for violin and piano, and nine violin duets.[10] Of these the Sonata in G Minor and the Duet in F (both 1805) are fine specimens of his talent. The former is not simply a promising work—it fulfils its promises. The first movement, marked *allegro moderato con espressione*, is passionate in mood, cogent in argument, and full of splendid thematic invention. The Adagio sostenuto e legato in E flat major which follows is even better. The violin is given a long sustained melodic line of very great beauty, which culminates in a cadence that sounds fifty years ahead of its time (ex. 17.1). It could be argued that the concluding rondo, in G major, is something of an anti-climax; unlike the first two movements it aims only to please. This it succeeds in doing agreeably enough, and as the music flows amiably along there is always some

*See below, pp. 400–14.

Ex. 17.1   George F. Pinto, Violin and Piano Sonata in G minor (c. 1805): 2nd movement

(Adagio sostenuto e legato)

(*P:* Mrs Sanders, c. [1806])·

unexpected twist (usually harmonic) to hold one's attention. The Duet is also a most accomplished piece of work; but, such are the limitations of the medium, it is almost certainly more fun to play than to listen to.

Pinto's friend Field did live long enough to find his own individual style, but he seldom directed his attention to writing chamber music (although he enjoyed playing quartets). Apart from a few transcriptions of piano solos, there are only two Divertissements and a Quintet in A Flat, all for piano and string quartet.[11] Only the last can be counted among his major achievements. Written as one single continuous slow movement, it is in fact (though not in name) an extended nocturne, whose mood Patrick Piggott rightly describes as one of entranced, unruffled calm. This is secured by means that in any other context would have certainly resulted in monotony—unambitious string writing (confined mostly to dialogue with the piano or the occasional accompaniment), lack of any well-defined thematic contrast, and virtually no variety of key. But here the composer's deliberate restraint justifies itself; far from boring the listener, Field imperceptibly hypnotizes him.

Two other composers produced isolated works which are also very considerable achievements. In 1826, when he was sixty, Samuel Wesley wrote a Trio in F for two flutes and piano. This is a very individual blend of Mozartian elegance and Bachian counterpoint, and has deservedly been reprinted. There are two movements. The first is an energetic sonata-allegro, prefaced by an introduction in a pastoral mood; the second presents a rather gentle theme which is the subject of four variations of great resource and inventiveness. Wesley is particularly skilful in obtaining contrasts of texture from a combination of instruments which has strictly limited possibilities. The variations make (as is customary) increasing demands on the virtuosity of the players until the final page is reached; there the thick clouds of demisemiquavers are dispersed, and Wesley returns to the simple mood of the original theme with ravishing effect.

The other work of distinction is the String Quartet in C Minor of Henry Bishop, composed in 1816. Nicholas Temperley has justly written of it: 'This is a most attractive and vigorous work; it is, like so much English music of its period, in the style of Mozart, but has none of the feeble collapses that spoil many works in imitation of that composer. It keeps up a steady flow of musical invention throughout, and preserves a nice proportion.'[12] The cantabile passages for the viola and, in the recapitulation, for the cello are a very attractive feature of the slow movement; the many corrections in the manuscript testify to the care which Bishop took over this composition. It has, as yet, never been printed; the composer's holograph is in the British Library.[13]

Among the more conservative, Mozart continued to exert a powerful attraction for a very long time. As late as 1868 Ouseley published two string quartets which follow very competently in the master's footsteps. It is a pity that the finale of No. 1 in C pays quite such an obsequious tribute to the 'Jupiter' Symphony; but No. 2 in D Minor begins more enterprisingly with a subject that alternates two contrasting tempos (*allegro moderato* and *adagio*). To anyone who is untroubled by anachronisms, these quartets might still give pleasure.

A different influence is at work in the music of Cipriani Potter (1792–1871). As a student in Vienna he became greatly attached to Beethoven*; and the three Grand Trios, op. 12 (1835) owe that master a debt which is charmingly acknowledged on the title page of the third: 'très humblement dedié à L. van Beethoven par son ami et grand admirateur'. Reading these works one is struck by the virile themes and strong rhythmic interest, especially in the scherzo movements; the piano tends to dominate the ensemble, with a good deal of virtuoso writing in the manner of the London School. A strong candidate for revival is the first of the set, a four-movement work in E flat major. Here the piano is partnered not by violin and cello (although alternative parts are provided for that purpose) but clarinet and bassoon. This would make a very valuable addition to the limited woodwind repertoire. Potter also published an unusual 'Sonata di bravura' for horn and piano, in E flat (c. 1825).

Potter's most famous pupil at the Academy was William Sterndale Bennett (1816–75). Although Bennett's reputation as the first great English composer of chamber music in the nineteenth century is justly earned, it rests on only three completed works. (A juvenile string

*In 1815 Beethoven had another English visitor, Charles Neate (1784–1877), who is also credited with the composition of several piano trios.

quartet, written as one of his earliest Academy exercises, should be disregarded.) First in order of composition is the Sextet in F Sharp Minor for piano, string quartet, and double bass, op. 8, written in 1835. The piano plays perhaps rather too prominent a concertante role for the work to be entirely satisfactory as chamber music, but it is full of good things and would make a capital companion piece to Schubert's 'Trout' Quintet. The first movement is marked by Bennett's very fresh and individual brand of lyricism which—contrary to popular belief—is as different from Mendelssohn's as Arne's is different from Handel's.[14] Also most attractive are the Andante grazioso and the scherzo, whose chordal trio makes an excellent foil to the unexpected starts and stops of the scherzo's first subject (ex. 17.2).

Ex. 17.2   William Sterndale Bennett, Sextet in F sharp minor, op. 8 (1835)

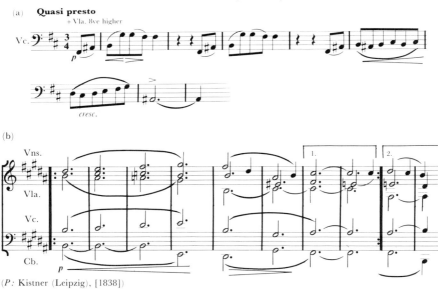

(*P:* Kistner (Leipzig), [1838])

In the Chamber Trio in A, op. 26,[15] the partnership between piano and stringed instruments is perfectly handled. Especially noteworthy is the central 'Serenade', where the pizzicato of the violin and the cello either combines with the pianist's staccato, or contrasts with a single legato line which was so much a feature of Bennett's own playing that 'an eminent Leipzig pianoforte teacher came to him . . . and begged to be initiated into the secret'.[16] The music 'rings with lovely melodies as over-richly as a nest of nightingales' (to borrow a phrase originally applied to the Fantasia in A, op. 16).[17] But its execution is classical—never two notes where one will do. This gives the work a deceptively simple appearance which has sometimes led to its being undervalued, though it was a favourite of the composer and his contemporaries.

We know from a letter of Bennett's in the possession of the family that there should have been a companion Trio in E minor. It seems probable that he completed one movement of such a work; and rather than waste it when the original project (for whatever reason) collapsed, he transcribed it for piano solo and published it as Scherzo, op. 27, in 1845. It is easy to imagine how well such a passage as example 17.3 would have sounded scored for piano and strings.

Ex. 17.3   Bennett, Scherzo for piano solo, op. 27 (1845)

(S: Kistner (Leipzig), 1845)

Bennett's masterpiece is the Sonata Duo, op. 32, for cello and piano,[18] completed in 1852 when the composer was under intolerable pressure owing to a teaching programme of inhuman proportions.[19] This work, above all, reveals Bennett's mastery of large-scale design. The first movement is a sonata-allegro in A minor framed by an Adagio

Sostenuto in A major. This is followed by a 'Minuetto caractéristique', a movement that might be said to foreshadow some of Elgar's delicate light miniatures, and an exuberantly lyrical rondo.

Both the Trio and the Sonata Duo were played (together with music by Bach, Mozart, Beethoven, and Weber) at Bennett's series of forty 'Classical Chamber Concerts' given between 1843 and 1856.[20] Among other important pioneers of the chamber concert at this time were Joseph Dando, whose string quartet concerts were given (like Bennett's) in the Hanover Square Rooms, from 1836 to 1859; and the partnership of Mori and Lindley, which began operations at the Horn Tavern, Doctors Commons, in January 1836. Later, and longer lasting, series were John Ella's Musical Union (1845–80)[21] and the celebrated 'Pops'—Popular Concerts of Chamber Music managed by Chappell & Co. which ran once weekly from 1859, and twice weekly from 1865 until they ceased in 1898.[22] Their 'popularity' seems to have been secured by confining the repertory almost entirely to the music of Germany, though from time to time an English composer did manage to obtain an isolated hearing.

Bennett's pre-eminence as a composer is emphasized by the flatness of the surrounding countryside. His solitary rival was George Macfarren (1813–87), who concentrated on the string quartet. He composed six,* of which only the second, a rather attractive-looking work in F major, was published. Temperley regards the First Quartet in G minor as 'admirable', but considers that 'the later ones are increasingly marked by the quirks and oddities that are present in most of his later works'.[23] The quirks and oddities could equally well be called sparks of originality that prevent his later music from being imitative and uninteresting. Macfarren certainly had a real feeling for the string quartet medium, as is shown both by the all-pizzicato scherzo of the First Quartet, and by the corresponding movement of the Second (ex. 17.4).

Macfarren also published a Quintet in G Minor which he wrote in 1843. This has a number of unusual features. The scoring is for piano, violin, viola, cello, and double bass; the second movement is a barcarolle and the third a bolero with two trios. Other publications include a Duo and a Trio, both featuring the flute; and a *Romanza and Allegro* for piano trio. Two violin sonatas remain in manuscript: the Sonata in A Major, lyrical in feeling and ably written for the instrument, reads the better of the two, but like so many works of the period it outstays its welcome. Recapitulation *in extenso* is all very well when the composer is Sterndale Bennett; he needed a large canvas and knew how to fill it. But

---

*Condemned unheard on second-hand evidence as 'already obsolete' and as displaying 'good musicianship but very little charm.' (Cobbett, II, 108.)

Ex. 17.4 George A. Macfarren, String Quartet No. 2 in F major, op. 54 (performed 1844)
(Vivace capriccioso)

(*P:* Kistner (Leipzig), [1846?])

for others, this practice seems to have been just a matter of thoughtless routine.

Several other composers were encouraged to compose chamber music for the concerts of the Society of British Musicians. Charles Stephens (1821–92) studied, like Bennett, with Cipriani Potter; op. 1 is a Piano Trio, op. 2 a Piano Quartet, both in four movements. Although these works are competently written (and had some success in their day), they contain little to excite interest, chiefly owing to the limpness of the melodic invention which borders dangerously on the sentimental. But the scherzos of both works are an exception, and are enlivened by a very effective use of cross accents. Nothing exceptional occurs to arouse enthusiasm in the duo-sonatas of Charles Edward Horsley (1822–76), for cello, flute, and violin (respectively) with piano, all dating from the 1840s. He was the son of a talented and deservedly popular writer of glees, William Horsley, and like his father was a close friend of Mendelssohn—whose influence, unfortunately, he was quite unable to shake off. Edward Loder (1813–65) composed several string quartets, but they are lost; an impressive Sonata for Flute and Piano in E flat survives only in a manuscript with the last page missing.[24]

Bennett had two pupils who shared his interest in chamber music, and one of them, Francis Edward Bache (1833–58), might have grown into a composer of real stature had he not died in his twenties. He had already published (in Germany) a Piano Trio in D Minor, in which technical mastery and spiritual immaturity go hand in hand. 'Facile' would be too harsh a term, but its merits lie close to the surface. Alice Mary White (née Smith) (1839–84) wrote four piano quartets and three string quartets, but none of them were published—nor, to judge from the state of the manuscripts,* were they ever prepared for publication. One of the latter is, unusually, a programmatic work entitled *Tubal Cain*, containing some cyclic elements as well as quasi-vocal recitative passages for the individual string instruments. Apart from this one venture, however, she could not escape from the overpowering influence of her teacher; the only work of hers which stands any chance of revival today is the Sonata in A for clarinet and piano in three movements, written in 1870—a fluent, fully professional piece which could well be a useful addition to the repertory.

If the work of most of Bennett's pupils and contemporaries causes a certain disappointment, two composers seemingly unlikely to be much interested in chamber music provide a pleasant surprise. And yet perhaps there is nothing odd about Michael Balfe (1808–70) writing for a handful of instruments after a lifetime of working in the theatre, when one recalls the case of Verdi's string quartet and the fact that Balfe began his career as a professional violinist. One's first reaction to Balfe's Sonata in A Flat for cello and piano is likely to be one of amusement; the opening phrase of the principal theme is so very operatic, even to the extent of ending with a loud chord on an off-beat that cries out for full orchestra and bass drum. But soon amusement turns to interest, then to appreciation, and finally to enthusiasm as Balfe's richness of melodic invention and professional skill carry all before them. At the heart of the work is a thoughtful Adagio written—

*These were very kindly put at my disposal by the Rev. Humphrey Kempe, the composer's grandson.

389

many years before Tchaikovsky—in 5/4 time.* The concluding
Allegro vivace contains some nimble counterpoint and, like the rest of
the sonata, is splendidly written for both instruments. It is perhaps a
pity that the coda tries quite so obviously to drum up applause (but
theatrical habits die hard).

Balfe's Piano Trio in A was given its first performance posthumously
in 1877 at a Saturday 'Pop' by Marie Krebs (piano), Joachim, and
Piatti—and well deserved such distinguished performers. As with the
Cello Sonata, the best of the work is to be found in the slow movement
(in character, if not in name, a cavatina). Unlike the Sonata, the Piano
Trio includes a scherzo, in which one commentator (though not this
one) has found 'some reminders of [Balfe's] Irish nationality'.[25] The
only weakness in an otherwise delightful composition is that the subject
matter of the finale—agreeable enough in itself—is rather four-square
in its phrasing; interest consequently flags and the work seems overlong.

The Duo Concertante (1868) for cello and piano by Arthur Sullivan
has a less ambitious design. It is a single-movement work in which an
Andante in G minor introduces a sonata-form Allegro moderato in G
major. Much of what has been said about Balfe's work could be said of
Sullivan's; there is considerable melodic interest, the writing fits the
instruments like a glove, and the craftsmanship is masterly. To give an
example of the latter, the development section of the Allegro moderato
confines its modulations entirely to the flat keys, so that the eventual
return of the sharp key of G major gives extra brightness to the
recapitulation. Equally effective is the blurring of the tonality and the
interruption of the rhythmic flow just before the onset of the coda. An
alternative view of the work is that it is 'an overlong piece [which] also
shows Sullivan's irresolution in development . . . the mechanical
details of formal design are so evident that they effectively prevent any
coherence of idea'.[26]

One further isolated work must be considered before moving on to
our next two major masters, Parry and Stanford. This is a comparatively early composition by one of their contemporaries, Alexander
Mackenzie (1847–1935): his Piano Quartet in E Flat, op. 11 (1874). It
is unlike theirs in that the presiding genius is certainly Schumann. It
aroused von Bülow to such enthusiasm, when he saw the work in proof
at the publishers (Kahnt of Leipzig), that he sought out the composer
to congratulate him and subsequently performed the quartet himself at
Hanover. It has been called in a recent article 'a charming if shallow
work',[27] yet surely it is a composer's job to make his music sound both

*This device was anticipated by, among others, William Shield, in a string trio of 1796.

effortless and entertaining, *if he can*. After a serious Allegro ma moderato (Schumannesque in its melodic outlines, though not in its avoidance of unnecessary doublings) and a brisk scherzo, there follows a set of six variations in C minor. Mackenzie's imagination and resource in treating a theme which in itself does not appear particularly promising can scarcely be too highly praised. Neither can the vitality of the finale; marked *allegro molto e con brio*, it crowns the work with a splendid display of rhythmic and contrapuntal energy.

The Cult of Brahms

If, as is commonly supposed, the middle of the century in Britain was the era of Mendelssohn, then the end of the century was the age of Brahms. Everyone at the time, except perhaps Bernard Shaw, thought that this was a change for the better; but in reality all that had been accomplished was the substitution of one idol for another (just as today the worship of Schoenberg has been succeeded by the worship of Stockhausen).

The chamber music of Hubert Parry (1848–1918) dates from his early years, when his admiration for Brahms was to some extent tempered by an enthusiasm for Wagner,* and when he showed that his natural inclination and genius were for instrumental music first and choral music second. It is a thousand pities that the harsh reality of English musical life compelled him (as it did Elgar) to write so many cantatas: a composer had the chance of a public hearing at one of the big choral festivals, or none at all.

Parry's early chamber works were brought out at semi-private gatherings organized by his teacher, Edward Dannreuther.[28] His published works include two Piano Trios, in E minor (1878) and B minor (1884); a Piano Quartet (1879); a Cello Sonata (1880); and a String Quintet (1884). Three string quartets which he worked at when he was barely out of his teens remain in manuscript, as do a third Piano Trio in G major and a Nonet. (The Third String Quartet was completely rewritten in 1878;† it was performed but never published.)

Reading the scores of the published trios, one is immediately struck by the unusual tonal and rhythmic features which occur in No. 1 (the slighter work of the two). In the opening Allegro appassionato the key

*The original writer of the programme notes for the first performance (probably J. W. Davison) smelt Wagnerian heresy in the Piano Quartet in A Flat. See Cobbett, I, 209.
†Data given by H. C. Colles. Stephen Banfield implies that the revision was not completed until 1880, the year of the first performance. See Banfield, 213.

centre of the first group is E minor, whereas that of the second group is A flat; during the latter section the basic three-crotchet beat is relegated to the background, and over it a conflicting beat of three minims is superimposed. This trio was (surprisingly) Fuller Maitland's favourite.[29] One would have expected the preference to be given to No. 2 in B minor, a virile work with cyclic elements. The first movement begins with a *maestoso* section which recurs (along with other material) as the introduction to the fourth. The second movement, marked *lento*, is a magnificent achievement; in it Parry's gift for sustaining a broad singing line until it grows into a great arch of melody is given the fullest scope. The Lento is separated from the finale by an attractive Allegro vivace in that characteristic 'English' vein which was to reappear in the later suites for string orchestra. The work ends convincingly with an expansive coda in the major key.

The Cello Sonata is a three-movement composition full of good ideas. Unfortunately these eventually grow wearisome owing to an incessant thickness of texture, relieved only by the occasional merciful ascent of both the pianist's hands into the treble register. (One such interlude occurs in the coda of the opening sonata-allegro.) The central Andante sostenuto has been praised as 'one of the finest slow movements in the cello repertory'.[30] Parry himself was the sonata's severest critic: 'it all sprawls about and is too long and indefinite.'[31]

The Piano Quartet in A Flat is arguably Parry's chamber music masterpiece, a spacious, fully cyclic work whose finale brings together elements from all three of the previous movements. The work begins with an introduction which foreshadows the opening march theme of the Allegro molto (ex. 17.5); this returns at the end of the movement to provide a coda of serene beauty. The scherzo, 'one of the small group of highly original scherzos written since Beethoven',[32] is marvellously athletic, and has a slower trio built over a pedal bass. (Pedals also underpin the climax of the slow movement and the principal theme of the finale, a feature which contributes to the work's strongly unified character.) Banfield sees the beneficial influence of Wagner in the Andante, both in the opening theme itself and in the composer's resolute avoidance of full closes. It is a movement of great lyrical warmth and deep feeling. The cyclic finale provides in every way a satisfying conclusion; the return of the march theme from the first movement is no mere contrivance, but the logical consequence of all that has gone before. The balance between the instruments is here—unlike the Cello Sonata—perfectly managed; only the legato second subject of the finale (written for the three strings alone) is difficult to bring off with the exact rhythmic definition required.

Ex. 17.5 C. Hubert H. Parry, Piano Quartet in A flat (1879): 1st movement

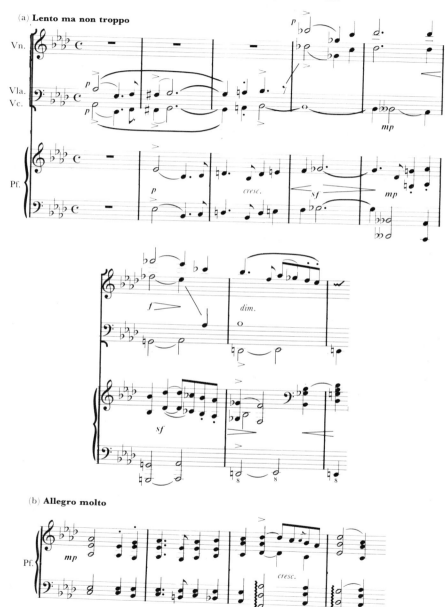

(P: Novello, 1884)

Bernard Shaw diagnosed Stanford (1852–1924) as a case of split personality.* In the right circumstances such tensions can be very fruitful; unfortunately chamber music was for Stanford the Holy of Holies, into which nothing profane or vulgar must be allowed to enter. Consequently the struggle was completely one-sided, with the Professor first and the 'Aboriginal Celt' generally nowhere. The first two String Quartets, op. 44 in G and op. 45 in A minor, written as a pair in August 1891, provide the utterly delightful exceptions to this rule. Both are thoroughly imbued with the spirit of Schubertian lyricism, and sound as if they were undertaken in the relaxed mood of a summer vacation—the musical equivalent, so to speak, of building sandcastles on the beach.

The first Quartet begins with an Allegro assai; Stanford's handling of sonata form is traditional, but without a trace of academicism. Typical is the carefree way in which he prepares for the return of the main key at the recapitulation by modulating through D flat and B major (ex. 17.6). There follows a lilting intermezzo (to all intents and purposes a waltz) with two *presto* interludes, and a warm Largo con espressione in E flat major. The finale is a dashing Irish jig, whose headlong triplets are occasionally, and most effectively, changed into pairs of quavers.

The *molto moderato* movement with which the Second Quartet begins makes one wonder whether Stanford had recently been keeping company with another quartet in A minor, Beethoven's op. 132. Be that as it may, this is a thoroughly unconventional sonata structure, whose opening theme—it later proves to be a 'motto' for the whole quartet—is presented in a variety of polyphonic textures. Transitions are kept to the minimum or omitted altogether, so that the movement is at one and the same time unhurried and concise. The scherzo is quite brilliant, and the contrasting trio has a dance-like quality which, though worthy of Schubert, is entirely Stanford's own. The beautifully scored Andante espressivo grows out of the motto theme; an ideal contrast to this is provided by the unevenly phrased and cleverly varied finale, suggestive of a village fiddler from Stanford's native Leinster. Just before the end the tempo changes to *molto moderato*; with absolute inevitability the slowed-down fiddler's theme gradually gives way to the 'motto' from the first movement—only to reappear faster and wilder than before in a brief, dazzling coda.

The string quartets are the core of Stanford's chamber music. Of the remaining six, only two more were published: No. 3 in D minor and No. 5 in B flat. The Third Quartet still has some attractive and uncommon features. The first movement, *allegro moderato ma appassionato*, is admir-

*See above, p. 374.

Ex. 17.6   Charles V. Stanford, String Quartet in G, op. 44 (1891): 1st movement

(*S:* Eulenberg, 1891)

ably terse, confining its exposition to a mere forty-odd bars. The main theme of the third movement, described as 'Andante quasi fantasia', consists of expressive arabesques for the first violin culminating in *sforzando* chords for the rest of the players. This seems to anticipate the Irish lament which forms the centrepiece of the later clarinet sonata, and certainly leads very convincingly into the energetic Irish reel with which the work ends. But the Aboriginal Celt is altogether banished from the Fifth Quartet, written in 1907 in memory of Joachim. This is unified by using as the final cadence of each movement a little phrase which Joachim apparently used to play to himself in the dressing-room before appearing on the concert platform. But however poignant its

395

associations, the phrase is not sufficiently interesting to justify its inclusion on purely musical grounds. Much the best of the quartet is to be found in the Adagio pesante in F sharp minor, a movement of controlled but real emotional power. The last half-dozen bars of the work, soaring into the upper register, are also genuinely touching.

By the time Stanford had reached the Seventh and Eighth Quartets (written, like the first two, consecutively), composing had become largely a matter of habit. Like Stravinsky he 'began with technique'; unfortunately he ended only intermittently with inspiration. In performance, the scherzo of No. 7 in C minor emerges as much the best movement. This is really vital music, and a welcome change from the Brahmsian type of intermezzo for which (beginning at the time of the third quartet) Stanford had conceived a fatal passion. The slow movement of No. 8 in E minor, entitled 'Canzona', is also a very fine piece of string writing.

Much of the rest of Stanford's chamber music involves the piano (exceptions being the two String Quintets and an unpublished Serenade); all of it is haunted by the ghost of Johannes Brahms. So pervasive is this influence that it reaches right to the smallest details of a composition: characteristic harmonies, triple-time cross-rhythms, even the layout of the piano part. Despite this, some worthwhile music resulted, particularly in the early stages of his career before the machine began to run itself of its own accord. In his own day the Piano Quintet in D Minor, op. 25, was comparatively often played—and deservedly so, for it is superbly laid out for the instruments. The climax in the last movement, where the piano hammers out a rhythmic ostinato in major seconds, might excite even a twentieth-century audience.

Of the three Piano Trios, No. 1 in E flat, op. 35, is a very amiable work, with a finale that handles an unconventional tonal argument vigorously and with conviction. (It begins in C minor and ends in E flat major.) No. 3 in A, op. 158, subtitled 'Per aspera ad astra', was written in memory of five friends killed during the first world war. This has aroused very different reactions, from Thomas Dunhill's '[it] has but little to commend it'[33] to John Porte's 'one of the finest of all Stanford's works'.[34] Dunhill acknowledges, a little grudgingly, that the composer's technique is still in working order, and certainly the cyclic construction is skillfully carried out. (The initial five-note motif becomes, in inversion, the principal feature of a finale in Stanford's bluff 'Devonian' manner.) It is a pity that the work is so incurably conservative in outlook and, perhaps for this reason, so obstinately refuses to stay in the memory.

Of the sonatas, the best is again a comparatively early work, the Sonata No. 2 in D Minor for cello and piano, op. 39 (1893). This improves as it goes on. After a rather easy-going start, the central movement proves to be a minuet-like theme with two variations; these enclose two intermezzos, and are themselves enclosed by three appearances of a recitative-like prelude, producing the musical equivalent of a series of Chinese boxes. This imaginative piece is followed by a splendidly buoyant Allegro giusto, which never loses the impetus given it by the first polyphonic statement of the principal theme. From the Clarinet Sonata, op. 129 (1911), only the justly famous Caoine (or Irish lament) should be preserved. It is prefaced by an Allegro moderato and followed by an Allegretto grazioso, both of a blandness quite intolerable in our day—and, one would like to think, in Stanford's too.

This survey does not exhaust the whole catalogue of Stanford's chamber compositions (there are also two piano quartets, two violin sonatas, and two late sonatas for 'violin accompanied by piano'); nor does it take into account what is perhaps his chief service to chamber music, teaching the greater men who were to follow him. Their work properly belongs to the next volume of this History. But two composers who were not destined to live much beyond the nineteenth century should perhaps be briefly mentioned here—Samuel Coleridge-Taylor, who in 1895 produced a Clarinet Quintet which was warmly received at the time, and William Hurlstone, whose Piano Quartet in E Minor (1906) was, by a tragic irony, given its first performance on the day of his funeral. This magnificent work, and also a very attractive Piano Trio, make one bitterly regret yet another irreparable loss to British music. Stanford has been criticized as a teacher for trying to put his pupils into a musical straitjacket; but this allegation is scarcely borne out by John Ireland's account of the very personal (though strict) treatment he received at Stanford's hands.[35] In any case, his methods cannot have been so very misguided if they could produce such diverse musical personalities as Ireland himself, Vaughan Williams, Frank Bridge, Eugene Goossens, and Herbert Howells.

This chapter would not be complete without a mention of two more composers, both of whom were notable (if for nothing else) for phenomenal industry. John Lodge Ellerton (1801–73)—he was born John Lodge and added the name Ellerton later—composed, at the last count, 54 string quartets, as well as string trios, piano trios, and sonatas for various combinations of instruments. It is tempting to dismiss his entire output as 'mediocre work [which] received some attention from amateurs',[36] and the composer himself as an amateur; but this would be to do Ellerton less than justice. Anyone who looks at the scores of the quartets will see at once that they are perfectly professional affairs, written (admittedly) in a style at least fifty years out of date at the time. It would be truer to say that their content is elementary, so that a single playing of one of his quartets gives considerable pleasure, which then diminishes with each subsequent performance.

The case of Algernon Ashton (1859–1937) is rather sadder. He had high ideals and a certain talent which might have matured into something worthwile if he had not gone to Frankfurt to study, and there fallen hopelessly in love with German music of the most turgid kind. The trouble is not just that his output is so vast (over 150 published compositions) as to be unmanageable, but that his works are so remorseless in their length and so stuffed with notes. He had no powers of self-criticism. He often begins well; one starts to read with interest, only to fall back stunned and exhausted within five minutes. Of his chamber work—there are in the British Library three piano trios, two piano quartets, two piano quintets, and eight sonatas for piano and various stringed instruments—Adolph Mann singled out the Violin Sonata No. 2 in E, op. 38, as particularly worthy of attention,[37] but it is hard to see that it differs greatly from its companions. It might be a better idea to try to revive the Viola Sonata in A Minor, op. 44, if only because the viola repertory is so limited.

Emphasis on the viola is a distinctive characteristic of much British chamber music of the early twentieth century, and here Ashton's Sonata (1891) was a pioneering work. Several players actively promoted the viola as a solo instrument in the '90s, but the most important figure was Lionel Tertis (1876–1975). Because of his eminence as the leading violist in the world, he was able to persuade many composers to write for his instrument, including Bax, Bliss, Bloch, Bowen, Bridge, Dale, Holbrooke, Holst, McEwen, and Vaughan Williams. Benjamin Dale even contributed an *Introduction and Andante* for six violas (1911); York Bowen, though himself a pianist, wrote two viola sonatas and at least ten other works with prominent solo viola parts.[38] Tertis's many pupils continued the tradition and completed his self-appointed task of raising the viola's status to that of a recognized solo instrument. In this development, according to Thomas Tatton, 'composers on the continent were some five to fifteen years behind England'.[39]

The recognition of the viola was part of a more general rise in the prestige of chamber music which was an important aspect of the 'renaissance'. Beginning in 1893, chamber music began to play a part in the growing competition festival movement.[40] Though the Monday and Saturday Popular Concerts ceased in 1898, their place was filled and expanded by a growing number of other chamber music series, including the Musical Artists' Society (1873–99), the South Place Concerts (1887–), the Musical Guild (1889–98), the Broadwood Chamber Concerts (1902–12), and series organized individually by Ernest Fowles, Granville Bantock, Josef Holbrooke, and Thomas Dunhill among others.[41] All these groups actively sought out contemporary British compositions, in the new spirit of musical nationalism, and hundreds of chamber works by British composers were performed by them. The most significant patron of all was Walter Cobbett (1847–1937), a wealthy business man who virtually devoted his life and resources to the promotion of chamber music, and more particularly of chamber music by British composers. From 1905 he ran a series of composition competitions 'designed to bring to light the talents of young British composers'.[42] The first of these required the composition of a 'Phantasy' for string quartet, which Cobbett conceived as a 'modern analogue of the old English Fancy or Fancie', clearly designed to encourage a break with ossified sonata forms by resurrecting methods of an earlier time. No less than sixty-seven manuscripts were received: the winner was William Hurlstone, and the six leading entries were published by Novello & Co.[43] Cobbett also directly commissioned a number of chamber works, including a String Quintet by Vaughan Williams (1911) and a Piano Quintet by Donald Tovey (1912), and encouraged the composition of chamber music in many other ways, such as the periodical *Chamber Music* (1913–16) and the monumental *Cyclopedic Survey of Chamber Music* (1928).[44] As a direct result of his efforts, it was possible for Dunhill to write in 1927 that 'today the revival of chamber music is perhaps the most striking feature on the [British] musical landscape'.[45]

Chapter 18

PIANO MUSIC: 1800–1870

NICHOLAS TEMPERLEY

The 'London Piano School' (1790–1830)

The pianoforte was invented in 1709 by an Italian, Bartolommeo Cristofori. It was not until the 1740s that it began to be widely used, especially in Germany, and it was only in the 1760s that large numbers of German square pianos began to appear in England.[1] From then on there was a steady development of the instrument, which changed radically during the next eighty years before settling down into the approximate form we know today. In this development English manufacturers such as Broadwood and Clementi played a leading part, especially before 1860, when British mass-production, marketing techniques and processed materials (such as steel) enjoyed a decisive superiority over those of other countries. The Broadwood piano was later overtaken by the new technology of the American Steinway, and Britain lost its lead in piano manufacture.[2]

In the period before 1800 the piano gradually replaced the harpsichord, first in the drawing-room, then on the concert platform, finally in the opera house for the accompaniment of recitatives. In this development, also, England was clearly in the lead. German players were still attached to the clavichord at the end of the eighteenth century (Türk recommended it as a beginner's instrument even in the 1802 edition of his *Klavierschule*); while in France the harpsichord remained popular well after 1800.[3] In London, Kirkman is said to have continued to make harpsichords until 1809, but the latest surviving instrument by him is dated 1800, while the latest by Shudi & Broadwood, the other principal manufacturer, is of 1793.[4] In the earlier decades the piano still had about it an aura of novelty and romance, which was kept alive by the almost annual tone improvements, compass extensions, and promotional devices such as harp stops and 'Turkish' percussion effects. Two types of piano, the English and the Viennese, were generally recognized and distinguished. Hummel compared them in his method

400

of 1827.[5] The English pianos were more brilliant in their tone (due to
iron reinforcements and later the all-iron frame), and had greater
sustaining power, but their heavy touch made them less suited to rapid
passage work.

In the 1790s and early 1800s London was the scene of advanced
developments in keyboard composition and performance as well as in
piano manufacture and sale. An important group of composers, many
of them foreign-born, was exploiting the greater power of British-made
instruments, both for virtuoso display and for new artistic effects of a
kind that would later be called 'romantic'; the group has been called
'the London Pianoforte School'.[6] Muzio Clementi (1752–1832), resident in England since 1767, had during his years of isolated study built
up a playing technique that surpassed all rivals (as even Mozart
grudgingly conceded). In his Opus 2 set of solo sonatas,* with their
chains of rapid octaves and thirds, he opened a new epoch in virtuoso
keyboard writing which probably earned him the sobriquet 'Father of
the Pianoforte'.[7] In later life he developed a more profound and highly
individual style of composition, deeply affected by the music of Bach,
and in turn greatly influencing Beethoven: it is at its most impressive in
his last three Sonatas, op. 50 (composed probably in 1804–5,[8] published 1821) and in the *Gradus ad Parnassum* (1817). Jan Ladislav Dušík
(1760–1812), known in England as Dussek, was resident at London
from 1790 to 1800; he was Haydn's chief rival as concert pianist in
1791–2 and 1794–5 and developed his own extraordinarily prophetic
style of writing for the piano during his London years, nowhere better
displayed than in his Sonata in E Flat, 'The Farewell', op. 44, dedicated
to Clementi (1801).[9] Other notable foreign pianist-composers who
resided in London during this period include Daniel Steibelt,
1796–1800 and 1802–5; Joseph Woelfl, 1805–12; Ferdinand Ries,
1813–24; Friedrich Kalkbrenner, 1814–23; and Ignaz Moscheles,
1826–46. All contributed to the English school of the pianoforte.

The English heirs of Clementi and Dussek in the early nineteenth
century were a group of composers of diverse background, each interesting in himself, though hardly together adding up to a cohesive
'school'. Among them were Clementi's leading pupils, John Baptist
Cramer (1771–1858), who came to London as a small infant and
remained there for most of his long career, and the Irish-born John
Field (1782–1837), who made his career in Russia after 1802; the
short-lived George Frederick Pinto (1785–1806) and the long-lived
Cipriani Potter (1792–1871); and, of an older generation and with more
indigenous roots, Samuel Wesley (1766–1837). Between them these

*Alan Tyson has established that this famous work was published in 1779 (Tyson c, 14–15).

men kept up a valuable tradition of serious art music for the pianoforte in a period when popular music held the field; and they paved the way for the modest but accomplished Victorian school of piano music led by Sterndale Bennett. The contributions of each of these five composers will be separately considered.

There was a distinction at this time between concert and domestic piano music. On the concert platform a star pianist such as Cramer or Dussek was most likely to appear in a concerto or other work for piano and orchestra, or in a concertante with a group of string or wind instruments. Concert sonatas, however, on the model of Clementi's Op. 2 were still sometimes to be heard in 1800, though by 1810 they were almost a thing of the past, and for the next two decades pianists rarely played solos of any sort at London concerts.[10] For the home (which, naturally, provided the market for published music) a simpler variety of sonata was produced, with or without optional 'accompaniments' for violin, flute, or cello. In the early years of the century there was still a market for serious solo sonatas, which stimulated a short and brilliant flowering in the sonatas of Field and Pinto. But arrangements of orchestral and operatic music and collections of popular tunes were much easier to sell. Already publishers were trying to popularize the sonata by commissioning ones in which the latter movements, or even all the movements, were based on popular tunes. After 1810 the only serious sonatas composed, without hope of commercial success, were for the benefit of a small band of 'serious' musicians.[11] London was already experiencing the degeneration of keyboard music of which Schumann would complain in Leipzig in the 1830s: in concert music, empty virtuosity; in domestic music, triviality and popularization.*

The steep decline in the demand for serious piano music in England between about 1805 and 1830 is to be accounted for, no doubt, by the fact that piano playing was an adjunct to the rapid rise in social status of the newly rich, which was not yet being experienced to the same degree on the Continent. All the main English keyboard composers of the early nineteenth century, like most of their continental counterparts including Beethoven, wrote popular as well as serious music for the piano. In England it must be assumed that the popular music was written for profit and the serious chiefly for reputation.

Cramer's large output can be rather clearly divided into serious and popular portions. Until about 1810 his works with opus numbers (opp. 1–47) were largely sonatas, with or without accompaniments for violin, flute, etc., and ensemble pieces including concertos. After about 1800 he tended to distinguish between 'grand sonatas', of more serious

*See also Chapter 6.

402

intent, and 'sonatas' introducing popular tunes. The former were frequently dedicated to fellow composers, for instance Op. 22 to Haydn, Op. 29 to Dussek, Op. 36 to Clementi. After 1820 he published only eight more sonatas, all conceived on a large scale, but many works with popular titles such as 'Characteristic Diversion', op. 71 (1824); 'The Banks of the Liffey: Grand Fantasia on Favourite Irish Airs', op. 76 (1827); Capriccio, 'Les Adieux de Baden', op. 83 (1835); 'Convalescence and Hope: Characteristic Impromptu', op. 105 (c. 1845); he lived long enough to publish '12 Characteristic Pieces: Homage to the Memory of Mendelssohn', op. 111 (1848).* Not all such pieces were exclusively popular in intention, but it is clear that Cramer no longer felt it worth his while to publish much purely abstract music such as sonatas. Another class of piano music was his teaching pieces, beginning with the famous Studies (1804–10) which he supplemented at various times, and including several sets of Preludes in all keys, for introducing longer pieces. Cramer had a flourishing practice as a piano teacher and was renowned as a leading exponent of a 'classical' English school of piano playing, with Clementi at its head. In the later part of his life he was regarded in England as 'a great musical bulwark; he prevents the inundation of bad taste by which we are threatened from overwhelming us'.[12] Some of his most interesting music is in his later sonatas, in which he had ceased to try and attract popularity by introducing well-known tunes, and was frankly appealing to serious tastes.[13] Sometimes he wrote in an emotional vein that seems to look ahead to Mendelssohn, as in the last movement of the Sonata in E Minor, op. 59 (1817) (ex. 18.1).

By far the most influential work of Cramer's was his *Studio per il Piano Forte: Consisting of Forty Two Exercises, Intended to Facilitate the Progress of Those who Study That Instrument*, op. 30 (London, [1804]), and its sequel, op. 40 [1810]. These eighty-four *studies* occupy a position of great historical importance. They were the first of their kind: indeed the word 'study' ('étude') appears to have acquired its modern meaning through them, although in Cramer's title it was used in the singular as a name for the whole collection. No comprehensive collection of teaching pieces for the piano, as opposed to other keyboard instruments, had yet appeared, though there had been several 'methods', incorporating brief examples in a book of instructions: for example Clementi's *Introduction to the Pianoforte* (1801).[14] In Cramer's work each study explores a technical problem by many repetitions and sequences of the same melodic pattern, but in a form that makes a performable piece of music, with sufficient variety and harmonic interest and in appropriately balanced form. Clementi himself was preparing such a work under the title of

*The word 'characteristic' in these titles implies nationalistic or programmatic elements.

Ex. 18.1 John Baptist Cramer, Piano Sonata in E minor, 'Les Suivantes', No. 3;
op. 59 (1817): last movement

(S: Clementi, [1817?])

'Studio' and was incensed by his pupil's action in stealing a march on
him: his own *Gradus ad Parnassum* did not appear until 1817.[15] But
whatever the ethics of the situation, Cramer's work was the first in fact,
and became the model for many later collections of studies, though
none excelled it in the opinion of such diverse judges as Beethoven,
Fétis, and von Bülow. Its influence on Beethoven was profound: in
playing the studies one is constantly meeting familiar ideas which,
when pursued, can be traced to Beethoven works of later date. The
most blatant example is the opening phrase of the Study in F Minor, op.
30, no. 16, which Beethoven used wholesale in the last movement of the
Appassionata Sonata.[16]

The other frequent reminiscence is of Bach's 'Well-Tempered
Clavier', and it is abundantly clear that Cramer (as Clementi's pupil)
knew this work thoroughly and had it constantly in mind when composing his studies. Prelude No. 2 of Book One is recalled specifically in
several of the studies, and its stormy mood more generally pervades
many of the minor-key studies. A calmer type of Bach texture occurs in
others, and it is not surprising that Cramer found in the late baroque
period rather than his own the best models for a type of piece that was
necessarily based on pervasive figuration. He seems to have learned
from Bach how to stretch a single pattern through a complete piece by

404

means of sequential passages in which the figuration conceals a full harmonic progression with dissonances and resolutions (ex. 18.2). But even in this type of movement Cramer is still generally tied to the four-bar phrase. In some of the studies he exploits specifically pianistic features, such as the sustaining pedal and the power to 'bring out' a melody against an accompaniment in the same hand, qualities soon to become commonplace, but rarely found in keyboard writing before 1810.

Ex. 18.2   Cramer, *Studio per il Piano Forte*, op. 30 (1804): no. 20, in G major

(*S:* Schirmer (New York), 1904)

Field had an even greater influence on romantic piano music than Cramer. The number of editions of his music, particularly in France and Germany, exceeded that of most contemporaries,[17] and his great influence on later composers, above all Chopin, has been frequently pointed out.[18] In some ways he was a less English composer than the German-born Cramer. Born in Dublin in 1782, he spent the formative years between 1793 and 1802 in London, but during that time was under the shadow of Clementi. He had only two active seasons as a pianist in London, those of 1800 and 1801; then he embarked with Clementi on a world tour, but stayed on in St Petersburg when his master returned home, and spent the rest of his life in Russia except for a not very successful tour of Western Europe in 1831–4.[19] He never enjoyed anything like Cramer's position in London's musical life. His

London apprenticeship as a composer culminated in his Three Sonatas, op. 1 (1801). The very different style of his nocturnes was apparently evolved in Russia; its origins are not altogether clear, but it has no obvious connection with the styles developed in London in the 1790s. The First Piano Concerto is usually held up as a demonstration of Field's early mastery of pianistic writing.[20] But, although the work published as 'Premier Concerto' in 1814 was undoubtedly the same work as that performed on 7 February 1799 at the King's Theatre, London, there is no knowing how extensively the piano part had been revised in the meantime.

The few pieces of Field's that were published in London before 1800 were short rondos and variations of a popular kind, and contain no suggestion of what was to come. The Opus 1 Sonatas, however, mark their eighteen-year-old composer as a true son of the 'London Piano School', showing the influence of Clementi and Dussek in about equal quantities. They are two-movement works with serious first movements in sonata form followed by rondos of semi-popular character. The third is the most unlike Field's later music: it is taut, lean and passionate, very much in the manner of his master Clementi. This is the only movement in all three sonatas, perhaps in all of Field's works, in which there is enough creative drive to provide a true development section. The rondo of No. 1 was later published separately as a 'Rondo brillante'. The texture of its opening was quite original in 1801, with its tenth-leaps in the left hand.

The early years of Field's Russian period yielded no new publications of any importance, but towards the end of his first decade in Russia he began to produce pieces which show a momentous development of style. These include the variations on *Kamarinskaya* (1809), the *Fantaisie sur l'Andante de Martini*, op. 3 (1811), the first three nocturnes (1812), and the B Major Sonata (1813). The new style had no clear predecessors, though elements of it were anticipated by Dussek, Steibelt and Weber. It was presumably worked out by the composer, freed now from the domineering influence of Clementi, as he planned the improvisations for which he was becoming famous in the concert halls of St Petersburg and Moscow. With the end of the Napoleonic wars and the reopening of communications across Europe, his piano works were reissued by Western publishers, and their reputation and influence spread far and wide.

The pieces which made the greatest impression, and which have remained in favour to this day, were the *nocturnes*. The prevailing though not universal texture of these pieces was an expressive sustained melody, carried by the right hand alone, and a richly figured accompaniment in the left hand aided by the pedal. The style of melody and its ornamentation has often been compared with Bellini's vocal cantilenas (which, however, it anticipated by at least a decade). But the technical advance lay primarily in the method of accompaniment (ex. 18.3). Its ancestor was the Alberti bass, but this did not provide the richness of chord spacing that romantic composers desired, and which had been achieved in orchestral music. Field played a low bass note and caught it with the sustaining pedal, leaving the left hand free to fill in a rich accompaniment figure in the middle register until the harmony changed, while the right hand could concentrate solely on the expressive interpretation of the melody. On early pianos the pedal had only a slight sustaining effect on the upper half of the compass, so the melody could include passing notes and elaborate ornaments which would not blur too disagreeably. It was even possible to change the left-hand harmony while holding a pedal bass note with the sustaining pedal, an effect that cannot be precisely reproduced on a modern piano, though it can be approximated by using the middle pedal on a three-pedal Steinway.

This 'nocturne texture',[21] to which other composers were also groping their way at the time, placed at the pianist's command an entirely new range of effects, and Field was the first to exploit them fully. In place of the textures characteristic of the harpsichord, where each note was a clear and finite entity, it was possible to set up a kind of tone cloud through which some notes stood out clearly, others were only dimly perceived. It was analogous to the effect of the sustained winds backing up repeated string chords with such magical effect in some of Mozart's accompaniments. It exactly suited the romantic predilection for undefined feeling, for what Chateaubriand called 'le vague des passions', and it partly accounts for the excitement about the piano generally and about Field's nocturnes in particular. For the first time the amateur pianist, in his own music room, was able to evoke a dreamy world of sound hitherto restricted to the orchestra. He could hold and entrance the sensitive listener from first note to last. The 'sound envelope' was almost continuous; nothing was permitted to break the mood. It has been noticed by several critics that the nocturnes are formally unenterprising and often scarcely leave the home key. Field knew what he was doing. He was not, as in a sonata movement, taking the listener on a journey through largely familiar territory, pointing out landmarks, novelties and contrasts as he went. He was casting a spell. He was the first of the romantic keyboard dreamers, and no successor, not even Chopin, could quite recapture his simple magic.

It is evident from contemporary descriptions that Field's playing

407

Ex. 18.3 Field, Nocturne No. 4 in A major (first published 1817)

Poco adagio

(*S:* Augener, 1872)

contributed greatly to the effect of his compositions: 'his touch on the keys—the way his melodies sang—the easy, heavenly "floating" of his scales and passages';[22] 'singing phrases took on, under his fingers, a sweet and tender feeling that few virtuosi were able to achieve';[23] 'his fingers alone played, without any unnecessary movement of the hand and arm, each finger striking the key with such mechanical power and nicety, that he was enabled to produce the loudest as well as the softest tones, the shortest as well as the longest notes, with equal perfection, without the slightest visible effort.'[24] Clearly Field set up a new ideal of artistic expressiveness to replace the vulgar adulation of mere technical brilliance which had dominated early piano playing. Contemporaries like Spohr, Hummel, and Glinka, who had heard him play in his prime, contributed to the building up of a romantic legend which spread throughout Europe. The 'school of Field' was followed by such musicians as Friedrich Wieck, father and teacher of Clara Schumann, who regarded the 'so-called Viennese school' as 'entirely subordinate' to it.[25] Field was the archetype of the 'artistic' concert soloist, as his master Clementi had been of the 'cosmopolitan virtuoso'.[26] And his poetic miniatures not only had an obvious influence on Chopin, Mendelssohn and Liszt, as well as a host of minor composers of the same generation: echoes of them can be heard even in Fauré, Grieg, Gottschalk, Glazunow, Medtner, and Rachmaninov.

No such widespread influence can be claimed for Field's friend and contemporary, George Frederick Pinto (1785–1806). His reputation was barely established in Britain when he died, 'a martyr to dissipation',[27] at the age of twenty, and was soon forgotten except by a few fellow-musicians who had appreciated his extraordinary talents ('A greater musical genius has not been known'—Wesley; 'if he had lived ... England would have had the honour of producing a second Mozart'—Salomon).[28] These expressions are hardly exaggerated. There are few composers of any period or country whose achievement *before the age of twenty* matches Pinto's in quality and maturity: and 'as a "prophet" of keyboard things to come Pinto is virtually without peers'.[29]

Pinto's father's name was Samuel Saunders; he took his surname from his mother, who was the daughter of a prominent London-born Italian violinist, Thomas Pinto (1714–c. 1780). The violin was his first instrument, and from the age of eight he studied under Salomon. Later the piano became his favourite instrument, and he played both at many public concerts between 1798 and 1803: on one occasion in 1800 he played a violin and piano sonata with Field. His surviving piano music consists of six sonatas; a *Fantasia and Sonata* left incomplete and finished after his death by Joseph Woelfl; three sets of variations; and a few minor pieces.* The most important are the Two Sonatas, op. 3, in E flat minor and A major respectively, and the Sonata in C Minor dedicated to Field: all were published in 1803. As well as the influence of Haydn, Mozart and Dussek, one can see also a resemblance to Field's C Minor Sonata, op. 1, no. 3, especially in the finale of the E Flat Minor Sonata. There is no similarity with Field's mature style. 'Reminiscences' detected in Pinto's music turn out, more often than not, to be of later music—especially that of Beethoven, Schubert, and Schumann.

The arresting opening of the E Flat Minor Sonata plunges at once into romantic gloom: the mood is maintained with unremitting intensity, reaching even greater depths in the coda, and returns in the turbulent finale after a more tranquil slow movement. The A Major Sonata shows a completely contrasting side of Pinto's nature: its serene, pastoral mood is hardly disturbed until the climax of the last movement, but there is a wealth of lyrical invention. The second subject of the first movement contains modulations that remind one to an almost incredible degree of the mature Schubert. The slow movement, beginning on a dominant discord, has a middle section (ex. 18.4) remarkable

Ex. 18.4 George F. Pinto, Piano Sonata in A major, op. 3, no. 2 (1803): 2nd movement

(S: Author, [1893])

*For a detailed list see Temperley GFP, 266.

not only for its profound feeling but also for its technical advance, which looks ahead to the 'song without words' manner of Mendelssohn or Schumann. Pinto is here exploiting the touch discrimination possible on the piano by requiring the right hand simultaneously to bring out a melody and to subdue an accompaniment figure. The C Minor Sonata is again quite different in character, having some of Clementi's taut, 'classical' nervous energy. The last movement is perhaps the best. Pinto did not, like some late-classical composers, suffer from weak last movements; all three contain outbursts of controlled passion that bring the preceding movements to a climax of intensity.

The Three Sonatas, op. 4 (1804–5), are relatively trivial works containing popular movements, and the posthumous *Fantasia and Sonata* has splendid moments but obviously needed revision by the composer. Of the three variation sets, which according to a memoir were his earliest work (they were published as op. 2 in 1802 or 1803), only the second is worthy of Pinto's best efforts. It is on an original theme in E minor, of great pathos, characteristically intensified in the coda (ex. 18.5) with the help of an interrupted cadence. The Minuet in A Flat and Rondo in E Flat may have been movements of another mature sonata. They were published in *The Harmonicon* by William Ayrton, who said that 'either would do credit to the name of the greatest composer that ever lived'.[30]

Samuel Wesley's gifts were not primarily pianistic: his greatest achievements were in choral and organ music.* On the whole he used the piano for popular music that would reach a ready market. His Sonata *The Siege of Badajoz* (c. 1812) was no better or worse than others in the series of battle pieces that began with Kotzwara's *Battle of Prague*. But he cultivated serious sonatas as long as they were publishable. His *Four Sonatas and Two Duets*, op. 5 (1801), are modest, workmanlike pieces in the Clementi tradition. The most remarkable work is *A Sonata . . . in which is Introduced a Fugue from a Subject of Mr. Salomon* (1808), where Wesley shows a restless searching after possible innovations of style that he never pursued again in piano music. The disturbingly emotional slow introduction is quite Pintoesque in places (ex. 18.6), while its double dots are a conservative feature. The main movement is the fugue, in which Wesley displays his great contrapuntal facility to the full. It may have been meant as a tribute to Bach, but the style is more reminiscent of Handel's fugues in its dramatic treatment of the entries and unfugal episodes, and of Mozart's in its aggressive dissonance. Of the fugue's 194 bars, 35 form an interlude in the tonic major, which are

*See pp. 210–12, 440–4.

Ex. 18.5 Pinto, *Three Favourite Airs with Variations*, op. 2 (1802–3): no. 2, in E minor

(*S:* Author, [1802–3])

followed by a frenetic stretto and coda. The whole is remarkable for stamina and inventiveness, and comes across as a series of spontaneous ideas rather than an integrated structure. The final Allegretto, in D major, is a quiet pastoral movement, and its calm is the more appreciated because of the prolonged tension of the fugue.

Ex. 18.6   Samuel Wesley, Piano Sonata in D minor (1808): introduction

(S: Birchall, [1808])

Cipriani Potter's output of piano works is modest. Much of his composing career was devoted to a quixotic effort to establish himself as a symphonist* and, in addition, he expended great energies as a performer, teacher and administrator.[31] He wrote at least four sonatas early in his career, a number of teaching pieces, and some variations and character pieces of various kinds. He succumbed infrequently to the temptation of writing popular piano music. A considerable curiosity is *The Enigma: Variations and Fantasia on a Favourite Irish Air* (1825) in which he provided a parody of the styles of several leading composers of the time.[32] Potter was a great admirer of Beethoven, whose influence is evident in his sonatas. His studies, including a set of twenty-four in all keys, written for the students of the Royal Academy of Music, show an assured technique, a command of technical difficulty, and an occasionally original manner, and are well worthy of the Clementi-Cramer

*See pp. 364–5.

413

tradition. But with all these virtues Potter's music lacks the qualities to make it memorable, above all the gift of melodic invention. His great importance is as an influence on his successors.

The Romantics (1830–1870)

In the next generation a new note enters the tradition of serious piano music in Britain. There is a strong element, now, of *consciously* preserving a tradition of refinement and artistic integrity against commercial pressures. Unlike their predecessors, the new school of composers disdained to write popular piano music, turning to other activities such as teaching, journalism, and administration as means of livelihood, while keeping their music pure and aloof from influences thought to be harmful. There is an obvious parallel here with the attitudes of Mendelssohn and Schumann. The English analogue of *Davidsbund* was a small group of young musicians trained at the Royal Academy of Music, who formed the nucleus of the Society of British Musicians. Their principal teacher, Cipriani Potter, implanted in them a sense of the importance of instrumental music and a reverence for the German classical composers, above all Mozart,[33] and they consciously sought to preserve and develop the classical ideal. It was only the Academy composers in this period who were serious about the piano as a vehicle for composition, and cultivated the artistic, quiet, intimate style of piano playing initiated by Field, in opposition both to popular domestic piano music and to the spectacular virtuosos such as Herz, Thalberg and Liszt who were successively lionized by the fashionable concert-going public. George Hogarth remarked in 1835 on the 'purity of the English School of the pianoforte', founded on the studies of Clementi and Cramer, which, in turn, were based on the 'old masters':

Students thus imbued with solid knowledge and good taste, are in little danger of being corrupted by the shallow and frivolous style which, springing from Vienna and Paris, is spreading itself over Europe. Our principal public performers, Mrs. Anderson, Neate, Potter, and Bennett and a great number of excellent teachers, not only in London, but all our principal towns, belong to the school of these great masters, and follow their footsteps in tuition.[34]

There is little doubt that the existence of this 'school' was largely due to the influence of Potter's teaching and example.[35] It was certainly centred on the Academy, where Lucy Anderson, Potter, and Bennett all taught the piano. The leading composers were William Sterndale Bennett (1816–75) and George Alexander Macfarren (1813–87). Their

414

close colleague and fellow Academician, James William Davison (1813–85), gave up composing after some early failures, but became a formidable champion of his friends' music in *The Times* and *The Musical World*. Other composers in the Academy group included Charles Lucas (1808–69), Thomas M. Mudie (1809–76), William H. Holmes (1812–85), Charles E. Stephens (1821–92), Kate F. Loder (1825–1904), and Macfarren's younger brother Walter (1826–1905). But the leader of them all was Sterndale Bennett, who alone gained the ultimate accolade of recognition in Germany.

This school of composers was typical of conservative romanticism in its conception of itself as the bearer of a special mission to preserve the high ideals of art. But it could not quite produce from within its own ranks a composer who would provide a sufficiently strong nucleus for its aspirations, and it was dependent on frequent infusions of creativity from its German counterparts, above all from Mendelssohn. The Society of British Musicians, which excluded foreign music from its concerts, was never taken seriously by the public, and the high points of Bennett's musical endeavours were his own Classical Chamber Concerts, in which his music and that of his colleagues took its place among established works of the Viennese classics or recent compositions of Mendelssohn and Spohr.

Bennett was orphaned as an infant, and brought up by his grandfather, a lay-clerk of King's College, Cambridge.[36] He entered the R.A.M. in 1826 (before his tenth birthday) and his most productive period as a composer began in 1832, when he came under Potter's influence. Greatly encouraged by Mendelssohn's praise of his first piano concerto, he continued for several years to produce major orchestral works, and he accepted Mendelssohn's invitations to visit him in Leipzig. There he soon became a recognized member of the school of composers of which Mendelssohn was the leader. Schumann, a prominent member of that circle, soon spotted Bennett's talent, and praised him highly in the *Neue Zeitschrift für Musik*: 'Were there many artists like Sterndale Bennett', he wrote in 1837, 'all our fears for the future progress of our art would be silenced.'[37] Bennett's reputation in Germany remained high throughout his life, but he refused the signal honour of the conductorship of the Gewandhaus concerts which was offered to him in 1853. Instead, he settled down to a long career of teaching and administration in England. His determination to maintain the high ideals he had set for himself, in the face of many discouragements, commands admiration.

Most of Bennett's piano music was composed in the years between 1834 and 1856, when he was regularly playing in public. Some, such as the Capriccio Scherzando, op. 27, the Toccata, op. 38, and the Rondeau à la Polonaise, op. 37, are clearly concert pieces of considerable technical difficulty; others, like the three pieces of op. 28 and the Rondeau 'Pas triste, pas gai', op. 34, are deliberately simple pieces dedicated to his pupils. (Similarly with the charming Three Diversions, op. 17, for piano duet.) In both cases the foundation of his style was clearly the *character piece*, a single movement in ternary or abridged sonata form which established and maintained a mood, in part by means of a persistent figure that could serve as both melody and accompaniment. In an illuminating paper on Bennett's piano music, Geoffrey Bush has identified the greatest works as the Sonata in F Minor, op. 13;[38] Three Romances, op. 14; and Fantaisie, op. 16—all dating from 1837—and the Suite de Pièces, op. 24,[39] published (though not necessarily composed) in 1841.[40] After that early peak his piano music shared in the general decline of his creative powers, though there were occasional revivals of his youthful strength, even in his last work of substance, the Sonata 'The Maid of Orleans', completed in 1873. But in these large-scale works there is rarely an attempt at large-scale forms. The Suite and Fantaisie are groups of independent movements in suitably related keys; and in individual movements Bennett, like most of his contemporaries, was more at ease repeating, varying and contrasting materials than developing them. His only really successful extended 'development' section is in the first movement of the F Minor Sonata. But it would be a mistake to assume that the delicate restraint of his more popular pieces is the only mood Bennett was able to evoke. The emotional range of his larger pieces is considerable, and Bush has convincingly refuted Hadow's opinion that Bennett was incapable of 'vehemence and passion'.[41] Few piano works by any composer are more passionate than the A minor finale of the A Major Fantaisie, whose coda (ex. 18.7) seems to anticipate in mood and idea the finale of Chopin's B Minor Sonata. (A lesser composer would have written a D, not a B flat, as the bass of the Neapolitan chord in this example.) If it is argued that the style of this passage is Mendelssohnian, it is well to remember its affinities with Cramer (compare ex. 18.1). The style could be purely English in origin.

Bennett was a master of piano texture. He was 'essentially a composer for the piano',[42] and was keenly alive to the limitations as well as the possibilities of the instrument. He never, for example, overstrained its powers of sustaining a melody: the delicious 'second subject' of his Impromptu, op. 12, no. 1 (ex. 18.8) has the tune placed in the resonant tenor register, and its longest notes are given every chance to last out their allotted time by an avoidance of chord changes, and by keeping

Ex. 18.7   William Sterndale Bennett, Fantasie in A major, op. 16 (1837): finale

(Presto agitato)

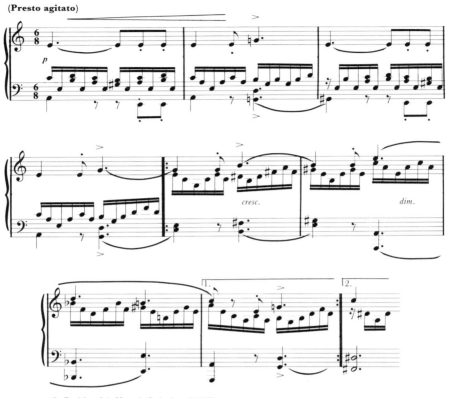

(S: Breitkopf & Härtel (Leipzig), [1837])

the accompaniment in a remote pitch register and light texture. Typical of Bennett is the subtle way in which the right hand imperceptibly
takes over the melodic lead. Also characteristic are certain harmonic
asperities, such as the inverted tonic pedal, the evaded resolution, and
what might be termed harmonic anticipation.[43] These and many other
unobtrusive details give Bennett's style a distinction and an individuality, so that, as Schumann pointed out, it has a 'remarkable family
resemblance' to the style of Mendelssohn, '. . . but with a difference'.[44]
    At the same time it is idle to deny this resemblance, which is not a
matter of plagiarism but a natural similarity between contemporaries
who were remarkably at one in their musical backgrounds and ideals.
And, after all, resemblance to the style of Mendelssohn is not in itself a

Ex. 18.8 Bennett, Three Impromptus, op. 12 (1836): no. 1
(Andante espressivo)

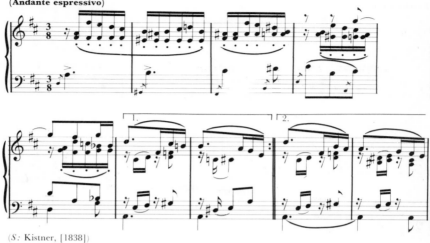

(*S:* Kistner, [1838])

disgrace. The fairylike staccato which was one of Mendelssohn's trademarks was also successfully exploited by Bennett, in such works as the Presto Agitato (no. 5 of the *Suite*) or 'The Fountain', op. 10, no. 3, 'but with a difference'. The 'song without words' texture was at least as much English as German in its antecedents, as we have seen; and Mendelssohn wrote no more beautiful or original example than Bennett's Romance, op. 14, no. 2 in E flat major, full of unexpected dissonances and harmonic ambiguities that mitigate the sweetness of this style. Bennett also shared some of Mendelssohn's weaknesses, including a distressing tendency to drop an accompaniment figure when it is most needed, and fall back weakly on plain chords (e.g., op. 18, bars 55–6; op. 37, bars 31–2).

Schumann was right in crediting Bennett with the technical command and the inventiveness to make a composer of the first rank. That he did not, in the end, manage to do so has been explained in various ways: by the unfavourable musical climate of England (from which, however, Bennett could have escaped if he had chosen); by the lack of opportunity to have his works performed; by exhaustion due to other demands on his time.[45] Much of the undoubted decline of his later years can be put down, however, to 'internal' causes. It must be remembered that Mendelssohn and Schumann, as well as Bennett, failed in their maturity to surpass the achievements of their youth and early middle age, and are unusual among the great composers in the fact that their later works are not, on the whole, so highly regarded as their earlier ones. This was indeed characteristic of this phase of romanticism (compare Wordsworth). All three composers consciously set themselves against many of the current developments in music, and set out to keep alive techniques and styles that no longer had real vitality. Their self-inflicted deafness to current musical sounds required a degree of conscious restraint that in the end interfered with spontaneous expression. With Bennett there may have been an additional psychological factor: an exceptionally intense need for encouragement and reassurance caused by the early loss of both parents. During the 1830s he was exhilarated by the admiration of Mendelssohn and Schumann among others, but both showed their disappointment with Bennett's failure to increase his stature as a composer, and by 1850 neither was in a position to help him. Later he was depressed by a series of professional quarrels on matters of principle. After 1850 he generally required the stimulus of a specific commission to set him to work, and even then there is evidence that the act of composition cost him tremendous efforts of self-discipline. Loneliness and defeat speak from the dispiriting pages of the late songs and piano pieces, and from *The Woman of Samaria*. Fortunately, however, Bennett had already in his earlier years produced a body of works that establish his position as a minor master.

Macfarren was a much tougher character than Sterndale Bennett, and was less easily discouraged from his goal of maintaining classical ideals. For example he did not, like Bennett, give up orchestral music after his time as a student at the Academy, but persisted in writing symphonies for the rest of his life; most of them were lucky if they received one performance. He also achieved much in opera and oratorio. Similarly he persevered in the classical sonata,[46] when this was hardly a way of acquiring a reputation. He modelled his style on Mozart and, more noticeably, Beethoven. If his natural talent was smaller than Bennett's he was capable of calculated boldness which occasionally gave his themes the stamp of originality, and his development technique was considerable. The Sonata No. 1 in E flat (1842), first played at Macfarren's and Davison's concert the following year, is a large-scale four-movement work. Its first two movements both contain strong reminiscences of Beethoven's sonatas (e.g. his op. 7 and op. 28), but also a number of innovative ideas; the fiercely dissonant scherzo must have been unacceptable to most ears in its time. Sonata No. 2 in A (1843), subtitled 'Ma Cousine', is a gentler work, its slow movement virtually a song without words. No. 3 was written some time

later for the prominent pianist Agnes Zimmermann, and its first
movement in G minor has a fine Mozartian tragic sweep with some
astounding modulations.

No significant composer outside Academy circles devoted himself to
serious composition for the piano. But two, whose main energies were
directed to other kinds of music, each produced one remarkable composition for the instrument. Samuel Sebastian Wesley (1810–76), who
was a notable pianist especially in his earlier years, claimed to be a
representative of the school of Clementi, Cramer, Kalkbrenner, and
Moscheles.[47] Apart from youthful efforts his piano works are said to
consist of a set of three quadrilles entitled 'Jeux d'esprit' (1846), written
satirically 'in the style of Herz', a Rondo in G (1839), and a March and
Rondo (1842). I have only been able to trace a copy of the last of these.
It is a piece of such formidable energy and difficulty as to suggest that
Wesley, if he had not had his mind set on church music, could have
been one of the great pianist-composers of the age. The march proceeds
at a hectic pace (♩ 168) and is as terrifying as Berlioz's 'Marche au
supplice', even though it contains late echoes of Mozart's C minor
Fantasia—it is in the same key. Both the main section and the C major
trio return with driving triplet accompaniment. The rondo (*allegro con
spirito*, C major) is a huge sonata-allegro, with a Dussekian profusion of
ideas, a main subject (ex. 18.9 (a)) that promises continuous energy

Ex. 18.9 Samuel Sebastian Wesley, March and Rondo in C minor and major (1842): Rondo

Allegro con spirito (♩ = 120)

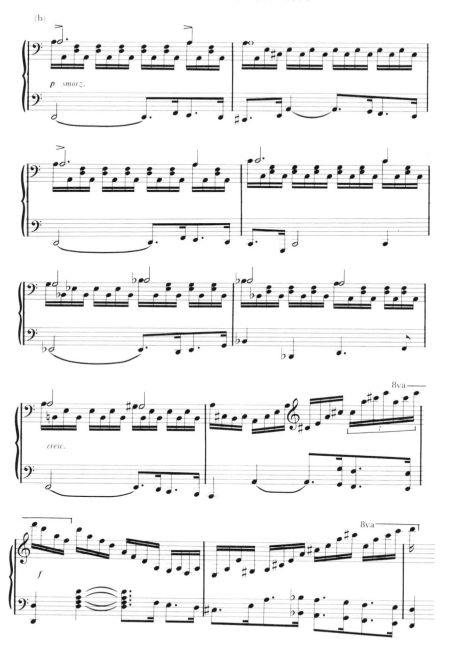

(*S:* [Hawes?], 1842, repr. Novello, Ewer, n.d.)

421

and bustle (a promise that is not belied), but also many moments of lyrical passion. The second subject (which does not return in the recapitulation) sounds like an addition to Mozart's variations on 'Ah, vous dirai-je, Maman'; but during a lull in the tumultuous development section there appears a splendid tune in D minor recalling Weber or even Wagner, first *sotto voce* low in the piano compass and then in a wildly pianistic variation (the whole of the former and the beginning of the latter are shown in ex. 18.9 (b)). The piece winds up to a bravura coda and a big C major ending that betrays its origin or destination in the concert hall. There is not a trace in this brilliant piece of the organ loft, a locale which critics are inclined to detect any time a church composer tries his hand at secular music; and it would well repay any pianist bold enough to tackle it.

Only one piano work by Henry Hugo Pierson (1815–73) has survived. 'Musical Meditations: Three Romances for the Piano Forte' was published in 1844 when the composer was still calling himself 'Professor of Music in the University of Edinburgh',[48] and was dedicated to 'the illustrious Meyerbeer'. Pierson headed each Romance with a quotation. The first, subtitled 'Lost Happiness', has the same excerpt from Dante's *Inferno* that would later be used by Stanford for his Rhapsody, op. 92, no. 1.* It alternates a pathetic E minor strain with a lyrical passage in E major; the two are mixed in the central development section, but the major passage ends the piece (oddly, considering the title and implied programme). The other two carry less personal messages, No. 2 a descriptive quotation about dawn from Lamartine, and No. 3 merely 'O primavera, gioventù dell'anno' (Guarini). Though both have interesting passages, and are again reminiscent of Dussek,† their alternations of mood and metre, and their frequent surprises, do not always make musical sense, and are not explained by any stated programme.

The important advances in European piano music in this period were made not by those such as Mendelssohn who adhered to classical ideals, but by those such as Chopin and Liszt who boldly grasped the popular demand for spectacular virtuosity and made something new and great out of it. No English composer participated significantly in these developments, though Wesley might have done; and hence English piano music dropped out of the European mainstream, in which it

---

*See below, p. 429.

†Curiously enough No. 3, like Wesley's March, has a section that quite explicitly recalls Berlioz's 'Marche au supplice'. The *Symphonie fantastique* had not yet been performed in England: Pierson could have heard Berlioz conduct it at Dresden in February 1843, or earlier at Paris; Wesley could only have seen Liszt's piano transcription, published in 1834.

had a leading position earlier in the century. Thus, despite Bennett's individual achievements, the early Victorian period must be regarded as a decline after the collective importance of the London Piano School.

Chapter 19

PIANO MUSIC: 1870–1914

JOHN PARRY

New musical thought and pianistic innovation in the romantic period came from the pen of composers who were incidentally gifted pianists, but more particularly from professional virtuosos who could play their own music to enthusiastic and often idolatrous audiences. For whatever reason, Britain did not produce specimens of this breed of virtuoso-composer; but the British public was willing to pay well for the privilege of hearing the leading continental examples. Some, like Moscheles and Thalberg, made fortunes in London; others, such as Agnes Zimmermann (1857–1925), to whom many compositions by prominent British composers were dedicated, and Charles Hallé (1819–95), who did much to popularize Beethoven's sonatas,[1] made England their home.

Thus the bulk of the enormous expenditure on piano music went into the hands of foreign musicians and their publishers. For the young composer with an English name, however talented and impeccably trained he might be, financial reward and popularity could only be attained by composing small pieces for gifted amateur pianists and drawing-room songs for musical evenings around the piano. (Such music has been dealt with in Chapter 6.) A few British-born composers turned their hand occasionally to piano music of serious intent, but it was not until after 1900 that a British composer again produced works of lasting importance.

Among Sterndale Bennett's pupils at the Royal Academy of Music was a personable young man of Irish extraction who admired the strength of his teacher's fingers, lazily reflecting perhaps that it must have taken a lot of practice to achieve such a fine technique. His studies continued in Leipzig, and it was thanks to his teacher, Moscheles, that the young man, Arthur Sullivan, became as he himself admitted 'a tolerably good pianist'. Ten short pieces are his total surviving output for the piano, all written between 1861 and 1867 following his return from Leipzig.² They are all simple in form and content and, with the exception of the Allegro Risoluto in B flat minor published for the first time in 1976, do not call for exceptional skill at the keyboard. Their source of inspiration, as might be expected, is Mendelssohn. It was in miniatures like these that he could excel: *The Musical Times* noted in its reviews of the six pieces entitled 'Daydreams', op. 14, that 'there is no power more rare than that of producing trifles impressed with special value and marked character: and of this power Mr. Sullivan seems to possess a considerable share'.³ Each 'Daydream' has attractive features: the ambiguous D flat at the end of the first (*andante religioso*) which almost forces a change of key from F to A; the unexpected French sixth at the end of the fifth (*andante con molto tenerezza*); and the constant play between major and minor which is a characteristic of the third, fourth, and sixth. The best of the group is the fourth, a lively waltz, in which he shows how easily he could move from key to key. It ends, as does the 'A l'Hongroise' which concludes the set, on an effective cascade of notes.

There is a sunny Schubertian start to the first of two charming *Thoughts*, op. 2, while the second has an opening reminiscent of Schumann. But the best of his compositions for piano is undoubtedly the evocative nocturne *Twilight*, whose feline turn of phrase and tonal variety have a simplicity not lacking in subtlety. The Allegro Risoluto was perhaps intended as a companion piece to *Twilight*, being in its relative minor and written at about the same time. Its restless inner chromatic semiquaver movement presents technical difficulties which make it a useful study; but the stern melody with which it opens never gets any thematic development, and its brevity is therefore perhaps a disappointment.

Hubert Parry (1848–1918) worked and practised hard for many years at the piano, but seldom did himself justice when playing in public. In private with a few congenial friends he was a delightful and exhilarating performer, especially in the works of Bach, Beethoven, Schumann, and Chopin, which he studied for many years with Edward Dannreuther. In his early years he excelled in improvisation. The three sets of *Sonnets and Songs without Words* (1869–79) are dull, with only 'Gnome' and 'Owlet' from the first set showing any trace of originality. The seven *Charakterbilder* (1872) are more substantial but flat and uninspired. These early pieces were played at musical soirées held by Dannreuther.

The *Grosses Duo* (1877) for two pianos shows the influence of J. S. Bach so strongly that, were it not for the grotesque fugal subject of the last movement, it could be mistaken for an original work by Bach himself, brilliantly arranged for the modern piano perhaps by Busoni:

it is extremely well laid out for the two instruments. Parry's 15 Variations and Finale on an air in E minor by Bach, composed 1873–5, were
never published. The theme of another set of variations, in D minor,
which he published in 1885, could well be by Bach also, but in fact is
original. The variations follow an interesting course: most of them
overlap, and it is impossible to count them as they go by. Even Parry,
when challenged to number them, gave up the attempt after twice
getting different answers.[4] They represent an attempt to solve problems
which he mastered later in the Symphonic Variations. The theme is
immediately followed by three variations in D minor, dissolving into a
lyrical D major. By means of a weak canonic link, a Brahmsian section
in A major is introduced, followed by three variations in A minor. The
writing here is particularly original (ex. 19.1), and builds up to a
ferocious climax in double octaves. Perhaps bearing in mind Macfarren's comment that harsh passages in Bach are followed by ones of
unequalled beauty,[5] this climax is succeeded by a sensuous passage in F
major. A martial transformation of the theme brings us to the final
pages, which start quietly over a pedal bass, building until the theme
appears as a grandiose tune (which Elgar would surely have marked
nobilmente). This dies away into a thematic inversion, and with a final
crescendo the work is over.

Ex. 19.1   C. Hubert H. Parry, Theme and Variations in D minor (completed 1885)
(Allegro non troppo)

(*S:* Stanley Lucas, 1885)

426

Parry's two Sonatas (1877, 1878) are very disappointing: he was not happy working in this form. Both are very conservative works, with the usual classical four movements, and the occasionally sentimental ideas are developed in an academic manner. The piano writing is competent but uninspired, the layout sometimes reminiscent of organ writing. The best movement in either sonata is the scherzo of No. 1; it was published separately in later years. A much later but still academic work is the Suite *Hands Across the Centuries* (1918): the pieces observe all the traditions of every dance, such as the sarabande and gavotte, harmonized in what was then a modern style. The courante was rewritten several times in order to get the proper curve up to the climax and a just balance of keys.[6]

The ten pieces in the album of *Shulbrede Tunes* (1914) constitute Parry's best pieces for piano: he obviously had a deep personal affection for the home of his daughter, her husband and their children, and his pranks at children's parties have been described by his son-in-law.[7] The opening piece 'Shulbrede' with its surging arpeggio figuration might well be his excitement on arriving there. 'Elizabeth' and 'Matthew' are probably likenesses of the two grandchildren and there are two pieces called 'Dolly'. There is vigour in the arresting opening of 'Children's Pranks' (ex. 19.2) and humour in the dénouement of the 'Bogies and Sprites that Gambol by Nights'. Here, in the middle of the

Ex. 19.2 Parry, *Shulbrede Tunes* for Piano (1914): No. 7, 'Children's Pranks'

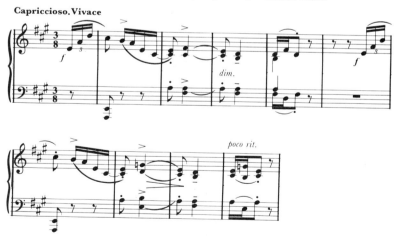

(*S:* Augener, 1914)

427

night, the ticking of the grandfather clock and the first three notes of a well-known nursery rhyme grow into terrifying proportions. After much scampering around and much play of being frightened the cause is revealed by the rest of the nursery rhyme—'Three Blind Mice'. The mice have the last word with a final squeak. There is a quiet nocturne 'Prior's Chamber by Firelight' and a diatonic and very English 'In the Garden—with the Dew on the Grass'. A feature of most of the group is the introduction of the key of the flattened sixth before the end, as in the concluding 'Father Playmate'. This is a passacaglia and an uproarious portrayal of the tricks he would get up to with his young friends.

Mention must also be made of the excellent two sets of *Characteristic Popular Tunes of the British Isles* for piano duet (1885) intended for young performers which are easy to play and provide much fun, and of the *Five Miniatures* (published 1926), notably 'Little Christmas Piece' and 'Capriccio'.

The imagination and wit that Parry showed in such pieces were amply possessed by Charles Stanford, and are displayed in the early Suite, op. 2, and the sparkling, if somewhat Germanic, Toccata, op. 3, which was written when Weber's 'Perpetuum mobile' was the *ne plus ultra* of piano technique. The manuscript of Stanford's unpublished Piano Sonata in D Flat, op. 20, has disappeared, but a contemporary review called it 'one of the most important compositions for piano solo produced within the present generation'.[8] Also lost are a group of Six Pieces, op. 42, and a Scherzo in B Minor. The 'Ten Dances Old and New', op. 58, are excellent. Written like Parry's 'Shulbrede Tunes' with young people in mind, they offer no great difficulties to the young enthusiastic pianist and they illustrate very well the characteristics of each dance. The set is up to date, as it includes a polka and a galop as well as a mazurka, a morris dance, and a waltz.

Stanford in 1904 published Three Rhapsodies, op. 92, composed in 1875, and dedicated them to Percy Grainger. They were yet another reason why for seventeen years Stanford never spoke to Elgar. In 1905, in his inaugural lecture as first professor of music at the University of Birmingham, Elgar mocked the writers of rhapsodies and some of the English music written since 1880: 'Twenty, twenty-five years ago, some of the Rhapsodies of Liszt became popular. I think every Englishman since has called some work a Rhapsody. Could anything be more inconceivably inept? To rhapsodize is one thing Englishmen *cannot do* . . . It points a moral showing how the Englishman always prefers to imitate.'[9] Stanford took this as a personal attack: the rhapsodies were his best and most difficult piano pieces.

These tone poems—for that is what they are—have as their inspiration Dante's *Inferno*, and our hopes rise when we see a quotation at the head of the first, 'Francesca':

> Nessun maggior dolore,
> Che ricordarsi del tempo felice
> nella miseria.   (Canto V)

It tells of the fateful love of Francesca for the brother of her crippled husband and of her death. This is a most moving piece, without a doubt the best of the group, and one that can very well stand by itself. The second is 'Beatrice' (from Canto II), the embodiment of heavenly truth, who guides Dante eventually through Paradise to the presence of God. She is depicted in a flowing 9/8 in B major with a contrasting middle section in which an insistent bell-note is heard. It is a warm gentle piece contrasting well with the last of the group, 'Capaneo':

> Se Giove stanchi'l suo fabbro . . .
> E me saetti con tutta sua forza;
> Non ne potrebbe aver vendetta allegra.   (Canto XIV)*

Here we plunge into a development of symphonic proportions. The battle of Thebes is portrayed in a lusty C major, the music also depicting Capaneo's climb to the top of the walls of the beleaguered city, his blasphemy against Jove, and the thunderbolt that strikes him down. The middle section finds him still unrepentant in the seventh circle of Hell. Broad flakes of fire fall on him and set the sandy ground alight. After a reprise the final page concludes with a broad melody marked *nobilmente*. As Stanford believed and explained in a treatise of Musical Composition that it was not necessary to depict an ugly character or situation by illustrating it with ugly music,[10] this is naturally the least successful of the rhapsodies. He seems almost afraid to expose any great feeling. Bernard Shaw commented (in another context): 'As a professional man with a certain social position to keep up, it would be bad form to make a public display of savage emotion. But as it is, Mr Stanford is far too much the gentleman to compose anything but drawing-room or class-room music.'[11]

Stanford's writing for the piano is professional and idiomatic, almost to the extent of being facile. No exceptional demands are made on the performer, although he presupposes a complete command of the instrument. His disdain for virtuoso display is the more surprising as he was himself an excellent pianist. To him the body of the music was the main thing, not the clothes in which it was dressed. But this dislike of empty piano figuration occasionally militates against him in the Five

---

*Stanford's arrangement of both quotations has been reproduced here.

Capriccios, op. 136, published in 1913. The opening march would sound better in the orchestra, as would the scherzo-like third piece. The most dramatic of the group, the second, has a broad melody in octaves, which would be better sustained by brass instruments, but it is also remarkable for some striking exploitation of piano sonorities. This is followed four bars later by a passage of great beauty (ex. 19.3), where rising and falling semiquavers support a flowing melody which is joined eventually by another. This is lovely writing, typical of Stanford at his best. The lyricism is also well illustrated by the opening melody of the fourth capriccio in B flat. It is perhaps the best of the set, despite the weakened climaxes, and has some good pianistic writing. The last, a charming 'Tempo di Valse' in A flat, steers a course between Brahms and Chopin. His later piano music relies more and more on Brahms and has few moments of real imagination or originality.

Elgar was not completely at home with the piano and did not seem to enjoy writing for it. 'In Smyrna' (1905) is one of the better compositions, a souvenir of a month's holiday spent on a cruise in the Mediterranean, a haunting piece which paints a mood of sadness. There is an interesting cadenza towards the end, but the shimmering effect of a *tremolando* open fifth might be even more effective on violins, and the opening melody seems ready-made for a French horn; Elgar thought orchestrally. His Concert Allegro (1901) was likened by Richter to a marriage between Bach and Liszt.[12] As might be expected from this comment it is an odd, unsatisfactory piece, and the state of the autograph suggests that Elgar planned to revise it with orchestral accompaniment. Apart from a lovely and idiomatic second subject and its march-like continuation, this piece is not the composer's best. The two-movement Sonatina is a late work (1932), a thoroughly professional piece of little difficulty. There are also some original pieces of a more popular type—'Adieu', 'Serenade', 'Salut d'amour' (originally for violin and piano), 'Rosemary', and 'May Song'.

Samuel Coleridge-Taylor (1875–1912) studied under Stanford and was befriended at the outset by Elgar. His strength lay in small unpretentious compositions. His collection of Twenty-Four Negro Melodies, op. 59, which includes such favourites as 'Deep River', 'Steal away', and 'Sometimes I feel like a motherless child' is probably the first work by a British-trained composer to draw attention to Afro-American songs. He emphatically rejected ragtime music, however, as combining the most vulgar elements of white and negro music.[13]

Around the turn of the century there was a strong new turn of interest in British folksong, which stimulated a number of composers of piano music. The Australian pianist Percy Grainger (1882–1961) collected

Ex. 19.3   Charles V. Stanford, Five Capriccios, op. 136 (1913): No. 2

(S: Stainer & Bell, 1913)

and arranged for piano many British folksongs. The famous Handker-chief Dance ('Country Gardens'), the 'Sussex Mummers' Christmas Carol', the 'Londonderry Air', 'Scotch Strathspey' (which combines Scottish and Irish folk melodies with 'What shall we do with a drunken sailor?') 'Molly on the Shore', 'Shepherd's Hey', 'Died for Love', 'The Merry King', 'Knight and Shepherd's Daughter' were all arranged with great skill by him, and are minor classics. Alexander Mackenzie (1847–1935), George Butterworth (1885–1916), and Hamish McCunn (1868–1916) also contributed to this nationalist school of piano music.

John McEwen (1868–1948), a composer more in the academic line of Parry and Stanford, who was to succeed Mackenzie in 1924 as principal of the R.A.M., wrote a Sonata in E Minor in 1901 that was evidently successful (it was reprinted several times). It is well worked out and contrasted, but the constant stream of semiquavers in every movement but the second, a funeral march, does not make for satisfying listening: one of the few outstanding passages is the aggressive start to the last movement. Later in life McEwen moved with the times, and though the Sonatina (1919) is generally dull, the last movement indulges in bitonality and is delightfully thin in texture. More reminiscent of Holst, however, are the Three Preludes (1920). These are mysterious pieces; in the first the restless rippling accompaniment in B major supports a tune in B minor; the second wanders through strange keys and odd dissonances, with big leaps to the melody and chromatic sliding chords; the short third prelude (marked *presto*) is in 6/8 with a bass sometimes in 3/4, full of sudden crescendos, and has a discordant end.

We come finally to the outstanding piano work of the English neo-romantic period, Benjamin Dale's precocious Sonata in D Minor, op. 1. Its bold upward thrusts have been compared to those of Richard Strauss,[14] its changing harmony to Max Reger's.[15] It has been called the best sonata in Europe since that of Franz Liszt:[16] a work well in the mainstream of European musical thought and the first by any British composer to show great understanding of the modern instrument for which it was written and of its potential. Written while Dale (1885–1943) was still a student, and dedicated to his teacher, York Bowen, himself a young and brilliant pianist and gifted composer, it covers sixty-two pages in print and takes some forty-five minutes to play. The rhapsodic piano writing is rich, well varied, and full of interest, and its harmony and flexible form were new enough to puzzle one German reviewer.[17] Though it breaks no new ground in piano technique, it is as practical to play as Liszt's sonata and nearly as difficult. There is a broad organization: the first movement is well drawn out and the ideas are well contrasted and developed. A theme

Ex. 19.4 Benjamin Dale, Piano Sonata in D minor, op. 1 (1905): transition to last movement

with seven variations follows, the slow movement consisting of the theme and the first four variations, the scherzo comprising variations five to seven. This leads without a break into the finale, which is in rondo form; the whole work ends quietly and sadly in the home key of D minor. It is a difficult task to select any single passage from this sonata to convey a complete picture: example 19.4, from the substantial passage which links variation seven to the finale, shows his basically Wagnerian language, but also his originality, impeccable phrasing, and carefully wrought climaxes.

Dale's *Night Fancies*, op. 3 (1909), is an atmospheric piece that flows naturally through its constantly changing time and key signatures. The opening section moves imperceptibly into a *scherzando* middle section, dying away again into a reprise of the opening. The outbreak of war in 1914 caught Dale in Germany, and he was interned until 1918 in Ruhleben, where *Prunella* was written as incidental music to a performance of a play of that name (a performance that however did not take place): it is a piece of great charm.

As Edwin Evans put it in Grove's Dictionary (1929): 'a certain fastidiousness prevents his output from becoming considerable, but also ensures the maintenance of a high standard, which caused [Frederick] Corder once to claim that Dale had [in 1918] written "fewer and better works than any English composer of his generation."'[18] This view has been endorsed by more impartial critics.[19]

Chapter 20

ORGAN MUSIC

NICHOLAS TEMPERLEY

Organ music in Britain in the early nineteenth century was more indigenous in its traditions and character than other kinds of instrumental music. This was partly because most of it catered to the needs of the Church of England, but also because the instrument itself was notably different in character from either the German or the French organ. In the course of the century, English organs were redesigned so as to be capable of playing music of the great continental schools; and a corresponding change took place in organ music by British composers, which became directly imitative of continental styles.

Last Years of the Old English Organ

In 1800 the English organ was generally based on an F or G compass (that is, the lowest note on each manual was F or G, rather than C as on the German organ); it was still tuned in meantone temperament; and it had two or three manuals (Great, Choir, Swell). The open and stopped diapasons, which were the foundation of the instrument's tone, had a characteristically 'silvery' quality that differed from French or German organ tone. In many cases the Choir and Swell manuals did not possess a fully independent range of stops, but were used primarily for background or echo effects, or for occasional solos.[1] Pedals were extremely rare; facility in playing them was unknown. When in 1809 Samuel Wesley and Karl Friedrich Horn brought out the first English edition of Bach's organ sonatas, the preface stated that these pieces were 'performed by the matchless Author in a very extraordinary manner. The first and second Treble Parts were played with both Hands on two Sets of Keys, and the Base (wonderful as it appears) he executed entirely upon Pedals, without assistance.' As late as the 1830s there were still only half a dozen organists who could give an unassisted performance

435

of Bach's organ works;[2] they were sometimes played as organ duets,[3] or with the pedal part arranged for double-bass by Dragonetti.[4] The conservatism of the older school of organists resisted the introduction of pedals, as well as equal temperament and the C compass. Sir George Smart (1776–1867), who had 'presided at the organ' at the coronations of William IV and Victoria, was asked to play on one of the pedal organs exhibited at the Great Exhibition in 1851. 'My dear Sir,' he replied witheringly, 'I never in my life played upon a *gridiron.*'[5] It is not surprising that pedal parts in most English organ music before 1850 are either rudimentary or altogether lacking.

Secular organ music was not unknown in the earlier nineteenth century. Many houses possessed small chamber organs. They were mainly used to accompany singing, to play piano music and arrangements of operatic and orchestral works, and to play chamber music;[6] but from time to time composers wrote pieces specially for domestic organs. Samuel Wesley did so, and his son Sebastian's most important organ works, despite his lifelong career in the church, consisted of two sets of *Pieces for a Chamber Organ*, published in 1842 with a dedication to Lady Acland of Killerton Park, Devon.[7]

Organ music of the 'public' kind remained a tradition throughout the period. The organs at the King's, Covent Garden and Drury Lane Theatres were used not only in oratorios and (when occasion required) in operas, but also for the performance of organ concertos, a peculiarly English genre invented by Handel. Some of the last published examples* of the Handelian organ concerto were three by William Crotch (about 1805)[8] and three by Matthew Camidge (about 1815): Camidge in his preface admitted that he was writing in the 'ancient style'. Samuel Wesley composed several concertos, and also a grand organ duet (four hands, no feet) which he performed with Vincent Novello at the Hanover Square Concert Rooms in 1812. He wrote another duet as an introduction to Bach's 'St Anne's' Fugue, also for concert use.

The great quality that the nineteenth century demanded of organs was their ability to imitate the orchestra. As early as 1806 Joseph Woelfl excited admiration by his performance of the overture to 'The Magic Flute' on the organ at the King's Theatre 'without an accompaniment',[9] and a very interesting article on organ playing in 1840 stated that 'the two great and peculiar qualities of the organ [are] . . . disposition of harmony and orchestral effect', and praised the arrangements of orchestral music for the organ that were then in vogue.[10] At a recital given in 1840 by Thomas Adams (1785–1858) to

---

* T. A. Walmisley's manuscript 'Second Organ Concerto' is dated 1831. In 1910 the idea was revived, when a concerto by Basil Harwood was performed at the Gloucester Festival.

open a new organ in Exeter Hall, twelve out of sixteen items in the programme were arrangements of orchestral, vocal and choral music, one was a fugue by Bach (but this may well have been one of the '48'), and the other three were extemporizations. The monster organ called 'The Apollonicon', built by Flight & Robson in the years 1812–17 and housed in a special hall in St Martin's Lane, was purposely constructed to imitate an orchestra, and was fitted with pipes imitating strings, woodwind and brass, and even with a pair of kettledrums mechanically struck. It had five manuals (but no pedals) and could be played either by a performer or by a pin barrel. Regular concerts on the Apollonicon continued until about 1840. Adams and the blind John Purkis (1781–1849) performed symphonies, operatic selections, a motet by Bach, a selection from Pergolesi's *Miserere*, and all manner of other music on this extraordinary instrument.

It is notable that in many of the surviving programmes of public organ recitals from this period, the only music not arranged from some other medium was extemporized. The art of extemporization was, indeed, more strongly associated with organ playing than with any other branch of music, and it seems to have preserved some elements of the 'learned' contrapuntal style of an earlier era. All the leading organists of the time, including both Wesleys, were renowned extemporizers. In the absence of direct evidence it appears that works entitled 'pieces' (as opposed to 'voluntaries') were generally intended as models for such improvised playing in organ concerts. Adams's *Six Organ Pieces*, published about 1825, are fully-fledged sonatas in several contrasting movements, each including at least one fugue and displaying other learned devices. In the fugue from No. 2 the final stretto combines inversion and augmentation of the subject, then abandons counterpoint for enharmonic modulation at the climax (ex. 20.1: the subject starts in the upper voice). The apparently innocent 'Pastorale' which begins this piece exhibits specimens of invertible counterpoint at the octave, tenth and twelfth; imitation by inversion; and various species of canon. But the effect is of a melodious and well-knit movement, in which three manuals are admirably contrasted. Other movements in these excellent pieces (only one of which has a pedal part) have sustained, florid melodies on a solo manual.

But the organ remained primarily an instrument of the Church, and in the earlier nineteenth century this meant the Church of England: it was not until late Victorian times that Catholic or Nonconformist churches had either the need or the resources to rival the Anglican hegemony in this field. Liturgical organ music was at a low ebb in 1800. The nearest

Ex. 20.1 Thomas Adams, Six Organ Pieces (c. 1825): No. 2, fugue
(Allegro ♩ = 96)

(S: Novello, [c. 1825])

thing to the German chorale prelude had been the elaborate *givings-out and interludes* for use with psalm tunes. Several sets were published between 1700 and 1770,[11] but by 1800 these had degenerated into trivial sets of all-purpose interludes, unrelated to any specific psalm or hymn tune, and sets of preludes in all useful keys, to be played before hymns or anthems. Such collections continued to be published in the nineteenth century. Elaborate settings of hymn tunes occasionally appeared. William Horsley published an interesting set in 1828;[12] Sebastian Wesley's *Selection of Psalm Tunes No. 1* (1838) was specially designed to train young organists in the independent use of pedals and the left hand, and the composer acknowledged the influence of Bach in his preface.[13] Henry Smart still used the old term 'givings-out' when in 1855 he printed, by way of models, four elaborate settings of the hymn tune LONDON NEW in an appendix to his *Choral Book*.[14] A still greater rarity was a set of twelve organ fugues based on Anglican chants, composed by Crotch and published in 1836–7.[15]

Tune-based organ music, then, never quite died out in England. But by far the most important kind of organ music used in church was the *voluntary*. An essay on voluntary playing by William Mason, printed in 1795, makes it clear that most voluntaries were improvised. Those played before the service, before an·anthem, during communion, or before the first lesson* still retained a liturgical function of preparing the congregation for worship and prayer, and Mason recommended either music in the older learned style or else 'a merely melodious or harmonical movement' which 'glides, as it were, through the ear, awakens a transient pleasing sensation, but leaves behind it no lasting impression'.[16] Voluntaries in these positions were necessarily of uncertain length, and hence could not have a well-defined form. Nevertheless, examples were occasionally provided. Among the more distinguished were those of Samuel Wesley, published in 1831: *Six Introductory Movements for the Organ, Intended for the Use of Organists as Soft Voluntaries, To be Performed at the Commencement of Services of the Established Church, To Which is Added a Loud Voluntary with Introduction and Fugue.*[17] The distinction is made explicit in this title.

For the voluntary after the service, such restrictions did not apply. As Mason pointed out, 'these lullaby strains' need not be 'exclusively adhered to, except when preparative to devotion'.[18] There was no problem about length or form; a substantial and arresting piece could be employed, and it could come to a loud, imposing finish. Although after-service voluntaries, too, were normally extemporized, the more prominent organist-composers published many models for use and imitation by their less accomplished colleagues. This was the function of the sets of published voluntaries which had appeared from the 1720s onwards and continued to appear in the early nineteenth century. No standard form had ever been firmly established, but many voluntaries were in two movements, one slow and sustained, the other quicker and generally fugal. Such a scheme was obviously well adapted to a position at the end of the service, avoiding too harsh a break with the contemplative mood of the concluding prayers. It was the organist's best chance to display his powers.

The most important composer of after-service voluntaries, and indeed the greatest English organ composer of our period, was Samuel Wesley (1766–1837), who maintained almost single-handed the great

*See above, p. 180.

English tradition of organ music for manuals which had been continuous since the sixteenth century. Wesley[19] composed prolifically in every main branch of music except opera, and was highly appreciated in his own day, though by a relatively small group of fellow musicians. His friend Vincent Novello considered him 'a real genius (who, like Purcell, was an honour to the country where he was born)'.[20] After his death his music was quickly forgotten, and at the beginning of the present century Ernest Walker astonishingly failed to mention the organ music at all,[21] though John Fuller Maitland thought it 'so fine in conception and so dignified in style, that it is well worth the trouble of adapting it to the modern pedal organ'.[22] In recent times there have been signs of rehabilitation. His Latin church music* has begun to be explored, and the importance of his contribution to the Bach revival is now recognized. Editions of some of his organ works have appeared. To Francis Routh, in particular, we owe the dawning realization that we have in Wesley an English composer not merely of promise, but of true greatness in his actual accomplishment.[23]

He was the son of the great hymn writer, Charles Wesley, and the nephew of John Wesley, founder of Methodism. As a young man he was briefly converted to the Roman Catholic church. Thus his connection with the Church of England was tenuous. Despite his reputation, he never secured an important church appointment, and his enforced free-lance career made his living a hazardous one. Many of his voluntaries may have been first played at the Surrey Chapel, where his friend Benjamin Jacob was organist from 1794, or at the chapel at the Portugese Embassy, where Novello was organist from 1797. His greatest collection was published in separate numbers by W. Hodsoll between 1802 and 1815, and then reissued in two sets of *Six Voluntaries* (op. 6, books 1 and 2). Two books of *Three Voluntaries* dedicated to John Harding appeared in about 1825. A projected set of *Preludes and Fugues* dedicated to Adams did not continue beyond 'No. 1' in C minor, published 1826. Several voluntaries were published separately, or attached to sets of shorter pieces, and *Six Voluntaries for the Use of Young Organists* appeared as op. 36 in the last year of his life, 1837. Others remained in manuscript.

Wesley's voluntaries, according to Francis Routh, 'exploit the expressive power of the eighteenth-century organ up to the very limit—if not beyond'.[24] They make full and imaginative use of the available varieties of tone colour, setting off one manual against another. Although he was evidently quite at ease working within the normal structures of the day—the sonata-allegro, the rondo, the theme and

*See above, p. 210.

440

variation—he rarely used them strictly or mechanically, always reserving the possibility of surprise. He was often unconventional in his choice of models or of ideas to spark his invention. For example the three movements of Op. 6, no. 4 are all based on the old canon *Non nobis Domine* (traditionally attributed to William Byrd); no. 5 in the same opus is principally a set of variations on a theme of Stephen Paxton (1735-89). He felt free to add movements to the normal two-movement form, or to vary the weight and balance between those two movements.

Nowhere is Wesley's self-confidence and individuality more convincingly expressed than in his ornate melodies, firmly based in late-baroque idiom and yet showing, in every twist and turn, the composer's delight in ranging freely over the highways and byways of the diatonic and chromatic scales (ex. 20.2). More often than not Wesley used a lean, two-part texture, both acknowledging and taking advantage of the limitations of his instrument; he had mastered Bach's art of making his melodies adumbrate at least two harmonic parts, while his basses always formed the foundation of a strong and well directed harmony.

Another great strength in Wesley's voluntaries is his command of counterpoint—a weak spot in the equipment of his contemporaries (Adams was an exception). His fugal technique perhaps owed more to Handel than to Bach, often relying on the dramatic qualities of the subject itself. In a voluntary dedicated to Thomas Attwood and published in 1829, Wesley builds up to the fugue in three movements of gradually increasing tempo and registration, then, after some powerful chordal writing for full organ, introduces what Routh has aptly termed a 'strutting' fugue subject[25] with a compass of an octave and a half and a clearly marked contrast between its two parts (ex. 20.3(a)). In the course of the brilliant working-out of this fugue Wesley not only brings in the 'pull-down' pedals but also exploits the full G compass of the manual (ex. 20.3(b)).

'Wesley was as much a master of the short piece as he was of the extended one.'[26] There are two published collections. *Twelve Short Pieces with a Full Voluntary Added* (1816) actually contains thirteen pieces in addition to the voluntary: they are arranged in groups of pieces all in one key (the keys are G major, A minor, F major and D major), which points to a possible liturgical use for the catholic Mass, though the word 'piece' may suggest a secular use. Wesley gives each piece a strong individuality within its small compass, often with the help of a characteristic solo stop or with bold chromatic harmonies. The *Six Introductory Movements* (1831), as already mentioned, were published for use as voluntaries before service. The three that also survive in manuscript are each headed 'A Desk Voluntary' in the autograph,[27] which has led

441

Routh to speculate that they were originally 'written for a desk or chamber organ': if so, this would be a very unusual use of the word 'voluntary' for a secular organ piece. All six are quiet and contemplative in character. Wesley also wrote many short preludes, and a number of small pieces equally suited to piano or chamber organ; some

Ex. 20.2   Samuel Wesley, Six Voluntaries, op. 6, book II; no. 10 (c. 1807), 1st movement
Andante Larghetto

(*S:* Hodsoll, [c. 1807])

442

ORGAN MUSIC

Ex. 20.3   Wesley, Voluntary in B flat (1829)
Fuga (Allegro moderato)

(*S*: London, Royal College of Music, MS 4025)

of these are collected in a book which he gave to his daughter Eliza on 6 May 1837.[28] They are full of charm and humour, and some, such as 'Gavotta' in G minor and an Andante grazioso in A major, have considerable substance.

The organ music of Wesley's contemporaries pales in comparison. Apart from Adams the only one worth individual attention is William Russell (1777–1813), who was appointed organist at the Foundling Hospital in 1805. He composed much choral music, including several oratorios, and a Mass in C minor[29] which must have been written for one of the Embassy chapels. He published two sets of *Twelve Voluntaries* in 1804 and 1812. They are planned on a large scale, are often original in effect, and pay unusual attention to organ registration.[30]

Victorian Organ Music

It has been said that the Great Exhibition of 1851 marked the decisive break with the earlier English tradition of organ music.[31] The instruments displayed there, which included examples by prominent continental builders such as J. F. Schulze and Aristide Cavaillé-Coll, not only eclipsed the older English organ but manifested a new and ominous interest in size and power for its own sake. Many English organists, led by Henry Gauntlett (1805–76) but opposed by Sebastian Wesley, supported the change to C compass, independent pedals and full choruses on the Choir and Swell. One of the chief reasons was their wish to perform the music of Bach and other German composers. But organ-builders were also influenced by the spirit of industrial rivalry and vulgarity which was so strong in the Exhibition. They stimulated a demand for gigantic organs of unprecedented power, particularly from city corporations, who wished to install them in the town hall. Henry Willis's organ (117 stops, 8,000 pipes) at St George's Hall, Liverpool (1855) and Gray and Davison's (119 stops, 6,093 pipes) at Leeds Town Hall (1858)[32] were typical of the new trend. They were imitated in many other towns; and, inevitably, the new ideal came to influence cathedral and even parish-church organs. The organ at Holy Trinity, Hull was enlarged no less than six times between 1845 and 1900;[33] at Doncaster, a new parish church built in 1858 was installed with a *five*-manual organ built by Schulze (1862).

With the new kind of organ came a new kind of player—the professional recitalist, often with a salaried position on a corporation payroll, who was expected to give weekly or fortnightly organ concerts that would display the powers of the instrument to best advantage. The audience had little sense of the historical repertory of the English organ, and wanted to hear arrangements of orchestral, vocal and even operatic music, which came to dominate the programmes to the exclusion of all else, except an occasional organ work of Bach and sometimes the traditional extemporization. The new professional standing of the organist, independent of the Church, was recognized by the foundation in 1864 of the College of Organists (made 'Royal' in 1893).

Typical of the new breed of organists was William Thomas Best (1826–97), who held only brief and minor church appointments and made his career as a city recitalist: his chief appointment was as organist at St George's Hall, Liverpool at £300 a year (later £400). It was said of Best: 'To the organ student he is best known by his "Arrangements from the Scores of the Great Masters", . . . in which he showed that the organ is itself capable of reproducing orchestral effects, without transcending its proper functions and descending to trickery.'[34] Not all musicians were pleased with the organ's function as imitator of the orchestra; there was an exchange on the subject between Henry Chorley and Henry Smart in *The Athenaeum* in the 1850s, and another between Best and Sir Walter Parratt in 1891–2.[35] Parratt (1841–1924), who was organist of St George's Chapel, Windsor from 1882, was a staunch upholder of the 'legitimate' in organ playing, and deplored 'the tendency . . . to make the instrument a mere caricature of the orchestra'.[36]

In church as well as in concert, the Victorians used the organ for arrangements much more than for original music. Large numbers of collected 'voluntaries' appeared, tailored to the varying abilities of organists, and made up almost entirely of adaptations from other media. Novello & Co. headed the list of publishers catering to this need, with such collections as *Melodies for the Soft Stops*: their *Cathedral Voluntaries* were arrangements of anthems. Many organ publications still used two staves only, for small parish-organs or for harmoniums, which were increasingly popular after 1860. (A few composers, among them Macfarren, took the trouble to write original music specifically for the harmonium.)

Of the 'legitimate' school of organist-composers perhaps the most famous in the mid-Victorian period was Henry Smart (1813–79), who was renowned above all for his powers as an accompanist, and hence made his career chiefly as an organist of large parish churches, notably that of St Pancras.[37] He composed in many branches of music, including church music, partsongs and opera, but it was his organ music that acquired a reputation that now seems astonishing. He remains perhaps the only English composer who has had a book (admittedly, a small one) devoted entirely to his organ music.[38] Example 20.4(a), from a Prelude he published in *The Organist's Quarterly Journal* in 1869, is representative of Victorian organ style, with its 'mushy', unarticulated opening phrase over a tonic pedal; a later transitional passage in the same piece (ex. 20.4(b)) has a mildly enterprising texture and harmony. But it is hard to see anything that could remotely justify John Broadhouse's panegyric of this prelude as a 'masterpiece', still less the claim of Smart's biographer that his organ music was 'second only to Bach, and quite equal to Mendelssohn'.[39]

Two contemporaries of Smart may well have reached greater heights in organ composition, but, for different reasons, we cannot adequately assess their achievement. Samuel Sebastian Wesley (1810–76) was a champion of his father's ideals and wished to continue them, even to the extent of opposing equal temperament and the C compass and continuing to write on two staves. His powers of extemporization were legendary. Hubert Parry wrote after hearing him play a concluding voluntary at Gloucester cathedral in 1865:

He began the accompaniment in crotchets alone, and then gradually worked into quavers, then triplets and lastly semiquavers. It was quite marvellous. The powerful old subject came stalking in right and left with the running accompaniment wonderfully entwined with it—all in the style of old Bach.[40]

But Wesley left practically no models of his improvisations. The custom of publishing sets of original voluntaries was out of date, and his jealous character may have led him to deny others the opportunity to master his techniques. It seems certain that the few pieces he did publish are quite insufficient to represent his genius. Six of them, as already mentioned, were pieces for chamber organ, the best being the Andante in F Major. An imposing Introduction and Fugue in C Sharp Minor appeared as No. 1 of *A Studio for the Organ* in 1836, but no subsequent numbers in this series were printed. He composed one 'recital' piece, the Fantasia in G Major, which was first performed at the Birmingham Festival of 1849 and later used for the inauguration of Willis's organs at St George's Hall, Liverpool (1855) and the London Exhibition of 1862.[41]

Thomas Attwood Walmisley (1814–56), another distinguished organist and composer of cathedral music, left a quantity of organ music in manuscript, much of which passed eventually into the hands of Frederick Fertel, who edited a Larghetto in F Minor, published in 1933. The rest was dispersed after his death a few years later. Judging from the other two organ pieces that have survived, this is a serious loss.

Ex. 20.4 Henry Smart, Organ Prelude in A major (1869)

Molto moderato ($\flat$ = 69)

(a)

Ch. Salicional

[16 ft. + Ch. to Ped.?]

(b)

Sw.

[Ch.]

tr

(Broadhouse, 40–1)

447

A Voluntary in C Minor and Major[42] written in 1831 shows a certain freshness of melodic ideas, while the Prelude and Fugue in E Minor, published in 1839, is one of the first English works clearly and successfully modelled on the music of Bach.

Serious English organ music of the later nineteenth century was based on German models, the chief of which were Bach, Mendelssohn, and Rheinberger. The revival of Bach's chorale preludes came rather later than that of his other organ works, and it led, in England, to a new spurt of compositions based on psalm and hymn tunes. The results were assessed by Charles Pearce in a lecture to the College of Organists in 1885.[43] He gave examples of tune-based works of all types; of the 'chorale prelude' type he singled out Smart's, Wesley's and a set of twelve by Best. Among variations on hymn tunes he mentioned Adams's on ADESTE FIDELES, C. E. Stephens's on ST JAMES, and George Macfarren's on WINDSOR. He commended fugues based on hymn tunes by several composers, especially Best's Fantasia and Fugue in E Minor on 'Ravenscroft's OLD 81ST' (actually OLD 104TH) and Edouard Silas's Fantasia on ST ANNE. All these, it may be noted, were based on English tunes, although the treatment, especially in the post-1850 examples, is heavily indebted to Bach.

The trend continued after the time of Pearce's lecture, and produced more distinguished results in the chorale preludes of Basil Harwood, Charles Wood, and above all Hubert Parry. Harwood's *Short Postlude for Ascensiontide* (op. 15, no. 4) is a richly flowing 'chorale prelude', which could also be used as an accompaniment, to the austere psalm tune OLD 25TH. He wrote several other such pieces, and also *Three Preludes on Anglican Chants* (op. 15, no. 17). Parry's two sets of seven *Chorale Preludes* (1912, 1916) and three *Chorale Fantasias* (1915), all based on well-known English tunes, are still full of reminiscences of Bach, and yet have a romantic warmth and individuality that have made several of them favourites with organists.

The other new development of this period was the organ sonata. Curiously enough, the first significant works to appear with that name were originally commissioned as voluntaries, when the London publisher Coventry wrote to ask Mendelssohn to give the English public the benefit of his ability as an improviser. Mendelssohn wrote back that he preferred the term 'sonatas'; he did not know precisely what 'voluntary' meant.[45] Coventry & Hollier published the six sonatas in 1845, at first using the title *Mendelssohn's School of Organ Playing* for the collection. But, as Newman has pointed out, they were hardly sonatas in the usual meaning of the time, being highly irregular groups of movements which hardly ever approach 'sonata form' but include imitative preludes, fugues, variations, and (in four cases) chorale-based movements.[46] The organ sonata idea caught on in France and Germany as well as England. The most important German successors were the twenty organ sonatas of Rheinberger, which come much closer to traditional sonata form and use no chorales (Rheinberger was from Catholic Munich), although many of them contain fugues. Rheinberger was highly influential on late Victorian composers: Harvey Grace ranked his organ music as second only to Bach's.[47]

A surprisingly large crop of English organ sonatas appeared between 1860 and 1920: Newman mentions fifty-five by twenty-two composers.[48] They follow the German lead rather than English predecessors such as the Adams pieces. Among the earliest were one in G major (1862) by Best, and one in G minor by Henry Hiles (1826–1904) that won a prize in 1868 from the College of Organists. Well-known composers such as Macfarren and Ouseley contributed to the repertory. Alan Gray (1855–1935), organist of Trinity College, Cambridge, published four 'superior' sonatas in 1890;[49] Charles Stanford turned to the form late in his career, composing five sonatas between 1916 and 1921.[50]

The most significant sonatas in this group are those of Basil Harwood and Edward Elgar. Harwood (1859–1949) was organist of Ely Cathedral from 1887 to 1892, then of Christ Church, Oxford until 1907, when he retired from professional activity but continued to compose in many forms. His organ works, numbering more than thirty pieces, include two sonatas, not mentioned by Newman: Op. 5, in C sharp minor (1886), and Op. 26, in F sharp minor (1912). The passionate opening of the C Sharp Minor Sonata (ex. 20.5) shows how far the 'symphonic' influence had thickened the texture of English organ music; how completely independent the pedals had become; and how the style in general was now more or less indistinguishable from German models, such as (in this case) Rheinberger's. But it also shows an English composer in thorough control of this style, and able to use it in a way that arrests the audience's attention. In the working-out of this sonata that attention is held and rewarded. A fugal development near the end leads suddenly into a chorale-like treatment of a plainsong theme, which is stated first quietly, then *grandioso*, with the full resources of the late Victorian organ. Such a climax was usual in organ sonatas, matching perhaps the finale of a Bruckner symphony, but no English composer handles it with greater distinction than Harwood. His other sonata, though headed 'for a chamber organ', also calls for three manuals and pedals, with a Solo Tuba stop, and reaches a similarly grand climax. Among Harwood's shorter pieces the

Ex. 20.5 Basil Harwood, Organ Sonata No. 1, op. 5 (1866):1st movement

Allegro appassionato

(*S:* Schott, 1886)

Dithyramb, op. 7 (1892), a fantasia 'Christmastide', op. 34, and a Rhapsody, op. 38, are worth special mention.

Elgar was organist of St George's Roman Catholic church, Worcester, from 1885 to 1889 in succession to his father, a position that brought forth one liturgical composition, the *Eleven Vesper Voluntaries*, published in 1891. His Organ Sonata in G Major, op. 28 (1895), is by contrast a thoroughly secular work, first performed at a congress of American organists, with no use of plainsong or hymn tunes, and without even the traditional fugal movement. It is very much like the conventional piano sonata, in four movements, the two outer ones in sonata form; but with full, chordal textures not unlike Harwood's, clearly written for a large contemporary instrument.

PART IV

Writings On Music

Chapter 21

AESTHETICS AND CRITICISM

STEPHEN BANFIELD

Aesthetics

At the end of the eighteenth century William Mason (1725–97), pre-centor of York, published *Essays, Historical and Critical, on English Church Music*, which give a good impression of current attitudes to music. Many of Mason's ideas were borrowed from his hero Rousseau, whose timely emphasis on nature as the source of aesthetic laws had by this time outstayed its welcome and was in danger of degenerating into the platitude that art should imitate nature. Viewing music in this light, it is not surprising that in Mason's opening gambit he ranked music 'as an imitative art', 'so much below poetry and painting, that, in my own opinion, which I have found confirmed by many late writers of the best judgement, it can hardly be so termed with propriety'.[1] He continued: 'Notwithstanding this, it has certain qualities, so analogous to those which constitute metre or versification, such as accent, rhythm, pause, and cadence, that it thereby becomes, equally with poetry, an object of criticism.'[2]

We see here evidence of two attitudes that were to dominate nineteenth-century musical aesthetics. One is the fondness for drawing analogies between the arts. The cross-fertilization of artistic disciplines was of course a major force in the later romantic movement, resulting repeatedly in *Gesamtkunstwerk* theory and practice (and it is interesting to see Skryabin's use of colour prophesied by Haweis in *Music and Morals* of 1871). But the attempt to justify an aesthetic view of one art because it was appropriate to another was to lead all too invitingly to groundless speculations. These were often, as with George Field's *Outlines of Analogical Philosophy* (1839)—not to mention his many other books—redolent merely of an outworn classical desire for a closed, contained system of knowledge, more familiar through the sterile researches and philosophizings of Mr Casaubon in George Eliot's *Middlemarch*. Mason's own analogy is, however, quite reasonably

455

explained as a similarity of 'modern' (i.e., classical) melody's variety of accent and phrase structure to those of a verbal sentence. This too is from Rousseau.

The second seminal attitude becomes clear when Mason, still prompted by Rousseau, explains how music can be not just 'natural' (we would say 'absolute') but 'imitative'. This imitative music does not depict 'particular sounds, motions, &c. of a corporeal kind', but rather 'by its eloquent vocality expresses all kinds of passions; paints, as it were, all sorts of objects, and represents the various situations of the human mind . . . and thus strikes us even to the heart with every sentiment capable of giving it emotion'.[3] Music expresses passions, which produce emotions. The ellipsis has here not quite been made, but the idea of music expressing emotions was no newcomer in the romantic era. It was, rather, a Renaissance tenet, resulting from the break-up of mediaeval thought and the new association of music with the art of rhetoric rather than the sciences of the *quadrivium*; Hanslick, in wishing to circumscribe the notion, was able to cite plenty of statements of it from the eighteenth as well as the nineteenth centuries.[4] We leave Mason with the observation that he ascribed music's 'imitative' power to its 'eloquent vocality'; here and in the earlier analogy with verbal structures, he followed Rousseau in regarding music as essentially a heightened form of speech. Vocal music was still supreme.

A few years later William Crotch (1775–1847) began the delivery of a series of lectures on music in his capacity as professor at the University of Oxford; they were later repeated in London, and published in 1831. Well-written, elegant, informed, and always thoughtful, they retained something of the elevating common sense of Dr Johnson. Crotch, like Mason, did not rate music's pictorial capabilities very highly, and as a painter himself (he was constantly referring to Sir Joshua Reynolds's *Discourses*) was at pains to point out that music 'conveys no imagery',[5] or can only focus on isolated aspects of an image:

In setting the words, 'When thou hadst overcome the sharpness of death,' which is the musical composer to lay hold of? He cannot convey an idea of 'overcome'; he therefore adapts the expression 'sharpness of death' to appropriate discords. Great musicians have been censured for this.[6]

Again, like Mason, it is the emotional power of music which he sees as pre-eminent:

Music can awaken the affections by her magic influence, producing at her will, and that instantly, serenity, complacency, pleasure, delight, ecstasy, melancholy, woe, pain, terror, and distraction.[7]

456

However, he also is addicted to analogizing. He argues carefully enough for the process:

All arts having the same general end, which is to please, and addressing themselves to the same faculties through the medium of the senses, it follows that their rules and principles must have as great an affinity as the different materials, and the different organs or vehicles by which they pass to the mind, will permit them to retain.[8]

It is when he begins to compartmentalize works of art into three categories, the *sublime*, the *beautiful*, and the *ornamental*, that his conservatism is revealed. (The categories themselves are a compound of Longinus, Uvedale Price, Burke, Harris, and Reynolds, all of whom discoursed on one or more of them.) The three styles, approximating to degrees of *antico* and *moderno*, are ranked in descending order of greatness. Church music belongs to the sublime; church music is on the decline; therefore music is on the decline. Most modern music is characterized by a mixture of the beautiful and the ornamental. Roughly speaking, the beautiful is represented by classical elements (compared to 'a small, perfect, Grecian temple, or a landscape of Claude Lorraine'[9]), the ornamental by romanticism ('aged heads, old hovels, cottages, or mills, ruined temples or castles, rough animals, peasants at a fair, and the like, are picturesque. In music, eccentric and difficult melody; rapid, broken, and varied rhythm; wild and unexpected modulation, indicate this third style.').[10] The general impression is of a conception limited by the antiquarian's mind, viewing the baroque, classical, and romantic styles as alternatives rather than recognizing that each had been superseded by the other. Crotch has no concern with evolution.

In 1832, however, William Gardiner (1770–1853) published *The Music of Nature: or, An Attempt to Prove that what is Passionate and Pleasing in the Art of Singing, Speaking, and Performing upon Musical Instruments, is Derived from the Sounds of the Animated World*. He provided 'curious illustrations', ranging from the amusing transliteration on to staff notation of the cries of animals, birds, and insects to tables of the 'colours' of different instrumental timbres (e.g., the French horn is violet), all jumbled up with musical examples of complete airs, descriptions of orchestral instruments and famous singers' voices, gobbets of gossip and sound lore, dubious harmonic rules, and emotional descriptions of different keys. Like Rousseau and Mason, he took it for granted that for the purposes of analysing expression a line of vocal melody can be equated with a line of speech; there was no wider concept of *melos* as yet. But there was a speculative interest in evolution. Gardiner did not

457

see music as an emotionally heightened form of speech, but traced the expression of emotions and the communication of experiences back to a more primitive use of sound out of which both music and speech grew:

Children have no difficulty in expressing their wants, their pleasures, or pains, long before they can speak or understand the meaning of a word. In the dawn of society, ages may have passed away with little more converse than what these efforts would produce; but as the mind developed, and our wants increased, means would be suggested by the articulating powers, to break these instinctive tones into particles of imitative sound; and in all probability the first words that were uttered bore some resemblance to the things described, as the boisterous roar of the sea would call for a boisterous expression. The limited number of these sounds would at first lead men to describe many things with different degrees of force; and these varieties, added to an animated gesture, would render the primitive language a sort of musical declamation.[11]

The best part of another generation passed before this sort of speculation came of age. The next landmark, Herbert Spencer's article on 'The Origin and Function of Music', appeared in *Fraser's Magazine* for October 1857. In the meantime Wagner had published a number of his prose works on art theory, and Darwin had completed his biological researches for *The Origin of Species*, though they were not written up until 1858–9. Spencer (1829–1903) was from this time onwards somewhat of a Mephistophelian shadow to Darwin, a visionary enthusiast with a dangerous capacity for cashing in on the implications of his theories and extending them into a romantically world-embracing system of sociology. The present article illustrates this. His argument hinges on the by now familiar tenet, 'All music is originally vocal'. Music developed as an exaggeration of the intonation principles of speech, themselves resulting from muscular contractions and relaxations consequent on the experiencing of pain or pleasure (this convenient polarization is typical). 'Thus . . . song employs and exaggerates the natural language of the emotions',[12] and various types of musical figure express different emotional states (e.g., staccato, determination or a confident sharpness; legato, gentle feelings and caresses). Primitive music, he says, is monotonous because it has hardly developed out of speech. (In his obsession with melody he appears unaware of the rhythmic subtleties in much 'primitive' music.) But, he continues—and here his argument reflects Wagner's apotheosis of the symphonic *melos*, his 'endless melody'—as Western music evolves further, its refinement of vocal melody into less overt instrumental textures leads the hypersensitive composer (he cites Mozart, Beethoven, Chopin, and Mendelssohn) to express 'feelings we never had before . . . dormant sentiments of which we . . . do not know the meaning; or, as Richter says—tells us of things we have not seen and shall not see'.[13]

However specious Spencer's biological argument, he went much further than the English writers examined so far in recognizing and attempting to account for music's extraordinary rising power, at the hands of Beethoven and Wagner, over the subconscious. In a crescendo of evolutionary optimism he not only, by placing music at the head of the arts, reversed the position accorded to it by Crotch and Mason; he also placed it at the head of society:

In its bearings upon human happiness . . . this emotional language which musical culture develops and refines, is only second in importance to the language of the intellect: perhaps not even second to it. For these . . . feelings . . . are the chief media of *sympathy* . . . There is . . . growing up a language of sympathetic intercourse—a language through which we communicate to others the happiness we feel, and are made sharers in their happiness. . . . Feelings of a higher and more complex kind, as yet experienced only by the cultivated few, will become general; and there will be a corresponding development of the emotional language into more involved forms. . . . Those vague feelings of unexperienced felicity which music arouses—those indefinite impressions of an unkown ideal life which it calls up, may be considered as a prophecy, to the fulfilment of which music is itself partly instrumental. . . . Music must take rank as the highest of the fine arts—as the one which, more than any other, ministers to human welfare.[14]

Spencer's article carried reverberations for the next fifty years. Darwin's differing view, published in *The Descent of Man* (1871), that the origin of music lay in courtship rituals was also adopted by Edmund Gurney in an article 'On Some Disputed Points in Music' in the *Fortnightly Review* for July 1876, in which he criticized Spencer, and in his later book *The Power of Sound*. By the time Spencer replied, in a lengthy footnote of 1890 (almost longer than the original article and printed with it in his collected *Essays*), both Gurney and Darwin were dead. However, he took the opportunity to point out that he had originally been merely trying to elucidate the *origin* of music, and went on anew to define its constituent aesthetic elements, which he saw as the *sensational* (concerned with the intrinsic beauty, congruity, and variety of tones), the *perceptional* (involving contrast, repetition, and symmetry in intellectually pleasing and challenging arrangements), and the *emotional* (the domain of his previously expounded 'idealized emotion'). Indefatigably, he went on to answer more objections in his *Facts and Comments* (1902), where he challenged Ernest Newman's refutation of Wagner's similar theory of the origin of music voiced in *A Study of Wagner* (1899).[15] Newman had the last word, upbraiding

Spencer posthumously in an essay entitled 'Herbert Spencer and the Origin of Music'.[16] The nineteenth century pursued its conceptual issues unflaggingly.

One further humanistic exponent of the emotional theory deserves mention. Hugh Haweis (1838–1901) is remembered for *Music and Morals* (1871), a curious but lively mixture of sense and sentimentality which passed through twelve editions in as many years. Haweis's life is of interest. After graduating from Cambridge he travelled in Italy, associating with Garibaldi and Victor Emmanuel. Then, much under the progressive influence of *Essays and Reviews*, and later of Jowett and Colenso, he entered the Church and took a parish in Bethnal Green where he fostered concerts for the poor.

His approach to aesthetic questions, though uneven in quality, was serious in tone. He saw music as the emotional art *par excellence*, and went further than his predecessors in regarding the processes of intellectual perception only as channels for emotional experiences.

Once raise a thought to its highest power, and it not only is accompanied by the strongest emotion, but, strange to say, actually passes out of the condition of a thought altogether into the condition of an emotion, just as hard metal raised to a sufficient power of heat evaporates into the most subtle and attenuated gases.[17]

From this he proceeded, in *My Musical Life* (1884), to construct fascinating 'emotional programmes' of musical works, analysing for the purpose Mendelssohn's *Lied ohne Wörte*, II, No. 4.[18] He viewed the development of emotional responses through intellectual perception not as an indulgence, but as a moral discipline (and condemned 'as immoral the deliberate cultivation of unbalanced emotions merely for the sake of producing pleasure'[19]); like Spencer he looked upon music as having a millennial significance:

We are, when we hear music intelligently and sympathetically, *actually cultivating abstract habits of mind which may afterwards be transferred as trained forces to the affairs of daily life*. . . . The time is not distant when this great truth will be understood and practised in connection with our toiling masses—our artisans, our poor, our labourers, our degraded denizens of back streets, cellars, and foul alleys.[20]

A reaction to such a panaceatic view of music was inevitable. Hanslick, in *The Beautiful in Music*, had already argued, with more of the repetitious persuasion of the law student than the balanced tone of the philosopher, that beauty in music consisted purely in the intellectually pleasing arrangement of tones; he did not belittle music's ability to induce an emotional response, but saw that response as conditioned by the aesthetic value of the work in question. As a critic he was concerned with music's structural organization rather than its ethical possibilities; the dichotomy between form and content was beginning to come into focus.

In England the awareness of this dichotomy was strongest in the writings of James Sully (1842–1923) and Edmund Gurney (1847–88). Sully, in his article 'Aesthetics' in the eleventh edition of the *Encyclopaedia Britannica* (1910–11)—an unusually lucid introduction to the subject—gave a creditably detached exposition of the problems and scope of the science, which he defined as 'the contemplative enjoyment of beauty'. He sympathetically explained the split between 'formalists' and 'expressionalists'. But in the chapters on music in his earlier *Sensation and Intuition: Studies in Psychology and Aesthetics*, partisan views had been more freely expressed. His appreciation of 'formalist' criteria, worked out in a section on 'Aspects of Beauty in Musical Form', appears barren and simplistic, not going beyond the resistless conception of beauty lying in architectonic symmetry.

In the chapter 'On the Nature and Limits of Musical Expression', however, Sully took Spencer's ideas further. He endorsed Spencer's three aesthetic constituents in music—the acoustic, the intellectual, and the emotional—as well as his theory of the vocal origin of music. He added an explanation of how the processes of musical representation and communication work in three ways, firstly by vocal action ('the conscious play of muscular energy'), secondly thereby reviving 'varieties of emotional agitation, such as usually vent themselves in like vocal sounds', and thirdly in that 'these re-awakened feelings are projected in fancy behind the musical tones, so that these seem to be the utterances of another soul stirred to emotional movement'.[21] But if the conviction of this third stage appears rather vague, elsewhere he comes close to Deryck Cooke's starting-point[22] for an investigation of the *semantics* of tonal music:

We may readily understand how it happens that we attribute a vocal significance to the elaborate relations of key, regarding each note of the scale as the equivalent of a certain vocal transition from the medium and normal pitch of quiet customary expression.[23]

He was, however, aware—more aware than Spencer—of the difficulties of fixing a specific emotional programme on a piece of music. He saw music, as the above passage implies, rather as an art of rhetoric, in which an interplay of emotional tension and relaxation is only the means to an aesthetic end. The acoustical studies of Helmholtz (whose *Lehre von dem Tonempfindungen* had appeared in 1862 and was translated into English by A. J. Ellis in 1875) were greatly influential at this time; Sully subscribed to his view 'that music produces not definite emotions but rather moods or emotional frames of mind'.[24] His panegyrics of music's power and influence were similar in tone to Spencer's, but he was more specific about the superior evolutionary status of instrumental music:

The extended range of tone supplied by artificial instruments, together with their variety of force and timbre, and the magnitude and complexity of structure of which this branch of music is susceptible, supply a vast field for the idealization of natural vocal expression, and for the revival, in faint pulsations, of myriads of slumbering emotional forces.[25]

In returning to a question by-passed by Spencer—can music provide concrete images?—Sully betrayed another German influence (possibly imbibed through Wagner), that of Schopenhauer. Schopenhauer, he said, found music a non-representational art, all Will and no Idea. But this view ignored music's trigger-response of evocation, important to Sully:

The most constant intellectual accompaniment of a deep emotion is the thought of its exciting cause, or objective source. Hence, under the influence of an impressive piece of music, the mind is strongly predisposed to look for recognizable causes of its strange agitations; and by this means suggestions of external events, which otherwise would scarcely rise into consciousness as distinct ideas, become intense and luminous images.[26]

He did not, however, suggest that the conjured images in the minds of composer and listener should be expected to be the same, a point similarly inconclusive in the aesthetic of Impressionism soon to develop in France.

By far the most substantial English treatise of the century is Edmund Gurney's *The Power of Sound*, published in 1880 and fabricated largely out of articles published previously in various general periodicals. Lengthy, laborious and, unlike Hanslick (whose views Gurney often echoed), not argued from a single premise, it retains little sense of immediacy to-day, and reads meagrely as literature. Yet by a framework of careful and unbiased consideration it takes many specific questions on aesthetics further than the other writings of the era. The severe tone adopted acts as a counterweight to the more metaphysical flights of fancy of some of his contemporaries.

Gurney was not a Wagnerian (in fact he showed no knowledge of any of Wagner's scores after *Lohengrin*). He criticized Ruskin's confusion of musical tones with colours. In effect he threw a wet blanket over Walter Pater's celebrated statement, in *The Renaissance* of 1873, that 'All art constantly aspires towards the condition of music' by painstakingly limiting 'the condition of music'. And he was perhaps consciously thinking of Spencer's euphoric view of music's subtleties when he said, in his preface, that music 'has a unique message for the uncultivated and ignorant, for the publicans and sinners; and not in the millennium, but now; not after but before they cease to be uncultivated and ignorant'.[27] Music, he stated later, should be a popular art, memorable and assimilable by the common people, who alone hold the key to its chief ingredient, melody. Harmony is subservient to it. We are right back with Rousseau.

Yet at the same time the preoccupation with *melos* in a broader sense—'ideal motion' as Gurney later termed it—is typical of the period; it also anticipated, if only obliquely, the linear analytical approach of Schenker. Moreover, Gurney was far from wishing to keep alive Rousseau's views on the speech-origin of melody (or indeed of music in general—he preferred Darwin's courtship-origin theory): melody was seen rather as the simplest distillation of form, and 'the world of Beauty is pre-eminently the world of Form'.[28] Material and form were placed above colour, to whose modern usurpations he took the same moralistic attitude as Parry:

The opportunities, and I fear the taste, for finely-toned noise have . . . increased and may yet increase; and it is, and always will be, infinitely easier to use any amount of such noise than to write a single piece of noble tune.[29]

Nevertheless, his concept of form is a gratifyingly broad one. He saw a musical entity not as an agglomerative crystal but as an organism whose pattern of growth and size depend, as an inner necessity, on its nature, not on any fixed law of proportion. In the chapter on 'The relations of reason and order to beauty', he rejected the notion of aesthetic beauty being co-extensive with scientific cognition (e.g., of the relation of parts to a whole); he did not accept the intellectual auton-omy of artistic values, and concluded:

The perception of unity under variety, merely as such . . . cannot make good its claim to a truly aesthetic character. . . . The spectator is treated as though he were a sudden importation from another sphere, gifted with the perception of relations of fact, but without any emotional history or nature; not as the product of slow development in a certain environment, a being whose percep-tions in certain directions are saturated with emotion, and whose feelings, however interfused and transformed, have their primaeval roots in simple experiences, and in associations whose ingredients are usually easy enough to surmise.[30]

Gurney's aesthetic shows two major weaknesses, both common to other writers of his time. One is an addiction to schematic comparisons of the nature and properties of music with those of other arts, which mars a good deal of the early parts of the book. The other arises in trying to define the role of the emotions in an aesthetic system. He divides music's effects into the impressive and the expressive (equivalent to Sully's formalist/expressionalist distinction); both involve the emotions (the one manufacturing, the other reflecting them), yet only the first is seen as the domain of aesthetics.

John Stainer (1840–1901), possessing one of the clearest and most well-read minds on the subject (he had assimilated Locke, Kant, Hegel, Helmholtz, Spencer, Sully, Gurney, and others), in his Oxford professorial lecture of 8 June 1892, *Music in its Relation to the Intellect and the Emotions*, more acceptably put aesthetics back into the emotional province, but carefully avoided the fraught distinction between the production and representation of emotions:

As all musical productions have always been and still continually are under process of analysis by hearers and critics, it follows that methods of melodic progression, treatment of chords, and the outlines of Form and Construction are constantly added to Treatises on Music, until at last certain progressions become as familiar and as necessary in music as *idioms in speech*, and similarly, musical Forms become known and open to recognition. But as all these gradually cease to be new, and as they become incorporated as part of the syntax of music, so do they come within the scope of intellect; in other words, as the Unknown in the Art becomes known and systematized, so in proportion the field of the operation of the Intellect is extended, and the effect on the Emotions is pushed farther back. Emotions are not evoked by parsing and scanning a Poem. . . . It is evident then that Art cannot be said to exist unless there is an appeal to the Emotions by means of the Intellect. If the thing created appeals *only* to the Intellect, it is not a work of art.[31]

What it seems, in retrospect, that Stainer, Gurney, and their predecessors lacked (though Haweis, and later Parry in *The Art of Music*, came close to it) was a grasp of the manner in which musical thought builds up an ebb and flow of tension and relaxation through the conflict and balance of opposing forces. These terms of reference, hackneyed enough today, were simply not available in the pre-Freudian aestheticians' world. Had they been, theorists might have applied them to the properties of tonality to produce a semantic theory—such as expounded in our own century by Deryck Cooke—of the *language* of music, in which aesthetics could at least have been defined more clearly as the use made of that language. Stainer recognized the basis of the language, but he seems to have viewed the aesthetic realm as something imposed upon it from without rather than inherent in its usage.

464

Nevertheless, Cooke and other twentieth-century theorists, including Stravinsky and Hindemith, have but heaped coals upon the ever-burning question of whether music expresses emotions.

Criticism

In volume, if not always in incisiveness, English musical criticism, still at this time a relatively young discipline, flourished in the nineteenth century. A new form, the periodical devoted solely to music,* emerged, one of the earliest examples being *The Quarterly Musical Magazine and Review* (1818–28), edited by Richard M. Bacon, music critic of *The Norwich Mercury* and also a political pamphleteer. William Ayrton's *The Harmonicon* (1823–33) was similarly short-lived but influential. Others, such as George Hogarth's *Musical Herald* (1846) and Ashton Ellis's Wagner review, *The Meister* (1888–95), came and went, but a number of periodicals, showing greater powers of endurance, provided the foundations of modern journalism in England. *The Musical World*, founded by Charles Cowden Clarke in 1836 and subsequently edited by Edward Holmes, George Macfarren (father of the composer), James W. Davison, Edgar F. Jacques, and Francis Hueffer, survived until 1891, *The Musical Standard* from 1862 to 1933. *The Monthly Musical Record*, edited for its first three years by Ebenezer Prout and then by John Shedlock, ran from 1871 to 1960; *Musical Opinion and Music Trades Review*, begun in 1877, still survives.

The most important venture was *The Musical Times and Singing-Class Circular*, founded by Joseph Novello in 1844 and numbering among its succession of editors and contributors Holmes, Leigh Hunt, Mary Cowden Clarke (wife of Charles), Henry C. Lunn, William A. Barrett, Jacques, and Frederick G. Edwards. *The Musical Times* has often suffered, as did *The Musical Standard*, from a bias towards the commercial aspects of church music, and in its earliest years penetrating essays in criticism are found interspersed with patronizing dross betraying an over-zealous approach to musical education. On the whole the century's critical heritage is best preserved in the non-musical daily papers and weekly magazines. Despite Crowest's disapproval[32] of editors of weekly and bi-weekly journals for employing *feuilletonistes* with no musical knowledge (he names none), the criticisms of men of letters not primarily musicians, including Leigh Hunt, Thomas Love Peacock and, above all, George Bernard Shaw, if occasionally wide of the mark, are nevertheless of permanent value in removing music from the

*For a full list of British music periodicals, see Grove, article 'Periodicals'.

465

demands of trade journalism and viewing it in a broader cultural context. And, after all, criticism is a literary genre.

The music critic's position was, in the nineteenth century as today, a tenuous one. Only Davison (1813–85), who ran a short-lived weekly, *The Musical Examiner* (1842–4), contributed occasionally to *The Saturday Review*, *The Pall Mall Gazette*, and *The Graphic*, and performed his chief service in *The Times* (1846–79) and *The Musical World* (1844–85), seems to have been a composer *manqué*. Several others approached their task from a literary standpoint, but rarely stood unsupported as creative writers. Joseph Bennett (1831–1911) (music critic of *The Daily Telegraph* and contributor to *The Sunday Times*, *The Pall Mall Gazette*, and *The Graphic*) wrote librettos for Mackenzie's *The Dream of Jubal* and *The Rose of Sharon*, Sullivan's *The Golden Legend*, and Cowen's *Ruth*, none of which distinguished him. The German-born Francis Hueffer (1843–89: *The Times* music critic, 1879–89, and assistant editor of *The Academy* from about 1871), with Edward Dannreuther Wagner's chief advocate in England, and an authority on troubadour music, successfully re-translated Verdi's *Otello* into Shakespeare's English but courted mediocrity in providing librettos for Mackenzie's *Colomba* and *The Troubadour* and Cowen's *The Sleeping Beauty*. Henry F. Chorley (1808–72), whose journalistic career with *The Athenaeum* began when he was asked to provide an account of the opening of the Liverpool-Manchester railway in 1830, wrote dramatic criticisms, librettos, and words for songs by Sullivan and Gounod, and nourished aspirations as a novelist; but they remained aspirations.

A number of critics performed their most important services to music outside the columns of journalism. William Ayrton (1777–1858), who, in addition to running *The Harmonicon* and *The Musical Library* (1834–6), wrote for *The Examiner* (1837–51) and *The Morning Chronicle* (1813–26), was a founder member and subsequent director of the Philharmonic Society, and as director of the King's Theatre introduced *Così fan tutte*, *Die Zauberflöte* and *Don Giovanni* to English audiences. John Ella (1802–88), music critic of *The Morning Post* and contributer to *The Athenaeum*, ran his chamber music society, the Musical Union, from 1845 to 1880. John A. Fuller Maitland (1856–1936), music critic of *The Pall Mall Gazette* (1882–4), *The Guardian* (1884–9), and *The Times* (1889–1911), is chiefly remembered for his edition of the Fitzwilliam Virginal Book.

In general, with Hueffer the most notable exception, these men represented the forces of conservatism. Neither Chorley nor Davison had much time for Wagner when he conducted the Philharmonic in 1855. Davison wrote a severe review of the season in *The Times*,[33] which like Chorley's vitriolic notices (e.g., of Spohr) remind us that the barbed tongues of the eighteenth century were not quite extinct. For the freshest criticisms of the age, however, away from the jaded atmosphere of the musical profession, we must turn to Hunt, Peacock, and Shaw.

Leigh Hunt (1784–1859), as its editor, wrote music criticisms for *The Examiner* (1808–12 and 1815–21). Occasionally (as when describing Paganini) he adopted over-romantic attitudes or lapsed into platitudes, but he generally articulated issues close to him with a persuasive enthusiasm. Mozart was his greatest love. He said of 'The Magic Flute':

It has 'eyes of youth.' It is even more; it anticipates for us something of the good, which the human mind, as long as it is worth anything, is so anxious to realize, something of a brighter and more innocent world, in which the good-natured and flowery will is gratified. . . . It is to Mozart's other works what *The Tempest* is to the most popular of Shakespeare's comedies.[34]

As an opera critic he had a high concern for the balance of drama and music, and where the partnership failed, as in a new mock-melodrama with words by Dibdin, his remarks could be scathing; he fixed on the unfortunate librettist's apologetic image with a relentless grip:

The author, it is said, intends his composition for nothing but a vehicle to the music and scenery . . . [but] I really do not see the right which any dramatist possesses to give a bad vehicle to good music . . . I am sure that Messrs. Longman and Brodrip would never send home one of their pianos on a brewer's sledge; and why should a dramatist be allowed to jolt and destroy good music by any wretched vehicle he chooses? . . . I have very good reasons for supposing that the authors of these wretched pieces regard themselves . . . as legitimate dramatists.[35]

As for *L'Italiana in Algieri* by Rossini—not a composer whom he took to initially—he found the less said about the plot the better.[36] Like Rossini himself, he deplored excessive ornamentation, and called for singers to show an interpretative appreciation of the music and words they were singing, not just in dramatic contexts but in oratorio:

The character . . . of Haydn's beautiful song, 'With verdure clad,' is a gradual and as it were plastic benevolence, expressive of the growth of the herbs and plants and their genial effect upon the senses; but Mrs Dickons took every opportunity of interspersing it with ornament, and frisked and fluttered about like a romp in a hayfield, instead of expressing the fine, intellectual enjoyment of a soul contemplating creation.[37]

Most of the music criticism and reviews of Thomas Love Peacock (1785–1866) appeared in *The Globe and Traveller* in 1830 and *The*

Examiner from 1831 to 1834; a review of Lord Mount Edgcumbe's *Musical Reminiscences*, from which a number of the following quotations are taken, and his novel *Gryll Grange* also contain characteristic musical opinions. Peacock's is an urbane, classical disposition, sharp and satirical; in raising a timely voice against the fulsome romanticisms of song poetry, for instance, he sounds almost like F. R. Leavis; ballad writers later in the century would have done well to heed his censure:

Our old English songs were models of simplicity, but our modern songs are almost all false sentiment, overwhelmed with imagery utterly false to nature . . . Mr. Moore, with his everlasting 'brilliant and sparkling' metaphors, has contributed to lead the *servum pecus* into this limbo of poetical vanity; but the original cause lies deeper: namely, in a very general diffusion of heartlessness and false pretension.[38]

He too, as a connoisseur of Italian opera (especially of Bellini) who acted as Shelley's mentor for the genre, was seriously concerned with it as a dramatic entity. When he stressed that singers should work together as a team and not as egotistic stars he was demanding standards of production still by no means universally adopted today. He denigrated the impresarios of his day with a sarcasm which looked forward to Shaw.[39] Similarly Shavian was his quizzical interest, not only in opera performers, but in opera audiences, whose outlandish attire both satirized.[40] Like Hunt, he rated Mozart above all others (and again compared him to Shakespeare); in writing of the English premiere of 'The Barber of Seville' in 1818, however, he showed a more enthusiastic appreciation of Rossini:

We saw at once that there was a great revolution in dramatic music. Rossini burst on the stage like a torrent, and swept everything before him except Mozart, who stood, and will stand, alone and unshaken, like the Rock of Ages, because his art is like Shakespeare's, identical with nature, based on principles that cannot change till the constitution of the human race itself be changed, and therefore secure of admiration through all time, as the drapery of the Greek statues has been through all the varieties of fashion.[41]

Peacock was unusual in England in his day for preferring the classical balance of the complete, authentic *Don Giovanni* to the romanticized, circumcised morality made familiar to his compatriots:

Don Juan's first introduction to a modern English audience was in a pantomime (at Drury Lane we believe), which ended with the infernal regions, a shower of fire, and a dance of devils. Mozart's opera has, properly, no such conclusion. . . . The opera is wound up by a fugue in D major . . . one of the very finest things in dramatic music, and the most appropriate possible termination of the subject; and yet is this most noble composition, this most

AESTHETICS AND CRITICISM

fitting and genuine conclusion, sacrificed to a dance of devils flashing torches
of rosin, for no earthly reason but that so ended the Drury Lane pantomime.[42]

George Bernard Shaw (1856–1950), in his preface to a collected
volume of his music criticisms, once described something of the effect of
his columns on the critical world: 'I sparkled every week . . . in a
manner so absolutely unlike the conventional musical criticism of the
time that all the journalists believed that the affair was a huge joke, the
point of which was that I knew nothing whatever about music.'[43] In fact
Shaw, though in no sense an academic, knew quite enough about
music's technicalities, and far more about the human condition than
most of his fellow critics. It was the combination of the two which made
his criticism unique; for instance, his short article commemorating the
Mozart centenary[44] communicates a rare understanding of the man
and his music, perfectly expressed.

Shaw owed his musical background to his stepfather, a remarkable
Irishman, G. J. Vandeleur Lee, who had developed an unorthodox but
principally sound method of voice production and taught it to Shaw's
mother. Lee also gave Shaw his first critical assignments, ghosting for
him in *The Hornet* between November 1876 and September 1877. It is
remarkable to observe that his critical faculties and inimitable style
burst more or less fully-fledged on a surprised and often outraged world
at this period. In January 1877 he was vigorously attacking the
royalty-ballad system and the journals put out by publishing houses,
and by March Messrs. Boosey & Co. had declined to advertize further
in *The Hornet* as a result. Shaw's journalistic career entered on its
second, most vital phase in 1885, when he began a three-year post as
reviewer of books for *The Pall Mall Gazette*, later functioning concurrently as art critic of *The World* (1886–9), both at the instigation of
William Archer. In 1888 he began writing occasional articles on music
in *The Star*, a new evening paper, and provided a regular weekly column
as 'Corno di Bassetto' from February 1889 to May 1890, when he
transferred back to *The World* until the death of its editor, Edmund
Yates, in 1894. His regular journalistic career ended with an influential
period (1895–8) of dramatic criticism in *The Saturday Review*, although
occasional articles, including a number on music, were contributed to
various periodicals during the next fifty years. It is important to realize
that his output of plays had only just begun in the 1890s.[45]

Shaw's upbringing gave him an astute grasp of voice production and
a broad, loving acceptance of nineteenth-century Italian opera. These
were joined by a passion for Wagner, as much for his visionary drama-
tization of mythology as for his musical achievements; an energetic

469

practical commitment to Fabian socialism; and a very highly developed ironic wit. His equipment as a reforming critic was indeed formidable.

Reform was central to his purpose, and the demands he made of the critic in this capacity, which he knew that he himself fulfilled, were tough:

It is an important part of a critic's business to agitate for musical reforms; and unless he knows what the reforms will cost, and whether they are worth that cost, and who will have to pay the bill, and a dozen other cognate matters not usually included in treatises on harmony, he will not make any effective impression on the people with whom the initiative rests—indeed he will not know who they are. Even his artistic verdicts will often be aimed at the wrong person.[46]

He was deeply concerned with music's accessibility to the poorer people—as were the aestheticians from Spencer onwards, who saw music as playing a part in schemes of sociological idealism. He called for a series of cheap concerts independent of fashionable 'seasons'. His confidence in the cultural craving and stamina of working men—the 'shilling public'—was unusually well-informed: 'the labourers', he argued, 'are so enormously numerous that the absolute number of their exceptional men—men who will buy books out of 13s. a week in the country and 18s. in a town, and find time to read them while working 12 hours a day—is considerable.' Yet at the same time he cunningly rounded on the hypocrisy of those calling comfortably for 'music for the people':

What we want is not music for the people, but bread for the people, rest for the people, immunity from robbery and scorn for the people, hope for them, enjoyment, equal respect and consideration, life and aspiration, instead of drudgery and despair. When we get that I imagine the people will make tolerable music for themselves, even if all Beethoven's scores perish in the interim.[47]

There was but a thin barrier between Shaw the critic and Shaw the socialist orator, as another member of the critical profession, Francis Hueffer, must have discovered when Shaw disagreed with him 'about 15 seconds after the opening of our first conversation' on whether the English upper classes cared in the least for music. Later, Shaw spotted Hueffer among the audience whilst he was 'perched on the gunwhale of a wagon in Hyde Park, filling up some ten minutes of a "demonstration" with the insufferable oratorizing which is the only sort feasible on such occasions'.[48] He was by no means averse to owning up to his political activism in his writings: 'The three Anabaptists [in Meyerbeer's *Le Prophète*] rather interested me when they started an open-air revolutionary agitation, as I am a bit of an amateur in that line myself; but when they turned out badly in the end . . . I affirm that . . . Scribe's history is trash.'[49] He even recommended 'oratorizing' to other critics as an occasional means of sampling reality.[50] On the other hand he was quite capable of advocating private enterprise instead (e.g., in the printing of cheap analytical concert programmes to undercut official ones)[51] when he saw the need for it. What he could not tolerate was humbug, social or religious—especially religious. The oratorio—similarly condemned by Ruskin for 'withering the life of religion into dead bones on the Syren sands'[52]—was anathema to him; throughout his journalistic career he inveighed against it:

What a day Sunday must be for the children of the oratorio public! It was prime, no doubt, at the Crystal Palace on Saturday, to hear the three thousand young ladies and gentlemen of the choir, in their Sunday best, all shouting 'Stone him to death: stone him to death'; and one could almost hear the satisfied sigh of Mr. Chadband as St Paul's 'God shall surely destroy them' was followed in due time by the piously fugal 'See what love hath the Father bestowed on us.' But to me, constitutional scoffer that I am, the prostitution of Mendelssohn's great genius to this lust for threatening and vengeance, doom and wrath, upon which he should have turned his back with detestation, is the most painful incident in the art-history of the century. . . . The worst of it is that Mendelssohn's business is still a going concern, though his genius has been withdrawn from it. Every year at the provincial festivals some dreary doctor of music wreaks his counterpoint on a string of execrable balderdash with Mesopotamia or some other blessed word for a title.[53]

English composers, notably Parry and Stanford, and Brahms, all suffered from his oratorio- and cantata-hating pen, which would beat the genre with any stick. 'It turned out', he wrote of the Brahms *Requiem*'s appearance in a concert programme, 'a clever device of Mr Stanford's to make his setting of Tennyson's Revenge seem livelier by force of contrast. But it would have needed half a dozen actual funerals to do that.'[54] His withering criticism of Parry's *Job*[55] is well known; *Judith* fared no better, the melody since become famous through the hymn 'Dear Lord and Father of Mankind' being singled out for, as he saw it, its particular lack of originality:

one popular number in the form of a ballad which consisted of the first line of The Minstrel Boy, followed by the second line of Tom Bowling, connected by an 'augmentation' of a passage from the finale of the second act of Lucrezia Borgia, with an ingenious blend of The Girl I Left Behind Me and We Be Three Poor Mariners. It will be understood, of course, that the intervals—except in the Lucrezia Borgia case—are altered, and that the source of

471

Mr Parry's unconscious inspiration is betrayed by the accent and measure only.[56]

If his critical methods here seem unprincipled, his aim—to stamp out oratorio and release Parry's 'genius from an unnatural venal alliance' for it to fly 'back to the noble poetry that was its first love'—was not.[57]

Shaw's style was framed by his devious and devastating wit, and by his intense love of London, on whose bustle and noise and general familiarity he would draw for his images and his humour. He upset many people—though the majority of these seem to have been private readers, not those criticized—by his blatant lack of 'impartiality', a quality for which he had little use:

Never in my life have I penned an impartial criticism; and I hope I never may. As long as I have a want, I am necessarily partial to the fulfilment of that want, with a view to which I must strive with all my wit to infect everyone else with it. . . . One must, of course, know the facts, and that is where the critic's skill comes in; but a moral has to be drawn from the facts, and that is where his bias comes out.[58]

Retrospectively, his most serious limitation can be seen as an inability to say 'Hats off, gentlemen: a genius' of any composer active during the half-decade or so in which he was. Wagner was his god, and Wagner was dead. Nationalism, the use of native accents and folk idioms, irritated him: forty years before Constant Lambert he pointed out the incompatibility, in the work of Stanford, of sonata procedure with folk material,[59] and of Grieg he wrote with unanswerable finality, 'His music does not remind me of Norway, perhaps because I have never been there.'[60] He seems to have found no outstanding merit in two masterpieces, Tchaikovsky's Sixth and Dvořák's Seventh Symphonies,[61] when first heard in London. Brahms was for years a strategic blind spot. And if British music was coolly received, satirized, or even insulted (though he was remarkably charitable to some mediocrities), it was not because he, like so many of those around him, had no faith in Britain's musicality, but that his convictions as to the course British music must take would allow him neither to hail the young lights of his day, such as Eugen d'Albert and Hamish MacCunn, as saviours, nor to overestimate the questionable achievements of Parry, Stanford, Mackenzie, Cowen, and even Sullivan:

If we would only give a chance to every potential Wagner among our millions—that is, secure him adequate schooling and adequate grub—we should have an actual one in two generations at latest . . . . We cannot count on another Purcell; but in my opinion England's turn in art is coming, especially since there is a growing disposition among us to carry our social aims further than providing every middle-class dog with his own manger as soon as he is able to pay for it . . . We must have an English Wagner; perhaps he is starving somewhere whilst I write.[62]

He was, hyperbolically speaking, and before long Shaw recognized in Elgar the messiah of whose coming he had preached in the wilderness.

Chapter 22

MUSIC THEORY

G. LARRY WHATLEY

The study of music theory was considered indispensable to the British musician's training in the nineteenth century. One indication of this is the presence at each major educational institution of a succession of men who taught theory, composition, and related subjects, individuals now counted among the most prominent British musicians of the century. The large number of books about music theory published by British authors in the nineteenth century is another indication of how significant music theory was in educating the serious musician.

There were two main approaches to theoretical matters during this period. One was a continuation of Rameau's concern with natural acoustical phenomena as a scientific explanation of music. The other was an exclusively practical approach which emphasized the learning of 'musical grammar', giving little attention to the scientific basis for it. Most nineteenth-century theorists, in fact, made a distinction between the theory of harmony and such practical skills as counterpoint, orchestration, and form analysis. Even though theorists wrote about both theoretical and practical matters, most of them made little attempt to show the correlation between theory and practice which dominates musical thought today.

Theories of Harmony

The more systematic treatments of theoretical subjects are found chiefly in books on harmony. They are often as interesting for their omissions as for their contents. A general characteristic is the emphasis placed on rules, which appeared mainly in negative terms, prohibitions designed to guide students in 'correct' writing and to preserve 'purity' of style. The authors strongly conveyed the idea that they had developed the only true explanation of music theory, though they seldom either attempted a formal proof or revealed the source of their knowledge and ideas.

Along with the rules are found copious examples, certainly a time-honoured feature of theory books. Most of these, however, were composed by the authors, and comprised abstract chord progressions illustrating specific theoretical points. It was rare before the last decades of this period to find excerpts from the music of representative composers, although frequent verbal references to compositions do occur.

The nineteenth-century British theorists were primarily concerned with formulating a *theory of harmony*, to explain the origins of chords in terms of natural acoustical phenomena. In this endeavour, their theories are all descended from those of Rameau, but sometimes show striking, even novel, extensions of the famous French theorist's ideas. They usually made little effort to acknowledge Rameau's influence, although it is evident in most instances; most of them professed their ideas to be new and original, superior to any other explanation.

Considerable similarity may also be noticed between British theorists and their contemporaries on the Continent, mainly in Germany and France. Indeed, most significant advances in nineteenth-century music theory came rather from the Continent than from Great Britain, and, in retrospect, the importance of the British theorists is mainly local. Cherubini's *Cours de contrepoint et de fugue* (1835) was published in English translation in 1841 and was adopted for use at the Royal Academy of Music, replacing Crotch's book.

In 1845, however, a startlingly original book on music theory was published by a British author: *A Treatise on Harmony* by Alfred Day (1810–49). It was highly controversial, and when it was introduced in Academy classes by George Macfarren there was a dispute which led to Macfarren's resignation in 1848.[1] Day, who was by profession a homeopathic physician, took his basic premises from Rameau, but pushed them to a point at which their incompatibility with intuitive understanding of music was too glaring to be overlooked.

According to Day, chords are generated from certain notes taken as roots, the notes of a chord being selected from the harmonic series derived from each root. Day claimed that 'the harmonics from any given note (without taking the order in which they arise, but their practical use), are, major third, perfect fifth, minor seventh, minor or major ninth, eleventh, and minor or major thirteenth'.[2] He believed that only three notes of the scale—tonic, dominant, and supertonic—may serve as roots, and that from these arise all of the chromatic harmonies of the key. His distinction between diatonic and chromatic harmony is that diatonic discords require preparation, while chromatic discords are 'prepared by nature'. According to him, the dominant discords were the first which were used without preparation, later followed by supertonic discords, and even later by tonic discords. Further, only the chromatic notes produced by the overtones of the tonic, dominant, or supertonic could be allowed in any given key; chromatic notes other than these imply a change of key.

The effect of Day's theory was that most chords now taken for granted, and certainly to be found in the music of the nineteenth century, were given novel and curious identifications. For example, Day identified the subdominant chord as the upper three notes (seventh, ninth, and eleventh) of the dominant-eleventh chord, claiming that the root of the chord, although absent for the moment, was the dominant. Similarly, he claimed that the submediant chord consisted of the ninth, eleventh, and thirteenth of the dominant-thirteenth chord. He derived the augmented-sixth chord from *two* roots, the lower note as the minor ninth of the primary root (the dominant) and the upper note as the major third of the secondary root (the supertonic); the remaining notes of the chord came from the secondary root. He did not employ the customary names (Italian, French, and German) for the variants of the augmented-sixth chord.

The basic premises of Day's theories appear with few substantive changes in the writings of both George Macfarren (1813–87) and Frederick Ouseley (1825–89). Macfarren, the chief advocate and defender of Day's theories, returned to the Academy in 1851 and later became professor of music at Cambridge University. His major books on theory, *Rudiments of Harmony* (1860) and *Six Lectures on Harmony* (1867), were intended to disseminate Day's ideas. In addition to these books, he edited and annotated a second edition (1885) of Day's *Treatise on Harmony* which had first appeared in 1845.

Although Macfarren's writings were mainly a restatement of Day's thories, some differences exist in his derivation of chords. Unlike Day, he acknowledged consonant triads built on the second, fourth, and sixth degrees of the scale as *concords*, not considering them to be 'natural discords' springing from the dominant root. Also, he considered the subdominant to be a chord related to the tonic by a fifth below (analogous to the dominant a fifth above the tonic), not part of the dominant-eleventh chord. Thus he came a little closer to generally accepted ideas, though his explanation of more complex harmonies, such as the augmented-sixth chord, was essentially identical with Day's.

In his *Treatise on Harmony* (1868), Ouseley echoed much of Day's theory. One difference was his emphasis on the dominant-ninth and the

476

tonic as the two principal chords, both being required to generate harmonic 'motion' in which the characteristically unstable dominant resolves to tonic. He, like Day, derived fundamental discords from overtones occurring above the tonic and dominant roots; although drawing mainly upon the first sixteen overtones, he sometimes had to select tones much higher in the series. He also used Day's double-root theory to account for the augmented-sixth chord, and he did speak of Italian, French, and German augmented-sixth chords, referring to the use of these names by such earlier writers as William Crotch, in *Elements of Musical Composition* (1812).

A point of view radically different from that of Day, Macfarren, and Ouseley is found in *Theory of Harmony, Founded on the Tempered Scale* (1871), by John Stainer (1840–1901). Stainer abandoned the overtone series as the source for chords, considering the tempered scale to be the basis for harmony. He constructed chords by adding thirds until all notes of the tempered scale had been used, e.g., C, E, G, B, D, F, A (in major) and C, E♭, G, B, D, F, A♭ (in minor). He then derived the various chords of diatonic and chromatic harmony from these stacks of thirds. In some details, however, Stainer's theory was influenced by Day's, especially in his explanations of the subdominant and of augmented-sixth chords.

Ebenezer Prout (1835–1909), in his *Harmony: Its Theory and Practice* (1889), outlined a theory of harmony quite similar to Day's. According to Matthew Shirlaw, Prout advocated 'the selection of certain sounds of the scale, major or minor, as roots or generators; the building up of chords by means of added thirds; and the arbitrary selection for this purpose of sounds from the harmonic series'.[3] Prout also derived discords from tonic, supertonic, and dominant roots, and he derived the augmented-sixth chords from double roots. In some matters, particularly in drawing chord members from overtones very high in the series, Prout was at first almost more arbitrary and pedantic than Day.

But in the sixteenth edition of his book (1901) he made a sharp turn away from Day's theory. He abandoned the harmonic series, and acknowledged an aesthetic basis for composers' selection of musical materials, instead of the traditionally recognized scientific basis. He now considered chromatic harmony to be 'subordinate to the diatonic, . . . chromatic chords . . . being borrowed from neighbouring keys'.[4] He discarded the 'fundamental discords' on the tonic and supertonic but retained the discords based on the dominant root. Prout also recognized the subdominant chord, along with the tonic and dominant, as one of the three primary triads in the key.

British theorists, like their colleagues on the Continent, attempted to explain the origin of the minor triad. Unlike the major triad, which can easily be derived from the first six partials of the harmonic series, the minor triad yields to no easy explanation. The question has always baffled those theorists who claim a scientific basis for harmonic theory, and the British theorists were no more successful in solving this problem than were any others.

As with the theory of chord generation, most theorists have explained minor harmony in a manner similar to Rameau's. Day, for instance, explained the third of the minor triad as an arbitrary sound, used instead of the major third, and he considered the tonic triad in minor keys to be *major*! Because of his theory of chord generation, he considered the only viable form of the minor scale to be the harmonic. Although Macfarren's system was quite similar to Day's, he did concede that the tonic triad in minor keys was *minor*. While he claimed that a major key and its relative minor have different keynotes, he considered the true relative minor of a major key to be the *tonic* minor, saying that 'the variations of major and minor are modifications of the one same key, not of the two relative keys'.[5] According to Shirlaw, the contradiction is left unresolved in Macfarren's writings.

Ouseley gave a different (and original) explanation, deriving the minor triad from harmonics high in the overtone series; he maintained that the harmonic ratio 16:19:24 (C, E♭, G) yields a minor triad which is enough in tune to be usable. He rejected the E-minor triad, represented by the ratio 10:12:15, because he considered C to be the root of the whole series, and he claimed that C cannot be the root of the E minor triad. In agreement with Day and Macfarren, however, he recognized only the harmonic form of the minor scale. Still another approach to minor harmony was Stainer's construction of chords by adding successive thirds from scale degrees, forming the minor triad by stacking in thirds the notes of the minor scale. Prout, in the first edition of his book, had adopted Ouseley's explanation of the origin of the minor triad; in the sixteenth edition he abandoned this explanation.

Most nineteenth-century theorists were frustrated by the problem of intonation in developing a theory of harmony. In the natural overtone series, many of the higher partials, beginning with the seventh, are noticeably out of tune; the difficulty was to achieve a reconciliation between the 'faulty' intonation of the overtone series and the various systems of tuning prevalent at that time. Equal temperament, if accepted at all, was acknowledged with reluctance, and theorists laboured diligently to find usable ratios which would yield the purest intonation. Although a subject far too complex to be treated in full in a survey such as this, the concern with intonation should be recognized

478

as a primary reason for the somewhat bizarre explanations of harmonic phenomena found in the writings of British theorists.

The approach to the theory of harmony taken by Prout in 1901 was the signal of a broader change of emphasis in studying music. While earlier theorists wrote almost exclusively about harmony, its origin, and the rules for writing it correctly, Prout (and, to a certain extent, Macfarren before him) became more concerned with the practice of music than with its theory. While many earlier theorists had virtually ignored such matters as musical form, melodic construction, orchestration, and contrapuntal techniques (Hamilton is a notable exception), Prout wrote extensively about such topics. His approach centred upon analysing the construction and design of actual musical compositions, rather than constructing abstract chord progressions and forming *a priori* theories.

Although it may be argued that Prout was pedantic and rigid, he was less so than most of his predecessors. His writings, in fact, indicate a turning point in the thinking of British theorists. It is true, of course, that theorists in other countries were more influential in creating what the modern theorist would consider an enlightened point of view. In Britain, however, it was Prout who made the first advance in this direction.

Practical Musicianship

The discrediting of the more artificial and dogmatic kind of music theory was in the end perhaps more thorough in Britain than on the Continent. It took place as the older theories became more and more obviously out of step with the rapid changes in musical style at the end of the nineteenth century, and as knowledge of older styles grew. The new approach to music theory came not from harmony books, but from several other literary forms whose goals were more closely tied to practical musicianship. These forms covered areas of musical study which are now regarded as part of the theory of music, but which had been traditionally ignored in theoretical treatises.

Many books used for practical instruction were descended from the *thorough-bass primers* of earlier periods. They usually summarized the 'grammar of music', with passages on the origins of music (mainly the overtone series, without detailed consideration of acoustics), notation, scales, chords, and figured bass. A good example was William Crotch's *Practical Thorough-Bass* (c. 1825), which included rules for writing four-part harmony. Another was Johann Bernhard Logier's *A System of the*

Science of Music and Practical Composition (1827), which combined theoretical and practical instruction. The German-born Logier (1777–1846)
was mainly a pianist: a highly controversial figure, he was widely
accused of being a charlatan more interested in making money than in
serious instruction. He stated that he did not 'arrogate to himself the
discovery of new principles of harmony', but merely endeavoured to
'develop a method simple and efficacious, by which the principles
already established may be more easily comprehended and effectually
put into practice'.[6]

One popular format for instructional books was the *catechism*, in
which questions were posed and then answered, obviously a variation
of the dialogue between master and student common in mediaeval
books and familiar from Fux's *Gradus ad Parnassum*. James Hamilton
(1785–1845) was a popular nineteenth-century writer who used the
catechism format in a variety of books on musical subjects. His theory
books were clearly designed for the less well educated reader.

Two other literary forms have some importance for the music theory
that they frequently incorporated. One was the musical *dictionary* of the
comprehensive type, such as the one begun but never completed by
John Wall Callcott (1766–1821). Thomas Busby's *Musical Dictionary*,
first published in 1786, was reprinted many times in the nineteenth
century; of the many similar works, one of the most significant was John
Stainer and William Barrett's *Dictionary of Musical Terms* (1876). Encyc-
lopaedias also frequently contained articles of theoretical importance.
Abraham Rees's *Cyclopedia* (1819) had musical articles by Charles
Burney, while successive editions of the *Encyclopaedia Britannica* repay
study for their efforts to bring music theory up to date. The eleventh
edition of 1910–11 was distinguished by a number of articles by Donald
Tovey on such terms as 'Music', 'Harmony', 'Sonata Forms', and
'Contrapuntal Forms', in which a refreshingly original point of view
was often brought to bear upon a well-tried subject. These articles have
been reprinted in book form.[7]

The *annotated programme* served, in the Victorian period, to educate
the concert-going middle-class public in many branches of music
theory, more particularly in formal analysis, a topic that was neglected
by most writers of theory books. Scholes has found a few isolated
examples of annotated programmes from the eighteenth century,[8] but
the first regular programme notes in Britain seem to have been provided by John Thomson (1805–41) at the Reid Concerts in Edinburgh
from about 1835. John Ella's Musical Union concerts from 1845 had
elaborate 'synoptical analyses' of the works performed, with quotations
in music notation.[9] Important analytical programme notes were pro-

vided anonymously for the Monday and Saturday Popular Concerts by James W. Davison, and for the Crystal Palace Concerts by George Grove (from 1856 to 1896). Again the culminating point was reached in the work of Tovey. His famous programme notes, made for the Reid Concerts and various other occasions, were eventually collected into his six volumes of *Essays in Musical Analysis* (1935–9).

Indeed it was in the writings of Tovey (1875–1940) that these different strands of 'practical' music theory found their first comprehensive, though not necessarily systematic, treatment. Composer, conductor, pianist, essayist, and professor, he brought to the study of music an insight which is legendary, and which should be emphasized perhaps more than it is today. His election in 1914 as Reid Professor of Music at Edinburgh University provided a base from which he exerted tremendous influence upon British musical life through his concerts, writings, and teaching.

Tovey is not usually considered to be a theorist. His fame rests principally upon his prolific writings about music, but he was a theorist in the best sense of the word: for the charm of his literary style and avoidance of pedantry, jargon, and unnecessary technicality conceal his profound understanding of every branch of music theory. His intimate knowledge of music, supported by a broad historical perspective, provided a background for some of the finest writings about eighteenth- and nineteenth-century composers and their music to be found anywhere. On another level his writings have even greater significance: his attitudes and observations reflect insight and perspective extending far beyond the music about which he wrote, and his point of view is highly instructive even in the study of music composed after his time.

Tovey's writings contain many technical details, and he frequently explained his terminology. By his own admission, however, he explained only those aspects of theory which he needed in any given instance to illustrate a more general musical point. Because of this, and because of his conversational writing style, one can find in his works no such systematic theory as that found in the books of Prout, Stainer, Ouseley, Macfarren, or Day. His views about theoretical matters are thoroughly intermixed with his ideas about musical style, practice, and aesthetics, matters with which conventional theorists had had little concern.

He spoke forcibly about the dangers of forming *a priori* ideas about music, especially with regard to musical form. One of his recurring themes is that each composition is a unique, individual work of art which must be met on its own terms. Connected with this idea is his approach to analysing and listening to music: he advocated a phrase-by-phrase description of musical events, maintaining that 'a true analysis takes the standpoint of a listener who knows nothing beforehand, but hears and remembers everything'.[10] His primary concern was the evaluation and criticism of music, designed to facilitate the listener's appreciation; for him, theory was a tool, a means to an end.

Tovey also commented on the theorists of the nineteenth century, including those discussed earlier in this survey. He had little patience with pedantry and was highly critical of most theorists; he described many of their ideas as 'humbug' which had little to do with actual musical practice and style. He maintained that music selects from acoustics the materials necessary for its purposes, and that almost every acoustical fact applicable to music is quickly transcended in the complexities of musical aesthetics.

Although many of his comments are general criticisms of 'the textbooks', the authors of which remain unnamed but may be assumed to include most of those mentioned above, Tovey occasionally mentioned some of the more prominent theorists by name, such as Day, Macfarren, and Prout. His attitudes toward them and their ideas were expressed very clearly and forcibly:

The beginning of the nineteenth century was unfortunately the beginning of an age of humbug in musical education. One consequence is that many a musical revolt purports to revolt against the classics when its nearest contact with classical forms has been the perky generalizations of textbooks by writers who regarded the great masters as dangerous, and who deduced their rules from the uniform procedures of lesser composers.[11]

Tovey's writings—especially his programme notes—filled a need that had not existed before the nineteenth century: to explain and justify the ways of composers for the benefit of persons who sought to enter the ranks of the *cognoscenti*. But in a broader sense they may be classified as music theory, rather than criticism, in that they accept on subjective grounds the aesthetic validity of a body of art works and provide an exegesis of them, both individually and in general. With the self-confidence born of his prodigious musical talent and impeccable classical education, he was able to voice an unashamedly British approach to the profound mysteries of harmony, musical form, and musical expression. Building on the work of predecessors such as Grove and Prout, he succeeded in showing the informed music-lover that music theory was not necessarily the coldly abstract or obscurely Teutonic science that it had often seemed to be before his time.

Chapter 23

MUSICOLOGY

VINCENT DUCKLES

Musicology today is clearly an international discipline, the joint product of the work of a community of scholars devoting themselves to common problems regardless of national boundaries. As we look back from the twentieth century, however, certain differences become apparent from one country to the next. Much has been written about national styles in musical composition and performance, comparatively little about styles in musical learning. In the early part of the nineteenth century, France, which had been culturally dominant throughout the preceding century, was entering into a kind of renaissance in the wake of the Napoleonic wars. The reemergence of French musical scholarship was brought about primarily through the efforts of one man, François-Joseph Fétis (1784–1871), and one institution, the Paris Conservatoire. At the same time, Germany was on the threshold of an outburst of energy that touched nearly all areas of musical productivity (theory, composition, performance, scholarship); while in Italy, by contrast, the last vestiges of an earlier supremacy survived in a few isolated individuals and locations: Baini and Santini in Rome, Caffi in Venice, Florimo in Naples, and so on. In Britain musical scholarship was beginning to develop its own traditions, traditions that were chiefly based, naturally enough, on the rediscovery of its own resources from the past: the madrigal, the glee, the anthem and oratorio. Its patterns were influenced to a considerable extent by the tastes of a mercantile society set within a well-defined class structure. The image of the musical scholar in British life was not that of the professional musician, but rather of the gentleman amateur, best represented by the country clergyman quietly pursuing his own antiquarian interests, or by the semi-retired engineer or business man returning to an interest neglected since his youth.

Musicology, in whatever terms we choose to describe it, is a complex and diversified activity utilizing methods drawn from both the natural and cultural sciences. It differs from its neighbours in the humanities in the fact that it is of comparatively recent origin. The historical and comparative study of art and literature, language, philosophy and religion, had all won their places in the academic hierarchy by the time musicology appeared on the scene. The establishment of the discipline was further delayed in Britain by a certain reluctance to accept the terminology of modern musical scholarship. France had its *musicologie*, Germany its *Musikwissenschaft*, long before the existence of an equivalent term in the English language. In fact full acceptance for 'musicology' as such did not come until at least the middle of the present century. Even Edward Dent, who probably did more to stimulate musical research in British universities than any other individual, referred to musicology somewhat contemptuously as 'musical excavation'. The truth of the matter is that Englishmen, in their thought about music, have always taken greater interest in the *artistic* than in the *scientific* aspect of their discipline. They have never ceased to regard music as a realm of concrete experience, not a field for philosophical speculation. There have been exceptions to this, but the prevailing attitude has been, and still is, on the side of music-making rather than system-building.

Schools of Thought in Musical Scholarship

At the beginning of modern musical scholarship in England there were two outstanding figures who can be said to represent opposing attitudes toward the discipline. Roger North (1653–1734) was a dilettante, a moderately skilled amateur performer of noble birth, who thought seriously about his art, filling numerous notebooks with 'memoirs' (observations) on the history of music, on the nature of musical 'air', on the principles of music aesthetics and criticism.[1] Though he had little direct influence on his contemporaries, yet he exemplified the views of an increasing number of them, particularly those who had encountered the empirical philosophies of Descartes and Locke, who sought the meaning of music within their own experience rather than between the covers of dusty books. The name of Charles Burney (1726–1814) stands foremost among North's spiritual descendants. By contrast, John Christopher Pepusch (1667–1752), a German-born theorist and composer, carried the weight of a professional reputation on his shoulders: according to Burney his sole ambition in later life was 'the obtaining of a reputation of a profound theorist, preferably skilled in the music of the Ancients'.[2] He was the prototype of the tradition-bound scholar for whom the music of his own day held little interest. He assembled a distinguished music library which included the Fitzwilliam Virginal Book and other early manuscripts.[3] He prepared editions of Corelli's sonatas and concertos that do not fall far short of modern standards of textual criticism. His attitudes to musical scholarship were passed on to Burney's great rival, John Hawkins (1719–89).

It is easy to make invidious comparisons between the two men, as it is to treat Burney and Hawkins in utterly opposing terms. What is important is that both approaches be recognized as legitimate avenues to scholarship. The polarity between music as an art and music as a science runs throughout the nineteenth century. The contrast is expressed frequently in terms of a contest between the speculative or contemplative approach on the one hand and practical musicianship on the other. But either predisposition if carried too far can lead to abuses. Interest in performance alone can easily degenerate into a superficial display of technique; speculative music, however, can just as easily descend into pedantry and pretence. One early nineteenth-century musician who was particularly conscious of this dichotomy was Edward Hodges (1796–1867),[4] the author of an interesting series of essays printed in *The Musical World* (1836) under the title 'On the Objects of Musical Study'. Hodges wrote in a rich Victorian prose, and was obviously carried away by his own rhetoric as he pictured the consequences of too much emphasis on performing techniques at the expense of musical understanding:

If it be a fact that the *ne plus ultra* of musical attainment is the power of scampering over the greatest possible number of notes in a given time; occasionally with the velocity of lightning, flitting from the north to the south poles of the gamut; now dashing, here and there, through all the known and unknown scales, backwards and forwards, right and left, with all the fantastic coruscations of a 'troubled meteor'; now with the animus of a huntsman scouring the diatonic plains, leaping chromatic five-barred gates, and clearing enharmonic ditches . . . If this be the perfection of music, then in heaven's name let us at once drop all pretensions to *science*; let us take our place with the shoemakers and blacksmiths, or rather with less usefully employed mechanics.[5]

When an early nineteenth-century musician concerned himself with 'the science of music', he usually had in mind the subject matter of acoustics.[6] No educated man of the time could fail to be aware of the impact of the natural sciences on human life and thought. It was inevitable that students in the cultural fields (art, music, history, religion) should seek to emulate scientific methods as far as possible. During the spring of 1835, Charles Wheatstone (1802–75), professor of experimental philosophy at King's College, London, gave a course of eight lectures at the college on the physics and physiology of sound that attracted a great deal of public interest.

Mr Wheatstone got up his course in a most complete manner; his models, machinery, diagrams, etc. were abundant and perfect; his matter was good, much of it new, and his experiments, with an exception or two, very successful. . . . They gave a general view of our present knowledge of the laws of sound, including the recent discoveries of Chladni, Savart, Cagniard de la Tour, Weber, Willis, Faraday, etc.; the application of these laws to the construction of musical and acoustic instruments, acoustic buildings, etc., as well as to the mechanism of the organs of hearing, voice and speech; and the intimate analogies between the undulatory theory of light and that of sound were clearly pointed out.[7]

Acoustics continued to stimulate the interest of scholars throughout the century. Further impetus was furnished by the work of Hermann von Helmholtz, whose *Die Lehre von den Tonempfindungen* (1863) was translated into English in 1875 by Alexander J. Ellis (1814–90) under the title *On the Sensations of Tone*. Helmholtz's views exercised considerable influence on nineteenth-century English music theory. Ellis, in collaboration with A. J. Hipkins, made basic studies of the phenomenon of musical pitch. Another musical scientist was William Pole (1814–1900) whose book *The Philosophy of Music* (1879) went through many editions as a popular introduction to acoustics.

Concepts regarding the nature and content of musical learning were frequently propagated and defined in the musical periodicals that burgeoned in Britain during our period. The first to be established on a long-term basis was *The Quarterly Musical Magazine and Review* (1818–28), edited by Richard Bacon of Norwich, which contained a number of articles of a scholarly and speculative nature in addition to comments and criticisms on the day-to-day musical life of the time. Still more important were *The Harmonicon* (1823–33) and its successor *The Monthly Supplement to the Musical Library* (1834–7), both edited by William Ayrton (1777–1858). From a sampling of titles of articles in *The Harmonicon* one can already observe configurations of meaning taking shape that would in the course of a generation or two become significant strands of research activity. They can be grouped under six headings that reflect pre-musicological interests:

1. *Ethnic or folk music*: 16 titles, such as 'The State of Music in Calcutta', 'Capt. Parry on the Music of the Exquimaux, with Copies of the Airs', 'Burmese Musical Instruments', 'Music of the Bretons'.
2. *Historical studies*: 12 titles, including 'An Essay on the Gregorian

Chant', 'Origin and History of the *Concert Spirituel*', 'The *Miserere* of Allegri', 'Origin and History of the Organ'.

3. *Descriptions of libraries and reference tools*: 4 titles, such as 'Musical Discoveries in Ambrosian Library', 'M. Fétis on Musical Dictionaries'.

4. *Manuscripts and other primary sources*: 5 titles, such as 'Some Account of a Latin Ms. on Music, by the Celebrated Tinctor', 'Account of some Newly Discovered Original MSS of Mozart'.

5. *Acoustics*: 11 titles, including 'On Concert Pitch', 'On the Ratios of the Diatonic and Chromatic Intervals', 'On the Phenomenon of the *Third Sound*'.

6. *Music theory and aesthetics*: 9 titles, such as 'On the National Characteristics of Music', 'On Unity and Variety in Music, and on the Fugue', 'On the Power of Association in Works of Art', 'Outline of a System of Modern Harmony', 'A Treatise on Melody', 'Thoughts or Ideas in Music'.

Later musical journals like *The Musical World* (1836–91) and *The Musical Times* (1844–   ) also carried frequent articles concerned with the various branches of musical scholarship, though this was not their primary function. A less familiar periodical, *The Choir and Musical Record* (1863–78), had a stronger bias towards scholarship and a broader range of subject matter than its title might suggest. In addition to promoting 'the art of church music', it promised to reproduce 'those choral works of the great masters which are at present in the hands of the very few, comprising the best choral examples of secular music, facsimiles of Ancient Mss., etc. and to reprint rare treatises on the Art of Music'. No editor is mentioned but it is clear that one of the principal contributors was Edward F. Rimbault. He was responsible for a long serialized transcription of John Case's *The Praise of Musicke* (1586) as well as an edition, also serialized, of Purcell's *Dido and Aeneas*. Other representative articles are 'Music and Musical Instruments, a Course of Lectures being Delivered by Professor Hullah at the Society of Arts', 'On the Early Ages of English Music and Song', by William Chappell, 'Dr Campion's *Treatise on Counterpoint*', and so on.

In spite of their incipient research interest most of the articles printed in the above-mentioned periodicals were addressed to amateurs. British musical scholarship did not acquire a professional journal in its own right until the publication of *The Musical Antiquary* (1909–13). Its editor was G. E. P. Arkwright, who with a group of colleagues, including Dent, W. H. Grattan Flood, W. J. Lawrence, and E. W. Naylor, achieved a standard of scholarly excellence equal to anything produced elsewhere in Europe. In this context one should also mention the *Proceedings of the Musical Association*, not strictly a periodical but a yearbook devoted to the printing of research papers read by its members. This series began in 1874, preserving an unbroken record of distinguished scholarship from that date to the present day.

Historical Lectures

In a sense the founding of the Musical Association was the culminating point of the development of public lectures on musical history and other scholarly subjects, which had been in vogue throughout the century as a means of bringing musical culture to the otherwise well educated, or even to the 'general public'. Music more than any other art bears an aura of expertise that is both baffling and intriguing to the layman. Along with a desire to understand the structure of the art is an even more far-reaching curiosity about the nature of its history.

The pioneer in English lectures on music history was William Crotch (1775–1847), who began his public lecture-recitals at Oxford as early as 1798 and repeated them in London and Oxford for the next thirty years or more. Eventually he published *The Substance of Several Courses of Lectures on Music Read at the University of Oxford, and in the Metropolis* (1831). Here he made it clear that his intent was not to advance Science but to improve Taste. Thus he was in the North-Burney rather than the Pepusch-Hawkins line. His audiences were made up not of philosophers, composers, or scholars, but of music lovers and performers. Crotch was no profound thinker; most of his ideas on musical style were warmed-over concepts taken from Burke or Reynolds. But he did exercise a profound influence on his contemporaries. The music he used to illustrate his lectures was collected in his famous *Specimens of Various Styles of Music*, published in three volumes in 1801. Perhaps the most significant part was the section in Volume I devoted to 'national music'. Crotch himself spoke as a recent convert to this branch of musical investigation:

Having thus concluded these imperfect remarks on the National Airs contained in this volume, it may seem necessary to apologize for having dedicated so large a portion of this work to a subject hitherto considered of but little importance: it is a subject, however, which I am not disposed to view in that light; one wherein much remains to be discovered, and the study of which every lover of music may prosecute.[8]

The second and third volumes of Crotch's anthology are concerned with what he calls 'specimens of scientific music'—that is, music controlled by the laws of tonality. Here one finds a variety of examples from the polyphonic period to the present day, all reduced to keyboard score. But again, his purposes were to improve taste, to facilitate performance, and to provide models for the student of composition. The faithful restoration of early music through a critical examination of its sources was conspicuously absent from his mind.

Other lecturers announced readings from time to time. R. J. S. Stevens (1757–1837), a well-known composer of glees, was elected to the Gresham professorship of music in 1801. Between that year and 1837 he read frequent lectures on musical subjects, copies of which are preserved in the Guildhall Library. Stevens's successor in the Gresham Professorship was Edward Taylor (1784–1863), a civil engineer by profession and a successful musician in later life.[9] Two of his lecture series were reported in the *Monthly Supplement to the Musical Library*, one devoted to 'The Early English Opera', and the other to 'English Vocal Harmony'. Here is the editor's comment on them:

These lectures exhibited considerable research, a full knowledge of the subject, great decision of opinion, an intrepid vindication of English Composers, a warm and deserved panegyric on many of them, and some bold and biting remarks on the tendency of fashion in this country to despise and neglect its native musical produce, and to lend a willing ear only to the productions of the newest and weakest of foreign composers.[10]

Henry J. Gauntlett (1805–76), a prolific hymn writer and an advocate of improvements in the construction of English organs, gave a series of six lectures on 'The Rise and Progress of Ecclesiastical Music', which, according to a report in *The Musical World* (1837), were full-scale productions involving the participation of a chorus, solo voices, and instruments to illustrate the lecturer's observations. Samuel Wesley (1766–1837) was another musician who joined the parade of music lecturers. His remarks, delivered in Bristol and London between 1825 and 1830, are forthright and practical and at the same time full of fascinating information on a remarkable musician and the musical practices of his time.[11] The chief sponsor for public lectures in the first half of the century was the London Institution at Moorfields, built in 1819—a pioneering body in the history of adult education. Among the many subjects it covered in the arts, sciences, and 'manufactures and the useful arts', one of the most popular was music: 120 lectures on music were given under its auspices between 1819 and 1854, including series by Crotch, Wesley, Gauntlett, Vincent Novello, Taylor, Henry Bishop, and William H. Monk.[12]

About the middle of the century an institution was formed for the sole purpose of conducting meetings for scholarly lectures and discussion on musical topics; it was probably the first of its kind in the world. The Musical Institute of London, founded in 1851 with John Hullah as president, had among its aims 'the cultivation of the art and science of music', 'the holding of conversazioni, for the reading of papers upon musical subjects', and 'the publication of transactions'.[13] It failed in 1853, probably because even with over two hundred paying members it could not afford the rent of the permanent premises in Sackville Street, Piccadilly. Another organization along similar lines, the Musical Society of London, existed from 1858 to 1867.[14]

The foundation of the Musical Association was first proposed by John Stainer during a visit to Oxford of Dr William Pole in 1867. Shortly after moving to London as organist of St Paul's cathedral in 1872 Stainer took the initiative in the founding of the society by calling 'a meeting of influential musicians, practical and scientific', as he put it in a memoir:[15] in fact the opening meetings in 1874 were dominated by men of learning such as Pole, Spottiswoode, and Wheatstone (all Fellows of the Royal Society), and at least sixteen founding members of the Institute were included. Practical musicians such as Stainer himself were also represented. The first president was the Reverend Professor Sir Frederick Gore Ouseley, Bart. (1825–89), whose impeccable social position gave the Association the standing it needed to take its place among the established learned societies. The early Proceedings record lengthy and sometimes interesting discussions following each lecture, and give a vivid idea of both the strengths and the deficiencies of British musical scholarship of the time. The best speakers, like Stainer himself, combined excellent general knowledge in the sciences or the humanities or both with a good intuitive sense of musical style; but few had, as yet, much idea of a rigorous scholarly discipline appropriate to the systematic study of music. The prefix 'Royal' was not conferred upon the Association until 1944. From 1899 to 1914 it fulfilled an additional function as the British section of the International Musical Association, and the third meeting of the I.M.A. was held in London in 1911.

Histories of Music

In the publication of comprehensive histories of music Britain had won a clear lead with the appearance in the last quarter of the eighteenth century of the massive works of Burney and Hawkins. For some time these tended to act as a deterrent to original historical research and writing. Instead of a continuing advance toward the frontiers of musical knowledge, we find a variety of music histories for 'the man in the street' containing information that was an undisguised dilution and updating of Burney and Hawkins. This could be said of George Hogarth's *Musical History, Biography, and Criticism* (London, 1835), his *Memoirs of the Musical Drama* (1838), and Thomas Busby's *General History of Music* (London, 1819). One work that presented a somewhat different emphasis was William C. Stafford's *History of Music* (Edinburgh, 1830), which devoted an unusual amount of space to a discussion of the music of exotic cultures, ancient and primitive. It was this feature that attracted the attention of Fétis, who, though critical of some aspects of Stafford's book, thought highly enough of it to encourage his wife to translate it into French. Grove's *Dictionary* describes Stafford's work as 'chiefly noted for its inaccuracy', but it deserves better than that. It can, in fact, be regarded as a significant early document in the literature of ethnomusicology.

There were two important foreign histories that made considerable impact in translation on English musical thought of the first half of the nineteenth century. One was Etienne Alexandre Choron's *Sommaire de l'histoire de la musique* (1810), which was translated and inserted into Sainsbury's popular *Dictionary of Musicians* in 1824.[16] An even more influential work was Raphael Georg Kiesewetter's *Geschichte der europäisch-abendländische oder unserer heutigen Musik*, published in English in 1848. This was a distinctly innovative work. It did not attempt to treat the history of music exhaustively from antiquity to the present; rather, it focussed on the modern period, dividing historical time into seventeen epochs each identified with the work of one or more major composers. Kiesewetter was not concerned with biographical detail; his interest was directed toward musical forms and structures.

John Pyke Hullah (1812–83) was a leading spirit in the promotion of all forms of music education. He was a prolific editor and lecturer on musical subjects, including history. Two volumes of historical studies issued from his pen: *The History of Modern Music, a Course of Lectures Delivered at the Institute of Great Britain* (1862) and *The Third or Transition Period of Musical History* (1865). These volumes, though directed toward popular taste, contain an extraordinary amount of information. Hullah divided music history into four periods, the first ending about 1400, the second covering the fifteenth and sixteenth centuries, the third or 'transition period' extending from 1601 to 1750, and the fourth from 1751 onwards. Presumably he intended to publish a volume devoted to each of these four periods, but only the last two were completed. In any case, the volume concerned with the 'transition period', covering the

491

interval between Monteverdi and Bach, can justly be described as the first history of baroque music in the English language.

Other volumes of history appeared during the course of the century, but English historical writing did not come into its own until the early years of the twentieth century with the publication of the *Oxford History of Music* (1901). This was a composite work enlisting contributions from Harry Wooldridge, Hubert Parry, John Fuller Maitland, Henry Hadow, Edward Dannreuther, and H. C. Colles. An introductory volume was added to the second edition (1929) in belated recognition of the importance of peripheral fields that lay outside the traditional historical boundaries (plainsong, folksong, notation, iconography, etc.). The editor was Percy C. Buck (1871–1947). It was inevitable that a work of this kind should be uneven in quality. Undoubtedly the strongest volume in the set was that prepared by Wooldridge under the title of 'The Polyphonic Period'. This deserves special mention for its pioneer investigation of the music of the *ars antiqua*. With the publication of the *Oxford History* English musical scholarship gained an equal footing with the work accomplished by scholars on the Continent. It is significant that in 1911, when Guido Adler's *Der Stil in der Musik*, a basic document in the historiography of Western music, was published, Parry issued his *Style in Musical Art*, a study that traversed much of the same ground.

The Revival of Early Music

Another area in which Britain led the rest of Europe was in the publication of editions of early music. In this case the impetus came, as might be expected, directly from the performing organizations: from cathedral choirs, for which Boyce's *Cathedral Music* (1760–78) served a practical need; from secular societies such as the Catch Club, the Madrigal Society, the Academy of Ancient Music, and the Concert of Ancient Music, which sought new titles to add to their repertories of old music. This brought about a wave of historicism that swept through the late eighteenth century and on into the nineteenth, restoring the madrigal, the motet, and the anthem to life. Of course the greatest obstacle to an Englishman's reconciliation with his musical past was the formidable presence of Handel. In 1789 the composer Samuel Arnold (1740–1802), who had already edited a revised and expanded version of Boyce's *Cathedral Music*, published in 1790, issued proposals for a complete edition of Handel's works, to be published by Longman & Co. He proposed an edition of

492

the works of Handel in score: correct, uniform, and complete; consisting of his oratorios, operas, duets, anthems, concertos, lessons, Te Deums, trios, fugues, etc., elegantly engraved on large folio plates, under the immediate direction and inspection of Dr. Arnold, organist and composer to His Majesty.

The set, issued under the patronage of the King, continued through 180 instalments (1787–97). Arnold's standards of accuracy, uniformity, and completeness were not high, but his Handel edition can be cited as the first effort anywhere to compile a complete edition of the works of a major composer.

A late eighteenth-century edition of even greater interest was compiled by Edmund Thomas Warren (c. 1730–c. 1794: he later changed his name to Warren-Horne), secretary of the Noblemen's and Gentlemen's Catch Club. In the pursuit of his duties in that office he edited a series of volumes containing some 652 pieces from the club's repertory, including, in addition to the expected catches and glees, a considerable number of early madrigals and other partsongs, English and Italian. But the most significant product of Warren-Horne's editorial industry was interrupted short of publication. This was a projected anthology of 'Ancient Music' to be issued in six volumes, each of one hundred plates. The publisher, Peter Welcker, who undertook the task of seeing the work through the press, died shortly after the plates for the first volume had been engraved, and his widow, Mary Welcker, followed him to the grave four years later without having advanced the project any further. All that remains of this promising historical anthology, surely the first of its kind, is a set of uncorrected proof sheets for the first volume. They were sold at auction in 1797 by Leigh and Sotheby, along with the remainder of Warren-Horne's library, and eventually found their way into the collection of the British Library. The proofs are quite remarkable as to their contents. They include works by Josquin, Isaac, Compère, Crequillon, Clemens non Papa, de Rore, and other sixteenth- and seventeenth-century musicians. All are presented in score and bear annotations as to the sources from which they were taken. Had it ever reached publication, 'Ancient Music' would have constituted a milestone in the history of musical scholarship.[17]

What Warren-Horne did not achieve was accomplished in some measure by John Stafford Smith (1750–1836) in his *Musica Antiqua* (1812). The chief interest of this collection resides in the fact that many of the pieces (there are some 190 of them) are transcribed from early English sources, some of them taken from Smith's own rich private collection. As an historian Smith subscribed to a rather naïve version of the idea of Progress, in company with most of his contemporaries. For him, the chief purpose in recovering early music was to demonstrate the superiority of the present over the past: 'By raising from the dust, compositions of great merit in their day, we are able to trace the nice gradations by which music has advanced to its present state of perfection.' Smith's contribution was to direct the attention of his readers to the importance of source studies. He was probably the first to publish transcriptions from the Mulliner Book, the Ritson Manuscript, and some of the sources of the early English carol.

It has been suggested that the revival of early English music was closely allied to the activities of London's musical clubs. Many of these institutions accumulated rich music libraries over the years. The Sacred Harmonic Society, for example, could boast of remarkable holdings of English and Italian madrigals in their original editions.[18] In 1808 Richard Webb, a minor canon of St Paul's Cathedral, scored and edited a small collection of early polyphonic music on behalf of the Madrigal Society.[19] In 1816 William Hawes brought out a modern edition, in score, of Morley's tribute to Elizabeth I, *The Triumphs of Oriana*. The Motett Society sponsored the publication of *A Collection of Ancient Church Music, consisting of Selections from the Works of Composers of the 16th and 17th Centuries* (3 vols., 1842). Editions of this kind could not fail to make the British public more conscious of its native musical heritage, nor could such publications have been undertaken without the co-operation of British music publishers.

One firm in particular, the house of Novello, played a major role in recovering and reviving early music in England. Vincent Novello (1781–1861) was a man whose contribution to British musicology of the nineteenth century cannot be overrated. He was an astute business man, but one who placed service to the art of music above his commercial interests. The firm was founded in 1811, and by 1825 he had brought out a splendid five-volume set of early Italian sacred music taken from the collection of the Fitzwilliam Museum in Cambridge.* An even more impressive publication was his edition of Purcell's Sacred Music, begun in 1828 and completed in five volumes (seventy-two numbers) by his son, Joseph Alfred Novello, in 1832. Appended to the edition itself is an extraordinary biographical essay presenting a vast amount of information pertaining to the composer: his career, his music, his portraits, his contemporaries, along with selected critiques of his work. Throughout the century the fortunes of Purcell research were closely tied to the interests of Novello & Co. The publisher's imprint is to be found on all the volumes of Purcell's Complete Works from 1878 to 1962.

*For the contents of *The Fitzwilliam Music* and other nineteenth-century sets, see Heyer.

Clearly there is a distinction between the editing of early music for the delectation of amateurs, on the one hand, and for the purpose of sharing knowledge among specialists, on the other. English scholarship, especially in the early years, stressed the former purpose; it was concerned with the popularization of knowledge. But in the second quarter of the nineteenth century the character of editorial work in music began to change. Editors began to show more respect for the integrity of their sources, and to treat their facts within the proper historical context. A transitional figure in this respect was Edward Francis Rimbault (1816–76). His outlook was a blend of antiquarianism and critical analysis. Rimbault was completely captivated by the English musical past. He was an avid collector not only of information but of the actual documents of early English music. His personal library, sold by Sotheby, Wilkinson and Hodge in 1877, contained some 2,359 items, including such rarities as the Mulliner Book, the Sambrooke Manuscript, and John Gamble's Commonplace Book. Rimbault's research technique was largely philological; that is to say it consisted of extended glosses or annotations to his source materials. One can follow this method in the lengthy introductions he provided to such works as *The Rounds, Catches, and Canons of England* (1865?), his edition of Roger North's *Memoirs of Musick* (1846), and, above all, *Bibliotheca madrigaliana, a Bibliographical Account of the Musical and Poetical Works Published in England during the 16th and 17th Centuries* (1847). He was a genuine lover of books, and invited his readers to share that affection with him, 'becoming conversant with the books themselves, so as to give to each some sort of personal identity'.[20]

Rimbault's love of books evidently carried him beyond the bounds of propriety. There is a librarian's 'horror story' that has never been laid to rest to the effect that certain rare music books formerly part of the collection of Christ Church Library, Oxford, but missing for some time, eventually turned up in the British Museum having passed through the hands of Dr Rimbault.[21] He must have been a rather pretentious and unengaging figure to have attracted the vicious lampoon in the form of a fictitious book auction sale catalogue, *A Catalogue of the Extensive Library of Doctor Rainbeau, F.R.S., F.S.A., A.S.S.* (1862).

Yet one should not underestimate the role played by Rimbault in British musical scholarship of his day. He conducted important studies of English church music, and published, with E. J. Hopkins, an authoritative work on *The Organ, its History and Construction* (1855). He was only twenty-four years old when he founded, with William Chappell, the Musical Antiquarian Society, and he served as honorary secretary during the life of the organization. He was also active in the

Percy Society and in the Motett Society. In short, he was in the foreground of nearly every enterprise connected with musical scholarship in his time.

A substantial figure in the intellectual life of the early Victorian period was William Chappell (1809–88), a member of the family that owned the music publishing house of Chappell & Co. More than any other individual, he was responsible for establishing the study of folk and popular music on a firm scholastic basis. His initial publication in this field was *A Collection of National English Airs, Consisting of Ancient Song, Ballad and Dance Tunes . . . Preceded by an Essay on English Minstrelsy* (1838). The avowed purpose of this work in Chappell's words was 'to give practical refutation to the popular fallacy that England has no national music'. Chappell was writing at a time when the 'national music' of Ireland, Scotland, and (to a lesser extent) Wales was internationally known and appreciated, while that of England was virtually a closed book,* and he was inclined to blame the *Specimens* of Dr Crotch for this misunderstanding.

Chappell's great work was *The Ballad Literature and Popular Music of the Olden Time* (1855–9). It was an expansion of his earlier collection with extensive commentary and a presentation of both the literary and musical texts. Frederick Sternfeld has made a valid assessment of Chappell's contribution: 'With the great editors of Shakespeare in the 19th century Chappell has created for himself a lasting place in the chain of generations. We cannot accept his judgements as the final word, but to ignore his materials and his assessments of them would be a distinct loss to scholarship.'[22]

As has already been mentioned, Chappell was a prime mover, with Rimbault, of the Musical Antiquarian Society, founded in 1840 for the purpose of editing and publishing the works of the English school of composers of the sixteenth and seventeenth centuries. In the seven years of its existence the Society produced an incredible amount of work, no less than nineteen folio volumes containing, among other things, transcriptions of Purcell's *Dido and Aeneas*, *Bonduca*, and *King Arthur*, as well as of *Parthenia*, Gibbons's Three-Part Fantasias, East's *Whole Book of Psalms*, and many other items of historical interest. The Society ceased publication in 1847 and its place was taken, after an interval of over forty years, by The Old English Edition (25 volumes, 1889–1902) edited by Godfrey Edward Pellew Arkwright (1864–1944),

---

*An honourable, if ineffectual, effort to do justice to English 'national song' had been made earlier in the century by the physician and amateur musician William Kitchiner. He claimed to have collected 250 volumes of English songs in manuscript, but his proposed edition of *English Melodies* never appeared: there was only a two-volume collection, *The Loyal and National Songs of England* (1823). See Kitchiner, fol. E5[V].

one of the best informed specialists in early English music. The most significant editorial work of the last decades of the nineteenth century was produced by the Plainsong and Mediaeval Music Society. This organization was founded in 1888 with the following objectives in mind:

1. To be a centre of information in England for students of plainsong and mediaeval music, and a means of communication between them and those of other countries.
2. To publish facsimiles of important manuscripts, translations of foreign works on the subject, adaptations of the plainsong to the English use, etc.
3. To form a catalogue of all plainsong and measured music in England, dating not later than the middle of the eighteenth century.
4. To form a thoroughly proficient choir of limited numbers, with which to give illustrations of plainsong and mediaeval music.

In actual practice, the society's publications were of two kinds: chants for special services and manuals of the technique of plainchant; and critical editions and facsimiles. The publications in the second group[23] are of outstanding importance. The editions of mediaeval polyphony, for which the society is best remembered, extended over the next fifty years. Included among the facsimiles are the Sarum Antiphonal and Gradual edited by Walter Howard Frere (1863–1938, from 1923 Bishop of Truro). Frere was also responsible for the sole effort to realize the third objective in the above outline, 'to form a catalogue of all plainsong and measured music in England'. This was his *Bibliotheca musico-liturgica. A Descriptive Handlist of the Musical and Latin-Liturgical MSS. of the Middle Ages Preserved in the Libraries of Great Britain and Ireland* (1901–32). Although it has been superseded in many respects, it remains a valuable guide to the manuscript sources of mediaeval music in British libraries.

Parallel to the Plainsong and Mediaeval Music Society publications was an independent set bearing the title 'Early Bodleian Music'.[24] The principal editor was John Stainer (1840–1901), assisted by his son and daughter. The most noteworthy product of this family collaboration was *Dufay and his Contemporaries* (1898), which brought to light the secular compositions in the manuscript Oxford, Bodleian Library, Canonici misc. 213.

In 1899 there appeared *The Fitzwilliam Virginal Book*, the single most important source of English music for the virginals. The editors were John A. Fuller Maitland (1856–1936) and William Barclay Squire (1855–1927), but the collection was issued by Breitkopf & Härtel in

Leipzig, symbolizing the complete merger of British and continental musical scholarship at the highest level.

The vitality of English historical scholarship can be measured in terms of its treatment of three major composers: Purcell, Handel, and Bach. Purcell was universally recognized throughout the nineteenth century as the pride of English music, in Burney's judgement 'a great and original genius'. Attention has already been drawn to Vincent Novello's role in keeping the composer's reputation alive through the publication of an edition of his Sacred Music in five volumes (1832) including a rich supply of biographical information. Rimbault explored another area of Purcell's output in editing thirty-four of his rounds and catches in a volume of *Rounds, Catches, and Canons of England* (1865?). The world had to wait until 1881 to gain an independent biography of the composer. The author was William H. Cummings (1831–1915), one of the founders of the Purcell Society, which sponsored a complete edition of Purcell's works in thirty-two volumes (1878–1962).

Handel, the godfather of British music, was almost too close for criticism. In the latter part of the eighteenth century he was accorded what virtually amounted to royal protection because of the King's championship of his works. Despite the existence of Arnold's edition, in the early nineteenth century the oratorios, with the exception of *Messiah*, were known in fragmented form; that is, favourite arias and choruses performed at the Lent Oratorio Concerts or the Concert of Ancient Music, not to mention countless local festivals throughout the country. The operas were known only by a few favourite arias. From 1832 the Sacred Harmonic Society began to explore the little-known oratorios. A Handel Society was formed in London in 1843, and between that year and 1858 published fourteen volumes of oratorios. In the meantime, however, the Deutsche Händel-Gesellschaft, headed by Friedrich Chrysander, had been founded (1857) and began publication of *Georg Friedrich Händel's Werke*, a set that would eventually reach ninety-six volumes. Thus Germany had overtaken England's early lead in the publication of Handel's works.

The Bach revival in England had somewhat greater definition. It took its start from the activity of two German musicians who established themselves in London early in the century. They were August F. C. Kollmann (1756–1839) and Karl Friedrich Horn (1762–1832). It was Kollmann who provided the first English translation of Johann Nikolaus Forkel's biography of Bach (*On J. S. Bach's Life, Genius, and Works*, 1820) while Horn joined with Samuel Wesley to produce the first English edition of the 'Well-Tempered Clavier'. It was the keyboard music that first attracted the attention of British musicians, largely through the efforts of Muzio Clementi, who enriched his own style of composition with reflections of Bach's canons and fugues and transmitted that influence to some of his most famous pupils, notably John Cramer and John Field. The roster of English Bach enthusiasts grew rapidly to include such figures as George Pinto, Benjamin Jacob, Vincent Novello, and William Crotch. The latter printed the E Major Fugue of the second set of the '48' as the first entry in Volume III of his *Specimens*; he was also the first to play the 'St Anne Fugue' in public (as a piano piece). There was nothing in the English Bach revival quite so striking as the first modern performance of the St Matthew Passion that took place in Berlin in 1829 under Mendelssohn's direction. That event had its London counterpart in 1854, when Sterndale Bennett directed a performance at the Hanover Square Rooms in April of that year. Bennett had been instrumental in founding an English Bach Society in 1849, one year before the Bach Gesellschaft was established in Germany. The English Society, however, did not include among its objectives the publication of a critical edition of the composer's works.

Although editorial activity occupied the foreground of British musical scholarship in general, there were other areas that were given serious attention. Among these were the study of musical instruments coupled with the revival of early techniques of performance. This interest was stimulated by the presence of a number of notable collectors of early instruments such as Carl Engel (1818–82) and Thomas W. Taphouse (1838–1905), a one-time mayor of Oxford whose large collection was dispersed in 1898. Another rich collection was bequeathed to the Royal Manchester College of Music by Dr Henry Watson (1848–1911). The collection of Adam Carse (1878–1958), strong in wind instruments, found its way into the Horniman Museum at Forest Hill, London; that of Francis W. Galpin (1858–1945) was transported to Boston, Massachusetts, where it became part of the Leslie Lindsey Mason Collection of the Boston Museum. Galpin's interests as an instrument collector and scholar have been preserved in the Society that bears his name, which was founded in 1946.

The English were characteristically less interested in instruments as artifacts or museum pieces than in the opportunity they afforded to restore the original quality of early music. It was this kind of intuitive approach to the past that marked the work of Arnold Dolmetsch (1858–1940), a leader in the movement to bring authenticity to the performance of early music:

The student should first try and prepare his mind by thoroughly understanding what the Old Masters *felt* about their own music, what impressions they wished to convey, and generally what was the *Spirit of their Art*, for on these points the ideas of modern musicians are by no means clear.[25]

As early as 1889 Dolmetsch was giving concerts of old music performed on restored instruments or on replicas built to the specifications of the original models. He was a skilled craftsman as well as a creditable performer on a variety of early instruments: lute, recorder, viol, harpsichord, clavichord, and so on. Furthermore, he produced one of the first historical monographs on performance practice, *The Interpretation of the Music of the XVII and XVIII Centuries* (1915), a book that created a new discipline within the framework of historical musicology. For all his learning, Dolmetsch remained essentially an amateur with some of the weaknesses as well as the strengths implied by that term. Much of his scholarship has been superseded, but few scholars have been more successful in recreating the 'Spirit of the Art' of the musicians of the past.

Musical Dictionaries

The nineteenth century was an age of dictionary making. It could be said that an interest in lexicography is one of the marks of a rationalistic society. One can trace it from its beginnings in the eighteenth century, each country following a somewhat different pattern of emphasis.

English music dictionaries followed an eclectic path during most of the nineteenth century. Their borrowing goes back as far as 1740 when James Grassineau translated and expanded Brossard's dictionary of terms (1703) for English use. In 1814 appeared the first major English biographical dictionary of music, William Bingley's *Musical Biography*, which relied partly on invited autobiographical contributors.[26] This was followed, ten years later, by J. Sainsbury's *A Dictionary of Musicians*. It leaned heavily on Bingley, on Choron and Fayolle's *Dictionnaire historique des musiciens* (1810–11), and on Ernst Ludwig Gerber's *Historisch-biographisches Lexikon der Tonkünstler* (1790–2 and 1812–13), but it also contained new autobiographical material pertinent to the British scene. A continuing force in British music lexicography was Burney, who concluded his long career by contributing the music entries to Rees's *Cyclopaedia*, a forty-five-volume general reference work. As Percy Scholes observed, 'his articles, were they extracted and separately published, would constitute a large and comprehensive cyclopaedia of musical knowledge as it was up to that date'.[27] Actually no comprehensive, self-contained dictionary or encyclopaedia of music was produced in England until near the end of the century, but there is ample evidence of a recognized need for such a reference tool. Callcott, Ayrton, and Bacon all projected works of this kind, although nothing ever came of them.

A final synthesis was achieved in the publication of *A Dictionary of Music and Musicians (A.D. 1450–1880) by Eminent Writers, English and Foreign, with Illustrations and Woodcuts*, edited by George Grove. Already, by the time of publication, the planned two volumes had expanded to four, which appeared between 1879 and 1890, and the editor's assertion that 'the limit of the history has been fixed at A.D. 1450, as the most remote date to which the rise of modern music can be carried back' had been abandoned. It is clear that the main thrust of the work lay in the direction of historical studies, for the light they could throw on musical performance and appreciation. To quote from the preface: 'The limits of the work have necessarily excluded disquisitions on Acoustics, Anatomy, Mechanics, and other branches of science connected with the main subject which though highly important are not absolutely requisite in a book concerned with practical music . . . Similarly all investigations into the music of barbarous nations have been avoided, unless they have some direct bearing on European music.' There was no place for what we now call *systematic musicology* in the list of subjects covered in the first edition of Grove. But there is no doubt that the editing of the dictionary served as a major catalyst to historical research throughout the country. The great majority of the contributors were British, as might be expected, but there was a sprinkling of foreign scholars in evidence. Among the Germans were Max Friedländer, specialist in German song, and Philipp Spitta, the Bach authority. Also present was Carl Ferdinand Pohl, best known for his work on Mozart and Haydn. A few Americans were represented: Colonel Ware of the Boston Public Library, and Alexander Thayer, the biographer of Beethoven. Some French topics were handled by Gustave Chouquet of the Paris Conservatoire, and Adolphe Jullien, critic and biographer of Berlioz. The first issue of the dictionary contained an appendix, unfortunately omitted from later issues, consisting of an 'Index to the Four Volumes' and a 'Catalogue of Articles Contributed by each Writer'. In scanning the 'Catalogue' one encounters some rather unexpected areas of special interest. Who, for example, would expect to find that J. R. Sterndale Bennett (son and biographer of the composer) was the author of most of the biographical entries for Franco-Flemish composers of the fifteenth and sixteenth centuries? The 'Catalogue' furnishes a splendid overview of the range of scholarly expertise in music in the last decades of the nineteenth century.

Grove died in 1900 at the age of eighty. His life span paralleled the progress of musical scholarship in England from its antiquarian beginnings to the high level of authority it reached by the end of the century. This remarkable man[28] was trained as an engineer, served as chief administrator of the Crystal Palace at Sydenham, and was the first director of the Royal College of Music. He was editor of *Macmillan's Magazine* for fifteen years, and collaborated with William Smith on a *Dictionary of the Bible* before he accepted the responsibility of editor of the *Dictionary of Music and Musicians* that bears his name. As a musician he was largely self-taught, yet he acquired a mastery of the music of Beethoven, Mendelssohn, Schumann, and Schubert that few of his contemporaries could equal.

Like every scholarly discipline, musicology has continued to grow, taking on new configurations and emphasis. In the end it was through the efforts of Sir George Grove that British musicology achieved its nineteenth-century synthesis and definition.

NOTES

Introduction

1 Burrows
2 *Athenaeum*, 1833, 284
3 Boetticher, 227
4 Hitchcock, 36–73
5 Glennon, 243–53

Chapter 1
The Artist and Society

1 Emerson, 251, n.l.
2 *MT* 116 (1975), 439, 625, 877
3 B. Shaw PW, v
4 Emerson, 112
5 Hueffer, ch. 3
6 Hueffer, 2–3
7 P. Young H, 495
8 R. Williams, 16–18
9 Batley; Sutcliffe Smith; S. de B. Taylor
10 Weber, 160, table 3; Foster PSL
11 Weber, 63
12 Weber, esp. 68–9
13 J. Turner, 30, qtd Rainbow LWM, 156–7
14 Fuller Maitland EM, 128
15 Rainbow LWM, 30–1
16 Arnold CA, 112
17 Nettel MFT, 108
18 Temperley IM, 90
19 Weber, 163–5, tables 12, 13, 16
20 Trilling, 222
21 Weber, 19
22 Weber, 10
23 Rutland, ch. 1
24 Annan
25 Wakefield
26 *Athenaeum*, 1834, 753
27 Temperley HHP
28 Midgley, 21–2, qtd P. Young H, 509
29 B. Shaw PW, 29
30 Bax, 28
31 Temperley HHP, 30
32 Temperley HHP, 1218
33 P. Young H, 463
34 M. Clarke
35 Fenner, 32
36 E. Wesley, 29–30
37 S. S. Wesley, FW, 60–1
38 S. S. Wesley FW, 68–9
39 Rainbow CR, 143–61
40 Chadwick, I, 70 and n.3
41 Charlton, 76
42 Hogarth PSL, 92–3
43 *DNB*, art. 'Sheppard, E. S.'
44 Sheppard, II, 98
45 Graves, I, 48
46 Trilling, 162–5
47 Arnold SGC
48 Arnold EC, I, 236, qtd Trilling, 373
49 Arnold EC, II, 283
50 G. Eliot DD, ch. 22; Haight
51 Saddlemeyer, 19–21
52 Hurd

Chapter 2
Music in Education

1 Tuckwell, 71
2 Rennert, 50
3 Crotch L, 4
4 Bumpus H, 446–54
5 Tuckwell, 71

6 Parker, 106
7 Joyce, 138–55
8 Joyce, 148–9; Scholes MM, 653–4
9 *Musical Standard*, 28 April 1889;
  Havergal, 27
10 Scholes MM, 645–57
11 Scholes MM, 654
12 W. Glover, 37
13 Grove, 1st edn, IV, 379
14 Sterndale Bennett, 266
15 Sterndale Bennett, 249–50
16 Sterndale Bennett, 261
17 Scholes MM, 663
18 Grove, 1st edn, III, 713
19 Joyce, 140
20 Grove, 1st edn, IV, 33
21 Grove, 1st edn, I, 483
22 Grove, 1st edn, I, 483
23 Scholes MM, 663
24 Oakeley, 121
25 Scholes MM, 665
26 Bridge WP, 195
27 Scholes MM, 667–8
28 Scholes MM, 674–5
29 Scholes MM, 678–9
30 Scholes MM, 679
31 Grove, 1st edn, I, 346–7
32 Gardiner MF, 647–8
33 G. Macfarren AL, 149
34 G. Macfarren AL, 167
35 Corder RAM, 3
36 Corder RAM, 10–11
37 Society of Arts; Corder RAM, 12
38 Scholes BMT, I, 269
39 Gardiner MF, 806–7
40 Banister, 19–24
41 Banister, 23; G. Macfarren P
42 Banister, 24
43 Society of Arts
44 Sterndale Bennett, 418–21
45 Scholes MM, 695–704
46 Grove, 1st edn, II, 447
47 Scholes MM, 698
48 Scholes MM, 700; Grove, 1st edn,
  IV, 158
49 G. Warrack, 8–9
50 G. Warrack, 11
51 G. Warrack, 12–22

52 G. Warrack, 23–4
53 Scholes MM, 701–2
54 G. Warrack, 45
55 Grove, 1st edn, I, 436–8
56 Scholes MM, 709
57 Pollard
58 Rainbow LWM
59 Hullah WM, iv
60 Hullah WM, vi
61 *Westminster Review* 38 (1842), 1–43
62 J. Curwen TM, 382–4
63 J. Curwen TM, 377–8; S. Glover;
  Rainbow LWM, 43–53
64 J. Curwen TM, 385
65 Chesterfield, Letter 175 (April,
  1749); Locke, para. 197
66 Rainbow CR, ch. 12
67 Parkin, I, 306–9
68 Ivimey, 27–8
69 Ivimey, 4
70 *Nature* 10 (1874), 395
71 Kamm
72 Scholes MYCM, 17; Macpherson AC,
  29–32; Rainbow MLU
73 Scholes MM, 362
74 Crowest, 157

Chapter 3
Music Publishing

1 *MT* 5 (1852), 5–6
2 *MT* 17 (1876), 371–2
3 *MT* 22 (1881), 296
4 *MT* 17 (1876), 394–5
5 Boosey, 112–21, 145–57, 174–9
6 *MT* 25 (1885), 266
7 Batley, 281
8 Tyson AEEB
9 Qtd Rothenberg, 101n.
10 Boosey, 23
11 *MT* 17 (1876), 458
12 Stanford PUD, 221
13 S. S. Wesley FW, 33
14 Clarke & Clarke, 202
15 *MT* 20 (1879), 140
16 Chicago, Newberry Library, MS
  Case fV209.58

Chapter 4

Popular Music of the Lower Classes

1 Parry IA
2 Vicinus VPC
3 Lloyd FSE, 23–36; Maróthy, 131–44; Wiora
4 Lloyd F
5 R. Palmer, 94
6 Lloyd SE, 41–2
7 Lee, 106
8 Sharp, 4th edn, 133, 150–1
9 A. Williams, 9–29
10 Sharp, 4th edn, 133
11 Thompson, 69–75
12 Lee, 117
13 Lloyd SE, 51; Lloyd FSE, 320; A. Williams, 9–29
14 Lloyd SE, 34–8
15 Mayhew, I, 226–8, 272–80; R. Palmer, 10–17; Pearsall VPM, 211–14; Lloyd FSE, 28–34
16 Vicinus IM, 241–2
17 Lee, 110–12
18 Mayhew, III, 163–4; Thompson, 128–9, 327
19 Pearsall VPM, 215
20 Thompson, 39, 197–200
21 Sharp, 4th edn, 133
22 Sharp, 4th edn, 138–9
23 Thompson, 69
24 Thompson, 501–2
25 Nettel SSE, 190–1
26 Sharp, 4th edn, 35–7, 72–3, 140–7
27 P. Davison, 20–3
28 Chilton, 16–17
29 Howes FMB, 168–72
30 Lloyd FSE, 54, 319
31 Lloyd FSE, 31
32 Mayhew, I, 275
33 Kidson TT, 19; Howes FMB, 166
34 Pulling, 20
35 Hindley
36 Lloyd FSE, 29–30; Shepard, 74–5
37 Vicinus IM, 22–5, 52; J. Wilson; Allan's, 54–7, 235–55; R. Palmer, 8–10; Harland

38 Mayhew, I, 306–9; III, 196
39 Ashton, v, ix; Henderson, 10–12
40 Mayhew, I, 226–8, 272–9; III, 195–7
41 Vicinus IM, 20–1; Lloyd SE, 20
42 Lloyd SE, 41–2
43 Lloyd FSE, 30
44 Mayhew, I, 273, 298; III, 194–7; Lunn
45 Mayhew, I, 278
46 Mayhew, III, 190–1; Henderson, 19
47 Vicinus IM, 19
48 Mayhew, I, 227; R. Palmer, 302
49 Repr. Vicinus, 295; another version, R. Palmer, 62
50 Kidson TT, 170–1
51 R. Palmer, 28–30
52 Lloyd FSE, 317–20; Maróthy, 263–412
53 Vicinus IM, 48–53
54 Ritson; repr. Lloyd CAY, 20
55 Repr. Lloyd CAY, 28
56 Repr. Lloyd FSE, 321; Vicinus IM
57 Repr. Vicinus IM, 287
58 Repr. Lloyd FSE, 325
59 Repr. McColl, 4
60 Lloyd CAY; Lloyd FSE, 339ff.
61 Repr. Lloyd FSE, 339
62 Repr. Lloyd FSE, 345
63 Repr. P. Davison, 46
64 Repr. Lloyd FSE, 370
65 Repr. Lloyd FSE, 371
66 Repr. Lloyd CAY, 107
67 Repr. Lloyd FSE, 374
68 Repr. Lloyd CAY, 26, 125, 132
69 *Tonic*, March 1864, 219, qtd Nettel SSE, 204–7
70 Lloyd CAY, 78–80; Lloyd FSE, 356–7, 361–2
71 Repr. Lloyd FSE, 378
72 Repr. Lloyd FSE, 384
73 Maróthy, 263–412
74 Disher VS, 139–40; Vicinus IM, 321; Mayhew, I, 278, 298
75 Mayhew, III, 194–7; Lunn, 292–3
76 Repr. Lloyd CAY, 83
77 Mayhew, III, 158–90

78 Crowest, 112–41; see also Pearsall
   VPM, 189–95; Pearsall EPM, 146–9
79 Qtd Pearsall VPM, 194
80 Pearsall VPM, 98–106
81 Mander & Mitchinson BMH;
   Pulling, 166–235; Senelick,
   Vicinus IM, 238–66
82 Dickens SB, ch. 14
83 Speaight
84 W. Taylor, 131
85 Disraeli, ch. 10
86 Repr. Chilton, 60
87 Repr. Chilton, 2
88 Repr. Chilton, 72
89 Corvan
90 Repr. Harker, 43
91 Repr. Harker, 33
92 Repr. P. Davison, 192; Gammond,
   46; Sixty Old Time, 72
93 Repr. Sixty Old Time, 10
94 Repr. Sixty Old Time, 13
95 Repr. Sixty Old Time, 51
96 Repr. Sixty Old Time, 46, 100
97 Repr. Sixty Old Time, 18
98 Repr. Gammond, 37
99 Repr. P. Davison, 13
100 Vicinus IM, 263–6; Pope, 211–12;
   Pulling, 201; MacInnes, 36–7;
   Senelick, 394–5; T. S. Eliot; Jacob
101 T. S. Eliot, 456, 457
102 Jacob, 110–11
103 T. S. Eliot, 458
104 T. S. Eliot, 458
105 Qtd Whitcomb, 20, 154
106 E. S. Walker, 1
107 E. S. Walker
108 Repr. Sixty Old Time, 130
109 T. S. Eliot, 458–9

Chapter 5
Music of the Popular Theatre

1 Short, 10; Sherson, 80–6; Pearce
2 Croker & Tucker, II, 66–7
3 E. Watson, 339
4 Hayter, 14
5 Burnand, 35

6 Hibbert, 38
7 Nevill, 104
8 Burnand, 134
9 The Era, 19 Nov. 1865, qtd Mander
   & Mitchenson LT, 394
10 Hollingshead, 93
11 Nevill, 105–7
12 Knapp & Chapman, 131
13 Schönherr, 494
14 Bantock & Aflalo
15 The Era, 21 Oct. 1893
16 Keller, 420
17 J. Glover, 270–1
18 Pope, 411–16
19 Coates, 86–92
20 Boosey, 159
21 Nicoll, IV, 154
22 Hayter, 17
23 Guest AB
24 Guest EB

Chapter 6
Ballroom and Drawing-Room Music

1 P. Richardson, 29
2 P. Richardson, 34, 109
3 Byron, The Waltz (pub. 1813)
4 G. Eliot DD, ch. 11
5 Gronow, I, 32–3
6 Musical World 17 (1842), 324, 329,
   339
7 Dickens CC, stave 2
8 P. Richardson, 69, 85
9 P. Richardson, 106
10 P. Richardson, 117
11 Pearsall VPM, 124
12 Lamb, 8
13 Carse J
14 Pearsall VPM, 129
15 K. Young, 26–7
16 Austen, ch. 6
17 G. Eliot M, I, ch. 7
18 Forster, ch. 3
19 Pianiste, 30 Jan. 1835, 48: qtd
   Weber, 35

20 *Harmonicon*, 1823, 167; see also
  Musical World 20 (1845), 275;
  Novello & Co., 20n.
21 Langley
22 Grove, 1st edn, III, 541
23 Hitchcock, 65–73
24 *Harmonicon*, 1824, 146
25 *Times*, 15 Dec. 1877
26 Simpson, 81–2; Scholes MM, 292–3
27 M. Turner, 233
28 Simpson, 4
29 M. Turner, 216
30 Schmitz; *MT* 116 (1975), 439, 625,
  877
31 *Athenaeum*, 1838, 715
32 M. Turner, 143
33 M. Turner, 144
34 Simpson, 121
35 Temperley PC, II, ex. 83
36 M. Turner, 329
37 B. Shaw LM, 351
38 Simpson, 289
39 Simpson, 295
40 Simpson, 327

Chapter 7
Band Music

1 Hind, 184
2 Russell & Elliot, 60
3 Farmer RDMM, 58
4 Farmer MM, 43–4
5 Farmer RDMM, 114–15
6 Grove, 3rd edn, IV, 463
7 *Stalybridge*; Hampson; Millington;
  P. Young H, 488–9
8 *Stalybridge*, 12
9 Grove, 5th edn, I, 915
10 Carse ASDF, 195
11 Cook, 33
12 Russell & Elliot, 80–3
13 Carse J, 132
14 Russell & Elliot, 103
15 Zealley, 569
16 Russell & Elliot, 171
17 Sandall et al., I, 211; II, 118; IV,
  190

18 Sandall et al., IV, 238
19 Sandall et al., IV, 191–2
20 Wiggins, 12
21 Wiggins, 20
22 Wiggins, 25
23 Wiggins, 21
24 Russell & Elliot, 213

Chapter 8
Parochial and Nonconformist Church Music

1 Porteus, 244
2 Porteus, 242
3 Temperley PC, I, 215
4 Temperley PC, I, 208
5 Temperley G, 20–8
6 Dibb
7 Latrobe, 267
8 Rainbow CR
9 Redhead & Oakeley
10 See MS Life of William Dyce by his
  son, Aberdeen Art Gallery ABDAG:
  200
11 Dyce, Appendix, fol. 22
12 Rainbow CR, 58–73
13 *Parish Choir* 3 (1850–1), 1
14 *British Critic* 28 (1840), 388–9
15 *Ecclesiologist* 3 (1843), 2
16 *Parish Choir* 1 (1846–7), 37
17 *Parish Choir* 3 (1850–1), 148
18 Jebb, 298–9; S. S. Wesley FW, 75
19 Hullah P, preface
20 Worley, 137
21 Daniel, 150
22 Spark S, 22–3
23 Foster AAC, 161–96
24 Bridges
25 Crowest, 67–108
26 Box
27 J. S. Curwen SWM 2nd ser.
28 Crowest, 84
29 Crowest, 73
30 Cox, 7
31 J. S. Curwen SWM 2nd ser., 182
32 Temperley PC, I, 196–201, 239–42
33 Patrick, 149–61

34 Patrick, 193–5
35 M. Frost, 305
36 Guilbert; Fétis b, article 'Mainzer';
  Scholes mm, 3–10
37 Patrick, 197
38 Scholes ocm, 832
39 Brown & Stratton, 187
40 Brown & Stratton, 79; Carnie
41 J. S. Curwen swm 1st ser., 85
42 Rainbow lwm, 181–3
43 J. S. Curwen mjc
44 J. S. Curwen swm 1st ser., 220–1
45 Lightwood mmhb, hymn 909
46 Minshall, 48–68
47 Whitley, 129–30; Buckley;
  Humphreys, IV, 459–60
48 J. S. Curwen swm 1st ser., 209
49 Scholes ocm, 83
50 J. S. Curwen swm 1st ser., 29
51 Lightwood mmec, 26–40
52 Lightwood mmhb, 79–80
53 J. S. Curwen swm 2nd ser., 53
54 J. S. Curwen swm 1st ser., 39
55 M. Frost, 336
56 Jackson, 93–7
57 Benson, 487
58 Sandall et al., I
59 *Rambler* 3 (1849), 311–17
60 Pugin
61 *Parish Choir* 3 (1850–1), 171; *Rambler*
  3 (1849), 494
62 Terry, 116
63 Terry, 115

Chapter 9

Cathedral Music

1 Davies, III, 58
2 P. Barrett; E. Taylor
3 Rainbow cr, 220–42
4 Hackett, vii; 'Historical'; Lewer;
  Alderson & Colles
5 Torrington, II, 400
6 *Musical World* 4 (1837), 37
7 P. Barrett, 17; Dickson fy, 16
8 Bumpus ocpc, 187–9
9 W. Russell, 18–19

10 Close, 3
11 Flindall, 3
12 Parl. Papers (1854), XXVI, 1ff.,
  XXXIV, 81ff.; P. Barrett, 15
13 Sinclair, 400–21
14 Bumpus ocpc, 187–9, 193–4
15 P. Barrett, 34
16 Rainbow cr, 274–5
17 Bumpus ocpc, 190n.
18 York Minster MS Add. 157/1,
  p. 325
19 Routley, 228, 245
20 Jebb, II
21 *Church Choirmaster* 1 (1867), 142; W.
  Frost, 31
22 J. S. Curwen swm 1st ser., 101
23 M. Richardson, 101–2
24 Peace, 60–6, cited Rainbow cr, 251
25 *Quarterly* 4 (1822), 176
26 Rimbault cc, preface
27 J. Marsh I, preface
28 Temperley g
29 P. Barrett, 27
30 Bridges
31 Bumpus ocpc, 160
32 Bridge oa, 18
33 P. Barrett, 19
34 *Quarterly* 6 (1824), 26–7, 310–17
35 Rainbow cr, 329–43
36 *Forty Years*
37 J. Clarke, II, preface
38 *MT* 39 (1898), 544
39 *MT* 106 (1965), 886
40 W. Frost, 52–3
41 Baden Powell, 154
42 *Read & Others*
43 Baden Powell, 154
44 York Minster Library, bound
  service lists
45 Kitton, 23–4, 72
46 Yeats-Edwards, 168–72
47 Stubbs
48 Spink
49 *Treasury*, IV, 21
50 *Treasury*, IV, 26
51 Temperley moi, 314–15
52 Temperley pc, I, 214
53 Temperley pc, II, ex. 48

54 Fellowes, 1st edn, 203
55 Crotch L, 71, 72n.
56 Bumpus H, 367–71
57 British Library, shelfmark H.2182
58 Hunt, 106–9
59 *Treasury*, IV, 62
60 *Treasury*, IV, 69
61 Temperley w
62 *Treasury*, IV, 109
63 W. Shaw w
64 Temperley MOI, 314–15
65 Sterndale Bennett, 455–60
66 *Treasury*, IV, 136
67 *Treasury*, IV, 130
68 Spark MM, 96–8; P. Chappell, 57, 147
69 Bumpus H, 480–1
70 *Musical World* 2 (1836), 81, 97
71 *Times*, 2 July 1910, repr. Colles, 131–5
72 *Treasury*, IV, 94
73 *Treasury*, IV, 89
74 *Treasury*, IV, 81
75 Spark MM, 90
76 *Treasury*, IV, 73
77 Fellowes, 1st edn, 208
78 Hadow CM, 205
79 Fuller Maitland EM, 71–4, 100; Fellowes, 1st edn, 220–2
80 Rainbow CR, 270
81 Scholes MM, 556
82 Temperley PC, I, 302, 308
83 Fellowes, 1st edn, 221
84 Davies, V, 119
85 Spark s, 22–3
86 *Treasury*, IV, 100
87 *MT* 14 (1873), 556, qtd Rainbow CR, 271
88 Fellowes, 1st edn, 224–5
89 Qtd Long, 363
90 Weinandt & Young, 262–8
91 *MT* Supp., Dec. 1973
92 *Treasury*, IV, 158
93 *Treasury*, V, 1
94 *Treasury*, IV, 181
95 Long, 374
96 Fellowes, 1st edn, 239
97 *Treasury*, V, 15

98 *Treasury*, V, 39
99 Long, 414
100 *Treasury*, IV, 194
101 *Treasury*, V, 57
102 Hogan, 157
103 *Quarterly* 5 (1823), 204
104 J. Marsh II
105 Musica Britannica 41
106 *Treasury*, IV, 29
107 Both repr. in S. S. Wesley FW (1961)
108 *Athenaeum*, 1834, 17
109 *Church Choirmaster* 3 (1868), 134; J. S. Curwen SWM 1st ser., 184
110 Spark MR, 86; see also G. Smith, 133–5
111 Sutcliffe Smith, 92
112 Andrews, 41
113 Andrews, 88
114 Andrews, 138
115 Roman Catholic Church, *List*, 86
116 Andrews, 132; Hudson, 57
117 *Treasury*, V, 9

Chapter 10

Oratorios and Cantatas

1 Stanford PUD, 196
2 E. Walker, 1st edn, 245
3 Rennert, 43–7
4 Crotch L, 71
5 *S*: Novello, 1855, 44
6 P. Young H, 418
7 *K*: Novello, 1872, 8
8 J. Bennett FYM, 89–90
9 E. Newman MS, 89
10 *DNB*, article 'Pierson'
11 Sullivan & Flower, 74
12 *K*: Cramer, 1873, preface
13 P. Young s, 218
14 Fuller Maitland EM, 73
15 Milne, II, 35
16 P. Young H, 530, n.2
17 Mrs E. F. Dent, *Sunday Telegraph*, 25 July 1976
18 A. Jacobs in Stevens, 155, qtd Howes EMR, 17

19 B. Shaw MIL, I, 93
20 *K*: Novello, 1891, 17
21 *K*: Novello, 1891, 10
22 Fuller Maitland MPS
23 Martin Cooper, *Daily Telegraph*, 21 Aug. 1976
24 *K*: Harmonie Verlag (Berlin), 1907, 56–80
25 *S*: Boosey & Hawkes, 1939, 73

3 Moore VM, preface
4 Temperley GFP, 270
5 E. Walker, 1st edn, 277
6 Temperley SBL, 961
7 Temperley SBL, 1061
8 E. Walker, 3rd edn, 310
9 Temperley HHP, 33
10 Greene, 206–13
11 Threlfall

Chapter 11
Glees, Madrigals, and Partsongs

1 Grove, 1st edn, I, 322–3
2 W. Barrett EGP
3 Baptie
4 Hogarth MH, 231–3; Hullah MH, 16–18
5 Davey, 376
6 W. Barrett EGP, 211
7 G. Macfarren ENMP
8 Fuller Maitland EM, 80
9 W. Barrett EGMW, 35; Fuller Maitland EM, 79
10 W. Barrett EGP
11 Holmes, V, 3
12 Opheim, 190
13 Hunt, 45
14 Opheim, 51–3
15 London, Royal College of Music, MS 2265; Oxford, Bodleian Library, Dep Tenbury 959
16 Opheim, 50–1
17 Opheim
18 Holmes, V, 3
19 Scholes MM, 637
20 Routley, 175
21 Routley, 152
22 *Oxford Carols*, xvii
23 Routley, 231

Chapter 12
Songs

1 *Harmonicon*, 1826, 245
2 *New York Mirror*, 16 Oct. 1841

Chapter 13
Theatre Music, 1800–1834

1 *Theatrical Recorder* (1805–6), I, 214, qtd Mackerness LHMJ, 214
2 Arundell SW, 157
3 W. Smith; Ebers; Chorley
4 Winston, 9
5 Fiske, 280–1
6 Northcott, 44; Washington, Folger Library, MS T.a.7
7 Carse OBB, 53
8 Nicoll, IV, 246–7
9 Genest, IX, 49
10 Winston, 98
11 Washington, Folger Library, MS Y.d.S2. (245.)
12 London, British Library, MS Egerton 2159
13 Odell, II, 131–44
14 Corder B, 92
15 Northcott, 10
16 G. Macfarren BG, 409
17 Hughes S, 142–3
18 Planché, I, 79–80
19 Corder B, 95–6
20 Murray
21 S. Carr
22 *Times*, 29 Oct. 1834
23 *Athenaeum*, 1834, 644–5, qtd Cox, I, 305–6
24 Macmillan, 303
25 Oldman
26 Kelly, 346
27 Kelly, x
28 Washington, Folger Library, MS 152.Y.c.605(7)

29 J. Warrack, 308–47
30 Hogarth MMD, II, 456
31 Genest, VIII, 612–13
32 Ebers, 73
33 Northcott, 34
34 Kelly, 270, 282

Chapter 14
Opera, 1834–1865

1 W. Barrett B
2 Banister
3 Temperley RA
4 White, 245–54
5 B. Carr
6 Berlioz E, 366–76
7 See also J. Klein
8 Forsyth, 179
9 Arundell CO, 328

Chapter 15
Opera, 1865–1914

1 Baily, 171
2 Sullivan & Flower, 124
3 Stedman
4 P. Young S, 82
5 P. Young S, 229–31
6 P. Young S, 231
7 P. Young S, 237–40
8 H. Klein, qtd Baily, 358
9 Sullivan & Flower, 205
10 Baily, 369
11 *Saturday Review*, 19 Oct. 1893
12 *K*: Duff & Stewart, 1878, 42–3
13 Baily, 301
14 Howes EMR, 64
15 White, 285–6
16 Fuller Maitland MPS, 80
17 Fuller Maitland MPS, 87
18 *K*: Matthias & Strickland, 1894, 27
19 Redwood, 233

Chapter 16
Orchestral Music

1 Milligan
2 Temperley BLCL
3 Hogarth PSL, 2
4 *Harmonicon*, 1832, 247; Northcott, 13
5 Foster PSL, 5
6 Burgh, III, 454
7 Carse OBB, 212–18
8 Tyson C, 121–2; C. Bennett
9 *Allgemeine musikalische Zeitung* 19 (1817), 461–2; Plantinga, 251–6
10 Temperley IME, 171–4
11 Rennert, 104–5
12 Anderson, II, 759
13 Peter, 260–3
14 *Harmonicon*, 1826, 151
15 London, British Library, MS Add. 31783
16 Wagner, II, 630
17 Westrup, 43–4
18 *Northern Daily Times*, 19 March 1855
19 *Neue Zeitschrift* 69 (1873), 508
20 Rogers, 102
21 Legge & Hansell, 182
22 Carse HO, 288–9, 308–9
23 London, Royal College of Music, MS 4050
24 Greene, 15
25 Howes EMR, 153–4
26 B. Shaw ML, II, 306
27 P. Young E, 336
28 Kennedy, 74

Chapter 17
Chamber Music

1 Temperley DM, 35
2 Gardiner MF, II, 831
3 Haddock, 16
4 Hullah MH, 24
5 Temperley IM, 92–103
6 Guynemer, 10
7 Temperley IM, 394–6, 400–3, 409–10
8 *Musical World* 8 (1838), 50
9 Weber, 53–69

10 Temperley GFP, 269
11 Piggott, 265
12 Temperley DM, 36
13 S: London, British Library, MS Add. 34725
14 Bush, 86
15 Musica Britannica 37
16 Sterndale Bennett, 79
17 Schumann MM, 219
18 Musica Britannica 37
19 Sterndale Bennett, 194–201
20 Sterndale Bennett, 211
21 Record; Weber, 65–8; Cobbett, II, 232–5
22 Monday Popular Concerts
23 Temperley DM, 36
24 S: London, Royal College of Music, MS 2272
25 Cobbett, I, 57
26 P. Young s, 81
27 Banfield, 212
28 Fuller Maitland EM, 195
29 Cobbett, II, 210
30 Banfield, 213
31 Graves, I, 204
32 Cobbett, II, 210
33 Cobbett, II, 453
34 Porte, 117
35 Schafer, 27
36 Cobbett, I, 378
37 Cobbett, I, 27
38 Tatton, 77–91, 133–7
39 Tatton, 118
40 MT 34 (1893), 279–80
41 Tatton, 29–43
42 Cobbett, I, 284
43 MT 46 (1905), 791; 47 (1906), 489; 52 (1911), 242–3
44 Tatton, 58–63; Howes EMR, 335–6
45 Dunhill CVS, 51

Chapter 18
Piano Music, 1800–1870

1 Loesser, 219–23
2 Ehrlich SEIP
3 Parrish, 41–6

4 Boalch, 85, 94, 163
5 Hummel, 64–5, qtd Harding, 153
6 Ringer; Graue
7 Plantinga, 43, 291–3
8 Plantinga, 216–17
9 W. Newman, 658–75; Craw
10 Temperley IM, 37–8, 107–10
11 Harmonicon, 1827, 228
12 Harmonicon, 1829, 146
13 Temperley MEI, 226
14 Brocklehurst, 258
15 Plantinga, 284–5, n. 106
16 Brocklehurst, 261
17 Hopkinson, vii
18 Blom; Branson
19 Piggott
20 Merrick, xiii
21 Temperley F
22 Piggott, 102
23 Piggott, 78
24 Musical World 5 (1837), 70–2
25 Piggott, 100
26 Plantinga, 295
27 Sainsbury, II, 294
28 Temperley GFP, 266
29 Ringer, 755
30 Harmonicon, 1828, 216n.
31 Peter
32 W. Newman, 572
33 Banister, 220–1; Sterndale Bennett, 23–6; Musical World 22 (1847), 422
34 Hogarth MH, 266
35 G. Macfarren P
36 Sterndale Bennett
37 Schumann WSB; trans. Schumann MM, 214
38 Musica Britannica 37
39 Musica Britannica 37
40 Bush, 91–4
41 Bush, 93
42 Bush, 89
43 Temperley MEI, 231
44 Schumann MM, I, 142–3
45 Sterndale Bennett; Hadow; Grove, 3rd edn, I, 342
46 W. Newman, 580
47 P. Chappell, 96
48 Temperley HHP, 1218

Chapter 19
Piano Music, 1870–1914

1 Hallé, 103
2 P. Young s, 272–3
3 *MT* 13 (1868), 261
4 Fuller Maitland MPS, 26
5 Graves, I, 134
6 Graves, II, 175
7 Graves, II, 113–15
8 *MT* 25 (1884), 147
9 Elgar FEM, 51–3
10 Stanford MC, 186
11 B. Shaw LM, 377
12 *MT* 110 (1969), 137
13 Sayers, 262–3
14 W. Newman, 594
15 H. Redlich in *MGG* 2 (1954), col. 1871
16 Demuth, 121
17 A. Leitzmann in *Die Musik*, VI/4 (1906–7), 306
18 Grove, 3rd edn, II, 2
19 W. Newman, 593–4

Chapter 20
Organ Music

1 Sumner, 181–2; Routh, 265–9
2 C. W. Pearce PO, 63
3 Grove, 3rd edn, I, 183
4 Grove, 3rd edn, II, 92
5 C. W. Pearce PO, 57
6 F. Hodges, 13
7 P. Chappell, 50–1, 181–2
8 Temperley IM, 188–9; Rennert, 86–8
9 *Times*, 28 May 1806
10 *Musical World* 13 (1840), 315
11 Temperley PC, I, 129–30; II, 54–8
12 Howes DP
13 P. Chappell, 38, 156
14 Temperley PC, I, 274; II, 186–7
15 Rennert, 86, 105–6
16 Mason (1795), 311–13
17 Reviewed, *Harmonicon*, July 1831
18 Mason (1795), 313

19 Lightwood w
20 Lightwood w, 187
21 E. Walker, 3rd edn
22 Fuller Maitland EM, 89
23 Routh, 215–43
24 Routh, 230–1
25 Routh, 233
26 Routh, 237
27 London, British Library, MS Add. 35007, fol. 51ʳ
28 London, British Library, MS Add. 35006
29 London, Royal College of Music, MS 550
30 Routh, 214
31 Routh, 272
32 Spark & Bennett, 22
33 G. H. Smith, 27–41
34 Lahee, 204
35 Lahee, 219–24
36 Parratt, 604
37 Temperley PC, 274–5; Curwen (1880), 167–71
38 Broadhouse
39 Broadhouse, 40–2; Spark MM, 299
40 Graves, I, 56–7
41 P. Chappell, 183
42 MS at Addington Place, Croydon
43 C. W. Pearce TEHT
44 Coleman
45 Edwards, 2
46 W. Newman, 306
47 W. Newman, 354
48 W. Newman, 580–90, 600–1
49 W. Newman, 600
50 W. Newman, 586

Chapter 21
Aesthetics and Criticism

1 Mason, 3
2 Mason, 3–4
3 Mason, 49–50, n.
4 Hanslick, 17–19
5 Crotch L, 45
6 Crotch L, 55
7 Crotch L, 64

8 Crotch L, 27
9 Crotch L, 35
10 Crotch L, 35–6
11 Gardiner MN, 31–2
12 Spencer OFM, 401
13 Spencer OFM, 404
14 Spencer OFM, 407–8
15 E. Newman SW, 161–77
16 E. Newman MS, 189–218
17 Haweis MM, 16
18 Haweis ML, 204–7
19 Haweis MM, 42
20 Haweis ML, 207
21 Sully, 228
22 Cooke
23 Sully, 227
24 Sully, 232
25 Sully, 243
26 Sully, 239
27 Gurney, vii
28 Gurney, 14
29 Gurney, 303
30 Gurney, 190–1
31 Stainer MRIE, 16, 18
32 Crowest, 11
33 *Times*, 26 June 1855
34 *Examiner*, 30 May 1819; Houtchens, 216–18
35 *Examiner*, 10 April 1808; Houtchens, 14
36 *Examiner*, 31 Jan. 1819; Houtchens, 212
37 *Examiner*, 20 Feb. 1812; Houtchens, 63
38 Peacock, IX, 234
39 Peacock, IX, 236–7
40 Peacock, IX, 407
41 Peacock, IX, 244–5
42 Peacock, IX, 238–9
43 B. Shaw LM, 6
44 *Illustrated*, 12 Dec. 1891; B. Shaw HBMC, 195–200
45 Pearson, 194–212
46 B. Shaw HBMC, 5
47 *Star*, 31 May 1889; B. Shaw LM, 132–3
48 *Star*, 6 Dec. 1889; B. Shaw LM, 264–5

49 *World*, 2 July 1890; B. Shaw MIL, I, 30
50 *World*, 16 Sept. 1891; B. Shaw MIL, I, 254
51 B. Shaw HBMC, 107–12
52 Ruskin, 83
53 *World*, 25 June 1890; B. Shaw MIL, I, 22
54 *Star*, 16 May 1890; B. Shaw LM, 377
55 *World*, 3 May 1893; B. Shaw MIL, II, 297–303
56 *Star*, 12 Dec. 1888; B. Shaw LM, 44
57 *World*, 10 Dec. 1890; B. Shaw MIL, I, 93
58 *World*, 6 July 1892; B. Shaw MIL, II, 129–30
59 *World*, 10 May 1893; B. Shaw MIL, II, 305–8
60 *Star*, 16 Mar. 1889; B. Shaw LM, 79
61 *World*, 7 Mar. 1894; B. Shaw MIL, III, 169–70; B. Shaw HBMC, 83–4
62 *Star*, 2 May 1890; B. Shaw LM, 366

Chapter 22
Music Theory

1 Banister, 112–13
2 Day, 60
3 Shirlaw, 442
4 Prout, 16th edn, x
5 Shirlaw, 430
6 Logier, xvi
7 Tovey MAEB
8 Scholes OCM, 39–40
9 *Record*
10 Tovey E, I, 67–8
11 Tovey MAEB, 124–5

Chapter 23
Musicology

1 North
2 Rees, XXVI, fol. 4N1ᵛ
3 King BCM, 15
4 F. Hodges
5 E. Hodges, 40

514

6 E. Hodges, 38
7 *Monthly Supplement* 2 (1835), 101
8 Crotch s, I, 13–14
9 Squire
10 *Monthly Supplement* 2 (1835), 68–9
11 *Musical World* 5 (1837), 20, 45, 61, 77, 94, 109
12 London Institution, 9, 62–3
13 King MI, 221
14 King MI, 222
15 *MT* 42 (1901), 91
16 Sainsbury, I, v–lxxii
17 King BCM, 20–1
18 Sacred Harmonic Society
19 Webb
20 Rimbault BM, xiii
21 King BCM, 62
22 W. Chappell (1965 reprint), ix
23 Contents in Heyer, 253–7
24 Contents in Heyer, 97
25 Dolmetsch, vii
26 Ritchey, 53–4
27 Grove, 5th edn, I, 1030
28 P. Young G

BIBLIOGRAPHY

This list is meant to be fairly comprehensive for books, monographs and articles relating to the music of this period. It also includes primary printed sources, including periodicals, novels, collections of programmes, and collections of printed music actually referred to in the text. Official publications are listed by the name of the institution, other anonymous or collective works by title.

Manuscripts are not included here, but are supplied with complete references when cited in footnotes or as the sources for music examples. The same applies to printed editions of individual musical works (see page xii above).

ABRAHAM, GERALD. *A Hundred Years of Music.* 2nd edn. London 1949.
ALDERSON, MONTAGUE F. and COLLES, HENRY C., eds. *History of St Michael's College, Tenbury.* London 1943.
Allan's Illustrated Edition of Tyneside Songs and Readings. Newcastle upon Tyne 1891.
ANDERSON, EMILY, ed. and tr. *The Letters of Beethoven.* 3 vols. London 1961.
ANDREWS, HILDA F. *Westminster Retrospect: a Memoir of Sir Richard Terry.* London 1948.
ANNAN, NOEL G. 'The Intellectual Aristocracy' in J. H. Plumb, ed. *Studies in Social History* (London 1955), 241–87.
ARNOLD, MATTHEW. (CA) *Culture and Anarchy (1869)* repr. in R. H. Super, ed. *The Complete Prose Works of Matthew Arnold* (Ann Arbor 1973), vol. 5.
— (EC) *Essays in Criticism.* I (1865) repr. in R. H. Super, ed., *The Complete Prose Works of Matthew Arnold* (Ann Arbor 1973), vol. 3. II (1888) repr. in Super, vol. 9.
— (SGC) 'Stanzas from the Grande Chartreuse', in Arnold, *New Poems* (London 1867), 208–19.
ARUNDELL, DENNIS. (CO) *The Critic at the Opera.* London 1957.
— (SW) *The Story of Sadler's Wells.* London 1965.
ASHTON, JOHN, ed. *Modern Street Ballads.* London 1888.
Assumed Copyright in Foreign Authors: Judgment in the Case of Boosey v. Purday. London [1849].
ASTOR & CO. *G. Astor & Co.'s Collection of Twelve Country Dances, with their Basses—For the Year 1807 . . . As they are Performed at Court, Bath, and All Public Assemblies.* London [1807].
The Athenaeum. Weekly journal, 1828–1921.
ATTWOOD, THOMAS. *Cathedral Music,* ed. T. A. Walmisley. London [1852].
AUSTEN, JANE. *Pride and Prejudice.* London 1813.
BACHE, CONSTANCE. *Brother Musicians: Reminiscences of Edward and Walter Bache.* London 1901.
BADEN POWELL, J. *Choralia: A Handy Book for Parochial Precentors and Choirmasters.* London 1901.
BAILY, LESLIE. *The Gilbert and Sullivan Book.* London 1966.

BIBLIOGRAPHY

Bandmaster Brass Band Journal. Periodical, 1878–82.

BANFIELD, STEPHEN. 'British Chamber Music at the Turn of the Century: Parry, Stanford, Mackenzie' *MT*, 115 (1974), 211–13.

BANISTER, HENRY C. *George Alexander Macfarren: His Life, Works and Influence.* London 1891.

BANTOCK, GRANVILLE and AFLALO, FREDERICK G. *Round the World with 'A Gaiety Girl'.* London 1896.

BAPTIE, DAVID. *Sketches of English Glee Composers.* London [1896].

BARNETT, JOHN F. *Musical Reminiscences and Impressions.* London 1906.

BARRETT, GEORGE S., ed. *The Congregational Church Hymnal.* Sponsored by the Congregational Union of England and Wales. London 1887.

BARRETT, PHILIP. 'English Cathedral Choirs in the Nineteenth Century' *Journal of Ecclesiastical History*, 25 (1974), 15–37.

BARRETT, WILLIAM A. (B) *Balfe: His Life and Work.* London 1882.

—(EGMW) *English Glee and Madrigal Writers.* Two Lectures read at the London Institution . . . 1877. London [1877].

— (EGP) *English Glees and Partsongs.* London 1886.

BARZUN, JACQUES. *Berlioz and the Romantic Century.* Boston 1950.

BATES, FRANK. *Reminiscences and Autobiography of a Musician in Retirement.* Norwich 1930.

BATLEY, THOMAS, ed. *Sir Charles Hallé's Concerts in Manchester . . . Also the Whole of the Programmes of Concerts from . . . 1858 to . . . 1895.* Manchester (1896).

BAUGHAM, EDWARD A., ed. *Sixty Years of Music.* London 1897.

BAX, ARNOLD. *Farewell, my Youth.* London 1943.

BEATY, RICHARD W., ed. *The Hymns and Psalms, &c. &c. As Sung in the Magdalen Asylum, Leeson Street, [Dublin] . . . Harmonized . . . and Arranged . . . by the Late David Weyman.* Dublin (1825).

BEECHAM, THOMAS. *Frederick Delius.* London 1959.

BENNETT, ALFRED and MARSHALL, WILLIAM. *Cathedral Chants.* London (1829).

BENNETT, CLIVE. 'Clementi as Symphonist' *MT*, 120 (1979), 207–10.

BENNETT, JOSEPH. (FYM) *Forty Years of Music 1865–1905.* London 1908.

— (STHC) *A Story of Ten Hundred Concerts . . . The Monday Popular Concerts.* London 1887.

BENNETT, J. R. STERNDALE. See Sterndale Bennett.

BENSON, LOUIS F. *The English Hymn: Its Development and Use in Worship.* Richmond (Virginia) 1915. Repr. 1962.

BERLIOZ, HECTOR. (E) *Evenings with the Orchestra* [*Les Soirées de l'Orchestre*, 1852], tr. J. Barzun. New York 1956.

— (M) *The Memoirs of Hector Berlioz*, tr. David Cairns. London 1969.

BINGLEY, WILLIAM. *Musical Biography.* London 1814. Repr. London 1834, New York 1971.

BLOM, ERIC. 'John Field' *The Chesterian*, 11 (1930), 201–7, 233–9.

BOALCH, DONALD H. *Makers of the Harpsichord and Clavichord 1440–1840.* 2nd edn. Oxford 1974.

BOETTICHER, WOLFGANG. *Robert Schumann.* Berlin 1941.

BOOSEY, WILLIAM. *Fifty Years of Music.* London 1931.

BOOTH, EDWARD, ed. *The Wesleyan Psalmist . . . Chiefly Selected from the Compositions of the Old Masters.* London 1843.

517

BIBLIOGRAPHY

BOOTH, MICHAEL R. *English Melodrama*. London 1965.

BOSTON, NOEL and LANGWILL, LYNDESAY G. *Church and Chamber Barrel-Organs*. Edinburgh 1967.

BOX, CHARLES. *Church Music in the Metropolis*. London 1884.

BRAMLEY, HENRY R. and STAINER, JOHN, eds. *Christmas Carols, New and Old*. London 1871; 2nd edn. London 1878.

BRANSON, DAVID. *John Field and Chopin*. London 1972.

BRIDGE, J. FREDERICK. (OA) *Organ Accompaniment of the Choral Service*. London [1885].

— (WP) *A Westminster Pilgrim*. London (1918).

BRIDGES, ROBERT. 'English Chanting' *Musical Antiquary*, 2 (1910–11), 125–41; 3 (1911–12), 74–86.

The British Critic. Quarterly journal, 1793–1853.

BROADHOUSE, JOHN. *Henry Smart's Compositions for the Organ*. London 1880.

BROCKLEHURST, J. BRIAN. 'The Studies of J. B. Cramer and his Predecessors' *Music and Letters*, 39 (1958), 256–61.

BROWN, JAMES D. and STRATTON, STEPHEN S. *British Musical Biography*. Birmingham 1897.

BROWN, MAURICE J. E. 'Chopin and his English Publisher' *Music and Letters*, 39 (1958), 363–71.

BRUCE, J. COLLINGWOOD and STOKOE, JOHN. *Northumbrian Minstrelsy*. Newcastle upon Tyne 1882. Repr. 1965.

BUCK, PERCY C., MEE, JOHN H. and WOODS, F. C. *Ten Years of University Music in Oxford, . . . 1884–94*. Oxford 1894.

BUCKLEY, A. 'The "Deighn Layrocks"' *Baptist Quarterly*, n.s.4 (1928), 43–8.

BUMPUS, JOHN S. (H) *A History of English Cathedral Music, 1549–1889*. London 1908. Facs. repr. 1972.

— (OCPC) *The Organists and Composers of S. Paul's Cathedral*. London 1891.

BUNN, ALFRED. *The Stage: Both Before and Behind the Curtain, from 'Observations Taken on the Spot'* London 1840.

BURGH, A. *Anecdotes of Music, Historical and Biographical, in a Series of Letters from a Gentleman to his Daughter*. 3 vols. London 1814.

BURNAND, FRANCIS C. *Records and Reminiscences*. London 1904.

BURNEY, CHARLES. *A General History of Music*. 4 vols. London 1776–89; ed. F. Mercer, 2 vols. New York 1957.

BURROWS, DAVID. 'Music and the "Nausea delle cose cotidiane"' *Musical Quarterly*, 57 (1971), 230–40.

BUSBY, THOMAS. *A Grammar of Music*. London 1818.

BUSH, GEOFFREY. 'Sterndale Bennett: the Solo Piano Works' *Proceedings of the Royal Musical Association*, 91 (1964–5), 85–97.

CARNIE, WILLIAM. *Psalmody in Scotland*. A Lecture Delivered to the Aberdeen Young Men's Literary Union and Early-Closing Association, in the Free West Church, 25 January 1854. Aberdeen 1854.

CARR, BRUCE. 'The First All-Sung English 19th-Century Opera' *MT*, 115 (1974), 125–6.

CARR, SHERWYN T. 'Bunn, Byron and *Manfred*' *Nineteenth Century Theatre Research*, I (1973), 15–27.

CARSE, ADAM. (ASDF) 'Adolphe Sax and the Distin Family' *Music Review*, 6 (1945), 193–201.

BIBLIOGRAPHY

— (J) *The Life of Jullien.* Cambridge 1951.

— (OBB) *The Orchestra from Beethoven to Berlioz.* Cambridge 1948.

The Cathedral Psalter . . . Set to Appropriate Chants. London [1878].

CAZALET, WILLIAM W. *A History of the Royal Academy of Music.* London 1854.

A Century and a Half in Soho: A Short History of the Firm of Novello. London 1961.

CHADWICK, OWEN. *The Victorian Church.* 2 vols. London 1966–70.

CHAPMAN, ERNEST, comp. *John Ireland: A Catalogue of Published Works.* London 1968.

CHAPMAN, SHADRACH. *Sacred Music for Two, Three, and Four Voices, Designed for Public and Family Worship.* London 1838.

CHAPPELL, PAUL. *Dr. S. S. Wesley 1810–1876: Portrait of a Victorian Musician.* Great Wakering 1977.

CHAPPELL, WILLIAM. *The Ballad Literature and Popular Music of the Olden Time.* 2 vols. London 1859. Facs. repr. 1965.

CHARLTON, PETER. 'The Life and Influence of Sir John Stainer' Ph.D. dissertation, University of East Anglia, 1976.

CHESTERFIELD, PHILIP D. STANHOPE, 4th Earl of. *Letters . . . to his Son.* London 1803.

CHILTON, CHARLES, ed. *Victorian Folk Songs.* London 1962.

The Choir, and Musical Record. Weekly journal, 1863–78.

CHORLEY, HENRY F. *Thirty Years' Musical Recollections.* London 1862.

The Church Choirmaster. See *The Organist.*

The Church Congress: Reports of Proceedings. Annual publication, 1861–1925.

CLARK, KENNETH. *The Gothic Revival.* 2nd edn. London 1950.

CLARK, RICHARD, ed. *The Words of the Most Favourite Pieces, Performed at the Glee Club, the Catch Club, and Other Public Societies.* London 1814.

CLARKE, CHARLES COWDEN and CLARKE, MARY V. COWDEN. *Recollections of Writers.* London 1878.

CLARKE (later CLARKE-WHITFELD), JOHN. *A Morning and Evening Service with Six Anthems.* 3 vols. London 1805.

CLARKE, MARY COWDEN. *The Life and Labours of Vincent Novello.* London 1864.

CLOSE, FRANCIS. *Thoughts on the Daily Choral Services in Carlisle Cathedral.* 3rd edn. London 1865.

COATES, ERIC. *Suite in Four Movements.* London 1953.

COBBETT, WALTER W., ed. *Cobbett's Cyclopedic Survey of Chamber Music.* 2 vols. London 1929–30.

COLE, WILLIAM. *A View of Modern Psalmody.* Colchester 1819.

COLEMAN, HENRY. *Hymn-Tune Voluntaries for the Organ: An Index of Organ Pieces by British Composers.* London 1930

COLLES, HENRY C. (EL) *Essays and Lectures.* London 1945.

— (RCM) *The Royal College of Music. A Jubilee Record.* London 1933.

Concordia. Fortnightly journal. 2 vols., 1875–6.

Congregational Church Music: A Book for the Service of Song in the House of the Lord (with a preface by Thomas Binney). London (1853).

'Congregational Psalmody' [general review]. *British Quarterly Review*, 70 (April 1862), 366–94.

CONNOLLY, LEONARD W. and WEARING, J. P. *English Drama and Theatre 1800–1900: A Guide to Information Sources.* Detroit 1978.

COOK, KENNETH. *The Bandsman's Everything Within.* London 1950.

519

BIBLIOGRAPHY

COOKE, DERYCK. *The Language of Music.* London 1959.

CORDER, FREDERICK. (B) 'The Works of Sir Henry Bishop' *Musical Quarterly*, 4 (1918), 78–97.

— (RAM) *A History of the Royal Academy of Music from 1822 to 1922.* London 1922.

CORVAN, EDWARD. *Corvan's Song Book.* Newcastle [upon Tyne] [c. 1860].

COWAN, WILLIAM and LOVE, JAMES. *The Music of the Church Hymnary.* Edinburgh 1901.

[COX, JOHN E.] *Musical Recollections of the Last Half-Century.* 2 vols. London 1872.

CRAW, HOWARD A. 'A Biography and Thematic Catalog of the Works of J. L. Dussek (1760–1812)' Ph.D. dissertation, University of Southern California, 1964.

CROKER, THOMAS F. DILLON and TUCKER, STEPHEN, eds. *The Extravaganzas of J. R. Planché.* 5 vols. London 1879.

CRÓSSE, JOHN. *An Account of the Grand Musical Festival, Held in September, 1823, in the Cathedral Church of York.* York 1825.

CROTCH, WILLIAM. (C) ed. *A Collection of 72 Original Single and Double Chants.* London 1842.

— (E) *Elements of Musical Composition: Comprehending the Rules of Thorough Bass and the Theory of Tuning.* London 1812.

— (L) Substance of Several Courses of Lectures on Music. London 1831.

— (PTB) *Practical Thorough Bass, or, the Art of Playing from a Figured Bass.* London [c. 1825].

— (S) *Specimens of Various Styles of Music.* 3 vols. London 1808.

CROWEST, FREDERICK J. *Phases of Musical England.* London 1881.

CURWEN, JOHN. (HOH) *How to Observe Harmony, with Exercises in Analysis.* 7th edn. London 1872.

— (TM) *The Teacher's Manual.* London 1875.

CURWEN, JOHN SPENCER. (MJC) *Memorials of John Curwen.* London 1882.

— (MQA) *Music at the Queen's Accession.* London 1897.

— (SWM) *Studies in Worship Music.* [1st series], London 1880. 2nd series, London 1885.

(DNB) A Dictionary of National Biography. 22 vols. London 1908–9.

DAHLHAUS, CARL, ed. *Studien zur Trivialmusik des 19. Jahrhunderts.* Regensburg 1967.

D'ALMAINE & CO. *A Day at a Music Publishers.* London [1848?]. (Copies: British Library, Dept. of Prints and Drawings, Crace Portfolio XXIX, Sheet 21, no. 6*; New York Public Library, Drexel 2206.4.)

DANIEL, RICHARD B. *Chapters on Church Music.* London 1894.

DAVEY, HENRY. *History of English Music.* London 1895.

DAVIES, HORTON. *Worship and Theology in England.* 5 vols. Princeton (New Jersey), 1961–75. III (1690–1850). IV (1850–1900). V (1900–1965).

DAVISON, HENRY, comp. *Music During the Victorian Era. From Mendelssohn to Wagner: Being the Memoirs of J. W. Davison.* London 1912.

DAVISON, PETER, ed. *Songs of the British Music Hall.* London 1971.

DAY, ALFRED H. *A Treatise on Harmony.* London 1845; 2nd edn. (rev. G. A. Macfarren), London 1885.

DEMUTH, NORMAN. *Musical Trends in the 20th Century.* London 1952.

DIBB, JOHN E. *Key to Chanting. The Psalter . . . Appointed to be Sung or Chanted, With a Peculiar Arrangement to Facilitate the Practice.* London 1831.

DICKENS, CHARLES. (CC) *A Christmas Carol.* London 1843.

— (SB) *Sketches by Boz.* London 1836.

DICKSON, WILLIAM E. (FY) *Fifty Years of Church Music (1820–70).* Ely 1894.

BIBLIOGRAPHY

— (LDE) *A Letter to the Dean of Ely, on the Present State of Cathedral Music in England.* Ely 1860.

A Dictionary of National Biography. 22 vols. London 1908–9. (*DNB*)

DISHER, MAURICE WILLSON. (VS) *Victorian Songs, From Dive to Drawing Room.* London 1955.

— (WC) *Winkles and Champagne. Comedies and Tragedies of the Music Hall.* London 1938.

DISRAELI, BENJAMIN. *Sybil.* 3 vols. London 1845.

DOLMETSCH, ARNOLD. *The Interpretation of the Music of the XVII and XVIII Centuries.* London [1915?].

DUNHILL, THOMAS. (CVS) 'Charles Villiers Stanford' *Proceedings of the Musical Association* (1926–7), 41–65.

— (SCO) *Sullivan's Comic Operas.* London 1928.

DYCE, WILLIAM, ed. *The Order of Daily Service . . . with Plain-Tune.* London 1843.

EBERS, JOHN. *Seven Years of the King's Theatre.* London 1828.

The Ecclesiologist. Monthly journal, 1841–68.

EDWARDS, FREDERICK G. 'Mendelssohn's Organ Sonatas' *Proceedings of the Musical Association*, 21 (1894–5), 1–14.

EHRLICH, CYRIL. (P) *The Piano: A History.* London 1976.

— (SEIP) *Social Emulation and Industrial Progress—The Victorian Piano.* The Queen's University of Belfast New Lecture Series, no. 82. (Belfast) 1975.

ELGAR, EDWARD. (FEM) *A Future for English Music, and Other Lectures*, ed. P. M. Young. London 1968.

— (LN) *Letters to Nimrod . . . 1897–1908*, ed. P. M. Young. London 1965.

ELIOT, GEORGE. (DD) *Daniel Deronda.* London 1876.

— (M) *Middlemarch.* Edinburgh 1872.

ELIOT, THOMAS STEARNS. 'Marie Lloyd' in Eliot, *Selected Essays* (London 1951), 456–9.

ELKIN, ROBERT. *The Old Concert Rooms of London.* London 1955.

ELVEY, GEORGE J. *Life & Reminiscences of George J. Elvey Knt*, ed. Lady Elvey. London 1894.

EMERSON, RALPH W. *English Traits.* Boston 1856.

FARMER, HENRY G. (BMCA) 'British Musicians a Century Ago' *Music and Letters*, 12 (1931), 384–92.

— (HMS) *A History of Music in Scotland.* London [1948].

— (MM) *Military Music.* New York 1950.

— (RAB) *Memoirs of the Royal Artillery Band.* London 1904.

— (RDMM) *The Rise and Development of Military Music.* London [1912].

FAWCETT, TREVOR. 'Bishop and Aladdin' *MT*, 113 (1972), 1076–7.

FELLOWES, EDMUND H. *English Cathedral Music from Edward VI to Edward VII.* London 1941; 5th edn. (rev. J. A. Westrup), London 1969.

FENNER, THEODORE. *Leigh Hunt and Opera Criticism: The "Examiner" Years, 1808–1821.* Lawrence (Kansas) 1972.

FÉTIS, FRANÇOIS J. (B) *Biographie universelle des musiciens.* 8 vols. Paris and Brussels 1835–44.

— (SML) 'State of Music in London' [Letters, originally pub. *Revue musicale* 5 (1829), 313–567; tr. anon.] *Harmonicon*, 1829, pp. 181–6, 214–20, 241–6, 275–81.

FIELD, GEORGE. *Outlines of Analogical Philosophy.* 2 vols. London 1839.

FISKE, ROGER. *English Theatre Music in the Eighteenth Century.* London 1973.

BIBLIOGRAPHY

FITZBALL, EDWARD. *Thirty-Five Years of a Dramatic Author's Life*. London 1859.

FLINDALL, ROY P. *The Church of England 1815–1948: a Documentary History*. London 1972.

FLOOD, WILLIAM H. GRATTAN. *William Vincent Wallace: A Memoir*. Waterford 1912.

FOREMAN, R. 'The British Musical Renaissance: A Guide to Research' F.L.A. thesis, Cambridge University, 1972.

FORSTER, EDWARD MORGAN. *A Room with a View*. London 1908.

FORSYTH, CECIL. *Music and Nationalism. A Study of English Opera*. London 1911.

Forty Years of Cathedral Music. Church Music Society Occasional Papers, no. 13. London 1940.

FOSTER, MYLES B. (AAC) *Anthems and Anthem Composers*. London 1901.

— (PSL) *The History of the Philharmonic Society of London 1813–1912*. London 1912.

FOWLER, JOSEPH T., ed. *The Life and Letters of John Bacchus Dykes*. London 1897.

FRERE, WALTER H., ed. *Bibliotheca musico-liturgica. A Descriptive Handlist of the Musical and Latin-Liturgical MSS. of the Middle Ages Preserved in the Libraries of Great Britain and Ireland*. 2 vols. London 1901–32.

FROST, MAURICE, ed. *Historical Companion to Hymns Ancient & Modern*. London 1962.

FROST, WILLIAM. *Early Recollections of St. Paul's Cathedral*. London 1926.

FULLER MAITLAND, JOHN A. (EM) *English Music in the XIXth Century*. London 1902.

— (MPS) *The Music of Parry and Stanford*. Cambridge 1934.

GAMMOND, PETER, ed. *Music Hall Song Book*. Newton Abbot 1975.

GANZ, WILHELM. *Memories of a Musician*. London 1913.

GARDINER, WILLIAM. (MF) *Music and Friends; or, Pleasant Recollections of a Dilettante*. 3 vols. London 1838–53.

— (MN) *The Music of Nature; or, An Attempt to Prove that What is Passionate and Pleasing in the Art of Singing, Speaking, and Performing upon Musical Instruments, is Derived from the Sounds of the Animated World*. London 1832.

GARDNER, GEORGE L. and NICHOLSON, SYDNEY H. *A Manual of English Church Music*. London 1936.

GAUNTLETT, HENRY J. *The Choral Use of the Book of Common Prayer, for Choirs and Places Where They Sing*. London [1852].

GEARY, ELEANOR M. *Musical Education; With Practical Observations on the Art of Piano-Forte Playing*. London 1841.

GENEST, JOHN. *Some Account of the English Stage*. 10 vols. Bath 1832.

GILBERT, DAVIES. *Some Ancient Christmas Carols*. London 1822.

GLENNON, JAMES. *Australian Music and Musicians*. Adelaide 1968.

GLOVER, JAMES M. *Jimmy Glover His Book*. London 1911.

GLOVER, SARAH. *A Scheme for Rendering Psalmody Congregational*. London and Norwich 1835.

GLOVER, WILLIAM. *The Memoirs of a Cambridge Chorister*. 2 vols. London 1885.

GOOCH, BRYAN N.S. and THATCHER, DAVID S. (EMV) *Musical Settings of Early and Mid-Victorian Literature: A Catalogue*. New York and London 1979.

— (LVM) *Musical Settings of Late Victorian and Modern British Literature: A Catalogue*. New York and London 1976.

GRAHAM, GEORGE F. *An Account of the First Edinburgh Musical Festival*. Edinburgh 1816.

GRASSINEAU, JAMES. *A Musical Dictionary; being a Collection of Terms and Characters; as well Ancient as Modern*. London 1740.

BIBLIOGRAPHY

GRAUE, JERALD. 'Muzio Clementi and the Development of Pianoforte Music in Industrial England' Ph.D. dissertation, University of Illinois, 1971.

GRAVES, CHARLES L. *Hubert Parry. His Life and Works.* 2 vols. London 1926.

GREENE, HARRY PLUNKET. *Charles Villiers Stanford.* London 1935.

GRIERSON, MARY. *Donald Francis Tovey.* London 1952.

GRONOW, REES H. *The Reminiscences and Recollections of Captain Gronow . . . 1810–1860.* 2 vols. London 1892.

GROVE, GEORGE. ed. *A Dictionary of Music and Musicians.* London 1879–89; 2nd edn. (ed. J. A. Fuller Maitland), London 1904; 3rd edn. (ed. H. C. Colles), London 1927–8; Supplementary Volume, London 1945; 5th edn. (ed. E. Blom), London 1954–61.

GUEST, IVOR. (AB) *The Alhambra Ballet.* London 1959.

— (EB) *The Empire Ballet.* London 1962.

GUILBERT, ARISTIDE. *A Sketch of the Life and Labours of Joseph Mainzer,* tr. A. Park. Glasgow 1844.

GURNEY, EDMUND. *The Power of Sound.* London 1880.

GUYNEMER, C. *Essay on Chamber Classical Music.* London 1846.

HACKETT, MARIA. *A Brief Account of Cathedral and Collegiate Schools.* [London] 1827.

HADDOCK, GEORGE. *Some Early Musical Recollections of G. Haddock.* London 1906.

HADOW, W. HENRY. (CM) 'Church Music' in Hadow, *Collected Essays* (London 1928), 191–212.

— (SMM) *Studies in Modern Music.* 2 series. London 1893, 1895.

HAIGHT, GORDON. 'George Eliot's Klesmer' in M. Mack and I. Gregor, eds., *Imagined Worlds* (London 1968), 205–14.

HALLÉ, CHARLES. *The Life and Letters of Sir Charles Hallé,* ed. C. E. and Marie Hallé. London 1896.

HAMILTON, JAMES A. *A Catechism of the Rudiments of Harmony and Thorough-Bass.* London 1833.

HAMPSON, J. N. *History of the Besses O' the Barn Band.* Northampton 1893.

HANSLICK, EDUARD. *The Beautiful in Music,* tr. G. Cohen. New York 1957.

HARDING, ROSAMUND E. M. *The Piano-Forte: Its History Traced to the Great Exhibition of 1851.* Cambridge 1933. Facs. repr. 1973.

HARKER, DAVID, ed. *George Ridley, Gateshead Poet and Vocalist.* Newcastle upon Tyne 1973.

HARLAND, JOHN, ed. *The Songs of the Wilsons* [i.e., of M. T. and A. Wilson]. London 1865.

HARLEY, JOHN. 'Music at the English Court in the Eighteenth and Nineteenth Centuries' *Music and Letters,* 50 (1969), 332–51.

HARTNOLL, PHYLLIS ed. *Shakespeare and Music.* London 1964.

HAVERGAL, FRANCIS T. *Memorials of Frederick Arthur Gore Ouseley.* London 1889.

HAWEIS, HUGH R. (ML) *My Musical Life.* London 1884.

— (MM) *Music and Morals.* London 1871.

HAWKINS, JOHN. *A General History of the Science and Practice of Music.* 5 vols. London 1776.

HAYTER, CHARLES. 'Some Victorian Precursors of Gilbert and Sullivan' *The Savoyard,* 17 (1978), 13–18.

HELMHOLTZ, HERMANN VON. *On the Sensations of Tone,* tr. (with additions) A. J. Ellis. London 1875.

523

HELMORE, FREDERICK. *Memoir of the Reverend T[homas] Helmore.* London 1891.

HELMORE, THOMAS. *On Church Music.* London 1868.

HENDERSON, WILLIAM, ed. *Victorian Street Ballads.* London 1937.

HEYER, ANNA H. *Historical Sets, Collected Editions, and Monuments of Music: A Guide to their Contents.* 2nd edn. Chicago 1969.

HIBBERT, HENRY G. *Fifty Years of a Londoner's Life.* London 1916.

HILL, JOHN. Review of Pietro Spada's edition of Clementi's Symphonies. *Journal of the American Musicological Society*, 32 (1979), 577–86.

HIND, HAROLD C. 'The British Wind-Band' *Hinrichsen's Musical Year Book*, 7 (1952), 183–94.

HINDLEY, CHARLES. *The Catnach Press.* London 1869.

HIRST, THOMAS. *The Music of the Church . . . including . . . Notices, Biographical and Critical, of the Most Popular Hymnic Authors.* London and Nottingham 1841.

'Historical and Statistical Details Relating to the Cathedrals of the United Kingdom' *Cathedral Quarterly*, 1 (1913), 27–36.

A History of the Bristol Madrigal Society. Reprinted, with additions, from the 'Clifton Chronicle' of January 12, 1887. Clifton (1887).

HITCHCOCK, H. WILEY. *Music in the United States: A Historical Introduction.* Englewood Cliffs 1974.

HODGES, EDWARD. 'On the Objects of Musical Study' *Musical World*, 1 (1836), 37–41, 85–8, 149–52, 203–6; 2 (1836), 145–8.

HODGES, FAUSTINA. *Edward Hodges, Doctor in Music.* New York 1896.

HOGAN, ITA M. *Anglo-Irish Music, 1780–1830.* Cork 1966.

HOGARTH, GEORGE. (MH) *Musical History, Biography, and Criticism.* London 1835.

— (MMD) *Memoirs of the Musical Drama.* 2 vols. London 1838.

— (PSL) *The Philharmonic Society of London, from its Foundations, 1813, to its Fiftieth Year, 1862.* London 1862.

HOLLINGSHEAD, JOHN. *Gaiety Chronicles.* London 1898.

HOLMES, EDWARD. 'English Glee and Madrigal Composers' *MT*, 4 (1851), 281–2, and six later instalments, ending at 5 (1852), 22.

HOPKINS, EDWARD J. and RIMBAULT, EDWARD F. *The Organ, its History and Construction.* London 1855.

HOPKINSON, CECIL. *A Bibliographical Thematic Catalogue of the Works of John Field.* London 1961.

HOPKINSON, CECIL and OLDMAN, CECIL B. 'Thomson's Collections of National Song, with Special Reference to the Contributions of Haydn and Beethoven' *Edinburgh Bibliographical Society Transactions*, 2 (1940), 1–64; 3 (1954), 121–4.

HOUTCHENS, LAWRENCE and HOUTCHENS, CAROLYN. *Leigh Hunt's Dramatic Criticism 1808–31.* New York 1949.

HOWES, FRANK. (DP) 'The Dead Past' *Music and Letters*, 22 (1941), 257–60.

— (EMR) *The English Musical Renaissance.* London and New York 1966.

— (FMB) *Folk Music of Britain—and Beyond.* London 1969.

HUDSON, FREDERICK. 'A Catalogue of the Works of Charles Villiers Stanford (1852–1924)' *Music Review*, 25 (1964), 44–57.

HUEFFER, FRANCIS. *Half a Century of Music in England 1837–1887. Essays Towards a History.* London 1889.

HUGHES, GERVASE. (CO) *Composers of Operetta.* London 1962.

— (S) *The Music of Arthur Sullivan.* London 1960.

HULLAH, JOHN P. (G) *A Grammar of Musical Harmony.* London 1852.

— (H) *The History of Modern Music.* London 1862.

— (L) *A Course of Lectures on the Third or Transition Period of Musical History* [i.e., 1601–1750]. London 1865.

— (MH) *Music in the House.* London 1877.

— (P) ed. *The Psalter.* London 1843.

— (WM) ed. *Wilhelm's Method of Teaching Singing.* 2 vols. London 1842.

HUMMEL, JOHANN N. *A Complete Theoretical and Practical Course of Instruction on the Art of Playing the Piano Forte.* London 1827.

HUMPHREYS, ARTHUR L. *Materials for the History of the Town and Parish of Wellington in the County of Somerset.* 4 vols. London 1908–14.

HUMPHRIES, CHARLES and SMITH, WILLIAM C. *Music Publishing in the British Isles.* London 1954.

HUNT, EDGAR. *Robert Lucas Pearsall: the 'Compleat Gentleman' and his Music (1795–1856).* Chesham Bois 1977.

HURD, MICHAEL. *Immortal Hour: The Life and Period of Rutland Boughton.* London 1962.

HUTCHINGS, ARTHUR. (CM) *Church Music in the Nineteenth Century.* London 1967.

— (D) *Delius: A Critical Biography.* London 1948.

Hymns Ancient and Modern, ed. W. H. Monk. London 1861. Appendix, 1868; revised edn. 1875; supplement 1889; revised edn. 1904.

The Illustrated London News. Weekly journal, 1842–.

IMESON, WILLIAM E. *Illustrated Music-Titles and their Delineators: A Handbook for Collectors.* London 1912.

IVIMEY, JOHN W. *Boys and Music.* Marlborough 1936.

JACKSON, GEORGE PULLEN. *White and Negro Spirituals.* Locust Valley (N.Y.) 1943.

JACOB, NAOMI. *'Our Marie' (Marie Lloyd): A Biography.* London 1936; repr. Bath 1972.

JACOBI, ERWIN R. *Die Entwicklung der Musiktheorie in England nach der Zeit von J. P. Rameau.* 2 vols. Strasbourg 1957–60.

JARMAN, THOMAS. *Sacred Music. The Northamptonshire Harmony.* 4 books. London [c. 1810–22].

JEBB, JOHN. *The Choral Service of the United Church of England and Ireland.* 2 vols. London 1843.

JOHNSTONE, ARTHUR G. W. *Musical Criticisms.* Manchester 1905.

JOYCE, FREDERICK W. *The Life of Rev. Sir F. A. G. Ouseley, Bart., M.A., Mus.D., etc. etc.* London 1896.

JULIAN, JOHN. *A Dictionary of Hymnology.* 2nd edn. London 1907; repr. 1957.

K: see p. xi above.

KAMM, JOSEPHINE. *How different from Us: A Biography of Miss Buss and Miss Beale.* London 1958.

KASSLER, JAMIE CROY. *The Science of Music in Britain, 1714–1830: A Catologue.* 2 vols. New York 1979.

KELLER, OTTO. *Die Operette in ihrer geschichtlichen Entwicklung.* Vienna 1926.

KELLY, MICHAEL. *Reminiscences*, ed. Roger Fiske. London 1975.

KEMP, E. S. and MEE, JOHN H. *Ten More Years of University Music in Oxford.* London 1904.

KENNEDY, MICHAEL. *Portrait of Elgar.* London 1968.

KENNEY, CHARLES L. *A Memoir of Michael William Balfe.* London 1875.

KIDSON, FRANK. (BMP) *British Music Publishers.* London 1900.

BIBLIOGRAPHY

— (TT) *Traditional Tunes*. Oxford 1891.

KING, A. HYATT. (BCM) *Some British Collectors of Music*. Cambridge 1963.

— (EPM) 'English Pictorial Music Title-Pages, 1820–85: Their Style, Evolution, and Importance' *The Library*, 5th ser., 4 (1950), 262–72.

— (MCL) 'Music Circulating Libraries in Britain' *MT*, 119 (1978), 134–8.

— (MI) 'The Musical Institute of London and its Successors' *MT*, 117 (1976), 221–3.

KITCHINER, WILLIAM. *Observations on Vocal Music*. London 1821.

KITTON, FREDERICK G. *Zechariah Buck*. London 1899.

KLEIN, HERMANN. *Thirty Years of Musical Life in London, 1870–1900*. London 1903.

KLEIN, JOHN W. 'Vincent Wallace (1812–65): A Reassessment' *Opera*, 16 (1965), 709–16.

KNAPP, BETTINA and CHAPMAN, MYRA. *That Was Yvette*. London 1966.

KNEPLER, GEORG. *Musikgeschichte des 19. Jahrhunderts*. Berlin 1961.

KOLLMANN, AUGUST F. C. *An Essay on Musical Harmony*. London 1796.

KRUMMEL, DONALD W. *English Music Printing, 1553–1700*. London 1975.

LAHEE, HENRY C. *The Organ and its Masters*. Boston 1903.

LAMB, ANDREW. 'Viennese Dance Styles in Victorian England' *Dreivierteltakt* (Journal of the Viennese Light Musical Society [of Great Britain]), V/1 (1970), 6–9.

LANGLEY, GEORGE. 'The Pianoforte Works of Francis Edward Bache' *Monthly Musical Record*, 35 (1905), 83–4.

LATROBE, JOHN A. *The Music of the Church Considered in its Various Branches, Congregational and Choral*. London 1831.

LEE, EDWARD. *Music of the People. A Study of Popular Music in Great Britain*. London 1970.

LEGGE, ROBIN H. and HANSELL, W. E. *Annals of the Norfolk and Norwich Triennial Musical Festivals*. London 1896.

LEWER, DAVID. *A Spiritual Song: the Story of the Temple Choir and a History of Divine Service in the Temple Church*. London 1961.

LIGHTWOOD, JAMES T. (CDM) *Charles Dickens and Music*. London 1912.

— (MMEC) *Methodist Music of the Eighteenth Century*. London 1927.

— (MMHB) *The Music of the Methodist Hymn Book*. Rev. edn. London 1955.

— (W) *Samuel Wesley, Musician*. London 1937.

LLOYD, ALBERT L. (CAY) *Come All Ye Bold Miners. Ballads and Songs of the Coalfields*. London 1952.

— (F) 'Foreword' to L. Shepard, *The Broadside Ballad* (London 1962).

— (FSE) *Folk Song in England*. London 1967.

— (SE) *The Singing Englishman. An Introduction to Folk Song*. London 1944.

LOCKE, JOHN. *Some Thoughts Concerning Education*. Cambridge 1889.

LOESSER, ARTHUR. *Men, Women and Pianos: A Social History*. New York 1954.

LOGIER, JOHANN B. *A System of the Science of Music and Practical Composition*. London 1827.

London Institution. *A Descriptive Catalogue of the Lectures Delivered at the London Institution ... From the Opening of the Theatre ... 1819 to ... 1854*. London 1854.

LONG, KENNETH R. *The Music of the English Church*. London 1972.

LUMLEY, BENJAMIN. *Reminiscences of the Opera*. London 1864.

LUNN, HENRY C. 'Musings of a Musician' *Musical World*, 20 (1845), 3–4, and later instalments.

526

BIBLIOGRAPHY

(*MGG*) *Die Musik in Geschichte und Gegenwart*, ed. F. Blume. In progress. Kassel 1949–.

(*MT*) *The Musical Times*. Monthly journal, 1844–.

MCCOLL, EWAN, ed. *The Shuttle and the Cage*. London 1954.

MACDERMOTT, KENNETH H. *Sussex Church Music in the Past*. Chichester 1922.

MACFARREN, GEORGE A. (AL) *Addresses and Lectures*. London 1888.

— (BG) 'Bishop's Glees' *MT*, 11 (1864), 257–9, and later instalments to 12 (1865), 25–9.

— (E) 'On Editing' *MT*, 16 (1874), 707–9.

— (ENMP) 'The English are Not a Musical People' *Cornhill Magazine*, 18 (1868), 344–63.

— (IN) *Fifty-two Introits or Short Anthems*. London 1866.

— (LH) *Six Lectures on Harmony, Delivered at the Royal Institution of Great Britain*. London 1867.

— (P) 'Cipriani Potter: His Life and Work' *Proceedings of the Musical Association*, 10 (1883–4), 41–56.

— (R) *The Rudiments of Harmony, With Progressive Exercises*. London 1860.

MACFARREN, WALTER. *Memories: An Autobiography*. London 1905.

MACINNES, COLIN. *Sweet Saturday Night*. London 1967.

MACKENZIE, ALEXANDER C. *A Musician's Narrative*. London 1927.

MACKERNESS, ERIC D. (LHMJ) 'Leigh Hunt's Musical Journalism' *Monthly Musical Record*, 86 (1956), 212–22.

— (SH) *A Social History of English Music*. London 1964.

MACMILLAN, DOUGALD. *Catalogue of the Larpent Plays in the Huntington Library*. San Marino (Calif.) 1939.

MACPHERSON, (CHARLES) STEWART. (AC) *The Appreciation Class*. London 1923.

— (P) *A Plea for the Teaching of Music as a Language and Literature*. London 1908.

MACQUEEN-POPE, W. J. *see* Pope, W. J. M.

MAINZER, JOSEPH. (ME) *Music and Education*. London and Edinburgh 1848.

— (SM) *Singing for the Million*. London 1841.

MAIR, CARLENE. *The Chappell Story, 1811–1961*. London 1961.

MANDER, RAYMOND and MITCHENSON, JOE. (BMH) *British Music Hall. A Story in Pictures*. London 1965.

— (LT) *The Lost Theatres of London*. London 1968.

— (MC) *Musical Comedy*. London 1969.

— (R) *Revue*. London 1971.

MAPLESON, JAMES H. *The Mapleson Memoirs, 1848–1888*. London 1888.

MARETZEK, MAX. *Sharps and Flats*. New York 1890.

MARÓTHY, JÁNOS. *Music and the Bourgeois, Music and the Proletarian*. Budapest 1974.

MARR, ROBERT A. *Music for the People . . . With an Account of the Rise of Choral Societies in Scotland*. Edinburgh and Glasgow 1889.

MARSH, JOHN I (1752–1828). *The Cathedral Chant Book*. London 1804.

MARSH, JOHN II (fl. 1975). 'The Latin Church Music of Samuel Wesley' D.Phil. dissertation, York University, 1975.

MASON, WILLIAM. *Essays, Historical and Critical, on English Church Music*. York 1795. Repr. in *The Works of William Mason* (London 1811), III.

MAYHEW, HENRY. *London Labour and the London Poor*. 4 vols. London 1861–2. Facs. repr. 1967.

MEDICI, NERINA and HUGHES, ROSEMARY. *A Mozart Pilgrimage* [by Vincent and Mary Novello, 1829]. London 1955.

MERRICK, FRANK, ed. *John Field: Piano Concertos Nos. 1–3.* Musica Britannica XVII (1961).

MIDGLEY, SAMUEL. *My 70 Years' Musical Memories (1860–1930).* London 1934.

MILLIGAN, THOMAS B., JR. 'The Concerto in London, 1790–1800' Ph.D. dissertation, Eastman School of Music, 1978.

MILLINGTON, WILLIAM. *Sketches of Local Musicians and Musical Societies.* Pendlebury 1884.

MILNE, BASIL. *Elgar, His Life and Works.* 2 vols. London 1933.

MINSHALL, EBENEZER. *Organs, Organists, and Choirs.* London (1886).

MITCHELL, JEROME. *The Walter Scott Operas.* University (Alabama) (1977).

Monday Popular Concerts. *Catalogue of Works Performed . . . 1859 . . . [to] 1892.* London 1892.

The Monthly Supplement to the Musical Library. Monthly journal, 1834–7.

MOORE, THOMAS. (LMP) *Notes from the Letters . . . to his Music Publisher, James Power.* New York [1854].

— (VM) *A Collection of the Vocal Music of Thomas Moore Esq.* London and Dublin [1820?].

MORTIMER, CHARLES G. 'Leading Music Publishers'. 17 articles in *Musical Opinion* 62–3 (Sept. 1938–Jan. 1940), rev. and reissued as 'The Music Publisher of Tradition' *Musical Opinion*, 64–5 (June 1941–May 1942).

MOSCHELES, CHARLOTTE, ed. *Life of Moscheles with Selections from his Diaries and Correspondence, by his Wife,* tr. A. D. Coleridge. London 1873.

MOUNT EDGCUMBE, RICHARD, 2nd Earl of. *Musical Reminiscences.* 4th edn. London 1834.

MUIR, PERCY H. 'Thomas Moore's Irish Melodies, 1808–1834' *The Colophon,* 15 (1933), unpaginated.

MURRAY, CHRISTOPHER. 'Robert William Elliston's Production of *Faust,* Drury Lane, 1825' *Theatre Research,* 11 (1971), 102–13.

Musica Britannica: A National Collection of Music. London, 1951–.
17 (1961): John Field, *Piano Concertos,* ed. Frank Merrick.
37 (1972): William Sterndale Bennett, *Piano and Chamber Music,* ed. Geoffrey Bush.
41 (1978): Samuel Wesley, *Confitebor tibi, Domine,* ed. John Marsh.
43 (1979): *English Songs 1800–1860,* ed. Geoffrey Bush and Nicholas Temperley.

The Musical Standard. Weekly journal, 1862–1933.

The Musical Times. Monthly journal, 1844–. (*MT*)

The Musical World. Weekly journal, 1836–91.

Die Musik in Geschichte und Gegenwart, ed. F. Blume. Kassel, 1949–. (*MGG*).

NEALE, JOHN M. 'English Hymnology, its History and Prospects' *The Christian Remembrancer,* 18 (1850), 302–43.

NEALE, JOHN M. and HELMORE, THOMAS, eds. *Carols for Christmas Tide.* London 1853.

NEIGHBOUR, OLIVER W. and TYSON, ALAN. *English Music Publishers' Plate Numbers in the First Half of the Nineteenth Century.* London 1965.

NETTEL, REGINALD. (MFT) *Music in the Five Towns, 1840–1914: A Study of the Social Influence of Music in an Industrial District.* London 1944.

— (SSE) *Sing a Song of England. A Social History of Traditional Song.* London 1954; new edn. London 1969.

NEVILL, RALPH. *Night Life.* London 1926.

NEWMAN, ERNEST. (MS) *Musical Studies.* London 1905.

BIBLIOGRAPHY

— (SW) *A Study of Wagner*. London 1899.

NEWMAN, WILLIAM S. *The Sonata Since Beethoven*. Chapel Hill 1969.

NICOLL, ALLARDYCE. *A History of English Drama 1660–1900*. 6 vols. London 1952–9.

NIKOLAYEV, ALEXANDER. *John Field*. Moscow 1960.

NORTH, ROGER. *Roger North on Music*, ed. J. Wilson. London 1959.

NORTHCOTT, RICHARD. *The Life of Sir Henry R. Bishop*. London 1920.

NOVELLO, CLARA. *Reminiscences*. London 1910.

NOVELLO & CO. (CHS) *A Century and a Half in Soho*. London 1961.

— (CS) 'The Novello Centenary Supplement' *MT*, 52 (1911), Supp.

— (CTA) *Novello's Collection of Thirty-One Anthems, Intended Principally for the Use of Parish Choirs, Set to Music by Modern Composers*. London [1861].

— (SHCM) *A Short History of Cheap Music*. London 1887.

OAKELEY, EDWARD M. *The Life of Sir Herbert Stanley Oakeley*. London 1904.

ODELL, GEORGE C. D. *Shakespeare from Betterton to Irving*. 2 vols. New York 1966.

OLDMAN, CECIL B. 'Attwood's Dramatic Works' *MT*, 107 (1966), 23–7.

OLIPHANT, THOMAS. *A Short Account of Madrigals, from their Commencement up to the Present Time*. London 1836.

OPHEIM, VERNON. 'The English Romantic Madrigal' Ph.D. dissertation, University of Illinois, 1971.

The Organist (1866), *The Church Choirmaster* (1867–8), *The Choirmaster* (1869), *The Musician* (1869–70). Monthly journal.

OULTON, WALLEY C. *A History of the Theatres of London . . . from . . . 1795 to 1817*. London 1818.

OUSELEY, FREDERICK A. G. (ECC) 'The Education of Choristers in Cathedrals' in Howson, John S., ed., *Essays on Cathedrals* (London 1872), 209–34.

— (H) *A Treatise on Harmony*. Oxford 1868.

— (MEM) 'Modern English Music,' in: E. Naumann, *History of Music*, tr. F. Praeger (London 1886), V, 1274–1314.

The Oxford Book of Carols, ed. P. Dearmer, R. Vaughan Williams and M. Shaw. London 1928.

P: see p. iv above.

PALMER, BESSIE. *Musical Recollections*. London and Newcastle upon Tyne 1904.

PALMER, ROY, ed. *A Touch on the Times: Songs of Social Change 1770–1914*. Harmondsworth 1974.

The Parish Choir. Monthly journal 1846–51.

PARKE, WILLIAM T. *Musical Memoirs; . . . An Account of the General State of Music in England, from . . . 1784, to . . . 1830*. 2 vols. London 1830

PARKER, JOHN H. *A Hand-Book for Visitors to Oxford*. Oxford 1847.

PARKIN, GEORGE R. *Edward Thring . . .: Life, Diary and Letters*. 2 vols. London 1898.

Parliamentary Papers, 1854. Report of the Cathedral Commissioners: XXVI, 1ff.; XXXIV, 81ff.

PARRATT, WALTER. 'Music' in *The Reign of Queen Victoria*, ed. T. H. Ward (London 1887), II, 593–620.

PARRISH, CARL. *The Early Piano and its Influence on Keyboard Technique and Composition in the Eighteenth Century*. Research Microfilm Publishers Studies in Musicology, series A, no. 1. Superior (Wisconsin) 1953.

PARRY, C. HUBERT H. (AM) *The Art of Music*. London 1893.

— (IA) 'Inaugural Address to the Folk Song Society' *Journal of the Folk Song Society*, 1 (1899), 2–3.

PATRICK, MILLAR. *Four Centuries of Scottish Psalmody*. London 1949.

[Peace, John.] *An Apology for Cathedral Service*. London 1839.

PEACOCK, THOMAS L. *The Works of Thomas Love Peacock*, ed. H. F. B. Brett-Smith & C. E. Jones. 10 vols. London 1924–34.

PEARCE, CHARLES E. *Madame Vestris and her Times*. London 1923.

PEARCE, CHARLES W. (ESFS) 'English Sacred Folk Song of the West Gallery Period (circa 1695–1820)' *Proceedings of the Musical Association*, 48 (1921–2), 1–27.

— (H) *The Life and Works of Edward John Hopkins*. London [1910].

— (PO) *The Evolution of the Pedal Organ*. London 1927.

— (TEHT) 'On the Treatment of English Hymn Tunes in Organ Music.' College of Organists, *Lectures 1885–6* (London 1886), 15–41.

PEARSALL, RONALD. (EPM) *Edwardian Popular Music*. Newton Abbot 1975.

— (VPM) *Victorian Popular Music*. Newton Abbot 1973.

PEARSON, HESKETH. *Bernard Shaw: A Biography*. London 1961.

PETER, PHILIP H. 'The Life and Work of Cipriani Potter (1792–1871)' Ph.D. dissertation, Northwestern University, 1972.

PHILLIPS, HENRY. *Musical and Personal Recollections During Half a Century*. London 1864.

PIGGOTT, PATRICK. *The Life and Music of John Field, 1782–1837, Creator of the Nocturne*. London 1973.

PLANCHÉ, JAMES R. *The Recollections and Reflections of J. R. Planché*. London 1872.

PLANTINGA, LEON. *Clementi: His Life and Music*. London 1977.

POLE, WILLIAM. *The Philosophy of Music*. London 1879. [An introduction to acoustics.]

POLLARD, HUGH M. *Pioneers of Popular Education*. London 1956.

POPE, WALTER J. MACQUEEN. *The Melodies Linger On*. London 1950.

PORTE, JOHN F. *Sir Charles Villiers Stanford*. London 1921.

PORTEUS, BEILBY, bishop of London. 'A Charge Delivered to the Clergy of the Diocese of London . . . in 1790' in *Works* (ed. R. Hodgson, London 1811), 239–46.

POTTER, P. CIPRIANI H. 'Companion to the Orchestra' *Musical World*, 3 (1836), 97–101; 4 (1836–7), 1–5, 177–81.

PROUT, EBENEZER. *Harmony: Its Theory and Practice*. London 1889; 16th edn. London 1901.

PUGIN, AUGUSTUS W. *An Earnest Appeal for the Revival of the Ancient Plainsong*. London 1850.

PULLING, CHRISTOPHER. *They Were Singing, and What They Sang About*. London 1952.

The Quarterly Musical Magazine and Review. Quarterly journal 1818–28.

RAINBOW, BERNARR. (LWM) *The Land Without Music: Musical Education in England 1800–1860 and its Continental Antecedents*. London 1967.

— (CR) *The Choral Revival in the Anglican Church 1839–1872*. London 1970.

— (MLU) 'Mary Langdale Unappreciated' *Music Teacher*, 38 (1979), 16–17.

RANNIE, ALAN. *The Story of Music at Winchester College 1394–1969*. Winchester (1969).

Read & Others v. The Bishop of Lincoln (1890). *Law Times* n.s. 64 (1891), 170–3.

Record of the Musical Union. Periodical 1845–80.

REDHEAD, RICHARD and OAKELEY, FREDERICK. *Laudes diurnae*. London 1843.

REDLICH, HANS F. 'The Bach Revival in England (1750–1850)' *Hinrichsen's Musical Year Book*, 7 (1952), 287–300.

BIBLIOGRAPHY

REDWOOD, CHRISTOPHER, ed. *A Delius Companion*. London 1976.

REES, ABRAHAM. *The Cyclopaedia; or Universal Dictionary of Arts, Sciences, and Literature*. London 1819.

REEVES, J. SIMS. *My Jubilee*. London 1889.

RENNERT, JONATHAN. *William Crotch (1775–1847): Composer, Artist, Teacher*. Lavenham 1975.

RICE, CHARLES. *The London Theatre in the Eighteen-Thirties*, ed. A. C. Sprague. London 1950.

RICHARDSON, A. MADELEY. *Modern Organ Accompaniment*. London 1907.

RICHARDSON, PHILIP J. S. *The Social Dances of the Nineteenth Century in England*. London 1960.

RIMBAULT, EDWARD F. (BM) *Bibliotheca madrigaliana*. London 1847.

— (CC) *Cathedral Chants of the 16th, 17th, and 18th Centuries*. London 1844.

RINGER, ALEXANDER L. 'Beethoven and the London Pianoforte School' *Musical Quarterly*, 6 (1970), 742–58.

RITCHEY, LAWRENCE I. 'The Untimely Death of Samuel Wesley; or, The Perils of Plagiarism' *Music and Letters*, 60 (1979), 45–59.

RITSON, JOSEPH. *The Northumberland Garland*. Newcastle upon Tyne 1793.

ROGERS, CLARA KATHLEEN [BARNETT]. *Memories of a Musical Career*. Boston 1919.

Roman Catholic Church. Archdiocese of Westminster. *List of Approved Church Music*. London 1907.

ROTHENBERG, STANLEY. *Copyright and Public Performance of Music*. The Hague 1954.

ROUTH, FRANCIS. *Early English Organ Music from the Middle Ages to 1837*. London 1973.

ROUTLEY, ERIC. *The English Carol*. London 1958.

RUBIN, E. 'The English Glee from William Hayes to William Horsley' Ph.D. dissertation, University of Pittsburgh, 1968.

RUSKIN, JOHN. *Ruskin on Music*, ed. A. M. Wakefield. London 1894.

RUSSELL, JOHN and ELLIOT, JOHN H. *The Brass Band Movement*. London 1936.

RUSSELL, WILLIAM. *St. Paul's in the Early Nineteenth Century . . . Based on Extracts from the Diary and Correspondence of the Late William Hale Hale*. London 1920.

RUTLAND, WILLIAM. *Thomas Hardy: A Study of his Writings and their Background*. Oxford 1938.

S: see p. iv above.

SACHS, CURT. *The Commonwealth of Art: Style in the Fine Arts, Music and the Dance*. New York 1946.

Sacred Harmonic Society. *Catalogue of the Library of the Sacred Harmonic Society*. London 1862.

SADDLEMYER, ANN. 'The Cult of the Celt: Pan-Celticism in the Nineties' in R. Skelton and A. Saddlemyer, eds., *The World of W. B. Yeats: Essays in Perspective* (Dublin 1965), 19–21.

[SAINSBURY, JOHN, ed.] *A Dictionary of Musicians*. 2 vols. London 1825. Repr. New York 1966.

ST. JOHN, CHRISTOPHER M. *Ethel Smyth, A Biography*. London 1959.

The Salvation Army Hymn Book. London 1931.

SANDALL, ROBERT, WIGGINS, ARCH R., and others. *The History of the Salvation Army*. In progress. London, 1947–.

SANDYS, WILLIAM. *Christmas Carols, Ancient and Modern*. London 1833.

531

BIBLIOGRAPHY

SAYERS, W. C. BERWICK. *Samuel Coleridge-Taylor, Musician: His Life and Letters.* London 1915.

SCHAFER, R. MURRAY. *British Composers in Interview.* London 1963.

SCHMITZ, OSCAR A. *Das Land ohne Musik.* Munich 1914.

SCHÖNHERR, MAX. *Carl Maria Ziehrer: sein Werk, sein Leben, seine Zeit.* Vienna 1974.

SCHOLES, PERCY A. (BMT) ed. *Dr. Burney's Musical Tours in Europe.* 2 vols. London 1959.

— (MM) *The Mirror of Music, 1844–1944.* London 1947.

— (MYCM) *Music, the Young Child and the Masterpiece.* London 1935.

— (OCM) *The Oxford Companion to Music.* 9th edn. London 1955.

SCHUMANN, ROBERT. (MM) *Music and Musicians* (tr. Fanny R. Ritter) 1st series. 5th edn. New York 1895.

— (WSB) 'Wm. Sterndale Bennett' *Neue Zeitschrift für Musik*, 6 (1837), 2–3.

SCOTT, WILLIAM H. *Edward German.* London 1932.

SCOTT, WILLIAM S. *Green Retreats: The Story of Vauxhall Gardens, 1661–1859.* London 1955.

SENELICK, LAWRENCE. 'A Brief Life and Times of the Victorian Music Hall' *Harvard Library Bulletin*, 19 (1971), 375–98.

SHARP, CECIL. *English Folk Song: Some Conclusions.* London 1907; 4th edn, rev. M. Karpeles, Wakefield 1972.

SHAW, G. BERNARD. (HBMC) *How to Become a Musical Critic*, ed. D. H. Laurence. London 1960.

— (LM) *London Music in 1888–89 As Heard by Corno di Bassetto.* London [1937].

— (MIL) *Music in London 1890–94.* 3 vols. London 1932.

— (PW) *The Perfect Wagnerite.* 4th edn. London 1923.

SHAW, H. WATKINS. (ME) ed. *Musical Education: A Symposium.* London 1946.

— (TCF) *The Three Choirs Festival.* Worcester 1954.

— (W) 'Thomas Attwood Walmisley 1814–1856' *English Church Music*, 27 (1957), 2–8.

SHEPARD, LESLIE. *The Broadside Ballad.* London 1962.

[SHEPPARD, ELIZABETH S.]. *Charles Auchester.* 3 vols. London 1853.

SHERSON, ERROLL. *London's Lost Theatres of the Nineteenth Century.* London 1925.

SHIRLAW, MATTHEW. *The Theory of Harmony.* London 1917.

SHORT, ERNEST. *Fifty Years of Vaudeville.* London 1946.

SILANTIEN, JOHN J. 'The Part-Song in England, 1837–1914' Ph.D. dissertation, University of Illinois, 1980.

SIMPSON, HAROLD. *A Century of Ballads 1810–1910.* London 1910.

SINCLAIR, WILLIAM M. *Memorials of St. Paul's Cathedral.* London 1909.

SITWELL, SACHEVERELL. *Morning, Noon, and Night in London.* London 1948.

Sixty Old-Time Variety Songs. With an Introduction by Charles Coborn and an Appreciation by George Robey. London 1937.

SMART, GEORGE T. *Leaves from the Journals of Sir George Smart*, ed. H. B. and C. L. E. Cox. London 1907.

SMITH, G. H. *A History of Hull Organs and Organists.* London [1910?].

SMITH, JOHN STAFFORD, ed. *Musica antiqua.* 2 vols. London 1812.

SMITH, WILLIAM C., comp. *The Italian Opera and Contemporary Ballet in London, 1789–1920.* Society for Theatre Research, Publications. London 1955.

SMYTH, ETHEL. *Impressions that Remained.* 2 vols. London 1919.

532

BIBLIOGRAPHY

Society for the Encouragement of Arts, Manufactures, and Commerce. *First Report of the Committee . . . [on] Musical Education, At Home and Abroad.* London 1866.

SPARK, FREDERICK R. and BENNETT, JOSEPH. *History of the Leeds Musical Festivals 1858–1889.* Leeds and London 1892.

SPARK, WILLIAM. (MM) *Musical Memories.* London 1888.

— (MR) *Musical Reminiscences.* London 1892.

— (S) *Henry Smart: His Life and Works.* London 1881.

SPEAIGHT, GEORGE. *Bawdy Songs of the Early Music Hall.* Newton Abbot 1975.

SPENCER, HERBERT. (FC) *Facts and Comments.* London 1902.

— (OFM) 'The Origin and Function of Music' *Fraser's Magazine,* 56 (1857), 396–408.

SPINK, GERALD W. 'Walter Scott's Musical Acquaintances' *Music and Letters,* 51 (1970), 61–5.

SPOHR, LOUIS. *Louis Spohr's Autobiography,* tr. anon. London 1865.

SQUIRE, W. BARCLAY. 'Edward Taylor's Gresham Lectures' *MT,* 54 (1913), 581–4, 647–50.

STAFFORD, WILLIAM C. *A History of Music.* Edinburgh 1830.

STAINER, JOHN. (FWC) *A Few Words to Candidates for the Degree of Mus.Bac., Oxon.* London 1897.

— (MRIE) *Music in its Relation to the Intellect and the Emotions.* London 1892.

— (PMC) 'The Principles of Musical Criticism' *Proceedings of the Musical Association,* 7 (1880–1), 35–52.

— (TH) *A Theory of Harmony Founded on the Tempered Scale.* London 1871.

STAINER, JOHN and BARRETT, WILLIAM A. *A Dictionary of Musical Terms.* London 1876.

Stalybridge Old Band . . . A Record of a Hundred Years 1814–1914. Stalybridge 1914.

STANFORD, CHARLES V. (IRR) *Interludes: Records and Reflections.* London 1922.

— (MC) *Musical Composition. A Short Treatise for Students.* London 1911.

— (PUD) *Pages from an Unwritten Diary.* London 1914.

— (SM) *Studies and Memories.* London 1908.

STANFORD, CHARLES V. and FORSYTH, CECIL. *A History of Music.* London 1916.

STEDMAN, JANE W. 'From Dame to Woman: W. S. Gilbert and Theatrical Transvestism' *Victorian Studies,* 14 (1970–1), 27–46.

STERNDALE BENNETT, J. R. *The Life of William Sterndale Bennett.* By his Son. Cambridge 1907.

STEVENS, DENIS, ed. *A History of Song.* London 1960.

STOCKLEY, WILLIAM C. *Fifty Years of Music in Birmingham.* Birmingham 1913.

STUBBS, G. EDWARD. *Practical Hints on the Training of Choir Boys.* London [1897].

SULLIVAN, HERBERT and FLOWER, NEWMAN. *Sir Arthur Sullivan: His Life, Letters & Diaries.* London 1927.

SULLY, JAMES. *Sensation and Intuition: Studies in Psychology and Aesthetics.* London 1874.

SUMNER, WILLIAM L. *The Organ: Its Evolution, Principles of Construction and Use.* 4th edn. London 1973.

SUTCLIFFE SMITH, J. *The Story of Music in Birmingham.* Birmingham 1945.

Taphouse Ltd. *The Story of a Music Shop, 1857–1957.* Oxford [1957?].

TATTON, THOMAS. 'English Viola Music 1890–1937' D.M.A. dissertation, University of Illinois, 1976.

[TAYLOR, EDWARD]. *The English Cathedral Service, its Glory, its Decline, and its Designed Extinction.* London 1845.

533

TAYLOR, S. 'Musical Life in Derby in the 18th and 19th Centuries' *Derbyshire Archaeological and Natural History Society Journal*, 1947, 1–54.

TAYLOR, STAINTON DE B. *Two Centuries of Music in Liverpool*. Liverpool (1976).

TAYLOR, WILLIAM COOKE. *Notes on a Tour in the Manufacturing Districts of Lancashire*. London 1842.

TEMPERLEY, NICHOLAS. (BLCL) 'Beethoven in London Concert Life, 1800–1850' *The Music Review*, 21 (1960), 207–14.

— (DM) 'Domestic Music in England 1800–1860' *Proceedings of the Royal Musical Association*, 85 (1958–9), 31–47.

— (ERO) 'The English Romantic Opera' *Victorian Studies*, 9 (1966), 293–301.

— (F) 'John Field and the First Nocturne' *Music and Letters*, 56 (1975), 335–40.

— (G) *Jonathan Gray and Church Music in York*. Borthwick Institute of Historical Research: St Anthony's Hall Publications, no. 51. York 1977.

— (GFP) 'George Frederick Pinto' *MT*, 106 (1965), 265–70.

— (HHP) 'Henry Hugo Pierson, 1815–73' *MT*, 114 (1973), 1217–20; 115 (1974), 30–4.

— (IM) 'Instrumental Music in England 1800–1850' Ph.D. dissertation, Cambridge University, 1959.

— (MEI) 'Mendelssohn's Influence on English Music' *Music and Letters*, 43 (1962), 224–33.

— (MOI) 'Mozart's Influence on English Music' *Music and Letters*, 42 (1961), 307–18.

— (PC) *The Music of the English Parish Church*. 2 vols. Cambridge 1979.

— (RA) 'Raymond and Agnes' *MT*, 107 (1966), 307–10.

— (SBL) 'Sterndale Bennett and the Lied' *MT*, 116 (1975), 958–61, 1060–3.

— (W) 'A List of T. A. Walmisley's Church Music' *English Church Music*, 27 (1957), 8–11.

TENNYSON, ALFRED and SULLIVAN, ARTHUR. *The Window: Or, The Songs of the Wrens*. London 1871.

TERRY, RICHARD R. *A Forgotten Psalter and Other Essays*. London 1929.

TERTIS, LIONEL. *Cinderella No More*. London 1953.

THOMPSON, FLORA. *Lark Rise to Candleford*. Harmondsworth 1973.

THRELFALL, ROBERT. Introduction to Frederick Delius, *Ten Songs* (London, 1973).

The Tonic Sol-Fa Reporter. Monthly journal, 1851 and 1853–88.

TORRINGTON, JOHN BYNG, 5th Viscount. *The Torrington Diaries (1781–1794)*, ed. C. B. Andrews. 4 vols. London 1934–8.

TOVEY, DONALD F. (E) *Essays in Musical Analysis*. 6 vols. London 1935–9.

— (MAEB) *Musical Articles from the Encyclopaedia Britannica*, ed. H. J. Foss. London 1944.

— (SES) *Some English Symphonists*. London 1941.

The Treasury of English Church Music, ed. Gerald H. Knight and William L. Reed. 5 vols. London 1965.

TRILLING, LIONEL. *Matthew Arnold*. London 1939.

TUCKWELL, WILLIAM. *Reminiscences of Oxford*. London 1900.

TURNER, JOHN. *A Manual of Instruction in Vocal Music*. London 1833.

TURNER, MICHAEL, ed. *The Parlour Song Book*. London 1972.

TYSON, ALAN. (AEEB) *The Authentic English Editions of Beethoven*. London 1963.

— (C) *Thematic Catalogue of the Works of Muzio Clementi*. Tutzing 1967.

VENABLES, LEONARD C. *The School Teacher's Music Guide*. London 1911.

VICINUS, MARTHA. (IM) *The Industrial Muse*. London 1974.

BIBLIOGRAPHY

— (VPC) 'The Study of Victorian Popular Culture' *Victorian Studies*, 18 (1974–5), 473–83.

'Victorian Music' *MT*, 28 (1887), 329–32, 396–8, 464–6.

Victorian Society. Second Conference Report: 'The High Victorian Cultural Achievement', ed. Paul Thompson. London 1965.

WAGNER, RICHARD. *My Life*, tr. anon. 2 vols. London 1911.

WAKEFIELD, A. MARY, ed. *Ruskin on Music*. London 1894.

WALKER, EDWARD S. *English Ragtime: A Discography*. Mastin Moor 1971.

WALKER, ERNEST. *A History of Music in England*. Oxford 1907; 3rd edn, rev. J. A. Westrup, Oxford 1952.

WALMISLEY, THOMAS A. *Cathedral Music*, ed. T. F. Walmisley. London 1857.

WARRACK, G. 'The Royal College of Music; the First Eighty-Five Years.' (Typescript, distributed to several libraries, c. 1975).

WARRACK, JOHN. *Carl Maria von Weber*. London 1968.

WATSON, ARTHUR. 'Reprints' *Musical News*, 6 (1894), 177–8.

WATSON, ERNEST B. *Sheridan to Robertson*. New York 1963.

WEATHERLY, FRED E. *Piano and Gown*. London and New York 1926.

WEBB, RICHARD, ed. *A Collection of Madrigals for Three, Four, Five, and Six Voices, Selected from the Works of the Most Eminent Composers of the 15th and 16th Centuries*. London 1808.

WEBER, WILLIAM G. *Music and the Middle Class: The Social Structure of Concert Life in London, Paris, and Vienna, Between 1830 and 1848*. London 1975.

WESLEY, ELIZA, ed. *Letters of Samuel Wesley to Mr. Jacobs . . . Relating to the Introduction into this Country of the Works of John Sebastian Bach*. London 1875.

WESLEY, SAMUEL SEBASTIAN. (FW) *A Few Words on Cathedral Music*. London 1849. Facs. repr. 1961.

— (R) *Reply to the Inquiries of the Cathedral Commissioners*. London 1854.

The Westminster Review. Quarterly journal, 1824–87; monthly, –1914.

WESTRUP, JACK A. *An Introduction to Musical History*. London 1955.

WHATLEY, GEORGE L. 'Donald Francis Tovey and His Contributions to the Study of Harmony and Counterpoint' Ph.D. dissertation, Indiana University, 1974.

WHITCOMB, IAN. *After the Ball*. London 1972.

WHITE, ERIC W. *The Rise of English Opera*. London 1951.

WHITLEY, WILLIAM T. *Congregational Hymn-Singing*. London 1933.

WIENANDT, ELWYN A. and YOUNG, R. H. *The Anthem in England and America*. New York 1970.

WIGGINS, ARCH R. *Father of Salvation Army Music: Richard Slater*. London 1945.

WILLIAMS, ALFRED. *Folk Songs of the Upper Thames*. London 1923. Repr. Wakefield 1971.

WILLIAMS, B., comp. *Popular Dance Music Arranged for a Full Orchestra*. Parts. London [1857–8].

WILLIAMS, CHARLES F. ABDY. *A Short Historical Account of the Degrees in Music at Oxford and Cambridge*. London [1894].

WILLIAMS, FLORIAN. 'After Forty Years: Recollections of a Music Publisher'. 13 articles in *Musical Opinion*, 63–4 (Feb. 1940–Feb. 1941).

WILLIAMS, RAYMOND. *Culture and Society 1780–1950*. Harmondsworth 1961.

WILLIAMS, THOMAS. *A Treatise on Singing.* London 1834.

WILLIAMSON, AUDREY M. *Gilbert and Sullivan Opera*. London 1953.

BIBLIOGRAPHY

WILSON, ALEXANDER and WILSON, M. T. *Songs of the Wilsons*. Manchester [1842?]. See Harland, J.

WILSON, CHRISTOPHER. *Shakespeare and Music*. London 1922.

WILSON, JOHN, ed. *Songs of Joseph Mather*. Sheffield 1862.

WILSON, THOMAS. *Analysis of the London Ball-Room*. London 1825.

WINSTON, JAMES. *Drury Lane Journal: Selections from James Winston's Diaries*, ed. A. L. Nelson and G. B. Cross. London 1974.

WIORA, WALTER. *European Folk Song*, tr. R. Kolben. London 1967.

WODEHOUSE, PELHAM G. and BOLTON, GUY. *Bring On the Girls*. New York 1953.

WOLFE, RICHARD J. *Secular Music in America 1801–1825*. 3 vols. New York 1964.

WORLEY, GEORGE. *The Catholic Revival*. London 1894.

Worshipful Company of Musicians. *English Music 1604 to 1904, being the Lectures given at the Music Loan Exhibition of the Worshipful Company of Musicians*. London 1906.

WYNDHAM, H. SAXE. (AM) *August Manns and the Saturday Concerts*. London 1909.

— (CG) *Annals of Covent Garden Theatre*. London 1906.

— (S) *Arthur Seymour Sullivan*. London 1926.

YEATS-EDWARDS, PAUL. *English Church Music: a Bibliography*. London 1975.

YOUNG, KENNETH. *Music's Great Days in the Spas and Watering-Places*. London 1968.

YOUNG, PERCY M. (E) *Elgar, O. M.* London 1955.

— (G) *George Grove 1820–1900: A Biography*. London 1980.

— (H) *A History of British Music*. London 1967.

— (S) *Sir Arthur Sullivan*. London 1971.

ZEALLEY, ALFRED. 'The Great British Brass Band Movement' *Etude*, 66 (1948), 534–5, 568–9.

INDEX

537

INDEX

introts 181–2
other music 179–80, 181
cathedral music (Roman Catholic) 166, 172, *210–13*
Cathedral Psalter 150, 178
cathedrals 172–4, 212
Cavaillé-Coll, Aristide 444
Cecil, Rev. Richard 187
Cellier, Alfred *339*; stage pieces 340
cello, concertos 27, 371; sonatas 386–7, 389, 392, 397 Duo
  Concertante 390; in the orchestra 372
Celtic nationalism *25–6; see also* Ireland, Scotland, Wales
chamber concerts 5, 13, 382, *387*, 399
chamber music *382–99*; performed 5, 13, 359, *381–2, 398–9*
'Champagne Charlie' *83–4*, 95
chanting, Anglican 145–50, 151, *176–8*; nonconformist 157,
  159, *160–1*, 164
chants, Anglican 148, 157, 159–62, 164, *179*, organ music
  based on *439*, 448; Gregorian *147–8*, 173, 179, 194
Chapman, Shadrach 151–3
Chappell, William 42, 68, 125, 487, 495, *496*
Chappell & Co. 54, 55, 58, 387, 496
character pieces 403, *416*, 422, 425, 427–8, 434
characterization, musical 297–300, 301, 318, 321, 336, 351
Charlotte, Queen 305
Charlotte of Wales, Princess 186
Chartist movement 18, 21, 22, 41
Chateaubriand, F. R. de 407
Cheltenham 109
'Cherry ripe' *93*, 123, 266, 271, 294
Cherubini, Luigi 151, 301, 475
Chester cathedral 177
Chesterfield 42
children, music for 286, 427–8
chiroplast 35
choirs, cathedral *172–4*; parochial 144, *146–50*; nonconformist
  161; Roman Catholic 212–13
Chopin, Frédéric 53, 56, 408, 416, 422; Field's influence on 7,
  360, 405, 409; influence of 323
choral ballads 236–7
choral music, cathedral *175–213*; parochial 151–3; in schools
  and colleges 171–2; for chorus and orchestra *214–41*; partsongs *242–67*
choral societies 41, 51, 233, 243, 254
chorale melodies, used in English compositions 218, 219, 356
chorale preludes *448*
choristers (boys) 173, *183*
Chorley, Henry Fothergill 17, 18, *466*; as critic 17, 125, 445,
  466–7; librettos 220, 228, 320
Choron, Etienne Alexandre 491, 500
chorus, in promenade concerts 114–15; on stage 96, 99, 107,
  292–3, 303, 319, 320, 346
chorus girls 100, 102
Christmas carols *263–5*; pantomime 104
Chrysander, Friedrich 498
Church, Richard 174
Church Hymnary 157
Church of England (and Ireland) 172, 214, 437; choral foundations *172–4*; Evangelical movement 109, *144–5*, 151, 164, 174;
  Oxford movement 5, 21, 42, *146–8*, 153, 173, 179
Church of Scotland 156–7
churches (buildings), Victorian 149
Cimador, Giambattista 358
cinema 88, 293
circulating libraries 49, 113
clarinet, music for 374–5, 384, 389, 397; in bands 135, 136, 139;
  in the orchestra 372
Clarke, Cuthbert 107
Clarke (-Whitfield), Dr John 181, *183*; cathedral music *183–5*;
  oratorio 217; songs 268–9
class (social): distinctions in musical tastes *14–18, 64–5*, 78–80,
  109, *117–19*; problems and conflicts 19, 27, 65, 73–4
Classical Chamber Concerts 387, 415
'classical' repertory 12, 16, 359, 381–2, 415
classicism 333, 357, 457
clavichord 400, 500
Clay, Frederic *339–40*; stage works 340; *Lalla Rookh* 226–8; 'I'll
  sing thee songs of Araby' *130–3*, 226
Clementi, Muzio 382, *401*, 403, 405, 409, 498; influence 404,
  406, 411, 414, 420, 498; piano music 401, 403–4; symphonies
  359–60
Clementi & Co. 49
Clifton, Harry, 'Work, Boys, Work' 77, *82*
Coates, Eric 103–4

Cobbett, Walter *399*
cockney song 82–3
Cocks & Co. 49
Coleridge, Mary 284
Coleridge, Samuel Taylor 221
Coleridge-Taylor, Samuel *232*, 374, 375; choral music 232–3;
  clarinet quintet 397; orchestral *Ballade* 375; partsongs 263;
  piano music 430
collects, as anthems 184; as songs 274
college chapels 30, 31, 171, 174, 208
Colles, H. C. 492
'Come-All-Ye' song type 76
comic opera 96, 98, 99, 100, 330–3, 336–42
comic songs 72, 81–2, 86, 133; in stage works 292
communion service 147, 171; choral settings 174, *181–2*, 201,
  203, 205, 210
Comte, Auguste 17
Concentores Sodales 211, 242
'concert-household song' 122
Concert of Ancient Music 13, 210–11, 291, 492, 498
concert organizations 13–14, *358–9, 369*, 375–6, 399
concertante 402
concertina 79
concertos, performed 358, 360, 364, 402, 436; composed, for
  cello 27, 371, clarinet 374–5, organ *436*, piano 119, *360–1*,
  369, 372, 374, 402, violin 374
concerts, public 13–14, 15–16, 122, 387, 402; promenade concerts 113–15
Conder, Joseph 158
conducting 115, 359, 376
congregational anthem 159, 162
Congregational Church 158–61, 164
congregational singing 40, 145–9, 151, 156–66, 167
Connell, Jim 78
conservatism, political 18, 22; musical 180, 218, 382, 427
conservatories *34–9*
conviviality, songs of 86
Cooke, Deryck 461, 464
Cooke, Tom 289, *304*, *305*; theatre music 305
Cooper, George *164*
Cooper, Martin 240
Coote family 113
copyright 49 (Table 1), 50–3; international 52, 121
Corder, Frederick 12, *347*, 434
cornet (cornopean) 79, 114, 335n.; in bands 136, 139, 140, 141
Cornwall, Barry 255, 276
Costa, Sir Michael 200, *225*, 331, 359, 369; oratorios *225–7*
cotillion 109
'Cotton Lords of Preston' *72*
country dances 109, *110*, 111, 112
court (royal) 358
Covent Garden Theatre 122, 288, 307, 310, 343n., *436*;
  promenade concerts 116
Coventry & Hollier 448
Cowden Clarke, Charles 465; Mary 465
Cowell, Sam 82
Cowen, Sir Frederic 280, *342*; operas 342–4; oratorio 232;
  partsongs 261; songs 280
Cramer, Franz 358, 359
Cramer, John Baptist 358, 359, 382, *401*, 405, 499; influence
  403, 404, 414, 416, 420; concertos *360*; piano music *402–3*,
  Studio per il Piano Forte 403–5
Cramer & Beale 57, 58
Crimean War 137
criticism 7, *465–73*, 482
Cristofori, Bartolommeo 400
Crook, John *105*
Crotch, Dr William 17, 30, 36, 37, 217, *456*, 499; lectures 30,
  456–7, 488, 489; writings 456–7, 475, 477, 478; antiquarian-
  ism *187–8*, 215, 457; influence 187–8, 218, 488
    anthems 184, 217
    chants *179*
    orchestral music 363–4
    organ concertos 217, *436*, fugues 439
    Palestine 215–17
    psalm tunes 150
    Specimens 488–9, 496, 499
Crowe, Alfred Gwyllym *116*
Crowest, F. J. 79, 151, 465
Crystal Palace 140, 142, 259, *369*, 471, 502; orchestral concerts
  369, 371, 481
Cummings, William H. 264, *498*

539

541

INDEX

INDEX

INDEX

INDEX

N₁